# BARRON'S

# american slang

## Dictionary and Thesaurus

D0309721

# BARRON'S
# american slang

# Dictionary and Thesaurus

## Mary Elizabeth, M.Ed.

Educational Product Developer
Adjunct Faculty
University of Vermont
Burlington, Vermont

Dedicated to Wendy, a master of words and
wordplay and a gem of a sister.

With thanks to those whose personal vocabularies have brought new words into
my life, including Nan and Dan and Ann and Daniel and Mike and Zippy and James
and Hans-Christoph and Neil and Bill; and to Tanya and Lyn, dear friends who provide
a haven of repose from the struggle, sweat, and verve of slang.

Special appreciation also goes to the Barron's Editorial team,
and especially to Debby Becak in Production and Rosemary Sause
in Proofreading and typesetter Karen Watson.

*All inquiries should be addressed to:*
Barron's Educational Series, Inc.
250 Wireless Boulevard
New York, NY 11788
**www.barronseduc.com**

ISBN-13: 978-0-7641-3861-4
ISBN-10: 0-7641-3861-8
Library of Congress Control Number 2009934705

Printed in Canada
9 8 7 6 5 4 3 2 1

# CONTENTS

## TYPES OF PEOPLE • 411

## TYPES OF THINGS • 456

**PATTERNS OF LANGUAGE ILLUSTRATIONS**

## TEACHING WITH SLANG • 585

# PREFACE

When I was eleven, I knew someone who seemed to be doing everything imaginable to make my life as difficult as possible. And having received a diary for my birthday and having had a particularly bad day, I urgently wanted to write something to express my anger, frustration, and outrage. But I didn't have the words.

I wrote "I hate X," and it neither made me feel better nor expressed how deeply bitter my pre-teen soul felt. My 6th-grade teacher had given me a thesaurus at the beginning of the school year—the first time I had ever encountered one—and now, for the first time, I opened it and looked up *hate*, which I found under *hatred*, and read:

V. **hate**, abhor, abominate, detest, loathe, despise; shudder, recoil, shrink.

Even at eleven, I knew that *shudder, recoil,* and *shrink* had more to do with fear than loathing. And perhaps that caused the doubt that led me not to wish to use *abominate* or *loathe* without knowing what they meant (never mind how to pronounce them). Flipping to the appropriate pages in the thesaurus yielded nothing, and while that helped me to understand how thesauruses work, it also made me realize that I couldn't use the thesaurus by itself: I was going to need a dictionary. So I sighed (I didn't much care for the tedious task of looking up words anyway, and what thoroughly upset child wants to work on alphabetization skills?) and found my student dictionary ... and it didn't have either of those words.

My wish to write was being thwarted by the reference books that were supposed to be specially designed to help me. There was the possibility of finding an "adult" dictionary, but I was too frustrated. I simply wrote:

I hate, abhor, abominate, detest, loathe, and despise X!!!!!!

and closed my diary for the day.

My frustration with reference books in general and thesauruses in particular was exacerbated by further experience. Thesauruses still group words that aren't synonyms, but are just sorta-kinda related in meaning, even mixing in different parts of speech—with the result that they require a great deal of prior knowledge to be useful. They don't have pronunciations or definitions, so one frequently needs to resort to a dictionary. They don't put the words they include in a context: that is, they don't include the full range of language—they're either slang and nothing else or standard English with a bit of informal language. They require a great deal of verbal skill to know anything at all about a word, and they are prescriptive simply by being non-inclusive. But this book—which I privately refer to as a *dictionasaurus*—was conceived to change all that.

# GUIDE TO THIS BOOK

This book is designed to be used to look up a single word or phrase or browsed to gain a broader sense of the slang element of American English. It is formatted to serve experienced users of English and word buffs, as well as students of English including non-native speakers.

Because this reference contains both a dictionary and a thesaurus, you can look up words in alphabetical order or by topic. If you've heard or read some slang that's unfamiliar, you can search alphabetically in the dictionary section. If you're trying to choose the best word to express your meaning, you can search thematically in the thesaurus.

The lists of non-slang synonyms at the end of each thesaurus section contextualize the slang entries, as do the Patterns of Language Illustrations, which reveal relationships between and among slang words and phrases. The use of styling to designate the registers of both the slang entries and the non-slang synonyms helps you grasp at a glance whether a word or phrase is potentially offensive slang, slang, informal, formal, or non-registered language, the last of which is adaptable to any context. This guide introduces the major features of this book, many of which will be familiar from your experience with other reference books, and some of which are unique.

# WHAT IS SLANG?

Read two references, and you will find two differing definitions of slang. With no general agreement on what slang is, each slang reference is compelled to present a rationale for its contents. Part of what must be addressed is the relationship of slang to other elements of language that are sometimes defined as being, or overlapping with, slang. I am not as interested in the historical meanings of each term as creating an internally consistent system that allows a clear discussion of the elements of language and maintains the gist of expert opinion. I will begin with other categories of language in order to clear the way for the definition of slang used in this book:

- **Jargon** is the technical language of a profession or field that is necessary or useful for the practice of that field. It may refer to materials, jobs, tools, situations, roles, etc. Jargon is not a set of replacement terms substituted for other language, but the primary names of these items. Also, clever jargon is not slang on account of its humor (*black hole*) if it is the primary accepted term for something.
- **Argot** and **cant** are interchangeable names for the language that is intended to be used by a group's insiders only, and not meant to be commonly understood. As such, it is commonly used as a shibboleth to distinguish insiders from outsiders.
- **Dialect** is generally the language of a particular region. It includes differences in diction (*hero* vs. *submarine* vs. *po'boy sandwich*), as well as differences in pronunciation.

- **Doublespeak** and **doubletalk** are names for language that is only truly understood by a few and intended to obscure, rather than reveal, meaning for everyone else, either through deception or equivocation.
- **Informal language** is casual and familiar. It tends to differ from formal language in that it uses contractions and allows for different rules of negation (e.g. double negatives, *ain't*) and agreement. It includes abbreviations and language deletions (sentence fragments) not allowed in formal use, and it has different diction, some of which is slang, but some of which is informal without being slang. In this book, because of its slang focus, informal language that is not slang is distinguished from slang. (For more about informal language, see "Language Registers" on page 587.)
- **Standard English** is a range of language from formal to informal, used by educated speakers and including some informal language, but excluding slang, which is considered nonstandard. Here is an illustration:

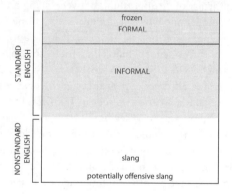

- **Slang**, then, is nonstandard and nontechnical English, used at the extreme end of informal language and across the population, most often as a substitute when one or more Standard English words are available. It is often playful, sometimes outspoken, and frequently adds emotional intensity to discourse. It is sometimes euphemistic (making things sound better or less unpleasant) and sometimes dysphemistic (making things sound worse or more unpleasant) than Standard English would. Slang's vocabulary comes from re-use of Standard English or words from other languages, as well as from shortening; adding prefixes, suffixes, or infixes; changing pronunciation; or from newly-minted words. Some slang has broken free from the niches of jargon, argot and cant, and/or dialect and made its way into general use. Slang can be perfectly integrated into discourse or used self-consciously, with a slight change of tone or mien calling attention to its use. Philosopher Ted Cohen in his book *Jokes: Philosophical Thoughts on Joking Matters* suggests that sharing jokes can lead to "the attainment of a very special kind of intimacy." I believe that, in a smaller way, sharing slang can sometimes do the same.

# THE SCOPE OF THIS BOOK

Since slang finds much to speak of at the extremes of meaning, those areas more often have abundant slang, while subjects with less intensity have little or none. Note, however, that what is extreme depends on how concepts are formulated. If one looks at the range Love–Hate, then one might expect little coverage of indifference, but one could also conceive of a range Passionate–Indifferent that makes indifference an extreme.

The scope of slang changes constantly, both from the introduction of new slang and from slang going in and out of fashion. It is likely that the connections between people fostered by the Internet, the rise of websites that invite slang definitions, and the large number of non-native speakers have all had an impact on the life-cycle of slang. But whatever the causes, it has always been true that some slang has lasted longer than other bits, and some slang has faded from view only to make a strong comeback. Couple this with the difficulty of distinguishing between slang and other informal language, and you will understand why only an approximation of the current compass is possible at any given time. Nevertheless, better and worse approximations are possible. Flying in the face of the evidence, Philip B. Corbett, the deputy news editor of *The New York Times*, in his article "The Chitchat Patrol" (January 27, 2009) writes, "Even the dated 'swanky' has made 34 *Times* appearances in the past year. Swanky?" Hello, Mr. Corbett: if *swanky* has made 34 appearances in *The Times* (and how many dozens? hundreds? thousands? of appearances elsewhere) in the past year, then—whatever you want to believe about it—it's not "dated," it's current! The same goes for *cool, groovy,* and many others. My choice is to include words rather than report their demise prematurely. You may, therefore, find some words in this book that you consider to be outdated or that you think are from the range of informal language that is not slang. I'm afraid that this is unavoidable.

With the flux of slang and the need for every entry to appear both in the dictionary and the thesaurus, it was not possible to include all American slang and still have a volume of a reasonable size. In the interests of a reference that is broadly useful, the following groups of slang were omitted: very new words that may or may not attain the breadth to be considered general slang; slang not currently in general use; slang having to do with illegal activities and referring to body parts and bodily functions; and so-called *slang* that would be better termed jargon, since its use is limited to particular fields like sports, journalism, medicine, technology, business, politics, etc. Note that since slang words naming body parts and bodily functions are incorporated into slang with other meanings and uses, such words do appear in this book.

The categories used here were derived from the slang after it was collected, rather than pre-conceived. Nevertheless, any categorization of language is a contrivance imposed for convenience, and not inherent in the language itself.

Multiple spellings are included within reason. When myriad spellings exist, only the most often used are included.

## ENTRY OVERVIEW

Each entry, whether in the thesaurus section or the dictionary section includes the following elements, as applicable:

- **entry word or phrase and alternate spellings**
- **pronunciation**
- **part of speech**
- **definition**
- **origins**
- **usage info**
- **usage alert**

Entries are words or phrases that have a slang meaning, although they may have standard English meanings as well. Virtually identical slang that is alphabetically in place may be indicated in the entry with a slash, or bulleted at the end. When the slang includes an element that is filled in by the user in context, a placeholder such as *sb, st,* or *sb/st*—standing for *somebody* or *something* or both—or the name of a part of speech such as <pronoun> is used.

In the thesaurus section, each category places slang in the context of its synonyms—slang words or phrases with the same part of speech and very similar meanings. In addition, a list of non-slang synonyms is generally provided at the end of each section. Placing slang in context is important for two reasons. The first has to do with a basic premise of how we understand anything. Anthropologist Gregory Bateson makes this point in his book *Mind and Nature: A Necessary Unity* (1979), offering a compelling argument that a true definition tells not only what a thing is "in itself" but shows it in relationship to other, related things in order to really make headway in clarifying its nature. Second, since slang, by definition, exists in contrast to other language choices, we cannot understand slang without looking at the language it is chosen to replace. In comparing the "fragrant" slang **bullshit** to the refined, formal **mendacity**, or the picturesque blister or wart to the more theoretical **vexation**, we can better appreciate what slang is and what it does for us in our communications.

## TEXT STYLING

As a reading clinician, I've observed that people who are still developing vocabulary—whether they are younger native speakers or non-native language learners—are at a deficit when using reference books that communicate entirely through verbal means. Both for them, and for visual learners and anyone else who wants to know more about the words they use, styling is used in this book to give an approximate read on the register of each entry word or phrase and each non-slang synonym (to understand more about registers, see "Language Registers" on page 587). This means that even without reading the text, one has a beginning sense of the language choices and their inter-relationships.

While all entries are red to help readers pick them out quickly on the page, you will notice that some entries are bolder than others. The bolder font is reserved for any entry word or phrase that has strong potential for being objectionable in and of itself, regardless of the meaning being expressed. Such entries are referred to in this book as *potentially offensive words* or *PO words* for short—it is both red and ultra. That is, **PO SLANG** is slang that may be found offensive by people who may agree with your meaning, but strenuously object to the way you have chosen to express it, and it is called out for your consideration. Slang that may be (and is often intended to be) insulting or abusive in *meaning* is treated under the USAGE ALERT heading. An entry that is both PO slang and insulting or abusive will both be bold and have a USAGE ALERT.

The styles are as follows. Notice that the register extremes—PO slang and formal language—are both bold, and that non-registered language has the least styling.

- **Potentially Offensive Slang**
- Slang
- <u>Informal Language</u>
- Non-registered Language
- **Formal Language**

Keep in mind that the styling is only a guide. As a reference book, this book describes language use so that you can consider this information—along with other factors—in making your personal language choices. The use of styling to show register is meant as a rough guide, subject to your understanding of the various contexts in which you use language. As I cannot know your context, I cannot possibly suggest which words or phrases you need for your purposes. If you read this book as prescriptive, you will be employing it for a job that it was not intended to perform.

Also, it's important to note that part of sorting language by registers is looking at the available language for a certain meaning and seeing what is more and less formal in the context of what the choices are. That is, the word use that will be considered formal or slang will be determined in part by the standards, but also in part by the available words for the specific concept. It is also the case that words formed with initials are generally considered less formal than their written-out counterparts.

## ENTRY ELEMENTS

## Pronunciation

The pronunciation is designed to give you a fairly close approximation of the sounds that make up the word or phrase and a general indication of the stress in multi-syllabic words and phrases. Only an approximation is aimed at because the vowels produced by Americans vary markedly by region and background and the stress in phrases depends to a certain extent on context. In addition, for simplicity's sake, only two stress levels are shown, the stronger level indicated by capitalization.

In order to make reading the pronunciation as easy as possible, the various sounds of American English are primarily provided by letter combinations, rather than diacriticals. Here is the pronunciation key, followed by a few notes:

## PRONUNCIATION KEY

| | | | | |
|---|---|---|---|---|
| a | bat | h | had |
| ā | bate, bait | j | jade, ridge, giraffe |
| ah | bot, bother | k | cat, kangaroo |
| aw | bought, bawl, for, all, father | l | lad |
| e | bet | 'l | needle |
| ē | beet | m | mad |
| i | bit | n | nap |
| ī | bite | 'n | sudden |
| ō | boat | p | pad |
| u | but | r | rad |
| o͝o | put, good | s | sad, cell |
| ū | boot, to, truth | t | tad |
| yū | beaut, you | v | vat |
| oi | boil, boy | w | wag |
| ou | bow, bound | y | yen |
| ahr | bar | z | zen |
| er | bear, bare | ch | chat |
| ir | beer | kh | chutzpah |
| awr | bore, or | sh | shell |
| ur | bur, bird | th | thin |
| b | bad | *th* | the, this |
| d | bad | zh | decision, garage |
| f | fad, fluff, phase | ng | lung |
| g | gad | hw | what |

- Short vowels are usually the vowel by itself: **a, e, i, o, u**—but *o* is represented by **ah**
- Long vowels have a macron: **ā, ē, ī, ō, ū**, and **yū**
- The vowel sound in *good* has the scoop over two *o*'s: **o͝o**
- *Th* pronounced as in *thin* is Roman, but *th* as in *this* is italic: **th, th**

With this scheme in place, the definite article usually shows up as |*thu*| (occasionally |*thē*|) and the indefinite article as |u|. And may be |and| or |und|. Since *sb, st,* and *sb/st* and parts of speech that the user fills in are unknowns, the abbreviations, rather than a pronunciation, are used.

The entries in this book include slang formed from the initials of words in a phrase. Although these words are referred to loosely as *acronyms,* most of them are actually *initialisms,* meaning that they are pronounced by saying the letter names in order. A few of them, though, are actually *acronyms,* words formed of initials but pronounced as words. Entries for initialisms are limited to definitions, but acronyms have pronunciations as well. Initialisms are usually considered more informal than the phrase or sentence they represent.

# Part of Speech

The part of speech indicates how the entry word or phrase is used. The parts of speech are slightly adapted in some cases to fit the way that slang appears, as defined here:

*n* for noun—a word or phrase that names a person, place, or thing

*adj* for adjective—a word or phrase that modifies a noun

*v* for verb—an action word (main verb) or a phrase that functions as a predicate

*adv* for adverb—a word that modifies a verb or an entire sentence

*a/a* for adjective and adverb—a word that can fulfill either function

*excl* for exclamation—for a word or group of words that stands alone, often a sentence fragment or single word, but also whole sentences that have an expressive function

*phr* for phrase—for expressions that do not fit any other category, including constructions that are grammatically clauses

*pfx* for prefix—a word part added to the beginning of a word

*sfx* for suffix—a word part added to the end of a word

*ifx* for infix—a word added into the middle of a word

Because of the easing of grammatical rules in informal language, there are a number of cases in which what appear to be two different forms of a word have the same grammatical function. For example, both forms **awful** and **awful(ly)** are slang adverbs, and the two forms **damn** and **damn(ed)** can both be either slang adjectives or adverbs. Such words are labeled by their function.

# Definition

Definitions only cover slang meanings of the entries. Standard English meanings (i.e., meanings in informal language that is not slang, language that is not tied to one particular register, or formal English) are not referenced except in ORIGINS, and then only if they are known and provide insight into how the slang word arose and/or is used. This is limiting as far as knowing the entire breadth of a word's meanings, but necessary for length. Definitions are divided (and numbered, if they are the same part of speech) in cases in which the meanings are in separate places in the thesaurus.

# Origins

ORIGINS covers how the word arose. Since the history of slang words is not always known and often disputed—with different sources providing definitive, but conflicting, etymologies—the more general approach implied by *origins* seemed appropriate. In addition, the purposes of this book would not be served by precise, etymological detail, even when it is available. Important cultural connections that have either popularized a slang word or phrase or strongly impact the associations that many people have with the slang are noted because they can have an important effect on the word's connotations. Euphemistic terms are noted in ORIGINS, but it is essential to understand that just because a word or phrase *can* be used as a euphemism for a PO term does not mean that it *is*, in fact, used with the intention of evoking the more volatile term in every case.

## Usage Info

When there is something noteworthy in the way a slang word or phrase is usually used or a need to let you know about grammatical peculiarities, the USAGE INFO provides helpful information and appropriate examples. For the most part, these examples are from real discourse.

## Usage Alert

Most people would agree that if you're going to offend someone, it's better to do it knowingly. Though the information provided on why certain slang can be offensive or objectionable may make the USAGE ALERTs tedious for some readers under some circumstances (for which, my sincere apologies), for other readers, they may prove valuable. For readers who are not native speakers, they may prove useful in detailing why an audience might react to the diction rather than, or in addition to, the meaning you're trying to make using these particular slang words and phrases. Words that are usually used with intent to offend or be rude and understood as such are noted.

## Non-Slang Synonyms

Synonyms from other registers help put the slang vocabulary in context. These synonyms are included to both augment understanding of the meaning and use of the slang, as well as provide alternatives for situations where you, say, have a burning desire to call someone a *dork* or *dumbass*, but think that it would probably be a good idea to use a less loaded word. Non-slang synonyms are omitted in a few cases in which it doesn't make sense to include them.

## Section Introductions

Each of the twelve major sections begins with a brief introduction that concludes with a mini table of contents for the section. Other short introductory material is provided as needed.

## Patterns of Language Illustrations

Fourteen illustrations help to capture and highlight slang tropes: patterns of meaning that run through the American English slang lexicon.

# DICTIONARY OF SLANG

## PRONUNCIATION KEY

| | | | | |
|---|---|---|---|---|
| a | bat | h | had |
| ā | bate, bait | j | jade, ridge, giraffe |
| ah | bot, bother | k | cat, kangaroo |
| aw | bought, bawl, for, all, father | l | lad |
| e | bet | 'l | needle |
| ē | beet | m | mad |
| i | bit | n | nap |
| ī | bite | 'n | sudden |
| ō | boat | p | pad |
| u | but | r | rad |
| o͞o | put, good | s | sad, cell |
| ū | boot, to, truth | t | tad |
| yū | beaut, you | v | vat |
| oi | boil, boy | w | wag |
| ou | bow, bound | y | yen |
| ahr | bar | z | zen |
| er | bear, bare | ch | chat |
| ir | beer | kh | chutzpah |
| awr | bore, or | sh | shell |
| ur | bur, bird | th | thin |
| b | bad | *th* | the, this |
| d | bad | zh | decision, garage |
| f | fad, fluff, phase | ng | lung |
| g | gad | hw | what |

N.B. The definite article usually shows up as |*thu*| (occasionally |*th*ē|) and the indefinite article as |u| (occasionally |ā|). And may be |and| or |und|. Since *sb, st,* and *sb/st* and parts of speech that the user fills in are unknowns, the abbreviation or part of speech label, rather than a pronunciation, is used.

## REGISTER STYLING

- **Potentially Offensive Slang**
- • Slang
- • <u>Informal Language</u>
- • Non-registered Language
- • **Formal Language**

## ALPHABETIZATION

- • Words in parentheses are optional.
- • In definitions with *be* following, *be* is most often a placeholder for *am, is, are,* or contractions of those words, and therefore is not included in the pronunciation.

**A**

**\<number> ways to/from/'til Sunday** |\<number> wāz tū SUN dā / \<number> wāz frum SUN dā / \<number> wāz til SUN dā| *adv* To an extreme degree; extremely well. ORIGINS: **Six ways for Sunday** comes from as early as 1886, when it appears in the novel *Tracy Park* by US author Mary Jane Holmes. Repopularized by the 1997 film *Six Ways to Sunday* and the song "Six Ways 'Til Sunday" by Rise Against (from their album *The Unraveling*, 2001). USAGE INFO: Though it often appears as **six ways to Sunday**, perhaps influenced by the film, the number, the preposition, and the day of the week can all vary as in, for example, **four ways from Sunday**, **six ways from Wednesday**, etc. USAGE INFO: Used as an adverb as in "we beat them six ways to Sunday."

**\<Proper noun> FTL** \<Proper noun> for the loss.

**\<Proper noun> FTW** \<Proper noun> for the win. *See* \<PROPER NOUN> FOR THE WIN!

**\<Proper noun> for the loss!** |\<Proper noun> fawr *thu* LOSS| *excl* An alternative cry of victory by naming the other person as the loser; an acclamation of the poor quality of an item. ORIGINS: From computer games. The idea is that choosing/using this item will result in a figurative loss to you. Altered from \<Proper noun> for the win!

**\<Proper noun> for the win!** |\<Proper noun> fawr *thu* WIN| *excl* A self-congratulatory announcement of victory in which the winner fills in his or her own name; an acclamation of the value or attractiveness of *sb/st*, e.g., a brand. ORIGINS: Said by the announcer of the winner in *The Hollywood Squares* game show (1966–1981).

**10-4** *excl* Message received and understood. ORIGINS: From US Police 10-codes.

**404** |FAWR ō FAWR| No information.

**4COL** For crying out loud!

**AMF** Adios, mother fucker!

**AYBABTU** All your base are belong to us.

**a \<noun> and a half** |u \<noun> and u HAF| *n* A great amount of whatever is referenced.

**A-list** |Ā list| *adj* A highly-regarded celebrity. ORIGINS: From the celebrity ranking system invented by journalist James Ulmer and known as the Ulmer scale. It uses a 100-point system to rank a star's bankability. The most bankable stars are referred to as **A-list**.

**A-OK, A-okay** |Ā ō KĀ| *adj* Fine; well-done. USAGE INFO: Some definitions say "satisfactory," but that suggests a minimal meeting of requirements, and **A-OK** is actually superior to simply **OK** or **okay**.

**Abso-fucking-lutely!** |ab su FUK ing lūt lē| *excl* Certainly! ORIGINS: SE absolutely with added emphasis from the infix **fucking**. USAGE INFO: Other spellings are also used. USAGE ALERT: The use of **fucking** in this phrase will make it objectionable in some contexts and to some people.

**Abso-goddamn-lutely! Abso-goddam-lutely!** |ab su GAH DAM LŪT lē| *excl* Certainly! ORIGINS: SE absolutely with added emphasis from the infix **goddamn**. USAGE INFO: Other spellings are also used. USAGE ALERT: The use of **goddamn** in this phrase will make it objectionable in some contexts and to some people.

**Absotively-posilutely!** |AB su tiv lē PAH zu lūt lē| *excl* Certainly! ORIGINS: An exchange of syllables in the SE words **absolutely** and **positively** to form two portmanteau words.

**Abyssinia!** |ab u SIN ē u| *excl* I'll be seeing you! ORIGINS: Shortened and altered form of "I'll be seeing you," rendered humorous by assuming the form of another word, the former name of the country now known as *Ethiopia*.

**ace** |ās| *n* An outstanding person, noteworthy for qualifications, skills, or character traits. ORIGINS: From the ace's role as the highest-ranked playing card.

**ace** |ās| *adj* The best. ORIGINS: From the ace's role as the highest-ranked playing card. Recently popularized through an episode of CollegeHumor's video series *Jake and Amir* entitled "Ace," in which Jake pretends that he made up the words **ace** and **gullies**.

**ace (it)** |ās / ĀS it| *v* To perform superbly, especially on an examination. ORIGINS: From the ace's role as the highest-ranked playing card.

**ace in the hole** |ĀS in *thu* HŌL| *n* A concealed asset that insures a win. ORIGINS: From the ace's role as the highest-ranked playing card and the role in poker of the "hole card," kept face-down until the showdown.

**Ack!** |ak| *excl* A sound to express disgust or dismay.

**act up** |AK tup| *v* To cause trouble; to malfunction. USAGE INFO: Used of *sb/st* who or that can or has in the past acted appropriately/functioned well.

**acting up** |AK ting up| *adj* Causing trouble; malfunctioning. USAGE INFO: Used of *sb/st* who or that can or has in the past acted appropriately/functioned well.

**addlebrain*** |AD 'l brān| *n* A person suffering from confusion; a foolish person. ORIGINS: Addle comes from a Middle English word related to the German **adele**, which means "liquid manure." It can be followed by several synonyms for *head*. USAGE INFO: The current usage is gentler than its etymology suggests: this word is not the equivalent of **shithead**. The etymology of **addle** is not widely known, so people are not likely to connect the word with excrement. Still, it is usually used with intent to denigrate or insult and understood as such.
• addlehead |AD 'l hed|
• addlepate |AD 'l pāt|

**Adios, MOFO!** |ah dē ŌS MŌ fō| *excl* Goodbye, mother fucker. ORIGINS: From Standard Spanish **adios** meaning "goodbye" and **MOFO**, an abbreviation of **mother fucker**, a general term of extreme abuse. USAGE INFO: **Mother fucker** is considered one of, if not *the,* worst insults one can make to a man, since it suggests that he has an incestuous relationship with his mother. The phrase seems to have experienced an increase in popularity after it was used by Texas Governor Rick Perry in speaking to a reporter on June 21, 2005. A video of the incident was posted on YouTube, Governor Perry made several "Quote of the Day" lists, and he inspired a tee-shirt with the quotation and his likeness. USAGE ALERT: This word carries implications not only about the person referred to, but also about his mother. The inclusion of **MOFO** will make this phrase objectionable in some contexts and to some people. Usually used with intent to denigrate or insult and understood as such.

**Ahoi-hoi! Ahoy-hoy!** |u HOI HOI| *excl* Hello! ORIGINS: Of debatable origins, but commonly used as a nautical greeting and as a general greeting by the eighteenth century. *Ahoy* was Alexander Graham Bell's preferred word for a telephone greeting, but Thomas Edison's preferred word—*hello*—became the actual standard. Ahoy-hoy has had a recent surge in popularity due to its use as a telephone greeting by (Charles) Montgomery Burns, a character on the television show *The Simpsons*.

**Aight! Aiight!** |ī ĪT| *excl* A casual greeting; an exclamation of agreement. ORIGINS: From elision of alright. USAGE INFO: Usually used in speech, so its spelling is not standardized. There are a number of other spellings in use besides those listed.

**airbrain**\* |ER brān| *n* A stupid person. ORIGINS: Suggests that a person has air—that is, nothing—in his/her head, rather than brains, and so is empty-headed. USAGE ALERT: Usually used with intent to denigrate or insult and understood as such. • airhead |ER hed|

**all about that, be** |awl u BOUT THAT| *v* To accept "that" as crucially important or central to one's being.

**all-fired** |AWL FĪRD| *adv* Extremely. ORIGINS: Either refers to propulsion through the firing of engines or can be a euphemism of **hell-fired**. USAGE INFO: Used as an adverb ("so all-fired smart"). Don't confuse it with the similar looking "all fired up," in which **all** is an adverb modifying the phrasal verb **fired up**.

**All foam, no beer.** |AWL fōm NŌ bir| *phr* Unintelligent. ORIGINS: Though foam and beer would both be expected when beer is poured into a glass, the proportions are important. Foam is mainly air, while beer is the substance. This phrase then, suggests that the person is an airbrain. USAGE ALERT: Usually used with intent to denigrate or insult and understood as such.

**all that** |awl THAT| *adj* Of the highest quality, sophistication, or hotness possible. ORIGINS: Either All that and a bag of chips is a superlative of all that or all that is a shortened form of the longer phrase. Popularized by the movie *She's All That* (1999) based on *Pygmalion* by George Bernard Shaw, a book *All That and a Bag of Chips* (2002) by Darrien Lee, and a rock band of the same name from Oslo, Norway.

USAGE INFO: Used in phrases such as "S/he thinks s/he's all that" to suggest that a person has a false sense of being hot and/or sophisticated.

**All your base are belong to us.** |awl yŏŏr BĀS ar bu lawng tū US| *phr* ORIGINS: From the (poorly done) English translation of the Japanese video game "Zero Wing" (1991).

**Amen to that!** |ā MEN tū *that*| *excl* Expression of strong agreement. ORIGINS: From standard response to prayer indicating agreement.

**amoeba-brain** |u MĒ bu brān| *n* An extremely stupid person. ORIGINS: An amoeba is a one-celled animal that has no brain. USAGE ALERT: Usually used with intent to denigrate or insult and understood as such.

**Amscray!** |AM skrā| *excl* Go away! ORIGINS: This is a rendering of slang **scram** meaning "Go away!" in pig Latin, a simple, coded language used primarily by children. USAGE ALERT: Usually used with intent to be rude and understood as such.

**And how!** |AND HOU| *excl* Exclamation of enthusiastic agreement.

**And I care because?** |and Ī ker bē CUZ| *phr* I don't care.

**And I care why?** |and Ī ker WĪ| *phr* I don't care.

**ante (up)** |AN tē / AN tē up| *v* To pay. ORIGINS: From the practice in poker of making an initial bet as the first step in participating in a round.

**antsy** |ANT sē| *adj* Nervous; fidgety. ORIGINS: Possibly related to the ceaseless movement of ants and the slang phrase **have ants in one's pants**.

**apple polisher** |AP ul PAH lish ur| *n* One who seeks favor; a sycophant. ORIGINS: Reference to the practice of a student presenting a shiny apple to a teacher, trying to gain an advantage in grades by being pleasant. USAGE INFO: Despite the positive image, this term is disparaging.

**Are we on the same sheet of music?** |ahr wē ahn *thu* SĀM SHĒT uv MYŪ zik| *phr* Do we share a common understanding? ORIGINS: From the situation of musicians performing from individual parts and having to pay careful attention to make sure that they are playing in sync with each other.

**Are we on the same wavelength?** |ahr wē ahn *thu* SĀM WĀV lengkth| *phr* Are we understanding things in a similar way? ORIGINS: From radio waves carrying a broadcast. Being on the same wavelength means hearing the same thing, and thus being "in tune" with others.

**Are you fucking kidding me?** |AR yū FUK ing KID ing mē| *excl* I can hardly believe what you're saying! ORIGINS: From slang **fuck** meaning "to engage in sexual intercourse," used here as a sentence modifier to intensify the whole sentence. USAGE ALERT: This use of a form of **fuck** will be objectionable in some contexts and to some people.

**Are you nuts?** |ar yū NUTS| *excl* What you're saying is crazy. ORIGINS: A comment on *sb's* soundness of mind, couched as a question, but not seeking an answer.

**Are you tuned in?** |ahr yū tūnd IN| *phr* Are you getting the fine points? ORIGINS: Tuning in a radio is the exercise in achieving the best and clearest reception of a station. So *sb* who is "tuned in" is making a real effort to achieve understanding.

**armchair general** |AHRM cher GEN ur ul| *n* A person without power or position who pontificates on how the world or a war should be run from the comfort of his/her overstuffed chair at home.

**armchair strategist** |AHRM cher STRAT u jist| *n* A person without power or position who pontificates on how the world or a war should be run from the comfort of his/her overstuffed chair at home.

**around the bend** |u ROUND *thu* BEND| *adj* Crazy; insane. USAGE ALERT: Often used with intent to denigrate or insult and understood as such. This way of speaking about *sb's* mental health may be considered insensitive and therefore objectionable in some contexts and by some people.

**Arrgh!** |ahrg| *excl* Sound to indicate irritation. ORIGINS: Popularized by its use in Talk Like a Pirate Day celebrations and related events and materials. USAGE INFO: Arrgh is spelled in a variety of ways.

**arrive** |u RĪV| *v* To attain success.

**artist** |AHR tist| *sfx* An expert in something (often illegal, unpleasant, or not likely to gain respect). ORIGINS: Extended from SE **artist** to apply to other fields, sometimes ironically. USAGE INFO: Usually follows a noun, e.g., con **artist**, **bullshit artist**.

**as < adjective> as a bastard** |az <adjective> az u BAS turd| *adj* Intensifies the named adjective to an extreme degree. ORIGINS: From **bastard** meaning "a mean or nasty person" or "a problematic situation," by extension of SE bastard, meaning "an illegitimate child." USAGE ALERT: The inclusion of the word **bastard** in the phrase will render this phrase objectionable in some contexts and to some people.

**as < adjective> as a bitch** |az <adjective> az a BICH| *adj* Intensifies the named adjective to an extreme degree. ORIGINS: From **bitch** meaning "an unpleasant, offensive, difficult person of either sex" or "extremely difficult," extended from SE bitch, meaning "a female dog." USAGE ALERT: The inclusion of the word **bitch** in the phrase will render it objectionable in some contexts and to some people.

**as < adjective> as all creation** |az <adjective> az awl krē Ā shun| *adj* Intensifies the named adjective to an extreme degree.

**as < adjective> as all get out** |az <adjective> az awl GET out| *adj* Intensifies the named adjective to an extreme degree.

**as < adjective> as anything** |az <adjective> az EN ē thing| *adj* Intensifies the named adjective to an extreme degree.

**as < adjective> as blazes** |az <adjective> az BLĀ zuz| *adj* Intensifies the named adjective to an extreme degree. ORIGINS: Euphemism for **as <adjective>**

**as hell**. Blazes is a euphemism for **hell** from SE hell meaning "the alternative to heaven; the realm of the devil." Blazes to the fires of hell. USAGE ALERT: The euphemism blazes in this phrase will soften it somewhat, but it may still be objectionable in some contexts and to some people.

**as <adjective> as can be** |az <adjective> az kan BĒ| *adj* Intensifies the named adjective to an extreme degree.

**as <adjective> as heck** |az <adjective> az HEK| *adj* Intensifies the named adjective to a moderate degree. ORIGINS: Euphemism for **as <adjective> as hell**. Heck is a euphemism for **hell** from SE hell meaning "the alternative to heaven; the realm of the devil." Heck has a similar-sounding start, but its substitution tends to lessen the intensity of the comparison. USAGE ALERT: The euphemism **heck** in this phrase will soften it somewhat, but it may still be objectionable in some contexts and to some people.

**as <adjective> as hell** |az <adjective> az HEL| *adj* Intensifies the named adjective to an extreme degree. ORIGINS: Figurative use of SE hell meaning "the alternative to heaven; the realm of the devil." USAGE ALERT: The inclusion of the word **hell** in this phrase will render it objectionable in some contexts and to some people.

**as <adjective> as shit** |az <adjective> az SHIT| *adj* Intensifies the named adjective to an extreme degree. ORIGINS: From **shit** meaning "excrement." USAGE ALERT: The inclusion of the word **shit** in this phrase will render it objectionable in some contexts and to some people.

**as <adjective> as they come** |az <adjective> az *th*ā KUM| *adj* Intensifies the named adjective to an extreme degree.

**ask for trouble/it** |ASK fawr TRU bul / ASK fawr it| *v* Take an unnecessary risk; do something despite knowing the (unpleasant) consequences. USAGE INFO: *Trouble* can be substituted by *it* as in "You asked for it."

**ass** |as| *n* A foolish, incompetent person. ORIGINS: From SE ass meaning "a donkey," but commonly used as slang to refer to the rear end or buttocks. USAGE INFO: Can also, depending on context, mean "an unpleasant, vain, pompous, or offensively stupid person," or—on the other hand—be used affectionately of someone who is silly or characteristically blunders, as in "You silly ass!" USAGE ALERT: All words containing **ass** will be found objectionable in some contexts and by some people. Usually used with intent to denigrate or insult and understood as such.

**-ass(ed)** |as / ast| *sfx* The suffix **-ass** can combine with an SE noun (candy) or adjective (sad) to form a noun (**candy-ass**, **sadass**) or an adjective (crazy) to form an adjective (**crazy-ass**). The suffix **-assed** can combine with a noun or adjective (candy, sad) to form an adjective (**candy-assed**, **sadassed**). ORIGINS: From SE ass meaning "a donkey," but commonly used as slang to refer to the rear end or buttocks. USAGE INFO: Note that both the noun and the adjective form are used as adjectives. Intensifies the word it follows to an extreme degree, as in: **candy-ass** ("a sissy; not up to expectations"); **crazy-ass** ("an eccentric, a fool, or an out-of-control person"); **hard-ass** ("an uncompromising or mean person"—

beyond <u>hardnose</u>); **raggedyass** ("a disreputable or impoverished person or place"); and **sadass** ("a depressed person"). *See* **BADASS**, **KICK-ASS**, and **SMART-ASS** for their idiosyncratic meanings. USAGE ALERT: All words containing **ass** will be found objectionable in some contexts and by some people.

**ass backward(s)** |AS BAK wurd / AS BAK wurdz| *adj* Chaotic; in a mess. ORIGINS: From SE ass meaning "a donkey," but commonly used as slang to refer to the rear end or buttocks. Thus **assbackward(s)** means "back-to-front," but has the extended figurative meaning of "confused." USAGE ALERT: All words containing **ass** will be found objectionable in some contexts and by some people.

**ass-kiss** |AS kis| *v* To seek favor through flattery; to be a sycophant or toady. ORIGINS: From SE ass meaning "a donkey," but commonly used as slang to refer to the rear end or buttocks. USAGE ALERT: The use of the word **ass**, the graphic image, and the implied insult will make this phrase objectionable in some contexts and to some people.

**ass-kisser\*** |AS KIS ur| *n* One who seeks favor; a sycophant. ORIGINS: From SE ass meaning "a donkey," but commonly used as slang to refer to the rear end or buttocks. USAGE INFO: **Kiss-ass** is a separate, synonymous word that has the words in the reverse order. USAGE ALERT: The use of the word **ass** and the graphic image will make this phrase objectionable in some contexts and to some people. Usually used with intent to denigrate or insult and understood as such.
• **ass-licker** |AS LIK ur|

**asshole** |AS hōl| *n* A nasty or despicable person. ORIGINS: From SE ass meaning "a donkey," but commonly used as slang to refer to the rear end or buttocks. Thus, with SE **hole**, a reference to the anus. USAGE ALERT: All words containing **ass** will be found objectionable in some contexts and by some people. **Asshole** is stronger than **ass**, and considered more objectionable. Usually used with intent to denigrate or insult and understood as such.

**at the helm, be** |at *thu* HELM| *v* To lead; to set the direction. ORIGINS: From the sphere of the navy in which the **helm** is the mechanism for steering a boat or ship.

**awesome** |AW sum| *adj* Outstanding, impressive, excellent. ORIGINS: Used in SE to characterize something that inspires or expresses awe, the word lost its spiritual side and gained popularity following its slang use in popular culture, such as the language of the Teenage Mutant Ninja Turtles, beginning with their debut in 1984, and the movie *Bill & Ted's Excellent Adventure* (1989). USAGE INFO: Because of the juvenile associations with its origins, the slang use of **awesome** may be self-mocking, to show that the user is not immature.

**awful(ly)** |AW ful / AW flē| *adv* Very. USAGE INFO: Notice that the adjective and adverb forms are both used in an adverbial sense, but using the adjective form (**awful**) in a context where an adverbial modifier (**awfully**) is expected may be considered grammatically incorrect, even in a context in which slang is acceptable. So "I'm awfully sick" may be viewed as more acceptable than "I'm awful sick," though both are used.

**axe** |aks| *v* To fire or terminate unceremoniously. ORIGINS: From the hand tool. The sharp edge and violent potential of the axe lend this particular term a sense of cruelty.

**Ay yi yi! Ai yie yie!** |ī yī YĪ| *excl* Oh no! ORIGINS: This is not the same expression used by the Frito Bandito in Frito-Lay® advertisements. USAGE INFO: Always used with either 2 or 4 yi's following the Ay.

**B4N** Bye for now.

**BB4N** Bye-bye for now.

**BBFN** Bye-bye for now.

**BBIAB** Be back in a bit.

**BBIAF** Be back in a few [minutes].

**BBIAS** Be back in a sec[ond].

**BBIAW** Be back in a while.

**BBL** Be back later.

**BFN** Bye for now.

**BHOM** Beats the hell/heck out of me.

**BI5** Back in five [minutes].

**BIOYE** Blow it out your ear.

**BLBBLB** Back like bull, brain like bird.

**BMGWL** Busting my guts with laughter.

**BMOTA** Bite me on the ass.

**BRB** Be right back.

**BSOM** Beats the shit out of me.

**BTDT** Been there, done that.

**BTHOOM** Beats the hell/heck out of me.

**BTSOOM** Beats the shit out of me.

**BWL** Bursting with laughter.

**b.s., bs** |BĒ ES| *n* Lies; words or actions meant to be deceptive. ORIGINS: An abbreviation of **bullshit**; from the SE name of male cattle (**bull**) and the slang word for their dung (**shit**). USAGE INFO: Spelled both with and without periods. USAGE ALERT: Despite the attempt to soften by abbreviation, the graphic reference referred to by this phrase makes it objectionable in some contexts and to some people.

**b.s., bs** |BĒ ES| *adj* Inferior; worthless; rubbishy. ORIGINS: An abbreviation of **bullshit** from the SE name of male cattle (**bull**) and the slang word for their dung (**shit**). USAGE INFO: Spelled both with and without periods. USAGE ALERT: Despite the attempt to soften by abbreviation, the graphic reference indicated by this phrase makes it objectionable in some contexts and to some people.

**babbler** |BA blur| *n* A person whose conversation is trivial, foolish, or revealing of things better left undisclosed. ORIGINS: It may be that the association of the SE word **babble** with the unceasing sound of flowing water, particularly a brook, adds to the denotation a suggestion of excess.

**babe** |bāb| *n* A particularly attractive woman or—in some contexts—man. USAGE INFO: Originally applied only to women, in the late 1980s the term also began to be applied to men.

**babelicious** |BĀB u LISH us| *adj* Used of a very beautiful or sexually attractive woman. ORIGINS: From the slang word babe plus the slang suffix -licious by extension of SE **delicious**. *See* **-LICIOUS**. USAGE ALERT: Apt to be considered an objectification of women by some, and therefore objectionable.

**baboon** |ba BŪN| *n* A crude, boorish person; a brute. ORIGINS: After SE **baboon**, a type of terrestrial monkey found in Africa and Asia, and its (stereotypically) conceived behavior patterns. USAGE ALERT: Usually used with intent to denigrate or insult and understood as such.

**Back in a bit/few/sec** |BAK in u BIT/FYŪ/SEK| *phr* I will return shortly. ORIGINS: From SE **bit** meaning "a short period of time"; few, short for "a few minutes" or "a few moments"; or slang sec, short for "a second."

**Back like bull, brain like bird.** |BAK līk BŌOL BRĀN līk BURD| *phr* Unintelligent. ORIGINS: One of a number of synonymous phrases in which the first part sets up an inference, and the second undercuts it. In this case, the first phrase creates the impression that the person being described is extraordinarily gifted, but the second part, drawing on the association of birds with lack of intelligence (*See* **BIRDBRAIN**) belies the initial conclusion. USAGE ALERT: Usually used with intent to denigrate or insult and understood as such.

**back off** |BAK AHF| *v* To retreat from a position of aggression. USAGE INFO: Also used as an imperative exclamation to request being left in peace.

**back-slap** |BAK slap| *v* To congratulate effusively, often in order to ingratiate oneself. ORIGINS: From the congratulatory gesture of patting the back of someone who has achieved a notable success.

**backseat driver** |BAK sēt DRĪ vur| *n* A person who persists in offering unwanted advice to the person in charge. ORIGINS: From the practice of motor vehicle passengers who second-guess the driver.

**backup, back-up** |BAK up| *n* A person or item relied on for support. ORIGINS: From SE **back-up** meaning "support or help."

**bad** |bad| *adj* Outstandingly good. ORIGINS: Akin to other words, in both English and other languages, that have taken on opposite meanings, i.e., become contronyms. In this case, the reversal has been traced to the origins of this usage in the Black community, which felt that its standards were at odds with the accepted/ establishment value system.

**bad job** |BAD JAHB| *n* A difficulty with no reasonable resolution. USAGE INFO: Often used in the phrase "give *st* up as a bad job."

**bad mouth, bad-mouth** |BAD mouth| *v* To attack verbally; to criticize unfairly.

**bad news** |BAD NŪZ| *n* Difficulties or trouble. USAGE INFO: Used of a person who is perpetually in trouble or who drags acquaintances into bad situations.

**bad rap** |BAD RAP| *n* False accusation; unjust condemnation; unfair punishment. ORIGINS: Extended from the earlier slang meaning of "a (serious) criminal charge." From SE **rap** meaning "a tap on the shoulder."

**bad scene** |BAD SĒN| *n* An unpleasant situation or one in which trouble is likely to befall.

**bad shit** |BAD SHIT| *n* Serious problems. ORIGINS: From slang **shit** meaning "excrement." USAGE ALERT: The use of the word **shit** will make this phrase objectionable in some contexts and to some people.

**badass** |BAD as| *n* An aggressive, tough, frightening person. ORIGINS: From slang **ass** meaning "the rear end or buttocks." *See* **-ASS(ED)** for more information about the suffix. USAGE INFO: **Badass** is a contronym. It can also mean "an admirable or formidably talented person." USAGE ALERT: The inclusion of **ass** will make this term objectionable in some contexts and to some people. Usually used with intent to denigrate or insult and understood as such.

**badass(ed)** |BAD as / BAD ast | *adj* First-rate; admirable. ORIGINS: From slang **ass** meaning "the rear end or buttocks." USAGE INFO: **Badass(ed)** is a contronym. It can also mean "aggressive, tough, and frightening." *See* **-ASS(ED)** for more information about the suffix. Note that both the noun and the adjective form are used as adjectives. USAGE ALERT: The inclusion of **ass** will make this term objectionable in some contexts and to some people.

**bafflegab** |BA ful gab| *n* Words intended to deceive and baffle. ORIGINS: A rare coined bit of slang originating in May 1952, **bafflegab** was invented by Milton Smith, assistant general counsel of the US Chamber of Commerce, to describe the baffling language commonly found in government regulations.

**bag** |bag| *v* To gain possession of; to steal.

**-bag** |bag| *sfx* A person. Combines with a noun (most often) to describe a person who is considered contemptible. ORIGINS: Similar to the idiom **bag of bones** to characterize a person. Terms with -bag often depict a person as a bag full of unpleasant or disgusting contents. USAGE INFO: *See* DIRTBAG, **DOUCHEBAG**,

**SCUMBAG**, SCUZZBAG, SLEAZEBAG, and SLIMEBAG, found grouped with SLIMEBALL.

**bag it** |BAG it| *v* To stop doing *st*; to abandon a project.

**Bag it!** |BAG it| *excl* Be quiet! ORIGINS: By extension of SE **bag** meaning "a holder" (used to remove something from active use) or slang **bag** meaning "to quit or abandon." USAGE ALERT: Often used with intent to denigrate or insult and understood as such.

**bag of wind** |bag uv WIND| *n* A person who talks too much and says little of value. ORIGINS: From the slang suffix -bag, here in a different position, but still functioning as a derogatory reference to a person. Wind here is similar to hot air: all breath and no substance. USAGE ALERT: Usually used with intent to denigrate or insult and understood as such.

**bag *sb/st*** |bag *sb/st*| *v* To abandon, get rid of, dismiss *sb* or *st*. USAGE INFO: Bag is a contronym: it can also mean "to capture or secure *st* for oneself."

**bag some *z*'s** |BAG sum zēz| *v* To take a nap. ORIGINS: Slang **bag** can mean "take" or "steal." *Z*'s are used as an onomatopoeic representation of sleep.

**bags** |BAGZ| *n* A great deal. ORIGINS: From SE **bag** in reference to the day's kill collected by hunters. Its use spread during WWI.

**-ball** |bawl| *sfx See* -BAG.

**ball-buster** |BAWL bus tur| *n* Extremely demanding and difficult problem. ORIGINS: From slang **balls** meaning "testicles," and SE **buster**, "someone or something that breaks things." USAGE INFO: Most often used by males. Can also be used of a person who is extremely demanding, in which case it can refer to a male or a female. USAGE ALERT: The use of **ball** in this phrase will make it objectionable in some contexts and to some people. Usually used with intent to denigrate or insult and understood as such.

**ball of fire\*** |BAWL uv FĪR| *n* A person possessed of great energy and drive. USAGE INFO: Notice that the phrase can be formed with the main words in either order. • fireball |FĪR bawl|

**ball up** |BAWL up| *v* To make a mistake; to ruin; to make a mess of. ORIGINS: Euphemism for **fuck up**. **Ball** means "testicle." USAGE INFO: Used of messes made by females as well as males. USAGE ALERT: This slang phrase is often somewhat less objectionable than **fuck up**, because a) it refers to sex organs, but not sexual activity, and b) ball has alternate SE meanings that are unrelated to sexuality.

**balled-up** |BAWLD up| *adj* Confused; in a mess. ORIGINS: From slang **balls**, euphemism for SE **testicles**. Entered the language after the verb form **ball up** and before the noun form **balls-up**. USAGE ALERT: The inclusion of **balled** in this phrase will make it objectionable in some contexts and to some people. **Fucked up** will be found more objectionable, **messed up** less so.

**Balls!** |bawlz| *excl* I don't believe it/you! ORIGINS: From slang **balls**, meaning "testicles." USAGE INFO: Usually used by men, with rare exceptions. USAGE ALERT: The reference to the male sex organs will render this phrase objectionable in some contexts and to some people.

**balls-up** |BAWLZ up| *n* An error or blunder. ORIGINS: From slang **balls** meaning "testicles." Originally a military usage. *See* **FUBAR** and **SNAFU**. USAGE ALERT: The inclusion of **balls** in this phrase will make it objectionable in some contexts and to some people.

**ballsy** |BAWL zē| *adj* Courageous, masculine. ORIGINS: Masculine traits are connected with the **balls**, meaning "testicles." Usually, but not always, used of males. USAGE ALERT: This form of **balls** will be objectionable in some contexts and to some people.

**ballyhoo** |BAL ē hū| *v* To publicize in a sensationalist way.

**bam** |bam| *v* To punch. ORIGINS: Imitative of the sound of a blow.

**bananas** |bu NAN uz| *adj* Crazy; insane. ORIGINS: May be referencing **go ape** in the sense of losing control and the common understanding that apes are extremely fond of bananas. USAGE ALERT: Often used with intent to denigrate or insult and understood as such. This way of speaking about *sb's* mental health may be considered insensitive and therefore objectionable in some contexts and by some people.

**bang heads together** |BANG HEDS tū ge*th* ur| *v See* KNOCK HEADS TOGETHER.

**bardacious** |bahr DĀ shus| *adj See* BODACIOUS, BODASHES.

**barking mad** |BAHR king MAD| *adj* Crazy; insane. ORIGINS: May be referencing the wild barking of mad dogs. USAGE ALERT: Often used with intent to denigrate or insult and understood as such. This way of speaking about *sb's* mental health may be considered insensitive and therefore objectionable in some contexts and by some people.

**barrel (along)** |BER ul / BER ul u LAWNG| *v* To move swiftly (in a motor vehicle). ORIGINS: From the SE **barrel into**, referring to a barrel rolling downhill. USAGE ALERT: **Barrel through** and **barrel ahead** also refer to speedy progress, but are more often used of situations that do not involve vehicular travel, for example, "barrel through an examination"; "barrel ahead with the treaty signing."

**bash *sb*** |BASH *sb*| *v* To hit *sb* a solid blow; to criticize harshly and with accusations and threats. ORIGINS: The meaning of verbal attack is a figurative extension of the physical attack.

**bash *sb* up** |BASH *sb* up| *v* To beat thoroughly using repeated strikes and/or kicks. ORIGINS: By extension of slang bash *sb*.

**bassackwards, bass-ackwards** |BAS ak wurdz| *adj* Chaotic; in a mess. ORIGINS: A euphemistic Spoonerism (reversing the initial letters of two major words) of the phrase **assbackwards**, to playfully make meaning in the way that concrete poetry does: by demonstrating its meaning graphically, with the confused letter order paralleling the confused state of affairs it denotes. Developed from slang **ass** meaning "the rear end or buttocks." USAGE ALERT: The use of the word **ass** will make this term objectionable in some contexts and to some people.

**bastard**[1] |BAS turd| *n* A mean or nasty person; an offensive or despicable person. ORIGINS: From SE **bastard** meaning "an illegitimate child." USAGE ALERT: The SE sense means that this word carries implications not only about the person referred to, but also about his or her mother. The words **SOB** and **son of a bitch** have a similar issue, as does **motherfucker**. In any case, in some contexts and to some people, the term **bastard** with any meaning will be considered objectionable. Usually used with intent to denigrate or insult and understood as such.

**bastard**[2] |BAS turd| *n* A very difficult problem. ORIGINS: From SE **bastard** meaning "an illegitimate child." USAGE ALERT: The term **bastard** will be considered objectionable in some contexts and by some people.

**bats** |bats| *adj* Crazy; insane. ORIGINS: Shortened form of **bats in the belfry**, which describes insanity as if it were an infestation of the brain, drawing an analogy between the belfry at the top of a church tower, and the head at the top of the body. USAGE ALERT: Often used with intent to denigrate or insult and understood as such. This way of speaking about *sb's* mental health may be considered insensitive and therefore objectionable in some contexts and by some people.

**bats in the belfry** |BATS in *thu* BEL frē| *adj* Crazy; insane. ORIGINS: Describes insanity as if it were an infestation of the brain, drawing an analogy between the belfry at the top of a church tower, and the head at the top of the body. USAGE ALERT: Often used with intent to denigrate or insult and understood as such. This way of speaking about *sb's* mental health may be considered insensitive and therefore objectionable in some contexts and by some people.

**batshit crazy** |BAT shit KRĀ zē| *adj* Extremely crazy; recklessly crazy. ORIGINS: From slang **bats** meaning "insane" and slang **apeshit** meaning "to lose control." USAGE ALERT: The inclusion of the word **shit** will render this phrase objectionable in some contexts and to some people. Often used with intent to denigrate or insult and understood as such. This way of speaking about *sb's* mental health may be considered insensitive and therefore objectionable in some contexts and by some people.

**batso** |BAT sō| *adj* Crazy; insane. ORIGINS: Combines **bats,** which is short for **have bats in the belfry** and the slang suffix -o used to create adjectives, including some others having to do with mental health, like **nutso, sicko,** and **wacko,** making them similar to abbreviated **schizo** and **psycho**. USAGE ALERT: Often used with intent to denigrate or insult and understood as such. This way of speaking about *sb's* mental health may be considered insensitive and therefore objectionable in some contexts and by some people.

**batty** |BAT ē| *adj* Crazy; insane. ORIGINS: Shortened form of **bats in the belfry**, which describes insanity as if it were an infestation of the brain, drawing an analogy between the belfry at the top of a church tower, and the head at the top of the body. USAGE ALERT: Often used with intent to denigrate or insult and understood as such. This way of speaking about *sb's* mental health may be considered insensitive and therefore objectionable in some contexts and by some people.

**bawl *sb* out** |bawl *sb* OUT| *v* To reprimand *sb* harshly. ORIGINS: From SE **bawl** meaning "to cry loudly."

**bazillion** |bu ZIL yun| *n* An unspecified, exceedingly large amount. ORIGINS: One of a group of made up numbers ending in *-illion* with pretty indistinguishable meanings, although additional elements may signal even larger amounts (i.e., a bazillion may be larger than a **zillion**).

**be in *sb's* corner** |BĒ in *sb's* KAWR nur| *v* To supply *sb* with whatever assistance they need. ORIGINS: From the role of a boxer's support staff in boxing matches.

**beans** |bēnz| *n* A small amount. USAGE INFO: Often in the phrase "I don't know beans about...."

**bear** |ber| *n* A difficult or unpleasant thing or situation. ORIGINS: Based on SE **bear**, the large, omnivorous, and sometimes aggressive mammals that can be dangerous to humans.

**beastly** |BĒST lē| *adj* Awful or extremely unpleasant.

**beat** |bēt| *adj* Worn out, as if from a beating.

**beat** |bēt| *v* To cheat by not paying. USAGE INFO: **Beat** can also be used for other forms of cheating and defrauding.

**beat a dead horse** |bēt u ded hawrs| *v* To refuse to drop a subject that has already been discussed thoroughly and completely.

**beat it** |BĒT it| *v* To leave in a hurry. ORIGINS: Possibly from a combination of SE **beat a path** and reference to the sound of rapidly retreating footsteps beating the floor/pavement.

**Beat it!** |BĒT it| *excl* To send away without ceremony. ORIGINS: Possibly from a combination of SE **beat a path** and reference to the sound of rapidly retreating footsteps beating the floor/pavement. USAGE ALERT: Usually used with intent to be rude and understood as such.

**beat *sb* to a pulp** |BĒT *sb* tū u pulp| *v* To beat *sb* until s/he is seriously injured. ORIGINS: Pulp is a shapeless, wet mass of material, and the slang term draws a comparison between that and the damage that is sustained by a severely beaten person.

**beat *sb's* ass** |BĒT *sb's* AS| *v* To beat *sb* up; to harass or annoy *sb*. ORIGINS: From slang **ass** meaning "the rear end or buttocks." USAGE INFO: Since spanking has been a standard punishment for some time, this expression does not seem as violating as **beat *sb's* balls**, for example. USAGE ALERT: The inclusion of **ass** will make this phrase objectionable in some contexts and to some people.

**B**

**beat *sb*'s balls** |BĒT *sb*'s BAWLZ| *v* To beat *sb* up; to harass or annoy *sb*. ORIGINS: From slang **balls** meaning "testicles." USAGE INFO: **Beat *sb*'s balls** is usually only used to refer to, or used self-referentially by, males. **Beat *sb*'s balls** may suggest a more personal and more violent attack than **beat *sb*'s ass**. USAGE ALERT: The inclusion of **balls** will make this phrase objectionable in some contexts and to some people.

**beat *sb*'s buns** |BĒT *sb*'s BUNZ| *v* To beat *sb* up; to harass or annoy *sb*. ORIGINS: Euphemism for **beat *sb*'s ass**. From slang **buns**, a euphemism for slang **ass**, meaning "the rear end or buttocks." USAGE INFO: Since spanking has been a standard punishment for some time, this expression does not seem as violating as **beat *sb*'s balls**, for example. USAGE ALERT: The reference to the human rear end or buttocks will render this phrase objectionable in some contexts and to some people. Some people will find **buns** less offensive than **butt**, which is, in turn, often considered less objectionable than **ass**.

**beat *sb*'s butt** |BĒT *sb*'s BUT| *v* To beat *sb* up; to harass or annoy *sb*. ORIGINS: Euphemism for **beat *sb*'s ass**. From slang **butt**, a euphemism for slang **ass**, meaning "the rear end or buttocks." USAGE INFO: Since spanking has been a standard punishment for some time, this expression does not seem as violating as **beat *sb*'s balls**, for example. USAGE ALERT: Although it is a euphemism, the inclusion of **butt** will make this phrase objectionable in some contexts and to some people.

**beat the crap out of *sb*** |BĒT *thu* KRAP out uv *sb*| *v* To beat severely. ORIGINS: Euphemism for **beat the shit out of *sb***. From slang **crap**, a euphemism for slang **shit**, meaning "excrement." USAGE ALERT: The reference to **crap** will make this phrase objectionable in some contexts and to some people, though some people will find **crap** less objectionable than **shit**.

beat the (living) daylights out of *sb* |BĒT *thu* (LIV ing) DĀ lītz out uv *sb*| *v* To beat severely. ORIGINS: From SE beat and slang daylights originally meaning "the eyes" and then "the insides."

**beat the shit out of *sb*** |BĒT *thu* SHIT out uv *sb*| *v* To beat severely. ORIGINS: From slang **shit** meaning "excrement." USAGE ALERT: The reference to **shit** will make this phrase objectionable in some contexts and to some people.

beat the stuffing out of *sb* |BĒT *thu* STUF ing out uv *sb*| *v* To beat severely; to undermine someone's confidence. ORIGINS: **Stuffing** is conceived as in a rag-doll: if it were to be taken out, there would just be a saggy cloth bag left.

beat the tar out of *sb* |BĒT *thu* TAR out uv *sb*| *v* To beat severely. ORIGINS: Perhaps because organic substances break down into tar eventually, in this expression tar is conceived of as the essence of a person.

Beats me! |bēts MĒ| *phr* I don't know! ORIGINS: Shortened from phrase "It beats me."

**Beats the hell out of me!** |bēts *thu* HEL out uv MĒ| *phr* I don't know! ORIGINS: Shortened from phrase "It beats the hell out of me." Figurative use of SE **hell** meaning "the alternative to heaven; the realm of the devil." USAGE ALERT: The inclusion of **hell** will make this expression objectionable in some contexts and to some people.

**Beats the shit out of me!** |bēts *thu* SHIT out uv MĒ| *phr* I don't know! ORIGINS: Shortened from phrase "It beats the shit out of me." From slang **shit** meaning "excrement." USAGE ALERT: The inclusion of **shit** will make this expression objectionable in some contexts and to some people.

**beaucoup** |bō KŪ| *adj* A lot; a large quantity of. ORIGINS: From the French **beaucoup** meaning "many." It became popular during the Vietnam War, during which US soldiers came in contact with speakers of French or French/Vietnamese pidgin.

**beef** |bēf| *v* To complain. ORIGINS: From an old meaning of **beef**: "to raise an alarm."

**Been there, done that.** |BIN *the*r DUN *that*| *excl* This is not new or interesting to me.

**beetlebrain** |BĒT 'l brān| *n* A stupid person. ORIGINS: The implication is that the person's brain is the size of a beetle's. USAGE ALERT: Usually used with intent to denigrate or insult and understood as such.

**behind the eight ball, behind the eightball** |bē HĪND *th*ē ĀT bawl| *phr* In trouble; in unfavorable or uncomfortable circumstances. ORIGINS: From a variation of Kelly Pool, in which players are assigned balls by number and those with a number higher than (i.e., "behind") the eight ball, have greatly reduced chances of winning the game.

**beige** |bāzh| *adj* Bland; uninteresting; boring. ORIGINS: From the perceived insipidity of the color beige.

**bejesus out of, the** |*thu* bi JĒ zus out uv| *adv* To a great extent. ORIGINS: From SE Jesus Christ, whom Christians hold to be the Son of God. USAGE INFO: Most often used with the verb *scare* and verbs related to fighting, e.g., *beat*, but can also be used with *confuse, bore* and other verbs that indicate someone being put at a disadvantage in some way. *See* **SCARE THE BEJESUS OUT OF** *SB*. USAGE ALERT: The use of the name **Jesus** in this manner will be considered blasphemous and found objectionable in some contexts and by some people.

**belly up** |BEL ē up| *adj* Bankrupt; failed; dead. ORIGINS: From the floating position of a dead fish. USAGE INFO: Often in the slang phrase **go belly up**, which is used more frequently of a business than of a personal financial failure. *See* GO BELLY UP.

**bellyache** |BEL lē āk| *v* To complain or moan as if one had a stomachache.

**bellyacher** |BEL ē āk ur| *n* A person who complains or moans as if s/he had a stomachache.

**bellyful** |BEL ē ful| *n* More than enough, specifically of something unpleasant.

**belt** |belt| *v* To strike a strong blow with a belt or one's fist.

**belt (along)** |belt / BELT u LAWNG| *v* To move with great speed or to hurry, usually in a vehicle.

**bench** |bench| *v* To remove *sb* from participation in some event. ORIGINS: From sports such as baseball and football in which players who are not actively participating watch the play from a bench at the side of the playing field

**bend over (for *sb*)** |bend ō vur / bend ō vur fur *sb*| *v* To submit. ORIGINS: A reference to a posture assumed for sex. USAGE INFO: Some people may not know the origins and may use this phrase innocently. USAGE ALERT: This phrase is not related to bend over backwards, which has inoffensive ORIGINS and a different meaning. The origins of and graphic image presented by this phrase will make its use objectionable in some contexts and to some people.

**bend over backwards** |BEND ō vur BAK wurdz| *v* To make a great effort. ORIGINS: From the difficulty of bending backwards in, for example, the game of limbo. USAGE ALERT: This phrase is completely distinct from **bend over (for)**.

**bend *sb*'s ear** |BEND *sb*'s IR| *v* To talk tediously.

**bent out of shape** |BENT out uv SHĀP| *adj* Very angry. ORIGINS: This phrase is conceived on the analogy of a person to a delicate object that can be damaged in two degrees: 1) bent out of shape; 2) broken. USAGE INFO: The phrase is sometimes abbreviated to bent. The comparable verb form **bend *sb* out of shape** is hardly ever used.

**bestest** |BES tist| *adj* A superlative superlative. ORIGINS: This word is constructed of two superlatives: best, the superlative of **good**, and the superlative ending -est. Since only one superlative element is needed and best is already ultimate, the result is humorous.

**bet the farm*** |BET *thu* FAHRM| *v* To risk everything. ORIGINS: Depending on which property is chosen—farm, house, or ranch—one is risking one's livelihood or one's residence—in any case, taking an enormous risk.
• bet the house |BET *thu* HOUS|
• bet the ranch |BET *thu* RANCH|

**biff** |bif| *v* To punch lightly. ORIGINS: Imitative of the sound of a blow.

**big boy** |BIG boi| *n* Person with power or influence; in particular, an organized crime boss. USAGE INFO: May be used ironically.

**big bucks** |BIG BUKS| *n* An unspecified, large amount of money. USAGE INFO: Because **money** is SE, while bucks is slang, big bucks is slangier than big money.

**big cheese** |BIG CHĒZ| *n* Person with power or influence; an important person or "the boss." ORIGINS: Suspected by some to have arisen from a British misapprehension of the Persian or Hindi or Urdu word chiz, meaning "thing," during the nineteenth century when many British were in India. USAGE INFO: Often used with *the*.

**big chief** |BIG CHĒF| *n* Person with power or influence; the most important of all the important people. USAGE INFO: Often used with *the*.

**big daddy (of them all)** |big DA dē / big DA dē uv *th*um AWL| *n* Predominant in impact, importance, or other ways; may refer to a person or thing. ORIGINS: From the father as the head of the family in a paternalistic society. USAGE INFO: Often used with *the*.

**big deal** |BIG DĒL| *n* Person with power or influence; an important person. ORIGINS: From SE big and slang deal meaning "an individual." USAGE INFO: Often used with *a*.

**Big deal!** |BIG dēl| *excl* I don't care; this is not important or interesting. USAGE INFO: Always said sarcastically with this meaning.

**big enchilada** |BIG en chu LAH du| *n* Person with power or influence. ORIGINS: Said to be modeled on other slang terms with *big*, such as **big cheese**. Popularized by its appearance in the White House tapes made public on account of the Watergate Scandal. USAGE INFO: Often used with *the*.

**big fellow** |BIG FEL ō| *n* Person with power or influence; in particular, an organized crime boss.

**big fish** |BIG FISH| *n* Person with power or influence. USAGE INFO: Often used with *a* as in the phrase "a big fish in a small pond."

**big gun** |BIG GUN| *n* Person with power or influence. ORIGINS: From military jargon big gun meaning "a large-caliber artillery piece." USAGE INFO: Often used in the plural.

**big guy** |BIG gī| *n* Person with power or influence or considered to be powerful or influential.

**big-headed** |BIG hed id| *adj* Arrogant; conceited. ORIGINS: From SE big and slang suffix -head.

**big man** |BIG MAN| *n* Person with power or influence; a major drug dealer.

**big money** |BIG MUN ē| *n* An unspecified, large amount of money. USAGE INFO: Because money is SE, while bucks is slang, big bucks is slangier than big money.

**big shot** |BIG shaht| *n* Person with power or influence, often one who is self-important or perceived as over-reaching. USAGE INFO: Can be used as a back-handed compliment or out of jealousy.

**big spender** |BIG SPEN dur| *n* Person who spends to impress. USAGE INFO: Used ironically of a cheapskate.

**big-time** |BIG tīm| *a/a* Important; complete; in a big way; completely. ORIGINS: May draw on the noun big time, which means "the highest level of success in a given field." USAGE INFO: Can be used as an adjective ("big-time loser"; "big-time lawyer") or as an adverb ("He's losing it big-time.").

**big wheel** |BIG WĒL| *n* Person with power or influence, particularly in the realm of business. ORIGINS: Possibly a reference to wheels and cogs one might imagine in the proverbial "engines of industry."

**big wig** |BIG wig| *n* Person with power or influence. ORIGINS: A reference to the large wigs once worn by influential and important men.

**biggie, biggy** |BIG ē| *n* Anyone or anything large, important, or successful. ORIGINS: By addition of an irreverent ending (one that usually serves to diminish) to SE **big**.

**bigmouth, big mouth** |BIG mouth| *n* A boaster; a gossip; a person who is indiscreet. ORIGINS: From drawing a connection between mouth size and the amount that a person says. USAGE ALERT: Usually used with intent to denigrate or insult and understood as such.

**bilge (water)** |BILJ / BILJ WAH tur| *n* Rubbish; untruths; lies. ORIGINS: By analogy to the foul water that collects in the bilge of a ship; along the same lines as calling a lie **shit** or **crap**. USAGE INFO: Despite the analogy, this term does not cause the type of offense that a term including the word **shit** or **crap** does.

**bimbette** |bim BET| *n* Vacuous, but notably attractive, person aspiring to be a bimbo. ORIGINS: May derive from the Italian **bimbo** meaning "baby." USAGE INFO: Often applied to a woman seeking to get rich by using her sexuality to gain economic support or who is perceived as doing so. USAGE ALERT: Usually used with intent to denigrate or insult and understood as such. The suggestion of trading sex for money and/or a perception that this word is disparaging to women will make this term objectionable in some contexts and to some people.

**bimbo** |BIM bō| *n* Vacuous, but notably attractive, person. ORIGINS: May derive from the Italian **bimbo** meaning "baby." USAGE INFO: Often applied to a gold-digger, a woman who uses her sexuality in order to gain economic support or who is perceived as doing so. USAGE ALERT: Usually used with intent to denigrate or insult and understood as such. The suggestion of trading sex for money and/or a perception that this word is disparaging to women will make this term objectionable in some contexts and to some people.

**bind** |bīnd| *n* Predicament or difficult situation.

**birdbrain** |BURD brān| *n* A person considered to be silly or stupid. ORIGINS: Draws on the perception that birds have low intelligence that one perceives in phrases like **running around like a chicken with its head cut off**. USAGE ALERT: Usually used with intent to denigrate or insult and understood as such.

**birdbrained** |BURD brānd| *adj* Ridiculous or preposterous. USAGE INFO: Often used of an idea that is absurd. USAGE ALERT: Often used with intent to denigrate or insult and understood as such.

**bitch**[1] |bich| *n* An unpleasant, offensive, difficult person of either sex. ORIGINS: From SE **bitch**, meaning "a female dog." It is Marge Dursley's use of the word bitch to describe Lily Potter that leads Harry Potter to make Marge inflate and to run away from the Dursley's home in *Harry Potter and the Prisoner of Azkaban*. USAGE INFO: Original meanings focused on sexuality; current meanings focus on the unpleasantness of a person's disposition. Can also mean an unspecified object or person, as in "Who's the bitch who took my shoes?" USAGE ALERT: This term will be objectionable in some contexts and to some people. Usually used with intent to denigrate or insult and understood as such.

**bitch**² |bich| *n* An extremely difficult or unpleasant problem. ORIGINS: From SE bitch, meaning "a female dog." USAGE ALERT: **Bitch** will be objectionable in some contexts and to some people.

**bitch** |bich| *v* To complain. ORIGINS: By extension from the slang noun **bitch** with the idea that this behavior would be typical of a **bitch**. USAGE ALERT: The reference to **bitch** in this phrase will make it objectionable in some contexts and to some people.

**bitch and moan** |BICH und MŌN| *v* To complain all the time. ORIGINS: By extension from the slang noun **bitch** with the idea that this behavior would be typical of such a person. USAGE ALERT: The reference to **bitch** in this phrase will make it objectionable in some contexts and to some people.

**bitching, bitchin, bitchen** |BICH ing / BICH un| *adj* Excellent; wonderful. ORIGINS: From SE bitch, meaning "a female dog." USAGE INFO: Note that forms of **bitch** are used with extremely negative as well as extremely positive meanings. The form **bitching** also means "complaining bitterly." USAGE ALERT: Despite their positive meaning, these forms of **bitch** will be objectionable in some contexts and to some people.

**bitchy** |BICH ē| *adj* Easily roused to anger; difficult to deal with. ORIGINS: From SE bitch, meaning "a female dog." USAGE ALERT: This term will be objectionable in some contexts and to some people. Usually used with intent to denigrate or insult and understood as such.

**Bite me!** |BĪT mē| *excl* A contemptuous dismissal. ORIGINS: Abbreviated form of slang phrase **Bite my ass!** USAGE ALERT: Usually used with intent to be rude and understood as such. Because **ass** is part of the phrase that is intended, even if it is not spoken, those who know what is meant may be offended by that as well as the graphic image (and the usually offensive tone in which it is said).

**Bite me on the ass!** |BĪT mē ahn *th*ē AS| *excl* A contemptuous dismissal. ORIGINS: From slang **ass** meaning "the rear end or buttocks." USAGE ALERT: Usually used with intent to be rude and understood as such. In addition, the inclusion of **ass** and the graphic image will make this expression objectionable in some contexts and to some people.

**Bite my ass!** |BĪT mī as| *excl* A contemptuous dismissal. ORIGINS: From slang **ass** meaning "the rear end or buttocks." USAGE ALERT: Usually used with intent to be rude and understood as such. In addition, the inclusion of **ass** and the graphic image will make this expression objectionable in some contexts and to some people.

**bite *sb's* head off** |BĪT *sb's* HED awf| *v* Attack verbally, used especially in cases in which the attack is objectively out of proportion to the situation. USAGE INFO: Despite the physical description in the phrase, it is not used for physical altercations.

**bite the dust** |BĪT *thu* dust| *v* To die; to be utterly defeated. ORIGINS: Although associated in many people's minds with US Westerns, the concept of dying in battle with one's face in the dirt goes back at least to Homer's *Iliad* (Book II, line 418, for example), and the phrase *bite the dust* was used in Samuel Butler's translation of *The Iliad* into English in 1898, at which time, it was not slang.

**bitty*** |BIT ē| *adj* Little, small; insignificant. ORIGINS: Diminutive of SE bit. USAGE INFO: Bitty is often combined into little bitty or itty bitty; bitsy may be combined to form itsy bitsy. Reduplication is common for small things, e.g., teensy-weensy and the children's finger-play song "The Eensy-Weensy Spider."
• bitsy |BIT sē|

**blab** |blab| *v* To talk about trivial things; to reveal information that shouldn't have been shared.

**blabber** |Bl AB ur| *v* To talk indiscreetly; to gossip.

**blabbermouth** |BLA bur mouth| *n* An indiscreet or gossiping person. ORIGINS: From slang blab, meaning "to reveal information that shouldn't have been shared." USAGE ALERT: Often used with intent to denigrate or insult and understood as such.

**blah** |blah| *adj* Without interest; boring. ORIGINS: Onomatopoeic sound of chatter; meaningless, uninteresting talk.

**blah-blaher** |blah BLAH ur| *n* A person who chatters continually and meaninglessly. ORIGINS: Onomatopoeic sound of meaningless, uninteresting talk. The -er suffix is applied to show that the word is naming the person who is chattering. USAGE ALERT: Often used with intent to denigrate or insult and understood as such.

**blahs** |blahz| *n* An occurrence of depression. ORIGINS: Extension of blah, which comes from the onomatopoeic sound of meaningless, uninteresting talk. USAGE INFO: Often follows *the*.

**blam** |blam| *v* To punch hard. ORIGINS: Imitative of the sound of a blow.

**blame(d)** |blām / blāmd| *a/a* Extreme; extremely; very; blameworthy; etc. ORIGINS: A euphemism for **damn(ed)**. USAGE INFO: Used as an adjective ("a blame(d) idiot") or an adverb ("traffic moving so blame(d) slow"; "a blame(d) fool thing to do"). USAGE ALERT: Euphemisms may still be objectionable in some contexts and to some people.

**blamedest** |BLĀM dist| *a/a* Worst; least; etc. ORIGINS: A euphemism for **damnedest**. USAGE INFO: Used as either an adjective ("the blamedest idea") or an adverb ("the blamedest little thing"). USAGE ALERT: Euphemisms may still be objectionable in some contexts and to some people.

**Blank it!** |BLANGK it| *excl* An interjection expressing anger, frustration, dismay, etc. ORIGINS: Euphemism for several PO exclamations, such as **Damn it!** and **Fuck it!** Refers to the blank space left in a text to replace a PO word. USAGE INFO: People do not ordinarily use blank alone ("Blank!"). USAGE ALERT: Euphemisms may still be objectionable in some contexts and to some people.

**blanked** |blangkt| *a/a* Extreme; extremely; very; etc. ORIGINS: Euphemism for **damned**. Refers to the blank space sometimes left in a text to replace a PO word. The *-ed* ending is in imitation of the past participles. USAGE INFO: Used as an adjective ("a blanked fool") or an adverb ("so blanked fancy"). USAGE ALERT: Euphemisms may still be objectionable in some contexts and to some people.

**blankety(-blank)** |BLANG ki tē / BLANG ki tē BLANGK| *a/a* Cursed; very; extremely. Also functions as a sentence modifier. ORIGINS: Euphemism for **damned** and other PO words. Refers to the blank space sometimes left in a text to replace a PO word. **Blankety** draws on an adjective suffix used in words like **persnickety, crotchety, fidgety,** etc. Although one might expect **blank** to replace one-syllable words and **blankety** or **blankety-blank** to replace multi-syllable words, this is not always the case. An increased number of syllables may, however, suggest a stronger word. Used as an adjective ("my blankety-blank job") or an adverb ("so blankety-blank often"). USAGE ALERT: Euphemisms may still be objectionable in some contexts and to some people.

**blanking** |BLANG king| *a/a* Extreme; extremely; very; etc. ORIGINS: Euphemism for **fucking** or **damned** or other PO words. Refers to the blank space sometimes left in a text to replace a PO word. The *-ing* ending is in imitation of present participles. Used as an adjective ("a blanking idiot") though **blinking idiot** is more common, or an adverb ("blanking good news"). USAGE ALERT: Euphemisms may still be objectionable in some contexts and to some people.

**blast** |blast| *v* To attack violently with a gun; to attack verbally with strong criticism or accusations.

**Blast (it)!** |blast / BLAST it| *excl* An interjection expressing anger, frustration, dismay, etc. ORIGINS: Euphemism for **Damn! Damn it!** USAGE ALERT: Euphemisms may still be objectionable in some contexts and to some people.

**blast *sb/st* out of the water** |BLAST *sb/st* OUT uv *thu* WAH tur| *v* To launch an attack of devastating proportions; to destroy. ORIGINS: The imagery comes from a naval battle.

**blasted** |BLAS tid| *a/a* Extreme; extremely; very; etc. ORIGINS: A euphemism for **damn(ed)**. USAGE INFO: Used as an adjective ("blasted mosquitoes") or an adverb ("blasted good time"). Note that the *-ed* is not optional for **blasted**. USAGE ALERT: Euphemisms may still be objectionable in some contexts and to some people.

**blat** |blat| *v* To talk shrilly.

**Bleah!** |bleh| *excl* A sound to express disgust.

**bleater** |blēt ur| *n* A person who often complains feebly or in a whining way. ORIGINS: Imitative of the sound of a sheep or goat.

**Blecch!** |blek| *excl* A sound to express disgust.

**Bleep (it)!** |blēp / BLĒP it| *excl* An interjection expressing anger, frustration, dismay, etc. ORIGINS: Euphemism for **Damn! Fuck! Shit! Damn it! Fuck it!** or other PO words. From the sound used to overdub obscenities in broadcasts. USAGE ALERT: Euphemisms may still be objectionable in some contexts and to some people.

**bleeped** |blēpt| *a/a* Extreme; extremely; very; etc. ORIGINS: Euphemism for **damn(ed)**. From the sound used to overdub obscenities in broadcasts. The *-ed* ending is in imitation of past participles. USAGE INFO: Used as an adjective ("bleeped fool") or an adverb ("bleeped stupid ass"). Note that the *-ed* is not optional for **bleeped**. USAGE ALERT: Euphemisms may still be objectionable in some contexts and to some people.

**bleeping** |BLĒP ing| *a/a* Extreme; extremely; very; etc. ORIGINS: Euphemism for **fucking**. From the sound used to overdub obscenities in broadcasts. The *-ing* ending is in imitation of present participles. USAGE INFO: Used as an adjective ("a bleeping fool") or an adverb ("bleeping cool movie"). USAGE ALERT: Euphemisms may still be objectionable in some contexts and to some people.

**blessed** |BLES id| *a/a* Extreme; extremely; very; etc. ORIGINS: Euphemism for **damned**. USAGE INFO: Literally means the opposite of **damned**, so becomes a contronym in this use. Used as an adjective ("not a blessed cent") or an adverb ("a blessed good thing"). USAGE ALERT: Euphemisms may still be objectionable in some contexts and to some people.

**blindside** |BLĪND sīd| *v* Attack unexpectedly or by surprise. ORIGINS: From the football term meaning "to attack an opponent from a point where his vision is obscured."

**blinking** |BLING king| *a/a* Extreme or extremely. ORIGINS: Originated as a euphemism for the British word **blooming**, itself a euphemism for **bloody**. The use of this term in the US may have been prompted by Shakespeare's phrase "the portrait of a blinking idiot" in II, ix, 57 of *The Merchant of Venice*. USAGE INFO: Used as an adjective ("blinking idiot") or an adverb ("blinking good idea"). USAGE ALERT: Speakers of British English are more likely than speakers of US English to know the actual origins of the word, but it may still be objectionable in some contexts and to some people.

**blip** |blip| *n* A small, easily amended problem; a temporary hiatus. ORIGINS: From technology jargon **blip**, which refers to the transient appearance of a small spot on a radar screen.

**blister** |BLIS tur| *n* A person who causes ongoing pain and annoyance. ORIGINS: Possibly by analogy to, say, the aggravation of walking with a blister on one's heel. USAGE ALERT: Usually used with intent to denigrate or insult and understood as such.

**blithering idiot** |BLI*TH* ur ing ID ē ut| *n* A stupid person who insists on spouting his or her ill-conceived ideas. ORIGINS: A variant of **blethering**, meaning "nonsense." USAGE ALERT: This is a harsher term than most synonyms for **stupid**, many of which could be said with pity or affection; this term is tinged with contempt. Usually used with intent to denigrate or insult and understood as such.

**blitz** |blitz| *v* To defeat utterly; to destroy; to overcome in a sudden and comprehensive attack. ORIGINS: From the German **blitzkrieg**, meaning "a violent surprise attack" (literally, "lightning war"), a strategy the Germans used in WWII.

USAGE INFO: Blitz is used figuratively for performing outstandingly on an examination, in which sense it is synonymous with **ace**, or the recent **pwn**.

**blivit, blivet** |BLIV it| *n* Something that is useless, annoying, or nameless. ORIGINS: A meaningless word used to set up a joke by inducing one's audience to ask, "what's a blivit?" The answer was/is a variant on "ten pounds of shit in a five pound bag."

**blockhead** |BLAHK hed| *n* A silly, unintelligent, or foolish person. ORIGINS: From SE **block**, as in a block of wood, and slang suffix -head. USAGE ALERT: Usually used with intent to denigrate or insult and understood as such.

**bloomer** |BLŪ mur| *n* A blunder. ORIGINS: **Blooming** is a British English substitute for **bloody**. Bloomer is said to combine slang **blooming** and SE **error**. USAGE ALERT: Speakers of British English are more likely than speakers of US English to know the actual ORIGINS of the word, and some of them may find it objectionable.

**blooper** |BLŪ pur| *n* An embarrassing verbal faux pas or other public mistake. ORIGINS: Possibly from extension of **oops** or from baseball jargon for a fly ball that goes over the infield but is too close in for the outfielders to catch.

**blow**[1] |blō| *v* To expose; to betray a secret. ORIGINS: Possibly shortened from longer slang phrases like blow the lid off (of) *st*. USAGE INFO: Can be a positive or a negative act, depending on the morality of keeping the secret.

**blow**[2] |blō| *v* To leave; to depart speedily. ORIGINS: May be by analogy with the blowing of the wind. USAGE INFO: Often incorporated in longer slang phrases, such as blow the joint, blow out of town.

**Blow (it)!** |blō / BLŌ it| *excl* An interjection expressing anger, frustration, dismay, etc. ORIGINS: Euphemism for **Damn! Fuck! Shit! Damn it!** or other words in the curse formula. USAGE ALERT. Euphemisms may still be objectionable in some contexts and to some people.

**blow it** |BLŌ it| *v* To botch, destroy, or ruin through ineptitude.

**Blow it out your ass!** |BLŌ it out yŏŏr AS| *excl* A contemptuous dismissal, often of something that's been said. ORIGINS: From the US military and slang **ass** meaning "the rear end or buttocks." USAGE ALERT: Usually used with intent to be rude and understood as such. In addition, the inclusion of **ass** and the graphic image will make this expression objectionable in some contexts and to some people.

**Blow it out your ear!** |BLŌ it out yŏŏr IR| *excl* A contemptuous dismissal, often of something that's been said. ORIGINS: Euphemism for **blow it out your ass**, which originated with the US military. USAGE ALERT: Usually used with intent to be rude and understood as such.

**blow off** |BLŌ awf| *v* To purposely miss an engagement; to skip out on something after committing. USAGE INFO: The object can be placed between the main verb and the particle as in "blow the meeting off," but is most often placed after the entire phrasal verb as in "blow off the meeting."

## blow off one's mouth/trap/yap |BLŌ ahf wunz MOUTH/TRAP/YAP|
*v* To praise oneself excessively; to reveal what was meant to be secret. ORIGINS: From slang **blow** meaning "boast or brag."

## blow one's bazoo |BLŌ wunz bu ZŪ| *v* To brag or boast. ORIGINS: From slang **blow** meaning "boast or brag" and slang **bazoo** meaning "mouth," which comes from Dutch **baizu** meaning "trumpet." *See* BLOW ONE'S OWN HORN/TRUMPET and TOOT ONE'S OWN HORN/TRUMPET.

## blow one's cool |BLŌ wunz KŪL| *v* To become angry; to lose control. ORIGINS: From extension of slang **blow** meaning "to squander or waste (money)" along with the conception of cool as a concrete possession that could be spent or lost.

## blow one's cork |BLŌ wunz KAWRK| *v* To explode with anger; to lose one's temper; to become furious. ORIGINS: By figurative extension of SE **blow** meaning "explode." **Cork** can be replaced with a number of other items that have to do with the topmost part of something: the word **top** itself, the closing mechanism at the top of a bottle (**stopper**), the highest part of a train engine (**stack**), or the item worn on top of the head (**wig**). USAGE INFO: *See* **BLOW THE LID OFF (OF)** *ST*, which has similar elements, but a quite different meaning.

## blow one's fuse* |BLŌ wunz FYŪZ| *v* To explode with anger. ORIGINS: A figurative use of the identical phrase from electrical engineering, which refers to the fact that a fuse is a device that protects electrical circuits from overloading. The fuse "blows" to interrupt the circuit and prevent damage. In other technical fields, such as plumbing, a gasket is used to prevent the escape of gas or fluid. If the gasket is "blown," the gas or fluid is released. This is also applied figuratively.
• blow one's gasket |BLŌ wunz GAS kit|

## blow one's mind |BLŌ wunz MĪND| *v* To become insane.

## blow one's own horn/trumpet |BLŌ wunz ōn HAWRN/TRUM pit| *v* To boast or brag. ORIGINS: From the practice of announcing important people with a fanfare played on brass instruments.

## blow one's stack |BLŌ wunz STAK| *v See* BLOW ONE'S CORK.

## blow one's stopper |BLŌ wunz STAH pur| *v See* BLOW ONE'S CORK.

## blow one's top |BLŌ wunz TAHP| *v See* BLOW ONE'S CORK.

## blow one's wig |BLŌ wunz WIG| *v See* BLOW ONE'S CORK.

## blow *sb* away |BLŌ *sb* u WĀ| *v* To kill by shooting with a firearm. ORIGINS: Possibly a reference to the projectile (bullet) being blown out of the gun due to the controlled explosion that is caused by firing.

## blow *sb/st* out of the water |BLŌ *sb/st* OUT uv thu WAH tur| *v* To launch a surprise attack of devastating proportions; to destroy. ORIGINS: Imagery comes from a naval battle. USAGE INFO: Can also mean to surprise pleasantly but utterly.

**blow smoke** |BLŌ SMŌK| *v* To promote an illusion or fantasy about oneself. ORIGINS: From slang **blow** meaning "boast or brag" and slang **smoke** meaning "illusion or fantasy—something beyond the reality."

**blow** *st* **sky-high** |BLŌ *st* SKĪ HĪ| *v* To destroy or ruin, often through a revelation of something that had been secret or concealed. USAGE INFO: This action can either be destructive or good (e.g., when done by a whistle-blower to expose illegal activity).

**blow** *st* **wide open** |BLŌ *st* WĪD Ō pun| *v* To make public something that had been secret. USAGE INFO: This action can either be destructive or good (e.g., when someone exposes a scandal).

**blow the coop** |BLŌ *thu* KŪP| *v* To leave suddenly; to escape from prison.

**blow the lid off (of)** *st* |BLŌ *thu* LID awf (uv) *st*| *v* To make public something that had been unknown or concealed. USAGE INFO: This action can either be destructive or good (e.g., when an expert makes great advances in a field of study, significantly changing its nature, or when someone exposes a scandal).

**blow the whistle on** *st* |BLŌ *thu* WIS ul ahn *st*| *v* To bring something to an end; to inform authorities about wrongdoing in order to stop it. ORIGINS: From the practice of a referee for a sporting event blowing a whistle to stop play when a rule is being violated.

**blow up**[1] |BLŌ up| *v* To lose control; to become enraged. ORIGINS: From SE **blow up** meaning "to explode," used figuratively.

**blow up**[2] |blō UP| *v* To make exaggerated claims. ORIGINS: From SE **blow up** meaning "to increase the size of by filling with air," used figuratively.

**blues** |blūz| *n* A fit of depression or unhappiness. ORIGINS: First recorded use in a letter by British actor David Garrick in 1741, using the spelling *Blews*. Also said to be short for an eighteenth century expression **blue devils**. USAGE INFO: Often with *the* as in "I've got the blues."

**bobble** |BAHB ul| *n* A mistake or blunder. ORIGINS: A generalization of the jargon of baseball and football for the mishandling or fumbled catch of the ball.

**bodacious, bodashes** |bō DĀ shus| *adj* Impressive. ORIGINS: Created by combining the SE words **bold** and **audacious**. Although its origins lie in the nineteenth century, the portmanteau word was popularized in the movie *Bill and Ted's Excellent Adventure* (1989). USAGE INFO: This word has great variety in its spellings, including **bowdacious**, and **bardacious**.

**bodylicious, bodilicious, bodelicious** |bahd i LISH us| *adj* Physically attractive. ORIGINS: From SE **body** and slang -licious; possibly a punning reference to bodacious.

**boil over** |BOIL Ō vur| *v* To become extremely angry. ORIGINS: From cooking.

**boiled up** |BOILD UP| *adj* To be very angry. ORIGINS: From cooking.

**boiling (mad)** | BOI ling / BOI ling MAD| *adj* To be very angry. ORIGINS: From cooking.

**bomb, the** |thu BAHM| *adj* The best; the most outstanding; the coolest.

**bone-breaker** |BŌN brā kur| *n* An extremely difficult problem. ORIGINS: Implying that the difficulty will literally break one's bones.

**bonehead** |BŌN hed| *n* An unintelligent person. ORIGINS: From SE **bone** and slang suffix -head, suggesting a head full of bone rather than brain, so not much thinking going on. USAGE ALERT: Often used with intent to denigrate or insult and understood as such.

**boner** |BŌN ur| *n* A mistake; a blunder. ORIGINS: The action of a **bonehead**. USAGE INFO: A **boner** may be mild or serious.

**bonk** |bahnk| *v* To hit, especially on the head. ORIGINS: From WWI military expression **bonk** meaning "to shell." Has an onomatopoeic element. USAGE INFO: Possibly because of the onomatopoeia, it is often used in jest or teasing.

**bonkers** |BAHN kurz| *adj* Crazy; insane. ORIGINS: Madness imagined as the result of a blow (**bonk**) to the head. USAGE ALERT: Often used with intent to denigrate or insult and understood as such. This way of speaking about *sb's* mental health may be considered insensitive and therefore objectionable in some contexts and by some people.

**boo-boo** |BŪ bū| *n* A mistake or blunder, often embarrassing. ORIGINS: Extended from **boob** meaning an error or blunder. USAGE INFO: The reduplication makes the word seem childish, thus it is often used self-consciously, employed when someone is acknowledging an embarrassing mistake, or used in an attempt to diminish the importance of another's misstep. **Boo-boo** is also a child's word for a minor injury.

**boob(y)** |būb / BŪ bē| *n* A stupid or foolish person; a dolt. ORIGINS: Possibly from the Spanish **bobo** meaning "a fool." **Boob** is an abbreviated form of **booby**. USAGE ALERT: Often used with intent to denigrate or insult and understood as such.

**boodle** |BŪ dul| *n* A large but unspecified amount of money. ORIGINS: Thought to be from Dutch **boedel** meaning "one's estate."

**boogie** |BOŎ gē| *v* To dance or move quickly. ORIGINS: From the dance called the boogie-woogie.

**book (it)** |BOŎK it| *v* To move quickly, especially when leaving. ORIGINS: From bookity-book, an obsolete slang word meaning "to run fast."

**boot (out)** |būt / BŪT out| *v* To fire; get rid of; throw out. ORIGINS: A reference to kicking someone out with a booted foot.

**bootlicker** |BŪT lik ur| *n* A servile flatterer; a toady or sycophant. ORIGINS: From the posture of groveling at *sb's* feet. USAGE INFO: May be used as a euphemism for **ass licker**. USAGE ALERT: Usually used with intent to denigrate or insult and understood as such.

**bootylicious** |bū tē LISH us| *adj* Physically attractive; possessing a shapely rear end. ORIGINS: From slang **booty** meaning "rear end or buttocks" and the slang suffix -licious from SE delicious. Originally negative and in contrast to bodylicious, it is now used as praise as well. USAGE ALERT: The reference to the rear end or buttocks in this term will make it objectionable in some contexts and to some people. Some people will also find it sexist.

**Booyah!** |BŪ yah| *excl* An exclamation of great success or victory.

**bop** |bahp| *v* To hit, strike. ORIGINS: An onomatopoeic word. USAGE INFO: Possibly due to the onomatopoeia, often used in jest.

**bore stiff** |BAWR STIF| *v* To be unbearably uninteresting.

**borked** |bawrkt| *adj* Broken; not functioning. ORIGINS: From the rejection of the nomination of Robert Heron Bork to the Supreme Court by the US Senate in 1987. Originally it meant "to savagely attack in order to prevent appointment to public office," but its use has broadened. Its use for **broken** may be particularly attractive because of the letters in common. USAGE INFO: Because this slang is only thirty years old, it may not be universally understood; nevertheless, it is widely used by people who have no idea of the connection to Robert Bork.

**bosh** |bahsh| *n* Worthless or untrue words. ORIGINS: Influenced by the slang noun bosh from the Turkish **bosh**, meaning "empty or worthless" and possibly reinforced by **bosh**, an artificial substitute for butter, some of which was manufactured at Hertogenbosch in Holland.

**boss** |baws| *adj* Outstanding; excellent; wonderful. ORIGINS: From a meaning of the slang noun boss, "an excellent person," which originates from the Dutch **baas**, meaning "master."

**boss (man)** |baws / BAWS man| *n* A leader of a company; the manager to whom one reports. ORIGINS: From the Dutch **baas**, meaning "master."

**Bother!** |BAH*TH* ur| *excl* An expression of mild irritation or annoyance. ORIGINS: Although more often used in British English, it is notable in fiction that is popular in the US, for example, the stories of Winnie-the-Pooh, which may have encouraged the US use. USAGE INFO: **Bother** is not linked to any particular PO word and is unlikely to offend for that reason. Nevertheless, it can be substituted for virtually any interjection denoting mild anger or frustration.

**Botheration!** |bah*th* u RĀ shun| *excl* An expression of irritation or annoyance. ORIGINS: Extended from SE **bother**. USAGE INFO: Due to length, it may register as a bit stronger than Bother!

**bottom-feeder** |BAHT um fē dur| *n* A despicable person. ORIGINS: From SE **bottom-feeder** meaning "a fish that feeds off the ocean floor"—i.e., on the waste created by other ocean life. Figuratively extended to mean "a scavenger; an opportunist who takes advantage of others' misfortune." From there it has been generalized to mean "a contemptible person." USAGE INFO: This phrase has no connection to the human rear end or buttocks. USAGE ALERT: Usually used with intent to denigrate or insult and understood as such.

**bottom line** |BAHT um LĪN| *n* A succinct summary of what's at stake; the essentials. ORIGINS: From SE **bottom line**, meaning "the profit/loss figure for an account."

**bounce** |bouns| *v* To fire; to expel by force. ORIGINS: Perhaps the force is so strong that the person who is expelled is imagined to bounce on the pavement.

**bounce back** |bouns BAK| *v* To recover quickly from adversity; to rebound. ORIGINS: From the concept of a ball or spring returning to its original position after a bounce.

**bow out** |BOU OUT| *v* To leave, resign, withdraw. ORIGINS: From the graceful gesture at the end of a performance, acknowledging the audience before the final curtain. USAGE INFO: Can indicate a gracious withdrawal or avoidance of an obligation. Can be used euphemistically to cover a more complicated/fraught situation.

**bowdacious** |bō DĀ shus| *adj See* BODACIOUS, BODASHES.

**bowl *sb* over**[1] |bōl *sb* Ō vur| *v* To take by surprise. ORIGINS: From the sport of cricket, in which the term means to retire a batsman by bowling in such a way that both bails are knocked off the wicket.

**bowl *sb* over**[2] |BŌL *sb* ō vur| *v* To overwhelm. ORIGINS: From the sport of cricket, in which the term means to retire a batsman by bowling in such a way that both bails are knocked off the wicket.

**bozo** |BŌ zō| *n* A clownish person; a fool; an incompetent person. ORIGINS: Recent US usage most likely influenced by the character of Bozo the Clown, popular in children's television in the last half of the twentieth century. The voice of Krusty the Clown on *The Simpsons* television show is said to be a nod to Bozo. USAGE ALERT: Usually used with intent to denigrate or insult and understood as such.

**brag oneself up** |BRAG wun self UP| *v* To boast about oneself.

**brain** |brān| *v* To hit on the head; to knock out. ORIGINS: Like **bean**, a slang verb that refers to the object of the action.

**brainiac** |BRĀN ē ak| *n* A very intelligent person. ORIGINS: From the D.C. Comics villain, Brainiac, whose name blends SE **brain** and **maniac**. USAGE INFO: The word can be used with no inference of villainy.

**brass** |bras| *n* High ranking officials or senior officers in business, government, or military settings. ORIGINS: From **brass hat**, a senior officer in the police, so named for the adornment (gold braid, for example) on their helmets. USAGE INFO: Can be singular, but usually plural.

**break one's ass** |BRĀK wunz AS| *v* To work very hard; to put in an enormous effort. ORIGINS: From slang **ass** meaning "the rear end or buttocks." USAGE INFO: Compare with **break *sb*'s ass**. USAGE ALERT: The reference to the human rear end or buttocks will render this phrase objectionable in some contexts and to some people.

**break one's balls** | BRĀK wunz BAWLZ | *v* To work very hard; to put in an enormous effort. ORIGINS: From slang **balls** meaning "testicles." USAGE INFO: Don't confuse this form with **break sb's balls** (that is, someone else's **balls**), which means "to beat up; to harass or annoy." **Break one's balls** is usually only used to refer to, or used self-referentially by, males. USAGE ALERT: The inclusion of **balls** will make this phrase objectionable in some contexts and to some people.

**break one's buns** | BRĀK wunz BUNZ | *v* To work very hard; to put in an enormous effort. ORIGINS: Euphemism for **break one's ass**. From slang **buns**, a euphemism for slang **ass**, meaning "the rear end or buttocks." USAGE INFO: Compare with **break sb's buns** meaning "to beat up; to harass or annoy." USAGE ALERT: The reference to the human rear end or buttocks will render this phrase objectionable in some contexts and to some people. Some people will find **buns** less offensive than **butt**, which is, in turn, often considered less objectionable than **ass**.

**break one's butt** | BRĀK wunz BUT| *v* To work very hard; to put in an enormous effort. ORIGINS: Euphemism for **break one's ass**. From slang **butt**, a euphemism for slang **ass**, meaning "the rear end or buttocks." USAGE INFO: Compare with **break sb's butt**, meaning "to beat up; to harass or annoy." USAGE ALERT: The reference to the human rear end or buttocks will render this phrase objectionable in some contexts and to some people.

**break one's chops** |BRĀK wunz CHAHPS| *v* To work hard; to talk ceaselessly. ORIGINS: From SE **break** and slang **chops**, which refers to the mouth. USAGE ALERT: In its first meaning, this phrase is synonymous with **break one's ass**, **buns**, or **butt**, but is less offensive because of the particular part of the body referenced. But also, unlike those phrases, it has a second meaning that ties explicitly to the mouth.

**break out** |BRĀK out| *v* To leave, escape. USAGE INFO: **Break out** is SE when referring to escaping from jail. It is likely to be considered slang when said, say, to one's employer in the course of suddenly leaving one's job.

**break sb up** |BRĀK sb up| *v* To make someone laugh heartily. USAGE INFO: **Break sb up** is a contronym and can also mean "to make someone extremely upset." **Break up** without an object means "to burst into laughter" or "to stop dating."

**break sb's ass** |BRĀK sb's AS| *v* To beat up; to harass or annoy. ORIGINS: From slang **ass** meaning "the rear end or buttocks." USAGE INFO: Don't confuse this form with **break one's ass** (that is, one's own **ass**), which means "to make a great effort; to work very hard." USAGE ALERT: The inclusion of **ass** will make this phrase objectionable in some contexts and to some people.

**break sb's balls** |BRĀK sb's BAWLZ| *v* To beat up; to harass or annoy. ORIGINS: From slang **balls** meaning "testicles." USAGE INFO: Don't confuse this form with **break one's balls** (that is, one's own **balls**), which means "to make a great effort; to work very hard." **Break sb's balls** is usually only used to refer to males. **Break sb's balls** may suggest a more personal and more violent attack than **break**

B

*sb's* **ass**. USAGE ALERT: The inclusion of **balls** will make this phrase objectionable in some contexts and to some people.

**break *sb's* buns** | BRĀK *sb's* BUNZ | *v* To beat up; to harass or annoy. ORIGINS: Euphemism for **break *sb's* ass**. From slang **buns**, a euphemism for slang **ass**, meaning "the rear end or buttocks." USAGE INFO: Since spanking has been a standard punishment for some time, this expression does not seem as violating as **break *sb's* balls**, for example. USAGE ALERT: The reference to the human rear end or buttocks will render this phrase objectionable in some contexts and to some people. Some people will find **buns** less offensive than **butt**, which is, in turn, often considered less objectionable than **ass**.

**break *sb's* butt** |BRĀK *sb's* BUT| *v* To beat up; to harass or annoy. ORIGINS: Euphemism for **break *sb's* ass**. From slang **butt**, a euphemism for slang **ass**, meaning "the rear end or buttocks." USAGE INFO: Don't confuse this form with **break one's butt** (that is, one's own **butt**), which means "to make a great effort; to work very hard." USAGE ALERT: Although it is a euphemism, the inclusion of **butt** will make this phrase objectionable in some contexts and to some people.

**break *sb's* chops** |brāk *sb's* CHAHPS| *v* To nag *sb*; to criticize *sb* harshly. ORIGINS: From SE **break** and **chops**, which refers to the mouth. USAGE INFO: Don't confuse this form with **break one's chops** (that is, one's own **chops**), which means "to make a great effort; to work very hard."

**break *sb's* head** |BRĀK *sb's* HED| *v* To deliver a violent blow to *sb's* skull (such that they are overcome); to defeat in a physical fight.

**break up** |BRĀK up| *v* To laugh heartily. USAGE INFO: **Break up** is a contronym and can also mean "to become extremely upset, hysterical," or "to stop dating." **Break *sb* up** with an object means "to cause to burst into laughter."

**breeze** |brēz| *n* Simple, easy to resolve or complete. ORIGINS: From analogy to wind in being able to "blow" through something. USAGE INFO: Often used in the phrase "It's a breeze."

**breeze** |brēz| *v* To move swiftly and effortlessly. ORIGINS: From analogy to the movement of unimpeded wind.

**bring off** |BRING awf| *v* To succeed, accomplish.

**bring *sb* down a peg (or two)** |BRING *sb* DOUN u peg / BRING *sb* doun u PEG awr tū| *v* To humiliate. ORIGINS: A counterpart to the slang phrase **come down a peg (or two)**.

**bring *sb* up to speed** |BRING *sb* up tū spēd| *v* To supply *sb* with all information that s/he is lacking. ORIGINS: Treats knowledge and understanding as if they were fuel which, once attained, allow full power to be reached. USAGE INFO: Usually used when *sb* is absent, comes late, or is a recent hire and needs to be made aware of what happened during his/her absence or prior to his/her arrival.

**brown (nose)*** |broun / BROUN noz| *n* An obsequious flatterer. ORIGINS: From the imagined behavior of a literal **ass-kisser**: **brown** refers to (the color of)

excrement. USAGE ALERT: The reference to excrement and the graphic image will make this term objectionable in some contexts and to some people. In addition, it is usually used with intent to denigrate or insult and understood as such.
• **brown noser** |BROUN nōz ur|

**brush off** |BRUSH awf| *v* To dismiss; to ignore; to treat with contempt. ORIGINS: From the SE brush off as in using the hand to flick a small piece of lint off of one's clothing.

**brute** |brūt| *n* An extremely large or difficult problem. ORIGINS: From SE **brute**. USAGE INFO: Often in the phrase "a brute of a...."

**bubblehead** |BUB ul hed| *n* A silly, careless, unintelligent person. ORIGINS: From SE **bubble** and slang suffix **-head**. Bubbles are full of air, so a **bubblehead** has an empty head. USAGE INFO: Similar to **airhead** in meaning. USAGE ALERT: Usually used with intent to denigrate or insult and understood as such.

**buck the system** |buk *th*u SIS tum| *v* To oppose or resist the standard approach. ORIGINS: Related to SE **buck**, meaning "to throw or toss by arching one's back." As a bucking bronco seeks to unseat a rider, **bucking the system** is done in an attempt to overthrow the current state of affairs.

**-bucket** |BUK it| *sfx See* -BAG.

**bucket of shit** |BUK it uv SHIT| *n* Falsehoods; untruths; lies. ORIGINS: From SE **bucket**, a container, and slang **shit** meaning "excrement." USAGE ALERT: Because this term includes the word **shit**, it will be considered objectionable in some contexts and by some people.

**buckle down** |BUK ul doun| *v* To get to work; to apply oneself diligently to a task. ORIGINS: Possibly from the practice of fastening one's buckles (on armor or a sandal) preparatory to engaging in a task. USAGE INFO: *See* KNUCKLE DOWN.

**buckle under** |BUK ul UN dur| *v* To give in; to consent reluctantly. ORIGINS: Related to SE **buckle** meaning "bending or warping under pressure." USAGE INFO: *See* KNUCKLE UNDER.

**bucks** |buks| *n* Unspecified amount of money in bills. ORIGINS: By extension from slang **buck** meaning "a dollar."

**buddy up** |BUD ē YUP| *v* To join together as friends in a pair.

**buff** |buf| *sfx* An amateur enthusiast. ORIGINS: From the uniform color (buff) of volunteer fire fighters in New York City at one time. Follows a noun or gerund, as in a sports buff, skiing buff.

**buffalo** |BUF u lō| *v* To pressure; to intimidate. ORIGINS: From the size and power of the SE **buffalo**.

**bug** |bug| *n* A malfunction, defect, or problem. ORIGINS: By extension from the annoyance of an SE **bug** ("an insect"). USAGE INFO: Frequently used of problems arising in computer software.

**bug** |bug| *v* To irritate; to annoy. ORIGINS: To act like an SE **bug** ("an insect").

**Bug off!** |bug AWF| *excl* Go away! ORIGINS: A reference to the experience of having bees or other insects hovering in an annoying way. USAGE ALERT: Often used with intent to be rude and understood as such.

**bug out** |bug out| *v* To leave or take off; to run away. ORIGINS: A reference to a flitting insect. USAGE ALERT: Another meaning of **bug out**, which extends the idea of a bug as irritating or annoying, is "to go insane; to be driven mad."

**buggy** |BUG ē| *adj* Crazy. ORIGINS: The idea is that one's mind has become infested with insects. USAGE ALERT: Often used with intent to denigrate or insult and understood as such. This way of speaking about sb's mental health may be considered insensitive and therefore objectionable in some contexts and by some people.

**build a fire under** *sb* |bild u FĪR un dur *sb*| *v* To urge or goad into action. ORIGINS: Based on the idea that a fire burning very close nearby would make even the laziest person anxious to get moving.

**bull** |bool| *See* BULLSHIT.

**bulldoze** |BOOL dōz| *v* To intimidate; to coerce; to force by using violence. ORIGINS: From the size and power of the SE **bulldozer**.

**bullshit** |BOOL shit| *n* Nonsense; untruths; lies. ORIGINS: From SE **bull** (the animal) and slang **shit**, i.e., bull excrement—which could be described as "worthless and having a stench"—applied figuratively to worthless or deceptive statements. USAGE ALERT: The reference to excrement will make this term objectionable in some contexts and to some people.

**bullshit** |BOOL shit| *adj* Inferior; worthless; rubbishy. ORIGINS: From SE **bull** (the animal) and slang **shit**, i.e., bull excrement—which could be described as "worthless and having a stench"—applied figuratively to things of poor quality. USAGE ALERT: The reference to excrement will make this term objectionable in some contexts and to some people.

**bully** |BOO lē| *adj* Excellent; first-rate; splendid. ORIGINS: Draws on the earliest slang meaning of **bully** as "a good person or companion." USAGE INFO: Used (most often ironically) in the phrase "bully for you."

**bum** |bum| *n* A contemptible person; a general term of abuse. ORIGINS: Expanded meaning and shortened form from slang **bummer** meaning "vagrant or tramp." **Bum** meaning "vagrant or tramp" now seems to be considered informal. USAGE ALERT: Usually used with intent to denigrate or insult and understood as such.

**bum** |bum| *adj* Malfunctioning; out-of-order; broken. ORIGINS: Possibly by analogy with slang **bum** meaning "vagrant or tramp" as someone who is not functioning within the standard expectations of society.

**bum** |bum| *v* To beg. ORIGINS: From the informal **bum**, meaning "vagrant or tramp." USAGE INFO: Unlike **beg**, **bum** does not require a preposition. Compare: "to beg for a meal"; "to bum a meal."

**bum** |bum| *sfx* A fan, usually of a sport. ORIGINS: Extension of informal **bum**, meaning "vagrant or tramp." USAGE INFO: Suggests obsession or unhealthy level of interest, possibly to the detriment of other (necessary) activities, particularly work; e.g., a person who devotes more than what the observer deems as enough time to surfing may be styled a beach bum.

**bum deal** |BUM DĒL| *n* A bad bargain; an agreement that falls through. ORIGINS: Slang bum meaning "broken" and SE **deal**.

**bum rap** |BUM RAP| *n* A false accusation; an unfair sentence. ORIGINS: From slang bum meaning "unfair" and slang rap meaning "a criminal charge or jail sentence."

**bummed (out)** |bumd / BUMD OUT| *adj* Depressed; miserable; very unhappy. ORIGINS: Extended from slang adjective bum meaning "bad for (you)."

**bump¹** |bump| *v* To glamorize; to adorn so as to increase value.

**bump²** |bump| *v* To dismiss someone from employment or a group. ORIGINS: Possibly by extension of SE **bump** meaning "to knock into; to shift to a new position; to push (out of the way)." USAGE ALERT: **Bump** is a contronym and can also mean "to promote."

**bump³, also bump off** |bump / BUMP AWF| *v* To kill; to murder; to shoot to death. ORIGINS: Expanded from SE **bump** meaning "to knock into; to shift to a new position; to push (out of the way)." USAGE INFO: By extension, bump oneself off means "to commit suicide."

**bun-buster** |BUN bus tur| *n* Extremely difficult, overwhelming, arduous, or punishing problem. ORIGINS: From SE **bust** meaning "to break" combined with slang for a core body part: **bun**, a euphemism for slang **ass** meaning "the rear end or buttocks." USAGE ALERT: Although **bun** is generally considered less objectionable than **ass** or **butt**, it will still be objectionable in some contexts and to some people. A less objectionable choice would be gut-buster.

**bundle** |BUN dul| *n* A large amount of money.

**bunk** |bungk| *n* Nonsense; worthless talk; untruths, lies. ORIGINS: Shortened from bunkum meaning "insincere or empty talk" from the characterization of a speech made by a congressman from Buncombe County, North Carolina.

**burn¹** |burn| *v* To cheat or swindle.

**burn², also burn up** |burn / BURN up| *v* To become very angry. ORIGINS: A number of slang terms for anger relate to heat.

**burn rubber** |BURN RUB ur| *v* To speed in a car, especially accelerating from a standstill to a very high speed. ORIGINS: From the effect on rubber tires caused by such driving.

**burn *sb* up** |BURN *sb* up| *v* To cause extreme anger. ORIGINS: A number of slang terms for anger relate to heat.

**burning up** |BUR ning up| *adj* Feeling extremely angry. ORIGINS: A number of slang terms for anger relate to heat.

**bursting at the seams with** |BUR sting at *thu* SĒMZ with| *adj* Extremely full of; containing an extraordinary number of. ORIGINS: From the results of overloading a bag with too many or too heavy items.

**bush league** |BOOSH lēg| *adj* Amateurish attempt; failure. ORIGINS: From baseball jargon meaning literally, "minor league"; figuratively, "unprofessional."

**bushed** |boosht| *adj* Extremely tired; exhausted. ORIGINS: As tired as if one had been wandering for a long time in the woods/bush.

**bushels** |BOOSH ulz| *n* A large, unspecified amount; a great deal. ORIGINS: From the SE unit of measure, a **bushel**.

**bushwhack** |BOOSH hwak| *v* Attack unexpectedly; ambush. ORIGINS: From SE **bushwhack**, meaning "to travel through a thickly wooded area by clearing away branches and bushes as one goes." Because an attack on *sb* emerging from thick woods is a technique of guerilla warfare, the word became connected with such an ambush.

**business end** |BIZ nis end| *n* The functional part; the part that really matters. ORIGINS: The part that does the business.

**bust** |bust| *v* To smash or break, especially using force; to render useless or inoperable.

**bust(ed)**[1] |bust / BUS tid| *adj* Bankrupt. ORIGINS: Equivalent to informal **broke** meaning "having no money," just as the past participle forms slang **busted** and SE **broken** are synonyms for "damaged in such a way as to render non-functional." In each case, the form of *bust* is the more slangy word.

**bust(ed)**[2] |bust / BUS tid| *adj* Broken; rendered non-functional. ORIGINS: Equivalent to SE **broken**. Notice the analogous relationship of slang **busted** and informal **broke**, synonyms for "having no money." In each case, the form of *bust* is the more slangy word.

**bust a gut** |BUST u gut| *v* To laugh very hard. USAGE INFO: This phrase also means "to work very hard; to put in an enormous effort."

**bust one's ass** |BUST wunz AS| *v* To work very hard; to put in an enormous effort. ORIGINS: From slang **ass** meaning "the rear end or buttocks." USAGE INFO: Compare with **bust sb's ass**. USAGE ALERT: The reference to the human rear end or buttocks will render this phrase objectionable in some contexts and to some people. Some people will find **buns** or **butt** less offensive than **ass**.

**bust one's balls** |BUST wunz BAWLS| *v* To work very hard; to put in an enormous effort. ORIGINS: From slang **balls**, euphemism for SE **testicles**. USAGE INFO: This phrase is usually only used self-referentially by males. USAGE ALERT: The reference to the male sex organs will render this phrase objectionable in some contexts and to some people.

**bust one's buns** |BUST wunz BUNZ| *v* To work very hard; to put in an enormous effort. ORIGINS: Euphemism for **bust one's ass**. From slang **buns**, a euphemism for slang **ass**, meaning "the rear end or buttocks." USAGE INFO: **Buns** is more apt than **butt** to be used coyly, with a wink and a nod, so to speak. USAGE ALERT: The reference to the human rear end or buttocks will render this phrase objectionable in some contexts and to some people. Some people will find **buns** less offensive than **butt**, which is, in turn, often considered less objectionable than **ass**.

**bust one's butt** |BUST wunz BUT| *v* To work very hard; to put in an enormous effort. ORIGINS: Euphemism for **bust one's ass**. From slang **butt**, a euphemism for slang **ass** meaning "the rear end or buttocks." USAGE INFO: Compare with **bust *sb's* butt**. USAGE ALERT: The reference to the human rear end or buttocks will render this phrase objectionable in some contexts and to some people. Some people will find **butt** less offensive than **ass**, but possibly more offensive than **buns**.

**bust one's chops** |BUST wunz CHAHPS| *v* To work hard; to talk ceaselessly. ORIGINS: Slang bust meaning "to break" and chops, which refers to the mouth. USAGE ALERT: In its first meaning, this phrase is synonymous with **bust one's ass**, **bust one's butt**, **bust one's buns**, and **bust one's balls**, but is less offensive because of the particular part of the body referenced. But also, unlike those phrases, it has a second meaning that ties explicitly to the mouth.

**bust one's gut** |BUST wunz GUT| *v* To laugh very hard. USAGE INFO: This phrase also means "to work very hard; to put in an enormous effort."

**bust one's hump** |BUST wunz HUMP| *v* To work very hard; to put in an enormous effort. ORIGINS: Generalized from SE **hump** meaning "a back deformity" to mean "the back." It has no relationship to the slang verb **hump** meaning "to engage in sex." USAGE INFO: The phrase is, roughly, a slang version of "doing back-breaking labor." USAGE ALERT: Because **hump** referring to the back is not in common use, this term may send people's minds toward the other slang meaning.

**bust out** |BUST out| *v* To escape (particularly, from prison). USAGE INFO: Synonymous with **break out**, but more slangy.

**bust *sb's* ass** |BUST *sb's* AS| *v* To beat up; to harass or annoy. ORIGINS: From slang **ass** meaning "rear end or buttocks." USAGE INFO: Don't confuse this form with **break** or **bust one's ass** (that is, one's own **ass**), which means "to make a great effort; to work very hard." USAGE ALERT: The inclusion of **ass** will make this phrase objectionable in some contexts and to some people.

**bust *sb's* balls** |BUST *sb's* BAWLZ| *v* To beat up; to harass or annoy. ORIGINS: From slang **balls** meaning "testicles." USAGE INFO: Don't confuse this form with **break** or **bust one's balls** (that is, one's own **balls**),which means "to make a great effort; to work very hard." **Balls** is usually only used to refer to, or used self-referentially by, males. USAGE ALERT: The inclusion of **balls** will make this phrase objectionable in some contexts and to some people.

**bust *sb's* buns** | BUST *sb's* BUNZ | *v* To beat up; to harass or annoy. ORIGINS: Euphemism for **beat *sb's* ass**. From slang **buns**, a euphemism for slang **ass**, meaning "the rear end or buttocks." USAGE INFO: Since spanking has been a standard punishment for some time, this expression does not seem as violating as **bust *sb's* balls**, for example. USAGE ALERT: The reference to the human rear end or buttocks will render this phrase objectionable in some contexts and to some people. Some people will find **buns** less offensive than **butt**, which is, in turn, often considered less objectionable than **ass**.

**bust *sb*'s butt** |BUST *sb's* BUT| *v* To beat up; to harass or annoy. ORIGINS: Euphemism for **bust *sb*'s ass**. From slang **butt**, a euphemism for slang **ass** meaning "the rear end or buttocks." USAGE INFO: Don't confuse this form with **break** or **bust one's butt** (that is, one's own **butt**), which means "to make a great effort; to work very hard." USAGE ALERT: The reference to the human rear end or buttocks will render this phrase objectionable in some contexts and to some people. Some people will find **butt** less offensive than **ass**.

**bust *sb*'s chops** |BUST *sb's* CHAHPS| *v* To nag *sb*; to criticize *sb* harshly. ORIGINS: Slang **bust** meaning "to break" and **chops**, which refers to the mouth. USAGE INFO: Don't confuse this form with **bust one's chops** (that is, one's own **chops**), which means "to make a great effort; to work very hard."

**bust-up¹** |BUST up| *n* A financial collapse. ORIGINS: The slang verb **bust** means "break" and a **bust-up** is the result of "breaking the bank."

**bust-up²** |BUST up| *n* A serious argument or quarrel, especially a relationship-ending one. ORIGINS: An incident of "breaking," in this case, applied to a relationship. *See* BUST-UP.

**but good** |but GŎOD| *adv* To a great degree or extent. USAGE INFO: Used after the word or phrase it modifies as in "I hope she beats him but good."

**butt in** |BUD IN| *v* To get in the way; to interfere. ORIGINS: From SE **butt** meaning "to push with the head or horns." USAGE INFO: This use of **butt** is not anatomical, although many people may not know that.

**butt-buster** |BUT bus tur| *n* Extremely difficult, overwhelming, arduous, or punishing problem. ORIGINS: From SE **bust** meaning "to break" combined with slang for a core body part: **butt**, a euphemism for slang **ass** meaning "the rear end or buttocks." USAGE ALERT: Although **butt** is generally considered less objectionable than **ass**, it will still be objectionable in some contexts and to some people. A less objectionable choice would be **gut-buster**.

**butter up** |BUT ur up| *v* To flatter; to curry favor. ORIGINS: From the SE noun **butter**, meaning "flattery." The conception is of smoothly spreading flattery.

**butterfingers** |BUT ur fin gerz| *n* A person who drops or fails to catch things. ORIGINS: From imagining a person whose fingers are covered with butter, therefore too slippery to maintain a grip. USAGE INFO: May be considered an insult, depending on context.

**butthead** |BUT hed| *n* An obnoxious, crude, and stupid person. ORIGINS: From slang **butt**, a euphemism for **ass**, meaning "the rear end or buttocks" and slang suffix -head. The concept is of a person who has a rear end or buttocks for a head. Popularized since the 1990s by the MTV television series *Beavis and Butthead*. USAGE ALERT: Because it refers to the human rear end or buttocks, this term will be considered objectionable in some contexts and by some people.

**buttinsky, buttinski** |bu TIN skē| *n* A meddler; someone who intrudes or interferes. ORIGINS: From slang **butt in** meaning "to intrude," from SE **butt** meaning "to push with the head or horns," combined with the **-ski /-sky** ending that is characteristic of many Slavic surnames. USAGE INFO: This use of **butt** is not anatomical, although many people may not know that. USAGE ALERT: Because it singles out a particular ethnic group, this term will be considered objectionable in some contexts and to some people. Usually used with intent to denigrate or insult and understood as such.

**buttload** |BUT lōd| *n* A large quantity. ORIGINS: On the model of the more oft-heard slang **shitload**, meaning "an unspecified large amount." At the same time, **buttload** is, in fact, a synonym for **shit**. From slang **butt** meaning "the rear end or buttocks" and acting as a euphemism for **ass**. USAGE ALERT: Because it mentions the human rear end or buttocks, refers to excrement, and presents a graphic image, this term will be considered objectionable in some contexts and by some people.

**Button your lip/face!** |BUT 'n yŏŏr LIP/FĀS| *excl* Be quiet! ORIGINS: The idea is that the mouth is sealed shut and no words can escape. USAGE ALERT: Often used with intent to denigrate or insult and understood as such.

**buy** |bī| *v* To accept completely.

**buy the farm\*** |BĪ *thu* fahrm| *v* To die, especially suddenly, or by violence. ORIGINS: From US Air Force slang referring to a scenario in which a jet pilot dies crashing into a farm and the farmer is awarded enough in damages to pay off the mortgage, with the result that the pilot has, in effect, bought the farm. USAGE INFO: *It* can replace either *farm* or *ranch*.
• buy the ranch |BĪ *thu* ranch|
• buy it |BĪ it|

**Buzz off!** |buz AWF| *excl* Go away! ORIGINS: A reference to the experience of having bees or other insects buzzing around annoyingly. USAGE ALERT: Often used with intent to be rude and understood as such.

**Bwa-ha-ha-ha!** |BWAH hah hah hah| *excl* Evil laugh. USAGE INFO: A variety of spellings exist.

**C&G** Chuckle and grin.

**C4N** Ciao for now!

**CBB** Can't be bothered.

**CSA** Cool, sweet, awesome. (Context should help distinguish from Confederate States of America.)

**CSG** Chuckle, snicker, grin.

**CSN** Chuckle, snicker, grin.

**CYA** See ya! Also Cover your ass!

**CYL** See you/ya later! Catch you later!

**cadge** |kadj| *v* To beg. ORIGINS: Possibly a back-formation from the noun **cadger**, meaning "a peddler." USAGE INFO: **Cadge** does not require a preposition: "cadge a meal."

**cage rattler** |KĀJ rat lur| *n* A person who stubbornly does something that causes annoyance to others (usually in the process of trying to achieve a higher end). ORIGINS: From imagining a caged animal in a zoo banging into the cage bars while seeking a change in conditions. USAGE INFO: This phrase is a synonym of **boat rocker**, i.e., someone who figuratively rocks the boat for others while seeking a change in the status quo.

**call down** |kawl DOUN| *v* To scold or reprimand. ORIGINS: Perhaps referring to the SE meaning of **down**, "from a higher to a lower place or position," since being called down damages one's status.

**call on the carpet** |KAWL ahn *thu* KAR pit| *v* To scold or reprimand. ORIGINS: Refers to a carpet that is placed in front of the boss's desk, so the suggestion is that one is called into the boss's office to be scolded or dressed down.

**call the shots** |kawl *thu* SHAHTS| *v* To lead; to dictate the strategy to be adopted. ORIGINS: From the sphere of gambling with dice.

**can** |kan| *v* To fire, abandon, or dismiss. ORIGINS: From the slang meaning of **can**—a euphemism for **ass** meaning "the rear end or buttocks"—in the phrase: **to toss out on one's can**. USAGE INFO: Sufficiently disconnected from its origins that it is unlikely to be objectionable.

**can of worms** |kan uv WURMZ| *n* A complex or serious problem. ORIGINS: The unappealing scenario of discovering a difficult problem is compared in the phrase to the sensation upon opening a can and unexpectedly finding it full of worms.

**candy-ass** |KAN dē as| *n* One who is afraid; a sissy. ORIGINS: From slang **candy** meaning "a cowardly, weak person." Note that both the noun and the adjective form are used as adjectives. *See* **-ASS(ED)** for more information about the suffix. USAGE ALERT: Because it contains the word **ass**, this phrase will be objectionable in some contexts and to some people. Usually used with intent to denigrate or insult and understood as such.

**can't cut the mustard** |KANT kut *thu* MUS turd| *v* To fail to perform adequately; to be unable to attain the set standard. USAGE INFO: More often found in the negative than the positive: you rarely, if ever, hear of people who *can* cut the mustard.

**Capiche? Capisce?** |ku PĒSH| *phr* Do you understand? ORIGINS: Adapted from Italian **capisci** meaning "Do you understand?" USAGE INFO: Numerous other spellings are used as well.

**Capiche! Capisce!** |ku PĒSH| *excl* I understand! ORIGINS: Adapted from Italian *capisco* meaning "I understand." USAGE INFO: Numerous other spellings are used as well. Note that it is often used as a response to the question **Capiche?** or **Capisce?** and hardly ever as a response to a question about understanding phrased another way.

**carry the ball** |KER ē *thu* BAWL| *v* To lead; to take charge; to take responsibility for the course of action. ORIGINS: From the sphere of football, rugby, and other sports in which players run with the ball to advance it toward a goal.

**cash in**[1] |KASH in| *v* To make a profit, especially by exploiting circumstances. USAGE INFO: Because it may carry the implication of exploitation, this phrase may imply criticism.

**cash in**[2], **also cash in one's chips** |KASH in / KASH in wunz CHIPS| *v* To die. ORIGINS: From the world of gambling: when one is withdrawing from a game, one exchanges one's chips for cash as one's final act before departing.

**cat's chance in hell** |KATS chans in hel| *n* No chance of achieving one's goal. ORIGINS: Figurative use of SE **hell** meaning "the alternative to heaven; the realm of the devil." USAGE INFO: Usually after the verb *have,* as in "He doesn't have a cat's chance in hell of winning *American Idol.*" USAGE ALERT: The inclusion of the word **hell** in the phrase will render it objectionable in some contexts and to some people.

**catbird seat, in the** |in *thu* KAT burd SĒT| *adj* In a privileged position; in a position of power or prominence. ORIGINS: Likely from the catbird's choice of the highest perch in a tree from which to sing. The phrase was popularized by US sports announcer Red Barber in his career from 1934–1966, and by author James Thurber who quoted Red Barber in the short story "The Catbird Seat" (1942), but has remained popular.

**catch it in the neck** |KACH it in *thu* NEK| *v* To be verbally attacked; to be punished or criticized severely. ORIGINS: A figurative interpretation of a phrase that was originally used literally and meant "to be killed or severely wounded." USAGE INFO: The location of the wound makes the attack seem particularly blameworthy and unjustified.

**catch on (to)** |kach AHN / kach AHN tū| *v* To come to understand.

**catch red-handed** |KACH red HAN did| *v* To catch in the act of doing something morally wrong or illegal. ORIGINS: The image of red hands comes from the Scottish law stating that blood-stained hands were required for the sheriff to act against a suspected murderer.

**catch *sb* with his/her pants down** |KACH *sb* with hiz/hur PANTS doun| *v* To catch *sb* in the act of doing something morally wrong or illegal. ORIGINS: The idea is of seeing *sb* commit the crime (the suggestion is adultery, rape, or something similar or—taken figuratively—of catching *sb* in an embarrassing and defenseless position), incontrovertible proof of guilt. USAGE INFO: Despite the image, this phrase can be used of any embarrassing, illegal, or immoral act, not just sex crimes.

**catch some z's** |KACH sum zēz| *v* To take a nap. ORIGINS: *Z's* are used as an onomatopoeic representation of sleep.

**catch with a hand in the cookie jar/till** |KACH with u HAND in *thu* KŎOK ē jar / KACH with u HAND in *thu* TIL| *v* To catch in the act of doing something morally wrong or illegal, especially theft or embezzlement. ORIGINS: The **cookie jar** is a place for storing goodies. The **till** is a place to store money. The idea is of seeing *sb* commit the crime, incontrovertible proof of guilt.

**catch with a smoking gun** |KACH with u smōk ing gun| *v* To catch in the act of doing something morally wrong or illegal. ORIGINS: The idea is of catching *sb* holding a firearm used in a crime, still giving off evidence of having been just fired (smoking).

**catch with the goods/merchandise** |KACH with *thu* GŎODZ / KACH with *thu* MUR chun dīz| *v* To catch in the act of doing something morally wrong or illegal. ORIGINS: The idea is of catching a thief or robber still in possession of the stolen items.

**Catch you later! Catch ya later! Catcha later! Catchya later!** |KA chū LĀ tur| *excl* See you later! ORIGINS: From slang catch meaning to meet in a casual social encounter.

**cave in** |CĀV in| *v* To yield to pressure. ORIGINS: The reference is to a cave roof collapsing. USAGE INFO: Often in the phrase "cave in to *sb/st*."

**cert** |surt| *n* A certainty. ORIGINS: Shortened from SE **certainty**.

**chance it** |CHANS it| *v* To take a risk. ORIGINS: Extension of SE **chance**.

**chatterbox** |CHAT ur bahks| *n* A person who doesn't know when to be quiet. USAGE ALERT: Usually used with intent to denigrate or insult and understood as such.

**chazzerei, chazerei** |KHAHZ ur ī| *n* See CHOZZERAI, CHOZERAI.

**cheapo** |CHĒ pō| *n* A mean or stingy person. ORIGINS: From SE **cheap**. USAGE ALERT: May be used jocularly or as an insult.

**cheapo¹** |CHĒ pō| *adj* Selling for a very small amount of money. ORIGINS: From SE **cheap**.

**cheapo²** |CHĒ pō| *adj* Produced cheaply; of inferior quality. ORIGINS: From SE **cheap**.

**cheapskate** |CHĒP skāt| *n* A mean, stingy person. ORIGINS: From SE **cheap** and slang skate, meaning "a mean or contemptible person." USAGE ALERT: Usually used with intent to denigrate or insult and understood as such.

**check out** |CHEK OUT| *v* To die. ORIGINS: From the practice of signing out just prior to leaving a hotel or other temporary residence.

**cheesy, cheezy** |CHĒ zē| *adj* Of poor quality; shoddy; cheap and nasty; corny. ORIGINS: Extending the literal meaning of "smelly cheese" to cover things that are figuratively stinky, because of poor quality.

**chew *sb* out** |CHŪ *sb* out| *v* To reprimand, scold. ORIGINS: From the figurative extension of SE chew to compare the scolding to being gnawed.

**chew *sb*'s ass (off)** |CHŪ *sb*'s AS / CHŪ *sb*'s AS awf| *v* To reprimand; to berate; to criticize severely. ORIGINS: From the figurative extension of SE chew to compare the scolding to being gnawed and SE **ass** meaning "a donkey," but commonly used as slang to refer to the rear end or buttocks. USAGE ALERT: The reference to **ass** and the graphic image evoked will make this phrase objectionable in some contexts and to some people.

**chicken** |CHIK un| *n* Someone who is afraid; a coward. ORIGINS: Chickens are typically characterized as easily frightened creatures.

**chicken feed** |CHIK un fēd| *n* A very small amount of money; small change. ORIGINS: From the very small size of grain required to make food digestible for poultry.

**chicken-hearted*** |CHIK un hahr tid| *adj* Cowardly. ORIGINS: From the association of chickens with fearfulness and the association of the heart and/or the liver as the seats of emotion.
• chicken-livered |CHIK un liv urd|

**chicken out** |CHIK un out| *v* To be too frightened to act; to back out. ORIGINS: From the association of chickens with fearfulness.

**chief** |chēf| *n* A boss. ORIGINS: From the SE use of chief to designate the head of a Native American or American Indian tribe—therefore, by extension, any head of any organization.

**chill (out)** |chil / chil OUT| *v* To calm down; to relax; to act cool. ORIGINS: When people get agitated or angry, they often become warm and flushed. So anger is associated with heat, and its opposite, being relaxed, is associated with a cool temperature.

**chilled out** |child OUT| *adj* Relaxed; calm. ORIGINS: When people get agitated or angry, they often become warm and flushed. Just as anger and being in a temper are associated with heat, being relaxed is associated with a cool temperature.

**Chinaman's chance in hell** |CHĪ nu munz CHANS in HEL| *v* No chance. ORIGINS: Said to be from the time of the US Gold Rush, during which Chinese prospectors, who were late to the scene, ended up having to work other people's abandoned mines, with little chance of finding anything of value. Figurative use of SE **hell** meaning "the alternative to heaven; the realm of the devil." USAGE ALERT: Today, this expression may be considered racist. The reference to **hell** will make it objectionable in some contexts and to some people, as well.

**chintzy** |CHINT sē| *adj* Of poor quality; shoddy; second-rate; inferior. ORIGINS: From the SE chintz, a fabric that was commonly used in the nineteenth century and widely disparaged.

**chinwagger** |CHIN wag ur| *n* An avid talker. ORIGINS: By extension from slang chinwag, meaning "a chat," from the motion of the jaw, chin when talking.

**chipper** |CHIP ur| *adj* Cheerful; in good spirits. ORIGINS: Thought to be from the British dialect term **chipper** meaning a cheerful song.

**chock-a-block/choc-a-block with** |CHAHK u BLAHK with| *adj* Crammed full; jammed full; stuffed. ORIGINS: From nautical jargon referring to a situation in which hoisting tackle have reached their limits.

**choke (*st*) off** |CHŌK AWF / CHŌK *st* AWF | *v* To stop in midstream; to end suddenly, as if by choking. ORIGINS: From SE **choke**; the reference is to a dog, stopped short by a choke collar.

**choke up** |CHŌK UP| *v* To be overcome with such strong emotion that one cannot speak.

**chowderhead, chowder-head** |CHOU dur hed| *n* A stupid or foolish person. ORIGINS: Likely a variation on the dialect slang form **jolterhead**, meaning "blockhead." USAGE ALERT: Usually used with intent to denigrate or insult and understood as such.

**chozzerai, chozerai** |KHAHZ ur I| *n* Junk; trashy stuff; inferior or worthless goods. ORIGINS: From Yiddish **chozzer** meaning "pig," hence **chozzerai** meaning "pig food; swill."

**Christ!** |krīst| *excl* An interjection. ORIGINS: SE **Christ** means "messiah" and is part of the name of Jesus Christ, whom Christians hold to be the Son of God. USAGE ALERT: Using the name of Jesus Christ in this way will be found objectionable and blasphemous in some contexts and by some people.

**Chuck it!** |CHUK it| *excl* Be quiet! ORIGINS: From slang **chuck** meaning "to quit or give up." USAGE ALERT: Often used with intent to denigrate or insult and understood as such.

**chuck out** |CHUK out| *v* To throw out a person; to discard an object. ORIGINS: From the slang **chuck**, meaning "to throw away."

**Chuck you, Farley!** |CHUK yū fahr lē| *excl* A contemptuous dismissal. ORIGINS: Spoonerism (exchange of first letters of two important words) in order to create a euphemistic version of the phrase **Fuck you, Charley!**, an extension of **Fuck you!** USAGE ALERT: Usually used with intent to be rude and understood as such. In addition, the inclusion of **fuck** will make this expression objectionable in some contexts and to some people.

**chucklehead** |CHUK ul hed| *n* A stupid, socially tactless person; a blockhead. ORIGINS: Possibly from SE **chuck** meaning "a cut of beef" and slang suffix -head which adds up to the approximate equivalent of **meathead**. USAGE ALERT: Usually used with intent to denigrate or insult and understood as such.

**chump** |chump| *n* A gullible person; someone who is easily taken in. ORIGINS: SE **chump**, meaning "a lump of wood." *See* **KLUTZ** and **BLOCKHEAD**. USAGE ALERT: Usually used with intent to denigrate or insult and understood as such.

**churn (*st*) out** |CHURN out / CHURN *st* out| *v* To produce large quantities on a regular schedule. ORIGINS: A reference to production with a butter churn. USAGE INFO: May imply efficiency or automatic and thoughtless production of a product that suffers from such an approach.

**Ciao for now!** |CHOU fawr NOU| *excl* Goodbye for now. ORIGINS: From Standard Italian **ciao** meaning "goodbye." USAGE INFO: The rhyme puts this in the slang category. **Ciao** by itself is used by people of Italian descent as well as others. However, note that unless one were Italian or there were Italians present, it would be unlikely in formal usage.

**cinch¹** |SINCH| *n* An easy to resolve problem. ORIGINS: By extension from SE **cinch** meaning "to grasp tightly" and derived from Spanish **cincha**, meaning "a saddle girth"—something that can be easily grasped. USAGE INFO: Always with the indefinite article, as in: "It'll be a cinch to fix."

**cinch²** |SINCH| *n* A certainty; a sure thing. ORIGINS: By extension from SE **cinch** meaning "to grasp tightly" and derived from Spanish **cincha**, meaning "a saddle girth"—something that can be easily grasped. USAGE INFO: Always with the indefinite article and often followed by a clause, with or without an introductory *that* as in: "It's a cinch that Wobbly Legs will win the third race."

**cinch** |SINCH| *v* To make conclusive. ORIGINS: By extension from SE **cinch** meaning "to grasp tightly" and derived from Spanish **cincha**, meaning "a saddle girth" in a figurative sense: something that has been obtained. USAGE INFO: Often in the phrase "cinch the deal." Compare with the very similarly spelled and sounding SE **clinch the deal**, with a virtually identical meaning.

**Clam up!** |KLAM up| *excl* Be quiet! ORIGINS: Based on the tightly shut shell of the bivalve, the idea is that the speaker should seal his or her lips. USAGE ALERT: Often used with intent to denigrate or insult and understood as such.

**claptrap** |KLAP trap| *n* Meaningless talk; incorrect or misinformed comments; untruths; lies. ORIGINS: By extension from theatre jargon **claptrap**, meaning "a theatrical trick (trap) to win audience applause (clapping)."

**clean *sb* out** |KLĒN *sb* OUT| *v* To steal; to take all of an opponent's money (in gambling); to ruin financially. ORIGINS: Figurative use of SE **clean**. USAGE INFO: Don't confuse with **clean *st* out** meaning "to empty of contents."

**clean up** |KLĒN up| *v* To make a large profit (in a short time). ORIGINS: Figurative use of SE **clean up**.

**clean up one's act** |KLĒN up wunz AKT| *v* To improve one's behavior or performance. ORIGINS: Figurative use of SE **clean up**.

**clean up one's shit** |KLĒN up wunz SHIT| *v* To improve one's behavior or performance; to organize one's possessions. ORIGINS: Figurative use of SE **clean up**. Extended from slang **shit** meaning "possessions." USAGE ALERT: The inclusion of **shit** will make this phrase objectionable in some contexts and to some people.

**cleaned out** |klēnd OUT| *adj* Broke. ORIGINS: Figurative use of SE **clean**.

**clear off/out** |KLIR awf / KLIR out| *v* To leave in a hurry; to depart. ORIGINS: By extension of SE **clear**, with the idea that one will "clear" a place of one's presence. USAGE INFO: Can be used as an imperative to signal dismissal.

**click¹** |klik| *v* To become friends; to hit it off. ORIGINS: From the behavior of machinery in good working order, for example, the sound that a metal piece makes when "clicking" into its proper place.

**click²** |klik| *v* To become interpretable or clear. ORIGINS: From the behavior of things fitting perfectly, for example, the sound that a metal piece makes when "clicking" into place.

**climb the wall(s)** |KLĪM *thu* WAWL / KLĪM *thu* WAWLZ| *v* To become angry; to lose one's temper; to lose one's mind. ORIGINS: The phrase may be an attempt to create an image of *sb* trying anything and everything to escape the situation s/he is in.

**climber** |KLĪM ur| *n* A person who aspires to be accepted by the upper class. ORIGINS: From the conception of social classes as a hierarchy or ladder. USAGE INFO: Sometimes used in the phrase "a social climber."

**clincher** |KLIN chur| *n* The decisive factor; the factor that seals the deal. ORIGINS: From SE **clinch**, a variation on SE **clench**.

**clinker** |KLINK ur| *n* A blunder; a muffed performance. ORIGINS: From baseball jargon for an error.

**clip** |klip| *n* An attempt; a try; a time; an occasion. USAGE INFO: Especially in the phrases "at one clip" or "at a clip."

**clip** |klip| *v* To hit sharply, often in passing.

**clobber¹** |KLAH bur| *v* To strike violently.

**clobber²** |KLAH bur| *v* To beat up or batter; to criticize harshly; to defeat soundly.

**clock** |klahk| *v* To hit (in the face). ORIGINS: By extension of slang **clock** meaning "a person's face or head," from SE **clock**.

**clock-watcher** |KLAHK wawch ur| *n* A person preoccupied with quitting time rather than work; a lazy, uncommitted worker. ORIGINS: A reference to a worker who is constantly checking the time.

**clod** |klahd| *n* A dull or stupid person; a rude or socially awkward person. ORIGINS: By figurative extension from SE **clod**, meaning "a lump of earth." USAGE ALERT: Usually used with intent to denigrate or insult and understood as such.

**clonk** |klahngk| *v* To hit. ORIGINS: By extension of onomatopoeic SE **clonk** meaning "to make a dull thud or metallic thud."

**close call/shave** |KLŌS KAWL / KLŌS SHĀV| *n* A very near thing (either positive or negative). ORIGINS: From the referee's call of, for example, a shot being in or out of bounds. USAGE INFO: Always perceived in retrospect.

**clout** |klout| *v* To strike a heavy blow.

**cluckhead** |KLUK hed| *n* A silly person; a fool. ORIGINS: From SE **cluck**, the sound a chicken makes, and slang suffix -head, with **cluck** evoking a chicken, which is generally thought of as being unintelligent. USAGE ALERT: Usually used with intent to denigrate or insult and understood as such.

**clunk** |klungk| *v* To strike or collide with. ORIGINS: Imitative of the sound of a blow.

**clunker** |KLUNGK ur| *n* A person, speech, product, or other item that is a complete flop; a failure. ORIGINS: Since **clunker** also refers to a badly working piece of machinery, often an aging automobile that may make "clunking" noises, so possibly by extension from that.

**clutch** |kluch| *n* A difficult or tense situation. ORIGINS: Popularized by, if not originating in, sports broadcasting, particularly the baseball term **clutch hitter**. USAGE INFO: Often in the phrase "in the clutch."

**cock up** |KAHK up| *v* To make a mistake; to ruin; to make a mess of. ORIGINS: Euphemism for **fuck up**. **Cock** means "penis." USAGE INFO: Used of messes made by females as well as males. USAGE ALERT: This slang phrase is often somewhat less objectionable than **fuck up**, because a) it refers to sex organs, but not sexual activity, and likely because b) on its own, SE **cock** has alternate meanings that are unrelated to sexuality.

**cockeyed** |KAHK īd| *adj* Mildly crazy; outlandish; ludicrous; absurd. ORIGINS: By extension from SE **cock**, meaning "to bend" and SE **eye**, meaning the eyes aren't level and focused. USAGE ALERT: Usually used with intent to denigrate or insult and understood as such. This way of speaking about *sb's* mental health may be considered insensitive and therefore objectionable in some contexts and by some people.

**cocksucker** |KAHK suk ur| *n* A nasty or despicable person. ORIGINS: From slang **cock** meaning "penis" and SE **suck**. USAGE ALERT: This word is considered one of the most offensive in English. Because of the reference to a sex act, and the graphic image, this term will be objectionable in some contexts and to some people. This term is most often used with specific intent to give offense and understood as such.

**codswallop** |KAHDZ wawl up| *n* Nonsense; lies.

**coin** |koin| *n* Unspecified amount of money in change.

**cold cash** |KŌLD KASH| *n* Ready money.

**coldcock** |KŌLD kahk| *v* To knock *sb* unconscious. ORIGINS: From SE **out cold** meaning "unconscious" and SE **knock cold**, meaning "to knock out." USAGE ALERT: Although this word has nothing to do with slang **cock** meaning "penis," some people may assume that it does.

**come across (with)** |kum u KRAWS / kum u KRAWS with| *v* To do or pay what's expected (reluctantly); to acquiesce and do what is required of one.

**Come again?** |kum u GEN| *phr* Could you repeat that? ORIGINS: In this case come means "speak."

**come apart at the seams** |kum u PAHRT at *th*u SĒMZ| *v* To lose control. ORIGINS: By analogy between physically and mentally falling apart.

**come back** |KUM bak| *v* To respond to *st* previously said.

**come clean** |kum KLĒN| *v* To tell the truth after not having told the truth (or the whole truth) previously.

**come down a peg (or two)** |kum DOUN u peg / KUM doun u PEG awr tū| *v* To experience humiliation. ORIGINS: The counterpart to the slang phrases take/bring *sb* down a peg (or two).

**come down hard (on)** |KUM doun HAHRD / kum doun HAHRD ahn| *v* To reprimand; to assault verbally.

**Come off it!** |kum AHF it| *excl* I don't believe it/you!

**come out on top** |kum out ahn TAHP| *v* To surpass in a contest of some kind; to overcome difficulties. ORIGINS: Draws on the concept of the highest being the best.

**come out swinging** |kum out SWING ing| *v* To go on the offensive from the very start. ORIGINS: SE **swinging** refers to the arm movement of a fighter who is throwing punches.

**come through with** |kum THRŪ with| *v* To deliver; to do what is wanted or required in a situation.

**come unglued** |kum un GLŪD| *v* To lose one's emotional or mental balance. ORIGINS: By analogy between physically and mentally falling apart.

**come unstuck** |kum un STUK| *v* To lose one's emotional or mental balance. ORIGINS: By analogy between physically and mentally falling apart.

**come up roses** |KUM up RŌ zis| *v* To have an auspicious or favorable result; to succeed. ORIGINS: Similar to "come up smelling of violets," the phrase suggests an attractive ending (even if the process was rocky). The "rose" version has been popularized by the song "Everything's Coming Up Roses," from the musical *Gypsy: A Musical Fable.*

**comp** |kahmp| *adj* Received without charge. ORIGINS: Short for SE **complimentary.** Complimentary tickets are given to VIPs and sometimes to friends and family of stars. They are also used to fill out an audience that might otherwise be lacking, in a move called **papering the house,** meaning "filling up an audience by giving away (paper) tickets."

**Comprende?** |kōm PREN de| *phr* Do you understand? ORIGINS: Adapted from Standard Spanish ¿Comprende? meaning "Do you understand?" USAGE INFO: The initial question mark used in Spanish is usually omitted in English.

**con** |kahn| *v* To deceive *sb* with a confidence trick or game, a type of swindle.

**Confound it!** |kun FOUN dit| *excl* An interjection expressing anger, frustration, dismay, etc. ORIGINS: Euphemism for **Damn it!** From SE confound meaning "to bring to perdition." USAGE ALERT: Euphemisms may still be objectionable in some contexts and to some people.

**confounded** |kun FOUN did| *a/a* Extreme; extremely; very; etc. ORIGINS: Euphemism for **damn(ed)**. From SE **confound** meaning "to bring to perdition." USAGE INFO: Used as an adjective ("confounded idiot") or as an adverb ("confounded good idea"). Note that the *-ed* is not optional for **confounded**. USAGE ALERT: Euphemisms may still be objectionable in some contexts and to some people.

**confuddled** |kun FUD uld| *adj* Extremely confused. ORIGINS: A portmanteau word, from combining **confused** with either **befuddled** or **muddled**. USAGE INFO: Used of people.

**confussed** |kun FUST| *adj* Confused and upset. ORIGINS: A portmanteau word, from combining **confused** and **fussed** meaning "upset." USAGE INFO: Used of people.

**conk** |kahngk| *v* To hit, particularly on the nose or in the head. ORIGINS: Onomatopoeic, from the sound of a blow and slang **conk**, meaning "the nose."

**conk out**[1] |KAHNGK OUT| *v* To fall asleep. ORIGINS: By extension from slang verb **conk** meaning "to knock out."

**conk out**[2] |KAHNGK OUT| *v* To die; to come to an end or give out. ORIGINS: Initially used of a machine giving out, and then by figurative extension from that to people.

**conked out** |kahngk'd OUT| *adj* Non-functioning; out-of-order. ORIGINS: The result of slang verb **conk out**.

**conniption (fit)** |ku NIP shun / ku NIP shun fit| *n* Fit of anger, panic, or anxiety.

**Consarn it!** |kun SAHRN it| *excl* An interjection expressing anger, frustration, dismay, etc. ORIGINS: Euphemism for **Damn it!** From SE **concern**. USAGE ALERT: Euphemisms may still be objectionable in some contexts and to some people.

**consarned** |kun SAHRND| *adj* Extreme; extremely; very; etc. ORIGINS: Euphemism for **damn(ed)**. From SE **concern**. USAGE INFO: Used as an adjective ("now wait a consarned minute") or an adverb ("consarned small thing to care about so much"). Note that the *-ed* is not optional for **consarned**. USAGE ALERT: Euphemisms may still be objectionable in some contexts and to some people.

**contraption** |kun TRAP shun| *n* An unspecified mechanical device; a gadget. ORIGINS: Possibly a portmanteau word from a combination of two or more of the SE words **contrivance, trap,** and **invention**.

**convulse** |kun VULS| *v* To cause overwhelming laughter; to laugh. ORIGINS: By extension from SE **convulse** and the similarity of the bodily effects of laughter to the involuntary muscle contractions of a convulsion.

**cook *sb*'s goose** |KOOK *sb*'s GŪS| *v* To kill *sb*; to ruin *sb*; to spoil *sb*'s chances. USAGE INFO: Can be used reflexively for *sb* who has ruined his/her own chances. Though it has a similar construction, it is different from **settle** *sb's* **hash**, which suggests getting revenge.

**cook the books** |KOOK *thu* BOOKS| *v* To falsify or manipulate records or documentation of financial transactions for the purpose of deceiving.

**cooking (with gas)** |KOOK ing / KOOK ing with GAS| *adj* Doing very well; performing wonderfully; making progress. ORIGINS: From an advertisement by the gas industry—"Now you're cooking with gas!"—to counteract the popularity of the electric range during the 1930s. Also used by jazz musicians to praise an exceptional performance. USAGE INFO: Sometimes appears as **cooking on gas**.

**cool** |kūl| *adj* Excellent; fine; first-rate. USAGE INFO: **Cool** is a contronym, with its early uses being negative, e.g., "emotionless," "cold-blooded." Positive uses emerged later.

**Cool beans!** |kūl BĒNZ| *excl* An exclamation of agreement, approval, or general satisfaction. ORIGINS: Apparently from the 1960s, the phrase was repopularized by the movies *Saving Private Ryan* (1998) and *Hot Rod* (2007).

**cool it/out** |KŪL it / kūl OUT| *v* To calm down; to stop what one is doing. ORIGINS: Plays on the concept of anger being hot and relaxation being cool.

**Cool it!** |KŪL it| *excl* Be quiet! Relax! ORIGINS: Related to the hot–cold trope for being excited, angry, and vociferous on the one hand or calm and soft-spoken on the other. USAGE ALERT: Sometimes used with intent to denigrate or insult and understood as such.

**cool million** |KŪL MIL yun| *n* A million dollars. ORIGINS: **Cool** seems to be emphasizing the sizeable amount. USAGE INFO: **Cool** can be used with other large sums, but usually only amounts formed by a one and following zeroes (hundred, thousand, million, etc.), and not less than a hundred, unless one is being ironic.

**cool one's jets** |KŪL wunz JETS| *v* To calm down; to relax. ORIGINS: Based on the behavior of jet engines, which get hot when they run and require cooling systems to prevent part failure. USAGE INFO: **Cool one's heels** may seem to be parallel, but it actually means "to be kept waiting."

**cop** |kahp| *v* To get possession of for oneself; to steal. ORIGINS: From Old French **caper** meaning "to seize."

**cop it** |KAHP it| *v* To die; to get into trouble. ORIGINS: From slang **cop** meaning "a beating" and SE **it** referring to trouble.

**cop out** |KAHP out| *v* To fail to fulfill what's promised; to give up; to renege. ORIGINS: Related to **cop a plea**, in which one takes less responsibility than one is actually accountable for.

**cop some z's** |KAHP sum zēz| *v* To take a nap. ORIGINS: Slang **cop** means "catch" or "steal." *Z's* are used as an onomatopoeic representation of sleep.

**copacetic, copasetic** |kō pu SET ik| *adj* Excellent; first-rate. ORIGINS: Bill "Bojangles" Robinson, a US entertainer in the early twentieth century, claims to have coined the word. Although this hasn't been proven, other etymological claims haven't plausibly refuted it.

**costing an arm and a leg** |KAWST ing an AHRM und u LEG| *adj* Offered for an extremely high price. ORIGINS: Figurative image of enormous sacrifices required for a purchase.

**cotton on (to)** |kaht'n AHN / kaht'n AHN tū| *v* To realize; to recognize; to arrive at understanding. ORIGINS: By extension of the meaning of slang **cotton to**. USAGE INFO: Can also mean "to become attached to."

**cotton-picking** |KAHT'n pik ing| *adj* Adjective that works as a sentence modifier. ORIGINS: Euphemism for **damn(ed)**. From the time when people, particularly slaves, picked cotton. USAGE INFO: Like **damn(ed)**, cotton-picking is an all-purpose term that usually intensifies the feeling of a whole sentence rather than specifically the word that it precedes and appears to modify; e.g., "Get your cotton-picking hand out of the cookie jar" is a condemnation of you-taking-a-cookie, not an attack on the quality of your hand. *See* **DAMN(ED)**. Often heard in the phrases "wait a cotton-picking minute" and "are you out of your cotton-picking mind?" USAGE ALERT: People who identify the reference as racist or who recognize it as a substitute for **damn(ed)** may find **cotton-picking** objectionable.

**cotton to** |KAHT'n tū| *v* To agree; to get on well together; to become mutually attached; to favor. USAGE INFO: Can also mean "to get to know about, or come to understand."

**couch potato** |KOUCH pu tā tō| *n* One who spends inordinate time on the couch watching television; one who lays around and is inactive. ORIGINS: Coined in 1976 from SE **couch** and **potato**, the latter used figuratively.

**cough up** |KAWF up| *v* To hand over (money), usually unwillingly or under duress; to relinquish; to confess.

**Cowabunga!** |kou u BUNG u| *excl* An exclamation of surprise or excitement. ORIGINS: From the exclamation spoken by Chief George "Capps" Thunderthud on the television series, *The Howdy Doody Show*. Used among surfers and repopularized in more recent popular culture, particularly by *The Teenage Mutant Ninja Turtles,* in whose use it is often followed by "Dude."

**cowboy** |KOU boi| *n* A reckless man; a reckless showoff. ORIGINS: From SE **cowboy**. USAGE INFO: This word is a contronym in that it can either condemn or praise adventurous behavior, as it can also mean "an adventurous hero."

**crack** |krak| *v* To suffer an emotional breakdown. ORIGINS: By analogy between physical and mental breakage.

**crack (at)** |krak / KRAK at| *n* An attempt. USAGE INFO: Often found in the phrase "take a crack at."

**crack down on** |krak DOUN awn| *v* To act with more force, usually in pressuring people or finding and punishing infringements.

**crack one's jaw** |KRAK wunz JAW| *v* To boast or brag. ORIGINS: From SE **crack** meaning "to make a sudden, loud noise."

**crack *sb* up** |KRAK *sb* UP| *v* To cause *sb* to laugh uproariously. ORIGINS: From SE **crack** meaning "to break" combined with the idea that one can "break" into laughter.

**crack the whip** |KRAK *thu* WHIP| *v* To lead in a domineering way; to be a demanding taskmaster. ORIGINS: From the era of horse-drawn carriages, when the drivers would exercise control over the horses with loud cracks of their whips.

**crack up**[1] |KRAK UP| *v* To laugh uproariously. ORIGINS: From SE **crack** meaning "to break" combined with the idea that one can "break" into laughter. USAGE INFO: Be careful to distinguish crack up from crack *sb* up.

**crack up**[2] |KRAK UP| *v* To suffer a nervous breakdown. ORIGINS: By analogy between physical and mental breakage. USAGE ALERT: This way of speaking about *sb's* mental health may be considered insensitive and therefore objectionable in some contexts and by some people.

**cracked** |krakt| *adj* Crazy; insane. ORIGINS: From SE **cracked** meaning "broken." USAGE ALERT: Often used with intent to denigrate or insult and understood as such. This way of speaking about *sb's* mental health may be considered insensitive and therefore objectionable in some contexts and by some people.

**crackerjack, crackajack** |KRAK ur jak, KRAK u jak| *adj* Excellent; first-rate. ORIGINS: Likely from SE **crack** meaning "excelling," as in "a crack shot."

**crackers** |KRAK urz| *adj* Crazy; insane. ORIGINS: From SE **cracked** meaning "broken." USAGE ALERT: Often used with intent to denigrate or insult and understood as such. This way of speaking about *sb's* mental health may be considered insensitive and therefore objectionable in some contexts and by some people.

**crackpot** |KRAK paht| *adj* Crazy or eccentric; outlandish; absurd; harebrained; foolish; unworkable. ORIGINS: By extension from SE **crack**, meaning "to break" and **pot** meaning "skull," i.e., the kind of suggestions one would expect from someone whose brains were not functioning properly. USAGE INFO: Often used of ideas, as well as of people. USAGE ALERT: When used of people, will usually be used with intent to denigrate or insult and understood as such. This way of speaking about *sb's* mental health may be considered insensitive and therefore objectionable in some contexts and by some people.

**crackup, crack-up** |KRAK up| *n* A collapse; a failure; a vehicle crash; a mental breakdown. ORIGINS: From SE **crack** meaning "to break."

**Cram it!** |KRAM it| *excl* Be quiet! ORIGINS: By extension of SE **cram** meaning to force something into a container, thus getting it out of the way. USAGE ALERT: Usually used with intent to denigrate or insult and understood as such.

**crap**[1] |krap| *n* An item or items that are estimated to be of the same value or quality as excrement. ORIGINS: From **crap**, a euphemism for slang **shit** meaning "excrement." USAGE ALERT: Because it refers to excrement, this term will be objectionable in some situations and to some people.

**crap², also crapola** |krap / kra PŌ lu| *n* Lies; untruths; nonsense; boasts. ORIGINS: From **crap**, a euphemism for **shit** meaning "excrement" and -ola, a slang intensifying suffix. USAGE ALERT: This term will be objectionable in some situations and to some people.

**crap³, also crapola** |krap / kra PŌ lu| *n* Unspecified "stuff." ORIGINS: Euphemism for **shit**. From **crap**, a euphemism for **shit** meaning "things" and **-ola**, a slang intensifying suffix. USAGE INFO: The use of **crap(ola)** to refer to items does not necessarily speak to the quality of the items being referred to nor the speaker's attitude. "I'll get my crap out of the living room in the morning" could refer to the speaker's laptop and DVDs, which s/he treasures. USAGE ALERT: This term will be objectionable in some situations and to some people.

**Crap!** |krap| Oh no! ORIGINS: From slang **crap**, a euphemism for slang **shit** meaning "excrement." USAGE ALERT: The reference to **crap** will make this phrase objectionable in some contexts and to some people, though some people will find **crap** less objectionable than **shit**.

**crap around** |krap u ROUND| *v* To fool around; to waste time. ORIGINS: From **crap**, a euphemism for **shit**, meaning "excrement." USAGE INFO: Along the lines of **fuck around**, **futz around**, **fart around**, etc. USAGE ALERT: This term will be objectionable in some situations and to some people.

**crap out** |krap OUT| *v* To stop working properly or at all. ORIGINS: By extension of the gambling jargon **crap out**, meaning "make a losing throw in the game of craps." USAGE ALERT: Some people may misconstrue this term as being related to excrement.

**crappy** |KRAP ē| *adj* Inferior; worthless; miserable; contemptible. ORIGINS: Euphemism for **shitty**. From **crap**, a euphemism for **shit**. USAGE ALERT: This term will be objectionable in some situations and to some people.

**crapshoot** |KRAP shūt| *n* A situation in which luck matters more than intelligence; a risky enterprise. ORIGINS: From gambling jargon **shooting craps**, a game of dice in which luck is the deciding factor. USAGE ALERT: Some people may misconstrue this term as being related to excrement.

**crash** |krash| *n* A sudden failure. ORIGINS: Perhaps originating with the stock market crash of 1929 and repopularized by computer jargon **crash**, indicating a failure of the hard drive.

**crash** |krash| *v* To find a place to sleep; to go to sleep; to collapse with tiredness. USAGE INFO: Often refers to a spell of sleep that is not in one's normal routine and sometimes decided upon on the spur of the moment.

**crash and burn** |KRASH und BURN| *v* To fail completely; to wipe out (fail). ORIGINS: From repeated incidents in airplane and car crashes. USAGE INFO: Usually depicts a more catastrophic event than simply crashing.

**crater** |KRĀ tur| *v* To fail; to be ruined. ORIGINS: Figurative use based on SE **crater**, meaning "a depression or pit."

**crazy¹** |KRĀ zē| *adj* Wonderful; amazing. USAGE INFO: **Crazy** is a contronym.

**crazy**[2] |KRĀ zē| *adj* Outlandish; weird; bizarre. USAGE INFO: Crazy is a contronym.

**crazy about** |KRĀ zē u BOUT| *adj* Enthusiastic about; keen on; very attracted to; in love with. ORIGINS: Takes the idea of SE **crazy** and narrows it to apply to a specific slice of life: that having to do with love.

**crazy as a bedbug** |KRĀ zē az u BED bug| *adj* Crazy or eccentric. USAGE ALERT: Often used with intent to denigrate or insult and understood as such. This way of speaking about *sb's* mental health may be considered insensitive and therefore objectionable in some contexts and by some people.

**crazy as catshit** |KRĀ zē az KAT shit| *adj* Extremely crazy. USAGE ALERT: The inclusion of a form of the word **shit** will render this phrase objectionable in some contexts and to some people. Often used with intent to denigrate or insult and understood as such. This way of speaking about *sb's* mental health may be considered insensitive and therefore objectionable in some contexts and by some people.

**cream** |krēm| *v* To beat up; to beat decisively in a sporting event or other competition. ORIGINS: The idea is that cream, being superior to milk, rises to the top.

**creampuff** |KRĒM puf| *n* A weakling; a person who is out of shape. ORIGINS: From the fragile-shelled pastry. USAGE INFO: Creampuff, which can also mean "an outstanding person," is a contronym. USAGE ALERT: When the negative meaning is the one referenced, usually used with intent to denigrate or insult and understood as such.

**creep** |krēp| *n* An unpleasant or repulsive person, sometimes with intimations of criminal involvement; someone who gives you **the creeps**. ORIGINS: From figurative extension of SE **creep**. USAGE ALERT: Usually used with intent to denigrate or insult and understood as such.

**creep *sb* out** |KRĒP *sb* OUT| *v* To cause fear by exhibiting the qualities of a creep, i.e., unpleasantness, repulsiveness, or some criminal connection. USAGE INFO: About the same as "give *sb* the creeps." USAGE ALERT: Be careful to distinguish creep *sb* out from **creep out**, meaning "to exit or sneak away quietly."

**creeps, the** |*thu* KRĒPS| *n* An attack of fear; a feeling of dread or repulsion. ORIGINS: The feeling of "creeping" in one's flesh when one is scared, horrified, or repulsed.

**cretin** |KRĒT'n| *n* An obnoxious or stupid person; an idiot. ORIGINS: By extension from the SE medical term **cretinism**, a disease of the thyroid. USAGE ALERT: Usually used with intent to denigrate or insult and understood as such. In addition, because this term implicitly makes fun of people with a medical disorder, it will be considered objectionable in some contexts and by some people.

**Cripes!** |krīps| *excl* An interjection expressing shock, surprise, dismay, etc. ORIGINS: Euphemism for **Christ!** An alteration of the name of **Jesus Christ** by changing letters. SE **Christ** means "messiah" and is part of the name of Jesus Christ, whom Christians hold to be the Son of God. USAGE ALERT: People who recognize it as a replacement for a name of God may find **Cripes!** objectionable and/or blasphemous. Some people will use it without realizing the connection.

**croak** |krōk| *v* To kill; to die. ORIGINS: Possibly onomatopoeic use of SE <u>croak</u> to invoke the sound of the death rattle.

**crock, a** |u KRAHK| *n* Falsehoods; untruths; lies. ORIGINS: Euphemism for **crock of shit**. From SE crock meaning "a large pottery container." USAGE INFO: Often occurs in the phrase "that's a crock." When **crock** is used by itself, the usage is the figure of speech called metonymy, specifically, using the name of the container to signify the thing contained. USAGE ALERT: Euphemisms may still be objectionable in some contexts and to some people.

**crock of shit** |KRAHK uv SHIT| *n* Falsehoods; untruths; lies. ORIGINS: From SE crock meaning "a large pottery container" and slang **shit** meaning "excrement." USAGE ALERT: Because this term includes the word **shit**, it will be considered objectionable in some contexts and by some people.

**cross-up** |KRAWS up| *n* A complete failure; an instance of confusion. ORIGINS: Likely related to the idiom "get one's signals crossed."

**crotchety** |KRAHCH i tē| *adj* Irritable; prone to anger; bad-tempered. ORIGINS: The expected behavior of someone with SE <u>crotchets</u>, idiosyncratic opinions and/or preference, thus, one who is very particular and easily put-out.

**crowd** |kroud| *v* To pressure someone; to try to force someone's hand. ORIGINS: Extension of SE crowd, in which one is jostled into a limited space.

**crown** |kroun| *v* To hit over the head. ORIGINS: By extension of SE crown, meaning "the top of the head." Like **bean** and **brain**, **crown** names the part of the body that receives the blow.

**cruddy** |KRUD ē| *adj* Dirt-encrusted; worthless; disgusting; inferior. ORIGINS: From slang **crud**, meaning "a coating of filth." USAGE INFO: Because the filth referred to by **cruddy** is not explicitly excrement, it can be substituted for **shitty**, **crappy**, etc. and be considered less objectionable.

**crumb** |krum| *n* A contemptible or mean person. ORIGINS: By extension of the original meaning, "a body louse."

**crumbs** |krumz| *adv* Sentence modifier. ORIGINS: Euphemism for **Christ!** An alteration of the name of Jesus Christ by changing letters. USAGE INFO: Often used to express disappointment, as in "Crumbs, what a small serving!" USAGE ALERT: People who recognize it as a replacement for a name of God may find **crumbs** objectionable and/or blasphemous. However, in the twenty-first century, most people will probably not make the connection.

**Crumbs!** |krumz| *excl* Expression of mild to moderate irritation, frustration, dismay, etc. ORIGINS: Euphemism for **Christ!** An alteration of the name of Jesus Christ by changing letters. SE **Christ** means "messiah" and is part of the name of Jesus Christ, whom Christians hold to be the Son of God. USAGE INFO: Can be used upon discovery of a mistake or problem. USAGE ALERT: People who recognize it as a replacement for a name of God may find **Crumbs!** objectionable and/or blasphemous. However, in the twenty-first century, most people will probably not make the connection.

**crummy, crumby** |KRUM ē| *adj* Shabby; miserable; lousy; inferior. ORIGINS: extension of the original meaning: "louse-infested."

**crunch-time** |KRUNCH tīm| *n* A critical moment calling for decisive action. ORIGINS: From SE **the crunch**.

**cry uncle** |KRĪ UNG kul| *v* To surrender. ORIGINS: Said to be from the Old Irish word **anacol**, meaning "safety; deliverance."

**crying** |KRĪ ing| *adj* To an extent that it would be justified to cry about it. USAGE INFO: Commonly found in the phrases "a crying shame," and "a crying need."

**cunt** |kunt| *n* A multi-faceted term of abuse for anyone considered contemptible: the foolish, unpleasant, unintelligent, and women. ORIGINS: From slang **cunt**, meaning "vagina." USAGE INFO: At one time, this was an accepted term, used in medical writing. Now, often found in a part-for-the-whole usage to refer to a woman. USAGE ALERT: **Cunt** is considered among the most objectionable terms in the English language. Using **cunt** is nearly always done with specific intent to give offense and will be understood as such.

**curtains** |KUR tunz| *n* Complete ruin; death. ORIGINS: From the drawing or dropping of the curtain at the end of a theatrical performance. USAGE INFO: Often in the phrase "It's curtains for...."

**cushy** |KO͞OSH ē| *adj* Extremely comfortable. ORIGINS: Often traced to the Hindu **khush**, meaning "pleasant," but its etymology isn't certain.

**cuss out** |KUS OUT| *v* To verbally abuse; to reprimand with swearing. ORIGINS: The word **cuss**, slang for "swearing" comes from SE **curse**.

**cussed** |KUS id| *a/a* Extreme; extremely; very; cursed. ORIGINS: Euphemism for **damn(ed)**. From SE **cursed**. USAGE INFO: Used as an adjective ("cussed fool") or an adverb ("cussed small serving"). USAGE ALERT: Euphemisms may still be objectionable in some contexts and to some people.

**cut (and run)** |kut / KUT und RUN| *v* To escape; to run away; to avoid a difficult situation by fleeing. ORIGINS: From nautical jargon **cut and run**, meaning "to cut the anchor cable and run before the wind."

**cut one's own throat** |KUT wunz ōn THRŌT| *v* To ruin one's own prospects. ORIGINS: Figurative interpretation of the words describing suicide.

**cut oneself off at the knees** |KUT wun self AWF at *thu* NĒZ| *v* To ruin one's own prospects. ORIGINS: Figurative interpretation of the words describing incapacitating oneself.

**cut *sb* a new asshole/one** |KUT *sb* u NŪ AS hōl / KUT *sb* u NŪ wun| *v* To attack *sb* savagely, physically or verbally. ORIGINS: The graphic image speaks to the violence of the attack. From slang **asshole** meaning "anus." USAGE ALERT: Because of the reference to the human rear end or buttocks, as well as the graphic depiction of violence (even if **asshole** is replaced with euphemistic **one**), this expression will be found objectionable in some contexts and by some people.

**cut *sb* down (to size)** |KUT *sb* DOUN / kut *sb* DOUN tū sīz| *v* To insult. ORIGINS: The concept is of trimming an oversized ego. USAGE INFO: The emphasis in this construction can vary quite a bit: THAT'LL cut him down to size. That'll cut HIM down to size. That'll cut him down to SIZE.

**Cut the cackle!** |KUT *thu* kak ul| *excl* Be quiet! Get serious! ORIGINS: A shortened form of the expression "Cut the cackle and get to the horses," comparing the more important livestock—horses—to the constant, meaningless noise of chickens. USAGE ALERT: Sometimes used with intent to denigrate or insult and understood as such.

**cut the crap** |KUT *thu* KRAP| *v* To stop goofing around; to stop talking nonsense or telling lies; to get serious. ORIGINS: Euphemism for **cut the shit**. From **crap**, a euphemism for **shit**, meaning "excrement." USAGE ALERT: The reference to excrement will make this phrase objectionable in some situations and to some people. People may find **crap** less objectionable than **shit**. Usually used with intent to be rude and understood as such.

**cut the funny business** |KUT *thu* FUN ē biz nis| *v* To get focused; to get serious; to stop dishonest practices.

**cut the shit** |KUT *thu* SHIT| *v* To stop goofing around; to stop talking nonsense or telling lies; to get serious. ORIGINS: From **shit** meaning "excrement." USAGE ALERT: The reference to excrement will make this phrase objectionable in some situations and to some people. People may find **crap** less objectionable than **shit**. Usually used with intent to be rude and understood as such.

**DILLIGAD** |DIL ē gad| Does it look like I give a damn? Do I look like I give a damn?

**DILLIGAF** |DIL ē gaf| Does it look like I give a fuck? Do I look like I give a fuck?

**DILLIGAS** |DIL ē gas| Does it look like I give a shit? Do I look like I give a shit?

**DQYDJ** Don't quit your day job.

**DWB** Don't write back.

**D-list** |DĒ list| *adj* A very minor celebrity. ORIGINS: From the celebrity ranking system invented by journalist James Ulmer and known as the Ulmer scale. It considers 100 points in order to rank a star's bankability. The most bankable stars are referred to as A-list. The phrase has been popularized in the twenty-first century by stand-up comedian Kathy Griffin, who has not only proclaimed herself to be on the **D-list**, but also hosts a television series, *My Life on the D-List*. USAGE ALERT: Usually used with intent to denigrate or insult and understood as such.

**D'oh!** |dō| *excl* Annoyed grunt of frustration, pain, or realization. ORIGINS: Although people have doubtless grunted throughout history, this particular spelling has been popularized through being the catchphrase of the character Homer Simpson in the television series *The Simpsons* (1989–).

**D**

**da bomb** |du BAHM| *adj* The best; the most outstanding; the coolest.

**dab hand** |DAB HAND| *adj* An expert; someone skilled at a particular task. USAGE INFO: Often used with *at* or *with*.

**Dad blame it! Dadblame it!** |dad BLĀM it| *excl* An interjection expressing anger, frustration, dismay, etc. ORIGINS: Euphemism for **Goddamn it!** Dad is a euphemism used in a number of curses to replace **God** in order to be less objectionable. Blame is a euphemism for **damn**. USAGE ALERT: Euphemisms may still be objectionable in some contexts and to some people.

**dad gum(med)/dadgum(med)** |DAD GUM / DAD GUM'D| *a/a* Extreme; extremely; very; blameworthy; etc. ORIGINS: Euphemism for **goddamn(ed)**. Dad is a euphemism used in a number of curses to replace **God** in order to be less objectionable. Gum is a euphemism for **damn(ed)**. USAGE INFO: Used as an adjective ("the dadgum(med) rat") or an adverb ("so dadgum(med) good"). USAGE ALERT: Euphemisms may still be objectionable in some contexts and to some people.

**Dad gum it! Dadgum it!** |dad GUM it| *excl* An interjection expressing anger, frustration, dismay, etc. ORIGINS: Euphemism for **Goddamn it!** Dad is a euphemism used in a number of curses to replace **God** in order to be less objectionable. Gum is a euphemism for **damn**. USAGE ALERT: Euphemisms may still be objectionable in some contexts and to some people.

**dadblame(d)** |dad BLĀM / dad BLĀM'd| *a/a* Extreme; extremely; very; blameworthy; etc. ORIGINS: Euphemism for **goddamn(ed)**. Dad is a euphemism used in a number of curses to replace **God** in order to be less objectionable. Blamed is a euphemism for **damn(ed)**. USAGE INFO: Used as an adjective ("dadblame(d) horse") or an adverb ("dadblame(d) awful time"). USAGE ALERT: Euphemisms may still be objectionable in some contexts and to some people.

**dadblasted** |DAD BLAS tid| *a/a* Extreme; extremely; very; blameworthy; etc. ORIGINS: Euphemism for **goddamn(ed)**. Dad is a euphemism used in a number of curses to replace **God** in order to be less objectionable. Blasted is a euphemism for **damn(ed)**. USAGE INFO: Used as an adjective ("the dadblasted thing") or an adverb ("dadblasted stupid person"). USAGE ALERT: Euphemisms may still be objectionable in some contexts and to some people.

**daddy of all** |DA dē uv awl| *adj* Especially large, problematic, impressive, etc. ORIGINS: From the father as the head of the family in a paternalistic society. USAGE INFO: *See* GRANDDADDY; MOTHER OF ALL.

**Dagnab (it)!** |DAG NAB / DAG NAB it| *excl* An interjection expressing anger, frustration, dismay, etc. ORIGINS: Euphemism for **Goddamn!** or **Goddamn it!** Dag is an altered form of **dad**, which is a euphemism for **God** in a number of replacement curses. Nab is a euphemism for **damn**. USAGE INFO: Used to express displeasure, anger, or frustration. USAGE ALERT: Euphemisms may still be objectionable in some contexts and to some people.

**dagnabbed** |DAG NAB'D| *a/a* Goddamn(ed). ORIGINS: **Dag** is an altered form of **dad**, which is a euphemism used in a number of curses to replace **God** in order to be less objectionable. **Nabbed** is a euphemism for **damn(ed)**. USAGE INFO: Used as an adjective ("the dagnabbed situation") or an adverb ("dagnabbed stupid person"). USAGE ALERT: Euphemisms may still be objectionable in some contexts and to some people.

**damn** |DAM it awl| *adv* Sentence modifier with various shades of meaning. ORIGINS: By extension from SE **damn**, which literally means "Send (it) to hell." USAGE INFO: Used to modify/intensify a whole sentence, as in "Damn, that's a gorgeous sunset!" USAGE ALERT: Although this use of **damn** is usually synonymous with a word like *wow* or *well*, nevertheless, people who take issue with cursing are likely to find it objectionable.

**Damn!** |dam| *excl* An interjection expressing anger, frustration, dismay, etc. ORIGINS: By extension from SE **damn**, which literally means "Send (it) to hell." USAGE ALERT: Usually used to relieve feelings without any intent to curse. Nevertheless, the use of the word **damn** will make it objectionable in some contexts and to some people.

**damn(ed)** |dam / dam'd| *a/a* Cursed; very; extremely; extreme. Also functions as a sentence modifier. ORIGINS: By extension from SE **damn**, which literally means "Send (it) to hell." USAGE INFO: Used as an adjective ("damn(ed) fool") or as an adverb ("damn(ed) good meal"). USAGE ALERT: Although these uses of **damn(ed)** are often simply equivalent to *very* or *extreme*, and not intended to mean "cursed," nevertheless, people who take issue with cursing are likely to find them objectionable.

**damn(ed)** |dam / dam'd| *adj* Adjective that works as a sentence modifier. ORIGINS: By extension from SE **damn**, which literally means "Send (it) to hell." USAGE INFO: Functions as a sentence modifier while positioned as an adjective ("Get in the damn(ed) house!"; "Why can't I find my damn(ed) wallet?"). USAGE ALERT: People who take issue with cursing are likely to find this use of **damn(ed)** objectionable.

**damn(ed) sight, a** |u DAM SĪT / u DAM'D SĪT| *adv* Much; a great degree or extent. ORIGINS: By extension from SE **damn**, which literally means "Send (it) to hell." USAGE ALERT: Even when used in a positive sense, as in "You're a damn(ed) sight smarter than he is," the use of **damned** will be objectionable in some situations and to some people.

**damn-all** |DAM awl| *n* Nothing at all. ORIGINS: By extension from SE **damn**, which literally means "Send (it) to hell." USAGE INFO: **Damn-all** is used for emphasis, as in "I've had damn-all to eat today." USAGE ALERT: This term with **damn** will be objectionable in some contexts and to some people.

**Damn and blast!** |DAM und BLAST| *excl* An interjection expressing anger, frustration, dismay, etc. ORIGINS: By extension from SE **damn**, which literally means "Send (it) to hell." USAGE ALERT: This term is usually used to relieve feelings without any other purpose. Nevertheless, **damn** and the similar, though euphemistic, **blast** will make it objectionable in some contexts and to some people.

**Damn it! Dammit! Damnit!** \* |DAM it| *excl* A curse. An interjection expressing anger, frustration, dismay, etc. ORIGINS: By extension from SE **damn**, which literally means "Send (it) to hell" or "May it be sent to hell." USAGE ALERT: Usually used to relieve feelings without any intent to curse. Nevertheless, people who take issue with cursing are likely to find these terms objectionable.
• **Damn it all!** |DAM it awl|

**Damn it to hell!** |DAM it tū HEL| *excl* A curse. An interjection expressing anger, frustration, dismay, etc. ORIGINS: By extension from SE **damn**, which literally means "Send (it) to hell," **hell** meaning "the alternative to heaven; the realm of the devil." USAGE ALERT: This term is usually used to relieve feelings without any intent to curse. Nevertheless, people who take issue with cursing are likely to find this term objectionable.

**damn well** |DAM WEL| *adv* Adverb that works as a sentence modifier. ORIGINS: By extension from SE **damn**, which literally means "Send (it) to hell." USAGE INFO: This phrase often modifies the word directly following ("I damn well *will*"; "He damn well *is* going to spend the rest of his life in jail!"). As the italics in the example sentences indicate, the word following the phrase usually receives the most emphasis. *See* FUCKING WELL. USAGE ALERT: The inclusion of **damn** will make this phrase objectionable in some contexts and to some people.

**damnedest** |DAM dist| *adj* Most of whatever is being expressed: most amazing, most difficult, etc. ORIGINS: Superlative of **damned**. By extension from SE **damn**, which literally means "Send (it) to hell." USAGE INFO: Often used in phrases such as "it was the damnedest thing"; "I had the damnedest time (finding the restaurant or whatever)". USAGE ALERT: The use of a form of **damn** will be objectionable in some contexts and to some people.

**dang** |dang| *adv* Sentence modifier. ORIGINS: Euphemism for **damn**. USAGE INFO: Sentence modifier showing disappointment or frustration, as in "Dang, we missed the bus." USAGE ALERT: Euphemisms may still be objectionable in some contexts and to some people.

**Dang (it)!** |dang / DANG it| *excl* An interjection expressing anger, frustration, dismay, etc. ORIGINS: Euphemism for **Damn! Damn it!** USAGE ALERT: Euphemisms may still be objectionable in some contexts and to some people.

**dang(ed)** |dang / dang'd| *a/a* Extreme; extremely; very. ORIGINS: Euphemism for **damn(ed)**. USAGE INFO: Used as an adjective ("dang(ed) idiot") or an adverb ("so dang(ed) stupid"; "dang(ed) good thing"). USAGE ALERT: Euphemisms may still be objectionable in some contexts and to some people.

**darn** |dahrn| *adv* Sentence modifier. ORIGINS: Euphemism for **damn**. USAGE INFO: Sentence modifier showing disappointment or frustration, as in "Darn, I wish I'd known." USAGE ALERT: Euphemisms may still be objectionable in some contexts and to some people.

**darn(ed)** |dahrn / dahrn'd| *a/a* Extreme; extremely; very. ORIGINS: Euphemism for **damn(ed)**. USAGE INFO: Used as an adjective ("darn(ed) cat") or an adverb ("darn(ed) good store"). USAGE ALERT: Euphemisms may still be objectionable in some contexts and to some people.

**Darn (it)!** |dahrn / DAHRN it| *excl* An interjection expressing mild to moderate displeasure, frustration, or irritation, etc. ORIGINS: Euphemism for **Damn! Damn it!** USAGE ALERT: Euphemisms may still be objectionable in some contexts and to some people.

**darnedest, darndest** |DAHRN dist| *adj* Most of whatever is being expressed: most amazing, most difficult, etc. ORIGINS: Euphemism for **damnedest**. Superlative of **darned**. USAGE INFO: Often used in phrases such as "It was the darnedest thing"; "I had the darnedest time (getting here)." USAGE ALERT: Euphemisms may still be objectionable in some contexts and to some people.

**Dash (it)!** |dash / DASH it| *excl* An interjection expressing mild to moderate displeasure, frustration, or irritation, etc. ORIGINS: Euphemism for **Damn! Damn it!** From the dashes used to replace the middle letters in **damn**, like this: *d--n,* in order to render it less objectionable in print. USAGE INFO: Often in the phrase "dash it all." USAGE ALERT: Euphemisms may still be objectionable in some contexts and to some people.

**dashed** |dasht| *a/a* Extreme; extremely; very. ORIGINS: Euphemism for **damn(ed)**. From the dashes used to replace the middle letters in **damn**, like this: *d--n,* in order to render it less objectionable in print. USAGE INFO: Used as an adjective ("dashed pigeons") or an adverb ("dashed good luck"). USAGE ALERT: Euphemisms may still be objectionable in some contexts and to some people.

**dead** |ded| *adj* Finished; through; over; lost. ORIGINS: By extension from SE **dead**, used of something that was alive.

**dead** |ded| *adv* Completely, very, extremely. USAGE INFO: Can have negative force, as in "dead broke" or positive, as in "dead right."

**Dead sure!** |DED shur| *excl* Absolutely certain! ORIGINS: From slang **dead** meaning "absolutely."

**decider** |du SĪD ur| *n* The person who gets to make the final decisions. ORIGINS: From President George W. Bush's comment in the Rose Garden on April 18, 2006, as he defended his decision to keep Donald Rumsfeld as secretary of defense: "I'm the decider and I decide what's best."

**deck** |dek| *v* To knock *sb* down. ORIGINS: Extended from SE **deck**, meaning "the floor or ground"—the end location of someone who is "decked."

D

**deep doo-doo** |dēp DŪ dū| *n* Serious trouble. ORIGINS: Euphemism for **deep shit**. From SE deep and slang **doo-doo**, a childish euphemism for **shit**. USAGE ALERT: The euphemism **doo-doo** in this phrase will soften it somewhat, but it may still be objectionable in some contexts and to some people.

**deep pockets** |dēp PAH kits| *n* A person with a large, steady amount of money. ORIGINS: From imagining someone reaching down into extensive pockets and bringing up more and more money.

**deep shit** |DĒP SHIT| *n* A serious situation. ORIGINS: From slang **shit** meaning "excrement." USAGE ALERT: The word **shit** may make this phrase objectionable in some contexts and to some people.

**deep-six** |DĒP SIKS| *v* To abandon; to get rid of. ORIGINS: From nautical jargon deep six meaning "to throw overboard," which itself derives from the use of the sea as a grave and the conventional depth of a dug grave being six feet.

**def** |def| *adj* Excellent; first-rate. ORIGINS: Possibly short for SE **definite** or alteration of **to death** meaning "excessively."

**dehire** |dē HĪR| *v* To lay off or terminate. ORIGINS: Prefix de- meaning "undo" and the SE verb **hire**, meaning "to employ."

**delish** |di LISH| *adj* Delicious; desirable. ORIGINS: Shortened and altered form of SE delicious.

**deliver (the goods)** |di LIV ur / di LIV ur *thu* GŌŌDZ| *v* To complete *st.*; to fulfill a promise. ORIGINS: Extended from the literal notion of SE **delivery**.

**deuced** |dūst| *a/a* Extreme; extremely; very. ORIGINS: Euphemism for **damn(ed)**. Originally a euphemism for the devil, possibly inspired by SE **deuce**, the lowest, least fortunate throw in games of dice. USAGE INFO: Used as an adjective ("deuced shame") or an adverb ("deuced lucky"; "a deuced good time"). USAGE ALERT: Euphemisms may still be objectionable in some contexts and to some people.

**devilishly** |DEV ul ish lē| *adv* Extremely. ORIGINS: From SE devil meaning "god's adversary." USAGE INFO: Despite origins, is often used light-heartedly as in, e.g., "devilishly delicious." USAGE ALERT: This use of **devil** will be objectionable in some contexts and to some people.

**dicey proposition** |DĪ sē prahp u ZISH un| *n* An untrustworthy or unreliable plan or proposal. ORIGINS: Based on imagery from gambling games in which dice are rolled.

**dick\*** |dik| *n* A contemptible or stupid person. ORIGINS: From slang **dick** meaning "penis." USAGE ALERT: The inclusion of a reference to sexual organs will make this phrase objectionable in some situations and to some people. In addition, it will be usually used with intent to denigrate or insult and understood as such.
• dickhead |DIK hed|

**dick around** |DIK u ROUND| *v* To waste time; to mess around. ORIGINS: From slang **dick** meaning "penis." USAGE ALERT: The inclusion of a reference to sexual organs will make this phrase objectionable in some situations and to some people.

**dick (around) with** *st* |DIK with *st* / DIK u ROUND with *st*| *v* To mess or fool around with *st*; to handle irresponsibly or without understanding. ORIGINS: From slang **dick** meaning "penis." USAGE ALERT: The inclusion of a reference to sexual organs will make this phrase objectionable in some situations and to some people.

**diddle** |DID'l| *v* To cheat or swindle.

**diddle (around) with** *st* |DID 'l with *st*/ DID 'l u ROUND with *st*| *v* To mess or fool around with; to handle irresponsibly or without understanding.

**diddley-shit, diddly-shit** |DID lē shit| *n* A small or worthless amount, particularly of money; nothing at all. ORIGINS: From slang **diddley** meaning "anything insignificant" and an extension of slang **shit** meaning "excrement" to use as an intensifier. USAGE INFO: Often used in constructions with an (implied) double negative: "I don't have diddley-shit." Abbreviated use with just the first word, spelled in any of the two ways: "I don't have diddley." USAGE ALERT: The use of **shit** will make this phrase objectionable in some situations and to some people.

**diddly-squat, diddlysquat** |DID lē skwaht| *n* Nothing at all. ORIGINS: Euphemism for **diddley-shit**. USAGE INFO: Often used in constructions with an (implied) double negative, as in "He doesn't have diddly-squat." Abbreviated by using just diddly or just squat. USAGE ALERT: The euphemism **squat** in this phrase will soften it somewhat, but it may still be objectionable in some contexts and to some people.

**die laughing** |DĪ LAF ing| *v* To laugh uproariously and uncontrollably. ORIGINS: Popularized by being a key plot element in the film *Who Framed Roger Rabbit?* (1988).

**dig¹** |dig| *v* To appreciate; to enjoy. ORIGINS: Jazz jargon.

**dig²** |dig| *v* To pay close attention to; to understand. ORIGINS: Jazz jargon.

**Dig (me)?** |dig / DIG mē| *phr* Do you both understand fully and agree with me?

**dime-a-dozen** |DĪM u DUZ un| *adj* Of limited value; common. ORIGINS: By extension of SE meaning of literal cost, to "inexpensive," and then to "cheap or low quality."

**dimwit** |DIM wit| *n* A stupid person. ORIGINS: From dim altered from slang **damn-all** meaning "none" and SE wits; therefore, "a brainless person." USAGE ALERT: Usually used with intent to denigrate or insult and understood as such.

**dinero** |di NER ō| *n* An unspecified amount of money. ORIGINS: From Spanish dinero meaning "money."

**ding-a-ling** |DING u ling| *n* A scatterbrained or eccentric person; someone who is insane. ORIGINS: From the onomatopoeic sound of a bell tied to the concept of a person who hears bells ringing in his/her head being disturbed in some way.

USAGE ALERT: Can be used affectionately, but often used with intent to denigrate or insult and understood as such.

**ding-dong** |DING dahng| *n* A fool; an empty-headed person; an insane person. ORIGINS: From the onomatopoeic sound of a bell tied to the concept of a person who hears bells ringing in his/her head being disturbed in some way. USAGE ALERT: Often used with intent to denigrate or insult and understood as such.

**dingbat** |DING bat| *n* A silly person or fool; an insane person. ORIGINS: Possibly from SE **ding** meaning "the sound of a bell" and slang bats in the belfry meaning "crazy." Popularized by Archie Bunker, who used it frequently of his wife, Edith, on the TV sitcom *All in the Family* (1968–1979, now in reruns). USAGE ALERT: Usually used with intent to denigrate or insult and understood as such.

**dingus** |DING us| *n* Any item the name of which can't be recalled. ORIGINS: From Dutch **ding** meaning "thing." USAGE INFO: Dingus is also used as a slang euphemism for SE **penis**, so there is the possibility for misinterpretation.

**dinky, dinkey** |DING kē| *adj* Tiny. ORIGINS: From Scotttish **dink** meaning "smart, neat," extended in railway jargon to name a small locomotive and in journalism jargon to name a 300-word piece of writing.

**dirt cheap** |DIRT CHĒP| *adj* Extremely inexpensive. USAGE INFO: Also cheap as dirt. This phrase may or may not imply that the product offered at that price is inferior or worthless.

**dirtbag** |DIRT bag| *n* A contemptible person; a vile person. ORIGINS: From SE **dirt** and the slang suffix -bag, which designates a person. USAGE ALERT: Usually used with intent to denigrate or insult and understood as such.

**dis, diss** |dis| *v* To disrespect; to disparage; to denigrate. ORIGINS: Shortening of SE **disrespect** or **disparagement**. USAGE INFO: Often refers to public humiliation.

**discombobulated** |dis kum BAHB yū lāt id| *adj* Confused; upset; in disarray. ORIGINS: Possibly by alteration of **discompose**. USAGE INFO: Used of people and things.

**dishy** |DISH ē| *adj* Attractive (of a thing); physically attractive (of a person). ORIGINS: Based on the concept that the person or thing is "good enough to eat, like a dish of food."

**ditch** |DICH| *v* To leave *sb* in the lurch; to discard. ORIGINS: Possibly by extension of jargon **ditch**, originating with the Royal Air Force and meaning "to land one's plane in the sea," usually in a body of water referred to as "the big ditch"—either the English Channel or the North Sea.

**ditz** |ditz| *n* A scatterbrained person; a fool. ORIGINS: Altered from SE **dizzy**. USAGE INFO: Most often used of women. USAGE ALERT: Usually used with intent to denigrate or insult and understood as such.

**do a 180** |DŪ u wun Ā tē| *v* To turn one's life around. ORIGINS: From the mathematical fact that turning 180° results in facing the opposite direction: by extension, a radical, complete change.

**do a bunk** |dū u BUNK| *v* To run away; to escape.

**do a hatchet job on** |dū u HACH ut jahb ahn| *v* To destroy by means of a false or malicious verbal attack. ORIGINS: By analogy to SE **hatchet** meaning a chopping tool that is meant for hacking *st* to pieces.

**do a job on** |dū u JAHB ahn| *v* To beat up; to harass or pressure; to cause trouble for.

**do a number on**[1] |dū u NUM bur ahn| *v* To subject to pressure, whether emotional blackmail or moral pressure. ORIGINS: From SE **number** meaning "a performance" extended to mean "an emotional outburst intended to manipulate."

**do a number on**[2] |dū u NUM bur ahn| *v* To thoroughly defeat; to purposefully humiliate. ORIGINS: From SE **number** meaning "a display."

**do a slow burn** |dū u SLŌ BURN| *v* To experience a gradually increasing sense or show of anger.

**do away with** *sb* |dū u WĀ with *sb*| *v* To murder *sb*. USAGE INFO: By extension, "do away with oneself" means "to commit suicide."

**do for** *sb* |DŪ fawr *sb*| *v* To murder *sb*.

**do-gooder** |DŪ gŏŏd ur| *n* A generous person who naively supports change. ORIGINS: From SE **do** and **good**. USAGE INFO: Often used ironically of (possibly) well-intentioned people who assist/interfere in matters and situations that they don't fully understand.

**do one's damnedest\*** |dū wunz DAM dist| *v* To do everything in one's power; to give one's utmost. ORIGINS: By extension from SE **damn**, which literally means "Send (it) to hell." USAGE ALERT: The use of **damnedest** will make this expression objectionable in some contexts and to some people.
  • **do one's darnedest** |dū wunz DAHRN dist|

**do** *sb* **in** |dū *sb* IN| *v* To murder *sb*. USAGE INFO: By extension, "do oneself in" means "to commit suicide."

**do** *sb* **out of** |DŪ *sb* OUT uv| *v* To cheat or swindle *sb*.

**do the heavy lifting** |DŪ thu hev ē LIF ting| *v* To take on tasks that require serious and devoted work.

**do the trick** |dū thu TRIK| *v* To do the thing that solves a problem, fixes what's broken, or puts things right; to succeed.

**Do you catch my drift?** |dū yu KACH mī DRIFT| *phr* Do you get the gist of my message? ORIGINS: Not about individual words, but about gist, a meaning of **drift** by the sixteenth century. *See also* DO YOU GET MY DRIFT?

**Do you get my drift?** |dū yu GET mī DRIFT| *phr* Do you understand the point I'm making? ORIGINS: Not about individual words, but about gist, a meaning of **drift** by the sixteenth century. *See also* DO YOU CATCH MY DRIFT?

**Do you read me?** |dū yu RĒD mē| *phr* Have you picked up my transmission? ORIGINS: From the language used in checking on the reception of radio and telephone transmissions, dating from about 1930.

**doctor** |DAHK tur| *v* To modify or alter for the sake of deception or for other purposes.

**D**

**dodgy** |DAHJ ē| *adj* Unreliable; risky; arousing suspicion.

**dodo** |DŌ dō| *n* A stupid person. ORIGINS: By extension from the large clumsy bird dodo that lived in Mauritius, but has become extinct. USAGE INFO: Sometimes used in the phrase "dumb dodo." USAGE ALERT: Often used with intent to denigrate or insult and understood as such.

**Does a bear shit in the woods?** |duz u BER SHIT in *thu* WOŌDZ| *excl* Sarcastic rhetorical question in response to a question whose answer is obviously "yes." ORIGINS: From the obvious fact that bears in the wild defecate in the woods. USAGE ALERT: The use of **shit** in this phrase will make it objectionable in some contexts and to some people.

**Does it look like I give a damn?** |duz it LOŌK līk Ī giv u dam| *excl* I don't give a damn! *See* I DON'T GIVE A DAMN!

**Does it look like I give a fuck?** |duz it LOŌK līk Ī giv u fuk| *excl* I don't give a fuck! *See* I DON'T GIVE A FUCK!

**Does it look like I give a shit?** |duz it LOŌK līk Ī giv u shit| *excl* I don't give a shit! *See* I DON'T GIVE A SHIT!

**dog it** |DAWG it| *v* To waste time; to shirk one's work. ORIGINS: Comparing human behavior to a stereotype of dog behavior.

**dog's chance** |DOGZ chans| *n* A very small chance. ORIGINS: From the perception of a dog's limited opportunities. USAGE INFO: Most often used in the negative, as in "doesn't have a dog's chance."

**dogass(ed)** |DAWG as / DAWG ast| *adj* Worthless; inferior. ORIGINS: The item so described is being compared to a dog's rear end or buttocks, where waste is excreted. From slang **ass** meaning "the rear end or buttocks." *See* **-ASS(ED)** for more information about the suffix. USAGE INFO: Note that both the noun and the adjective form are used as adjectives. USAGE ALERT: The reference to **ass** will make this expression objectionable in some contexts and to some people.

**doggone(d)** |dawg GAWN / dawg GAWN'D| *a/a* Extreme; extremely; very. ORIGINS: Euphemism for **damn(ed)**. USAGE INFO: Used as an adjective ("doggone(d) dog") or an adverb ("doggone(d) good thing"). USAGE ALERT: Euphemisms may still be objectionable in some contexts and to some people.

**Doggone (it)!** |dawg GAWN / dawg GAWN it| *excl* An interjection expressing anger, frustration, dismay, etc. ORIGINS: Euphemism for **Damn! Damn it!** USAGE ALERT: Euphemisms may still be objectionable in some contexts and to some people.

**dogshit** |DAWG shit| *n* An item or items that are estimated to be of the same value or quality as excrement. ORIGINS: From slang **shit** meaning "excrement." USAGE INFO: Whereas **bullshit** usually refers to lies, doublespeak, and other examples of false or untruthful communications, **dogshit** generally refers to physical items of extremely poor quality or extremely low value. USAGE ALERT: Because it refers to excrement, this term will be objectionable in some situations and to some people.

**dollop** |DAH lup| *n* A large lump or portion; a small amount. ORIGINS: Related to Norwegian **dolp** meaning "a lump."

**done for**[1] |DUN fawr| *adj* Dead. USAGE INFO: Meaning may be literal or figurative.

**done for**[2]**/in** |DUN fawr / DUN in| *adj* Exhausted; very tired.

**donkey** |DAHN kē| *n* A person who is obstinate to the point of stupidity. ORIGINS: From conventional characteristics of the SE **donkey**.

**Don't make a peep!** |DŌNT māk u PĒP| *excl* Be quiet! ORIGINS: SE **peep** was the collective noun for a brood of chickens and is used to mean "the smallest sound" in this phrase as well as in **hear a peep out of**.

**Don't mind if I do!** |dōnt MĪND if ī DŪ| *excl* A somewhat round-about statement of agreement. ORIGINS: Short for "I don't mind if I do." USAGE INFO: Most phrases starting with *don't* are imperative. In this case, the *I* is dropped, but the sense of a first person indicative expression is retained.

**Don't quit your day job!** |DŌNT kwit yŏŏr DĀ jahb| *excl* I can't believe your prospects are as good as you say: I'd wait and see.

**Don't sweat it.** |dōnt SWET it| *phr* Don't worry about it. ORIGINS: The idea is that the person offering thanks should not get so worked up about the obligation that s/he breaks into a sweat.

**Dontcha know? Doncha know?** |dōn chu NŌ| *phr* You know this, don't you? ORIGINS: Shortened form of **Don't you know?** USAGE INFO: Often used as a rhetorical tag question—a question tagged onto the end of a statement that may or may not be said with expectation of a response. Other spellings include: **Dont ya know? Don't ya know?**

**doo-doo head, do-do head** |DŪ dū hed| *n* A stupid person; an offensive, disgusting, or contemptible person. ORIGINS: From slang **doo-doo**, a childish euphemism for **shit**, and slang suffix **-head**. Thus, though literally a euphemism for **shithead**, it doesn't have the same impact. USAGE INFO: Because **doo-doo** is a childish word, this term may be used in teasing. USAGE ALERT: The reference to excrement will make this term objectionable in some contexts and to some people.

**doobob** |DŪ bahb| *n See* DOODAD.

**doodad, doodah, dooda, do-da** |DŪ dah| *n* Any nameless small object, or small object for which one cannot remember the name; often refers to a gadget. ORIGINS: May derive from people's efforts to recall a forgotten name. USAGE INFO: Exact sound and spelling vary too widely for all variations to be listed.

**doodley-squat, doodleysquat** |DŪD lē skwaht| *n* Nothing at all. ORIGINS: A variant euphemism for **diddley-shit**. USAGE INFO: Often used in constructions with an (implied) double negative, as in "He doesn't have doodly-squat." Abbreviated use with just **squat**. USAGE ALERT: The euphemism **squat** in this phrase will soften it somewhat, but it may still be objectionable in some contexts and to some people.

**doodly-shit, doodley-shit** |DŪD lē shit| *n* A small or worthless amount, particularly of money; nothing at all. ORIGINS: Variation on slang **diddley** meaning "anything insignificant" and an extension of slang **shit** meaning "excrement" to be an intensifier. USAGE INFO: Often used in constructions with an (implied) double negative: "I don't have doodley-shit." "I don't have doodley" is heard much less frequently than "I don't have diddley" (with whichever spelling). USAGE ALERT: The use of **shit** will make this phrase objectionable in some situations and to some people.

**doofus, dufus** |DŪ fus| *n* A person who is incompetent, foolish, or stupid. ORIGINS: May be related to slang **goofus** with a similar meaning. Doofus has been popularized by the character of Doofus Drake of Disney's *Duck Tales* (1987–1990) and Daggett Doofus Beaver in Nickelodeon's show *The Angry Beavers* (1997–2001). USAGE ALERT: Usually used with intent to denigrate or insult and understood as such.

**doohickey, dohickey, doohicky*** |DŪ hi kē| *n* Any nameless small object, or small object for which one cannot remember the name; often refers to a gadget. ORIGINS: May derive from people's efforts to recall a forgotten name. USAGE INFO: Exact sound and spelling vary too widely for all variations to be listed.
• doohinky |DŪ hing kē|

**doojigger, dojigger** |DŪ jig ur| *n* Any nameless small object, or small object for which one cannot remember the name; often refers to a gadget. ORIGINS: May derive from people's efforts to recall a forgotten name. USAGE INFO: Exact sound and spelling vary too widely for all variations to be listed.

**doormat** |DAWR mat| *n* A submissive person who gives in to the domination or mistreatment of others. ORIGINS: By extension from the abuse received by an SE doormat, a small rug that stands before a door and that is "walked all over."

**dope**[1] |dōp| *n* Reliable information; essential, important information. USAGE INFO: Often in the phrases "the inside dope" or "get the dope on . . . ."

**dope**[2] |dōp| *n* A fool; a stupid person. USAGE ALERT: Can be used affectionately, but often used with intent to denigrate or insult and understood as such.

**dopey** |DŌP ē| *adj* Silly; stupid. USAGE INFO: Often of an idea.

**dork** |dawrk| *n* A socially inept or stupid person. ORIGINS: Possibly an alteration from slang **dick**, supported by the fact that another meaning of **dork** is "penis." USAGE ALERT: Those who know the anatomical use of **dork** may find its use objectionable on those grounds. May be used in banter, but often used with intent to denigrate or insult and understood as such.

**dorkus maximus** |DAWRK us MAK si mus| *n* A complete idiot. ORIGINS: Fake Latin construction meaning "the ultimate dork," with **dork** meaning "a socially inept or stupid person." USAGE ALERT: Usually used with intent to denigrate or insult and understood as such.

**double-quick** |DU bul kwik| *adj* Extremely fast. ORIGINS: From SE **double** and SE **quick**.

**douchebag** |DŪSH bag| *n* A disgusting person; a worthless, obnoxious person. ORIGINS: From the SE **douchebag**, a device for cleaning the vaginal cavity and the slang suffix -bag. USAGE ALERT: The implied reference to sex and the sex organs in this term will make it objectionable in some contexts and to some people. Usually used with intent to denigrate or insult and understood as such.

**dough** |dō| *n* An unspecified amount of money. USAGE INFO: Both **dough** and bread are used to refer to money in the US.

**down** |doun| *adj* Depressed; dejected. ORIGINS: Based on the conceptualization of happy as being equivalent to up and sad being equivalent to down.

**down-and-out** |doun und OUT| *adj* Poor and homeless. ORIGINS: From the situation of being both "*down* in the gutter" and "*out* of luck."

**down for the count** |doun fawr *thu* KOUNT| *phr* A hair's breadth from complete failure. ORIGINS: From boxing jargon for the situation in which a boxer who is knocked down has till the end of the count to get up and return to the fight; otherwise the contestant left standing is declared the winner.

**down for the count, be** |doun fawr *thu* KOUNT| *v* To be defeated. ORIGINS: From boxing, for the situation in which a boxer who is knocked down has a count of 10 to arise and resume fighting; otherwise s/he loses.

**down in the dumps** |doun in *thu* DUMPS| *adj* Miserable; very unhappy or depressed. ORIGINS: An extension from slang **down** meaning "depressed."

**down in the mouth** |doun in *thu* MOUTH| *adj* Miserable; very unhappy or depressed. ORIGINS: The mouth of someone feeling this way has the corners turned down.

**down with** *st* |DOUN with *st*| *adj* To find something to be cool, enjoyable, or acceptable. ORIGINS: By extension of slang adjective **down** meaning "to be aware of." USAGE INFO: Not to be confused with "get down with," most of the meanings of which have to do with sexual activity.

**downer** |DOUN ur| *n* A bad situation; a situation that is worrisome or depressing. ORIGINS: By extension of slang **down** meaning "a state of depression."

**dragging** |DRAG ing| *adj* Feeling ill or lethargic; utterly exhausted. ORIGINS: From the movements of "dragging themselves around" made by people who feel this way.

**Drat (it)!** |drat / DRAT it| *excl* An interjection expressing anger, frustration, dismay, etc. ORIGINS: From the phrase "God rot it." Subsequently, a euphemism for **Damn! Damn it!** USAGE ALERT: Euphemisms may still be objectionable in some contexts and to some people.

**dratted** |DRAT id| *a/a* Extreme; extremely; very. Substitute for **damn(ed)**. ORIGINS: From the phrase "God rot it." Subsequently, a euphemism for **damn(ed)**. USAGE INFO: Used as an adjective ("dratted computer") or an adverb ("dratted awful insect"). USAGE ALERT: Euphemisms may still be objectionable in some contexts and to some people.

**dreadfully** |DRED ful ē| *adv* Very much; extremely. ORIGINS: Extended from SE **dreadful** meaning "inspiring dread, awe, or reverence." USAGE INFO: As in "I'm dreadfully sorry."

**dreamy** |DRĒM ē| *adj* So outstandingly attractive that one can hardly believe one is seeing it in real life.

**dreck** |drek| *n* An item or items that are estimated to be of the same value or quality as excrement. ORIGINS: From Yiddish **drek** and German **dreck** meaning "excrement" and "trash" respectively.

**dribs and drabs** |DRIBZ und drabz| *n* Small amounts (at irregular intervals).

**drip** |drip| *n* A weak, spineless, boring person. ORIGINS: From extension of SE **drip**, a weak, inadequate flow of water. USAGE ALERT: Usually used with intent to denigrate or insult and understood as such.

**drive *sb* crazy** |DRĪV *sb* KRĀ zē| *v* To exasperate *sb* to the point of distraction.

**drooly** |DROŌ lē| *adj* Desirable; sexy. ORIGINS: From the idea that an observer will drool with desire.

**drop** |drahp| *v* To knock *sb* down. ORIGINS: From SE **drop** meaning "to fall down," which is what the recipient of a drop does.

**drop-dead** |DRAHP DED| *adv* Impressively; enough to knock *sb* out. ORIGINS: From the imagined result of the observer dropping dead from the beauty seen. USAGE INFO: Often in the phrase "drop-dead gorgeous."

**Drop dead!** |DRAHP DED| *excl* A contemptuous dismissal. USAGE INFO: Although it may sound like a curse, the phrase is usually not meant literally. USAGE ALERT: Usually used with intent to be rude and understood as such.

**drop off** |DRAHP AWF| *v* To fall asleep. ORIGINS: A figurative use, perhaps playing on the idea of letting consciousness drop away.

**drop *sb* in it** |DRAHP *sb* IN it| *v* To do or say something that gets another person in trouble; to deliberately pass the responsibility. ORIGINS: As in other expressions, *it* can refer to trouble, but a parallel expression **drop *sb* in the shit** suggests that in some people's minds, **shit** might be the reference for it. USAGE ALERT: If the reference of *it* is **shit**, or if people think it is, this saying could be objectionable in some contexts and to some people.

**drop the ball** |DRAHP *thu* bawl| *v* To make a mistake at a telling moment. ORIGINS: From sports imagery that could apply to several sports, including baseball and football, in which it is legal to catch or carry the ball and losing hold of it can result in a penalty.

**drub** |drub| *v* To hit with repeated, heavy blows, often with a stick.

**Dry up!** |DRĪ up| *v* Be quiet! ORIGINS: This expression treats speech as if it were a flow of water, with drying analogous to being quiet. USAGE ALERT: Usually used with intent to denigrate or insult and understood as such.

**duck soup** |DUK sūp| *n* Easily resolved; simple. ORIGINS: Popularity boosted by the (still popular) 1933 Marx Brothers' film *Duck Soup*.

**ducky** |DUK ē| *adj* Excellent; delightful, charming, darling. ORIGINS: Possibly from the charm of ducklings. USAGE INFO: Often used ironically.

**duffer** |DUF ur| *n* An incompetent person.

**dum-dum** |DUM dum| *n* A stupid person. ORIGINS: Reduplication and alteration of **dumb**, possibly popularized by the lollipop named the *dum dum*, which may have been named with the British **dummy** meaning "pacifier" in mind. USAGE ALERT: *Dumb* has been used in English to refer to an inability to speak and to stupidity; it is now considered by some to be derogatory in any usage. Moreover, this term, while it may be used affectionately, is often used with intent to denigrate or insult and understood as such.

**dumb bastard** |DUM BAS turd| *n* An idiot; a person who is both stupid and obnoxious. ORIGINS: From slang **dumb**, meaning "lacking in intelligence" and **bastard**, meaning "a despicable, nasty person," extended from SE **bastard** meaning "an illegitimate child." USAGE ALERT: *Dumb* has been used in English to refer to an inability to speak and to stupidity; it is now considered by some to be derogatory in any usage. In addition, the inclusion of **bastard** in this term will make it objectionable in some contexts and to some people. Moreover, this term is usually used with intent to denigrate or insult and understood as such.

**dumb bunny** |DUM BUN ē| *n* A person who is both stupid and pathetic. ORIGINS: From slang **dumb**, meaning "lacking in intelligence" and **bunny**, meaning "a fool," based on the convention that bunnies are not too bright. USAGE INFO: *Dumb* has been used in English to refer to an inability to speak and to stupidity; it is now considered by some to be derogatory in any usage.

**dumb cluck** |DUM kluk| *n* A person who is both stupid and pathetic. ORIGINS: From slang **dumb**, meaning "lacking in intelligence" and **cluck** meaning "a dull person," based on the convention that chickens are not too bright. USAGE ALERT: *Dumb* has been used in English to refer to an inability to speak and to stupidity; it is now considered by some to be derogatory in any usage. Moreover, this term is usually used with intent to denigrate or insult and understood as such.

**dumb dodo** |DUM DŌ dō| *n* A very stupid person. ORIGINS: From slang **dumb**, meaning "lacking in intelligence" and **dodo**, meaning "a fool," based on the convention that the large, clumsy birds that are now extinct were not too bright. USAGE ALERT: *Dumb* has been used in English to refer to an inability to speak and to stupidity; it is now considered by some to be derogatory in any usage.

**dumb fuck** |DUM fuk| *n* An idiot who is also obnoxious. ORIGINS: From slang dumb, meaning "lacking in intelligence" and **fuck**, meaning "a despicable person," extended from **fuck**, meaning "sexual intercourse." USAGE ALERT: *Dumb* has been used in English to refer to an inability to speak and to stupidity; it is now considered by some to be derogatory in any usage. In addition, the inclusion of **fuck** in this term will make it objectionable in some contexts and to some people. Moreover, this term is usually used with intent to denigrate or insult and understood as such.

**dumb ox** |DUM ahks| *n* A very stupid, dull person. ORIGINS: From slang dumb, meaning "lacking in intelligence" and ox, meaning "slow and stupid," based on the convention that oxen are not too bright. USAGE ALERT: *Dumb* has been used in English to refer to an inability to speak and to stupidity; it is now considered by some to be derogatory in any usage. Moreover, this term is usually used with intent to denigrate or insult and understood as such.

**dumb shit** |DUM shit| *n* An idiot who is also obnoxious. ORIGINS: From slang dumb, meaning "lacking in intelligence" and **shit**, meaning "a despicable person," extended from **shit**, meaning "excrement." USAGE ALERT: *Dumb* has been used in English to refer to an inability to speak and to stupidity; it is now considered by some to be derogatory in any usage. In addition, the inclusion of **shit** in this term will make it objectionable in some contexts and to some people. Moreover, this term is usually used with intent to denigrate or insult and understood as such.

**dumbass** |DUM as| *n* An idiot; a stupid and obnoxious person. ORIGINS: From slang dumb, meaning "lacking in intelligence" and **ass**, referring to the portion of the anatomy in which the person's brains are estimated to reside. Slang **ass** is an extension of SE ass meaning "a donkey," but commonly used as slang to refer to the rear end or buttocks. USAGE ALERT: *Dumb* has been used in English to refer to an inability to speak and to stupidity; it is now considered by some to be derogatory in any usage. In addition, the inclusion of **ass** in this term will make it objectionable in some contexts and to some people. Moreover, this term is usually used with intent to denigrate or insult and understood as such.

**dumbbell, dumb-bell** |DUM bel| *n* A stupid person. ORIGINS: By extension from the SE **dumbbell**, originally an apparatus to strengthen aspiring bell-ringers employing weights which—not having clappers—functioned as "dumb bells" for the sake of the exercise. USAGE ALERT: *Dumb* has been used in English to refer to an inability to speak and to stupidity; it is now considered by some to be derogatory in any usage. Moreover, this term is usually used with intent to denigrate or insult and understood as such.

**dumbbutt, dumbutt** |DUM but| *n* An idiot; a stupid and obnoxious person. ORIGINS: A euphemism for **dumbass**. From slang dumb, meaning "lacking in intelligence" and **butt**, referring to the portion of the anatomy in which the person's brains are estimated to reside. Slang **butt** is a euphemism for **ass**, an extension of SE ass meaning "a donkey," but commonly used as slang to refer to the rear end or buttocks. USAGE ALERT: *Dumb* has been used in English to refer to an inability to speak and to stupidity; it is now considered by some to be derogatory in any usage. In addition, the inclusion of **butt** in this term will make it objectionable in some contexts and to some people. Moreover, this term is usually used with intent to denigrate or insult and understood as such.

**dumbhead** |DUM hed| *n* An idiot; a stupid and obnoxious person. ORIGINS: From slang **dumb**, meaning "lacking in intelligence" and slang suffix **-head**. USAGE ALERT: *Dumb* has been used in English to refer to an inability to speak and to stupidity; it is now considered by some to be derogatory in any usage. Moreover, this term is usually used with intent to denigrate or insult and understood as such.

**dumbo** |DUM bō| *n* A stupid person; a fool. ORIGINS: By extension of the slang **dumb** meaning stupid; possibly popularized by the taunting treatment of Dumbo in the Disney movie *Dumbo* (1941; but note that re-release in theaters and on VHS and DVD have extended its audience into the twenty-first century). USAGE ALERT: *Dumb* has been used in English to refer to an inability to speak and to stupidity; it is now considered by some to be derogatory in any usage. Moreover, this term is often used with intent to denigrate or insult and understood as such.

**dummkopf, dumkopf** |DUM kupf| *n* A stupid person. ORIGINS: From German **dumm**, meaning "dumb" and **kopf** meaning "head." USAGE ALERT: *Dumb* has been used in English to refer to an inability to speak and to stupidity; it is now considered by some to be derogatory in any usage. Moreover, this term is usually used with intent to denigrate or insult and understood as such.

**dummy** |DUM ē| *n* A stupid person; one who is socially inept. ORIGINS: By extension from SE **dumb** meaning "without speech." USAGE ALERT: *Dumb* has been used in English to refer to an inability to speak and to stupidity; it is now considered by some to be derogatory in any usage. Moreover, this term is usually used with intent to denigrate or insult and understood as such.

**dump** |dump| *v* To get rid of; to abruptly end a relationship with.

**dump on** |DUMP ahn| *v* To criticize unfairly or unexpectedly; to let loose one's emotional baggage on someone. ORIGINS: By extension of SE **dump**.

**dumps, the** |*thu* DUMPS| *n* A period of depression. USAGE INFO: Often in the phrase "down in the dumps."

**dunderhead** |DUN dur hed| *n* A stupid person. ORIGINS: Possibly from Dutch **donder** meaning "thunder" and slang suffix **-head**. USAGE ALERT: Usually used with intent to denigrate or insult and understood as such.

**Dunno.** |du NŌ| *excl* I don't know. ORIGINS: Shortened and altered from phrase I don't know.

**durn** |durn| *adv See* DARN.

**durn(ed)** |durn / durn'd| *a/a* Extreme; extremely; very. ORIGINS: Euphemism for **damn(ed)**. USAGE INFO: Used as an adjective ("durn(ed) contraption") or an adverb ("durn(ed) fine day"). USAGE ALERT: Euphemisms may still be objectionable in some contexts and to some people.

**Durn (it)!** |durn / DURN it| *excl* An interjection expressing mild to moderate displeasure, frustration, or irritation, etc. ORIGINS: Euphemism for **Damn! Damn it!** USAGE ALERT: Euphemisms may still be objectionable in some contexts and to some people.

**durndest, durnedest** |DURN dist| *adj* Most of whatever is being expressed: most amazing, most difficult, etc. ORIGINS: Superlative of **durned**. Euphemism for **damnedest**. USAGE INFO: Often used in phrases such as "he was the durnedest fool." USAGE ALERT: Euphemisms may still be objectionable in some contexts and to some people.

**dust** |dust| *v* To beat up; to thrash. ORIGINS: From the practice of beating the dust out of a carpet.

**dusting** |DUS ting| *n* A beating. ORIGINS: From the practice of beating the dust out of a carpet.

**dustup** |DUS tup| *n* A fight. ORIGINS: From military operations in which the interaction of men on horseback with each other raised a lot of dust.

**dweeb** |dwēb| *n* A socially inept person; someone at home in academics to the exclusion of having developed social graces. ORIGINS: Unknown, but popularity possibly influenced by the candy dweebs from the Willy Wonka Candy Company, and the CBS comedy *Dweebs* (1995). USAGE ALERT: May be used teasingly, but usually used with intent to denigrate or insult and understood as such.

**dynamite** |DĪ nu mīt| *adj* Especially fine; excellent; wonderful. ORIGINS: By extension of SE **dynamite** meaning "a powerful explosive."

**dynamo** |DĪ nu mō| *n* An energetic and aggressive person. ORIGINS: By extension of SE **dynamo** meaning "a power generator."

# E

**EL** Evil laugh.

**ESAD** Eat shit and die.

**eager beaver** |Ē gur BĒ vur| *n* An earnest and hard-working person; an especially industrious person. ORIGINS: From the conventional concept of the SE **beaver** as industrious.

**easy mark/touch** |Ē zē mahrk / Ē zē tuch| *n* An easily persuadable person; someone gullible. ORIGINS: From SE **easy** and slang **mark** or **touch** meaning "potential victim for a con."

**easy on the eyes** |Ē zē ahn *th*ē ĪZ| *adj* Extremely attractive. USAGE INFO: Usually used in ironic understatement (i.e., litotes) of *sb* with extraordinary good looks.

**eat crap** |ĒT CRAP| v To retract an error and accept public humiliation; to undergo humiliation. ORIGINS: Euphemism for **eat shit**. From slang **crap**, a euphemism for **shit**, meaning "excrement." From the imagined suffering of eating excrement. USAGE ALERT: The graphic image along with the use of **crap** will make this phrase objectionable in some contexts and to some people.

**eat crow** |ĒT KRŌ| v To publicly admit an error or mistake; to undergo humiliation. ORIGINS: First appeared in the phrase "eat boiled crow," but of uncertain origins. Apparently crow tastes awful, which adds to the imagined unpleasantness.

**eat dirt** |ĒT DIRT| v To retract an error and accept public humiliation; to undergo humiliation. ORIGINS: From the imagined suffering of eating dirt.

**eat for breakfast** |ĒT fawr BREK fust| v To criticize harshly; to deal with or defeat handily or easily.

**eat humble pie** |ĒT hum bul PĪ| v To be forced to admit an error and accept public humiliation; to undergo humiliation. ORIGINS: Humble pie is a make-believe food to describe the experience of humiliation, but also a pun on "the umbles," the entrails and organs that the huntsman and servants ate in a pie, while the nobles they served ate the venison.

**Eat it!** |ĒT it| excl A contemptuous dismissal. ORIGINS: Either it refers to the penis (in which case the speaker is male) or the phrase is a euphemism for **Eat shit!** (used by both men and women). USAGE ALERT: Usually used with intent to be rude and understood as such.

**eat one's hat** |ĒT wunz HAT| v To retract an error; to make a public admission of a mistake.

**eat sb/st up** |ĒT sb/st up| v To be obsessed with. ORIGINS: By extension of SE **eat up**, meaning to eat avidly and with delight.

**eat shit** |ĒT SHIT| v To retract an error and accept public humiliation; to undergo humiliation. ORIGINS: From slang **shit** meaning "excrement." From the imagined suffering of eating excrement. USAGE ALERT: The graphic image along with the use of **shit** will make this phrase objectionable in some contexts and to some people.

**Eat shit!** |ēt SHIT| excl A contemptuous dismissal. ORIGINS: From slang **shit** meaning "excrement." USAGE ALERT: Usually used with intent to be rude and understood as such. In addition, the inclusion of **shit** and the graphic image will make this expression objectionable in some contexts and to some people.

**Eat shit and die!** |ĒT SHIT and DĪ| excl A contemptuous dismissal. ORIGINS: From slang **shit** meaning "excrement." USAGE INFO: Although it may sound like a curse, the phrase is usually not meant literally. USAGE ALERT: Usually used with intent to be rude and understood as such. In addition, the inclusion of **shit** and the graphic image will make this expression objectionable in some contexts and to some people.

**eat st up** |ĒT st UP| v To accept completely.

**Eep!** |ēp| *excl* Sound to express fear.

**Eff off!** |EFF awf| *excl* Go away! Euphemism for **Fuck off!** ORIGINS: From initial letter of slang **fuck** meaning "to engage in sexual intercourse." USAGE ALERT: The reference to the word **fuck** will make this expression objectionable in some contexts and to some people.

**effing** |EF ing| *a/a* Extreme; extremely; very. ORIGINS: Euphemism for **fucking** using the initial letter and suffix. USAGE INFO: Used as an adjective ("effing asshole") or an adverb ("What took you such an effing long time?"). USAGE ALERT: Euphemisms may still be objectionable in some contexts and to some people.

**Egad(s)!** |ē GAD / ē GADZ| *excl* An interjection expressing mild anxiety, consternation, frustration, relief, etc. ORIGINS: Euphemism for blasphemous use of **Oh, god!**, i.e., not in prayer. USAGE INFO: Many people will not know the origins of this expression. USAGE ALERT: Euphemisms may still be objectionable in some contexts and to some people.

**egghead** |EG hed| *n* An intellectual; a very bright, intelligent person. ORIGINS: From SE **egg** and slang suffix -**head**.

**end of the line** |END uv *thu* LĪN| *n* The final part of something; the moment at which there is no going back. ORIGINS: Possibly from railway jargon, in which the end of the line is the termination of the service.

**energizer bunny** |EN ur gī zur BUN ē| *n* Extremely determined, persistent, and industrious. ORIGINS: From the brand symbol of Energizer Batteries, a bunny that "Keeps Going and Going and . . .®" no matter what.

**epic fail** |EP ik fāl| *n* A disastrous or total defeat.

**Epic win!** |EP ik win| *excl* I've just won an extremely impressive victory! USAGE INFO: The opposite is not "epic lose," as one might think, but **epic fail**.

**Erk!** |erk| *excl* Sound to indicate that one is pulled up short by something unexpected and not good.

**even the score** |Ē vun *thu* SKAWR| *v* To do something that one believes makes things even; to get revenge. ORIGINS: From sports jargon.

**evil** |Ē vul| *adj* Excellent; wonderful. ORIGINS: On the "bad is good" model. *See* BAD. USAGE INFO: Used to express admiration for a trait that is so outstanding as to arouse playful jealousy. Evil is a contronym.

**Ew! Eww!** |ēū| *excl* Sound expressing disgust.

**excessorize** |ek SES awr īz| *v* To add an excessive number of accessories, destroying the effect. ORIGINS: A punning portmanteau of SE **excess** and **accessorize**.

**exec** |ig ZEK| *n* An executive or executive officer. ORIGINS: Shortened form of SE executive.

**exit** |EG zit| *v* To die. ORIGINS: Possibly from an actor's exit in the theatre.

**eyeball** |Ī bawl| *v* To examine thoroughly; give a long stare; inspect. ORIGINS: From the role of the SE eye in many types of evaluation.

**eyewash** |Ī wahsh| *n* Words or actions meant to conceal reality rather than reveal it; lies or untruths. ORIGINS: Extending the original meaning of "a treatment of the eyes."

**FIIK** Fucked if I know.

**FINE** Freaked out; insecure; neurotic; emotional. ORIGINS: Popularized in the movie *The Italian Job* (2003). USAGE INFO: *F* is sometimes used to represent other words, such as fucked up, frustrated, or foggy.

**FMUTA** Fuck me up the ass!

**FOAD** Fuck off and die.

**FOFL** Falling on floor, laughing.

**FOMCL** Falling off my chair, laughing.

**FTASB** Faster than a speeding bullet.

**FTL** For the loss. *See* <Proper noun> FOR THE LOSS!

**FTLOG** For the love of God!

**FTW** For the win. *See* <Proper noun> FOR THE WIN!

**FUBAR** |FŪ bahr| *adj* Utterly botched or confused. ORIGINS: Acronym for the phrase f(ucked) u(p) b(eyond) a(ll) r(ecognition), used by the US military. The term is sometimes further euphemized by substituting fouled for **fucked**. Different than **foobar**, a word used as a placeholder in computer programming. USAGE ALERT: People who recognize that the acronym comes from a phrase that includes the word **fucked** may find it objectionable.

**fab** |fab| *adj* Fabulous; wonderful. ORIGINS: Shortened form of SE **fabulous**. Popularized by The Beatles. USAGE INFO: Sometimes used ironically now.

**face-off** |FĀS awf| *n* A confrontation. ORIGINS: From sports jargon in, e.g., hockey, in which two opponents face each other (face off) and attempt to gain control of the puck that is dropped in between them.

**fake out** |FĀK out| *v* To trick, deceive, or fool.

**fall down on the job** |FAWL DOUN ahn *thu* JAHB| *v* To fail to meet expectations; to fail to come through with required elements.

**fall flat** |fawl FLAT| *v* To fail completely. ORIGINS: From the concept conveyed by the literal meaning of the SE words.

**fall (flat) on one's face** |FAWL ahn wunz FĀS / fawl FLAT ahn wunz FĀS| v To fail completely; to fail completely and be publicly humiliated as well. ORIGINS: From the concept conveyed by the literal meaning of the SE words.

**fall for** *sb* |FAWL fawr *sb*| v To fall in love with *sb*. USAGE INFO: The idiom *fall for st* means "to become the victim of."

**fall for** *st* |fawl fawr *st*| v To be fooled into accepting/believing *st* meant to deceive.

**fall guy** |FAWL gī| n A gullible victim of a scheme; a dupe; a scapegoat.

**fall head over heels for** |FAWL HED ō vur HĒLS fawr| v To grow to be very much in love. ORIGINS: The concept is of someone tumbling over and over.

**fall on one's ass** |FAWL ahn wunz AS| v To fail completely; to fail completely and be publicly humiliated as well. ORIGINS: From the concept conveyed by the literal meaning of the SE words. From slang **ass** meaning "the rear end or buttocks." USAGE ALERT: The inclusion of the word **ass** will make this phrase objectionable in some contexts and to some people.

**fancy** *sb* |FAN sē *sb*| v To find *sb* attractive and/or desirable.

**fancy schmancy** |FAN sē SHMAN sē| adj A derisive recognition of *st* high class. ORIGINS: From a characteristic Yiddish speech pattern of showing contempt by using reduplication of a word, replacing the initial letters with *shm* or *schm* in the second instance.

**fantabulous** |fan TAB yu lus| adj Both fantastic and fabulous. ORIGINS: A portmanteau word made from two other words, SE **fantastic** and SE **fabulous**.

**fart** |fahrt| n An annoying or unpleasant person, usually older than the speaker, thus synonymous with **old fart**. ORIGINS: From slang **fart** meaning "to break wind." USAGE ALERT: This word will be objectionable in some contexts and to some people. In addition, it is usually used with intent to insult, and understood as such.

**fart around/about** |FAHRT u round / FAHRT u bout| v To waste time; to mess around. ORIGINS: Euphemism for **fuck around/about**. From slang **fart** meaning "to break wind." USAGE ALERT: Euphemisms may still be objectionable in some contexts and to some people.

**fart (around) with** *st* |FAHRT u round with *st*| v To use something irresponsibly or without understanding; to mess around with. ORIGINS: Euphemism for **fuck (around) with** *st*. From slang **fart** meaning "to break wind." USAGE ALERT: Euphemisms may still be objectionable in some contexts and to some people.

**fat cat** |FAT KAT| n A prosperous or wealthy individual. ORIGINS: From slang fat meaning "wealthy" and slang **cat** meaning "a male person." USAGE INFO: Can be used to imply that the person's wealth was ill-gotten.

**fat chance** |FAT CHANS| n Used sarcastically to mean "no chance."

fat lot |FAT LAHT| *n* Used sarcastically to mean "very little."

fat mouth |FAT mouth| *n* A boaster or braggart. USAGE ALERT: Usually used with intent to denigrate or insult and understood as such.

fathead |FAT hed| *n* A stupid person. ORIGINS: From SE fat and slang suffix -head. USAGE ALERT: This term is usually used with intent to denigrate or insult and understood as such.

feed *sb* a line |FĒD *sb* u LĪN| *v* To say *st* untrue, often to appease *sb*.

feel weak at the knees |fēl WĒK at *th*u NĒZ| *v* Become suddenly overcome with fear or another strong emotion. ORIGINS: From the physical feeling.

feeling the pinch |FĒL ing *th*u PINCH| *adj* To experience the effects of reduced income. ORIGINS: Metaphorical application of SE pinch, as also in penny-pinching.

feisty |FĪS tē| *adj* Full of spirit or courage. ORIGINS: From rarely used SE feist meaning "a small dog."

ferret out |FER it out| *v* Discover through painstaking searching. ORIGINS: In the fifteenth century, partially-tamed ferrets were used to keep down the rat population and to flush rabbits from their warrens, leading eventually to the slang use.

few beers short of a six-pack, a |u FYŪ BIRZ shawrt uv u SIKS pak| *adj* Unintelligent; crazy. ORIGINS: One of many synonyms of the term not all there, which indulge in wordplay by representing "all there" in a particular way and designating how the person in question fails to meet the criteria. In this case, "all there" is represented by a six-pack, a type of packaging in which beer is typically sold. If you're missing several beers, you do not, in fact, have a six-pack. USAGE ALERT: Usually used with intent to denigrate or insult and understood as such.

few cents short of a dollar, a |u FYŪ SENS shawrt uv u DAHL ur| *adj* Unintelligent; crazy. ORIGINS: One of many synonyms of the term not all there, which indulge in wordplay by representing "all there" in a particular way and designating how the person in question fails to meet the criteria. In this case, "all there" is represented by a dollar. If you're missing a few cents, you do not, in fact, have a dollar. USAGE ALERT: Usually used with intent to denigrate or insult and understood as such.

few fries short of a happy meal, a |u FYŪ FRĪZ shawrt uv u HAP ē mēl| *adj* Unintelligent; crazy. ORIGINS: One of many synonyms of the term not all there, which indulge in wordplay by representing "all there" in a particular way and designating how the person in question fails to meet the criteria. In this case, "all there" is represented by a McDonald's Happy Meal, a child-size meal that includes a main course, a drink, and a side-order, which is—in the stereotypical model—French fries. By a bit of a stretch, if you're missing several fries, you do not have a full-fledged Happy Meal. USAGE ALERT: Usually used with intent to denigrate or insult and understood as such.

few peas short of a casserole, a |u FYŪ PĒZ shawrt uv u CAS ur ōl| *adj* Unintelligent; crazy. ORIGINS: One of many synonyms of the term not all there, which indulge in wordplay by representing "all there" in a particular way and designating how the person in question fails to meet the criteria. In this case, "all there" is represented by a **casserole**, a baked meal-in-one-dish including—in the stereotypical conception—peas. By a bit of a stretch, without the peas, you do not have a full-fledged ideal casserole. USAGE ALERT: Usually used with intent to denigrate or insult and understood as such.

**few pecans short of a fruitcake, a** |u FYŪ pē KAHNZ shawrt uv u FRŪT kāk| *adj* Unintelligent; crazy. ORIGINS: One of many synonyms of the term **not all there**, which indulge in wordplay by representing "all there" in a particular way and designating how the person in question fails to meet the criteria. In this case, "all there" is represented by a **fruitcake**, a holiday cake made of flour, dried and candied fruit, and nuts (sometimes pecans), which—in the stereotypical model—are de rigeur (required). By a bit of a stretch, if you're missing several pecans, you do not have a full-fledged, authentic fruitcake. The relationship of nuts and fruitcake is also referenced in several slang phrases meaning crazy, such as **nutty as a fruitcake**. USAGE ALERT: Usually used with intent to denigrate or insult and understood as such.

**few sandwiches short of a picnic, a** |u FYŪ SAND wich iz shawrt uv u PIK nik| *adj* Unintelligent; crazy. ORIGINS: One of many synonyms of the term **not all there**, which indulge in wordplay by representing "all there" in a particular way and designating how the person in question fails to meet the criteria. In this case, "all there" is represented by a **picnic** spread, an outdoor meal including—in the stereotypical conception—sandwiches, side dishes, dessert, and drinks, often designed to be eaten with few or no implements. By a bit of a stretch, without enough sandwiches, you do not have a full-fledged ideal picnic. USAGE ALERT: Usually used with intent to denigrate or insult and understood as such.

**few slices short of a loaf, a** |u FYŪ SLĪ siz shawrt uv u LŌF| *adj* Unintelligent; crazy. ORIGINS: One of many synonyms of the term **not all there**, which indulge in wordplay by representing "all there" in a particular way and designating how the person in question fails to meet the criteria. In this case, "all there" is represented by a **loaf**, a typical way of preparing bread and packaging it for sale. If you're missing several slices, you do not, in fact, have a full loaf. USAGE ALERT: Usually used with intent to denigrate or insult and understood as such.

**few spokes short of a wheel, a** |u FYŪ SPŌKS shawrt uv u WĒL| *adj* Unintelligent; crazy. ORIGINS: One of many synonyms of the term **not all there**, which indulge in wordplay by representing "all there" in a particular way and designating how the person in question fails to meet the criteria. In this case, "all there" is represented by a **wheel** of the type found on a bicycle, with spokes connecting the outside edge to the hub. By a bit of a stretch, without enough spokes, you do not have a full-fledged ideal wheel. USAGE ALERT: Usually used with intent to denigrate or insult and understood as such.

**fiddle around** |FID ul u ROUND| *v* To fool around; to waste time. ORIGINS: From slang **fiddle** meaning "to shirk one's duty."

**fiddle (around) with** *st* |FID ul with *st*/ FID ul u ROUND with *st*| *v* To use something irresponsibly or without understanding; to mess around with. ORIGINS: From slang **fiddle** meaning "to shirk one's duty."

**fiddle-faddle** |FID ul fad ul| *n* Nonsense or untrue words. ORIGINS: Reduplication of fiddle.

**fiend** |fēnd| *sfx* An avid enthusiast; an addict; one who is obsessed by. ORIGINS: From SE **fiend** meaning "the devil." USAGE INFO: Despite origins, is used light-heartedly, as in, e.g., a tennis fiend.

**fiendishly** |FĒND ish lē| *adv* Extremely. ORIGINS: Euphemism for **devilishly**. From SE **fiend** meaning "the devil." USAGE INFO: Despite origins, is used light-heartedly as in, e.g., "fiendishly clever."

**fierce** |firs| *adj* Excellent; wonderful. ORIGINS: From SE **fierce** meaning "filled with vehemence," modified on the "bad is good" model. Repopularized in 2008 by Project Runway winner Christian Siriano, who uses **fierce** as a catchphrase.

**filch** |filch| *v* To furtively take *st*; to steal. ORIGINS: Popularized by the name of the character Argus Filch, Hogwarts' caretaker known for taking away students' possessions in the Harry Potter series.

**filthy** |FIL thē| *a/a* A general intensifier: very; extremely. ORIGINS: SE **filthy** meaning "very dirty." USAGE INFO: Used as an adjective ("filthy temper"), and very often connected with money, as in this adverbial use ("filthy rich").

**filthy rich** |FIL thē RICH| *adj* Having lots of money.

**filthy with <noun>** |FIL thē with <noun>| *adj* Full of; overloaded with. ORIGINS: From slang use of **filthy** as an intensifier. USAGE INFO: An example is the phrase "filthy with money."

**finagle** |fin Ā gul| *v* To cheat; to obtain deceitfully.

**finger** |FIN gur| *v* To inform on; to tip off about. ORIGINS: From the practice of pointing an accusing finger at someone.

**fink** |FINGK| *v* To inform against.

**fink out** |FINGk out| *v* To withdraw support; to renege.

**firewall** |FĪR wawl| *v* To accelerate maximally.

**fit to be tied** |FIT tū bē TĪD| *v* Enraged. ORIGINS: From the situation of someone so angry that s/he needs to be restrained (tied).

**fit to burst/bust** |fit tū BURST / fit tū BUST| *adj* To the greatest possible extent. ORIGINS: The concept is of having so much of *st* (emotion, for example) that no more is possible without destruction. USAGE INFO: Often used of displays of emotion, as in "laughing fit to bust."

**fit to kill** |fit tū KIL| *adj* To a great extent; to excess; in a striking manner. USAGE INFO: Often used in the phrases "dressed fit to kill" and "laughing fit to kill."

**fix** |fiks| *n* A predicament; a problematic situation. ORIGINS: The situation in which one is stuck or "fixed."

**fix *sb's* wagon** |FIKS *sb's* WAG un| *v* To get revenge; to thwart another's plans. USAGE INFO: A negative use of fix, which usually means to repair rather than to disable, making *fix* a contronym.

**fizzle (out)** |FIZ ul / FIZ ul out| *v* To fail; to slowly succumb to failure. ORIGINS: From the slang fizzle meaning "to fail" and (leak) out, calling to mind the sound of a slow air leak from a tire.

**flap one's gums/lips** |FLAP wunz GUMZ / FLAP wunz LIPS| *v* To talk about trivial things; to talk, but to no purpose.

**flapdoodle** |FLAP dū dul| *n* Foolish or nonsensical talk.

**flare-up** |FLER up| *n* Fit of anger; an eruption of strong feeling.

**flat broke** |FLAT BRŌK| *adj* Totally out of money. ORIGINS: From slang flat meaning "completely" and slang broke meaning "out of money."

**flatten** |FLAT un| *v* To knock *sb* down. ORIGINS: The word suggests the person who has been hit lying flat on the floor.

**flea short of an infestation, a** |u FLĒ shawrt uv an in fes TĀ shun| *adj* Unintelligent; crazy. ORIGINS: One of many synonyms of the term not all there, which indulge in wordplay by representing "all there" in a particular way and designating how the person in question fails to meet the criteria. In this case, "all there" is represented by an **infestation**, a large group of unwanted animals. By a bit of a stretch, without enough fleas, you do not have a full-fledged infestation. USAGE ALERT: Usually used with intent to denigrate or insult and understood as such.

**flea-bitten** |FLĒ bit un| *adj* Worn; seedy; dilapidated. ORIGINS: By extension of imagining the kind of place that would have a flea infestation.

**fleece** |flēz| *v* To defraud; to swindle. ORIGINS: The concept is of peeling off money as easily as the fleece is peeled off a sheep by an expert shearer.

**flip for *sb/st*** |FLIP fawr *sb/st*| *v* To become obsessed with *sb/st*; to become infatuated with *sb/st*. ORIGINS: By extension of slang flip meaning "to become overly excited about."

**flip one's lid/wig** |FLIP wunz lid / FLIP wunz wig| *v* To lose one's temper; to fly into a rage; to lose control emotionally; to go crazy. ORIGINS: From slang lid meaning "head."

**flip out** |FLIP out| *v* To become angry; to lose control. ORIGINS: By extension of slang flip meaning "to lose control."

**flipping** |FLIP ing| *a/a* Extreme; extremely; very. ORIGINS: Euphemism for **fucking**. USAGE INFO: Used as an adjective ("flipping idiot") or an adverb ("flipping good time"). USAGE ALERT: Euphemisms may still be objectionable in some contexts and to some people.

**floor** |flawr| *v* To knock *sb* down. ORIGINS: The concept is of the person who has been hit falling to the floor as a result.

**floor it** |FLAWR it| *v* To go really fast (in a vehicle). ORIGINS: From the action of someone driving a vehicle and pushing the accelerator pedal all the way down (to the floor).

**flop** |flahp| *v* To fail, particularly of a performance or a string of performances.

**flub** |flub| *v* To make a mess of; to bungle; to botch.

**fluff** |fluf| *v* To make a mistake; to bungle; to fail because of memory lapse. ORIGINS: From theatre jargon for actors who forget or confuse their lines.

**fluffhead** |FLUF hed| *n* A shallow, superficial person. ORIGINS: From SE **fluff** meaning "something with little substance" and the slang suffix -**head**. USAGE ALERT: Usually used with intent to denigrate or insult, and usually considered an insult.

**flummoxed** |FLUM ikst| *adj* Confused or perplexed. USAGE INFO: Used of people.

**flunk (out)** |flungk / FLUNGK OUT| *v* To fail an examination; to be dismissed from a school for academic failure.

**flunky** |FLUN kē| *n* A menial. ORIGINS: From SE **flunky** meaning "servant."

**flush** |flush| *adj* Having lots of money. ORIGINS: From SE **flush** meaning "overflowing."

**fly** |flī| *adj* Fashionable; stylish.

**fly by the seat-of-one's-pants** |FLĪ bī *thu* SĒT uv wunz PANTS| *v* To act based on intuition rather than a concrete plan; to improvise; to indulge in extremely risky behavior by choice. ORIGINS: From WWII aviators describing the experience of flying when instruments were not functioning or visibility was poor. USAGE INFO: The phrase can be merely a description of how someone behaves by necessity (when they run out of time, for example) or a condemnation of reckless behavior.

**fly in the ointment** |FLĪ in *thu* OINT munt| *n* Something small that nevertheless spoils an entire plan or project; a small setback; a detraction. From SE **fly** meaning "a flying insect" and SE **ointment** meaning "salve."

**fly off the handle** |FLĪ ahf *thu* HAN dul| *v* To become extremely angry; to lose control. ORIGINS: From what happens when an axe head becomes detached from the handle.

**fly the coop** |FLĪ *thu* KŪP| *v* To leave suddenly; to escape from prison.

**foaming at the mouth** |FŌM ing at *thu* MOUTH| *adj* Furious; enraged. ORIGINS: From the characteristics of a rabid dog.

**fold** |fold| *v* To shut down operations; to fail completely.

**food for squirrels** |FŪD fawr SKWURLZ| *adj* Crazy. ORIGINS: A euphemism for nuts. USAGE ALERT: Often used with intent to denigrate or insult and understood as such. This way of speaking about *sb's* mental health may be considered insensitive and therefore objectionable in some contexts and by some people.

**fool around** |FŪL u ROUND| *v* To act without aim or accomplishment; to waste time. USAGE INFO: Can also refer to sexual activity especially with someone who is not one's spouse or partner.

**fool (around) with** *st* |FŪL with *st* / FŪL u ROUND with *st*| *v* To use something irresponsibly or without understanding; to mess around with. USAGE INFO: Distinct from **fool around with** *sb*, which can refer to joint goofing off or to sexual activity.

**for a song** |fawr u SAHNG| *adv* For very little money; at a low price; cheaply.

**For Christ's sake!** * |fawr KRĪST sāk| *excl* Oh no! ORIGINS: From SE Jesus Christ whom Christians hold to be the Son of God. USAGE ALERT: The inclusion of the word Jesus in the phrase will make it seem blasphemous and objectionable in some contexts and to some people.
• **For Chrissake!** |fawr KRĪ sāk| *excl*

**For crying out loud!** |fawr KRĪ ing out loud| *excl* Oh no! ORIGINS: Euphemism of phrases **For Christ's sake!**, **Chrissake!** From SE Jesus Christ whom Christians hold to be the Son of God. USAGE ALERT: Most people will not recognize this phrase as a euphemism or know what phrase it comes from.

**for free** |fawr FRĒ| *adv* Essentially as a gift, with no recompense; with no strings attached.

**For fuck's sake!** |fawr FUK sāk| *excl* Oh no! ORIGINS: From slang **fuck** meaning "to engage in sexual intercourse." USAGE ALERT: The inclusion of **fuck** will make this expression objectionable in some contexts and to some people.

**For God's sake!** |fawr GAHD sāk| *excl* Oh no! ORIGINS: By extension from SE god meaning a being conceived as the divine Lord of the universe. USAGE ALERT: People who consider this use of **god** blasphemous are likely to find it objectionable.

**for nothing** |fawr NU thing| *adv* Essentially as a gift, with no recompense; with no strings attached.

**For Pete's sake!** |fawr PĒT sāk| *excl* Oh no! ORIGINS: Euphemism of phrase **For Christ's sake!**

**For real!** |fawr RĒL| *excl* Honestly; truly.

**For sure!** |fawr SHUR| *excl* Certainly.

**for the birds** |fawr *thu* BURDZ| *adj* Worthless; absurd; unacceptable. ORIGINS: Conveys the idea of something not appropriate for humans, but possibly acceptable to lesser beings.

**For the love of Mike!** |fawr *thu* LUV uv MĪK| *excl* Oh no! ORIGINS: Euphemism of phrase **For the love of God!**

**For the love of Pete!** |fawr *thu* LUV uv PĒT| *excl* Oh no! ORIGINS: Euphemism of phrase **For the love of God!**

**For true!** |fawr TRŪ| *excl* Truly! Honestly!

**Forget it.** |fur GED it| *phr* You don't need to feel obligated. ORIGINS: The idea is that the person offering thanks does not have to keep track of the obligation and remember to repay it.

**fork out/over** |FAWRK out / FAWRK ō vur| *v* To give out; to hand over, often reluctantly or under duress. ORIGINS: From slang **forks** meaning "hands."

**foul up** |FOUL up| *n* To make a mistake; to commit a blunder. ORIGINS: Euphemism for **fuck up**. From US military use. *See* **FUBAR** and **SNAFU**. USAGE ALERT: People who suspect euphemistic use may find this objectionable based on the phrase that hasn't been used.

**fouled up** |FOULD up| *adj* In a mess; chaotic. ORIGINS: Euphemism for **fucked up**. From US military use. *See* **FUBAR** and **SNAFU**. USAGE ALERT: People who suspect euphemistic use may find this objectionable based on the phrase that hasn't been used.

**fox** |fahks| *v* To outwit; to deceive with cunning. ORIGINS: From the common conception of the fox as a sly, clever creature.

**foxy** |FAHK sē| *adj* Sexy; attractive. ORIGINS: Based on a stereotype of behavior of foxes.

**frabjous** |FRAB jus| *adj* "Probably a blend of fair, fabulous, and joyous." ORIGINS: Definition from Lewis Carroll (Charles L. Dodgson), who coined this portmanteau word for his poem "Jabberwocky" which appeared in *Through the Looking-Glass, and What Alice Found There* (1871).

**fracture** |FRAK chur| *v* To make someone laugh heartily. USAGE INFO: **Fracture** is a contronym: it can also mean "to beat up."

**frag** |frag| *v* To wound or kill a fellow soldier or ally with an explosive, such as a fragmentation grenade. ORIGINS: Shortened from SE **fragmentation**.

**fraidy cat** |FRĀ dē kat| *n* One who's afraid; a coward. ORIGINS: From a childish shortening and alteration of SE **afraid** combined with SE **cat**, perhaps for their sometimes skittish behavior. USAGE INFO: Used in taunts by children; sometimes playfully or in teasing by adults, although it can be used to denigrate and insult.

**freak** |frēk| *sfx* Someone obsessed with or overly fond of something. ORIGINS: From the slang noun **freak**, meaning "someone who's obsessed." USAGE INFO: This word usually has negative connotations, as in "control freak."

**freak out** |FRĒK OUT| *v* To go crazy from fear; to lose control; to become greatly upset; to suffer an emotional breakdown. ORIGINS: From slang **freak** meaning "drug user"—developed from the volatile emotional state of someone who uses hallucinogenic drugs.

**freak *sb* out** |FRĒK *sb* OUT| *v* To cause *sb* to be afraid.

**freaking** |FRĒK ing| *a/a* Extreme; extremely; very. ORIGINS: Euphemism for **fucking**. A slang word that is related to sexuality and sounds very similar to **fucking**. In its denotative use (i.e., when it is not acting as an intensifier), **freaking** means "sexually perverse." USAGE INFO: Used as an adjective ("freaking moron") or an adverb ("freaking good meal"). Note that many users may think that this word is a sanitized version of the word **fucking**, not recognizing it as a real word with an independent existence. USAGE ALERT: People who know the denotative meanings of this word or suspect that it is being used as a euphemism for **fucking** are likely to find the terms objectionable.

**free lunch** |frē LUNCH| *n* Something obtained without the usual fee, transaction, exchange. ORIGINS: Free lunches were provided for paying customers at taverns in the nineteenth century. The term was popularized with the saying "There Ain't No Such Thing As A Free Lunch" (abbreviated with the acronym TANSTAAFL) by Robert Heinlein in a science fiction novel *The Moon Is a Harsh Mistress* (1966) and by economist Milton Friedman.

**free ride** |frē RĪD| *n* An (undeserved) easy time; something obtained without the expected or usual effort or cost.

**freebee, freebie** |FRĒ bē| *n* A free sample, promotion, or other item given without charge. ORIGINS: From SE **free**.

**freeze *sb* out** |frēz *sb* OUT| *v* To snub *sb*; to exclude *sb* from participation.

**freeze *sb*'s blood** |FRĒZ *sb*'s BLUD| *v* To terrify *sb*. To terrify so much as to paralyze.

**freeze up** |FRĒ zup| *v* To become paralyzed by fear; to be so afraid that one cannot move or speak.

**fricking** |FRIK ing| *a/a* Extreme; extremely; very. ORIGINS: Euphemism for **fucking**. A slang word that is related to sexuality and sounds very similar to **fucking**. In its denotative use (i.e., when it is not acting as an intensifier), **frick** (and **frack**) refers to the testicles. USAGE INFO: Used as an adjective ("fricking ass") or an adverb ("fricking beautiful"). Note that many users may think that this word is a sanitized version of the word **fucking**, not recognizing it as a real word with an independent existence. USAGE ALERT: People who know the denotative meanings of this word or suspect that it is being used as a euphemism for **fucking** are likely to find the terms objectionable.

**fried** |frīd| *adj* Exhausted; worn out; incapable of thought or action. ORIGINS: Figurative use of SE **fry**.

**Frig!** |frig| *excl* Exclamation of great displeasure. ORIGINS: Euphemism for **Fuck!** A slang word that is related to sexuality and sounds very similar to **fuck**. It means either "masturbating" or "intercourse." USAGE INFO: Note that many users may think that this word is a sanitized version of the word **fuck**, not recognizing it as a real word with an independent existence. USAGE ALERT: People who know the denotative meanings of this word or suspect that it is being used as a euphemism for **Fuck!** are likely to find the terms objectionable.

**frigging** |FRIG ing| *a/a* Extreme; extremely; very. ORIGINS: Euphemism for **fucking**. A slang word that is related to sexuality and sounds very similar to **fucking**.

In its denotative use (i.e., when it is not acting as an intensifier), **frigging** means either "masturbating" or "intercourse." USAGE INFO: Used as an adjective ("frigging shame") or an adverb ("frigging awful"). Note that many users may think that this word is a sanitized version of the word **fucking**, not recognizing it as a real word with an independent existence. USAGE ALERT: People who know the denotative meanings of this word or suspect that it is being used as a euphemism for **fucking** are likely to find the terms objectionable.

**frighten the living daylights out of** |FRĪT 'n *thu* LIV ing DĀ līts out uv| *v* To utterly terrify.

**frightfully** |FRĪT fu lē| *adj* Very; extremely. ORIGINS: From SE **frightfully**, meaning "horrifyingly." USAGE INFO: Originally British use; in the US, found mostly in puns, especially surrounding Halloween ("have a frightfully spooky Halloween"). The same (origins and beginning to be used in the US in puns) is true of **fearfully**, but it seems a bit less common.

**front office** |frunt AW fis| *n* The executive side of an organization; the policy makers; or the people in the organization who interact with customers. ORIGINS: From a frequently used location of the offices of such people.

**frost sb** |FROST *sb*| *v* To cause anger or upset; to cool off a relationship.

**fruitcakey** |FRŪT kāk ē| *adj* Crazy. ORIGINS: Fruitcakes are proverbially full of nuts, a reference to slang **nuts** meaning "crazy" or a reference to slang **fruity**, also meaning "nuts." USAGE ALERT: Often used with intent to denigrate or insult and understood as such. This way of speaking about *sb's* mental health may be considered insensitive and therefore objectionable in some contexts and by some people.

**fruity** |FRŪT ē| *adj* Crazy. ORIGINS: Possibly linked to slang **bananas**, an example of a fruit used to indicate craziness. USAGE ALERT: Often used with intent to denigrate or insult and understood as such. This way of speaking about *sb's* mental health may be considered insensitive and therefore objectionable in some contexts and by some people.

**fry** |frī| *v* To destroy an electronic device with heat or electrical current.

**fuck** |FUK| *adv* Sentence modifier with various shades of meaning. ORIGINS: From slang **fuck** meaning "to engage in sexual intercourse." USAGE INFO: Used to modify/intensify a whole sentence, as in "Fuck, that's a lot of money!" USAGE ALERT: This term will be objectionable in some contexts and to some people.

**Fuck!, also Fuck it!** |FUK / FUK it| *excl* An interjection expressing anger, frustration, extreme surprise, shock, realization of a mistake or error, etc. ORIGINS: From slang **fuck** meaning "to engage in sexual intercourse." USAGE ALERT: This term will be objectionable in some contexts and to some people.

**fuck-all** |FUK awl| *n* Nothing at all. ORIGINS: From slang **fuck** meaning "to engage in sexual intercourse." USAGE INFO: Used emphatically, as in "The will was read today, and I got fuck-all." USAGE ALERT: This term with **fuck** will be objectionable in some contexts and to some people.

**fuck around** |FUK u ROUND| *v* To waste time; to mess around. ORIGINS: From slang **fuck** meaning "to engage in sexual intercourse." USAGE INFO: Can also refer to sexual activity. USAGE ALERT: The inclusion of **fuck** will make this expression objectionable in some contexts and to some people.

**fuck (around) with** *st* |FUK with *st* / FUK u ROUND with *st*| *v* To use something irresponsibly or without understanding; to mess around with. ORIGINS: From slang **fuck** meaning "to engage in sexual intercourse." USAGE INFO: Distinct from **fuck around with** *sb*, which can either mean to goof around together, or refer to sexual activity. USAGE ALERT: The inclusion of **fuck** will make this expression objectionable in some contexts and to some people.

**Fuck it all!** |FUK it awl| *excl* An interjection expressing extreme anger or frustration. ORIGINS: From slang **fuck** meaning "to engage in sexual intercourse." USAGE ALERT: The inclusion of the word **fuck** will make this expression objectionable in some contexts and to some people.

**Fuck off!** |FUK awf| *excl* Go away! ORIGINS: From slang **fuck** meaning "to engage in sexual intercourse." USAGE ALERT: The inclusion of **fuck** will make this expression objectionable in some contexts and to some people.

**Fuck off and die!** |FUK ahf and dī| *excl* A contemptuous dismissal. ORIGINS: From slang **Fuck off!** which is, in turn, from slang **fuck** meaning "to engage in sexual intercourse." USAGE INFO: Although it may sound like a curse, the phrase is usually not meant literally. USAGE ALERT: Usually used with intent to be rude and understood as such. In addition, the inclusion of **shit** and the graphic image will make this expression objectionable in some contexts and to some people.

**fuck** *sb* **over** |FUK *sb* ō vur| *v* To cause huge problems for *sb*, often by deception. ORIGINS: From slang **fuck** meaning "to engage in sexual intercourse." USAGE ALERT: The inclusion of **fuck** will make this expression objectionable in some contexts and to some people.

**fuck** *sb* **up** |FUK *sb* up| *v* To hurt or injure severely. ORIGINS: From slang **fuck** meaning "to engage in sexual intercourse." USAGE ALERT: The inclusion of **fuck** will make this expression objectionable in some contexts and to some people.

**fuck** *st* **up** |FUK *st* up| *v* To ruin or destroy *st*; to make a complete mess of; to blunder; to make a mistake. ORIGINS: From slang **fuck** meaning "to engage in sexual intercourse." USAGE ALERT: The inclusion of **fuck** will make this expression objectionable in some contexts and to some people.

**fuck up** |FUK up| *v* To make a mistake; to ruin; to make a mess of; to blunder. ORIGINS: From slang **fuck** meaning "to engage in sexual intercourse." USAGE INFO: Unlike **fuck** *sb* **up** and **fuck** *st* **up**, **fuck up** does not take an object, as in "You know, you really fucked up!" USAGE ALERT: The inclusion of **fuck** will make this expression objectionable in some contexts and to some people.

**Fuck you!** |fuk YŪ| *excl* A contemptuous dismissal. ORIGINS: From slang **fuck** meaning "to engage in sexual intercourse." USAGE INFO: Often accompanied by the gesture referred to as "giving *sb* the finger." USAGE ALERT: Usually used with intent to be rude and understood as such. In addition, the inclusion of **fuck** and the graphic image will make this expression objectionable in some contexts and to some people.

**Fucked if I know!** |FUKT if Ī nō| *excl* I don't know! ORIGINS: Shortened from phrase **I'm fucked if I know!** From slang **fuck** meaning "to engage in sexual intercourse." USAGE ALERT: The inclusion of **fucked** will make this expression objectionable in some contexts and to some people.

**fucked up** |FUKT up| *phr* Messed up; botched; damaged; incapacitated. ORIGINS: From slang **fuck** meaning "to engage in sexual intercourse." USAGE ALERT: This term with **fucked** will be objectionable in some contexts and to some people.

**fucker**[1] |FUK ur| *n* An unspecified object, animal, or person. ORIGINS: From slang **fuck** meaning "to engage in sexual intercourse." USAGE INFO: This term can be used with no opprobrium or criticism attached or it can be used to provoke. USAGE ALERT: This form of **fuck** will be objectionable in some contexts and to some people.

**fucker**[2] |FUK ur| *n* A contemptible person; someone who harms others. ORIGINS: From slang **fuck** meaning "to engage in sexual intercourse." USAGE ALERT: This form of **fuck** will be objectionable in some contexts and to some people.

**fuckhead** |FUK hed| *n* A contemptible person. ORIGINS: From slang **fuck** meaning "sexual intercourse" and slang suffix -head meaning "person." USAGE ALERT: This form of **fuck** will be objectionable in some contexts and to some people.

**fucking** |FUK ing| *a/a* Very; complete; total; extremely. ORIGINS: From slang **fuck** meaning "to engage in sexual intercourse." USAGE INFO: Used as an adjective ("fucking asshole") or as an adverb ("fucking good time"). It was this type of use by Bono during the broadcast of the Golden Globe Awards in 2003—reported as "this is really, really fucking brilliant" or "this is fucking great"—that led to an obscenity complaint. However, such use was found *not* to be obscene by the Federal Communications Commission. There are many alternates and euphemisms for this emphatic use of **fucking**. USAGE ALERT: This use of **fucking** will be objectionable in some contexts and to some people.

**fucking** |FUK ing| *a/a* Adjective/adverb that works as a sentence modifier. ORIGINS: From slang **fuck** meaning "to engage in sexual intercourse." USAGE INFO: Used to modify/intensify a whole sentence, as in the phrase "Are you fucking kidding me?" or "Get in the fucking house." USAGE ALERT: This term will be objectionable in some contexts and to some people.

**Fucking ay, aye!** |FUK ing ā| *excl* Yes! Absolutely! Definitely! ORIGINS: From slang **fuck** meaning "to engage in sexual intercourse." USAGE INFO: This term is usually used without any intended provocation. USAGE ALERT: Nevertheless, the inclusion of a form of the word **fuck** will make this expression objectionable in some contexts and to some people.

**fucking well <auxiliary verb>** |FUK ing wel <auxiliary verb>| *excl* A violently emphatic agreement or disagreement. ORIGINS: From slang **fuck**

meaning "to engage in sexual intercourse," used as an intensifier. USAGE INFO: This expression picks up or employs an appropriate helping verb to respond emphatically to a statement or question, as in "Should we get some more gas?" "We fucking well should!"; "I'm not going skiing today." "I fucking well am!"; "I know she didn't take my car keys." "She fucking well did!" *See* DAMN WELL. USAGE ALERT: This phrase, which includes a form of **fuck**, will be objectionable in some contexts and to some people.

**fuckup** |FUK up| *n* An inept person (one who "fucks things up" for him/herself or others). ORIGINS: From slang **fuck** meaning "sexual intercourse." USAGE ALERT: This form of **fuck** will be objectionable in some contexts and to some people.

**fudge** |FUJ| *v* To stretch the truth; to fabricate.

**Fudge(nuts)!** |FUDJ / FUDJ nutz| *excl* Exclamation of moderate displeasure. ORIGINS: Euphemism for **Fuck!** From SE **fudge** meaning "chocolate candy" or slang **fudge** meaning "excrement." USAGE ALERT: Euphemisms may still be objectionable in some contexts and to some people.

**fugly** |FUG lē| *adj* Extraordinarily ugly. ORIGINS: Portmanteau of **fucking** and SE ugly.

**Fuhgeddaboudit! Fuhgedaboudit! Fuggeddaboudit! Fugedaboudit!** |fu GED u boud it| *excl* Don't even go there! It is not even worth considering. It's not going to happen. ORIGINS: The informal pronunciation of the phrase "Forget about it" captured in written form. There may be other spellings in use. USAGE INFO: Used in exchanges like: "I really wish the boss would give me a raise." "Fuhgeddaboudit!" Can also be used in reference to a further example for *st* already discussed and evaluated, to indicate that the further example is even more extreme—so much so that there's nothing to talk about. For example, "Have you seen the price of their lunch entrees? And dinner for two? Fuhgeddaboudit!"

**full monte, monty** |FUL mahn tē| *n* Everything. ORIGINS: Unknown. Popularized by the film *The Full Monty* (1997).

**full of baloney, be** |FUL uv bu LŌ nē| *v* To speak nonsense or untruths; to lie. ORIGINS: Euphemism for **full of bullshit**, possibly because of the nearly identical sound of the first syllables. USAGE ALERT: People who recognize it as a replacement for **bullshit** may find the expression objectionable.

**full of beans** |ful uv BĒNZ| *adj* Full of energy. ORIGINS: Said of a spirited horse, possibly because some kind of bean can form part of a horse's diet, providing protein; later applied to people. USAGE INFO: This phrase can also mean "mistaken; full of nonsense; lying" and with that sense is used as a euphemism for **full of shit**. *See* FULL OF BEANS, BE.

**full of beans, be** |ful uv BĒNZ| *v* To speak nonsense or untruths; to lie. ORIGINS: Euphemism for **full of shit**. Beans, being laxatives, are connected to excrement, and so are used to create an approximately synonymous euphemism for **full of shit**. USAGE ALERT: Euphemisms may still be objectionable in some contexts and to some people.

**full of boloney, be** |FUL uv bu LŌ nē| *v See* FULL OF BALONEY, BE.

**full of (bull)shit, be** |ful uv SHIT / ful uv BO͞OL SHIT| *v* To speak nonsense or untruths; to lie. ORIGINS: From slang **bullshit** meaning "excrement." USAGE ALERT: The inclusion of the word **bullshit** or the shortened form **shit** will make this phrase objectionable in some contexts and to some people.

**full of crap, be** |ful uv KRAP| *v* To speak nonsense or untruths; to lie. ORIGINS: Euphemism for **full of shit**. From slang **crap**, a euphemism for slang **shit** meaning "excrement." USAGE ALERT: Euphemisms may still be objectionable in some contexts and to some people.

**full of it, be** |FUL uv it| *v* To speak nonsense or untruths; to lie. ORIGINS: Euphemism for **full of shit**. While *it* is often used as a replacement for a word that's considered offensive in order to create a euphemism, in this case, the fact that **it** and **shit** rhyme may make it even more satisfactory as a substitute. USAGE ALERT: Euphemisms may still be objectionable in some contexts and to some people.

**full of pep** |FUL uv pep| *adj* Full of energy. ORIGINS: Pep is short for SE **pepper**.

**full of piss and vinegar** |FUL uv pis und VIN i gur| *adj* Full of energy. ORIGINS: Unknown. Slang **piss** means "urine." First use found in John Steinbeck's novel *The Grapes of Wrath* (1938). USAGE ALERT: The reference to urine will make this expression objectionable in some contexts and to some people.

**full of prunes, be** |ful uv PRŪNZ| *v* To speak nonsense or untruths; to lie. ORIGINS: Euphemism for **full of shit**. Prunes, being laxatives, are connected to excrement, and so are used to create an approximately synonymous euphemism for **full of shit**. USAGE ALERT: Euphemisms may still be objectionable in some contexts and to some people.

**funk** |fungk| *n* A state of depression; a bad mood. ORIGINS: From the Flemish **flonck** meaning "fear." USAGE INFO: Used with the indefinite article *a* unlike **the blues**.

**futz around/about** |FUTZ u round / FUTZ u bout| *v* To waste time; to mess around. ORIGINS: Euphemism for **fuck around/about**. From German **futz** meaning "fart." USAGE ALERT: Euphemisms may still be objectionable in some contexts and to some people.

**futz (around) with** *st* |FUTZ with *st* / FUTZ u round with *st*| *v* To use something irresponsibly or without understanding; to mess around with. ORIGINS: Euphemism for **fuck around with** *st*. From German **futz** meaning "fart." USAGE ALERT: Euphemisms may still be objectionable in some contexts and to some people.

**futzed up** |FUTST up| *adj* Spoiled; confused. ORIGINS: Euphemism for **fucked up**. From German **futz** meaning "fart." USAGE ALERT: Euphemisms may still be objectionable in some contexts and to some people.

**G2G** Got to go!

**G4N** Good for nothing.

**G8** Great.

**GFF** Go fucking figure.

**GFY** Go fuck yourself. (also, Good for you.)

**GGN** Gotta go now!

**GMAB** Give me a break!

**GOI** Get over it!

**GOYHH** Get off your high horse.

**GTFO** Get the fuck out.

**GTG** Got to go!

**GTH** Go to hell.

**GYHOOYA** Get your head out of your ass.

**gab** |gab| *v* To chat idly.

**gabber** |GAB ur| *n* A gossip; a person who speaks indiscreetly; someone who chatters. ORIGINS: From slang gab meaning "to talk a lot."

**gadzillion** |gad ZIL yun| *n* An unspecified, exceedingly large amount. ORIGINS: One of a group of made up numbers ending in *-illion* with pretty indistinguishable meanings, although additional prefixes may be indicating even larger amounts (i.e., a gadzillion may be larger than a zillion).

**gaga about/for/over** |GAH gah u bout / GAH gah fawr / GAH gah ō vur| *adj* Infatuated with. ORIGINS: From French gaga meaning "a senile person."

**gajillion** |gu JIL yun| *n See* GADZILLION.

**galley-west, gally-west** |gal ē WEST| *adj* Confused; scattered. ORIGINS: Considered to likely be from an alteration of Colleyweston, a village in England. USAGE INFO: Often used in the phrases "go galley-west"; "knock galley-west."

**galoot, galloot** |gu LŪT| *n* An awkward, clumsy, or uncouth person. USAGE INFO: Can be used affectionately.

**gamble** |GAM bul| *n* A risky situation. ORIGINS: From SE gamble. USAGE INFO: Often in the phrase "It's a gamble."

**gander** |GAN dur| *v* To look inquisitively. ORIGINS: From the behavior of the SE gander, stretching out one's long neck to view something.

**gasbag** |GAS bag| *n* A person who engages in excessive idle talk. ORIGINS: From slang gas meaning "idle talk" and slang suffix -bag meaning "a person."

**gasser** |GAS ur| *n* A talkative, chatty person. ORIGINS: From slang gas meaning "idle talk" and SE suffix -er meaning "one who."

**Gawd!** |Gawd| *excl* An exclamation of exasperation. ORIGINS: By alteration from SE god meaning a being conceived as the divine Lord of the universe. USAGE ALERT: People who consider this reference to god blasphemous are likely to find it objectionable.

**gawk** |gawk| *v* To stare stupidly; to gape.

**gazillion** |gu ZIL yun| *n See* GADZILLION.

**gee (whiz)** |gē / gē WIZ| *adv* Sentence modifier. ORIGINS: Euphemism for **Jesus** used as a sentence modifier—a figurative use of SE Jesus whom Christians hold to be the Son of God, but it is milder and is more likely to be positive. USAGE INFO: Used as a sentence modifier as in "Gee whiz, what a great movie!" USAGE ALERT: Even euphemized, this phrase will be considered objectionable in some contexts and by some people who may find it blasphemous.

**Gee (whiz)!** |gē / gē WIZ| *excl* An interjection used to express mild surprise, concern, disappointment, approval, etc. ORIGINS: Euphemism for **Jesus** used as a sentence modifier—a figurative use of SE **Jesus** whom Christians hold to be the Son of God, but it is milder. USAGE INFO: Notice that although it is a euphemism for **Jesus!** it is milder and more likely to be positive. USAGE ALERT: Even euphemized, this saying will be considered objectionable in some contexts and by some people who may find it blasphemous.

**geek** |gēk| *n* A physically or socially inept person, often one who is academically gifted or tech-savvy. ORIGINS: From Low German geck meaning "a fool." USAGE INFO: Used both jokingly and with intent to insult or denigrate.

**gelt** |gelt| *n* An unspecified amount of money. ORIGINS: From Yiddish gelt meaning "money" or German gelt meaning "gold."

**get** N.B. Many slang phrases beginning with *get* have a counterpart that begins with *give*. *See* entries beginning GIVE.

**get a bang out of** |get u BANG out uv| *v* To enjoy; to get a thrill from. ORIGINS: From slang **bang** meaning "a thrill."

**get a charge out of** |get u CHARJ out uv| *v* To enjoy very much. ORIGINS: From slang **charge** meaning "a feeling of excitement."

**get a kick out of** |get u KIK out uv| *v* To appreciate; to enjoy. ORIGINS: From slang kick meaning "a thrill" or "excitement." Popularized by the Cole Porter song, "I Get a Kick Out of You."

**get a lift out of** |get u LIFT out uv| *v* To experience an elevation of spirits. ORIGINS: From SE lift meaning "an elevation of one's spirits."

**get a line on** |get u LĪN ahn| *v* To secure information about; to understand. ORIGINS: From slang line meaning "a useful piece of information, often obtained confidentially."

**get a load of** *sb/st* |get u LŌD uv *sb/st*| *v* To take a look at; examine.

**get a move on** |get u MŪV ahn| *v* To hurry; to begin moving. USAGE INFO: Can be used as an imperative.

**get along** |get u LAWNG| *v* To make reasonable progress; to achieve minimum satisfaction.

**get an eyeful** |get an Ī ful| *v* To obtain a full view of *st*; to see something surprising.

**get at** |GET at| *v* To find a way to influence; to corrupt; to bribe; to coerce.

**Get away!** |get u WĀ| *excl* I can hardly believe what you're saying!

**get by** |get BĪ| *v* To achieve minimum satisfaction; to manage; to do acceptably well, but no better.

**get cold feet** |get kōld FĒT| *v* To become scared; to back out of a promise.

**get cracking** |get KRAK ing| *v* To start work on; to turn to with more zeal; to work quickly and efficiently; to hurry. USAGE INFO: Can be used as an imperative.

**get down on** *sb* |get DOUN ahn *sb*| *v* To develop a grudge against *sb*; to be abusive or hostile to *sb*.

**get even** |get Ē vun| *v* To get revenge; to punish a (perceived) wrong; to get back at someone.

**get going** |get GŌ ing| *v* To get started; to make a beginning.

**get his/hers/theirs** |get HIZ/HURZ/*THERZ*| *v* To get what one deserves; to die. ORIGINS: Possibly abbreviation of the phrase "get what's coming to one" or "to get what one deserves." USAGE INFO: Since "what one deserves" can be very good or very bad, this expression is a contronym.

**get in a wax** |get in u WAKS| *v* To become angry; to be in a rage. ORIGINS: From slang wax meaning "anger; temper."

**get in on the ground floor** |get in ahn *thu* GROUND FLAWR| *v* To be involved from the very beginning; to be in an advantageous position.

**get in** *sb's* **face** |get in *sb's* FĀS| *v* To be aggressively irritating. ORIGINS: From the close proximity to one's face of someone who is intruding into one's space.

**get in** *sb's* **hair** |get in *sb's* HER| *v* To annoy; to irritate. ORIGINS: From the situation of having lice in one's hair.

**get into a huff** |get in tū u HUF| *v* To get into a bad temper; to lose one's temper; to become offended.

**get into a lather** |get in tū u LA*TH* ur| *v* To get worked up about something; become anxious. ORIGINS: From the profuse sweating that can accompany anger and anxiety.

**get into a snit** |get in tū u SNIT| *v* To work oneself into a temper; to be so frustrated or angry that one takes it out on others; a state of agitation and irritation.

**get into a stew** |get in tū u STŪ| *v* To get worked up to the point of breaking out in a sweat; to be anxious or agitated.

**get into a sweat** |get in tū u SWET| *v See* GET INTO A LATHER.

**get it**[1] |GET it| *v* To receive and comprehend the message or material.

**get it**[2] |GET it| *v* To suffer the consequences; to be punished. USAGE INFO: Often in phrases like "You're really going to get it!"

**Get it?** |GET it| *phr* Do you understand? ORIGINS: Get is used here in the sense of "receive and comprehend."

**get it in one** |get it in WUN| *v* To succeed in grasping the issue at hand quickly or in the first attempt. USAGE INFO: Can be used for someone grasping some non-obvious dimension of a situation or succeeding in a difficult feat of brain power.

**get it in the neck** |GET it in *th*u NEK| *v* To be verbally attacked; to be punished or criticized severely. ORIGINS: A figurative interpretation of a phrase that was originally taken literally and meant "to be killed or severely wounded." USAGE INFO: The location of the wound makes the attack seem particularly blameworthy and unjustified.

**get it together** |get it tū GE*TH* ur| *v* To get focused; to get organized; to come to a decision; to pull oneself together.

**Get lost!** |get LAHST| *excl* Go away! ORIGINS: Ironic reversal of the usual situation of trying to *find* something that is lost. USAGE ALERT: Usually used with intent to be rude and understood as such.

**Get me?** |GET mē| *phr* Do you understand? ORIGINS: Get is used here in the sense of "receive and comprehend the message." USAGE INFO: Get me can be used as a verb phrase to mean "has a deep understanding of me as a person" as in "You might be surprised to hear it, but my mom really gets me."

**get moving** |get MŪ ving| *v* To hurry; to begin moving. USAGE INFO: Can be used as an imperative.

**Get off my back!** |get AWF mī BAK| *excl* Stop annoying me! Leave me alone! USAGE INFO: This is a response to the action of "getting on *sb's* back." USAGE ALERT: Usually used with intent to create distance and understood as such.

**Get off my case!** |get AWF mī CĀS| *excl* Stop annoying me! Leave me alone! ORIGINS: From slang **case** meaning "situation." USAGE INFO: This is a response to the action of "getting on *sb's* case." USAGE ALERT: Usually used with intent to be rude and understood as such.

**get off on** |get AWF ahn| *v* To experience pleasure or sexual arousal from. ORIGINS: From slang **get off** meaning "to have or bring to orgasm." USAGE ALERT: Because of the sexual reference, this term will be objectionable in some contexts and to some people.

**get off one's ass**\* |get awf wunz AS| *v* To get to work; to get moving; to stop sitting around, wasting time. ORIGINS: The idea is of a worker sitting around rather than working. From slang **ass** meaning "the rear end or buttocks." Slang **butt** is a euphemism for **ass**. Duff is either "even more euphemistic" or "generally less objectionable," depending on how you look at it. USAGE ALERT: The use of a reference to the rear end or buttocks will be objectionable in some contexts and to some people. When used as an imperative "get off your ass," the phrase is usually used with intent to be rude and understood as such.
• **get off one's butt** |get awf wunz BUT|
• get off one's duff |get awf wunz DUF|

**get off one's high horse** |GET ahf wunz hī HAWRS| *v* To cease acting superior; to stop being condescending. ORIGINS: The concept is of someone who has been under the impression that s/he is higher (read "better") than everyone else, but is undergoing a change of view.

**Get off your high horse!** |get AHF yŏŏr hī hawrs| *excl* Stop being so pretentious! ORIGINS: From a time when high-ranking people rode tall horses (while commoners walked).

**get on** |get AHN| *v* To do well enough to be satisfied; to achieve minimum satisfaction; to keep on keeping on.

**get on *sb's* back** |GET ahn *sb's* BAK| *v* To micromanage; to annoy with too much oversight.

**get on *sb's* case** |GET ahn *sb's* CĀS| *v* To criticize someone extensively; to persecute. ORIGINS: From slang **case** meaning "situation." USAGE INFO: Note how this differs from **be on the case**, which means "attending to what's needed in a particular situation."

**get on *sb's* nerves** |GET ahn *sb's* NURVZ| *v* To annoy or irritate a lot. USAGE INFO: Note that although you can ask *sb* to "get off my back" or "get off my case," there is no corresponding expression "get off my nerves."

**get on the ball** |GET ahn *thu* BAWL| *v* To become focused; to become active and aware of the needs of the situation. ORIGINS: From baseball jargon.

**get on the stick** |GET ahn *thu* STIK| *v* To get down to work. ORIGINS: From the gear shift in a car, also called "the stick," or the joystick of an airplane.

G

**get one's act together** |get wunz AKT tu ge*th* ur| *v* To get organized in working toward a goal; to get focused.

**get one's ass in gear** |get wunz AS in GIR| *v* To stop wasting time; to start operating with more drive and efficiency; to begin applying oneself in a useful way. ORIGINS: The reference is to one's body as a vehicle that is in neutral or park. From slang **ass** meaning "the rear end or buttocks." USAGE ALERT: Usually used with intent to denigrate or insult and understood as such.

**get one's ducks in a row** |get wunz DUKS in u RŌ| *v* To reach a satisfactory level of organization. ORIGINS: From the practice of lining like things up neatly. USAGE INFO: Also used in the negative to speak of disorganization or inability to organize.

**get one's finger out (of one's ass/butt)** | get wunz FIN gur out / get wunz FIN gur out uv wunz AS / get wunz FIN gur out uv wunz BUT| *v See* GET ONE'S THUMB OUT (OF ONE'S ASS/BUTT).

**get one's foot in the door** |get wunz FŌŌT in *th*u door| *v* To reach the initial stage in accomplishing something. ORIGINS: From the experience of crossing a threshold to enter a building.

**get one's head on straight** |get wunz HED ahn strāt| *v* To figure things out for oneself; to see one's situation clearly.

**get one's head out of one's ass/butt** |get wunz HED out uv wunz AS / get wunz HED out uv wunz BUT| *v* To stop acting stupidly. ORIGINS: The suggestion is of someone doing something thoroughly stupid. From slang **ass** meaning "the rear end or buttocks." From slang **butt** meaning "the rear end or buttocks" and acting as a euphemism for **ass**. USAGE ALERT: The crudeness of the image plus the reference to the buttocks or rear end will make this expression objectionable in some contexts and to some people.

**get one's head together** |get wunz HED tu ge*th* ur| *v* To become focused and centered after being scattered.

**get one's Irish up** |get wunz Ī rish up| *v* To become angry. USAGE ALERT: The association of anger with a particular cultural group will make this expression objectionable in some contexts and to some people.

**get one's own back** |get wunz ŌN bak| *v* To retaliate; to get revenge. ORIGINS: The concept is of someone taking back something that was taken from one.

**get one's shit together** |get wunz SHIT tu ge*th* ur| *v* To get focused and organized; to develop and carry out a plan for one's life. ORIGINS: From slang **shit** meaning "possessions" extended from slang **shit** meaning "excrement." USAGE ALERT: The inclusion of the word **shit** will make this expression objectionable in some contexts and to some people.

**get one's stuff together** |get wunz STUF tu ge*th* ur| *v* To get focused and organized; to develop and carry out a plan for one's life. ORIGINS: Euphemism for **get one's shit together**.

**get one's teeth into** |get wunz TĒTH in tū| *v* To get down to work; to eagerly engage with. ORIGINS: Figurative use of the experience of beginning a meal.

**get one's thumb out (of one's ass/butt)** |get wunz THUM out / get wunz THUM out uv wunz AS / get wunz THUM out uv wunz BUT| *v* To stop sitting around or messing around and get ready for serious action. ORIGINS: From slang **ass** meaning "the rear end or buttocks" or slang **butt**, a euphemism for **ass**. The suggestion is of someone doing something thoroughly worthless. USAGE ALERT: The crudeness of the image plus the reference to the buttocks or rear end will make this expression objectionable in some contexts and to some people.

**G**

**Get out!** |get OUT| *excl* I can hardly believe what you're saying!

**Get out of my face!** |get OUT uv mī FĀS| *excl* Leave me alone! Stop annoying me! USAGE INFO: The retort to the experience of having someone **get in one's face**. USAGE ALERT: Usually used with intent to be rude and understood as such.

**Get out of my hair!** |get OUT uv mī HER| *excl* Leave me alone! Stop annoying me! USAGE INFO: The retort to the experience of having someone **get in one's hair**. USAGE ALERT: Usually used with intent to be rude and understood as such.

**Get over it!** |get Ō vur it| *excl* Come to terms with whatever is bothering you and stop complaining/moping/etc.

**get physical** |get PHIZ i kul| *v* To move from a verbal interaction to a physical one, either for the sake of violence or of seeking physical intimacy.

**get pissed (off)** |get PIST / get PIST awf| *v* To become very annoyed. ORIGINS: From slang **piss**, meaning "urine." USAGE ALERT: The reference to urine will make this expression objectionable in some contexts and to some people.

**get *sb's* goat** |get *sb's* GŌT| *v* To purposely irritate; to provoke to the point of outburst.

**get shut/shot of** |get SHUT uv / get SHAHT uv| *v* To get rid of.

**get some shuteye** |get sum SHUT ī| *v* To go to sleep.

**get somewhere** |GET sum wer| *v* To succeed; to fulfill one's own dreams.

**get square** |get SKWER| *v* To get even; to get revenge; to retaliate.

**get the drift** |get *thu* DRIFT| *v* To understand another's words; to understand just the main points, but not the subtleties; to infer the whole story from subtle clues.

**Get the fuck out!** |get *thu* FUK OUT| *excl* A contemptuous dismissal. ORIGINS: From the sentence modifier **the fuck**, which makes figurative use of slang **fuck** meaning "sexual intercourse" to intensify sentences, and SE **Get out!** USAGE ALERT: Usually used with intent to be rude and understood as such. In addition, the inclusion of **fuck** will make this expression objectionable in some contexts and to some people.

**get the goods on** |get *thu* GŎODZ ahn| *v* To come into possession of previously secret or concealed information that is incriminating or otherwise damaging, with the intent of using it to one's advantage.

**get the hang of** |get *thu* HANG uv| *v* To learn how to (follow a procedure; use a tool; etc.); to become familiar with. ORIGINS: Was originally applied to learning to use a tool.

**Get the hell out!** |get *thu* hel OUT| *excl* An offensive dismissal. ORIGINS: From the sentence modifier **the hell**, which makes figurative use of SE hell meaning "the alternative to heaven; the realm of the devil." USAGE ALERT: The use of **hell** will make this expression objectionable in some contexts and to some people. In addition, this expression is usually used with intent to be rude and understood as such.

**get the idea** |get thē ī DĒ u| *v* To understand another's words; to understand just the overarching point, but not the subtleties; to infer the whole story from subtle clues.

**get the message** |get *thu* MES ij| *v* To understand fully what someone is trying to communicate.

**Get the message?** |get *thu* MES ij| *phr* Do you understand the point I'm making? ORIGINS: Not about individual words, but about gist.

**get the picture** |get *thu* PIK chur| *v* To understand; to appreciate the situation.

**Get the picture?** |get *thu* PIK chur| *phr* Do you understand the whole scope of what I'm saying? ORIGINS: Not about individual words, but about substance and implications.

**get the show on the road** |get *thu* SHŌ ahn *thu* RŌD| *v* To start; to set an operation in motion. ORIGINS: From show business tours.

**get to** *sb* |GET tū *sb*| *v* To irritate or annoy someone to the point at which they're seriously affected.

**get tough with** |get TUF with| *v* To intimidate; to act aggressively tough with.

**get under** *sb's* **skin** |get un dur *sb's* SKIN| *v* To irritate; to annoy; to pester. ORIGINS: To annoy like a splinter does.

**get up** *sb's* **nose** |get up *sb's* NŌZ| *v* To irritate; to annoy; to bother.

**get wise to** |get WĪZ tū| *v* To come to understand; to come to realize something that was previously not understood or was being actively concealed.

**get with it** |get WITH it| *v* To get ready for serious action; to accept the established conventions and act accordingly.

**get with the program** |GET with *thu* PRŌ gram| *v* To get ready for serious action; to accept the established conventions and act accordingly.

**Get your finger out (of your ass/butt)!** |get yŏŏr FIN gur out / get yŏŏr FIN gur out uv yŏŏr AS / get yŏŏr FIN gur out uv yŏŏr BUT| *excl See* GET YOUR THUMB OUT (OF YOUR ASS/BUTT)!

**Get your head out of your ass!** |get yŏŏr HED out uv yŏŏr AS| *excl* Stop being so self-involved! Quit being so wound up in your own little world! USAGE INFO: Tends not to drop the final prepositional phrase as in Get your finger/ thumb out!

**Get your thumb out (of your ass/butt)!** |get yŏŏr THUM out / get yŏŏr THUM out uv yŏŏr AS / get yŏŏr THUM out uv yŏŏr BUT| *excl* Stop sitting around or messing around and get ready for serious action. ORIGINS: From slang **ass** meaning "the rear end or buttocks" or slang **butt**, a euphemism for **ass**. The suggestion is of someone doing something thoroughly worthless. USAGE ALERT: The crudeness of the image plus the reference to the buttocks or rear end will make this expression objectionable in some contexts and to some people.

**G**

ginormous |gI NAWR mus| *adj* Very large. ORIGINS: A portmanteau word formed from SE **gigantic** and **enormous**.

**gip, gyp** |jip| *v* To cheat; to deceive; to avoid paying one's debts. ORIGINS: From the SE word **gypsy**. USAGE INFO: This word is considered an ethnic slur, but especially with the g-i-p spelling, many people who use it are unaware of the origins. USAGE ALERT: People who know that this word stereotypes Gypsies will unlikely find it objectionable.

give away |GIV u wā| *v* To reveal; to betray.

give her the gun |GIV her *thu* GUN| *v* To press hard on a vehicle's accelerator pedal; to drive a vehicle very fast. ORIGINS: From slang verb gun meaning "to rev an engine," which is done by pressing the accelerator.

give it a rest |giv it u REST| *v* To calm down; to pull back.

Give it a rest! |giv it u REST| *excl* Shut up! Take a break from talking about this topic! Stop nagging me! ORIGINS: Figurative use of Give *sb/st* a rest by allowing a break. USAGE INFO: Usually refers to spoken language.

give it all one's got |GIV it awl wunz GAHT| *v* To exert maximum effort; to put forth one's best effort.

give it one's all |GIV it wunz awl| *v* To exert maximum effort; to put forth one's best effort.

give it one's best (shot) |GIV it wunz BEST / GIV it wunz BEST SHAHT| *v* To exert maximum effort; to put forth one's best effort.

give it to *sb* |GIV it tū *sb*| *v* To hit, beat, or stab; to admonish severely.

Give me a break! |GIV mē u BRĀK| *excl* A plea for help, relief, or patience in the face of *st* annoying or frustrating, especially coming upon other difficult events or situations. ORIGINS: Reworking of the expression give *sb* a break meaning "to ease off, cut *sb* some slack, give another chance to *sb*, help *sb* out."

**Give me five!** |GI(V) mē FĪV| *excl* A request for a "high-five," a greeting or celebratory gesture of slapping hands (*five* refers to the number of fingers) "high" in the air—often above the head. ORIGINS: From African-American culture. Kept alive by the "Give me 5 for stroke" campaign of the Stroke Collaborative to encourage people to recognize the five most frequent stroke symptoms in order to seek timely assistance. USAGE INFO: May be pronounced as if spelled *gimme*.

**Give me some skin!** |GI(V) mē sum SKIN| *excl* A request for a "high-five," a greeting or celebratory gesture of slapping hands. ORIGINS: Refers to a greeting that involves skin contact (not just words). USAGE INFO: May be pronounced as if spelled *gimme*. *See* GIVE ME FIVE! and SLAP ME FIVE!

**give out** |GIV OUT| *v* To fail; to give up; to stop functioning.

**give over** |giv Ō vur| *v* To submit; to admit defeat.

**give *sb* a bad/hard time** |GIV *sb* u BAD TĪM / GIV *sb* u HAHRD TĪM| *v* To harrass *sb*; to make life difficult for *sb*.

**give *sb* a knuckle sandwich** |GIV *sb* u NU kul SAND wich| *v* To punch *sb* in the mouth. ORIGINS: The fist going into the opponent's mouth is being compared to a sandwich with the main ingredient being knuckles.

**give *sb* a line** |GIV *sb* u LĪN| *v* To say *st* untrue, often to appease.

**give *sb* a pain in the ass/butt** |GIV *sb* u PĀN in *thu* AS / GIV *sb* u PĀN in *thu* BUT| *v* To irritate someone. ORIGINS: From slang **ass** meaning "the rear end or buttocks." From slang **butt** meaning "the rear end or buttocks" and acting as a euphemism for **ass**. USAGE INFO: Comparison with **give *sb* a pain in the neck** shows that despite the difference in the body part in which one is pained (and that **neck** is less likely to be objectionable than **ass** or **butt**), there's not much difference in meaning. USAGE ALERT: The reference to the rear end or buttocks will make both versions of this expression objectionable in some contexts and to some people, though butt might be less objectionable to some than ass.

**give *sb* a pain in the neck** |GIV *sb* u PĀN in *thu* NEK| *v* To irritate someone. USAGE INFO: Sometimes purposely substituted for **pain in the ass/butt**, but may also be used in its own right.

**give *sb* a piece of one's mind** |GIV *sb* u PĒS uv wunz MĪND| *v* To reprimand forcefully; to tell off; to scold.

**give *sb* an earful** |GIV *sb* an IR foŏl| *v* To scold or reprimand *sb*.

**give *sb* flak** |GIV *sb* FLAK| *v* To berate with excessive or abusive criticism. ORIGINS: From an acronym for German Fl(ieger)a(bwehr)k(anone) meaning "aircraft defense gun."

**give *sb* grief** |GIV *sb* GRĒF| *v* To criticize *sb* in an angry way.

**give *sb* his/her marching orders** |GIV *sb* hiz/her MAR ching awr durz| *v* To dismiss someone from employment. ORIGINS: From military jargon, in which **marching orders** means "military orders to depart or move on."

**give _sb_ his/her walking papers** |GIV _sb_ hiz/her WAWK ing pā purz| _v_ To dismiss someone from employment. ORIGINS: From slang **walking papers** meaning "a notice of dismissal."

**give _sb_ (holy/merry) hell** |GIV _sb_ HEL / GIV _sb_ HŌ lē HEL / GIV _sb_ ME rē HEL| _v_ To injure seriously; to scold. ORIGINS: The concept is of making someone's life hellish, and from the slang intensifier **holy** from SE **holy** meaning "blessed by God." Figurative use of SE **hell** meaning "the alternative to heaven; the realm of the devil." USAGE INFO: Strangely, in this context **holy** and **merry** become intensifiers for the injurious behavior. USAGE ALERT: The inclusion of the word **hell** in this expression will make it objectionable in some contexts and to some people. The inclusion of the word holy in the phrase will make it seem blasphemous and objectionable in some contexts and to some people.

**give _sb_ the axe** |GIV _sb_ thu AKS| _v_ To fire or terminate unceremoniously; to discharge abruptly. ORIGINS: From SE **axe**, the hand tool. The sharp edge and violent potential of the axe lend this particular term a sense of cruelty. USAGE INFO: It is possible to both **give the axe** and **get the axe**, as well as **get axed**.

**give _sb_ the boot** |GIV _sb_ thu BŪT| _v_ To dismiss from employment; to end a romantic relationship. ORIGINS: From the mechanics of kicking someone with the toe of one's boot. USAGE INFO: It is possible to both **give the boot** and **get the boot**, as well as **get booted**

**give _sb_ the bum's rush** |GIV _sb_ thu BUMZ rush| _v_ To get rid of an unwanted person. ORIGINS: From slang **bum** meaning "a tramp or vagrant" and SE **rush** meaning "a sudden attack." Originated in the efforts of taverns who offered "free lunch" to paying customers to prevent non-paying "bums" from taking the food by expelling them from the premises. USAGE INFO: It is possible to both **give the bum's rush** and **get the bum's rush**

**give _sb_ the business** |GIV _sb_ thu BIZ nis| _v_ To reprimand; to criticize. ORIGINS: From slang **business** meaning "complaints." USAGE INFO: It is possible to both **give the business** and **get the business**.

**give _sb_ the chop** |GIV _sb_ thu CHAHP| _v_ To dismiss from employment. ORIGINS: By extension of SE **chop** meaning "to sever with a blow." USAGE INFO: It is possible to both **give the chop** and **get the chop**, as well as **get chopped**

**give _sb_ the chuck** |GIV _sb_ thu CHUK| _v_ To terminate employment; to end a relationship. ORIGINS: From slang **the chuck** meaning "an act of rejection." USAGE INFO: It is possible to both **give the chuck** and **get the chuck**, as well as **get chucked** (out)

**give _sb_ the cold shoulder** |GIV _sb_ thu KŌLD SHŌL dur| _v_ To ignore, avoid, or ostracize _sb_, intentionally and often without explanation. ORIGINS: From Sir Walter Scott's novel _The Antiquary_ (1816) in which a countess uses body language (turning her back on someone) as an act of dismissal.

**give *sb* the dickens** |GIV *sb thu* DIK uns| *v* To reprimand *sb* severely. ORIGINS: Slang **dickens** is an altered form of SE **devil**. USAGE ALERT: The inclusion of a reference to the devil will make this term objectionable in some contexts and to some people.

**give *sb* the dope** |giv *sb thu* DŌP| *v* To tell *sb* all the important information they need. ORIGINS: From slang **dope** meaning "essential information."

**give *sb* the gate** |GIV *sb thu* GĀT| *v* To abruptly end a relationship. ORIGINS: The reference is to being shown the exit. USAGE INFO: It is possible to both **give the gate** and **get the gate**.

**give *sb* the low down** |giv *sb thu* LŌ doun| *v* To tell *sb* all the inside information about *st*. ORIGINS: From slang **low down** meaning "the inside facts."

**give *sb* the (old) heave-ho** |GIV *sb thu* HĒV HŌ / GIV *sb thu* OLD HĒV HŌ| *v* To dismiss *sb* from employment; to end a relationship. ORIGINS: From slang **heave-ho** or **old heave-ho** meaning "rejection; ejection"; from nautical jargon **heave-ho**, a cry used to time the joint efforts when hauling the anchor cable, for example. Here, the work cry has been appropriated to the saloon bouncer's work of throwing an offending person out the door. USAGE INFO: It is possible to both **give the heave-ho** and **get the heave-ho**.

**give *sb* the once-over** |GIV *sb thu* wuns Ō vur| *v* To examine; to evaluate; to give a quick appraisal to. ORIGINS: From the slang noun **once-over** meaning "a quick glance." USAGE INFO: Differences in meaning depend on whether the focus is on *over*, in which case it tends toward thoroughness, or the focus is on *once*, which emphasizes speed and, perhaps, superficiality.

**give *sb* the poop** |giv *sb thu* PŪP| *v* To tell *sb* all the inside information about *st*. ORIGINS: From slang **poop** meaning "the inside information."

**give *sb* the push** |GIV *sb thu* PŌOSH| *v* To dismiss *sb* from a job; to end a relationship with *sb*; to eject *sb* (from a place of business). ORIGINS: From slang **the push** meaning "dismissal or ejection" by extension from SE **push** meaning "to shove." USAGE INFO: It is possible to both **give the push** and **get the push**.

**give *sb* the sack(eroo)** |GIV *sb thu* SAK / GIV *sb thu* SAK u rū| *v* To dismiss *sb* from a job; to reject a romantic partner. ORIGINS: From the situation of being handed one's possessions in a sack while being sent away. USAGE INFO: It is possible to both **give the sack** and **get the sack**, as well as **get sacked**.

**give *sb* the scoop** |giv *sb thu* SCŪP| *v* To tell *sb* all the current and/or exclusively obtained information about *st*. ORIGINS: From slang **scoop** meaning "exclusive news or the very latest information."

**give *sb* the shaft** |GIV *sb thu* SHAFT| *v* To reject; to treat unfairly; to cheat or deceive. ORIGINS: From slang **shaft** meaning "unfair treatment" by extension from SE **shaft** meaning "a projectile used to inflict injury, such as an arrow or spear." USAGE INFO: It is possible to both **give the shaft** and **get the shaft**, as well as **get shafted**.

**give** *sb* **the shivers** |GIV *sb thu* SHIV urz| *v* To make *sb* afraid, nervous, or terrified. ORIGINS: From SE **the shivers** meaning "an attack of shivering," or figuratively, an attack of fear.

**give** *sb* **the shove** |GIV *sb thu* SHUV| *v* To dismiss *sb* from a job; to end a romance. ORIGINS: From slang **the shove** meaning "dismissal" by extension from SE **shove** meaning "to push." USAGE INFO: It is possible to both **give the shove** and **get the shove**.

**give** *sb* **the works** |GIV *sb thu* WURKZ| *v* To hurt physically, ranging from a beating to murder; to attack verbally; to fill someone in on the whole picture, with both words and experiences; to put on one's best show for *sb*; to provide all the embellishments available. ORIGINS: From slang **the works** meaning "everything associated with a particular thing."

**give** *sb* **what-for, what for** |GIV *sb* what FAWR| *v* To beat up; to inflict serious pain; to let one's anger loose on *sb* verbally. ORIGINS: From slang **what-for** meaning "a punishment."

**give** *sb/st* **the up-and-down** |GIV *sb/st thu* up und DOUN| *v* To take a thorough look at; to scrutinize. ORIGINS: From slang **the up-and-down** meaning "a scrutinizing look; a look," based on how one's eyes would move in such a look.

**give** *st* **a miss** |giv *st* u MIS| *v* To skip an event or occasion.

**give the gaff** |GIV *thu* GAF| *n* To criticize; abuse; treat harshly.

**give TMFI** |giv TĒ EM EF Ī| *v* To give T(oo) M(uch) F(ucking) I(nformation). ORIGINS: An intensification of **give TMI**.

**give TMI** |giv TĒ EM Ī| *v* To give T(oo) M(uch) I(nformation). To talk about topics that the speaker's audience finds too intimate or too detailed for their relationship with the speaker and/or the social context.

**give up the ghost** |GIV up *thu* GŌST| *v* To die; to stop working or cease functioning (of a machine). ORIGINS: From the concept of the ghost/soul/spirit leaving the body upon death.

**giveaway, give-away** |GIV u wā| *n* Free samples.

**giveaway, give-away** |GIV u wā| *adj* Free; without charge.

**gizmo, gismo** |GIZ mō| *n* A gadget or device with an unknown or forgotten name.

**glam** |glam| *adj* Glamorous. ORIGINS: By shortening of SE **glamorous**.

**glam (up)** |glam / glam UP| *v* To glamorize; to take special care in preparing. ORIGINS: Shortened form of SE **glamorize**.

**glitch** |glich| *n* A minor malfunction; a small mishap or problem. ORIGINS: From Yiddish **glitsch** meaning "a lapse," from German **glitschen** meaning "to slip." Initially computer jargon and first used in writing by astronaut John Glenn (1962), it moved

**G**

from technical meanings related to power supply (loss of or spike in power) to more general meanings.

**glob** |glahb| *n* A roundish lump of something semi-solid; an indeterminate smallish amount. ORIGINS: From Middle English **globbe** meaning "a large mass," but related to **globe**.

**glom onto** |glom AHN tū| *v* To take over possession of; to steal.

**glop** |glahp| *n* A semi-solid, squishy substance; unappetizing (and unidentifiable) mushy mix of food. ORIGINS: Coined by Elzie Segar for use in the cartoon strip *Popeye the Sailor* from the onomatopoeic sound of mushy food being served, this word served initially as baby Swee'pea's entire vocabulary.

**gnarly** |NAHR lē| *adj* Wonderful; excellent. ORIGINS: From SE **gnarly** meaning "covered with knots or lumps," slang **gnarly** originally meant "disgusting" but on the "bad is good" model, came to have the opposite meaning. **Gnarly** was popularized in the film *Fast Times at Ridgemont High* (1982). USAGE INFO: **Gnarly** is a contronym. It is sometimes used self-mockingly to show that the user knows it is dated, although its continued use is attested, including in the phrase rendered either **gnarly, dude**, or **gnarly dude**.

**go** |gō| *n* An opportunity; a turn in a game; a try. USAGE INFO: Used in the phrases "all in one go" and "have a go at...."

**go** |gō| *v* To say. USAGE INFO: Often in present tense as in, "So then she goes, 'Do you want to see a movie?'"

**go all the way** |GŌ awl *th*u WĀ| *v* To see something through; to give one's best effort; in competition, to get to the finals, to win. USAGE ALERT: Also means "to have sexual intercourse."

**go along with** |gō u LAWNG with| *v* To agree to, but perhaps reluctantly or tentatively.

**go ape** |gō ĀP| *v* To become very angry; to lose one's temper; to lose control. ORIGINS: The conceived behavior of apes. USAGE INFO: Sometimes used to mean "to become happily excited."

**go ape for/over** |gō ĀP fawr / gō ĀP ō vur| *v* To become obsessed with; to become very excited about. ORIGINS: From the conceived behavior of apes.

**go ape shit** |gō ĀP SHIT| *v* To become very angry; to lose one's temper; to lose control. ORIGINS: From the conceived behavior of apes and slang **shit** meaning "excrement." USAGE ALERT: The inclusion of **shit** will make this expression objectionable in some contexts and to some people.

**go at it** |gō AT it| *v* To engage fully, either physically in a fight or love-making, verbally in a fight, or by engaging in some other activity with all one's energy.

**go AWOL** |gō Ā wahl| *v* To leave one's assigned position; to abandon one's duties. ORIGINS: From military slang acronym **AWOL** meaning "absent without leave," but carrying the implication that there is an intention to return, differentiating it from desertion.

**go back to square one** |gō BAK tū skwer WUN| *v* To restart; to resume from the beginning, often because of encountering problems or some kind of failure. ORIGINS: Possibly from the practice of a player being sent back in a board game in which the game path is drawn as a series of squares.

**go back to the drawing board** |gō BAK tū *thu* DRAW ing bawrd| *v* To restart; to return to the planning stage. ORIGINS: From SE **drawing board**, the desk used for drafting, as in drawing up architectural blueprints, etc.

**go ballistic** |gō bu LIS tik| *v* To lose one's temper; to become violently angry; to become extremely upset. ORIGINS: By extension from SE **ballistic** which refers to firearms, which operate by controlled explosion.

**go bananas** |gō bu NAN uz| *v* To be so angry one loses control. ORIGINS: Possibly extended from SE **bananas** going soft when they're overripe to "going soft in the head."

**go batty** |gō BAT ē| *v* To go insane. ORIGINS: Related to the phrase have bats in one's belfry. USAGE ALERT: This way of speaking about *sb's* mental health may be considered insensitive and therefore objectionable in some contexts and by some people.

**go belly up** |gō BEL lē up| *v* To die; to be ruined financially. ORIGINS: From the floating position of a dead fish. USAGE INFO: When speaking of finances, used more often of a business than of a personal financial failure.

**go crackers** |gō KRAK urz| *v* To go insane. ORIGINS: By extension of slang cracked. USAGE ALERT: This way of speaking about *sb's* mental health may be considered insensitive and therefore objectionable in some contexts and by some people.

**go crazy** |gō KRĀ zē| *v* To be so angry that one loses control.

**go down in flames** |gō doun in FLĀMZ| *v* To fail completely and suddenly. ORIGINS: Description of an aircraft falling to the ground and burning. USAGE INFO: See GO UP IN FLAMES.

**go down like a lead balloon** |gō DOUN līk u LED bu LŪN| *v* To fail. ORIGINS: From the conception of a (hot-air) balloon made of lead.

**go down the drain** |GŌ doun *thu* DRĀN| *v* To become irretrievably lost or destroyed; to be wasted. ORIGINS: The conception is of an emptying sink or bathtub.

**go down the tubes** |GŌ doun *thu* TŪB(Z)| *v* To fail completely; to collapse.

**go easy** |gō Ē zē| *v* To become calm.

**go easy on *sb*** |gō Ē zē ahn *sb*| *v* To limit one's hostility or anger when dealing with *sb*.

**go flat-out** |gō FLAT out| *v* To move at top speed.

G

**Go fly a kite!** |GŌ flī u KĪT| *excl* Go away! ORIGINS: Popularized in the film *Mary Poppins* (1964) in which, upon being terminated from his employment, Mr. Banks literally goes out to "fly a kite." USAGE ALERT: Usually used with intent to be rude and understood as such.

**go for** |gō fawr| *v* To invest oneself in; to feel attracted to.

**go for broke/it** |GŌ fawr BRŌK / GŌ fawr it| *v* To take a risk in order to accomplish something; to commit all of one's resources to a project or task. ORIGINS: By extension from slang **broke** meaning "bankrupt" to convey the idea that one risks losing everything.

**go for the jugular** |gō fawr *th*u JUG yū lur| *v* To criticize in the way that seems most likely to do damage. ORIGINS: From SE **jugular** meaning the large vein in the neck that carries blood to the heart and which, when severed, leads to a quick death.

**Go fuck yourself!** |gō FUK yŏŏr self| *excl* A contemptuous dismissal. ORIGINS: From slang **fuck** meaning "to engage in sexual intercourse." USAGE ALERT: Usually used with intent to be rude and understood as such. In addition, the inclusion of **fuck** and the graphic image will make this expression objectionable in some contexts and to some people.

**Go fucking figure!** |GŌ FUK ing FIG yur| *excl* Who would have thought! ORIGINS: From slang **fuck** meaning "to engage in sexual intercourse." USAGE ALERT: This use of a form of **fuck** will be objectionable in some contexts and to some people.

**go full blast** |GŌ ful blast| *v* To move forward with as much speed as possible. USAGE INFO: Also used of doing anything to the maximum level possible: as loud as possible; turned up to full power; with all of one's might; etc.

**go-getter** |GO get ur / GO GET ur| *n* An ambitious or enterprising person. ORIGINS: One who "goes and gets" what s/he desires.

**go great guns** |GŌ grāt GUNZ| *v* To progress well; to advance with great speed.

**Go hang!** |gō HANG| *excl* A contemptuous dismissal. USAGE INFO: Although it may sound like a curse, the phrase is usually not meant literally. USAGE ALERT: Usually used with intent to be rude and understood as such.

**go haywire** |gō HĀ wīr| *v* To malfunction; to fail to work properly.

**go home feet first** |gō HŌM fēt FIRST| *v* To die. ORIGINS: From the practice of being carried out of a place (because, being dead, one cannot leave under one's own power).

**go home in a box** |gō HŌM in u BAHKS| *v* To die. ORIGINS: The box is a coffin.

**go like a bat out of hell** |GŌ līk u BAT out uv HEL| *v* To go very fast. ORIGINS: Figurative use of SE **hell** meaning "the alternative to heaven; the realm of the devil." USAGE ALERT: The mention of **hell** will make use of this expression objectionable in some contexts and to some people.

**go like a shot** |GŌ līk u SHAHT| *v* To do something quickly. ORIGINS: The comparison is to a bullet shot out of a gun.

**go like blazes** |GŌ līk BLĀ zuz| *v* To go very fast. ORIGINS: Euphemism for **go like hell**. From slang **hell** as an intensifier. USAGE ALERT: Euphemisms may still be objectionable in some contexts and to some people.

**go like gangbusters** |GŌ līk GANG bus turz| *v* To achieve great success; forging ahead easily and without problems. ORIGINS: From a radio drama *Gangbusters* (1936–1957) featuring officers of the law who "busted" criminal gangs.

**go like greased lightning** |gō līk GRĒST LĪT ning| *v* To act very quickly. ORIGINS: The idea is that lightning would be even faster if grease was applied to it.

**go like hell** |gō līk HEL| *v* To go very fast. ORIGINS: Figurative use of SE hell meaning "the alternative to heaven; the realm of the devil." USAGE ALERT: The inclusion of **hell** will make this expression objectionable in some contexts and to some people.

**go like nobody's business** |gō līk NŌ bu dēz BIZ nis| *v* To go very quickly; to go very well. ORIGINS: From slang **nobody's business** meaning "something extraordinary."

**go like sixty** |gō līk SIK stē| *v* To go at a great speed; to do with great force or energy. ORIGINS: Possibly a comparison to the force/energy that sixty people could bring to bear.

**go like the deuce** |gō līk *thu* DŪS| *v* To go very fast; to do with great investment of effort. ORIGINS: Euphemism for **go like hell**, SE hell being the place where the devil resides and deuce being a euphemism for **devil**. USAGE ALERT: The inclusion of deuce will make this expression objectionable in some contexts and to some people, but usually less so than **devil**.

**go like the devil** |gō līk *thu* DEV ul| *v* To go very fast; to do with great investment of effort. ORIGINS: Euphemism for **go like hell**, SE hell being the place where the devil resides. USAGE ALERT: The inclusion of **devil** will make this expression objectionable in some contexts and to some people.

**go nuts** |gō NUTS| *v* To lose one's mind. ORIGINS: From slang noun nut meaning "an insane person." USAGE ALERT: This way of speaking about *sb's* mental health may be considered insensitive and therefore objectionable in some contexts and by some people.

**go nuts about/over** |gō NUTS u bout / gō NUTS ō vur| *v* To be attracted to; to be obsessed with. ORIGINS: From slang nuts meaning "fond of; attracted to."

**go off one's bean** |gō ahf wunz BĒN| *v* To lose one's mind. ORIGINS: From slang bean meaning "head." USAGE ALERT: This way of speaking about *sb's* mental health may be considered insensitive and therefore objectionable in some contexts and by some people.

**go off one's chump** |gō ahf wunz CHUMP| *v* To lose one's mind. ORIGINS: From slang chump meaning "head or face." USAGE ALERT: This way of speaking about *sb's* mental health may be considered insensitive and therefore objectionable in some contexts and by some people.

**go off one's head** |gō ahf wunz HED| *v* To lose one's mind. USAGE ALERT: This way of speaking about *sb's* mental health may be considered insensitive and therefore objectionable in some contexts and by some people.

**go off one's nut** |gō ahf wunz NUT| *v* To lose one's mind. ORIGINS: From slang nut meaning "head or brains." USAGE ALERT: This way of speaking about *sb's* mental health may be considered insensitive and therefore objectionable in some contexts and by some people.

**go off one's rocker** |gō ahf wunz RAH kur| *v* To go crazy. ORIGINS: From SE **rocking chair**; possibly a reference to a person who falls out of his or her rocker. USAGE ALERT: This way of speaking about *sb's* mental health may be considered insensitive and therefore objectionable in some contexts and by some people.

**go off the deep end** |gō ahf *thu* DĒP end| *v* To get out of one's depth, emotionally; to go crazy; to become so angry that one loses control. ORIGINS: Refers to the deep end of the swimming pool (and possibly to being in over one's head). USAGE ALERT: This way of speaking about *sb's* mental health may be considered insensitive and therefore objectionable in some contexts and by some people.

**go off with a bang** |gō ahf with u BANG| *v* To get off to a good start. ORIGINS: Perhaps referring to a firecracker successfully exploding.

**Go on!** |gō AHN| *excl* I can hardly believe what you're saying!

**go on (about)** |gō AHN / gō AHN u bout| *v* To talk about a topic beyond the point at which the audience loses interest.

**go on the lam** |gō ahn *thu* LAM| *v* To run away, often to escape from the police and a possible jail sentence. ORIGINS: From slang **lam** meaning "to run away." Repopularized by, for example, *The Simpsons* episode "Marge on the Lam" (1993).

**go out of one's gourd** |gō out uv wunz GAWRD| *v* To lose one's mind. ORIGINS: From slang **gourd** meaning "head." USAGE ALERT: This way of speaking about *sb's* mental health may be considered insensitive and therefore objectionable in some contexts and by some people.

**go out of one's skull** |gō out uv wunz SKUL| *v* To lose control; to go crazy. ORIGINS: The phrases **out of one's skull/mind/head/gourd**, etc. call up a contrast to the idiom **in one's right mind**, meaning "sane and in control."

**go over like a lead balloon** |gō Ō vur līk u LED bu LŪN| *v* To fail. ORIGINS: From the conception of a (hot-air) balloon made of lead. USAGE INFO: Often used for the reception of an idea or proposal.

**go overboard for** |gō Ō vur bawrd FAWR| *v* To become infatuated with; to become obsessed with. ORIGINS: Here, SE **overboard** meaning "over the side of a ship" has been adapted to characterize extreme behavior.

**go pfft** |gō PFFT| *v* To fizzle; to fail. ORIGINS: Perhaps referring to a failed firecracker that does not explode.

**Go piss up a rope!** |gō PIS up u RŌP| *excl* An offensive way to say go away! ORIGINS: The suggestion is for a futile act that will result in a mess for the person addressed. From slang **piss**, meaning "to urinate." USAGE ALERT: This phrase is usually intended to offend, and the graphic image as well as the use of the word **piss** will make it offensive in most contexts and to most people.

**go places** |GŌ plā siz| *v* To make good progress; to advance toward the desired goals.

**go postal** |gō PŌ stul| *v* To become extremely angry; to lose control. ORIGINS: This term refers to historical events of the late twentieth century in which there were several multiple shootings by postal workers of co-workers. USAGE INFO: Some people do not realize the historic background to this term and use it naively. USAGE ALERT: This phrase is offensive to postal workers and may also be to others who know its origins.

**Go soak your head!** |gō SŌK your HED| *excl* Go away! ORIGINS: This phrase suggests that the head in question is swollen (that is, the person is self-important) and soaking it (like soaking a finger or toe swollen by injury or infection) will bring the swelling down (i.e., give the person a more objective view of their own importance). USAGE ALERT: Usually used with intent to be rude and understood as such.

**go south** |gō SOUTH| *v* To become less successful; to lose value; to stop functioning; to be defeated. ORIGINS: Possibly from the practice of heading south of the southern US border to escape from accountability or from the law. *See* GO WEST.

**Go suck eggs!** |gō SUK EGZ| *excl* Go away! ORIGINS: The slang suck eggs is connected with old age ("teach your grandma to suck eggs") and bad manners. It's not clear exactly how **go suck eggs** fits in. USAGE ALERT: Usually used with intent to be rude and understood as such.

**go the distance** |gō *thu* DIS tuns| *v* To continue until a successful conclusion is reached. ORIGINS: From sports jargon in boxing and horse racing. USAGE INFO: Also used of having sexual intercourse.

**go the extra mile** |gō *thu* ek stru MĪL| *v* To make a greater effort than is expected or required.

**go the limit** |gō *thu* LI mit| *v* To give maximum effort. USAGE INFO: Also used of having sexual intercourse.

**go the whole hog** |gō *thu* HŌL HAWG| *v* To do something unreservedly; to do thoroughly; to do to the fullest extent possible.

**go the whole nine yards** |gō *thu* HŌL NĪN YAHRDZ| *v* To do something unreservedly; to do thoroughly; to do to the fullest extent possible.

**go through the roof** |gō thrū *thu* RŪF| *v* To lose one's temper; to become extremely angry. USAGE INFO: Also used of escalating prices.

**go to bat for** |gō tū BAT fawr| *v* To take *sb's* side. ORIGINS: From the practice of pinch hitting in baseball, where one player stands in for another.

**go to glory** |gō tū GLAW rē| *v* To die. ORIGINS: SE **glory** means "heaven," so this is a euphemism for dying and going to heaven.

**Go to hell!** |gō tū HEL| *excl* A contemptuous dismissal. ORIGINS: Figurative use of SE **hell** meaning "the alternative to heaven; the realm of the devil." USAGE INFO: Although it may sound like a curse, the phrase is usually not meant literally. USAGE ALERT: Usually used with intent to be rude and understood as such. In addition, the inclusion of **hell** will make this expression objectionable in some contexts and to some people.

**go to pieces** |gō tū PĒ siz| *v* To lose one's emotional or mental balance. ORIGINS: By analogy between physically and mentally falling apart.

**go to the dogs** |gō tū *th*u DAWGZ| *v* To become less successful; to go downhill; to be ruined; to decline in social status. ORIGINS: From the practice of once-famous race horses becoming dog food after death.

**go to the mat for** |gō tū *th*u MAT fawr| *v* To do one's utmost on behalf of something. ORIGINS: From the sport of wrestling, referring to a dispute that lasts until one side is victorious, i.e., pinned to the mat.

**go up in flames** |gō up in FLĀMZ| *v* To fail completely and suddenly. ORIGINS: Reference to the behavior of fire in a burning building. USAGE INFO: *See* GO DOWN IN FLAMES.

**go weak at the knees** |gō WĒK at *th*u NĒZ| *v* Become suddenly overcome with fear or another strong emotion. ORIGINS: From the physical feeling.

**go west** |gō WEST| *v* To fail; to die; to end. ORIGINS: From the sun setting in the west. *See* GO SOUTH.

**gob** |gahb| *n* A small lump of something mushy or slimy.

**gobble down** |GAWB ul DOUN| *v* To accept quickly and easily, without taking time for consideration or reflection.

**gobble up** |GAHB ul up| *v* To be strongly drawn to; to seek avidly. ORIGINS: From SE **gobble** meaning "to eat greedily."

**gobbledygook** |GAHB ul dē gook| *n* Unclear, incomprehensible language. ORIGINS: Imitative from the sound a turkey makes, written in English as **gobble**.

**gobs** |gahbz| *n* A large amount (often of money).

**god-awful** |GAHD aw ful| *a/a* Extremely bad; atrocious. ORIGINS: This term uses slang god as an intensifier. From SE **god** meaning a being conceived as the divine Lord of the universe. USAGE INFO: Used as an adjective ("a god-awful production of a play") or an adverb ("god-awful ugly uniform"). USAGE ALERT: Some people will consider this slang use of **god** blasphemous and therefore this phrase will be objectionable in some contexts and to some people.

**god dang, goddang, god-dang** |gahd DANG| *adv* Sentence modifier with various shades of meaning. ORIGINS: Euphemism for **goddamn**. From SE god meaning a being conceived as the divine Lord of the universe and dang, a euphemism for slang **damn**. USAGE INFO: Sentence modifier showing frustration, delight, etc., as in "God dang, that was awesome!" USAGE ALERT: People who take issue with cursing, or who view this use of god as blasphemy are likely to find this term objectionable.

**god dang(ed), goddang(ed), god-dang(ed)** |gahd DANG, gahd DANG'D| *a/a* Extreme; extremely; very. ORIGINS: Euphemism for **goddamn(ed)**. From SE god meaning a being conceived as the divine Lord of the universe and dang, a euphemism for slang **damn**. USAGE INFO: Used as an adjective ("god dang(ed) pain") or an adverb ("god dang(ed) pretty cat"). USAGE ALERT: People who take issue with cursing, or who view this use of god as blasphemy are likely to find this term objectionable.

**God dang (it)! Goddang (it)! God-dang (it)!** |GAHD dang / gahd DANG it| *excl* An interjection expressing anger, frustration, dismay, etc. ORIGINS: Euphemism for **Goddamn! Goddamn it!** From SE god meaning a being conceived as the divine Lord of the universe and dang, a euphemism for slang **damn**. USAGE ALERT: People who take issue with cursing or consider this use of god blasphemous are likely to find this term objectionable.

**goddamn, goddam** |GAHD dam| *adv* Sentence modifier with various shades of meaning. ORIGINS: By extension from SE **damn**, which literally means "Send (it) to hell," and SE god meaning a being conceived as the divine Lord of the universe. USAGE INFO: Used to modify/intensify a whole sentence, as in "Goddamn, you took a long time!" or "Goddamn, you look good!" USAGE ALERT: Although this use of **damn** is usually synonymous with a word like wow or well, nevertheless, people who take issue with cursing or consider this use of god blasphemous are likely to find it objectionable.

**Goddamn! Goddam! God-damn!** |GAHD dam| *excl* An interjection expressing anger, frustration, dismay, etc., interchangeable with **Damn!** ORIGINS: This term uses god as an intensifier. From SE god meaning a being conceived as the divine Lord of the universe, and by extension of SE **damn**, which literally means "Send (it) to hell." USAGE ALERT: People who take issue with cursing or consider this use of god to be blasphemous will likely find this term objectionable.

**Goddamn it! Goddam it! God-damn it!** |gahd DAM it| *excl* A curse. An interjection expressing anger, frustration, dismay, etc. Interchangeable with **Damn it!** ORIGINS: This term uses slang god as an intensifier. From SE god meaning a being conceived as the divine Lord of the universe and by extension from SE **damn**, which literally means "Send (it) to hell." USAGE INFO: *All* can be added at the end, as in **Goddamn it all!** USAGE ALERT: People who take issue with cursing or consider this use of god to be blasphemous will likely find this term objectionable.

**goddamn(ed), goddam(ed)** |GAHD dam / gahd DAM'D| *a/a* Cursed; very; extremely; extreme. ORIGINS: By extension from SE **damn**, which literally means "Send (it) to hell," and SE **god** meaning a being conceived as the divine Lord of the universe. USAGE INFO: Used as an adjective ("goddamn(ed) traffic") or as an adverb ("goddamn(ed) long time"). USAGE ALERT: Although these uses of **goddamn(ed)** are often simply equivalent to *very* or *extreme* and not intended to mean "cursed," nevertheless, people who take issue with cursing or consider this use of **god** blasphemous are likely to find them objectionable.

**goddarn, god-darn** |gahd DARN| *adv* Sentence modifier. ORIGINS: Euphemism for **goddamn**. From SE **god** meaning a being conceived as the divine Lord of the universe and darn, a euphemism for slang **damn**. USAGE INFO: Sentence modifier showing frustration, delight, etc., as in "Goddarn, that was a loud concert." USAGE ALERT: People who take issue with cursing, or who view this use of **god** as blasphemy are likely to find this term objectionable.

**goddarn(ed), god darn(ed)** |gahd DARN'D| *a/a* Extreme; extremely; very. ORIGINS: Euphemism for **goddamn(ed)**. From SE **god** meaning a being conceived as the divine Lord of the universe and darn, a euphemism for slang **damn**. USAGE INFO: Used as an adjective ("another goddarn(ed) test") or an adverb ("a goddarn(ed) funny joke"). USAGE ALERT: People who take issue with cursing, or who view this use of **god** as blasphemy are likely to find this term objectionable.

**Goddarn (it)! God-darn (it)!** |GAHD darn / gahd DARN it| *excl* An interjection expressing displeasure, frustration, or irritation, etc. ORIGINS: Euphemism for **Goddamn! Goddamn it!** From SE **god** meaning a being conceived as the divine Lord of the universe and darn, a euphemism for slang **damn**. USAGE ALERT: People who take issue with cursing or consider this use of **god** blasphemous are likely to find this term objectionable.

**gofer** |GŌ fur| *n* An assistant; someone whose role includes going on errands. ORIGINS: From the sending of such a person to "go for such-and-such," with **go for** becoming altered to gofer.

**gol dang, goldang** |gahl DANG| *adv* Sentence modifier. ORIGINS: Euphemism for **goddamn**. USAGE INFO: Sentence modifier showing frustration, delight, etc., as in "Gol dang, that mango was good." USAGE ALERT: Euphemisms may still be objectionable in some contexts and to some people.

**gol dang(ed), goldang(ed)** |gahl DANG / gahl DANG'D| *a/a* Extreme; extremely; very. ORIGINS: Euphemism for **goddamn(ed)**. USAGE INFO: Used as an adjective ("gol dang(ed) idiot") or an adverb ("a gol dang(ed) great article"). USAGE ALERT: Euphemisms may still be objectionable in some contexts and to some people.

**Gol dang (it)! Goldang (it)!** |GAHL dang / gahl DANG it| *excl* An interjection expressing displeasure, frustration, or irritation, etc. ORIGINS: Euphemism for **Goddamn! Goddamn it!** USAGE ALERT: Euphemisms may still be objectionable in some contexts and to some people.

**gold-brick** |GŌLD brik| *n* A slacker; a lazy person; a loafer; one who avoids working. ORIGINS: This meaning is from US military slang from around WWI. Goldbrick originally referred to the appointment of civilians with no experience to be officers, meaning that they were pretty worthless in their positions, and then—by extension—to refer to a soldier who tries to avoid assignments.

**goldarn, gol darn\*** |gahl DARN| *adv* Sentence modifier. ORIGINS: Euphemism for **goddamn**. USAGE INFO: Sentence modifier showing frustration, delight, etc., as in "Goldarn, I wish I'd known sooner." USAGE ALERT: Euphemisms may still be objectionable in some contexts and to some people.
• gol durn |gahl DURN|

**goldarn(ed), gol darn(ed)\*** |gahl DARN / gahl DARN'D| *a/a* Extreme; extremely; very. ORIGINS: Euphemism for **goddamn(ed)**. USAGE INFO: Used as an adjective ("goldarn(ed) mess") or an adverb ("a goldarn(ed) nice guy"). USAGE ALERT: Euphemisms may still be objectionable in some contexts and to some people.
• goldurn(ed) |gahl DURN / gahl DURN'D|

**Goldarn (it)! Gol darn (it)!\*** |GAHL darn / gahl DARN it| *excl* An interjection expressing displeasure, frustration, or irritation, etc. ORIGINS: Euphemism for **Goddamn! Goddamn it!** USAGE ALERT: Euphemisms may still be objectionable in some contexts and to some people.
• Gol durn (it)! |GAHL durn / gahl DURN it|

**golly** |GAH lē| *adv* Sentence modifier. ORIGINS: Euphemism for slang **god**. From SE god meaning a being conceived as the divine Lord of the universe. USAGE INFO: Sentence modifier showing frustration, delight, etc., as in "Golly, that was a lucky break!" Many people will not know the origins of this expression. USAGE ALERT: Euphemisms may still be objectionable in some contexts and to some people.

**Golly!** |GAH lē| *excl* An interjection expressing mild to moderate displeasure, frustration, or irritation, etc. ORIGINS: Euphemism for slang **god**. From SE god meaning a being conceived as the divine Lord of the universe. USAGE INFO: Many people will not know the origins of this expression. USAGE ALERT: Euphemisms may still be objectionable in some contexts and to some people.

**gomer** |GŌ mur| *n* A fool; a gullible and simple-minded person from a rural area. ORIGINS: From the main character in the television series *Gomer Pyle* (1964–1969), who had these attributes.

**gone on** |GAHN ahn| *adj* Infatuated with. Often used with an adverb such as *totally, completely,* etc.

**goo** |gū| *n* Sticky, semi-solid material.

**good and <adjective>** |GOOD und <adjective>| *adj* A flexible, fill-in-the-blank intensifier to which one can add an adjective. USAGE INFO: Can be used for such expressions as "I'll do it when I'm good and ready" (when I'm completely ready) or "Well, he's good and mad now" (he's extremely mad now), etc.

**good grief** |GOOD GRĒF| *adv* Sentence modifier with various shades of meaning. ORIGINS: Euphemism for **good god**. From SE god meaning a being conceived as the divine Lord of the universe. USAGE INFO: Used to modify/intensify a whole sentence, as in "Good grief, that was a narrow escape!" Many people will not know the origins of this expression. USAGE ALERT: Although this usage is usually synonymous with a word like *wow* or *well*, nevertheless, people who consider it blasphemy will find this term objectionable. Nevertheless, it has become more common and more accepted as time has passed.

**Good grief!** |GŎOD GRĒF| *excl* An interjection expressing mild to moderate displeasure, frustration, or irritation, etc. ORIGINS: Euphemism for **Good god!** From SE **god** meaning a being conceived as the divine Lord of the universe. USAGE INFO: Many people will not know the origins of this expression. USAGE ALERT: People who recognize it as a replacement for **god** and who consider it blasphemy will find this term objectionable, but it has become more common and more accepted as time has passed.

**goof¹, also goofball** |gūf / GŪF bawl| *n* A silly or incompetent person. ORIGINS: By several steps, from an obsolete English word **goff** meaning "fool," from an obsolete French word **goffe** meaning "stupid," and the slang suffix **-ball** meaning "a person not held in high regard." USAGE INFO: Can be used affectionately of, for example, a person who clowns around and makes others laugh.

**goof², also goof up** |gūf / GŪF up| *n* A silly or stupid mistake; a bungle. ORIGINS: By several steps, from an obsolete English word **goff** meaning "fool," from an obsolete French word **goffe** meaning "stupid."

**goof around** |GŪF u ROUND| *v* To squander one's time; to mess around; to avoid work. ORIGINS: By several steps, from an obsolete English word **goff** meaning "fool," from an obsolete French word **goffe** meaning "stupid."

**goof around with** *st* |gūf u ROUND with *st*| *v* To use something irresponsibly or without understanding; to mess around with. ORIGINS: By several steps, from an obsolete English word **goff** meaning "fool," from an obsolete French word **goffe** meaning "stupid."

**goof off** |GŪF AWF| *v* To squander one's time; to mess around; to avoid work. ORIGINS: By several steps, from an obsolete English word **goff** meaning "fool," from an obsolete French word **goffe** meaning "stupid."

**goof-off** |GŪF awf| *n* A person who squanders time, messes around, and/or avoids work. ORIGINS: By several steps, from an obsolete English word **goff** meaning "fool," from an obsolete French word **goffe** meaning "stupid."

**goofus** |GŪF us| *n* A stupid, blundering person. ORIGINS: By several steps, from an obsolete English word **goff** meaning "fool," from an obsolete French word **goffe** meaning "stupid." This particular form, however, has been popularized by the long running cartoon feature in *Highlights for Children* magazine, "Goofus and Gallant®" (1948–). USAGE ALERT: Usually used with intent to denigrate or insult and understood as such.

**goop** |gūp| *n* A sticky, but slippery, semi-solid substance. ORIGINS: Possibly an alternate form of **goo**.

**goose egg** |GŪS eg| *n* Zero; nothing; no points. ORIGINS: From the similarity in shape of the egg to a zero, possibly influenced by the cricket jargon **duck's egg** to indicate a score of nothing.

**gorilla** |gu RIL u| *n* A thug; a brutish man. ORIGINS: Stereotype of SE **gorilla** behavior.

**gosh** |gahsh| *adv* Sentence modifier. ORIGINS: Euphemism for slang **god**. From SE **god** meaning a being conceived as the divine Lord of the universe. USAGE INFO: Sentence modifier showing frustration, delight, etc., as in "Gosh, that was good." Many people do not know the origins of this expression. USAGE ALERT: People who consider this substitution for **god** as blasphemy will find this term objectionable, but it has become more common and more accepted as time has passed.

**Gosh!** |gahsh| *excl* An interjection expressing surprise, slight misgivings, and mild to moderate displeasure, frustration, or irritation, etc. ORIGINS: Euphemism for **God!** From SE **god** meaning a being conceived as the divine Lord of the universe. USAGE INFO: Many people will not know the origins of this expression. USAGE ALERT: People who consider this substitution for **god** blasphemous are likely to find this term objectionable, but it has become more common and more accepted as time has passed.

**gosh-awful** |GAHSH AW ful| *adj* Extremely bad; atrocious. ORIGINS: Euphemism for **god-awful**, with **gosh** being an alteration of SE **god**. USAGE INFO: Used as an adjective ("a gosh-awful mess") or an adverb ("gosh-awful bad memories"). Many people do not know the origins of this expression. USAGE ALERT: Some people will consider this substituted use of **god** blasphemous and therefore this phrase will be objectionable in some contexts and to some people; nevertheless, it has become more common and more accepted as time has passed.

**goshdarn(ed)** |gahsh DARN / gahsh DARN'D| *a/a* Extreme; extremely; very. ORIGINS: Euphemism for **goddamn(ed)**. USAGE INFO: Used as an adjective ("wait a goshdarn(ed) minute") or an adverb ("a goshdarn(ed) bad day"). USAGE ALERT: People who take issue with cursing, or who view the substituted use of **god** as blasphemy are likely to find this term objectionable; nevertheless, it has become more common and more accepted as time has passed.

**Goshdarn (it)!** |GAHSH darn / gahsh DARN it| *excl* An interjection expressing mild to moderate displeasure, frustration, or irritation, etc. ORIGINS: Euphemism for **Goddamn! Goddamn it!** USAGE ALERT: People who take issue with cursing or consider this substitution for **god** blasphemous are likely to find this term objectionable; nevertheless, it has become more common and more accepted as time has passed.

**Got it!** |GAHT it| *excl* I understand! ORIGINS: A form of **get** is used here in the sense of "receive and comprehend the message." Compare with **Gotcha!** USAGE INFO: **Got it!** is the usual response to **Got it?** or **Get it?** Sometimes used in the sequence—Person A: **Get it?** Person B: **Got it!** Person A: **Good.**—which originated in the 1956 Danny Kaye film, *The Court Jester*.

**Got it?** |GAH dit| *phr* Do you understand? ORIGINS: The past tense of get is used here in the sense of "receive and comprehend." Compare with **Get it?** USAGE INFO: **Got it?** as opposed to **Got me?** may be used in confirming understanding of something.

**Got me?** |GAHT mē| *phr* Do you understand? ORIGINS: **Get** is used here in the sense of "receive and comprehend." Compare with **Get me?**

**Gotcha!** |GAHCH u| *excl* I understand! ORIGINS: Altered form of "Got you!"—an expected response to **Got me?**

**Gotta go!** |GAH tu GŌ| *excl* I have to leave (immediately). ORIGINS: Shortened form of "I've got to go." USAGE INFO: In Instant Messaging (IM), may be used followed by an immediate departure without waiting for a response.

**gouge** |gouj| *v* To exact or extort a large amount of money; to swindle. ORIGINS: By extension of SE **gouge** meaning "to dig deep into something."

**granddaddy, grandaddy** |GRAN dad ē| *adj* The earliest; most respected; most outstanding; or largest of its kind. ORIGINS: From the role and circumstances of grandfathers in many families; having the largest size is an extension of the other traits.

**grandstander** |GRAND stan dur| *n* A show-off; one who acts ostentatiously in order to impress. ORIGINS: One who plays to the grandstands—seats at a stadium or racetrack.

**gravy** |GRĀV ē| *n* Money or profit acquired easily, especially tips or bonuses. ORIGINS: As **gravy** is used to adorn a food item that is very good in itself, like meat or a potato, tips, and bonuses that are considered gravy come in addition to good salary arrangements.

**green(backs)** |grēn / GRĒN baks| *n* An amount of money in bills. ORIGINS: From the color of US paper money.

**greenhorn** |GRĒN hawrn| *n* A novice; a beginner at something; a person who is new to a field or subject. ORIGINS: From SE **greenhorn** for a young ox with new horns; expanded by military use to describe new recruits; expanded from there to a beginner at anything.

**grind** |grīnd| *n* Difficult or demanding work, especially when it is unrelenting and academic. ORIGINS: By extension from SE **grind** meaning "to oppress continually." USAGE INFO: A **grind** is also a person who engages in such work. USAGE ALERT: **Grind** also refers to sexually provocative dance moves.

**gripe** |grīp| *v* To complain. ORIGINS: By extension from SE noun **gripes** meaning "the pain of colic," with the idea that this behavior would be a likely result.

**gripe sb's ass** |GRĪP sb's AS| *v* To anger sb. ORIGINS: By extension of slang **gripe**, meaning "to complain." From slang **ass** meaning "the rear end or buttocks." USAGE ALERT: The inclusion of the word **ass** will make this phrase objectionable in some contexts and to some people.

**griper** |GRĪP ur| *n* A person who complains in a petulant way. ORIGINS: By extension from SE noun **gripes** meaning "the pain of colic," with the idea that a person with this kind of pain would behave in this way.

**grok** |grahk| *v* To understand thoroughly; to experience completely. ORIGINS: Coined by Robert A. Heinlein in his novel *Stranger in a Strange Land* (1961).

**groove on** |GRŪV ahn| *v* To enjoy; to appreciate. ORIGINS: From slang groove meaning "to enjoy oneself." USAGE INFO: Groove on requires an object.

**groovy** |GRŪV ē| *adj* Wonderful; delightful. ORIGINS: Originally from jazz jargon, groovy had an initial spate of popularity in the early to mid-twentieth century, but has re-emerged into popular use again in the twenty-first century.

**Groovy!** |GRŪV ē| *excl* Wonderful! Delightful! Yes, I would enjoy that! Great! ORIGINS: An adjective appropriated to a term of approval. USAGE INFO: Cool and other adjectives are used similarly.

**gross** |grōs| *adj* Disgusting; repulsive. ORIGINS: From the slang adjective gross meaning "disgusting" which draws on the SE noun gross meaning "large."

**Gross!** |grōs| *excl* Disgusting! ORIGINS: From the slang adjective gross meaning "disgusting" which draws on the SE noun gross meaning "large." USAGE INFO: Sometimes the pronunciation is elongated into two syllables for effect: |gu RŌS|.

**gross out** |GRŌS out| *v* To cause disgust, repulsion, or strong dislike. ORIGINS: From the slang adjective gross meaning "disgusting" which draws on the SE noun gross meaning "large."

**grossed out** |GRŌST out| *adj* Feeling disgust, repulsion, or strong dislike. ORIGINS: From the slang adjective gross meaning "disgusting" which draws on the SE noun gross meaning "large."

**grotty, grody, groady, groddy, groaty** |GRŌ tē| *adj* Nasty; unattractive; disgusting. ORIGINS: Shortened from SE grotesque meaning "outlandish; bizarre; ludicrous" and popularized by The Beatles in their film *A Hard Day's Night* (1964).

**grouch** |grouch| *v* To complain. ORIGINS: By extension from SE noun **grouch** meaning "the pain of colic," with the idea that this behavior would be typical of such a person.

**grouchy** |GROU chē| *adj* Ill-tempered; prone to complaining. ORIGINS: Popularized by the character of Oscar the Grouch on the PBS television program *Sesame Street*.

**groupie** |GRŪ pē| *n* An avid follower; a fan who is obsessive. Sometimes especially applied to young women. ORIGINS: From SE **group** referring specifically to a rock or pop band.

**grouse** |grous| *v* To grumble and complain.

**grub** |grub| *v* To scrounge; to beg. ORIGINS: From SE grub meaning "to root in the dirt" extended to the search through garbage and other leavings.

**grumpy** |GRUM pē| *adj* Out of sorts and surly; ill-tempered and hostile.

**grungy** |GRUN gē| *adj* In poor or dirty, uncared for condition; seedy. ORIGINS: A portmanteau word from SE **grubby** meaning "dirty" and SE **dingy** meaning "darkened with dirt."

**grunt** |grunt| *n* An assistant; one who carries out menial tasks. ORIGINS: Probably onomatopoeic from SE **grunt** meaning "a deep guttural noise or moan." At one time in its history, referred specifically to members of the armed forces, but also has general use.

**guck** |guk| *n* Thick, messy, semi-solid stuff, usually a waste product or something perceived as dirty.

**gudgeon** |GUJ un| *n* An easily-duped person. ORIGINS: From SE **gudgeon** meaning "a small bait fish." Related to its role of being swallowed as bait—similarly, a gullible person will swallow deceptions. USAGE ALERT: Usually used with intent to denigrate or insult and understood as such.

**guff** |guf| *n* Lies; untruths; nonsense; sass.

**Guff!** |guf| *excl* I don't believe it/you!

**gulp down** |GULP DOUN| *v* To accept quickly and easily, without taking time for consideration or reflection.

**gummed up** |GUMD up| *adj* Messed up; stuck; confused; ruined. ORIGINS: Related to SE **chewing gum.**

**gun for *sb*** |GUN fawr *sb*| *v* To seek *sb* for a showdown confrontation; to pursue with the aim of destroying; to seek determinedly.

**gun *sb* down** |GUN *sb* DOUN| *v* To shoot *sb*, often killing the person.

**gung ho, gung-ho** |GUNG HŌ| *adj* Enthusiastic; exuberant and dedicated. ORIGINS: From the motto of the second Raider Battalion of the US Marine Corps, from the Chinese **kengo ho** (meaning disputed), introduced to them by Lieutenant Co. Evans F. Carlson in 1942.

**gunk** |gungk| *n* A thick or viscous substance. ORIGINS: From a proprietary name for cleansers used in 1932 by the A. F. Curran Company.

**gut-buster** |GUT bus tur| *n* Extremely difficult, overwhelming, arduous, or punishing problem. ORIGINS: From SE **bust** meaning "to break" combined with **gut**, which represents a person's essence (as in "I hate your guts").

**gutless (wonder)** |GUT lis / GUT lis WUN dur| *n* A coward. ORIGINS: Draws on the fairly standard connection between guts and courage.

**guts** |guts| *n* The essence of something. ORIGINS: By extension from slang **guts** meaning "stomach; a person's insides."

**gutsy** |GUT sē| *adj* Brave; spirited; courageous. ORIGINS: From slang **guts** meaning "courage; bravery."

**HAGD** Have a good day.

**HAGO** Have a great one!

**HAK** Hugs and kisses.

**HAND** Have a nice day.

**HIG** How's it going?

**HSIK** How should I know?

**HWGA** Here we go again!

**hack into** |HAK IN tū| *v* To use computer skills to gain unauthorized access to files or networks.

**hack it** |HACK it| *v* To succeed or manage; to handle whatever one is facing; to accomplish. ORIGINS: From SE hack meaning "to cut through." USAGE INFO: Used both positively and negatively.

**hacked (off)** |hakt / HAK tawf| *adj* Extremely angry. ORIGINS: From slang hack meaning "to irritate."

**hairy** |HER ē| *adj* Difficult; hazardous; concerning; scary. USAGE INFO: Carries the implication of *st* messy or complicated that is not easy to get a handle on.

**half sandwich short of a picnic, a** |u HAF SAND wich shawrt uv u PIK nik| *adj* Unintelligent; crazy. ORIGINS: One of many synonyms of the term not all there, which indulge in wordplay by representing "all there" in a particular way and designating how the person in question fails to meet the criteria. In this case, "all there" is represented by a **picnic** spread, an outdoor meal including—in the stereotypical conception—sandwiches, side dishes, dessert, and drinks, often designed to be eaten with few or no implements. By a bit of a stretch, without enough sandwiches, you do not have a full-fledged ideal picnic. USAGE ALERT: Usually used with intent to denigrate or insult and understood as such.

**half there** |HAF ther| *adj* Somewhat crazy. ORIGINS: A joking allusion to the term not all there, adding a quantification.

**half-ass(ed)** |HAF ass / HAF ast| *adj* Incompetent; poorly executed. ORIGINS: From slang **ass** meaning "the rear end or buttocks." *See* **-ASS(ED)** for more information about the suffix. Presumably the standard for competent and well-done is "whole-assed." USAGE INFO: Note that both the noun and the adjective form are used as adjectives: "half-ass approach"; "half-assed job." USAGE ALERT: The inclusion of **ass** will make this term objectionable in some contexts and to some people.

**half-baked** |HAF bākt| *adj* Incompletely thought out; ill-conceived. ORIGINS: By analogy to an incompletely cooked item or meal. USAGE INFO: Usually used of an idea, plan, or scheme, but can be applied to a person, in which case it means "having poor judgment; lacking common sense."

**hand in one's chips** |HAND in wunz CHIPS| *v* To die. ORIGINS: From the world of gambling: when one is withdrawing from a game, one exchanges one's chips for cash as one's final act before departing.

**hand *sb* his/her head on a plate*** |HAND *sb* hiz / hur HED ahn u PLĀT| *v* Destroy someone, physically or verbally. ORIGINS: From the New Testament story of King Herod's birthday celebration at which he promised Herodias's daughter anything she asked for after she danced, and at her mother's prompting she asked for the head of John the Baptist on a platter (Mark 6).
• hand *sb* his/her head on a platter |HAND *sb* hiz/hur HED ahn u PLA tur|

**hang in** |HANG IN| *v* To stick with something, overcoming fear or adversity.

**Hang it (all)!** |HANG it / HANG it awl| *excl* Exclamation of frustration or dismay. ORIGINS: From SE **hang**.

**hang loose** |hang LŪS| *v* To relax; to stay calm.

**hanging loose** |HANG ing LŪS| *adj* Staying relaxed or calm.

**happenin', happening** |HAP in in(g)| *adj* Fashionable; chic. ORIGINS: Slang usage of the 1960s. USAGE INFO: Today, often used ironically or self-consciously.

**happy as a pig in shit** |HAP ē az u PIG in SHIT| *adj* Extremely happy. ORIGINS: From slang **shit** meaning "excrement" and the idea that pigs enjoy rolling around in mud or manure. USAGE ALERT: The inclusion of the word **shit** in the phrase will render it objectionable in some contexts and to some people.

**hard-ass** |HAHRD as| *n* A person who is inflexible in following or enforcing rules; a person without kindness. ORIGINS: From slang **ass** meaning "the rear end or buttocks." USAGE ALERT: The inclusion of **ass** will make this term objectionable in some contexts and to some people. In addition, it is usually used with intent to denigrate or insult and understood as such.

**hard case** |HAHRD KĀS| *n* A tough or ruthless person.

**hard cash** |HAHRD KASH| *n* Immediately accessible sum of money in bills and coins. ORIGINS: *Hard* may refer to its tangible existence in paper and metal. USAGE INFO: In contrast to a check or other forms of payment.

**hard nut** |HAHRD NUT| *n* A determined or unpleasant person. ORIGINS: By extension from literal difficulty in getting a nut meat out of the shell. USAGE INFO: Sometimes used in a longer form, **a hard nut to crack**, but that generally means "a difficult problem to solve."

**hard-on** |HAHRD ahn| *n* A despicable, contemptible person. ORIGINS: By extension of the slang term **hard-on** meaning "an erection of the penis." USAGE INFO:

About equivalent to **prick**, **dick**, and similar terms. USAGE ALERT: The reference to sexual activity will make this term objectionable in some contexts and to some people. In addition, it is usually used with intent to denigrate or insult and understood as such.

**hard row to hoe** |HAHRD rō tū HŌ| *n* An extremely difficult task. ORIGINS: By analogy to farming.

**hard up** |HAHRD up| *adj* In need of funds; poor.

**hardhead** |HAHRD hed| *n* A stubborn person. ORIGINS: From SE **hard** and slang suffix -head, suggesting that a person's head is impermeable to the advice and ideas of others.

**hassle** *sb* |HAS ul *sb*| *v* To irritate or bother *sb*; to give *sb* a hard time.

**Hasta la vista, baby!** |AH stu lu VĒS tu BĀ bē| *excl* Casual farewell. ORIGINS: From *Standard* Spanish phrase **hasta la vista** meaning "see you later" and the slang term of address, **baby**. Initially popularized through the song *Looking for a New Love* by Jody Watley, released in 1987, but gained far more recognition from its use in instructing the Terminator in how to speak, and its subsequent use by the Terminator, played by Arnold Schwarzenegger in the 1991 movie *Terminator 2: Judgment Day*. Schwarzenegger has since become Governor of California and uses the phrase in his political career. It is number 76 on the American Film Institute's top 100 American cinema quotations.

**haul ass** |HAWL AS| *v* To move really quickly; to rush; to work really hard. ORIGINS: From SE **haul** and slang **ass** referring to the whole person as in the phrase "get your ass over here." Extended from slang **ass** to refer to the rear end or buttocks. USAGE ALERT: The inclusion of the word **ass** in the phrase will render it objectionable in some contexts and to some people.

**haul** *sb* **over the coals** |HAWL *sb* Ō vur *thu* KŌLZ| *v* To reprimand angrily. ORIGINS: Related to other phrases that link verbal attacks with heat, such as **make it hot for**. USAGE INFO: Sometimes seen as **drag over the coals**. *Also see* RAKE OVER THE COALS. *Drag* and *haul* just mean "pull," while *rake* means "scrape or scratch" and suggests more malice in the attack.

**have a case of the ass** |hav u KĀS uv thē AS| To feel extremely annoyed.

**have a catfit** |hav u KAT fit| *v* To have a tantrum.

**have a conniption fit** |hav u ku NIP shun fit| *v* To become violently angry or panicked.

**have a cow** |hav u KOU| *v* To become angry or upset; to throw a fit. ORIGINS: From the nervousness of an expectant mother animal. USAGE INFO: Often used in the negative imperative, e.g., "Don't have a cow!"

**have a crush on** *sb* |hav u KRUSH ahn *sb*| *v* To have a (usually temporary) infatuation with someone.

**have a fit** |HAV u FIT| *v* To become very angry; to have an angry outburst. USAGE INFO: Milder than **have forty fits**. *See also* THROW A FIT, which is stronger on account of the stronger verb.

**have forty fits** |hav FAWR tē FITS| *v* To become very angry; to have an angry outburst. USAGE INFO: Stronger than **have a fit**. *See also* THROW FORTY FITS, which is stronger on account of the stronger verb.

**have a go at** *st* |hav u GŌ at *st*| *v* To give something a try; to make an attempt.

**have a look-see, looksee** |hav u LOOK sē| *v* To examine briefly; to quickly survey; to glance at.

**have a shitfit** |hav u SHIT fit| *v* To throw a tantrum; to have an (angry) outburst. ORIGINS: From slang **shit** meaning "excrement" and SE **fit** meaning "a sudden outburst." USAGE ALERT: The reference to excrement will make this phrase objectionable in some contexts and to some people.

**have a short fuse** |hav u SHAWRT FŪZ| *v* To have quick temper; to be liable to anger.

**have a soft spot for** |hav u SAWFT spaht fawr| *v* To be moved by; to have tender feelings for.

**have a thing about/for** *sb* |hav u THING u BOUT *sb* / hav u THING fawr *sb*| *v* To be infatuated with *sb*; to like *sb* very much; to be very interested in *sb*. USAGE INFO: Can also mean the opposite: "to be unable to tolerate *sb*."

**have a yen for** *st* |hav u YEN fawr *st*| *v* To have a strong desire or yearning for; to have a craving for (food).

**have a/one's foot in the door** |hav u FOOT in *thu* door / hav wunz FOOT in *thu* door| *v* To reach the initial stage in accomplishing something. ORIGINS: From the experience of entering a building.

**have an itch for/to** |hav an ICH fawr / hav an ICH tū| *v* To desire or crave something or some activity.

**have balls** |hav BAWLS| *v* To have courage; to be presumptuous. ORIGINS: From slang **balls**, meaning "testicles," and, by extension, traditionally manly attributes such as courage. USAGE INFO: Usually used exclusively of men, with rare exceptions. USAGE ALERT: The reference to the male sex organs will render this phrase objectionable in some contexts and to some people.

**have chutzpah** |hav KHOOT spu| *v* To be audacious; to be impudent; to be recklessly courageous. ORIGINS: From Hebrew through Yiddish **khutspe** meaning "to be insolent." USAGE INFO: May be praise or criticism, depending on the situation.

**have cojones** |hav ku HŌ nās| *v* To have courage. ORIGINS: From Mexican Spanish **cojones**, the equivalent of US slang **balls**, meaning "testicles," and, by extension, traditionally manly attributes such as courage. Popularized first by Ernest Hemingway in his writings and more recently by Stephen Colbert on his television show *The Colbert Report* (2005–). USAGE INFO: Usually used exclusively of men, with rare exceptions. USAGE ALERT: The reference to the male sex organs will render this phrase objectionable in some contexts and to some people.

**have cold feet** |hav kōld FĒT| *v* To suffer from fear or timidity; to be unable to act on account of fear. ORIGINS: The concept is of someone whose feet are frozen in place. USAGE INFO: Often used of someone who has committed to a plan of action and then withdraws.

**have for breakfast** |HAV fawr BREK fust| *v* To criticize harshly; to deal with or defeat handily or easily.

**have gall** |hav GAWL| *v* To be outrageously insolent; to be arrogant or impudent. ORIGINS: From SE gall meaning "bitterness."

**have (got) it made** |HAV it mād / GAHT it mād| *v* To be in a situation in which success is guaranteed; to have acquired wealth and success. USAGE INFO: Note that this can refer to either (assured) potential for success or success that has been achieved already.

**have guts** |hav GUTS| *v* To have courage; to be audacious. USAGE INFO: The meaning of this term is similar to **have balls** and **have cojones**, but it is less objectionable because of the part of the body referenced.

**have it all over *sb/st*** |hav it AWL ō vur *sb/st*| *v* To surpass in a contest of some kind; to have *sb* at a disadvantage.

**have kittens** |hav KIT 'nz| *v* To become angry or upset; to throw a fit. ORIGINS: From the nervousness of an expectant mother animal. USAGE INFO: Often used in the negative imperative, e.g., "Don't have kittens!"

**have moxie** |hav MAHK sē| *v* To have courage, especially in the face of difficulties; to have energy; to be impudent; to have abilities. ORIGINS: From the soft drink Moxie, patented in 1924.

**have nerve** |hav NURV| *v* To have courage under pressure; to be bold; to be brazen and impudent. ORIGINS: From SE **nerve**. Popularized by the Cowardly Lion in *The Wizard of Oz*, who wished he had, as he pronounces it, "the noive." USAGE INFO: Often in the phrase "have the nerve to."

**have *sb* by the balls**\* |hav *sb* bī thu BAWLS| *v* To have *sb* at one's mercy. ORIGINS: From slang **balls**, meaning "testicles." **Short hairs** and **short and curlies** both refer to pubic hair. USAGE INFO: Also **have the world by the balls** (and similarly for the others listed on the next page). Usually used of males. USAGE ALERT: The inclusion of the word **balls** in the phrase will render it objectionable in some contexts and to some people.
- **have *sb* by the short and curlies** |hav *sb* bī thu SHAWRT und KUR lēz|
- **have *sb* by the short hair(s)** |hav *sb* bī thu SHAWRT HER(Z)|
- have *sb* by the tail |hav *sb* bī thu TĀL|

**have *sb* cold** |HAV *sb* KŌLD| *v* To have *sb* at one's mercy; to have caught *sb* doing something illegal or immoral. ORIGINS: From slang cold meaning "completely; absolutely."

**have *sb* in stitches** |HAV *sb* in STICH iz| *v* To cause riotous laughter.

**have *sb* on toast** |hav *sb* ahn TŌST| *v* To have in one's power or at one's mercy. ORIGINS: Along the lines of eat/have *sb* for breakfast, the meal at which toast is most often consumed.

**have *sb* over a barrel** |hav *sb* ō vur u BER ul| *v* To have someone in a weak position; to have someone at a disadvantage. ORIGINS: Reportedly from a practice for treating of victims of drowning.

**have spunk** |hav SPUNGK| *v* To have courage or spirit.

**have *st* on *sb*** |hav *st* AHN *sb*| *v* To be in possession of information or evidence that puts someone in one's power. USAGE INFO: Can be used of information that is incriminating, scandalous, etc.

**have steam coming out of one's ears** |hav STĒM kum ing out uv wunz irz| *v* To be extremely angry or upset. ORIGINS: Related to other phrases that figuratively convey anger with steam. *See* STEAM, STEAMED.

**have the final say** |hav *thu* FĪN ul SĀ| *v* To be the ultimate decision-maker.

**have the goods on** |hav *thu* GŌŌDZ ahn| *v* To be in possession of previously secret or concealed information that is incriminating or otherwise damaging with the intent of using it to one's advantage.

**have the last word** |hav *thu* LAST WURD| *v* To be the ultimate decision-maker.

**have the screaming meemies** |hav *thu* SKRĒM ing MĒ mēz| *v* To have an attack of nerves; to be extremely frightened. ORIGINS: From slang **meemies** meaning "hysteria," from WWII US military name **screaming meemies** for German mortars that were fired from a Nebelwerfer.

**having a screw loose** |hav ing u SKRŪ lūs| *adj* Insane. ORIGINS: The idea is that, like a mechanism with a loose screw, things in the brain are not working properly. USAGE ALERT: Often used with intent to denigrate or insult and understood as such. This way of speaking about *sb's* mental health may be considered insensitive and therefore objectionable in some contexts and by some people.

**having bats in one's belfry** |hav ing BATS in wunz BEL frē| *adj* Crazy. ORIGINS: Depicts insanity as an infestation of the brain, which is—like the belfry—the topmost part. USAGE ALERT: Often used with intent to denigrate or insult and understood as such. This way of speaking about *sb's* mental health may be considered insensitive and therefore objectionable in some contexts and by some people.

**having butterflies in one's stomach** |hav ing BUT ur flīz in wunz STUM uk| *adj* Feeling extremely nervous. ORIGINS: The physical sensation that can accompany nervousness.

**having one's ass in a sling** |hav ing wunz AS in u sling| *phr* To be in an awkward position and/or in trouble. ORIGINS: From slang **ass** meaning "the rear end or buttocks." USAGE ALERT: The inclusion of **ass** will make this term objectionable in some contexts and to some people.

**having one's work cut out for one** |hav ing wunz wurk kut OUT fawr wun| *phr* To have a challenging job ahead; to have as much as one can handle to do.

**hay** |hā| *n* A very small amount of money. USAGE INFO: Often appears in the phrase "that ain't hay" to indicate a notable sum of money.

**-head** |hed| *sfx* A fan, particularly of a music style. ORIGINS: SE **head** is used to represent the whole person. USAGE INFO: Forms a closed compound with the word it modifies, e.g., a **metalhead** is one who enthusiastically enjoys the music called *heavy metal*. **-head** is also combined with words to indicate foolishness or stupidity, as in blockhead.

**head honcho** |hed HAHN chō| *n* An important or influential person; the boss. ORIGINS: From Japanese **han'cho** meaning "group leader." Used by US military stationed in Korea.

**head up** |hed UP| *v* To be the head of.

**headache** |HED āk| *n* A serious or annoying problem or person. ORIGINS: Something capable of giving one a headache.

**heaps** |HĒPS| *n* A large amount; a great deal. ORIGINS: From SE **heap**.

**heart-throb** |HAHRT thrahb| *n* A male that many females find attractive. ORIGINS: From the association of the emotion of love with the heart.

**heavy hitter** |HEV ē HIT ur| *n* A person who is important or influential. ORIGINS: From the sport of boxing, someone who has a solid punch.

**heavy sledding** |HEV ē SLED ing| *n* A challenging problem. ORIGINS: In contrast to the usual smooth, quick movement of a sled over the snow.

**heavyweight** |HEV ē wāt| *n* A person who is very important or has a lot of influence. ORIGINS: From the sport of boxing, referring to a weight class or a boxer in that weight class.

**heck** |hek| *adv* Sentence modifier. ORIGINS: An altered form of and euphemism for **hell**. USAGE INFO: Sentence modifier showing frustration, delight, etc: "Heck, that was quite a ball game!" USAGE ALERT: Euphemisms may still be objectionable in some contexts and to some people.

**Heck!** |hek| *excl* An interjection expressing mild to moderate displeasure, frustration, or irritation, etc. ORIGINS: An altered form of and euphemism for **Hell!** USAGE ALERT: Euphemisms may still be objectionable in some contexts and to some people.

**heck of a, heckuva** |HEK uv u| *a/a* Extreme; extremely; very. ORIGINS: An altered form of and euphemism for **hell of a** or **helluva**. USAGE INFO: Used as an adjective ("a heckuva guy") or as an adverb ("one heck of a fine job"). Notice the use of **one**. USAGE ALERT: Euphemisms may still be objectionable in some contexts and to some people.

**heebie-jeebies** |HĒ bē JĒ bēz| *n* A fit of fright; nameless dread; a feeling of uneasiness; a case of the jitters. ORIGINS: Believed to have been coined by cartoonist identified both as Billy Derbeck and Billy DeBeck, in his strip *Barney Google* (1923).

**heel** |hēl| *n* A contemptible, ill-mannered person; someone (usually a man) who is dishonorable, especially where women are concerned.

**heeled** |hēld| *adj* Rich; moneyed. ORIGINS: By shortening of SE **well-heeled**.

**hefty** |HEF tē| *adj* A large size or amount. ORIGINS: From SE **heft** meaning "weight; heaviness."

**Heh!** |heh| *excl* An ironic or dry laugh.

**heist** |hīst| *v* To steal. ORIGINS: By variation of **hoist**, meaning "to shoplift, to rob."

**hell** |hel| *adv* Sentence modifier with various shades of meaning. ORIGINS: Figurative use of SE **hell** meaning "the alternative to heaven; the realm of the devil." USAGE INFO: Used to modify/intensify a whole sentence, as in "Hell, I wish I'd known!" USAGE ALERT: Although this use of **hell** is usually synonymous with a word like *wow* or *well*, nevertheless, people who take issue with cursing are likely to find it objectionable.

**Hell!** |hel| *excl* An interjection expressing anger, frustration, dismay, etc. ORIGINS: Figurative use of SE **hell** meaning "the alternative to heaven; the realm of the devil." USAGE ALERT: The use of the word **hell** will be objectionable in some contexts and to some people.

**hell of a, helluva** |hel uv u| *a/a* Extreme; extremely; very. ORIGINS: Figurative use of SE **hell** meaning "the alternative to heaven; the realm of the devil." USAGE INFO: Used as an adjective, as in "helluva guy," or as an adverb, as in "hell of a good sandwich." Also prefaced by *one* as in **one hell of a**. USAGE ALERT: Because this phrase includes the word **hell**, it will be objectionable in some contexts and to some people.

**Hell's bells!** |HELZ belz| *excl* An interjection expressing anger, frustration, dismay, etc. ORIGINS: Figurative use of SE **hell** meaning "the alternative to heaven; the realm of the devil." USAGE ALERT: Usually used to relieve feelings without any intent to curse. Nevertheless, the use of the word **hell** will make it objectionable in some contexts and to some people.

**hellacious** |hu LĀ shus| *adj* Extremely large or impressive. ORIGINS: From slang **hell** and SE **-acious** (as in **audacious**). Figurative use of SE **hell** meaning "the alternative to heaven; the realm of the devil." USAGE ALERT: This form of **hell** will be objectionable in some contexts and to some people.

**hell-bent for leather** |HEL bent fawr LE*TH* ur| *adj* Moving really quickly; traveling at break-neck speed. ORIGINS: From the sport of horseback riding, with the word **leather** referring to the harness. Figurative use of SE **hell** meaning "the alternative to heaven; the realm of the devil." USAGE INFO: There is a related phrase **hell for leather**. USAGE ALERT: The inclusion of the word **hell** in the phrase will render it objectionable in some contexts and to some people.

**hell-fired** |HEL fīrd| *a/a* Extreme; extremely; very. An intensifier. ORIGINS: From the concept of hell as a place with fire; literally "damned to the fires of hell." Figurative use of SE **hell** meaning "the alternative to heaven; the realm of the devil." USAGE INFO: Notice that **hell-fired** is used both as an adjective ("wrote hell-fired poetry") and as an adverb ("hell-fired mad"). USAGE ALERT: Because this phrase includes the word **hell**, it will be objectionable in some contexts and to some people.

**hellish** |HEL ish| *adj* Awful; reminiscent of hell; horrific. ORIGINS: By extension of descriptions of SE **hell**, "the alternative to heaven; the realm of the devil." USAGE ALERT: Because this word is a form of **hell**, it will be objectionable in some contexts and to some people.

**hellishly** |HEL ish lē| *adv* Extremely. ORIGINS: From SE **hell** meaning "the alternative to heaven; the realm of the devil." USAGE INFO: Unlike related words **devilishly** and **fiendlishly**, **hellishly** is always harsh and negative as in, e.g., "a hellishly difficult examination."

**helter-skelter** |HEL tur skel tur| *adj* Carelessly scattered; disorderly; haphazard. ORIGINS: From onomatopoeic beginnings, this word gained popularity through The Beatles song "Helter-Skelter" (1968) and murderer Charles Manson's use of the term in 1969 for what he believed to be an impending apocalypse.

**hen-pecked** |HEN pekt| *adj* Used of a male who is abused, persecuted, or under the thumb of the woman he lives with. ORIGINS: From the continuous pecking of a hen.

**hepped up** |HEPT up| *adj* Agitated; excited.

**het up** |HET up| *adj* Agitated; angry; tense. ORIGINS: From SE **heat** and the phrase "heated up."

**Hey!** |hā| *excl* A casual greeting; exclamation of delight, surprise, or warning. ORIGINS: Considered both a shortened version of "How are you?" as well as an alternative form of **hi.** At one time enjoyed more widespread use in the South, but is now found throughout the United States.

**Hey, man!** |HĀ man| *excl* Hello. USAGE INFO: Used mainly, but not exclusively, in greeting males. The comma is often omitted in non-formal writing.

**hiccup** |HIK up| *n* A minor difficulty or interruption. ORIGINS: SE **hiccup**.

**higgledy-piggledy** |HIG ul dē PIG ul dē| *adj* Disordered; jumbled. ORIGINS: Used by US author Nathaniel Hawthorne to describe pigs in his *American Notebooks* (1838): "Pigs, on a march, do not subject themselves to any leader among themselves, but pass on, higgledy-piggledy, without regard to age or sex."

**high** |HĪ| *adj* Filled with joy. ORIGINS: By figurative extension from the positive effect of some drugs on a person's mood.

**high as a kite** |HĪ az u KĪT| *adj* Very happy; stoned; high above the Earth.

**high end** |HĪ end| *adj* Extremely expensive and valuable.

**high-handed** |HĪ HAN did| *adj* Unnecessarily authoritarian.

**high muck-a-muck\*** |HĪ MUK u muk| *n* An important or self-important person. ORIGINS: From Chinook jargon **hiu muckamuck**, meaning "plenty to eat."
• high muckety-muck |HĪ MUK i tē muk|
• high mucky-muck |HĪ MUK ē muk|

**high on/off the hog** |HĪ ahn *thu* HAWG / HĪ awf *thu* HAWG| *adj* Living well; being extremely comfortable. ORIGINS: From the location on a pig of the best cuts of meat, such as bacon and chops, as opposed to the lower portions like trotters and jowls.

**high roller** |HĪ RŌ lur| *n* A person who is extravagant, careless with money, or takes serious risks with money, particularly in gambling.

**high-toned** |HĪ tōnd| *adj* Pretentiously elegant.

**high-wire act** |HĪ wīr akt| *n* A risky endeavor. ORIGINS: Generalized from the dangers of the tightrope act performed by an aerialist, in the context of a circus, for example.

**highfalutin', hi falutin'** |HĪ fu LOŌT'n| *adj* Pompous; pretentious.

**hightail (it)** |HĪ tāl / HĪ tāl it| *v* To go as quickly as possible; to flee.

**himself** |him SELF| *n* The boss.

**hinky** |HIN kē| *adj* Unusual, weird, or suspicious. ORIGINS: From law enforcement jargon, popularized by its use on television police procedurals *NCIS* and *CSI Miami*.

**hip** |hip| *adj* Fashionable or stylish. Sophisticated.

**hired gun** |HĪRD GUN| *n* A highly skilled person, not necessarily an assassin, who is brought in as a consultant to solve a particularly difficult problem. ORIGINS: By extension from hired killers (guns).

**his highness** |hiz HĪ nis| *n* A sarcastic title for a man whose greatness is all in his imagination. ORIGINS: From the title given to royalty.

**his nibs** |hiz NIBZ| *n* The boss. USAGE INFO: May be used sarcastically of someone self-important.

**hissy fit** |HIS ē fit| *n* A self-indulgent emotional outburst; a tantrum that is partly for show. ORIGINS: Possibly from SE **hysterical** or **hiss** (like a cat). USAGE INFO: More often used of females than males.

**hit it big** |hit it BIG| *v* To have an important success, financial or otherwise.

**hit it off** |hit it AWF| *v* To connect with; to be mutually attracted.

**hit *sb* up** |hit *sb* UP| *v* Ask or beg for something, especially money.

**hit *sb* where it counts** |HIT *sb* wer it KOUNTZ| *v* To strike a blow at a man's groin. ORIGINS: **Where it counts** is a euphemism for a male's groin. USAGE INFO: This phrase is commonly used in talking about self-defense for women. USAGE ALERT:

Despite the anatomical reference, when speaking of self-defense, this term is not likely to be found objectionable.

**hit the ceiling** |hit *thu* SĒ ling| *v See* HIT THE ROOF.

**hit the hay** |hit *thu* HĀ| *v* To go to bed; to go to sleep. ORIGINS: From SE **hit** and slang hay meaning "bed."

**hit the jackpot** |hit *thu* JAK paht| *v* To have an important success; to have great (unexpected) luck; to win a lot of money. ORIGINS: Possibly from the procedure in the game of draw poker.

**hit the panic button** |HIT *thu* PAN ik but'n| *v* A hasty or overly emotional response to an emergency situation. ORIGINS: From the button provided in case of emergency, in elevators, for example. Staples' recent "Easy Button" commercials play off the concept of a panic button.

**H**

**hit the road** |hit *thu* ROD| *v* To leave on a trip; to set out. USAGE INFO: Can be used as an imperative to send someone away.

**hit the roof** |hit *thu* RŪF| *v* To lose one's temper; to become explosively angry. ORIGINS: From the association of anger with explosions.

**hit the sack** |hit *thu* SAK| *v* To go to bed; to go to sleep. ORIGINS: From SE **hit** and slang sack meaning "bed."

**hit the skids** |hit *thu* SKIDZ| *v* To experience a decline in value; to run into difficulties that forecast a demise.

**hitch** |hich| *n* A malfunction; an impediment to progress; a delay.

**hoist** |hoist| *v* To shoplift or rob.

**hoity-toity** |HOI tē TOI tē| *adj* Pretentiously self-important; arrogant.

**hold one's horses** |hold wunz HAWR siz| *v* To cease activity; to calm down; to restrain oneself. USAGE INFO: Often used as an imperative: "Hold your horses!"

**hold *sb's* feet to the fire** |hōld *sb's* FĒT tū *thu* FĪR| *v* To try to influence *sb's* actions with pressure or by putting him/her under stress.

**hold the reins** |hōld *thu* RĀNZ| *v* To guide the direction forward. ORIGINS: A reference to the way one controls a horse.

**hole** |hōl| *n* A predicament; a difficult situation; a mess. USAGE INFO: Often appears in phrases such as in a hole meaning "in a fix" or in the hole, which can mean "at a disadvantage" or "short of money."

**holler uncle** |HAHL ur UN kul| *v See* CRY UNCLE.

**holy** |HŌ lē| *adj* An intensifier. ORIGINS: From the slang intensifier holy from SE **holy** meaning "blessed by God." USAGE INFO: Used as an intensifying adjective, as in the phrases "a holy terror" or "a holy mess." USAGE ALERT: The inclusion of the word holy as slang may make it seem blasphemous and objectionable in some contexts and to some people.

**holy** |HŌ lē| *pfx* Combining form to create interjections. ORIGINS: From the slang intensifier holy from SE **holy** meaning "blessed by God." USAGE INFO: Creates an interjection when combined with ordinary words, rhyming words, and PO words, as in Holy cow! Holy mackerel! Holy guacamole! Holy moly/moley! Holy smoke(s)! and **Holy fuck!** The phrases with rhyming words (such as *guacamole*) or oddball word choices (such as *mackerel*) have a touch of humor and are open to being used more light-heartedly. USAGE ALERT: The inclusion of the word holy as slang may make it seem blasphemous and objectionable in some contexts and to some people.

**Holy shit!** |HŌ lē SHIT| *excl* An interjection expressing anger, frustration, dismay, etc. ORIGINS: From the slang intensifier holy from SE **holy** meaning "blessed by God" and the slang **shit** meaning "excrement." USAGE ALERT: The reference to excrement, especially combined with a word connected to religion, will be objectionable in some contexts and to some people. The inclusion of a slang use of holy in the phrase will make it seem blasphemous and objectionable in some contexts and to some people.

**honcho** |HAHN chō| *n* An important or influential person; the boss. ORIGINS: From Japanese **han'cho** meaning "group leader." Used by US military stationed in Korea.

**hooey** |HŪ ē| *n* Nonsense; untruths; lies.

**hoof (it)** |hŏŏf / HŎŎF it| *v* To go by foot, walking or running; to dance. ORIGINS: From slang hoof meaning "the human foot."

**hooha, hoo-ha\*** |HŪ hah| *n* Any nameless object, or object for which one cannot remember the name. ORIGINS: May derive from people's efforts to recall a forgotten name.
• hoo-hoo |HŪ hū|

**hook** |hŏŏk| *v* To steal. ORIGINS: By extension of SE **hook** meaning "to snare st with a hook."

**hooked** |hŏŏkt| *adj* Captivated or addicted.

**hop to it** |hahp TŪ it| *v* To hurry; to make an energetic start on st; to get to work.

**hopped up** |HAHPT UP| *adj* Energized; agitated; excited. ORIGINS: By extension of the initial use, which referred to being under the influence of drugs.

**hornswoggle** |HAWRN swahg ul| *v* To cheat or swindle.

**horse's ass** |HAWR siz AS| *n* A stupid and incompetent person; a contemptible person. ORIGINS: From SE **horse** and slang **ass** meaning "rear end or buttocks." USAGE ALERT: The use of the word **shit** will be objectionable in some contexts and to some people. Can be used affectionately, but often used with intent to be rude and understood as such.

**horsefeathers** |HAWRS fe *thurz*| *n* Nonsense; untruths; lies. ORIGINS: Euphemism for **horseshit**, coined by Billy DeBeck in his comic strip *Barney Google*

(1928) and popularized by the Marx Brothers in their film *Horse Feathers* (1932). USAGE ALERT: Euphemisms may still be objectionable in some contexts and to some people.

**horseshit** |HAWRS SHIT| *n* Rubbish; untruths; lies. ORIGINS: From SE **horse** and slang **shit** meaning "excrement." Extended from the original meaning of "horse dung." USAGE ALERT: The use of the word **shit** will be objectionable in some contexts and to some people.

**hose** |hōz| *v* To kill with a firearm. ORIGINS: First used of a machine gun, perhaps because of the similarity of the motion of firing to that of using a hose to spray water from side to side on plants, for example.

**hot** |haht| *adj* Fashionable; interesting; exciting; attractive; popular; successful; skillful; on a lucky streak.

**hot-air artist** |HAHT ER ahr tist| *n* A person who talks a lot of nonsense.

**hot and bothered** |HAHT und BAH*TH* urd| *adj* In a state of excited expectation; agitated; flustered. ORIGINS: From the physical symptoms of such a state.

**hot dog** |HAHT dawg| *n* A person who shows off his or her (sometimes quite expert) skill to get attention; also, a risk-taker.

**Hot dog!** |haht DAWG| *excl* Delighted agreement. USAGE INFO: Alternate forms are Hot diggety dog! and Hot diggety!

**hot for/on** |haht fawr/ HAHT ahn| *adj* Enthusiastic about.

**hot potato** |haht pu TĀ tō| *n* A problem that is felt to be "too hot to handle"; a sensitive or politicized issue that people wish would go away. ORIGINS: From the earlier expression **drop like a hot potato**, which alludes to the heat-retaining properties of a baked potato. Popularized by the children's game Hot Potato.

**hot seat** |HAHT SĒT| *n* A difficult position, subject to scrutiny; a situation in which one is subject to harsh criticism. ORIGINS: By generalization of the slang **hot seat** meaning "the electric chair." USAGE INFO: Often in the phrase "in the hot seat."

**hot spot** |HAHT spaht| *n* An area of trouble; a difficult or dangerous situation.

**hot stuff** |HAHT stuf| *n* An expert; a particularly intelligent or capable person.

**hot under the collar** |HAHT UN dur *thu* KAH lur| *adj* Angry.

**hot water** |HAHT WAH tur| *n* A predicament; difficulties. USAGE INFO: Often in the phrases "in hot water" or "landed in hot water."

**hotshot, hot-shot** |HAHT shaht| *n* A person who is important or influential or expert. USAGE INFO: Used ironically of a self-important person.

**How do you mean?** |hou dū yū MĒN| *phr* How could this be? What do you mean?

**How's that?** |houz THAT| *phr* What do you mean? Could you explain your logic? ORIGINS: Can be a shortened form of "How is that possible?"

**How's tricks?** |houz TRIKS| *excl* How are you? USAGE INFO: Notice that although the subject of the sentence (*tricks*) is plural, the contracted verb (*is*) is singular. This is a hallmark of colloquial usage.

**Howdy!** |HOU dē| *excl* Hello, how are you? ORIGINS: A shortened form of the phrase "How do you do?"

**howl** |houl| *v* To laugh uproariously.

**howler** |houl ur| *n* A laughable mistake; a serious error. USAGE INFO: Two very different meanings, the first one a howl of laughter, the second, a howl of pain.

**huff** |huf| *n* A fit of ill temper or anger.

**huffy** |HUF ē| *adj* Bad-tempered; angry.

**Huh?** |hu| *phr* I don't have a clue what you're getting at.

**hulking** |HUL king| *adj* Of massive size; large and unwieldy; big. ORIGINS: From SE **hulk** meaning "a large person."

**humongous, humungous** |hū MAHN gus / hū MUN gus| *adj* Extraordinarily large; enormous; monstrous. ORIGINS: Thought to derive from SE **huge**, **monstrous**, and **tremendous**.

**hump** |hump| *v* To move really quickly; to hurry; to travel at great speed.

**hung up on** |hung UP ahn| *adj* Obsessing about; preoccupied with; in love with. ORIGINS: By generalization of slang **hung up** meaning "addicted to drugs."

**hunk** |hungk| *n* An attractive, well-built man.

**hunky-dory** |HUNG kē DAWR ē| *adj* Fine; wonderful. ORIGINS: Disputed.

**hustle** |HUS ul| *v* To sell by using pressure, aggressive techniques, or deceit, especially misrepresentation of oneself.

**hustler** |HUS lur| *n* An ambitious, hard-working person who inspires others to similar efforts; someone who cheats his or her way through life. USAGE INFO: A word to use carefully because of the very different impressions it might give.

**hype** |hīp| *v* To make exaggerated claims for the sake of promotion.

**hyped up** |HĪPT up| *adj* Tense and nervous. ORIGINS: By extension from slang hyped up meaning "under the influence of stimulants injected with a hypodermic needle."

**hyper** |HĪ pur| *adj* Over-stimulated; overly emotional; tense. ORIGINS: Shortened from SE **hyperactive**.

**IBIWISI** I'll believe it when I see it.

**IBTD** I beg to differ.

**IDC** I don't care.

**IDK** I don't know.

**IKWYM** I know what you mean.

**IOH** I'm outta here!

**ITA** I totally agree.

**IYD** In your dreams.

**I could care less!** |ī kōod ker LES| *excl* An interjection expressing complete indifference. ORIGINS: From **I couldn't care less!** with the negative removed. Logically, it means that one does care. Some say that the negative is covered by the phrase being said sarcastically. USAGE INFO: Those who do not believe that the tone covers removing the negative may find this expression to be grammatically incorrect. USAGE ALERT: Usually used with intent to be rude and understood as such.

**I couldn't care less!** |ī KŌOD'nt ker LES| *excl* An interjection expressing complete indifference. USAGE ALERT: Usually used with intent to be rude and understood as such.

**I don't buy it!** |ī dōnt BĪ it| *excl* I don't believe it/you!

**I don't give a care!** |ī dōnt GIV u ker| *excl* I don't care at all! USAGE INFO: May be used as a euphemism for other, stronger expressions of indifference. USAGE ALERT: Usually used with intent to be rude and understood as such.

**I don't give a crap!** |ī dōnt GIV u krap| *excl* An interjection expressing complete indifference. ORIGINS: Euphemism for **I don't give a shit!** Slang **crap** is a euphemism for **shit**. USAGE INFO: The intention is to express that the speaker does not even have the most minimal interest. USAGE ALERT: The reference to excrement will make this expression objectionable in some contexts and to some people. Usually used with intent to be rude and understood as such.

**I don't give a damn!** |ī dōnt GIV u dam| *excl* An interjection expressing complete indifference. ORIGINS: By extension from SE **damn**, which literally means "Send (it) to hell." USAGE INFO: The intention is to express that the speaker does not even have the most minimal interest. USAGE ALERT: The use of **damn** will make this expression objectionable in some contexts and to some people. Usually used with intent to be rude and understood as such.

**I don't give a darn!** |ī dōnt GIV u dahrn| *excl* An interjection expressing complete indifference. ORIGINS: Euphemism for **I don't give a damn!** and similar PO expressions. In this particular case, darn is said to serve as a euphemism for not giving a **crap**, **damn**, **fuck**, or **shit**. USAGE INFO: The intention is to express that the speaker does not even have the most minimal interest. USAGE ALERT: Euphemisms may still be objectionable in some contexts and to some people. Usually used with intent to be rude and understood as such.

**I don't give a fuck!** |ī dōnt GIV u fuk| *excl* An interjection expressing complete indifference. ORIGINS: From slang **fuck** meaning "sexual intercourse." USAGE INFO: The intention is to express that the speaker does not even have the most minimal interest. Notice that the use of **fuck** in this expression devalues sex. USAGE ALERT: The use of **fuck** will make this expression objectionable in some contexts and to some people. Usually used with intent to be rude and understood as such.

**I don't give a hill of beans!** |ī dōnt GIV u hil uv BĒNZ| *excl* An interjection expressing complete indifference. ORIGINS: Euphemism for similar expression with **crap**, **damn**, **fuck**, or **shit**. Beans are conceived to be a minimal item, as in the expression "I don't know beans about it." USAGE INFO: The intention is to express that the speaker does not even have the most minimal interest. USAGE ALERT: Euphemisms may still be objectionable in some contexts and to some people. Usually used with intent to be rude and understood as such.

**I don't give a hoot!** |ī dōnt GIV u hūt| *excl* An interjection expressing complete indifference. ORIGINS: Euphemism for similar expression with **crap**, **damn**, **fuck**, or **shit**. A hoot, the noise one makes in disgust, is conceived to be something without value. USAGE INFO: The intention is to express that the speaker does not even have the most minimal interest. USAGE ALERT: Euphemisms may still be objectionable in some contexts and to some people. Usually used with intent to be rude and understood as such.

**I don't give a rap!** |ī dōnt GIV u rap| *excl* An interjection expressing complete indifference. ORIGINS: Slang rap was a nickname in England for a halfpenny, a coin of very little value, the approximate equivalent of the US slang **red cent**. USAGE INFO:The intention is to express that the speaker does not even have the most minimal interest. USAGE ALERT: Usually used with intent to be rude and understood as such.

**I don't give a rat's ass!** |ī dōnt GIV u RATS AS| *excl* An interjection expressing complete indifference. ORIGINS: From slang **ass** meaning "the rear end or buttocks." USAGE INFO: The intention is to express that the speaker does not even have the most minimal interest. USAGE ALERT: The reference to **ass** will make this expression objectionable in some contexts and to some people. Usually used with intent to be rude and understood as such.

**I don't give a shit!** |ī dōnt GIV u shit| *excl* An interjection expressing complete indifference. ORIGINS: Slang **shit** means "excrement," but is figuratively used to mean "nothing" as in "I don't have shit." USAGE INFO: The intention is to express that the speaker does not even have the most minimal interest. USAGE ALERT:

The reference to excrement will make this expression objectionable in some contexts and to some people. Usually used with intent to be rude and understood as such.

**I don't give two fucks!** |ī dōnt GIV tū FUKS| *excl* An interjection expressing complete indifference. ORIGINS: From slang **fuck** meaning "sexual intercourse." USAGE INFO: The intention is to express that the speaker does not even have the most minimal interest. Notice that the use of **fuck** in this expression devalues sex. In this context, oddly, the word *two* acts as an intensifier of worthlessness. USAGE ALERT: The use of **fuck** will make this expression objectionable in some contexts and to some people. Usually used with intent to be rude and understood as such.

**I don't give two hoots!** |ī dōnt GIV tū hūts| *excl* An interjection expressing complete indifference. ORIGINS: Emphatic form of I don't give a hoot! Hoots, noises one makes in disgust, are conceived to be something without value. In this context, oddly, the word *two* acts as an intensifier of worthlessness. USAGE INFO: The intention is to express that the speaker does not even have the most minimal interest. USAGE ALERT: Euphemisms may still be objectionable in some contexts and to some people. Usually used with intent to be rude and understood as such.

**I don't have the foggiest.** |ī DŌNT hav *thu* FAW gē ist| *phr* I don't have any idea. I don't know the answer to your question. ORIGINS: From shortening of the phrase "I don't have the foggiest idea" and the obscuring property of fog that prevents clear vision.

**I don't know beans about it.** |ī dōnt nō BĒNZ u bout it| *excl* I don't know the subject. ORIGINS: From slang **beans**, which means a minimal amount of something, in this case, knowledge.

**I don't know <pronoun> from Adam.** |ī dōnt nō <pronoun> frum A dum| *excl* I don't know *sb/st*; I wouldn't recognize *sb/st*. ORIGINS: From slang **not know *sb* from**, which means "unable to recognize" and **Adam**, the name of the first man reported in Genesis in the Old Testament of the Bible.

**I own you!** |ī ŌN yū| *excl* I win: you lose! ORIGINS: From the victory cry uttered by players of first-person shooter games.

**I should worry!** |ī shŏŏd wur ē| *excl* An interjection expressing lack of concern. ORIGINS: From a Yiddish phrase. USAGE INFO: Sometimes said sarcastically.

**I wouldn't/won't say no!** |ī WŎŎD unt sā nō / ī WŌNT sā nō| *excl* An interjection offering a somewhat round-about statement of agreement. ORIGINS: This phrase employing a double negative logically ends up meaning "I would/ will say yes."

**I wouldn't know *sb/st* if I fell over <pronoun>.** |ī WŎŎD 'nt nō *sb/st* if ī FEL ō vur <pronoun>| *excl* I don't know *sb/st*; I wouldn't recognize *sb/st*, even up close.

**I wouldn't know *st* if it hit me in the face.** |ī WŎŎD 'nt nō *st* if it HIT mē in *thu* FĀS| *excl* I don't know *st*; I wouldn't recognize *st* even up close.

**I'll be jiggered!** |ī bē JIG urd| *excl* I'm shocked! ORIGINS: From jigger meaning "to shake."

**I'll drink to that!** |ĪL DRINGK tū *that*| *excl* An interjection expressing support for sb's idea/plan/decision. ORIGINS: Agreement in the form of a toast. From the niceties of drinking, taken out of context.

**I'm outta here!** |ĪM OU tu hir| *excl* I'm leaving this place (immediately)! USAGE INFO: In Instant Messaging (IM), may be used followed by an immediate departure without waiting for a response.

**I've had it!** |īv HAD it| *excl* I am losing my ability to cope! Cry of frustration, extreme annoyance, or exasperation. ORIGINS: Shortened version of the phrase I've had it with *sb/st* or I've had it up to here. USAGE INFO: Usually said after a series of events have built up the emotion prompting the exclamation.

**ice** |īs| *v* To defeat or kill; to murder.

**Ick!** |ik| *excl* A sound to express disgust. ORIGINS: A back-formation from slang icky.

**icky** |IK ē| *adj* Disgusting; unpleasant; distasteful. USAGE INFO: Can be applied to a semi-solid (gooey) substance, one's health, or something embarrassing.

**iffy proposition** |IF ē prahp u ZISH un| *n* A risky undertaking; a situation with an uncertain outcome. ORIGINS: From SE if plus the suffix -y.

**light! Ite!** |ī ĪT| *excl* See AIGHT!

**in** |in| *adj* Fashionable.

**in a dither** |in u DITH ur| *adj* So agitated that one cannot make up one's mind.

**in a doodah** |in u DŪ dah| *adj* In a state of nervous tension. ORIGINS: From the refrain of the Stephen Foster song "Camptown Races" (1850). USAGE INFO: This phrase (as opposed to its synonyms) is often used as an indication that the situation is not too serious.

**in a flutter** |in u FLUT ur| *adj* In a state of nervous excitement. USAGE INFO: May be positive or negative.

**in a funk** |in u FUNGK| *adj* Depressed; in a state of fear. ORIGINS: From Flemish **fonck** meaning "fear."

**in a hole** |in u HŌL| *phr* In a difficult situation; in debt. USAGE INFO: The same idea is expressed by the phrase in the hole.

**in a lather** |in u LATH ur| *adj* In a state of angry agitation; very anxious. ORIGINS: From the frothy sweat of an upset horse.

**in a pickle** |in u PIK ul| *phr* In a mess; in a difficult situation. ORIGINS: From slang pickle meaning "a predicament."

**in a state** |in u STĀT| *adj* Feeling extreme excitement or distress.

**in a sweat** |in u SWET| *adj* Agitated and worried or agitated and fearful.

**in a tight corner/spot** |in u TĪT KAWR nur / in u TĪT SPAHT| *phr* In a very difficult situation; facing a set of circumstances that will prove complicated to deal with. ORIGINS: From slang **tight** meaning "a tough, difficult to deal with situation."

**in a tizzy** |in u TIZ ē| *adj* In a panic; confused and undecided. ORIGINS: From slang **tizzy** meaning "panic."

**in clover** |in CLŌ vur| *adj* In very comfortable circumstances. ORIGINS: By comparison of wealthy people to cattle who favor clover, reportedly because it is tasty and fattening.

**in (deep) doo-doo** |in DŪ dū / in DĒP dū dū| *phr* In serious trouble. ORIGINS: Euphemism for **in deep shit**. **Doo-doo** is a childish euphemism for slang **shit** meaning "excrement." USAGE INFO: Because doo-doo is juvenile language, the phrase is often used self-mockingly. USAGE ALERT: The reference to excrement will make the phrase objectionable in some contexts and to some people.

**in deep shit** |in DĒP SHIT| *phr* In a serious situation. ORIGINS: From slang **shit** meaning "excrement." USAGE ALERT: The reference to excrement will make the phrase objectionable in some contexts and to some people.

**in great shape** |in GRET SHĀP| *adj* In excellent condition in terms of physical health, emotional well-being, financial outlook, or overall. USAGE INFO: Also used more specifically of athletes and others of being in prime physical condition.

**in hock** |in hock| *adj* In debt. ORIGINS: From **hock** meaning "a pledge in a pawnshop."

**in spades** |in SPĀDZ| *adv* Intensifier; to a great extent; to the greatest extent possible; extremely. ORIGINS: From the jargon of card games, in some of which, spades is the highest suit. USAGE INFO: Often of competition as in "we beat them in spades."

**in the bag** |in *thu* BAG| *adj* Guaranteed; made certain. USAGE INFO: Often used in forecasting the results of ventures.

**in the black** |in *thu* BLAK| *adj* Making a profit; doing well. ORIGINS: From the one-time accounting practice of using red ink for losses and black ink for profits.

**in the can** |in *thu* KAN| *adj* Finished; completed. ORIGINS: From the jargon of filmmaking, in which a completed roll of film is placed into a canister (can).

**in the dumps** |in *thu* DUMPS| *adj* Miserable or depressed; gloomy. USAGE INFO: Also forms part of the expression **down in the dumps**.

**in the money** |in *thu* MUN ē| *adj* Rich; wealthy. ORIGINS: From the horse-racing expression, "to run in the money," used of horses that place first, second, or third, thereby gaining a payoff for those who bet on them.

**in the money, be** |bē in *thu* MUN ē| *v* To profit by winning a wager. ORIGINS: From the horse-racing expression, "to run in the money," used of horses that place first, second, or third, thereby gaining a payoff for those who bet on them.

**in the red** |in *thu* RED| *adj* Broke; in debt. ORIGINS: From the one-time accounting practice of using red ink for losses and black ink for profits.

**in the soup** |in *thu* SŪP| *phr* In trouble.

**in whack** |in WAK| *adj* In good condition. ORIGINS: From SE **whack** meaning condition or state. USAGE INFO: *See* OUT OF WHACK.

**In your dreams!** |in yo͞or DRĒMZ| *excl* No! ORIGINS: The idea is that the content being responded to is completely unrealistic—only possible or valid in fantasy or the imagination.

**infernal** |in FUR nul| *adj* Extreme; complete. ORIGINS: From SE **infernal** meaning "of hell," used as a euphemism for **damn(ed)**. USAGE INFO: Used as an intensifier in negative contexts, as in "an infernal racket." USAGE ALERT: Euphemisms may still be objectionable in some contexts and to some people.

**infernally** |in FUR nu lē| *adv* Extremely; very. ORIGINS: From SE **infernally** meaning "fiendishly or diabolically," used as a euphemism for **damn(ed)**. USAGE INFO: Used as an intensifier in negative and positive contexts, as in "infernally difficult" or "infernally delicious." USAGE ALERT: Euphemisms may still be objectionable in some contexts and to some people.

**into** |IN tū| *adj* Attracted to, involved with.

**Is the pope Catholic?** |iz *thu* PŌP KATH lik| *excl* Sarcastic, rhetorical question in response to a question whose answer is obviously "Yes." ORIGINS: From the obvious fact that the pope, being the head of the Roman Catholic church is (by definition) Catholic.

**It won't wash!** |it WŌNT WAHSH| *excl* I don't believe it/you!

**It's Greek to me.** |its GRĒK tū MĒ| *phr* It's beyond my knowledge or understanding. ORIGINS: From slang **Greek** meaning "unintelligible." From a Latin proverb, "Graecum est, non potest legi" (It's Greek, therefore unreadable), but better known through the use in Shakespeare's 1599 play *The Tragedy of Julius Caesar* in which Casca says of Cicero's speech, "for mine own part, it was Greek to me," making a pun (I, ii). May allude to the fact that Greek not only is a different language from Latin, but also has a different alphabet.

**itchy** |ICH ē| *adj* Somewhat agitated; slightly anxious. ORIGINS: From the twitchy behavior of someone who has an itch. USAGE INFO: Usually used in a situation where the stakes are not high.

**itty-bitty** |IT ē BIT ē| *adj* Little, small; insignificant. ORIGINS: Probably related to SE **little**. USAGE INFO: Also itsy-bitsy. *See* BITTY.

**jabber** |JAB ur| *v* To chatter idly, unrestrainedly, or unintelligibly.

**jack (shit)** |jak / jak SHIT| *n* Nothing at all. ORIGINS: From slang jack meaning "fool," a shortening of SE jackass, and slang **shit** used as an intensifier. USAGE INFO: Often used in constructions with an (implied) double negative: "You don't know jackshit" or abbreviated to "You don't know jack." USAGE ALERT: The inclusion of **shit** will make this word objectionable in some situations and to some people.

**jack (up)** |jak / Jak UP| *v* To increase the price; to enhance. ORIGINS: Akin to SE jack meaning "a device to raise a car."

**jack around** |JAK u ROUND| *v* To mess around; to engage in useless/time-wasting activities. ORIGINS: By extension of slang jack, meaning fool and shortened from SE jackass.

**jack (around) with** *st* |jak with *st* / jak u ROUND with *st*| *v* To use something irresponsibly or without understanding; to mess around with. ORIGINS: Possibly from slang jack meaning "fool," a shortening of SE jackass, therefore a synonym for **fool (around) with**. USAGE ALERT: Because jack is used in phrases such as **jack off**, a euphemism for **jerk-off** meaning "to masturbate," and **jackshit** (see above), it's difficult to tell how this phrase may be received: as perfectly ordinary or as euphemistic and objectionable.

**jackass** |JAK as| *n* A foolish or stupid person who is loud, incompetent, and crude. ORIGINS: From SE jackass.

**jacked (up)** |jakt / jakt UP| *adj* Very excited or agitated; exhilarated. ORIGINS: Figurative version of slang jack up meaning "to inject narcotics" or "to drink coffee."

**jake** |jāk| *adj* Very satisfactory; fine.

**jamming** |JAM ing| *adj* Excellent; first-rate. ORIGINS: By extension of slang jam meaning "to have a good time."

**jaw** |jaw| *v* To chat.

**Jeepers!** |JĒ purz| *excl* An interjection expressing surprise, shock, dismay, etc. ORIGINS: Euphemism for **Jesus** used as an interjection—a figurative use of SE Jesus whom Christians hold to be the Son of God—but it is milder. USAGE INFO: Many people will not know the ORIGINS of this expression. USAGE ALERT: People who consider this substitution for Jesus blasphemous are likely to find this term objectionable.

**jeez** |jēz| *adv* Sentence modifier. ORIGINS: Euphemism for **Jesus** used as a sentence modifier—a figurative use of SE Jesus whom Christians hold to be the Son of God—but it is milder. USAGE INFO: Used as a sentence modifier to show frustration, relief, and other emotional responses, as in "Jeez, what a day!" Many people will not know the origins of this expression. USAGE ALERT: This saying will be considered objectionable in some contexts and by some people who may find it blasphemous.

**Jeez!** |jēz| *excl* An interjection expressing surprise, shock, dismay, etc. ORIGINS: Euphemism for **Jesus!** used as an interjection—a figurative use of SE Jesus whom Christians hold to be the Son of God, but it is milder. Many people will not know the origins of this expression. USAGE ALERT: This saying will be considered objectionable in some contexts and by some people who may find it blasphemous.

**jellyfish** |JEL ē fish| *n* A person who lacks strength of character; someone with no fortitude. ORIGINS: From perceived characteristics of the animal called a jellyfish.

**jerk(-off)** |jurk / JURK awf| *n* A contemptible person; an extremely offensive person. ORIGINS: From slang **jerk-off** meaning "to masturbate." USAGE ALERT: Many people use this word without reference to its origins and, often when using only jerk, without knowing them. This can lead to very different interpretations of acceptable use, especially when children are using the word or within earshot. Usually used with intent to denigrate or insult and understood as such.

**jerk *sb* around** |JERK *sb* u ROUND| *v* To take advantage of *sb*; to manipulate *sb*; to deceive *sb*; to treat *sb* badly. ORIGINS: Possibly related to the slang verb jerk meaning "to harass or deliberately annoy *sb*" or to jerk *sb's* chain (see the following entry). USAGE ALERT: Some people may connect this word to **jerk-off**, although they do not seem to be etymologically linked.

**jerk *sb's* chain** |JURK *sb's* CHĀN| *v* To purposely annoy or harass *sb*; to act in a way that one knows upsets *sb*. ORIGINS: From SE jerk meaning "to pull sharply." The reference is to using a leash and collar to curb a dog. USAGE INFO: *See* YANK *SB'S* CHAIN. USAGE ALERT: Some people may connect this word to **jerk-off**, although they do not seem to be etymologically linked.

**jerky** |JURK ē| *adj* Foolish; idiotic. ORIGINS: From slang jerk meaning "fool." It's not clear that it's tied to other meanings. USAGE ALERT: Some people may connect this word to **jerk-off**, although they do not seem to be etymologically linked.

**Jesus** |JĒ zus| *adv* Sentence modifier. ORIGINS: From SE **Jesus Christ** whom Christians hold to be the Son of God. USAGE INFO: Used as a sentence modifier to show anger, dismay, frustration, relief, and other emotional responses, as in "Jesus, what happened to my car!?" USAGE ALERT: The use of the word Jesus in this way will seem blasphemous and objectionable in some contexts and to some people.

**Jesus!** |JĒ zus| *excl* An interjection expressing anger or dismay, etc. ORIGINS: From SE **Jesus Christ** whom Christians hold to be the Son of God. USAGE ALERT: The use of the word Jesus in this way will seem blasphemous and objectionable in some contexts and to some people.

**jigger** |JIG ur| *n* Any nameless object, or object for which one cannot remember the name; often refers to a gadget. ORIGINS: Possibly short for watchamajigger or whatchamajigger or thingamajig or any of the very many other synonyms.

**jillion** |JIL yun| *n* An unspecified, exceedingly large amount. ORIGINS: One of a group of made up numbers ending in *-illion* with pretty indistinguishable meanings, although additional prefixes may be indicating even larger amounts (i.e., a **gajillion** may be larger than a jillion).

**jim-jams** |JIM jamz| *n* A fit of fear or apprehension; an episode of depression. ORIGINS: Broadened from slang **jim-jams** meaning "delirium tremens." USAGE INFO: Often used with *the*.

**jitters** |JIT urz| *n* A state of nervousness or agitation; emotional tension; stage fright. ORIGINS: Unlike jim-jams, jitters began with the broader use and was only later applied to delirium tremens. USAGE INFO: Often used with *the*.

**jittery** |JIT ur ē| *adj* Nervous; tense; feeling uneasy. ORIGINS: Based on slang jitters meaning "a state of nervousness or agitation."

**jive** |JĪV| *n* Deceptive talk; untruths; lies; nonsense. USAGE INFO: Jive is also the name of a type of slang.

**josh** |jawsh| *v* To tease good-naturedly. ORIGINS: From Josh Billings, the pseudonym of US humorist Henry Wheeler Shaw (1818–1885).

**jughead** |JUG hed| *n* A fool. ORIGINS: Possibly from the slang jughead for a mule, from SE jug and slang suffix head. Popularized by the character Jughead Jones in the Archie Comics (1941). USAGE ALERT: Usually used with intent to denigrate or insult and understood as such.

**jumbo** |JUM bō| *adj* A large, clumsy person. ORIGINS: Contrary to some suggestions, it seems that the term was used of people before being popularized with circus master P.T. Barnum's application of it to a large elephant in 1828.

**jump all over *sb*** |jump awl Ō vur *sb*| *v* To launch a verbal attack against *sb*; to berate *sb*.

**jump down *sb's* throat** |jump doun *sb's* THRŌT| *v* To launch a verbal attack—which could consist of an accusation, reprimand, criticism, or disagreement—against *sb*, often without any warning.

**jump on *sb*** |JUMP ahn *sb*| *v* To launch a verbal attack against *sb*; to berate *sb*.

**jumping** |JUMP ing| *adj* Filled with excitement. USAGE INFO: Used of a place, not a person.

**junkie, junky** |JUNG kē| *sfx* A person who is obsessively devoted to *st*; a person with a deep interest in *st*. ORIGINS: From generalizing slang junkie meaning "a heroin addict." USAGE INFO: Often spelled as an open compound, as in "sports junkie."

**junky** |JUNG kē| *adj* Fitting the category of junk; suitable for discarding; inferior; of poor quality. ORIGINS: From slang junk meaning "inferior."

**K** Okay.

**KMA** Kiss my ass.

**KWIM** Know what I mean?

**kabam** |ku BAM| *v* To punch. ORIGINS: Imitative of the sound of a blow.

**kahuna** |ku HŪ nu| *n Sb* or *st* important or large. ORIGINS: Generalized from Hawaiian **kahuna** meaning "wise man or priest." The initial slang meaning was "an expert surfer."

**kapow** |ku POU| *v* To punch. ORIGINS: Imitative of the sound of a blow.

**kaput, kaputt** |ku POŌT| *adj* Incapacitated: broken; non-functioning; out-of-order. ORIGINS: From German **kaputt** and French **être capot**, both of which are names for the situation of a player in the card game piquet who has not won any tricks.

**kayo** |KĀ Ō| *v* To incapacitate; to put out of commission. ORIGINS: Pronunciation of KO, the slang abbreviation for boxing jargon **knock out**, meaning "knock unconscious."

**keen on** |KĒN ahn| *adj* Intensely interested in; attracted to. ORIGINS: From SE **keen** meaning "ardent; eager."

**keep a tab on** |kēp u TAB ahn| *v* Watch with vigilance; keep a record of the actions of; keep under surveillance.

**keep on trucking** |kēp ahn TRUK ing| *v* To continue on with the (good) job or action one is doing; to keep moving. USAGE INFO: A phrase of encouragement when said to someone else. A statement of one's intent to continue in the same lines, when used of oneself.

**keep one's eyes peeled**\* |kēp wunz ĪZ PĒLD| *v* To stay visually alert; to be on guard. ORIGINS: The reference is to not allowing one's eyelids (peels/skins) to cover one's eyes, as they would if one fell asleep.
 • keep one's eyes skinned |kēp wunz ĪZ SKIND|

**keep one's pants/shirt on** |kēp wunz PANTS awn / kēp wunz SHURT awn| *v* To avoid becoming excited; to stay calm.

**keep tabs on** |kēp TABS ahn| *v* Watch with vigilance; keep a record of the actions of; keep under surveillance.

**key** |kē| *adj* Excellent; worthy of admiration. ORIGINS: By extension of SE **key** meaning "central; important."

**keyed up** |kēd UP| *adj* Agitated; excited; nervous. ORIGINS: From slang **keyed** meaning "drunk or under the influence of a drug."

**kibitzer** |KI bit sur| *n* A person who meddles in order to offer unsolicited and unwanted advice. ORIGINS: Through Yiddish **kibitsen**, from German **kiebitzen** meaning "to watch a card game without playing," from German **Kiebitz**, the name of a bird noted for being noisy and inquisitive. USAGE INFO: A kibitzer's advice is usually worthless.

**kick-ass*** |KIK ASS| *adj* Excellent; effective. ORIGINS: From slang **ass** meaning "the rear end or buttocks." USAGE INFO: **Kick-ass** can be used equally of negative and positive things: "a kick-ass getaway after the robbery" or "a kick-ass birthday party." USAGE ALERT: The inclusion of the word **ass** in the phrase will render it objectionable in some contexts and to some people.
• **kick-butt** |KIK BUTT|

**kick in** |kik IN| *v* To contribute a share in a group project (usually money); to take effect.

**kick off** |KIK AWF| *v* To die. ORIGINS: Possibly related to other slang terms for die with kick, like **kick the bucket**, **kick the wind**, and **kick the clouds**, the latter two of which are outdated terms referring to death by hanging.

**kick** *sb* **out** |kik *sb* OUT| *v* To force *sb* to leave; to eject *sb*.

**kick** *sb* **where it counts** |KIK *sb* wer it KOUNTZ| *v* To strike a blow at a man's groin using the foot. ORIGINS: **Where it counts** is a euphemism for a male's groin. USAGE INFO: This phrase is commonly used in talking about self-defense for women. USAGE ALERT: Despite the anatomical reference, when speaking of self-defense, this term is not likely to be found objectionable.

**kick** *sb*'s **ass/butt** |kik *sb*'s AS / kik *sb*'s BUT| *v* To beat *sb* in a fight; to achieve a success; to win a competition (such as a sports event) decidedly; to best *sb* in an argument. ORIGINS: From slang **ass** meaning "the rear end or buttocks." **Butt** is a euphemism for **ass**. USAGE ALERT: The reference to the rear end or buttocks will make this phrase objectionable in some contexts and to some people, though some people will find **butt** less objectionable.

**kick the bucket** |kik *thu* BU kit| *v* To die.

**kick the crap out of** *sb/st* |KIK *thu* KRAP out uv *sb/st*| *v* To beat up severely (with or without literal kicking). ORIGINS: Euphemism for **kick the shit out of** *sb/st*. Slang **crap** is a euphemism for **shit**. USAGE ALERT: The reference to excrement will make this phrase objectionable in some contexts and to some people, though some people will find **crap** less objectionable.

**kick the shit out of** *sb/st* |KIK *thu* SHIT out uv *sb/st*| *v* To beat up severely (with or without literal kicking). ORIGINS: From SE **kick** and slang **shit** meaning "excrement." USAGE ALERT: The reference to excrement will make this phrase objectionable in some contexts and to some people.

K

**kick the tires** |kik *thu* TĪ urz| *v* To examine; to check out before making a purchase. ORIGINS: In what some say is a fairly useless attempt to check for quality, people will sometimes kick the tires of a used car. Kick the tires has become a generalized term for making an assessment of something.

**kick up a fuss** |KIK up u FUS| *v* To respond unfavorably and vocally. ORIGINS: From slang kick up meaning "start or increase."

**kicker** |KIK ur| *n* A pitfall; a previously hidden or concealed difficulty or problem. ORIGINS: Seems logically (if not historically) connected to the effect of a poker player revealing his/her **kicker(s)**—an unmatched card or cards that can, nevertheless, play a role in winning a hand.

**kicking back** |KIK ing bak| *adj* Relaxing.

**kill** |kil| *v* To cause to laugh heartily; to delight.

**killer** |KIL ur| *adj* Impressive of its kind; terrific; effective.

**killing** |KIL ing| *n* An impressive (financial) success. USAGE INFO: Often in the phrase "make a killing."

**kingfish** |KING fish| *n* A political leader. ORIGINS: Used by Louisiana Governor and Senator Huey P. Long of himself, as well as being the name of a character in the *Amos and Andy* radio show. More recently popularized by Randy Newman in his song about Long, "Kingfish" (1974).

**kingpin** |KING pin| *n* The central or most important one in a group. ORIGINS: From SE **kingpin**, which refers to either the central pin or the headpin in bowling.

**kink** |kingk| *n* A malfunction; a difficulty; a flaw. ORIGINS: From SE **kink** meaning a bend in some material otherwise straight and meant to be straight. USAGE INFO: Kink can also mean a personal peculiarity of some kind.

**kiss-ass** |KIS AS| *n* One who seeks favor; a sycophant. ORIGINS: From slang **ass** meaning "the rear end or buttocks." USAGE INFO: **Ass-kisser** is a separate, synonymous word that has the words in the reverse order. USAGE ALERT: The use of the word **ass**, the graphic image, and the implied insult will make this phrase objectionable in some contexts and to some people.

**kiss goodbye** |KIS go͞od bī| *v* To end *st*.

**Kiss my ass!** |KIS mī as| *excl* A contemptuous dismissal. ORIGINS: From slang **ass** meaning "the rear end or buttocks." USAGE ALERT: Usually used with intent to be rude and understood as such. In addition, the inclusion of **ass** and the graphic image will make this expression objectionable in some contexts and to some people.

**kiss off** |KIS awf| *v* To dismiss or terminate *sb* from employment; to reject *sb*. ORIGINS: From the idea of a parting kiss.

**Kiss off!** |KIS awf| *excl* A contemptuous dismissal. ORIGINS: From the idea of a parting kiss, but possibly influenced by the similarity of sound to **Piss off!**, for which it may be used as a euphemism.

**kiss *sb's* ass** |KIS *sb's* AS| *v* To seek favor through flattery; to be a sycophant or toady. ORIGINS: From slang **ass** meaning "the rear end or buttocks." USAGE ALERT: The use of the word **ass**, the graphic image, and the implied insult will make this phrase objectionable in some contexts and to some people.

**klutz** |kluts| *n* A clumsy person; a stupid person; a person who is socially inept. ORIGINS: Through Yiddish **klots** from Middle High German **klotz** meaning "a lump of wood." *See* CHUMP and BLOCKHEAD.

**knock** |nahk| *v* To criticize; to find fault with. ORIGINS: Figurative extension of SE **knock** meaning "to hit."

**knock dead** |NAHK DED| *v* To impress to the highest degree: to astonish; to delight; to thrill; to amuse.

**knock for a loop** |NAHK fawr u LŪP| *v* To overcome. USAGE INFO: Don't confuse with **throw for a loop** meaning "to confuse."

**knock heads together** |NAHK HEDS tu ge*th* ur| *v* To use whatever means necessary to get people to stop quarreling or to stop working at cross purposes. USAGE INFO: Usually used as a threat, rather than as a description of an actual action, as in: "The new boss will knock heads together if she has to, to get the company out of this slump."

**Knock it off!** |NAHK it AWF| *excl* Stop (whatever you're doing)! ORIGINS: Extended from slang **knock off** meaning "to stop work." USAGE INFO: Often a request for *sb* to stop speaking in a certain way, e.g., nagging, pleading, teasing, etc.

**knock off** |NAHK AWF| *v* To kill; to murder.

**knock oneself out** |NAHK wun self OUT| *v* To put in a great effort; to work very hard. ORIGINS: By extension of slang **knock out** meaning "to knock unconscious." The idea is that one expends effort until one is in a similar state. USAGE INFO: Said to another person, as in "knock yourself out" either to give approval to the person doing something that is thought to be unnecessary or overkill or to sarcastically pass off a task to someone who has criticized the speaker's efforts. Also used as an exclamation to mean "have a good time."

**knock *sb* out** |NAHK *sb* OUT| *v* To knock *sb* unconscious; to kill *sb*; to best in a competition. USAGE INFO: Also used to mean "to amaze or impress."

**knock *sb's* block off** |NAHK *sb's* BLAHK awf| *v* To deliver a strong blow. ORIGINS: From slang **block** meaning "head." USAGE INFO: Used as a threat, rather than as a description of a particular action, as in, "If you say that again, I'm going to knock your block off."

**knock *sb's* lights out** |NAHK *sb's* LĪT zout| *v* To knock *sb* unconscious by any means (e.g., with a blow of the fist, by conking on the head with a pistol butt, etc.). ORIGINS: From slang **lights** meaning "eyes."

**knock the crap out of *sb/st*** |NAHK thu KRAP out uv *sb/st*| *v* To beat severely. ORIGINS: Euphemism for **knock the shit out of *sb/st***. Slang **crap**

is a euphemism for **shit**. USAGE ALERT: The reference to **crap** will make this phrase objectionable in some contexts and to some people, though some people will find **crap** less objectionable.

**knock the (living) daylights out of** *sb* |NAHK *thu* (LIV ing) DĀ lītz out uv *sb*| *v* To beat severely. ORIGINS: From SE knock and slang daylights originally meaning "the eyes" and then "the insides."

**knock the shit out of** *sb/st* |NAHK *thu* SHIT out uv *sb/st*| *v* To beat severely. ORIGINS: From SE knock and slang **shit** meaning "excrement." USAGE ALERT: The reference to **shit** will make this phrase objectionable in some contexts and to some people.

**knock the socks off** *sb*\* |NAHK *thu* SAHKS awf *sb*| *v* To overwhelm or defeat utterly. ORIGINS: Possibly a reference to cartoons in which someone hit by an uppercut flies out of his/her shoes and socks. USAGE INFO: Can also mean "to amaze or impress."
• knock *sb*'s socks off |NAHK *sb*'s SAHKS awf|

**knock the stuffing out of** *sb* |NAHK *thu* STUF ing out uv *sb*| *v* To beat severely; to undermine someone's confidence. ORIGINS: **Stuffing** is conceived as in a rag-doll: if it were to be taken out, there would just be a saggy cloth bag left.

**knock the tar out of** *sb* |NAHK *thu* tar out uv *sb*| *v* To beat severely. ORIGINS: Perhaps because organic substances break down into tar eventually, in this expression tar is conceived of as the essence of a person.

**knocked for a loop** |NAHKT fawr u LŪP| *adj* Surprised and disconcerted. USAGE INFO: Used of people.

**knockout** |NAHK out| *adj* An outstanding or excellent person or thing; a complete success.

**know-it-all** |NŌ it awl| *n* A person with an exaggerated view of his/her own intellectual capabilities; a person who is constantly putting his/her knowledge on display.

**know** *st* **backwards (and forwards)** |NŌ *st* BAK wurdz / NŌ *st* BAK wurd zund FAWR wurdz| *v* To know perfectly; to have complete command of; to have mastered *st*.

**know** *st* **inside out** |NŌ *st* IN sīd OUT| *v* To know perfectly; to have complete command of; to have mastered *st*.

**know** *st* **like the back of one's hand** |NŌ *st* līk *thu* BAK uv wunz HAND| *v* To know intimately; to have a complete understanding of.

**know the score** |NŌ *thu* SKAWR| *v* To have a grasp of an entire situation with all its ramifications; to understand the full situation. ORIGINS: From sports competitions.

**knuckle down** |NU kul doun| *v* To get to work; to apply oneself diligently to a task. ORIGINS: From the position of the hand in the game of marbles. USAGE INFO: *See* BUCKLE DOWN.

**knuckle under** |NU kul UN dur| *v* To give in; to consent reluctantly. ORIGINS: From the position of the knuckles coming close to the ground when a person stoops or kneels in submission. USAGE INFO: *See* BUCKLE UNDER.

**knucklehead** |NU kul hed| *n* An unintelligent person. ORIGINS: From SE **knuckle** and slang suffix -head, suggesting a head full of bone rather than brain, so not much thinking going on. USAGE ALERT: Often used with intent to denigrate or insult and understood as such.

**kopecks** |KŌ peks| *n* An unspecified amount of money. ORIGINS: From Russian **kopeika** meaning a Russian unit of currency. USAGE INFO: Used in very general terms, as in, "I don't have enough kopecks."

**kvelling** |KVEL ing| *adj* Feeling happy. ORIGINS: From Yiddish **kveln** meaning "to be delighted; to be pleased and proud."

**kvetch** |kvech| *n* A person who complains and whines continually. ORIGINS: From Yiddish **kvetshn** meaning "to complain."

**kvetch** |kvech| *v* To complain or nag. ORIGINS: From Yiddish **kvetshn** meaning "to complain."

# L

**L8R** [See you] Later.

**LMAO** Laughing my ass off.

**LMFAO** Laughing my fucking ass off.

**LONH** Light on, nobody home.

**LPOC** Lazy piece of crap.

**LPOS** Lazy piece of shit.

**la-di-da, lah-di-dah, la-de-da, lah-de-dah, lah-dee-dah** |lah dē DAH| *adj* Pretentious.

**laid back** |LĀD bak| *adj* Relaxed. ORIGINS: From the lounging posture commonly assumed when relaxing.

**lam(baste), lambast** |lam BAST/ lam BĀST| *v* To beat or thrash; to attack verbally: to scold or berate; to defeat in competition. ORIGINS: Related to Old Norse **lemja** meaning "to lame by beating."

**lame** |lām| *adj* Inadequate; worthless; incompetent; lacking substance. ORIGINS: By extension from SE **lame** meaning "disabled."

**lamebrain** |LĀM brān| *n* A foolish person; one who is dull-witted. ORIGINS: Just as slang **lame** is used in general to describe things that do not work properly or as expected or people who are incompetent, in **lamebrain** that meaning is applied specifically to a person's intellect. USAGE ALERT: Usually used with intent to denigrate or insult and understood as such.

**lamer** |LĀM ur| *n* An inept or ineffective person. ORIGINS: By extension of SE **lame** meaning "disabled." USAGE ALERT: Usually used with intent to denigrate or insult and understood as such.

**lap *st* up**[1] |LAP *st* up| *v* To be extremely fond of; to be completely accepting of *st*. ORIGINS: From SE **lap** meaning "to take in food or liquid by lifting it into the mouth with the tongue" (a description of how a dog or cat drinks, for example.)

**lap *st* up**[2] |LAP *st* UP| *v* To accept *st* eagerly and without question.

**lardhead** |LAHRD hed| *n* A stupid person. ORIGINS: From SE **lard** meaning "fat" and slang suffix -head. USAGE ALERT: This term is usually used with intent to denigrate or insult and understood as such.

**large order** |LAHRJ AWR dur| *n* An extremely difficult project or problem; an exceptionally demanding task.

**latch on(to)** |lach AHN / lach AHN tū| *v* Come to understand; grasp mentally.

**Later, gator!** |LĀ tur GĀ tur| *excl* See you later. ORIGINS: Shortened version of See you later, alligator! *See* SEE YOU LATER, ALLIGATOR!

**Laughing my ass off!** |LAF ing mī AS awf| *excl* A hearty, unrestrained laugh. ORIGINS: From slang **ass** meaning "the rear end or buttocks." USAGE ALERT: The inclusion of **ass** and the graphic image will make this expression objectionable in some contexts and to some people.

**lay an egg** |lā an EG| *v* To commit a social error; to make a mistake in public, such as in a performance. ORIGINS: From vaudeville slang.

**lay into** |lā IN tū| *v* To attack physically; to attack verbally.

**lay it on (with a trowel)** |lā it AHN / lā it AHN with u TROU ul| *v* To exaggerate; to concoct an elaborate deception or lie with far more detail than needed; to flatter shamelessly. ORIGINS: Presumably from the trades in which mortar or plaster is applied with a trowel.

**lay it on the line** |LĀ it ahn *thu* LĪN| *v* To speak with complete honesty; to clarify what's at stake.

**lay it on thick** |LĀ it ahn THIK| *v* To exaggerate; to concoct an elaborate deception or lie with far more detail than needed; to flatter shamelessly.

**Lay off!** |LĀ awf| *excl* Stop (whatever you're doing)! ORIGINS: Extended from slang lay off meaning "to take time off from work." USAGE INFO: Often a request for *sb* to stop speaking in a certain way, e.g., nagging, pleading, teasing, etc.

**lay *sb* (out) flat** |lā *sb* FLAT / lā *sb* out FLAT| *v* To knock *sb* down.

**lay them in the aisles** |LĀ *th*um in *th*ē ĪLZ| *v* To make people laugh uncontrollably (in a performance); to achieve a great success. ORIGINS: From show business.

**layabout** |LĀ u BOUT| *n* A person who is lazy or idle; a person who does nothing productive.

**lazy piece of crap/shit** |LĀ zē pēs uv KRAP / LĀ zē pēs uv SHIT| *n* A person judged to be worthless, possibly because s/he doesn't seem to accomplish anything, or just in general. USAGE ALERT: Usually used with intent to denigrate or insult and understood as such.

**lazy-bones** |LĀ zē bōnz| *n* A lazy person. ORIGINS: As in bone-lazy, the term suggests that the person is constitutionally lazy. USAGE INFO: Takes a singular verb.

**lead with one's chin** |LĒD with wunz CHIN| *v* To leave oneself vulnerable; to act without sufficient forethought; to act incautiously. ORIGINS: From the sport of boxing, in which leaving one's chin unprotected is dangerous.

**lean on** |LĒN ahn| *v* To pressure *sb* for a desired outcome; to attempt to influence *sb* through threats.

**Leave off!** |lēv awf| *excl* Stop (whatever you're doing)!

**leave *sb* holding the baby** |LĒV *sb* HŌL ding *th*u BĀ bē| *v* To leave *sb* else to solve or deal with a difficult situation; to shift responsibility and/or blame to *sb* else. USAGE INFO: The person who is the indirect object of the verb is then "left holding the baby."

**leave *sb* in the lurch** |LĒV *sb* in *th*u LURCH| *v* To abandon *sb* in a difficult situation; to desert a person in distress. ORIGINS: From the French **lourche**, a parlor game in which a player often lost with a score of nothing or next to nothing.

**leg it** |LEG it| *v* To run away; to escape on foot. ORIGINS: From slang leg meaning "to run."

**let fly at *sb*** |let FLĪ at *sb*| *v* To attack *sb* physically by throwing something; to attack *sb* verbally. ORIGINS: From loosing an arrow.

**let her rip** |LET hur RIP| *v* To set *st* in motion; to run *st* going at full speed. ORIGINS: Generalized from its use in steamboat races. At one time, it was customary to use the feminine singular pronoun to refer to ships and other vessels. USAGE INFO: Usually said quickly enough that the |h| is lost from the pronunciation.

**let it all hang out** |let it AWL hang out| *v* To act without regard for (social) restraints; to do whatever one wants. ORIGINS: Originally a musical term. USAGE INFO: This expression can be used to refer to being relaxed and at home; to being completely honest; or to defiantly disregarding constraints, whether or not they are legitimate.

**let loose on/at** |let LŪS ahn / let LŪS at| *v* To attack physically; to attack verbally.

**Let me breathe!** |let me BRĒ*TH*| *excl* Go away! Stop hanging over me! USAGE ALERT: Usually used with intent to be rude and understood as such.

**let on** |let AHN| *v* To allow *st* to be known or come to light. USAGE INFO: Most often in the negative, as in "Don't let on!"

**let *sb* have it** |let *sb* HAV it| *v* To administer a beating to *sb*; to scold *sb*; to punish *sb*.

**let *sb* in on** |LET *sb* IN ahn| *v* To share information that was heretofore not shared.

**let *st* ride** |LET *st* RĪD| *v* To hold off from taking expected action, such as punishment; to forgive or excuse *st*.

**level with** |LEV ul with| *v* To tell the truth; to share the full picture after not having done so; to confess.

**liberate** |LIB u rāt| *v* To steal. ORIGINS: Liberation applied to goods has roots in the actions of the WWII liberating forces as well as in anarchist thinking about property.

**-licious** |LISH us| *sfx* A delicious or enticing example of; an exceptional example of. ORIGINS: By extension of SE **delicious**. USAGE INFO: The first meaning occurs in constructions such as **babelicious** and **bootylicious**, relating to sexual attraction; the second, for example, in nonce situations like movie reviews, as in **grumpilicious**, describing a well-acted portrayal of a grumpy character.

**lick** |lik| *n* A small amount. USAGE INFO: Used with *a* as in, "he hasn't got a lick of sense."

**lick** |lik| *v* To defeat in a contest of some kind, either a physical fight or a competition. ORIGINS: From SE **lick** meaning "a blow."

**lick (*sb's*) ass** | LIK as / LIK *sb's* as| *v* To seek favor through flattery; to be a sycophant or toady. ORIGINS: From slang **ass** meaning "the rear end or buttocks." USAGE ALERT: The use of the word **ass**, the graphic image, and the implied insult will make this phrase objectionable in some contexts and to some people.

**lick at** |LIK at| *n* An attempt.

**lickety-split** |LIK i tē SPLIT| *adj* With great speed.

**lift** |lift| *v* To steal. ORIGINS: By extension of SE **lift** meaning "to alter *st's* position by moving it upwards."

**lift doesn't go to the top floor, the** |*thu* LIFT duz 'nt GŌ tū *thu* TAHP FLŌR| *phr* Unintelligent; crazy. ORIGINS: This slang phrase works in two ways. First, it sets up an expectation and then undercuts it: one would naturally expect a lift to go to all floors of a building. Second, it relies on an association between the head, at the top of the body, and the top floor of a building surmounting all the other floors. Thus, the phrase suggests that the person is completely functional, except for his/her brain. USAGE ALERT: Usually used with intent to denigrate or insult and understood as such.

**light a fire under** |lĭt u FĬR un dur| *v* To urge or goad into action. ORIGINS: Based on the idea that a fire burning very close nearby would make even the laziest person anxious to get moving.

**light into** *sb* |LĬT IN tū *sb*| *v* To attack physically; to attack verbally. ORIGINS: From SE **alight** meaning "to descend."

**light out** |LĬT OUT| *v* To set off hastily; to hurry away; to escape.

**lights are on, but nobody's home, the** |*thu* LĬTS ahr AHN but NŌ bahd ēz HŌM| *phr* Unintelligent; crazy. ORIGINS: This slang phrase works in two ways. First, it sets up an expectation and then undercuts it: one would naturally expect a light to signal the presence of a person. Second, it relies on an association between the absence of a person from a physical dwelling, and the failure of a person's intellect or mind, calling to mind an extension of the slang phrase **not all there**. USAGE ALERT: Usually used with intent to denigrate or insult and understood as such.

**lights out** |LĬTS out| *n* The end of something. ORIGINS: Possibly by extension of the saying "lights out" in military quarters, summer camps, dormitories, etc. to designate a prescribed bedtime.

**lightweight** |LĬT wāt| *n* A person without any strengths; a person who does not "pull his/her weight," i.e., do his or her part or make a significant contribution.

**like, be** |lĭk| *v* To say. USAGE INFO: Often used in present in reporting conversation ("So he's like, 'I'm much smarter than you,' and I'm like, 'No way!'")

**like a pig in shit** |lĭk u PIG in SHIT| *adj* Extremely happy. ORIGINS: From slang **shit** meaning "excrement" and the idea that pigs enjoy rolling around in mud or manure. This version of the expression, unlike **happy as a pig in shit**, requires the audience to infer that the pig is happy. USAGE ALERT: The inclusion of the word **shit** in the phrase will render it objectionable in some contexts and to some people.

**like anything** |lĭk EN ē thing| *adv* To the greatest extent possible; with total commitment.

**like crazy/mad** |lĭk KRĀ zē / lĭk MAD| *adv* To the greatest extent possible; with total commitment.

**like hell** |lĭk HEL| *adv* Very much; to a great extent. ORIGINS: Figurative use of SE **hell** meaning "the alternative to heaven; the realm of the devil." USAGE INFO: This can be an intensifier for something negative, as in "it hurts like hell," or it can be ironic and express disagreement as in: "Deal honestly? Like hell he does!" meaning that he doesn't. USAGE ALERT: The inclusion of **hell** in the phrase will render it objectionable in some contexts and to some people.

L

**Like hell (it is)!** |līk HEL / līk HEL it iz| *excl* I don't believe it/you! ORIGINS: Figurative use of SE **hell** meaning "the alternative to heaven; the realm of the devil." USAGE ALERT: The inclusion of the word **hell** in this phrase will render it objectionable in some contexts and to some people.

like **nobody's business** |līk NŌ bu dēz BIZ nis| *adv* Very quickly; very well.

**like the devil** |līk *thu* DEV ul| *adv* Very much; to a great extent (of whatever it is). ORIGINS: Euphemism for **like hell**, SE hell being the place where the devil resides. USAGE INFO: This phrase can modify a verb as **like hell** can, as in "run like the devil," but it does not share the second type of ironic use. USAGE ALERT: The inclusion of the word **devil** in the phrase will render it objectionable in some contexts and to some people.

**lily liver** |LIL ē liv ur| *n* A person who's afraid; a coward. ORIGINS: Extends the observation that a person's skin can turn pale with fear to suggest that all his/her organs do as well by using a lily, traditionally white, to convey the comparison. USAGE ALERT: Usually used with intent to denigrate or insult and understood as such.

**lily-livered** |LIL ē liv urd| *adj* Timid; cowardly. ORIGINS: Extends the observation that a person's skin can turn pale with fear to suggest that all his/her organs do as well by using a lily, traditionally white, to convey the comparison. USAGE INFO: Used by Shakespeare in *The Tragedy of Macbeth*, V, iii, 17 (1603) in Macbeth's abuse of the servant.

**line one's pockets** |līn wunz PAH kits| *v* To accept a bribe or other illicit funds; to make a large profit.

**liquidate** |LIK wi dāt| *v* To kill. ORIGINS: From Russian **likvidirovat**, a euphemism for killing used during Stalin's leadership in the USSR. A famous, popular, and punning use of the word occurs in the movie *The Wizard of Oz* (1939), released during the Stalinist era, in which the Wizard says to Dorothy after the inadvertent death of the Wicked Witch of the West by water, "Ohhh! You liquidated her, eh? Very resourceful."

**live wire** |LĪV WĪR| *n* A lively, energetic person; a vivacious person. ORIGINS: From slang live meaning "alert" and SE **wire**.

**livid** |LIV id| *adj* To be furious; to be filled with rage. ORIGINS: From SE **livid** meaning "ashen," that is white-faced; thus, an interesting contrast to other slang that connects anger with the color red and a red face.

**living daylights out of, the** |*thu* LIV ing DĀ līts out uv| *adv* To a great extent. ORIGINS: From slang **daylights** originally meaning "the eyes" and then "the insides." USAGE INFO: Most often used with verbs denoting fighting (*beat, knock, kick*) and terrifying (*scare*).

**living it up** |LIV ing it up| *adj* Enjoying oneself greatly; having a good time.

**load of shit** |LŌD uv SHIT| *n* Falsehoods; untruths; lies. ORIGINS: From SE **load**, meaning a large amount and slang **shit** meaning "excrement." USAGE ALERT: Because this term includes the word **shit**, it will be considered objectionable in some contexts and by some people.

**loaded** |LŌD ed| *adj* Rich; possessing a lot of money.

**loaded with <noun/pronoun>** |LŌD ed with <noun/pronoun>| *adj* Having a large amount of. USAGE INFO: Takes a plural or uncountable noun (like *money*).

**loads** |LŌDZ| *n* A large amount.

**loaf (around)** |lōf / LŌF u ROUND| *v* To hang around without accomplishing anything; to be idle.

**loafer** |lōf ur| *n* A person who loafs, i.e., one who is idle and accomplishes nothing.

**lob** |lob| *n* A clumsy person who is not bright. ORIGINS: From SE **lob** meaning "an awkward and rustic person."

**loco** |LŌ KŌ| *adj* Crazy. ORIGINS: Borrowed from Spanish **loco** meaning "crazy." USAGE ALERT: Often used with intent to denigrate or insult and understood as such. This way of speaking about *sb's* mental health may be considered insensitive and therefore objectionable in some contexts and by some people.

**L**

**lollygag, lallygag** |LAH lē gag| *v* To waste time; to putter around; to linger or lag behind.

**Long time, no see!** |long tīm nō SĒ| *excl* I haven't seen you for a long time. USAGE INFO: The ellipsis of a standard expression is a hallmark of colloquial language use.

**look alive** |lŏŏk u LĪV| *v* To hurry. USAGE INFO: Often used as an imperative.

**looker** |LŎŎK ur| *n* An extremely attractive person.

**looking up** |LŎŎK ing UP| *adj* Improving; becoming better. USAGE INFO: Often used of finances or prospects.

**loony** |LŪN ē| *adj* Crazy. ORIGINS: Short for SE **lunatic**. USAGE ALERT: Often used with intent to denigrate or insult and understood as such. This way of speaking about *sb's* mental health may be considered insensitive and therefore objectionable in some contexts and by some people.

**loopy** |LŪP ē| *adj* Crazy. USAGE ALERT: Often used with intent to denigrate or insult and understood as such. This way of speaking about *sb's* mental health may be considered insensitive and therefore objectionable in some contexts and by some people.

**loot** |lūt| *n* An unspecified amount of money or property, not necessarily gained by stealing. ORIGINS: From SE **loot** meaning "stolen goods" derived from a Hindi word meaning plunder.

**lose it** |lūz it| *v* To lose control; to become extremely angry.

**lose one's cool** |lūz wunz KŪL| *v* To become angry; to lose control. ORIGINS: From extension of SE **lose** along with the idea of cool being a concrete possession that could be lost.

**lose one's head** |lūz wunz HED| *v* To become angry; to lose control. ORIGINS: From extension of SE **lose** along with the idea of the head being the seat of rationality and balance.

**lose one's head over** *sb* |lūz wunz HED ō vur *sb*| *v* To become enamored of; to become obsessed with.

**lose one's marbles** |lūz wunz MAR bulz| *v* To go mad. ORIGINS: From slang **marbles** meaning "common sense." USAGE ALERT: This way of speaking about *sb's* mental health may be considered insensitive and therefore objectionable in some contexts and by some people.

**lose one's nerve** |lūz wunz NURV| *v* To lose courage or resolve; to become frightened.

**loser** |LŪZ ur| *n* A failure; a person perceived as worthless; a socially inept person.

**losingest** |LŪ zing ist| *adj* Less successful or losing more often than any others of its kind.

**lot, the** |*thu* LAHT| *n* All of whatever it is.

**lots** |LAHTS| *n* A large amount.

**loudmouth** |LOUD mouth| *n* A person who is noisy and tactless; a boaster; an indiscreet person. USAGE ALERT: Usually used with intent to denigrate or insult and understood as such.

**louse** |LOUS| *n* A despicable person; a mean, nasty person. ORIGINS: From SE **louse**, referring to the insect.

**louse up** |LOUS up| *v* To ruin; to make a mess of; to spoil. ORIGINS: From WWI military slang: the trenches were filled with lice (the plural of **louse**), who "loused up" things for the soldiers.

**lousy** |LOU zē| *adj* Awful; contemptible; inferior; worthless. ORIGINS: From SE **louse**, referring to the insect.

**lousy with <noun/pronoun>** |LOU zē with <noun/pronoun>| *adj* Having a great deal of. ORIGINS: From WWI military slang when soldiers in the trenches were lousy with lice. USAGE INFO: Takes a plural or uncountable noun (like *money*).

**lowdown, low-down, the** |*thu* LŌ doun| *n* Inside information.

**lummox** |LUM uks| *n* A large and clumsy or ungainly person; a stupid person. USAGE ALERT: Usually used with intent to denigrate or insult and understood as such.

**lunkhead** |LUNGK hed| *n* A stupid person; an incompetent person. ORIGINS: From SE **lump** and slang suffix **-head**. USAGE ALERT: Usually used with intent to denigrate or insult and understood as such.

**MITIN** More info than I needed.

**MTFBWY** May the Force be with you.

**MUBAR** |MŪ bahr| Messed up beyond all recognition.

**MYOB** Mind your own business.

**mad about** |MAD u bout| *adj* Infatuated with; immoderately fond of. ORIGINS: Takes the SE idea of **mad** and narrows it to a particular area of life. USAGE INFO: Also mad for, used by Shakespeare in *All's Well That Ends Well* (1598?) V, iii, 281.

**madder than a wet hen** |MAD ur *than* u WET HEN| *adj* Very angry. USAGE INFO: There have been a number of comparisons made to emphasize the extent of *sb's* anger. Mad as a hornet is another. Be careful to distinguish between comparisons in this form that refer to anger and those that refer to loss of sanity, such as **mad as a hatter** and **mad as a march hare**—both made popular in Lewis Carroll's (Charles L. Dodgson's) *Alice in Wonderland* (1865).

**madder than hell** |MAD ur *than* HEL| *adj* Enraged; furious. ORIGINS: The fires of hell are being referenced. Figurative use of SE **hell** meaning "the alternative to heaven; the realm of the devil." USAGE INFO: This phrase with the comparative form of mad associates anger with heat and fire, as do so many others. **Mad as hell** uses the positive form of the adjective, and so has a bit less force. USAGE ALERT: The inclusion of the word **hell** in the phrase will render it objectionable in some contexts and to some people.

**maggot** |MA gut| *n* A despicable person. ORIGINS: Builds on the common dislike and disgust surrounding SE **maggots**, fly larvae.

**majorly** |MĀ jur lē| *adv* To a very great degree; extremely. ORIGINS: From playful addition of the standard adverb ending -*ly* to a word that doesn't take that a suffix in Standard English. USAGE INFO: As in "He was majorly ticked off by her lateness."

**make a balls of** |māk u BAWL zuv| *v* To spoil; to ruin; to make a mistake. ORIGINS: From slang **balls** meaning "testicles." USAGE ALERT: The inclusion of the word **balls** in the phrase will render it objectionable in some contexts and to some people.

**make a big deal** |MĀK u big DĒL| *v* To exaggerate the importance of. ORIGINS: Treating *st* as if its priority and stature were those of an important business deal.

**make a big production** |MĀK u big pru DUK shun| *v* To exaggerate the importance of. ORIGINS: Treating *st* as if its importance were that of a major performance, a Broadway show, for example.

**make a (big) stink** |māk u STINGK / māk u BIG STINGK| *v* To complain in a way that attracts a lot of attention. ORIGINS: By figurative extension of SE **stink**.

**make a break for it** |māk u BRĀK fawr it| *v* To try to escape; to attempt to leave (often from prison).

**make a bundle** |māk u BUN dul| *v* To earn a great deal of money. ORIGINS: Slang **bundle** means "a roll of bills."

**make a fast buck** |māk u fast BUK| *v* To enjoy a quick financial success.

**make a federal case** |MĀK u FED ur ul KĀS| *v* To exaggerate the importance of. ORIGINS: Treating *st* as if its importance were that of a legal issue that deserved the attention of the highest (federal) courts.

**make a fool of** *sb* |māk u FŪL uv *sb*| *v* To purposely or accidentally do something that makes someone else look foolish or stupid.

**make a full-court press** |māk u FUL kawrt pres| *v* To make a vigorous response; to go on the offensive. ORIGINS: From basketball jargon, **full-court press** is a style of defense that engages the offense man-to-man from the moment of the inbound pass rather than picking up the defense at half court.

**make a go of it** |māk u GŌ uv it| *v* To succeed in spite of difficulties or poor odds.

**make a killing** |māk u KIL ing| *v* To clear a large profit by taking some kind of gamble; to make a great deal of money very easily. ORIGINS: From slang **killing** meaning "a great success, usually financial."

**make a muck of** |māk u MUK uv| *v* To add confusion or difficulty to a situation; to make a mess of *st*.

**make a patsy of** |māk u PAT sē uv| *v* A gullible person who is easily duped or swindled. ORIGINS: From slang **patsy** meaning "a gullible person; a person easily taken advantage of." There are suggestions that this word comes from Italian **pazzo** meaning "fool" or the Irish nickname for *Patrick*. USAGE ALERT: If the second etymology is true, or if people think that it is, this term may be viewed as a racial slur and therefore objectionable.

**make a pig's ear of** |māk u PIGZ IR uv| *v* To ruin or spoil *st*. ORIGINS: From slang **pig's ear** meaning "a mess."

**make hamburger of** |māk HAM bur gur uv| *v* To beat up; to destroy. ORIGINS: From the comparison of the appearance of the beat up person to chopped meat.

**make hash of** |māk HASH uv| *v* To confuse things; to make a muddle of things. ORIGINS: From SE **hash** meaning "a jumble."

**make it** |MĀK it| *v* To succeed.

**make it big** |māk it BIG| *v* To enjoy a notable success.

**make it hot for** |māk it HAHT fawr| *v* To reprimand; to punish; to make life unpleasant for someone.

**make it snappy** |MĀK it SNAP ē| *v* To be quick; to hurry.

**make mincemeat of** |māk MINS mēt uv| *v* To beat up; to destroy. ORIGINS: From the comparison of the appearance of the beat up person to chopped meat.

**make one sick** |māk wun SIK| *v* To cause disgust.

**make oneself scarce** |māk wun self SKERS| *v* To escape; to leave quickly.

**make out like a bandit** |māk out līk u BAN dit| *v* To make a very large profit. ORIGINS: The analogy to the bandit, who takes money without having to earn it, may suggest that the profit in question comes very easily.

**make sb's blood boil** |māk sb's BLUD boil| *v* To infuriate *sb*; to enrage *sb*. ORIGINS: An example of the association of anger and heat.

**make short work of** |māk SHAWRT wurk uv| *v* To complete quickly through expedience and skill; to consume quickly, often from greed.

**make the grade** |MĀK *thu* GRĀD| *v* To succeed; to qualify or meet the requirements of; to do really well. ORIGINS: From the concept of a system of standards in which one must reach a certain level in order to be judged acceptable.

**make tracks** |māk TRAKS| *v* To depart really quickly; to run away. ORIGINS: The tracks are the footprints left by the runner.

**Man!** |man| *excl* An expression of a variety of emotional states, from enjoyment to disappointment.

**Man (the)** |man / *thu* MAN| *n* The boss or person in charge; somebody important or powerful. ORIGINS: From the time when it was pretty inevitable that the boss was a man.

**man in the front office** |man in *thu* frunt AW fis| *n* The executives in an organization. ORIGINS: From the customary location of the executives (as opposed to production, research and development, etc.). USAGE INFO: Today, this term is often noticeable in sports reports on baseball and football, where most of these employees are, in fact, male.

**man up** |MAN up| *v* To take steps to display the courage that is considered the hallmark of a mature man.

**manage** |MA nij| *v* To achieve (at least) minimum satisfaction.

**mangy** |MĀN jē| *adj* Filthy; rundown; squalid. ORIGINS: From SE **mange** meaning "a severe, chronic skin disease that causes lesions and hair loss."

**mare's nest** |MERZ nest| *n* A serious problem; a very complex situation; a hoax. ORIGINS: Extended from slang **mare's nest** meaning "something imaginary" (i.e., mares don't build nests).

**mark** |mahrk| *n* A person chosen to be the the victim of a swindle; a dupe; someone gullible.

**marshmallow** |MAHRSH mel ō| *n* Someone who is timid; a fearful, ineffectual person. ORIGINS: From the SE **marshmallow**, a soft, white, not very flavorful confection.

**massacre** |MAS u kur| *v* To defeat convincingly; to spoil or ruin; to botch. ORIGINS: From SE **massacre** meaning "to kill."

**mastermind** |MAS tur mīnd| *n* A person of exceptional intelligence, able to successfully plan intricate, impressively difficult, and often illegal tasks or projects.

**mastermind** |MAS tur mīnd| *v* To direct or supervise. ORIGINS: By extension from the noun form **mastermind**.

**maul** |mawl| *v* To defeat resoundingly. ORIGINS: From SE **maul** meaning "to injure by beating." USAGE INFO: Often used in sports headlines with large score differentials.

**maven, mavin** |MĀ vun| *n* An expert; a connoisseur. ORIGINS: From Hebrew through Yiddish **meyvn**, meaning "to understand."

**May the Force be with you!** |mā *thu* FAWRS bē WITH yū| *excl* Go well! Good luck! ORIGINS: A secular equivalent of "God be with you," the phrase that is the source of the word **goodbye**. Spoken by Harrison Ford as Hans Solo's parting words to Luke Skywalker before the attack on the Death Star battle station in *Star Wars Episode IV: A New Hope* (1977). It is number 8 on the American Film Institute's top 100 American cinema quotations.

**mazuma** |mu ZŪ mu| *n* Unspecified amount of money. ORIGINS: From Hebrew through Yiddish **mazume** meaning "cash."

**mean** |mēn| *adj* Outstanding; excellent. ORIGINS: From slang **mean** meaning "in poor quality or condition" but turned around on the "bad is good" model. USAGE INFO: Used to praise skills or talents as in "plays a mean bass."

**meanie** |MĒ nē| *n* A person who is unkind, nasty, or ill-tempered. ORIGINS: A children's rendering of SE **mean**. USAGE INFO: On account of the association with children, **meanie** may be used self-mockingly, ironically, or in an attempt to gain sympathy.

**measly** |MĒZ lē| *adj* Contemptibly small.

**meat and potatoes** |MĒT und pu TĀ tōz| *n* The essence; the fundamentals. ORIGINS: From the conception of these two foods forming the essentials of a good sit-down meal.

**meatball** |MĒT bawl| *n* A stupid or clumsy person. ORIGINS: From SE **meatball**, a ball of ground meat and seasonings, associated with Italian, Swedish, and other cooking styles. USAGE ALERT: This term has been used in racist remarks directed at Italians and African Americans. Often used with intent to denigrate or insult and understood as such.

**meathead** |MĒT hed| *n* A stupid or clumsy person. ORIGINS: From SE **meat** and slang suffix -head, combined to create the idea that the person has something in his/

her head other than brains. USAGE ALERT: Often used with intent to denigrate or insult and understood as such.

**mega** |ME gu| *adj* Very large.

**megabucks** |ME gu buks| *n* A million dollars or a large unspecified amount of money; the name of a number of US state lotteries in which large amounts of money can be won.

**Meh!** |meh| *excl* A sound to express reservations, lack of interest, indifference, feeling poorly, etc. USAGE INFO: Given its meaning, it does not often take an exclamation point.

**mell of a hess** |MEL uv a hes| *n* A major predicament; a very bad situation. ORIGINS: A euphemistic Spoonerism (reversing the initial letters of two major words) of the phrase **hell of a mess**. USAGE ALERT: The underlying reference to **hell** may make this phrase objectionable in some contexts and to some people.

**mellow** |MEL ō| *adj* Relaxed; calm and in a good mood; to feel peaceful and content. ORIGINS: Generalized from slang mellow, which originally meant "drunk" and more recently referred to drugs, including pot (marijuana).

**mellow, be** |MEL ō| *v* To be calm and relaxed (even in the face of difficulties). ORIGINS: Generalized from slang mellow, which originally meant "drunk" and more recently referred to drugs, including pot (marijuana).

**mellow out** |MEL ō out| *v* To relax; to calm down; to become peaceful and content. ORIGINS: Generalized from slang mellow, which originally meant "drunk" and more recently referred to drugs, including pot (marijuana).

**meltdown** |MELT doun| *v* A breakdown: either an emotional breakdown or complete and sudden devastating collapse of some project, plan, enterprise, or situation. ORIGINS: From atomic energy jargon, **meltdown** means "severe overheating of the core of a nuclear reactor, leading to the core melting and radiation escaping."

**meshugaas, mishegaas, mishegoss** |mish u GAWS| *n* Nonsense; idiocy; crazy or senseless actions. ORIGINS: Through Yiddish **meshegas** from Hebrew.

**meshugah, meshugge, meshuga, meshuggah** |mu SHUG u| *adj* Crazy. ORIGINS: From Yiddish **mushuge** meaning "crazy." USAGE ALERT: Often used with intent to denigrate or insult and understood as such. This way of speaking about *sb's* mental health may be considered insensitive and therefore objectionable in some contexts and by some people.

**mess (around) with** *st* |MES with *st* / mes u ROUND with *st*| *v* To use something irresponsibly or without understanding. USAGE INFO: Mess with can also mean "to tease," as in "I'm just messing with you," or "to harass or interfere with," as in "You mess with the bull, you get the horns."

**mess around/about** |mes u ROUND / MES u BOUT| *v* To act without aim or accomplishment; to waste time.

**mess up** |MES UP| *v* To make a mistake, as on a test or in a presentation; to ruin *st*. ORIGINS: From SE mess.

**messed up** |MES Tup| *adj* Damaged or ruined: broken; thrown into disarray; beaten up; intoxicated or high; etc.

**Mickey Mouse** |MI kē mous| *adj* Use of *st* that fails to meet standards by a long shot: unimportant, unchallenging; poorly made or designed; silly or trivial. ORIGINS: From Walt Disney's cartoon character Mickey Mouse (1928–).

**miff** |mif| *v* To anger and offend; to annoy. ORIGINS: Onomatopoeic from a sniff of disgust.

**miffed** |mift| *adj* Annoyed and insulted; in a petulant bad mood. ORIGINS: Onomatopoeic from a sniff of disgust.

**miffy** |MI fē| *adj* Easily offended; supersensitive. ORIGINS: Onomatopoeic from a sniff of disgust.

**mill** |mil| *v* To fight with ones fists. ORIGINS: From the jargon of boxing.

**mind-fucker** |MĪND FUK ur| *n* A serious problem that tests one's mental abilities; a trick meant to deceive, confound, or disturb *sb*. ORIGINS: From slang **fuck** meaning "to engage in sexual intercourse." USAGE ALERT: The inclusion of a form of the word **fuck** in the phrase will render it objectionable in some contexts and to some people.

**mint** |mint| *n* A large amount of money. ORIGINS: Figurative application of SE mint meaning the place where coins are manufactured.

**mish-mash** |MISH mash| *n* A confused or jumbled collection of things. ORIGINS: Related both to Middle English **misse-masche** with a meaning something like "a soft mixture" and to Yiddish **mish-mash** with a meaning related to "to mix."

**miss the boat** |MIS *thu* BŌT| *v* To misunderstand; to miss an opportunity. ORIGINS: From the experience of being too late and arriving at the dock to find that the boat has departed.

**Mister Big** |MIS tur Big| *n* An important man; the head of a criminal organization. ORIGINS: Recently popularized by the character of Mr. Big in the books, television series, and movies, all called *Sex and the City* (1996–2008).

**mix it up** |MIKS it up| *v* To engage in a physical fight or competition; to launch an argument or other verbal attack; to cause trouble. ORIGINS: From slang mix meaning "to fight."

**MOFO** |MŌ fō| *n* Mother fucker; a general term of extreme abuse. ORIGINS: An abbreviation of **mother fucker**. USAGE INFO: **Mother fucker** is considered one of the, if not *the*, worst insults one can make to a man, since it suggests that he has an incestuous (i.e., sexual) relationship with his mother. Capitalization varies. USAGE ALERT: This word carries implications not only about the person referred to, but also about his mother. The inclusion of **MOFO** will make this phrase objectionable in some contexts and to some people. Usually used with intent to denigrate or insult and understood as such.

**Monday morning quarterback** |MUN dā MAWRN ing KAWR tur bak| *n* An amateur who feels confident in criticizing a professional's handling of things with the benefit of hindsight. ORIGINS: From the practice of sports fans who dissect the weekend's competitions after they're over.

**mondo** |MAHN dō| *a/a* Intensifier: great; greatly; extraordinary; extraordinarily. ORIGINS: From the use of the Italian word **mondo** meaning "large" in the title of the movie *Mondo Cane* meaning *A Dog's World* (1961). USAGE INFO: Used as an adjective, as in "a mondo burger," or as an adverb, as in the oft-used phrase "mondo bizarro" (also spelled "mondo bizzaro" by some).

**moneygrubber, money-grubber** |MUN ē grub ur| *n* A person whose sole focus is accumulating wealth.

**monkey around/about** |MUN kē u ROUND / MUN kē u BOUT| *v* To act without aim or accomplishment; to waste time. ORIGINS: From ideas about the behavior of monkeys. USAGE INFO: Unlike some other phrases about wasting time, this one can be playful.

**monkey around with** *st** |MUN kē u ROUND with *st*| *v* To use something irresponsibly or without understanding; to mess around with. ORIGINS: From (incorrect) ideas about the intelligence of SE monkeys.
• monkey with *st* |MUN kē with *st*|

**monster** |MAHN stur| *adj* Very large; enormous.

**monster** |MAHN stur| *sfx* A passionate fan of; a person who is devoted to. ORIGINS: From slang **monster** meaning "an outstanding example of (whatever it is)." Popularized by Cookie Monster, who is both a literal monster as well as the world's most devoted fan of cookies, on the television show, books, and films of *Sesame Street* (1969–).

**mooch** |MŪCH| *v* To obtain or try to obtain by begging. USAGE INFO: Often used of a friend trying to get some trivial item or small amount of money from another friend rather than of situations of deep and serious need and deprivation.

**mook** |mŏŏk| *n* A fool; an insignificant person.

**moola, moolah** |MŪ lah| *n* An unspecified amount of money.

**moon (about)** |mūn / MŪN u BOUT| *v* To wander about aimlessly while lamenting to oneself about love, often unrequited.

**mop the floor with** *sb* |MAHP *thu* FLAWR with *sb*| *v* To thrash; to beat convincingly. ORIGINS: Related to the Royal Navy slang **wipe the deck with** *sb*.

**mother of all** |MU *thur* uv awl| *adj* A situation, problem, delay, etc. that is especially large, difficult, critical, etc. USAGE INFO: *See* DADDY OF ALL and GRANDDADDY.

**motherfucker** |mu *th*ur FUK ur| *n* A person who is completely contemptible or despicable; *st* that is nasty or awful. ORIGINS: The literal meaning is a male who commits incest with his mother. From slang **fuck** meaning "to engage in sexual intercourse." USAGE ALERT: This is considered one of the most offensive words in English. **Motherfucker** carries implications not only about the person referred to, but also about his mother (it is most often used of males, though not exclusively; in any case, it has different overtones when used of a male). Almost always used with intent to denigrate or insult and understood as such.

**motherfucking** |MU *th*ur FUK ing| *a/a* Adjective/adverb that works as a sentence modifier. ORIGINS: The literal meaning is a male who commits incest with his mother. From slang **fuck** meaning "to engage in sexual intercourse." USAGE INFO: Used nominally as an adjective ("Get your motherfucking ass out of my chair!") or as an adverb ("What a motherfucking stupid idea!"). USAGE ALERT: Forms of **motherfucker** are considered among the most offensive words in English.

**motormouth** |MŌ tur mouth| *n* A person who talks continuously. USAGE ALERT: Usually used with intent to denigrate or insult and understood as such.

**mousy** |MOU sē| *adj* Timid and shy; quiet. ORIGINS: From the observed behavior of mice.

**mouth off** |mou*th* AWF| *v* To boast or brag.

**mow down** |MŌ DOUN| *v* To kill a large number (of people), most often using gunfire; to do violence to a number of things that were arrayed more or less in a row. ORIGINS: From SE **mow** meaning "to cut down large swaths of grass, leaving it to fall where it once stood."

**mucho** |MŪ chō| *n* Many. ORIGINS: From Spanish **mucho** meaning "many."

**muck about/around** |MUK u BOUT / MUK u ROUND| *v* To act without aim or accomplishment; to waste time.

**muck (around) with *st*** |MUK with *st* / muk u ROUND with *st*| *v* To use something irresponsibly or without understanding.

**muck *st* up** |muk *st* UP| *v* To spoil *st*; to ruin *st*.

**muck-up** |muk UP| *n* Something spoiled or ruined.

**muck up** |muk UP| *v* To damage or ruin. ORIGINS: Euphemism for **fuck up**.

**muckamuck** |MUK u muk| *n See* HIGH MUCK-A-MUCK.

**muddle through** |MU dul thrū| *v* To achieve something or get through something, despite confusion and/or difficulties.

**muddlehead** |MU dul hed| *n* A stupid or blundering person. ORIGINS: From SE **muddle** meaning "a mess; a confused situation" and slang suffix -head. USAGE ALERT: Often used with intent to denigrate or insult and understood as such.

**muff** |muf| *v* To fail because of memory lapse; to make a blunder; to make a mess.

**mug** |mug| *n* A fool or dupe. ORIGINS: From carnival jargon. USAGE ALERT: Often used with intent to denigrate or insult and understood as such.

**mule** |MYŪL| *nj* A person who is stubborn or unreasonably obstinate.

**Mum's the word!** |MUMZ *thu* WURD| *excl* Be quiet about this! Keep this a secret! ORIGINS: From imitative **mum** representing the kind of soft sound one might make if one was both trying to make a vocal signal and keep one's lips closed.

**mumbo jumbo** |MUM bō JUM bō| *n* Incomprehensible language; language that is meant to confuse or the meaning of which is purposefully left unclear.

**muscle in** |MUS ul IN| *v* To enter by force, often taking *sb* else's place.

**musclehead** |MU sul hed| *n* A well-built but stupid person, usually a man. ORIGINS: From SE **muscle** and slang suffix -head, suggesting that the muscle visible in the physique is also present in the head, replacing the brains. USAGE ALERT: Usually used with intent to denigrate or insult and understood as such.

**muthafucka** |MU *thu* FUK u| *n See* MOTHERFUCKER.

**muttonhead** |MU tun hed| *n* A stupid or foolish person. ORIGINS: From SE **mutton** and slang suffix -head. USAGE ALERT: Usually used with intent to denigrate or insult and understood as such.

**Mwahaha!** |MWAH hah hah| *excl* Evil laugh. USAGE INFO: Many other spellings are used.

**My ass!** |mī AS| *excl* I don't believe it/you! ORIGINS: From slang **ass** meaning "the rear end or buttocks." USAGE ALERT: The inclusion of **ass** will make this expression objectionable in some contexts and to some people.

**My eye!** |mī Ī| *excl* I don't believe it/you!

**My foot!** |mī FOŌT| *excl* I don't believe it/you! ORIGINS: Euphemism for **My ass!**

# N

**NADT** Not a damn thing.

**NBD** No big deal.

**NBIF** No basis in fact.

**NFI** No fucking idea.

**NFW** No fucking way.

**NHOH** Never heard of him/her.

**NIMBY** |NIM bē| Not in my backyard.

**NIMJD** [It's] not in my job description.

**NIMY** Never in [a] million years.

**NMP** Not my problem.

**NP** No problem.

**nabob** |NĀ bahb| *n* A wealthy or prominent person; someone of importance. ORIGINS: From the title of a governor in India during the Mogul Empire.

**nada** |NAH du| *n* Nothing. ORIGINS: Spanish nada meaning "nothing."

**nag** |nag| *n* A person who continually whines, complains, scolds, or criticizes.

**Nah!** |na| *excl* A sound expressing a negative response, but not a very strong one. USAGE INFO: Given its meaning, it does not often take an exclamation point.

**nail**[1] |nāl| *v* To do something perfectly, often something practiced and for which there is a standard, like a dive, a stage performance, a presentation, etc. ORIGINS: From SE **nail** meaning "to drive a nail with a hammer."

**nail**[2] |nāl| *v* To catch in the act. ORIGINS: From SE **nail** meaning "to make secure."

**nail**[3] |nāl| *v* To achieve understanding of. ORIGINS: From SE **nail** meaning "to make secure." USAGE INFO: Often in phrases like "nail the concept."

**nailed down** |NĀLD doun| *adj* Dealt with successfully; completed. ORIGINS: From SE **nail** meaning "to make secure."

**name of the game** |NĀM uv thu GĀM| *n* The essential part or quality.

**narrow shave/squeak** |ner ō SHĀV / ner ō SKWĒK| *n* A very near thing (either positive or negative). USAGE INFO: Always perceived in retrospect.

**Natch!** |nach| *excl* Naturally; of course; certainly. ORIGINS: From shortening of SE **naturally** meaning "of course."

**Neanderthal** |nē AN dur thawl| *n* A crude, stupid person; a boorish dolt. ORIGINS: From SE **Homo sapiens neanderthalensis**, an extinct human species that lived during the late Pleistocene Epoch. Popularized by Geico insurance advertisements (2004-). USAGE ALERT: Usually used with intent to denigrate or insult and understood as such.

**near miss/thing** |NIR MIS / NIR THING| *n* A near miss (whether negative or positive); a brush with disaster. USAGE INFO: Always perceived in retrospect.

**neat** |nēt| *adj* Great; terrific.

**nebbich, nebbish, nebish\*** |NE bish| *n* A person who's not worth noticing; a nobody; a pitifully insignificant person; an ineffectual loser. ORIGINS: From Yiddish **nebech** meaning "poor thing." USAGE ALERT: Usually used with intent to denigrate or insult and understood as such.
• nebbishe |NE bish u|
• nebbisher |NE bish ur|

**needle** |NĒ dul| *v* To provoke; to tease; to goad.

**nerd, nurd** |nurd| *n* An insignificant and boring person; a studious person who lacks social and athletic skills. ORIGINS: Widely believed to have been influenced by, if not derived from, the imaginary creature called Nerd in **If I Ran the Zoo** (1950) by Theodor Geisel (alias Dr. Seuss). USAGE ALERT: Usually used with intent to denigrate or insult and understood as such.

**nettle** |NE tul| *v* To vex; to annoy; to irritate. ORIGINS: From SE **nettle**, a plant with stinging hairs that cause skin irritation, therefore, "to irritate."

**neutralize** |NŪ tru līz| *v* To render harmless, especially by killing. ORIGINS: A euphemism for killing.

**Never in a million years!** |NEV ur in u MIL yun YIRZ| *excl* Emphatically no!

**newbie** |NŪ bē| *n* A newcomer or novice, particularly in military and online venues. ORIGINS: From SE **new**.

**nibble** |NIB ul| *n* A very small amount, used especially of food.

**nice hunk/piece of change** |NĪS HUNGK uv CHĀNJ / NĪS pēs uv CHĀNJ| *n* A large amount of money.

**nick** |nik| *v* To cheat by overcharging; to steal.

**nifty** |NIF tē| *adj* Capable; appealing; great; clever. USAGE INFO: Often used of small gadgets and technology.

**nincompoop** |NIN kum pūp| *n* A silly or foolish person; someone without common sense. USAGE ALERT: Usually used with intent to denigrate or insult and understood as such.

**ninny** |NIN ē| *n* A silly or foolish person; someone without common sense. USAGE ALERT: Usually used with intent to denigrate or insult and understood as such.

**nip** |nip| *v* To move quickly. USAGE INFO: Combined with a number of prepositions to form the phrases: nip along, nip into, nip out, etc.

**nitpicker** |NIT pik ur| *n* A person who focuses on the micro level, complaining about trivial matters.

**nitro** |NĪ trō| *adj* Excellent. ORIGINS: From shortening of chemical name **nitroglycerine** (used in dynamite).

**nitty-gritty** |NIT ē GRIT ē| *n* The most crucial or basic element.

**nitwit** |NIT wit| *n* A silly or stupid person. ORIGINS: Different etymologies are offered, one being SE **nit** meaning "louse" and SE **wit**, "brain," thus, "lousebrain." USAGE ALERT: Usually used with intent to denigrate or insult and understood as such.

**nix** |niks| *n* None. ORIGINS: From German **nichts** meaning "none."

**Nix!** |niks| *excl* No!

**no-account** |NŌ u kount| *adj* Worthless; undependable. ORIGINS: From SE **of no account** perhaps meaning "having no history to support a claim to respect, therefore, not worthy."

**N**

**No big deal.** |NŌ big dēl| *phr* It wasn't a major imposition. ORIGINS: The idea is that the person offering thanks has not incurred a major obligation.

**No biggie.** |nō BIG ē| *phr* It wasn't a major imposition. ORIGINS: Shortened version of No big deal.

**No buts about it!** |nō BUTS u bout it| *excl* Without a doubt. ORIGINS: Variation on the phrase **no ifs, ands, or buts**, which was originally in the form "ifs and ands" and had the same meaning.

**No clue.** |NŌ clū| *excl* I don't know.

**No dice!** |nō DĪS| *excl* No! ORIGINS: Refers to an unlucky toss of the dice.

**No duh!** |nō DU| *excl* No kidding! Scornful agreement with *st* the speaker thinks should go without saying.

**no end** |nō END| *n* A large amount of; lots. Used with *of* to modify a word or phrase as in "gave him no end of encouragement."

**no end** |NŌ end| *adv* To a great degree or extent; endlessly. USAGE INFO: Used before or after the word or phrase it modifies as in "annoyed him no end."

**No fear!** |NŌ FIR| *excl* Agreement with question posed in the negative: "You won't go without me, will you?" "No fear!" (i.e., you should have no fear that I will go without you).

**No fucking idea.** |nō FUK ing ī dē u| *excl* I don't know. ORIGINS: Shortened from phrase **I have no fucking idea.** From slang **fuck** meaning "to engage in sexual intercourse." USAGE ALERT: The inclusion of **fucking** will make this expression objectionable in some contexts and to some people.

**No fucking way!** |nō FUK ing wā| *excl* Emphatically no! ORIGINS: The slang phrase no way with the intensifier **fucking** added. USAGE ALERT: The use of **fucking** in this phrase, even though it is an intensifier, will make it objectionable in some contexts and to some people.

**no go** |NŌ gō| *n* A failed attempt; a prohibition.

**no great shakes** |NŌ grāt shāks| *adj* Inadequate; inconsequential.

**No idea.** |nō ī DĒ u| *excl* I don't know. ORIGINS: Shortened and altered from phrase I have no idea.

**no joke** |nō JŌK| *n* A serious, consequential, or important problem. USAGE INFO: Usually used in ironic understatement (i.e., litotes) of something extremely difficult; horrendously problematic; etc.

**no joy** |nō JOI| *n* No success. ORIGINS: From military aviation jargon, especially in radar location of targets.

**no-lose** |NŌ LŪZ| *adj* Certain to end happily or successfully for all participants.

**no picnic** |nō PIK nik| *n* A difficult, unpleasant problem that will allow neither enjoyment nor relaxation. ORIGINS: From standard conception of an SE **picnic**

as relaxing, enjoyable, etc. USAGE INFO: Usually used in ironic understatement (i.e., litotes) of something extremely difficult; horrendously problematic; etc.

**no problem** |nō PRAHB lum| *n* A problem that is easy to resolve. USAGE INFO: Also used as a twenty-first century substitute for "you're welcome," although some people find this problematic on the grounds that the response suggests that whatever it is was only done because it wasn't a major inconvenience, not out of some true desire to assist, help, support, etc.

**No problem.** |nō PRAHB lum| *phr* It did not cause me any trouble to help you out. ORIGINS: The idea is that the favor did not cause a major interruption in the helpful person's life.

**¡No problemo!** |nō prō BLĀM ō| *phr* No problem! ORIGINS: From Spanish meaning "no problem." USAGE INFO: Self-conscious, humorous use by a person who is not a native speaker of Spanish or of Spanish descent is what makes this slang. USAGE INFO: The initial exclamation mark used in Spanish is often omitted in English.

**No shit!** |nō SHIT| *excl* An interjection indicating surprised acceptance of an unexpected truth. ORIGINS: From slang **shit** meaning "excrement." USAGE ALERT: The inclusion of the word **shit** in the phrase will render it objectionable in some contexts and to some people.

**No siree (bob)!** |NŌ sur ē / NŌ sur e BAHB| *excl* Certainly not! ORIGINS: Extension of the phrase No, sir! The extra syllable on **siree** and the use of **bob** simply add emphasis.

**No skin off my ass/butt!** |nō skin ahf MĪ as / nō skin ahf MĪ BUT| *excl* An interjection signaling complete indifference: No problem! I don't care! It doesn't matter to me! ORIGINS: From slang **ass** meaning "the rear end or buttocks." From slang **butt**, a euphemism for **ass**. USAGE ALERT: The inclusion of the word **ass** or **butt** in the phrase will render it objectionable in some contexts and to some people.

**No skin off my nose!** |nō skin ahf MĪ nōz| *excl* An interjection signaling complete indifference: No problem! I don't care! It doesn't matter to me!

**No soap!** |nō SŌP| *excl* Certainly not! ORIGINS: Related to the phrase It won't wash, which also references cleaning and refers to disapproval.

**no sweat** |NŌ SWET| *n* A problem that is capable of being dealt with without hard work. ORIGINS: The expectation is that there is no need to break a sweat in order to fix <whatever it is>.

**No sweat.** |NŌ SWET| *phr* Don't worry about it. ORIGINS: Shortened and altered form of Don't sweat it.

**no tea party** |nō TĒ pahr tē| *n* A difficult, unpleasant problem that will allow neither enjoyment nor relaxation. ORIGINS: From standard conception of an SE **tea party** as relaxing, enjoyable, cultivated, etc. USAGE INFO: Usually used in ironic understatement (i.e., litotes) of something extremely difficult; horrendously problematic; etc.

N

**No way (José)!** |nō WĀ / nō WĀ hō ZĀ| *excl* An interjection signaling refusal or denial; interjection signaling surprise at hearing something very unexpected. ORIGINS: Shortened and altered from SE phrase **There is no way.**

**No worries.** |nō WUR ēz| *phr* Don't worry about it. ORIGINS: Shortened form of Don't worry about it.

**nod off/out** |nahd AWF / nahd OUT| *v* To fall asleep. ORIGINS: From the way people's heads nod as they fall asleep in an upright position. USAGE INFO: Most often refers to falling asleep unintentionally when in a sitting position and trying to stay awake for some purpose.

**non-starter** |NAHN STAHR tur| *n* An element that proves ineffective. ORIGINS: A person or horse entered in a race, but not participating.

**noodle** |NŪ dul| *n* A fool; someone weak and stupid. USAGE ALERT: Usually used with intent to denigrate or insult and understood as such.

**Nope!** |nōp| *excl* An interjection to signal denial or dismissal.

**nose** *st* **out** |NŌZ *st* out| *v* To discover something by detective work; to uncover something difficult to trace or purposely hidden. ORIGINS: From slang **nose** meaning "detective." USAGE INFO: Different from **nose out** which means "to win or best by a very small margin."

**. . . Not!** |naht| *excl* Rejection of whatever was said previously. USAGE INFO: A proposition is stated and, after a brief pause, the speaker uses this exclamation to reject the proposition, as in "Well *I* really love to watch watch bowling on television! . . . Not!" The pause is an essential part of the delivery.

**not all there**[1] |naht awl THER| *adj* Unintelligent. ORIGINS: The idea is that a portion of the person's brain is missing, resulting in a failure of intelligence. USAGE ALERT: Usually used with intent to denigrate or insult and understood as such.

**not all there**[2] |naht awl THER| *adj* Crazy. ORIGINS: The idea is that the person is lacking all the elements required for sanity. USAGE ALERT: Often used with intent to denigrate or insult and understood as such. This way of speaking about *sb's* mental health may be considered insensitive and therefore objectionable in some contexts and by some people.

**not get to first base** |naht get tū FURST BĀS| *v* To fail to make a promising beginning; to be unsuccessful in gaining initial success. ORIGINS: From baseball jargon in which getting to first base is the first step in scoring a run. USAGE INFO: Distinguish from **not get to first base with** *sb*, meaning "to receive a rebuff before having the opportunity to kiss."

**Not in my backyard!** |naht in MĪ bak yahrd| *excl* Opposition based on proximity, by people who may support a project theoretically, but not in their own neighborhood.

**Not in my job description!** |NAHT in mī JAHB du skrip shun| *excl* According to the terms of my contract, I don't have to do this, and I'm not going to. ORIGINS: An excuse/explanation for refusal.

**Not likely!** |NAHT LĪK lē| *adv* A denial or dismissal.

**not making the grade** |naht MĀK ing *thu* GRĀD| *adj* Failing when measured by a set standard.

**Not much!** |naht MUCH| *excl* Agreement with question posed in the negative: "You don't like television, do you?" "Not much." USAGE INFO: Also used ironically to mean "emphatically yes!" as in "You wouldn't want to go to Tahiti with me, would you?" "Not much!!!"

**Not on your life!** |naht ahn your LĪF| *excl* A strong denial or dismissal. USAGE INFO: The *on* construction makes this an oath form—though usually one swears by, for example, the Bible or one's own life.

**Not on your nelly!** |NAHT ahn yŏŏr NEL ē| *excl* Certainly not! ORIGINS: Shortening of a rhyming slang variant on **Not on your life!** The full phrase is **Not on your Nelly Duff!** which rhymes with **puff** meaning "breath of life." *Nelly* may also be spelled *Nellie*.

**not playing with a full deck** |naht PLĀ ing with u FUL DEK| *adj* Unintelligent; crazy. ORIGINS: One of many synonyms of the term **not all there**, which indulge in wordplay by representing "all there" in a particular way and designating how the person in question fails to meet the criteria. In this case, "all there" is represented by playing cards with a complete set of 52. Anybody who has tried to play a game of cards with less than the required number knows that it doesn't work really well. And herein lies the analogy to the mind or brain of the person who is **not playing with a full deck**. USAGE ALERT: Usually used with intent to denigrate or insult and understood as such.

**not the brightest bulb in the chandelier** |NAHT *thu* brī tist BULB in *thu* SHAN du lir| *adj* Unintelligent. ORIGINS: One of many synonyms of the term **not all there**, which indulge in wordplay by representing "all there" in a particular way and designating how the person in question fails to meet the criteria. In this case, "all there" is represented by being a bright lightbulb installed in a chandelier, and the person in question is "dim" by comparison, linking to slang terms such as **dimwit**. USAGE ALERT: Usually used with intent to denigrate or insult and understood as such.

**not the brightest light in the harbor** |NAHT *thu* brī tist LĪT in *thu* HAHR bur| *adj* Unintelligent. ORIGINS: One of many synonyms of the term **not all there**, which indulge in wordplay by representing "all there" in a particular way and designating how the person in question fails to meet the criteria. In this case, "all there" is represented by being a bright light, like a lighthouse, in a harbor, and the person in question is "dim" by comparison, linking to slang terms such as **dimwit**. USAGE ALERT: Usually used with intent to denigrate or insult and understood as such.

**not the sharpest knife in the drawer** |NAHT *thu* SHAHR pist NĪF in *thu* DRAWR| *adj* Unintelligent. ORIGINS: One of many synonyms of the term **not all there**, which indulge in wordplay by representing "all there" in a particular way and designating how the person in question fails to meet the criteria. In this case, "all there" is represented by being a well-sharpened knife, and the person in question is "dull" by comparison, linking to descriptions of unintelligent people as being **dull**. USAGE ALERT: Usually used with intent to denigrate or insult and understood as such.

**not too shabby** |NAHT tū SHA bē| *adj* Extremely excellent, lovely, delightful, etc. USAGE INFO: An example of litotes, ironic understatement used to indicate excess.

**not up to scratch** |NAHT up tū SKRACH| *adj* Inadequate; failing to meet requirements or standards; of less than required quality. ORIGINS: Figurative use of sports jargon from races in which **scratch** means "the line or marking indicating the starting line." USAGE INFO: *See* UP TO SCRATCH.

**not up to snuff** |NAHT up tū SNUF| *adj* Inadequate; failing to meet requirements or standards; of less than required quality. ORIGINS: Either from the quality requirements for tobacco to be used as snuff or from the stimulating effects of snuff usage. USAGE INFO: Used in constructions like, "He's been practicing, but his performance is not yet up to snuff." *See* UP TO SNUFF.

**Nothing doing!** |NU thing DŪ ing| *excl* A denial or dismissal.

**nudge, noodge, nudzh** |nŏŏj| *n* A person who is a pest; a persistently annoying person; an irritating person; a nag. ORIGINS: From Yiddish **nudyen** meaning "to pester or bore." USAGE ALERT: Usually used with intent to denigrate or insult and understood as such.

**nudge, noodge, nudzh** |nŏŏj| *v* To irritate; to pester; to nag or complain. ORIGINS: From Yiddish **nudyen** meaning "to pester or bore."

**nudnik, noodnik, nudnick** |NŎŎD nik| *n* A pest; a fool; a bore. ORIGINS: From Yiddish, **nudnik** from **nudyen** meaning "to pester or bore." USAGE ALERT: Usually used with intent to denigrate or insult and understood as such.

**Nuff said!** |NUF sed| *excl* Let's close this subject (lest *sb* overhear our discussion). ORIGINS: By shortening of the phrase "Enough said!"

**Nuh-uh! Nu-huh! Nuh-huh!** |NU U| *excl* USAGE INFO: In a family with negative rejoinder Uh-huh! Both **Uh-uh!** and **Nu-uh!** can be used to respond to Uh-huh!

**number one** |num bur WUN| *n* Oneself and one's personal interests; the best thing there is; the main person in one's life. ORIGINS: From Spanish **numero uno** or Italian **numero uno**, meaning "number one." USAGE INFO: Often in the phrase "Look out for number one."

**numero uno** |NŪ mu rō Ū nō| *n* Number one, meaning oneself and one's personal interests; the best thing there is; the boss. ORIGINS: From Spanish **numero uno** or Italian **numero uno**, meaning "number one."

**numskull, numbskull** |NUM skul| *n* A dull or stupid person; a fool. ORIGINS: From SE **numb** and **skull** meaning that the person's brains aren't operating at capacity. USAGE ALERT: Usually used with intent to denigrate or insult and understood as such.

**nut** |nut| *sfx* An enthusiast, often for a pastime or hobby. ORIGINS: Extended from slang **nut** "to be crazy" to "to be crazy about *st*." USAGE INFO: Follows the noun or gerund it modifies to form an open compound, as in "health nut."

**nuts about** |NUTS u bout| *adj* Wildly attracted to; infatuated with.

**nuts and bolts** |NUTS und BŌLTS| *n* The working parts of *st* (as opposed to cosmetic elements); the practical or essential parts of. ORIGINS: From the make-up of many machines, which are held together with nuts and bolts.

**nuts** |nuts| *adj* Crazy; insane. USAGE ALERT: Often used with intent to denigrate or insult and understood as such. This way of speaking about *sb's* mental health may be considered insensitive and therefore objectionable in some contexts and by some people.

**nutso** |NUT sō| *adj* Crazy. ORIGINS: From slang **nuts** and the slang suffix -o used to create adjectives, including some others having to do with mental health, like **batso**, **wacko**, and **sicko**, making them similar to abbreviated **schizo** and **psycho**. USAGE ALERT: Often used with intent to denigrate or insult and understood as such. This way of speaking about *sb's* mental health may be considered insensitive and therefore objectionable in some contexts and by some people.

**nutty** |NUT ē| *adj* Crazy; insane. USAGE ALERT: Often used with intent to denigrate or insult and understood as such. This way of speaking about *sb's* mental health may be considered insensitive and therefore objectionable in some contexts and by some people.

**nutty as a fruitcake** |NUT ē az u FRŪT kāk| *adj* Crazy; insane. USAGE ALERT: Often used with intent to denigrate or insult and understood as such. This way of speaking about *sb's* mental health may be considered insensitive and therefore objectionable in some contexts and by some people.

# O

**OIC** Oh, I see.

**OMDB** Over my dead body.

**OMG** Oh my God!

**ONID** Oh no I didn't!

**ONNA** Oh no: not again!

**-o** |ō| *sfx* Used to create adjectives, including some having to do with mental health, like batso, nutso, sicko, and wacko.

**oaf** |ōf| *n* A person who is large, clumsy, and dull. USAGE ALERT: Usually used with intent to denigrate or insult and understood as such.

**oceans** |ō shunz| *n* A very large amount.

**of sorts** |uv SAWRTS| *adj* Of a very poor sort; a poor example of. USAGE INFO: Used after a noun or noun phrase to undercut it. For example, "Yes, my uncle gave me a computer . . . of sorts" means that the computer was either very old, very inadequate, or was in fact an abacus.

**off** |ahf| *v* To kill; to murder. ORIGINS: Shortened from slang knock off meaning "to kill; to murder."

**off one's bean** |ahf wunz BĒN| *adj* Crazy. ORIGINS: From SE off and slang bean meaning "head." USAGE ALERT: Often used with intent to denigrate or insult and understood as such. This way of speaking about *sb's* mental health may be considered insensitive and therefore objectionable in some contexts and by some people.

**off one's chump** |ahf wunz CHUMP| *adj* Crazy. ORIGINS: From SE off and slang chump meaning "head or face." USAGE ALERT: Often used with intent to denigrate or insult and understood as such. This way of speaking about *sb's* mental health may be considered insensitive and therefore objectionable in some contexts and by some people.

**off one's head** |ahf wunz HED| *adj* Crazy. ORIGINS: From SE off and head. USAGE ALERT: Often used with intent to denigrate or insult and understood as such. This way of speaking about *sb's* mental health may be considered insensitive and therefore objectionable in some contexts and by some people.

**off one's rocker** |ahf wunz RAHK ur| *adj* Crazy. ORIGINS: From SE off and rocker, meaning "rocking chair"; perhaps the regular motion of the chair represents the smooth workings of sanity. USAGE ALERT: Often used with intent to denigrate or insult and understood as such. This way of speaking about *sb's* mental health may be considered insensitive and therefore objectionable in some contexts and by some people.

**off one's trolley** |ahf wunz TRAHL ē| *adj* Crazy. ORIGINS: From SE off and trolley tracks being used as a metaphor for the "grooves" in which sane people function. USAGE ALERT: Often used with intent to denigrate or insult and understood as such. This way of speaking about *sb's* mental health may be considered insensitive and therefore objectionable in some contexts and by some people.

**offload** |AHF lōd| *v* To get rid of; to (unfairly) pass on to *sb* else. ORIGINS: Extension of the concept in shipping or computer science of removing *st* from one locale to another.

**Oh my!** |ō MĪ| *excl* An interjection usually signaling mild to moderate surprise, dismay, delight, etc. ORIGINS: Shortened form of SE O, my God, which originally was a direct address to God at the opening of a prayer; later also an imprecation in which the use of God has no actual connection to the speaker's/writer's beliefs or lack thereof. USAGE INFO: This phrase is now unlikely to raise any objection.

**Oh my God!** |Ō mī GAHD| *excl* An interjection signaling strong surprise, dismay, delight, etc. ORIGINS: Secularized use of SE O, my God, which originally was a direct address to God at the opening of a prayer; also a slang imprecation in which the use of **god** conveys no information whatsoever about the speaker's/writer's beliefs. Derived from SE **god** meaning a being conceived as the divine Lord of the universe. USAGE INFO: For some speakers and writers, this formula is prayer and perfectly acceptable, though when that is the case, it is often followed by other words, as in "Oh, my God, help those poor people!" USAGE ALERT: Used without a religious sense, this phrase will be considered objectionable and blasphemous in some contexts and by some people.

**Oh, what the heck...!** |Ō wut *thu* HEK| *excl* Interjection signaling more or less reluctant acceptance of *st*. ORIGINS: An altered form of and euphemism for **Oh, what the hell...!** USAGE ALERT: The inclusion of a euphemistic reference to **hell** will make this term objectionable in some contexts and to some people.

**Oh, what the hell...!** |Ō wut *thu* HEL| *excl* An interjection signaling more or less reluctant acceptance of *st*. ORIGINS: Figurative use of SE **hell** meaning "the alternative to heaven; the realm of the devil." USAGE ALERT: The inclusion of **hell** will make this expression objectionable in some contexts and to some people.

**-ola** |Ō la| *sfx* Used as an intensifying suffix. USAGE INFO: As in **crapola**.

**old man** |ŌLD man| *n* A person of importance: one's father, boss, commanding officer, etc.

**on a roll, be** |bē ahn u RŌL| *v* To experience a winning streak or a period of repeated successes. ORIGINS: From the action of rolling the dice in gambling.

**on edge** |ahn EJ| *adj* Nervous; worried; agitated. USAGE INFO: The phrase "set one's teeth on edge" can mean both "to make one nervous" or "to be very irritating." In the second sense, it is often used of high pitched screeching noises, like fingernails on a blackboard.

**on the blink** |ahn *thu* BLINGK| *adj* Not functioning properly; out-of-order. ORIGINS: **Blink** is from blinking lights used to signal malfunction.

**on the double** |ahn *thu* DU bul| *adv* Very quickly. ORIGINS: From military jargon **double time** meaning "twice as fast as usual."

**on the fritz** |ahn *thu* FRITS| *adj* Not functioning properly; out-of-order. ORIGINS: The origin of **fritz** is not known.

**on the house** |ahn *thu* HOUS| *adv* Provided by the owner at no charge. ORIGINS: From SE **house** meaning "the establishment" whether a restaurant, bar, tavern, etc.

**on the rag** |ahn *thu* RAG| *adj* Irritable; angry and ready for a fight or an argument. ORIGINS: Probably connected to slang **rag** meaning sanitary napkin used during menstruation. USAGE ALERT: This phrase will be objectionable to people who believe that it suggests that women are unable to control their emotions due to hormonal changes, as well as for its graphic image.

**on the rocks** |ahn *thu* RAHKS| *adj* Likely to fail on account of serious problems; in trouble. ORIGINS: From the experience of a ship running aground and breaking up. USAGE INFO: Also means "on ice," with rocks referring to ice cubes.

**on the ropes** |ahn *thu* RŌPS| *phr* On the verge of being defeated. ORIGINS: From the situation in boxing in which one of the fighters is held against the ropes and pummelled.

**on the take, be** |ahn *thu* TĀK| *v* To accept bribes.

**on the up-and-up, be\*** |ahn *thu* UP und UP| *v* To be honest, legitimate.
• on the up and up, be |ahn *thu* UP und UP|

**on the warpath** |ahn *thu* WAWR path| *adj* Irritable; angry and ready for a fight or an argument. ORIGINS: From Native American **path to war** meaning "the route traveled to engage in battle." USAGE ALERT: Used today with no reference to its history, but will be objectionable to those who feel it is a racial slur, stereotyping Native Americans.

**one brick short of a load** |WUN BRIK shawrt uv u LŌD| *adj* Unintelligent; crazy. ORIGINS: One of many synonyms of the term not all there which indulge in wordplay by representing "all there" in a particular way and designating how the person in question fails to meet the criteria. In this case, "all there" is represented by a **load**, a large group of building materials. By a bit of a stretch, without enough bricks, you do not have a full-fledged load. USAGE ALERT: Usually used with intent to denigrate or insult and understood as such.

**one's ass off** |wunz AS awf| *adv* To the best of one's ability; with an intense effort. ORIGINS: From slang **ass** meaning "the rear end or buttocks." USAGE INFO: Follows a verb, as in "work one's ass off." USAGE ALERT: The inclusion of **ass** will make this phrase objectionable in some contexts and to some people.

**one's brains out** |wunz BRĀNZ out| *adv* To such an extent that one's sanity is affected. USAGE INFO: Used after the verb. Be careful to distinguish this adverbial usage from those in which *brains* is the object of the verb, as in **blow one's brains out** ("to shoot oneself in the head") or **beat one's brains out** ("to work hard at understanding something extremely difficult") or **beat** *sb's* **brains out** ("murder by blunt force trauma to the head").

**one's buns off** |wunz BUNZ awf| *adv* To the best of one's ability; with an intense effort. ORIGINS: Euphemism for **one's ass off**. From slang **buns**, a synonym for slang **ass** meaning "the rear end or buttocks." USAGE INFO: Follows a verb. USAGE ALERT: The inclusion of even the less objectionable **buns** will make this phrase objectionable in some contexts and to some people.

**one's damnedest** |wunz DAM dist| *adv* With one's maximum effort; with one's best effort. ORIGINS: Superlative of **damned**. By extension from SE damn, which literally means "Send (it) to hell." USAGE INFO: Often used in the phrase "do one's damnedest," as when one tries to ensure that *st* reaches completion, comes to pass, etc. USAGE ALERT: The use of a form of **damn** will be objectionable in some contexts and to some people.

**one's darnedest, darndest** |wunz DAHRN dist| *adv* With one's maximum effort; with one's best effort. ORIGINS: Euphemism for **one's damnedest**. USAGE INFO: Often used in the phrase "do one's darnedest," as when one tries to ensure that *st* reaches completion, comes to pass, etc. USAGE ALERT: Euphemisms may still be objectionable in some contexts and to some people.

**one's head off** |wunz HED awf| *adv* To such an extent that one's sanity is affected. USAGE INFO: Used after the verb. Used after the verb. Be careful to distinguish this adverbial usage from those in which *head* is the object of the verb, as in blow one's head off ("to shoot oneself in the head").

**oodles** |Ū dulz| *n* A great many; a large number or amount.

**oojah, oojar** |Ū ju / Ū jahr| *n* Any nameless small object, or small object for which one cannot remember the name; often refers to a gadget. ORIGINS: May derive from people's efforts to recall a forgotten name. USAGE INFO: Exact sound and spelling vary too widely for all variations to be listed.

**ooky** |Ū kē| *adj* Awful: can be applied to a semi-solid (gooey) substance, one's health, or something embarrassing. ORIGINS: From onomatopoeic slang **ook**, a sound signaling disgust.

**Oops!***  |ŪPS| *excl* A sound to signal discovery of a minor mistake (as in proofreading and discovering a typo) or the making of a blunder (such as dropping *st*; tripping; bumping into *sb/st*), sometimes conveying an implicit apology as well.
• Oopsie! |ŪP sē|

**open up** |Ō pun up| *v* To speak openly and fully after being less forthcoming (for any reason).

**open-and-shut case** |Ō pun und SHUT CĀS| *n* An issue with a foregone conclusion; a problem to which the solution is obvious. ORIGINS: The idea is that you do not have to keep the case file open very long, but can shut it virtually as soon as you open it, signaling that a solution or conclusion is at hand.

**operator** |AHP u rā tur| *n* An ambitious person who pursues success single-mindedly; a manipulative and ruthless person; a swindler.

**opt out** |AHPT out| *v* To cancel a previous decision; to indicate unwillingness to participate. ORIGINS: Shortened from SE **option**.

**ornery** |AWR nur ē| *adj* Disagreeble; liable to anger; mean-spirited. ORIGINS: From alteration of SE **ordinary**.

**out of one's gourd** |out uv wunz GAWRD| *adj* Crazy. ORIGINS: From slang **gourd** meaning "head." USAGE ALERT: Often used with intent to denigrate or insult and understood as such. This way of speaking about *sb's* mental health may be considered insensitive and therefore objectionable in some contexts and by some people.

**out of one's head/skull** |out uv wunz HED / out uv wunz SKUL| *adj* Crazy. ORIGINS: From SE **head** or **skull**. USAGE ALERT: Often used with intent to denigrate or insult and understood as such. This way of speaking about *sb's* mental health may be considered insensitive and therefore objectionable in some contexts and by some people.

**out of one's tree** |out uv wunz TRĒ| *adj* Crazy. ORIGINS: The idea is that the person referred to has fallen out of the tree. USAGE ALERT: Often used with intent to denigrate or insult and understood as such. This way of speaking about *sb's* mental health may be considered insensitive and therefore objectionable in some contexts and by some people.

**out of sight, outasight, outasite** |out uv SĪT / out u SĪT| *adj* Excellent; outstanding; exceptional. ORIGINS: From SE meaning "out of visual range," perhaps extended to mean that *st* is "beyond one's everyday, mundane expectations."

**out of this world** |OUT uv *th*is WURLD| *adj* Extraordinary; too good to be true. ORIGINS: From the idea that something is beyond mundane, everyday expectations.

**out of whack** |out uv WAK| *adj* Out of order; unbalanced; not functioning properly. ORIGINS: From SE **whack** meaning condition or state. USAGE INFO: See **IN WHACK**.

**out to lunch** |out tū LUNCH| *adj* Crazy. ORIGINS: If one is literally "out to lunch," one is absent from one's place of business. This is interpreted figuratively to play on the idea of being "not all there." USAGE ALERT: Often used with intent to denigrate or insult and understood as such. This way of speaking about *sb's* mental health may be considered insensitive and therefore objectionable in some contexts and by some people.

**outfox** |out FAHKS| *v* To win a battle of wits. ORIGINS: From the common conception of the fox as a sly, clever creature.

**Over my dead body!** |Ō vur MĪ DED BAHD ē| *excl* Interjection signaling strong refusal or denial. ORIGINS: Suggests that the speaker would die before allowing <whatever it is> to happen.

**overshare** |ō vur SHER| *v* To talk about topics that the speaker's audience finds too intimate or too detailed for their relationship with the speaker and/or the social context.

**Oy!** |oi| *excl* A sound to express sorrow, frustration, weariness, exasperation, dismay, disgust, etc. ORIGINS: Short for Yiddish phrase **oy vey/oy veh**, which expresses the same range of emotions. USAGE INFO: More frequently used in the shorter form by people who aren't Jewish by heritage.

**PDQ** Pretty damn quick.

**PEBCAC** Problem exists between chair and computer.

**PEBCAK** Problem exists between chair and keyboard.

**PITA** Pain in the ass.

**PML** Pissing myself laughing.

**PTB** Powers that be.

**pack it in** |PAK it in| *v* To close down work for the moment or the day; to give up on a project. ORIGINS: From the common need to pack up materials that one has been working with. USAGE INFO: *See* **PACK IT IN!**

**Pack it in!** |PAK it in| *excl* Stop (whatever you're doing)! ORIGINS: From SE **pack** meaning "to put away."

**pain** |PĀN| *n* An annoying person; a difficult, complex, and potentially time-consuming problem or development.

**pain in the ass**\* |PĀN in thē AS| *n* An annoying person; a difficult, complex, and potentially time consuming problem or development. ORIGINS: From slang **ass** meaning "the rear end or buttocks" or slang **butt**, a euphemism for **ass**. USAGE ALERT: A reference to the buttocks or rear end in any form will be objectionable in some contexts and to some people. Usually used with intent to denigrate or insult and understood as such.
• **pain in the butt** |PĀN in thu BUT|

**pain in the neck** |PĀN in thu NEK| *n* An annoying person; a difficult, complex, and potentially time-consuming problem or development. ORIGINS: A euphemism for **pain in the ass** and synonyms relating to the rear end or buttocks. USAGE ALERT: Often used with intent to denigrate or insult and understood as such.

**pain in the rear (end)**\* |PĀN in thu RIR / PĀN in thu RIR END| *n* An annoying person; a difficult, complex, and potentially time-consuming problem or development. ORIGINS: Euphemism for **pain in the ass**. Tush(y/ie) and rear (end) are euphemisms for **ass** meaning "the rear end or buttocks." USAGE ALERT: Tush(y/ie) and rear (end) are less in-your-face, but in some contexts and for some people, a reference to the buttocks or rear end in any form will be objectionable. Usually used with intent to denigrate or insult and understood as such.
• pain in the tush(y/ie) |PĀN in thu TUSH / PĀN in thu TU shē|

**palooka** |pu LŌŌ ku| *n* A large, stupid person; a boxer. ORIGINS: Popularized by the title character of the comic strip *Joe Palooka* (1930–1984), originally by Ham Fisher. USAGE ALERT: Often used with intent to denigrate or insult and understood as such.

**panic** |PA nik| *v* To cause to laugh uproariously.

**panjandrum** |pan JAN drum| *n* An important person; a person with an exaggerated view of his/her own importance. ORIGINS: From the character of the Grand Panjandrum in a nonsensical piece of prose by the dramatist and theatre director Samuel Foote (1754).

**pass in one's chips** |PAS in wunz CHIPS| *v* To die. ORIGINS: From the world of gambling: when one is withdrawing from a game, one exchanges one's chips for cash as one's final act upon leaving.

**paste** |pāst| *v* To hit hard. ORIGINS: Alteration of baste as in lambaste.

**pat oneself on the back** |PAT wun SELF ahn *thu* BAK| *v* To speak in a self-congratulatory way. ORIGINS: This slang phrase figuratively appropriates the gesture of patting on the back, usually used to acknowledge and honor *sb* else's accomplishments.

**patsy** |PAT sē| *n* A gullible person who is easily duped or swindled. ORIGINS: There are suggestions that this word comes from Italian **pazzo** meaning "fool" or the Irish nickname for **Patrick**. USAGE ALERT: If the second etymology is true, or if people think that it is, this term may be viewed as a racial slur and therefore be objectionable.

**payoff** |PĀ ahf| *n* The end result; the outcome of a project or plan.

**peabrain** |PĒ brān| *n* A foolish or stupid person. ORIGINS: Often considered to be related to the size of a pea, i.e., denoting a person with a pea-sized brain. USAGE ALERT: Usually used with intent to denigrate or insult and understood as such.

**peachy(-keen)** |PĒ chē / PĒ chē KĒN| *adj* Wonderful; excellent. ORIGINS: From slang peach meaning "*sb* or *st* especially fine."

**peanuts** |PĒ nuts| *n* A very small amount, especially of money; anything insignificant.

**pee oneself*** |PĒ wun self| *v* To be so terrified that one could (or does) urinate on oneself; to laugh riotously. ORIGINS: Euphemism for **piss oneself**. From slang **pee**, meaning "urine." USAGE ALERT: The inclusion of the word **pee** in this phrase will render it objectionable in some contexts and to some people. The usage of **pee** rather than **piss** in this phrase will soften it somewhat, but it may still be objectionable in some contexts and to some people. The versions with wet will be even less objectionable: *See* WET ONESELF; WET ONE'S PANTS.
  • **pee (in) one's pants** |PEE wunz pants / PEE in wunz pants|

**pee'd off** |PĒD AWF| *adj* Furious; extremely angry. ORIGINS: Euphemism for **pissed (off)**. From slang **pee**, a euphemism for slang **piss** meaning "to urinate." USAGE INFO: Unlike **pissed (off)** the particle off is rarely dropped from this phrase. USAGE ALERT: The inclusion of a word referring to urine in the phrase will render it objectionable in some contexts and to some people.

**peep** *sb/st* |pēp *sb/st*| *v* To have a look at; to check out. USAGE INFO: Notice that unlike SE peep, the preposition at is not used, e.g., "peep this."

**peg out** |PEG OUT| *v* To die.

**penny-pincher** |PEN ē pin chur| *n* A miser; a stingy person. ORIGINS: From the idea that someone has carried frugality to an extreme.

**peppy** |PEP ē| *adj* Energetic; cheerful and enthusiastic. From slang pep meaning "energy."

**perishing** |PER ish ing| *a/a* Extreme; extremely; very. ORIGINS: Euphemism for **damn(ed)**. USAGE INFO: Used as an adjective ("a perishing pity") or an adverb ("perishing cold"). Note that it is never "perishing hot." USAGE ALERT: Euphemisms may still be objectionable in some contexts and to some people.

**peter out** |PĒ tur out| *v* To fall short of expectations; to fail before reaching a successful conclusion; to tire.

**phat** |fat| *adj* Excellent; attractive; admirable. ORIGINS: Altered spelling of slang **fat** meaning "excellent."

**phon(e)y-baloney** |FŌ nē bu LŌ nē| *n* Nonsense; insincere talk; fake presentation or emotions. ORIGINS: From slang **phon(e)y** meaning "fake" and **baloney** meaning "nonsense." USAGE INFO: Other spellings are also used.

**Phooey!** |FŪ ē| *excl* I don't believe it/you!

**pick on** *sb* |PIK ahn *sb*| *v* To choose *sb* as the target for annoyance, irritation, insults, etc.

**pick up on** |pik UP ahn| *v* To catch on to; to come to understand; to grasp.

**pickle** |PIK ul| *n* A predicament; a problematic set of circumstances.

**picnic** |PIK nik| *adj* An easily dealt with issue; a straightforward and simple project. ORIGINS: From standard conception of an SE **picnic** as relaxing, enjoyable, etc. USAGE INFO: Usually used in the negative with ironic understatement (i.e., litotes) of something extremely difficult; horrendously problematic; etc. *See* NO PICNIC.

**piddle about/around** |PID'l u BOUT / PID'l u ROUND| *v* To waste time; to mess around. ORIGINS: From SE **piddle** meaning "to be busy with trifles." USAGE ALERT: Although this expression is unrelated to slang **piddle** meaning "to urinate," people may believe that it is a euphemism for **piss about/around**.

**piddling** |PID ling| *adj* Worthless; insignificant. ORIGINS: From SE **piddle** meaning "to be busy with trifles."

**pie** |pī| *n* An issue that is (apparently problematic but) easily dealt with; *st* that can be easily and efficiently handled. ORIGINS: Has to do with the ease of eating pie, rather than making it. USAGE INFO: Often, but not always, in the phrase "as easy as pie." **Pie in the sky** is something different—an empty promise.

**piece of cake** |PĒS uv CĀK| *n* An issue that is (apparently problematic but) easily dealt with; something that can be easily and efficiently handled. USAGE INFO: Often, but not always, used in "It's a piece of cake."

**piece of crap/shit** |pēs uv KRAP / pēs uv SHIT| *n* A person or thing judged to be of inferior quality or worthless. USAGE ALERT: When used of a person, usually used with intent to denigrate or insult and understood as such.

**piffle** |PIF ul| *n* Nonsense; shallow and insignificant talk.

**Piffle!** |PIF ul| *excl* I don't believe it/you! USAGE INFO: Usually used self-consciously.

**pig** |pig| *n* A person who is piglike: i.e., greedy, fat, dirty, ugly, repulsive. ORIGINS: From the conceived behavior and characteristics of pigs. USAGE ALERT: Usually used with intent to denigrate or insult and understood as such.

**pigeon** |PIJ un| *n* A person who is easy to dupe; a person who is gullible and easily taken advantage of. ORIGINS: Possibly shortening of slang clay pigeon—a device used for target practice by hunters—which has the same meaning.

**pile** |pīl| *n* A large amount of money.

**pile into** |pīl IN tū| *v* To attack physically; to attack verbally.

**pile it on** |PĪL it ahn| *v* To concoct an elaborate deception or lie with far more detail than needed; to flatter shamelessly.

**pile of crap** |PĪL uv KRAP| *n* Falsehoods; untruths; lies. ORIGINS: From SE pile meaning "a large amount" and slang **crap** meaning "excrement." USAGE ALERT: Because this term refers to excrement, it will be considered objectionable in some contexts and by some people. Unlike *crock*, *bucket*, and *load*, which are also combined with **shit** to denote lies, *pile* is more often heard with **crap**.

**pile of shit** |PĪL uv SHIT| *n* Falsehoods; untruths; lies. ORIGINS: From SE pile, meaning "a large amount" and slang **shit** meaning "excrement." USAGE ALERT: Because this term includes the word **shit**, it will be considered objectionable in some contexts and by some people.

**piles** |pīlz| *n* A large amount.

**pill** |pil| *n* An unpleasant person; a bore; a person who or a thing that is distasteful but not avoidable. ORIGINS: By comparison with unpleasantly-flavored medicine tablets.

**pimp (out/up)** |pimp / PIMP OUT / PIMP UP| *v* To improve the appearance and impressiveness of *st*; to improve the quality or functionality of *st* through modification or adding elements, like aftermarket accessories, in the case of a vehicle. ORIGINS: From slang pimp meaning "a procurer of customers for one or more prostitutes." USAGE ALERT: Some people will find the use of pimp in this phrase objectionable, possibly on the grounds that it may seem to be a glorification of pimping.

**pinch** |pinch| *n* A predicament; a problematic situation.

**pinch** |pinch| *v* To take what isn't one's own; to steal. ORIGINS: By extension of SE pinch meaning "to grasp and squeeze between the thumb and finger."

**pinhead** |PIN hed| *n* A foolish or stupid person. ORIGINS: From SE pinhead meaning "the head of a pin," suggesting a person with a very small head. USAGE ALERT: Usually used with intent to denigrate or insult and understood as such.

**pink slip** |PINK slip| *v* To fire or dismiss *sb* from employment. ORIGINS: The slang noun pink slip meaning "a notice of termination" (because that is the color paper they were printed on) has been turned into a verb.

**pipe** |pīp| *v* To notice; to take a look at; to look over.

**Pipe down!** |PĪP DOUN| *excl* Be quieter! USAGE INFO: Unlike most of the phrases in this section, Pipe down! can mean to be softer, rather than altogether silent.

**pipe up** |pīp up| *v* To speak after a long period of silence or when characteristically silent; to interrupt. ORIGINS: By extension of SE pipe.

**pipsqueak** |PIP skwēk| *n* An insignificant person. ORIGINS: From SE pip and squeak, both referring to small, high-pitched noises.

**piss about/around** |PIS u bout / PIS u round| *v* To fool around; to waste time. ORIGINS: From slang **piss** meaning "to urinate." USAGE INFO: Along the lines of **fuck around**, **futz around**, **fart around**. USAGE ALERT: The inclusion of the word **piss** in the phrase will render it objectionable in some contexts and to some people.

**piss and moan** |PIS und MŌN| *v* To complain repeatedly. ORIGINS: By figurative extension of slang **piss** meaning "to urinate" to mean "to complain." USAGE ALERT: The reference to urine in this phrase will make it objectionable in some contexts and to some people.

**Piss off!** |PIS awf| *excl* A contemptuous dismissal. ORIGINS: From slang **piss** meaning "urine." USAGE ALERT: Usually used with intent to be rude and understood as such. In addition, the inclusion of **piss** and the graphic image will make this expression objectionable in some contexts and to some people.

**piss on** *sb/st* |PIS ahn *sb/st*| *v* To denigrate; to treat with contempt. ORIGINS: Figurative interpretation of slang **piss on** meaning "the act of urinating." USAGE ALERT: The inclusion of the word **piss** in the phrase will render it objectionable in some contexts and to some people.

**Piss on you!** |PIS ahn YŪ| *excl* A contemptuous dismissal. ORIGINS: From slang **piss** meaning "urine." USAGE ALERT: Usually used with intent to be rude and understood as such. In addition, the inclusion of **piss** and the graphic image will make this expression objectionable in some contexts and to some people.

**piss one's pants**\* |PIS wunz pants| *v* To be so terrified that one could (or does) urinate on oneself; to laugh riotously. ORIGINS: From slang **piss**, meaning "urine." USAGE ALERT: The inclusion of the word **piss** in this phrase will render it objectionable in some contexts and to some people. *See* bullet under **PEE ONESELF** and the entry **WET ONE'S PANTS** for less offensive alternatives.
• **piss oneself** |PIS wun self|

**piss-** |pis| *pfx* Used as an intensifying prefix. ORIGINS: From slang **piss** meaning "urine." USAGE INFO: *See* **PISSANT**, **PISSHEAD**, **PISS-POOR**. USAGE ALERT: The inclusion of a form of **piss** joined to another word will render it objectionable in some contexts and to some people.

**piss** *sb* **off** |PIS *sb* awf| *v* To annoy or irritate. ORIGINS: From slang **piss** meaning "to urinate." USAGE ALERT: The inclusion of the word **piss** in the phrase will render it objectionable in some contexts and to some people.

**pissant, piss-ant** |PIS ant| *n* An insignificant person. ORIGINS: From slang **piss** meaning "urine." USAGE ALERT: The use of a form of the word **piss** will be objectionable in some contexts and to some people.

**pissed (off)** |pist / PIS tawf| *adj* Furious; extremely angry. ORIGINS: From slang **piss** meaning "to urinate." USAGE INFO: The two forms **pissed** and **pissed off** can be used interchangeably. USAGE ALERT: The inclusion of a form of the word **piss** in the phrase will render it objectionable in some contexts and to some people.

**pissed (off), be** |PIST AHF| *v* To feel extremely annoyed. ORIGINS: From slang **piss** meaning "to urinate." USAGE INFO: "He is pissed" and "He is pissed off" can be used interchangeably. USAGE ALERT: The inclusion of a form of the word **piss** in the phrase will render it objectionable in some contexts and to some people.

**pisser** |PIS ur| *n* A difficult task. ORIGINS: From slang **piss** meaning "to urinate," so *st* that makes one piss or perhaps that makes one pissed. USAGE ALERT: Use of a form of **piss** will be objectionable in some contexts and to some people.

**pisshead** |PIS hed| *n* An unpleasant, obnoxious person; a nasty individual. ORIGINS: From slang **piss** meaning "urine." Essentially the person is being referred to as "urinehead." USAGE ALERT: Use of a term with **piss** will be objectionable in some contexts and to some people. In addition, this word is usually used with intent to denigrate or insult and understood as such.

**pissing** |PIS ing| *a/a* Extreme; extremely; very. ORIGINS: From slang **piss** meaning "to urinate." USAGE INFO: Can be used as an adjective ("such a pissing idiot") or an adverb ("a pissing good joke"). USAGE ALERT: This use of **piss** will be objectionable in some contexts and to some people.

**piss-poor**[1] |PIS pŏŏr| *adj* Having very little money or other property. ORIGINS: From slang **piss** meaning "urine" and slang suffix -head, used here as an intensifier. USAGE ALERT: The inclusion of the word **piss** in the phrase will render it objectionable in some contexts and to some people.

**piss-poor**[2] |PIS pŏŏr| *adj* Of unbelievably poor quality; contemptible. ORIGINS: From slang **piss** meaning "urine," used here as an intensifier. USAGE ALERT: The inclusion of the word **piss** in the phrase will render it objectionable in some contexts and to some people.

**pitch into** |pich IN tū| *v* To attack physically; to attack verbally.

**pixilated** |PIK sul ā tid| *adj* Insane. ORIGINS: From SE **pixie**, *sb* whose mind has been taken over by sprites. USAGE ALERT: Often used with intent to denigrate or insult and understood as such. This way of speaking about *sb's* mental health may be considered insensitive and therefore objectionable in some contexts and by some people.

**plain vanilla** |PLĀN vu NIL lu| *adj* Without adornment or extra trimmings: uninteresting; bland.

**play hardball** |plā HAHRD bawl| *v* To use any means to reach one's end; to seek one's self interest without concern for others. ORIGINS: From sports: refers to the choice to play baseball (with its smaller, harder ball) rather than softball (with a larger, softer ball).

**play it cool** |plā it KŪL| *v* To keep one's temper in check.

**play up to** |plā up tū| *v* To curry favor with; to flatter. ORIGINS: From SE **play** meaning "to act."

**pleb** |pleb| *n* A plebian; a commoner; an inferior. ORIGINS: Short for SE **plebian** meaning "lower class." USAGE INFO: Don't confuse with **plebe**, the name for first-year students at the US Armed Forces Academies. USAGE ALERT: This word is usually used with intent to denigrate or insult and understood as such.

**plow into** |plou IN tū| *v* To attack forcefully, either physically or verbally. ORIGINS: From SE **plow**. USAGE INFO: Distinct from **plow through** meaning "to work diligently to get through a difficult, long, or complicated task."

**plucky** |PLUK ē| *adj* Spirited; courageous. ORIGINS: From slang **pluck** meaning "courage."

**plug** |plug| *v* To punch; to shoot with a gun. ORIGINS: From slang **plug** meaning "a blow."

**plunk down** |PLUNGK DOUN| *v* To pay. ORIGINS: From the sound of the money (presumably including some coins) hitting the table or counter. USAGE INFO: Also means "to wager."

**plush** |plush| *adj* Expensive; luxurious. ORIGINS: From SE **plush**, a soft, luxurious-feeling fabric.

**pocket one's pride** |PAHK it wunz PRĪD| *v* To accept humiliation; to admit being wrong or having made a mistake.

**poed, po'ed, p.o.'d** |PĒ ŌD| *adj* Furious; extremely angry. ORIGINS: Initialized euphemism for **pissed off**. From slang **piss** meaning "to urinate." USAGE ALERT: The reference to a form of the word **piss** in the phrase will render it objectionable in some contexts and to some people.

**point the/one's finger at** |POINT *thu* FIN gur at / POINT wunz FIN gur at| *v* To identify the guilty party; to accuse *sb* of responsibility for <whatever>.

**pointy-head** |POIN tē hed| *n* An intellectual. ORIGINS: From SE **pointy** and slang suffix -head. USAGE ALERT: Usually used with intent to denigrate or insult and understood as such.

**poison** |POI zun| *n* A serious problem; name for *sb/st* that should be avoided.

**poke one's nose into** *st* |PŌK wunz NŌZ in tū *st*| *v* To interfere in; to demonstrate nosy interest in; to snoop; to investigate what is not one's business.

**poke one's oar in** |PŌK wunz AWR in| *v* To join a discussion to which one hasn't been invited. ORIGINS: From the sayings "have an oar in every man's boat" and "put one's oar in every man's boat," the idea being that those with the oars are in charge both of the progress and direction of the vessel.

**polish off** |PAH lish ahf| *v* To defeat in a physical fight or a sports competition.

P

**pony up** |PŌ nē up| *v* To pay a debt that's due. ORIGINS: From slang **pony** meaning "money."

**pooh-bah** |PŪ bah| *n* A pompous official; someone in high office. ORIGINS: From the character of Pooh-bah, Lord High Everything Else in the Gilbert and Sullivan opera *Mikado or The Town of Titipu* (1885). Popularized in the twenty-first century by Nike with their Supa Pooh-Bah mountain bike shoes.

**poop** |pūp| *n* A fool; an annoying person. ORIGINS: Thought to be short for nincompoop. USAGE ALERT: People may connect this word with slang **poop** for excrement, in which case they will both understand it differently and possibly find it objectionable.

**poop out** |PŪP out| *v* To collapse; to stop from exhaustion; to stop functioning. ORIGINS: From slang **poop** meaning "to tire."

**poop, the** |*thu* PŪP| *n* Inside information; news; gossip.

**pooped** |pūpt| *adj* Worn out; exhausted. ORIGINS: From slang **poop** meaning "to tire."

**poopy** |PŪP ē| *adj* Unpleasant; irritating; disagreeable. ORIGINS: Figurative extension of slang **poopy**, a childish word for excrement, which may be onomatopoeic from the sound of defecation or passing wind. USAGE ALERT: The reference to excrement inherent in this word will render it objectionable in some contexts and to some people.

**pop** |pahp| *n* An attempt; a turn. USAGE INFO: Sometimes in a phrase that gives a price per try, as in "Bumper car rides are a dollar a pop."

**pop** |pahp| *v* To hit or punch.

**pop off** |PAHP AWF| *v* To die.

**pop one's cork** |pahp wunz KAWRK| *v* To lose one's temper; to become extremely angry. ORIGINS: From the association of anger with explosions.

**posh** |pahsh| *adj* Fashionable and elegant.

**posh up** |PAHSH up| *v* To make attractive and inviting; to accessorize; to glamorize.

**potchky, potchkie (around) with** *st* |PAHCH kē with *st* / PAHCH kē u ROUND with *st* | *v* To use something irresponsibly or without understanding; to mess around with. ORIGINS: From Yiddish **patsch** meaning "a slap."

**pour it on** |PAWR it ahn| *v* To move at maximum speed; to exert maximum effort.

**pow** |pou| *v* To deliver a solid punch. ORIGINS: Imitative of the sound of a blow.

**powder** |POU dur| *v* To defeat easily or notably. ORIGINS: From SE **powder** meaning "to reduce to powder."

**powerhouse** |POU ur hous| *n* An expert; an influential person.

**powers that be** |POU urz *that* BĒ| *n* The people in control or who have authority. ORIGINS: From the King James Bible version of Romans 13:1 "For there is no power but of God: the powers that be are ordained of God."

**prep** |prep| *v* To supply with all the necessary information. ORIGINS: Shortened form of SE **prepare**.

**press** *sb's* **buttons** |PRES *sb's* BUT'nz| *v* To behave in such a way as to gain the desired reaction; to act in a way that one knows will upset, anger, or frustrate *sb*.

**press-gang** |PRES gang| *v* To force or coerce into service, especially military or naval service.

**pricey, pricy** |PRĪ sē| *adj* Expensive.

**prick** |prik| *n* An extremely unpleasant, nasty person, usually male. ORIGINS: From slang **prick** meaning "penis." USAGE ALERT: Usually used with intent to denigrate or insult and understood as such. In addition, the inherent reference to sexual organs will make it objectionable in some contexts and to some people.

**prickly** |PRIK lē| *adj* Irritable.

**prime** |prīm| *v* To inform *sb* prior to the information being required.

**primo** |PRĒ mō| *adj* The best of its kind; excellent. ORIGINS: From Italian or Spanish **primo** meaning "first."

**pro** |prō| *n* A person who has expertise; a professional. ORIGINS: Shortening of SE **professional**.

**Problem exists between chair and computer.** |PRAHB lum ig ZISTS bu twēn CHER and cum PYŪT ur| *phr* User error. ORIGINS: From the language of technical support people, a humorous description of user error, the point being that the error is in how the user is operating the technology, not a hardware or software error. USAGE ALERT: In the tech support context, usually not said so that the user is aware of it. When said directly to *sb*, often used with intent to denigrate or insult and understood as such.

**Problem exists between chair and keyboard.** |PRAHB lum ig ZISTS bu twēn CHER and KĒ bawrd| *phr* User error. ORIGINS: From the language of technical support people, a humorous description of user error, the point being that the error is in how the user is operating the technology, not a hardware or software error. USAGE ALERT: In the tech support context, usually not said so that the user is aware of it. When said directly to *sb*, often used with intent to denigrate or insult and understood as such.

**psycho** |SĪ kō| *adj* Crazy. ORIGINS: Shortened from SE **psychotic**, rendering it similar to other words having to do with mental health, like **batso**, **nutso**, **schizo**, **sicko**, and **wacko**. USAGE ALERT: Often used with intent to denigrate or insult and understood as such. This way of speaking about *sb's* mental health may be considered insensitive and therefore objectionable in some contexts and by some people.

**pucker-assed** |PUK ur ast| *adj* Cowardly; timid; fearful. ORIGINS: From SE pucker meaning "wrinkled" and the slang suffix **-ass(ed)**. USAGE ALERT: The inclusion of a form of **ass** in this word will render it objectionable in some contexts and to some people.

**puffed up** |PUFT up| *adj* Arrogant; conceited.

**pull a fast one** |pool u FAST wun| *v* To successfully deceive *sb*.

**pull in** |POOL in| *v* To earn. USAGE INFO: Used with a "straight tone" for large sums and sarcastically of small sums.

**pull in one's horns** |PUL in wunz HAWRNS| *v* To retreat from a stance; to give in; to stop arguing and calm down. ORIGINS: From the action of a snail withdrawing into its shell.

**pull off** |PUL ahf| *v* To accomplish (despite the odds being against it); to succeed.

**pull *sb*'s chain** |POOL *sb*'s CHĀN| *v* To purposely annoy or harass *sb*; to act in a way that one knows upsets *sb*.

**pull *sb*'s leg** |POOL *sb*'s LEG| *v* To tease *sb*.

**pull *sb*'s strings** |POOL *sb*'s STRINGZ| *v* To behave in such a way as to gain the desired reaction; to act in a way that one knows will upset, anger, or frustrate *sb*.

**pull the plug on** |POOL *thu* PLUG ahn| *v* To purposely bring about the end of *st*; to stop a project or enterprise prior to completion.

**pull the rug out from under** |POOL *thu* RUG out frum UN dur| *v* To suddenly withdraw support from *sb*.

**pull up one's socks** |POOL up wunz SAHKS| *v* To get ready for serious action.

**Pull your finger out (of your ass/butt)!** |pool yoor FIN gur out / pool yoor FIN gur out uv yoor AS / pool yoor FIN gur out uv yoor BUT| *excl See* PULL YOUR THUMB OUT (OF YOUR ASS/BUTT)!

**Pull your thumb out (of your ass/butt)!** |pool yoor THUM out / pool yoor THUM out uv yoor AS / pool yoor THUM out uv yoor BUT| *excl* Stop sitting around or messing around and get ready for serious action. ORIGINS: From slang **ass** meaning "the rear end or buttocks" or slang **butt**, a euphemism for **ass**. The suggestion is of someone doing something thoroughly worthless. USAGE ALERT: The crudeness of the image plus the reference to the buttocks or rear end will make this expression objectionable in some contexts and to some people.

**pulverize** |PUL vur īz| *v* To demolish or annihilate in a physical fight, verbal battle, or competition.

**pump up** |PUMP up| *v* To exaggerate the qualities of *sb* or *st* for the sake of promotion.

**pumped (up)** |pumpt / PUMPT up| *adj* Excited; enthusiastic; energetic.

**punch sb's lights out** |PUNCH sb's LĪTZ out| *v* To knock *sb* unconscious with one or more punches. ORIGINS: From slang **lights** meaning "eyes."

**punk out** |pungk OUT| *v* To become afraid; to renege on *st* because of fear.

**punt** |punt| *v* To stop doing *st*; to give up on *st*. ORIGINS: From football, in which—on fourth down—a team will often punt the ball to the other team when they feel they are out of options, thus ending their drive for a touchdown or field goal.

**push off** |POŌSH awf| *v* To leave; to depart. ORIGINS: From the action of boaters pushing off from the dock.

**Push off!** |POŌSH awf| *excl* A dismissal. ORIGINS: From the action of boaters pushing off from the dock. USAGE INFO: Not as harsh as its counterpart **Shove off!**

**push one's luck** |POŌSH wunz LUK| *v* To risk previous accomplishments or successes by pursuing a risky path, either through actions or words. USAGE INFO: Sometimes used as an imperative, as in "Don't push your luck" to warn *sb* who is on the edge of making a serious mistake, tactical error, etc.

**push sb's buttons** |POŌSH sb's BUT unz| *v* To behave in such a way as to gain the desired reaction; to act in a way that one knows will upset, anger, or frustrate *sb*.

**push the panic button** |POŌSH thu PAN ik but'n| *v* To make a hasty or overly emotional response to an emergency situation. ORIGINS: From the button provided in case of emergency, in elevators, for example. Staples' recent "Easy Button" commercials play off the concept of a panic button.

**push up daisies** |POŌSH up DĀ zēz| *v* To die. ORIGINS: A reference to flowers growing on a grave.

**pushover** |POŌSH ō vur| *n* A dupe; a gullible person.

**pussy** |POŌS ē| *n* A cowardly weak man; an effeminate man. ORIGINS: From slang **pussy** meaning a woman, extended from meaning "the vagina"; from earlier affectionate name for a cat. USAGE INFO: Often used in taunting, as in "You pussy!" USAGE ALERT: This term may be found objectionable for the sexual reference, for the stereotyping of women, and for the stereotyping of men. Usually used with intent to denigrate or insult and understood as such.

**put a crimp in** |poōt u CRIMP in| *v* To thwart, limit, or interfere with, whether purposely or unintentionally. ORIGINS: From SE **crimp** meaning "to compress." USAGE INFO: Can be used with a personal subject as in, "His attitude put a crimp in my enjoyment of the evening" or an impersonal subject, as in "Well, the weather sure puts a crimp in our plans, doesn't it?"

**Put a sock in it!** |poōt u SAHK in it| *excl* Be quiet! ORIGINS: The suggestion is that one use a sock to stuff up one's mouth so that no sound can come out. USAGE ALERT: Usually used with intent to denigrate or insult and understood as such.

**put down** |POͦOT DOUN| *v* To insult; to denigrate. ORIGINS: From the general conception of down as bad and up as good.

**put in the dog house** |POͦOT in *thu* DAWG hous| *v* To shame; to ostracize. ORIGINS: From the practice of confining a dog to a separate doghouse, away from human company, as a punishment.

**put on the crap/shit list** |poͦot ahn *thu* KRAP list / poͦot ahn *thu* SHIT list| *v* To ostracize; to add to the list of people with whom one is greatly annoyed or displeased; to consider *sb* untrustworthy. ORIGINS: From slang **crap** or **shit** meaning "excrement," with *crap* usually considered less objectionable, and SE list. Possibly influenced by slang hit list, a list of potential targets for swindling or murder. USAGE ALERT: The inclusion of the word **crap** or **shit** in the phrase will render it objectionable in some contexts and to some people.

**put one's ass on the line** |POͦOT wunz AS ahn *thu* LĪN| *v* To take on responsibility; to accept responsibility for *st*; to take a huge risk. ORIGINS: From slang **ass** meaning "one's person," extended from slang **ass**, used to refer to the rear end or buttocks, and slang **on the line** from gambling jargon meaning "at stake." USAGE ALERT: The inclusion of the word **ass** in the phrase will render it objectionable in some contexts and to some people.

**put one's money on** |poͦot wunz MUN ē ahn| *v* To believe in. ORIGINS: From sports and games in which it refers to placing a bet.

**put one's oar in** |POͦOT wunz AWR in| *v* To join a discussion to which one hasn't been invited. ORIGINS: From the saying "have an oar in every man's boat" or "put one's oar in every man's boat," the idea being that those with the oars are in charge both of the progress and direction of the vessel.

**put one's two cents in** |POͦOT wunz TŪ SENS IN| *v* To join a discussion to which one hasn't been invited.

**put paid to** |poͦot PĀD tū| *v* To stop the progress or possibility of *st* immediately and without warning; to terminate; to quell *sb*'s plans. ORIGINS: From SE **pay off** meaning "to take revenge." USAGE INFO: Originally British only, but now showing up in US journalism, for example.

**put *sb* away** |poͦot *sb* u WĀ| *v* To knock out; to defeat in a physical fight.

**put *sb* in stitches** |POͦOT *sb* in STICH iz| *v* To cause riotous laughter.

**put *sb* in the picture** |POͦOT *sb* in *thu* PIK chur| *v* To provide the scope and depth of information that *sb* needs. ORIGINS: The concept is of stepping into a work of art or a photograph and seeing everything firsthand and up close.

**put *sb* on** |poͦot *sb* AHN| *v* To deceive *sb*; to say things that aren't truth; to lie to *sb*; to convince *sb* of *st* untrue as a joke. USAGE INFO: When one puts *sb* on for fun, one reveals the deception afterwards.

**put *sb* through the wringer*** |poͦot *sb* thrū *thu* RING ur| *v* To make things very difficult or unpleasant for *sb*. ORIGINS: Refers to the wringer used to

help squeeze water out of clothes before laundry was mainly done by machine. USAGE INFO: The agent can be personal, as in "Her boss is putting her through the wringer" or impersonal as "This lengthy divorce has really put him through the wringer."
• put *sb* through it |poot *sb* THRŪ it|

**put *sb* wise to** |poot *sb* WĪZ tū| *v* To inform *sb* about aspects or elements of *st* that are either not common knowledge and/or reveal potentially dangerous or sensitive attributes.

**put *sb's* nose out of joint** |poot *sb's* NŌZ out uv joint| *v* To offend and anger *sb*; to upset and annoy *sb*.

**put *st* on hold** |POOT *st* ahn HŌLD| *v* To postpone; to delay. ORIGINS: From the practice of putting one telephone call "on hold" in order to take another.

**put *st* on ice** |POOT *st* ahn ĪS| *v* To set aside a project idea for later use. ORIGINS: From slang on ice meaning "in reserve," possibly from the practice of using trays of ice to hold food for later, while maintaining its quality.

**put *st* on the back burner** |POOT *st* ahn *thu* BAK BURN ur| *v* To temporarily devote less attention to *st*; to deactivate *st* with the plan of starting it up again later; to lessen the priority of *st*.

**put the bite on** |poot *thu* BĪT ahn| *v* To try to get money from *sb*; to beg.

**put the finger on** |poot *thu* FIN gur ahn| *v* To inform on; to identify as the perpetrator; to betray.

**put the heat on** |poot *thu* HĒT ahn| *v* To pressure or threaten. ORIGINS: From slang heat meaning "pressure."

**put the kibosh on** |poot *thu* ku BAHSH ahn| *v* To spoil; to ruin; to prevent.

**put the pedal to the metal** |poot *thu* PET'l tū *thu* MET'l| *v* Move really quickly. ORIGINS: From vehicles in which the accelerator pedal makes the vehicle go at maximum speed when pushed as far down (to the metal of the floor) as possible.

**put the screws on** |poot *thu* SKREWZ ahn| *v* To pressure or threaten. ORIGINS: From SE **thumbscrew**, a torture device.

**put the skids on** |poot *thu* SKIDZ ahn| *v* To bring to an end. ORIGINS: From SE **skid** meaning "to brake a wheel" in order to stop a vehicle.

**put the squeeze on** |poot *thu* SKWĒZ ahn| *v* To attempt to influence through undue pressure.

**put the touch on** |poot *thu* TOUCH ahn| *v* To try to get or borrow money.

**put the wind up** |poot *thu* WIND up| *v* To frighten; to worry.

**putrid** |PŪ trid| *adj* A multi-purpose negative adjective: disgusting; loathsome; awful; repugnant; foul; etc. ORIGINS: From SE **putrid** meaning "the smell of decomposing flesh."

**putz** |putz| *n* A fool; an idiot. ORIGINS: From Yiddish **putz** meaning "penis." USAGE INFO: People may not know its original meaning. USAGE ALERT: The inclusion of a reference to sexual organs in this phrase will not often raise objections because most people don't make the connection.

**putz around** |PUTZ u ROUND| *v* To waste time; to mess around. ORIGINS: From Yiddish **putz** meaning "penis." USAGE INFO: Putz is also used to mean "fool," so people may not know its original meaning. In addition, the similarity of sound, spelling, and meaning to **putter** are likely to create associations with that word. USAGE ALERT: The somewhat distant reference to sexual organs in this phrase will not often raise objections because most people don't make the connection.

**putz (around) with** *st* |PUTZ with *st* / PUTZ u ROUND with *st*| *v* To mess or fool around with *st*; to handle irresponsibly or without understanding. ORIGINS: From Yiddish **putz**, meaning "penis." In addition, the similarity of sound, spelling, and meaning to **putter** are likely to create associations with that word. USAGE INFO: Putz is also used to mean "fool," so people may not know its original meaning. USAGE ALERT: The somewhat distant reference to sexual organs in this phrase will not often raise objections because most people don't make the connection.

**QYB** Quit your bitching!

**quibbler** |KWIB lur| *n* A person who raises petty and trivial arguments. ORIGINS: Repopularized as the name of the tabloid newspaper for which Rita Skeeter writes in the Harry Potter books by J.K. Rowling and the movies based on them.

**RCI** Rectal cranial inversion.

**RFR** Really fucking rich.

**ROFL** Rolling on floor, laughing.

**ROTFL** Rolling on the floor, laughing.

**ROTFLMAO** Rolling on the floor, laughing my ass off.

**ROTFLMFAO** Rolling on the floor, laughing my fucking ass off.

**ROTFLOL** Rolling on the floor, laughing out loud.

**RUFKM** Are you fucking kidding me?

**RUNTS** Are you nuts? USAGE INFO: Note that this is not formed in the usual maner of acronyms or initialisms: **are** and **you** are represented by letters that are homophones; **nuts** is abbreviated by leaving out the *u*. This manner of abbreviation forms the plural of an offensive slang term for a short or small person, **runt**.

**rad** |rad| *adj* Excellent; the best. ORIGINS: From shortening of slang **radical**, a term of approval, often used as an exclamation.

**radical** |RAD i kul| *adj* Excellent or wonderful.

**rafts** |rafts| *n* A vast amount.

**rag** |rag| *v* To annoy or tease repeatedly.

**raggedy-ass(ed)** |RA gi dē as / RA gi dē ast| *adj* Over-used; worn-out; pathetic; worthless. ORIGINS: From SE **ragged** and the slang suffix **-ass(ed)** meaning "a person," extended from slang **ass** meaning "the rear end or buttocks." USAGE INFO: Can be used of both things and people. USAGE ALERT: Usually used with intent to denigrate or insult and understood as such. The inclusion of the word **ass** in the phrase will render it objectionable in some contexts and to some people.

**railroad** |RĀL rōd| *v* To pressure; to threaten; to rush through *st* in the attempt to prevent dissent. ORIGINS: From the idea of going straight to some goal with no side trips.

**raise a stink** |RĀZ u stingk| *v* To complain in a way that attracts a lot of attention. ORIGINS: By figurative extension of SE **stink**.

**raise Cain** |RĀZ KĀN| *v* To create as troublesome a complaint as possible. ORIGINS: Euphemism for **raise Hell**. Cain, mentioned in the book of Genesis of the Old Testament, is the eldest son of Adam and Eve and the slayer of his brother Abel. USAGE ALERT: The appropriation of a Biblical reference in this phrase will make it objectionable in some contexts and to some people.

**raise (merry) hell** |RĀZ HEL / RĀZ mer ē HEL| *v* To object as forcefully and disruptively as possible. USAGE ALERT: The reference to **hell** in this phrase will make it objectionable in some contexts and to some people.

**rake it in** |RĀK it in| *v* To make a very large amount of money. ORIGINS: Presents the idea of having such large piles of money (like leaves) that a rake is the most effective way to move them.

**rake *sb* over the coals** |RĀK *sb* ō vur *thu* KŌLZ| *v* To reprimand angrily. ORIGINS: Related to other phrases that link verbal attacks with heat, such as make it hot for. USAGE INFO: Sometimes seen as **drag over the coals**. *See also* HAUL OVER THE COALS. *Drag* and *haul* just mean "pull," while *rake* means "scrape or scratch" and suggests more malice in the attack.

**rambunctious** |ram BUNGK shus| *adj* Boisterous; exuberantly unruly; noisily disorderly.

**ramshackle** |RAM shak ul| *adj* Shoddy; poorly-made; worn out and falling apart. ORIGINS: A back-formation from the rare SE ransackled meaning "to ransack." USAGE INFO: Usually used of structures, most often buildings, as in "a ramshackle old shack," but also of other structures, as in "a ramshackle plot" or "ramshackle government."

**rap *sb's* knuckles** |RAP *sb's* NU kuls| *v* To scold or reprimand *sb*. ORIGINS: From the traditional use of a ruler slap to the knuckles as a disciplinary tool in classrooms. USAGE INFO: Often used to refer to a minimal punishment (often when the speaker feels that a more substantial punishment is deserved), as in the phrase "let off with a rap on the knuckles."

**rarin' to go** |RER in tū GŌ| *adj* Eager to begin; excited; enthusiastic.

**Rats!** |rats| *excl* An interjection signaling an unpleasant surprise, disillusionment, frustration, etc.

**rattle *sb's* cage** |RAT ul *sb's* KĀJ| *v* To annoy or upset *sb* on purpose.

**rattlebrain\*** |RAT ul brān| *n* A foolish, chattering person; an empty-headed or scatterbrained person. ORIGINS: Either the person's jaw or brains are rattling around, or both. USAGE ALERT: This word is usually used with intent to denigrate or insult and understood as such.
• rattlehead |RAT ul hed|

**ratty** |RAT ē| *adj* Run-down; dilapidated; used; worn. ORIGINS: From negative associations with the behavior of rats.

**raunchy** |RAWN chē| *adj* Extremely dirty and uncared for; obscene.

**raw deal** |RAW DĒL| *n* Unfair or unjust treatment; extremely bad luck. ORIGINS: From slang raw meaning "unfair" and SE deal.

**razz** |raz| *v* To tease or deride. ORIGINS: Alteration and shortening of slang **raspberry**, a derisive spluttering sound made with the tongue and lips.

**Read me?** |RĒD mē| *phr* Have you picked up my transmission? ORIGINS: Shortened form of Do you read me? From the language used in checking on the reception of radio and telephone transmissions, dating from about 1930.

**read *sb/st* (like a book)** |RĒD *sb/st* / RĒD *sb/st* līk u BŎŎK| *v* To grasp *sb's* thoughts or feelings without having to be told; to discern where *sb's* coming from.

**read the riot act to** |rēd *thu* RĪ ut akt tū| *v* To reprimand severely. ORIGINS: From the historical practice of British law enforcement reading the legislation (the Riot Act, 1715) by the authority of which they acted to disorderly crowds before acting on it if the crowd failed to cooperate.

**reams** |rēmz| *n* Vast amounts. ORIGINS: From SE **reams** meaning "500 sheets of paper" applied to other amounts and other items.

**rectal cranial inversion** |REK tul CRĀN ē ul in VER zhun| *adj* Unintelligent. ORIGINS: The inversion suggests that the person's brains are in his/her bottom or rear end, while his/her head is full of excrement. USAGE ALERT: Usually used with intent to denigrate or insult and understood as such.

**retard** |RĒ tahrd| *n* A socially inept person; a stupid person; a person with a disability. ORIGINS: From the formerly acceptable SE **mentally retarded**, the use of which is considerably diminished and is now usually considered objectionable, even when speaking clinically about a disability. USAGE INFO: Often used in phrases like, "What are you: a retard?" USAGE ALERT: Usually used with intent to denigrate or insult and understood as such.

**rhubarb** |RŪ bahrb| *n* A heated debate; a quarrel; an argument with an umpire (in baseball). ORIGINS: From SE **rhubarb**, the plant.

**ride** |rīd| *v* To keep under constant pressure; to keep constant watch and pressure on. ORIGINS: From the rider's control over a horse when riding.

**ridiculous** |ri DIK yū lus| *adj* Outstanding; excellent.

**Right on!** |RĪT ahn| *excl* An interjection expressing strong approval and support.

**righteous** |RĪ chus| *adj* Wonderful; excellent. ORIGINS: Adaptation of SE **righteous** meaning "upright in the sight of God."

**Right-o!** |RĪT ō| *excl* An interjection expressing strong agreement.

**rile (up)** |rīl / RĪL up| *v* To make angry; to move to angry action. ORIGINS: From SE **roil**, meaning "to stir up."

**ringding** |RING ding| *n* A fool. USAGE ALERT: Usually used with intent to denigrate or insult and understood as such.

**riot** |RĪ ut| *n* An unrestrained physical fight.

**rip (into)** |rip / rip IN tū| *v* To verbally attack.

**rip off** |RIP awf| *v* To defraud; to swindle; to cheat; to steal from, often by charging an excessive amount.

**rip *sb* a new asshole/one** |RIP *sb* u NŪ AS hōl / RIP *sb* u NŪ wun| *v* To attack *sb* savagely, physically or verbally. ORIGINS: From slang **asshole** meaning "anus." USAGE ALERT: Because of the reference to the human rear end or buttocks, as well as the graphic depiction of violence (even if **asshole** is replaced with euphemistic **one**), this expression will be found objectionable in some contexts and by some people.

**rip shit** |RIP shit| *adj* Extremely angry. ORIGINS: From SE **rip** and slang **shit** meaning "excrement."

**ripper** |RIP ur| *adj* An excellent one of its type.

**risky business** |RIS kē BIZ nis| *n* A dangerous venture.

R

**roadkill** |RŌD kil| *n* A useless person; a person whose demotion or fall from power is best considered as collateral damage. ORIGINS: From slang **roadkill** for small animals accidentally killed by vehicles on the road (and *st* used for food). USAGE ALERT: Usually used with intent to denigrate or insult and understood as such.

**roar** |rawr| *v* To laugh heartily.

**rocket scientist** |RAHK ut SĪ un tist| *n* An extremely intelligent person. ORIGINS: From admiration given to "real" rocket scientists. USAGE INFO: Also used ironically of *sb* very stupid or of *sb* who always states the obvious; also used for an individual occasion of saying the obvious. USAGE ALERT: The ironic version is usually used with intent to denigrate or insult and understood as such.

**rocking** |RAHK ing| *adj* Outstanding; excellent: exciting.

**rolling in dough/it** |RŌL ing in DŌ / RŌL ing in it| *adj* Extremely wealthy. ORIGINS: The idea is that *sb* has so much money that it would fill a room enough that they could roll around in it.

**rolling in money** |RŌL ing in MUN ē| *adj* Extremely wealthy. ORIGINS: The idea is that *sb* has so much money that it would fill a room enough that s/he could roll around in it. USAGE INFO: **Rolling in money**, in which no word by itself is slang, is therefore less slangy than **rolling in dough**, in which **dough** by itself is slang.

**Rolling on the floor laughing!** |RŌL ing ahn *thu* FLAWR LAF ing| *excl* A hearty, unrestrained laugh.

**romp** |rahmp| *n* An easily accomplished task.

**rookie** |RŌOK ē| *n* A newcomer to a group, team, profession, or project. ORIGINS: Thought to be an alteration of SE **recruit**, which suggests it may come from military or law enforcement. USAGE INFO: Commonly used in sports jargon for athletes just starting their professional careers.

**rooter** |RŪT ur| *n* A supporter. ORIGINS: From fans who root for their team.

**ropy, ropey** |RŌP ē| *adj* Inferior; poor; lousy; second-rate.

**rosy** |RŌ zē| *adj* Promising; indicative of success.

**rotten egg** |RAHT'n eg| *n* A villain; a loser; a person who behaves in a nasty way. USAGE ALERT: Usually used with intent to denigrate or insult and understood as such.

**rough *sb* up** |RUF *sb* up| *v* To beat up; to use physical force to intimidate *sb*.

**roughhouse** |RUF hous| *v* To fight. USAGE INFO: Often used for the boisterous play-fighting of children as well.

**roughneck** |RUF nek| *n* A person with no manners; a person who is crude and violent. USAGE ALERT: Usually used with intent to denigrate or insult and understood as such.

**round the bend** |ROUND *thu* BEND| *adj See* AROUND THE BEND.

**row** |rō| *n* A fight.

**royal** |ROI ul| *adj* Extreme. ORIGINS: From SE **royal** meaning "pertaining to the/a royal family." USAGE INFO: Often in phrases like, "a royal mess" or "a royal pain."

**rub out** |RUB OUT| *v* To kill; murder.

**rub *sb*'s nose in it** |rub *sb*'s NŌZ in it| *v* To repeatedly force *sb* to review his/ her error; to not let a failure or mistake pass out of memory. ORIGINS: From a training technique used for housebreaking puppies.

**rubberneck** |RUB bur nek| *n* A snoop; a person who pries. USAGE ALERT: Usually used with intent to denigrate or insult and understood as such.

**rubberneck** |RUB bur nek| *v* To look or nose around in an obvious and unsubtle way; to snoop; to collect information about.

**ruckus** |RUK us| *n* A disturbance; a fight.

**rule the roost** |RŪL *thu* rūst| *v* To be the leader. ORIGINS: From the role of a rooster controlling which hens roost near him or the role of the cook who "rules the roast," an alternate spelling for some time.

**rumble** |RUM bul| *n* A gang fight; a large-scale brawl.

**rumpus** |RUM pus| *n* A commotion; a riot.

**Run along!** |RUN u lawng| *excl* An interjection of mild dismissal.

**run circles/rings around** |run SUR kulz u round / run RINGZ u round| *v* To surpass in a contest of some kind by a greater display of skill.

**run-in** |RUN in| *n* An argument; a fight, whether physical or verbal.

**run into the ground** |run IN tū *thu* GROUND| *v* To belabor a point.

**run off at the mouth** |run AHF at *thu* MOUTH| *v* To talk excessively; to talk without reference to the occasion or one's audience.

**run on empty** |run ahn EMP tē| *v* To be reaching the end of one's reserves of strength, patience, energy, money, or some other necessary item. ORIGINS: From the full–empty dichotomy presented by a gas gauge in a vehicle.

**run one's mouth** |RUN wunz MOUTH| *v* To talk without restraint; to gossip.

**run out of gas/steam** |run out uv GAS / run out uv STĒM| *v* To become too exhausted to continue *st.* ORIGINS: By analogy to a motorized engine that cannot run without fuel.

**run out on *sb/st*** |run OUT ahn *sb/st*| *v* To renege on a commitment, whether business or personal.

**run *sb* down** |RUN *sb* DOUN| *v* To insult *sb*; to denigrate *sb*.

**run scared** |run SKERD| *v* To flee in a panic; to harbor fears of failure or defeat.

R

**SFTTM** Stop fucking talking to me!

**SICL** Sitting in chair, laughing. ORIGINS: A smart-aleck response to ROTFL or similar.

**SLAP** Sounds like a plan.

**SNAFU** |sna FŪ| *n* An institutional mess; a situation of chaos and confusion. ORIGINS: From the military jargon acronym **Situation Normal All Fucked Up**. Fouled is sometimes substituted for **fucked** to create a euphemism. USAGE ALERT: The fact that the word **fucked** gets concealed within this acronym will soften the phrase somewhat, but it may still be objectionable in some contexts and to some people.

**S.O.B., SOB** |ESS Ō BĒ| *n* Short for son of a bitch; a contemptible, nasty person. USAGE ALERT: **Son of a bitch** and its abbreviations carry implications not only about the person referred to, but also about his (or, more rarely, her) mother. Usually used with intent to denigrate or insult and understood as such.

**SOIAR** Sit on it and rotate.

**SOL** Shit out [of] luck.

**STBY** Sucks to be you.

**STFU** Shut the fuck up!

**SWIM** See what I mean?

**SWIS** See what I'm saying?

**SYS** See you soon.

**SYT** See you tomorrow/tonight.

**sack** |sak| *v* To fire; to terminate from a job. ORIGINS: From slang the sack meaning "loss of employment" so that the ironic phrasing "give the sack" is actually not giving at all, but taking away.

**sack out** |SAK out| *v* To go to bed; to go to sleep. ORIGINS: From slang sack meaning "bed."

**sad-ass** |SAD as| *n* A pathetic person. ORIGINS: From SE sad and slang suffix **-ass**. *See* **-ASS(ED)** for more information about the suffix. USAGE ALERT: The inclusion of a form of **ass** in the phrase will render it objectionable in some contexts and to some people.

**sail into** |sāl IN tū| *v* To attack physically or verbally.

**sandbag** |SAND bag| *v* To hit a strong blow, as if with a sandbag. ORIGINS: From SE sandbag, a bag filled with sand used in fortification or as a weapon.

**sap** |sap| *n* An easily manipulated dupe; a gullible person.

**saphead** |SAP hed| *n* A fool. ORIGINS: From SE **sap** meaning "the liquid in a tree" and the slang suffix **-head**. USAGE ALERT: Usually used with intent to denigrate or insult and understood as such.

**Savvy?** |SAV ē| *phr* Do you understand? ORIGINS: From Spanish **sabe usted** meaning "you know." Popularized as a catchphrase spoken by Johnny Depp in the character of Captain Jack Sparrow in the *Pirates of the Caribbean* films (2003, 2006, 2007).

**Savvy!** |SAV ē| *excl* I understand! ORIGINS: From Spanish **sabe usted** meaning "you know"—an expected response to **Savvy?**

**say uncle** |sā UN kul| *v See* CRY UNCLE.

**Say what?** |sā WUT| *phr* Could you repeat that? ORIGINS: Alteration of the phrase **What did you say?**

**Sayonara!** |sī yu NAH ru| *excl* Casual farewell. ORIGINS: From the casual pronunciation of Japanese **sayonara**, which also has a different formal pronunciation. USAGE INFO: Is likely to be used self-consciously and for humorous effect (because it contrasts with the rest of the English words) by speakers who are not of Japanese descent and do not speak Japanese.

**scab** |scab| *n* A contemptible person. ORIGINS: From SE **scab**.

**scads** |scadz| *n* A large amount.

**scalp** |skalp| *v* To win a competition. ORIGINS: From SE **scalp** meaning "to remove an enemy's scalp as a war trophy." USAGE INFO: Often used in sports journalism when the winning team's name bears reference to Native Americans or American Indians, e.g., baseball: Atlanta Braves and Cleveland Indians; football: Kansas City Chiefs and Washington Redskins.

**scam** |skam| *v* To defraud or swindle.

**scare** *sb* **stiff** |sker *sb* STIF| *v* To frighten *sb* to the point that the person is paralyzed with fear.

**scare the bejesus out of** *sb* |sker *thu* bi JĒ zus out uv *sb*| *v* To terrify *sb*. ORIGINS: From the slang version of the SE exclamation "By Jesus!" From SE **Jesus Christ** whom Christians hold to be the Son of God. USAGE ALERT: The inclusion of the word **Jesus** in the phrase will make it seem blasphemous and objectionable in some contexts and to some people.

**scare the life out of** *sb* |sker *thu* LĪF out uv *sb*| *v* To terrify.

**scare the living daylights out of** *sb* |sker *thu* LIV ing DĀ lītz out uv *sb*| *v* To terrify. ORIGINS: From slang **daylights** originally meaning "the eyes" and then "the insides."

**scare the pants off of** *sb* |sker *thu* PANTS awf uv *sb*| *v* To terrify.

**scare the shit out of** *sb* |sker *thu* SHIT out uv *sb*| *v* To terrify. ORIGINS: From slang **shit** meaning "excrement," and from the fact that extreme fear can make people lose control of their excretory functions. USAGE ALERT: The inclusion of the word **shit** in the phrase will render it objectionable in some contexts and to some people.

**scared shitless, be** |skerd SHIT lis| *v* To be completely terrified. ORIGINS: From slang **shit** meaning "excrement," and from the fact that extreme fear can make people lose control of their excretory functions. USAGE ALERT: The inclusion of the word **shit** in the phrase will render it objectionable in some contexts and to some people.

**scared to death, be** |SKERD tū DETH| *v* To be extremely frightened.

**scaredy cat** |SKER dē cat| *n* A person who frequently exhibits fear. USAGE ALERT: Usually used with intent to denigrate or insult and understood as such.

**schiz(z) out** |skits OUT| *v* To lose control. ORIGINS: By shortening and alteration of SE **schizophrenia**. USAGE ALERT: This way of speaking about *sb's* mental health may be considered insensitive and therefore objectionable in some contexts and by some people.

**schizo** |SKITS ō| *adj* Crazy. ORIGINS: Shortened from SE **schizophrenic**, rendering it similar to other slang having to do with mental health, like **batso**, **nutso**, **psycho**, **sicko**, and **wacko**. USAGE ALERT: Often used with intent to denigrate or insult and understood as such. This way of speaking about *sb's* mental health may be considered insensitive and therefore objectionable in some contexts and by some people.

**schlemiel, shlemiel** |shlu MĒL| *n* A fool; an inept person; a bungler. ORIGINS: From Yiddish **shlemil**. USAGE ALERT: Usually used with intent to denigrate or insult and understood as such.

**schlep, shlep** |shlep| *n* An ordinary worker (as opposed to anyone with privilege or entitlement); a person who drearily drags him- or herself and/or things from place to place.

**schlock** |schlahk| *n* Items of inferior quality; worthless goods. ORIGINS: Possibly from Yiddish **shlak** meaning "evil."

**schlocky** |SHLAHK ē| *adj* Cheap; inferior; in poor taste. ORIGINS: From Yiddish **schlock**.

**schloomp, schlump** |shlump| *n* A stupid person; a slob. ORIGINS: From Yiddish **shlump** meaning "sloppy." USAGE ALERT: Usually used with intent to denigrate or insult and understood as such.

**schlub, shlub** |shlub| *n* A coarse, stupid person; a loser. ORIGINS: From Yiddish **schlub**. USAGE ALERT: Usually used with intent to denigrate or insult and understood as such.

**schmegegge, schmegeggy** |shmu GEG / shmu GEG ē| *n* A contemptible person; an incompetent person. ORIGINS: From a Yiddish word that also means "nonsense." USAGE ALERT: Usually used with intent to denigrate or insult and understood as such.

**schmendrik, shmendrik** |SHMEN drik| *n* A fool; an idiot. ORIGINS: From the name and title character of Abraham Goldfaden's Yiddish operetta *Shmendrik, or the Comical Wedding* (1877). USAGE ALERT: Usually used with intent to denigrate or insult and understood as such.

**schmo, shmo** |shmō| *n* A fool; a loser. ORIGINS: Invented as a euphemism for **schmuck**, from Yiddish **schmok**, meaning "penis." USAGE ALERT: Usually used with intent to denigrate or insult and understood as such.

**schmooze, shmooze** |shmūz| *v* To use flattery and ingratiation as a modus operandi; to become intimate for self-serving ends. ORIGINS: From Yiddish **shmuesn**.

**schmuck, shmuck** |shmuk| *n* A nasty, cruel, petty person. ORIGINS: From Yiddish **shmok** meaning "penis." USAGE ALERT: Usually used with intent to denigrate or insult and understood as such. This term will also be objectionable in some contexts and to some people.

**schnook, shnook** |shnŏŏk| *n* A gullible person; a dupe; an easy mark. ORIGINS: From Yiddish **shnuk** meaning "nose." USAGE ALERT: Usually used with intent to denigrate or insult and understood as such.

**scoop, the** |the SKŪP| *n* The latest information. ORIGINS: From journalism, in which it refers to an exclusive news story published before the information is reported by anyone else.

**scoot** |skūt| *v* To move along at a good pace.

**Scoot!** |skūt| *excl* An interjection signaling gentle dismissal. USAGE INFO: Often used simply as encouragement to get moving, softened by context.

**scope out** |skōp OUT| *v* To examine or investigate: to research. ORIGINS: From Greek **skopos** meaning one's goal or target.

**scorch**[1] |skawrch| *v* To reprimand severely; to criticize harshly.

**scorch**[2] |skawrch| *v* To move at great speed.

**score** |skawr| *v* To succeed.

**score, the** |*thu* SKAWR| *n* The essential element(s); the important part. USAGE INFO: Often used in the phrase "to know the score."

**Scram!** |skram| *excl* A threatening dismissal.

**scrap** |skrap| *n* A fight. ORIGINS: From boxing jargon.

**scrape** |skrāp| *n* An embarrassing situation; trouble.

**scrape along/by** |SKRĀP u lawng / SKRĀP BĪ| *v* To get by; to just manage what is needed.

S

**scrappy** |SKRAP ē| *adj* Quarrelsome; prone to fights. ORIGINS: From slang **scrap** meaning "to fight or box."

**scratch** |skrach| *v* To get rid of; to give up on. ORIGINS: From SE **scratch** meaning "to take a dog or horse out of a race in which it was scheduled to run."

**screw around** |SKREW u round| *v* To waste time; to mess around. ORIGINS: Euphemism for **fuck around**. From slang **screw**, a euphemism for **fuck**. USAGE INFO: Can also refer to sexual activity. USAGE ALERT: The euphemism **screw** in this phrase will soften it somewhat, but it may still be objectionable in some contexts and to some people.

**screw (around) with** *st* |SKREW with *st* / SKREW u round with *st* | *v* To use something irresponsibly or without understanding; to mess around with. ORIGINS: Euphemism for **fuck (around) with** *st*. From slang **screw**, a euphemism for **fuck**. USAGE INFO: Distinct from **screw around with** *sb*, which can either mean "to goof around together," or refer to sexual activity. USAGE ALERT: The euphemism **screw** in this phrase will soften it somewhat, but it may still be objectionable in some contexts and to some people.

**screw (over)** |skrū / skrū Ō vur| *v* To mistreat; to cheat. ORIGINS: Euphemism for **fuck (over)**. From slang **screw**, a euphemism for **fuck**. USAGE ALERT: The euphemism **screw** in this phrase will soften it somewhat, but it may still be objectionable in some contexts and to some people.

**screw (*sb/st*) up** |SKRŪ UP / SKRŪ *sb/st* UP | *v* To spoil; to ruin; to cause another person severe psychological distress. ORIGINS: Euphemism for **fuck (*sb/st*) up**. From slang **screw**, a euphemism for **fuck**. USAGE INFO: Can be used with or without an object. USAGE ALERT: The euphemism **screw** in this phrase will soften it somewhat, but it may still be objectionable in some contexts and to some people.

**Screw you!** |SKRŪ yū| *excl* A contemptuous dismissal. ORIGINS: A euphemism for **Fuck you!** From slang **screw**, a euphemism for **fuck**. USAGE ALERT: Usually used with intent to be rude and understood as such. Although the euphemistic alteration of this phrase will soften it somewhat, it may still be objectionable in some contexts and to some people.

**screwed up** |SKRŪ dup| *phr* In serious trouble of one sort or another. ORIGINS: Euphemism for **fucked-up**. From slang **screw**, a euphemism for **fuck**. USAGE ALERT: The euphemism **screw** in this phrase will soften it somewhat, but it may still be objectionable in some contexts and to some people.

**screwup, screw-up**[1] |SKRŪ up| *n* A person who characteristically ruins things, either for him- or herself or for others as well; an inept person. ORIGINS: Euphemism for **fuckup, fuck-up**. From slang **screw**, a euphemism for **fuck**. USAGE ALERT: Usually used with intent to denigrate or insult and understood as such. The euphemism **screw** in this phrase will soften it somewhat, but it may still be objectionable in some contexts and to some people.

**screwup, screw-up**[2] |SKRŪ up| *n* An error. ORIGINS: Euphemism for **fuckup, fuck-up**. From slang **screw**, a euphemism for **fuck**. USAGE ALERT: The euphemism screw in this phrase will soften it somewhat, but it may still be objectionable in some contexts and to some people.

**screwy** |SKRŪ ē| *adj* Crazy. ORIGINS: Shortened form of have a screw loose. USAGE ALERT: Often used with intent to denigrate or insult and understood as such. This way of speaking about *sb's* mental health may be considered insensitive and therefore objectionable in some contexts and by some people.

**scrounge** |skrounj| *v* To obtain by begging or borrowing, usually from friends and with no serious intent to repay.

**scrub** |skrub| *v* To cancel.

**scruffy** |SCRUF ē| *adj* Uncared for; untidy.

**scrumptious** |SKRUMP shus| *adj* Delicious; desirable.

**scum (of the earth)** |skum / SKUM uv thu IRTH| *n* A person or group regarded as worthless. ORIGINS: From SE scum, which refers to, for example, the filmy layer that forms in a bathtub and means "refuse." USAGE ALERT: Usually used with intent to denigrate or insult and understood as such.

**scumbag** |SKUM bag| *n* A despicable, contemptible person. ORIGINS: By extension of slang **scumbag** (from slang **scum** meaning "semen" and SE **bag**), meaning "used condom." USAGE ALERT: Many people use this word without knowing its origins, associating it with SE **scum**, which refers to the filmy layer that forms in a bathtub. This can lead to very different interpretations of proper use, especially when children are using the word or are within earshot. Usually used with intent to denigrate or insult and understood as such.

**scummy** |SKUM ē| *adj* Utterly contemptible or disgusting.

**scupper** |SKUP ur| *v* To put an end to; to call off. ORIGINS: From SE **scupper** meaning "to pour down the drain (of a boat)."

**scuzz, scuz** |SKUZ| *n* A repulsive person. USAGE ALERT: Usually used with intent to denigrate or insult and understood as such.

**scuzzbag*** |SKUZ bag| *n* A repulsive or contemptible person. ORIGINS: From slang scuzz and slang suffix -bag, -ball, or -bucket meaning "a person." USAGE ALERT: Usually used with intent to denigrate or insult and understood as such.
• scuzzball |SKUZ bawl|
• scuzz bucket |SKUZ buk it|

**scuzzy** |SKUZ ē | *n* Dirty; disreputable.

**Search me!** |surch MĒ| *excl* I have no idea. I don't know the answer to your question.

**see red** |SĒ RED| *v* To become extremely angry.

**see where *sb's* coming from** |SĒ wer *sb's* KUM ing frum| *v* To understand another's viewpoint.

S

**See you later, alligator!** |sē yu LĀ dur al i GĀ dur| *excl* A casual farewell, often responded to with the rejoinder, **After while, crocodile!** ORIGINS: From a catch phrase that was popularized by Bill Haley and His Comets' 1955 rock-and-roll rendition of the song "See You Later, Alligator," originally by Robert Charles Guidry. USAGE INFO: Though **See you later, alligator!** may be used without the response, the response is never used without **See you later, alligator!** being spoken.

**sell down the river** |SEL doun *thu* RIV ur| *v* To betray. ORIGINS: From the historical practice of selling recalcitrant slaves to a harsher master whose plantation happened to be down river.

**sell out** |sel OUT| *v* To betray one's principles, beliefs, or commitments.

**sell *sb* a bill of goods** |SEL *sb* u BIL uv GOOODZ| *v* To deceive *sb*; to cheat *sb*; to lie to *sb*. ORIGINS: From slang **bill of goods** meaning "false promises" from SE **bill of goods** meaning "a consignment of items being sold."

**sell *sb* a lemon** |SEL *sb* u LEM un| *v* To sell defective or damaged goods. ORIGINS: From slang **lemon** meaning "anything disappointing."

**send** |send| *v* To cause delight.

**send *sb* packing** |SEND *sb* PAK ing| *v* To dismiss *sb* either in a business or personal setting.

**send *sb* to the cleaners** |SEND *sb* tū *thu* KLĒN urz| *v* To trick *sb* out of all his/her money.

**send *sb* to the showers** |SEND *sb* tū *thu* SHOU urz| *v* To dismiss; to remove from the action. ORIGINS: From sports jargon.

**serious** |SIR ē us| *adj* Intensifier. USAGE INFO: Used in phrases such as "he was doing some serious drinking" or "that's some serious money."

**set about** |set u BOUT| *v* To attack. USAGE INFO: The weapon used is often named in a following prepositional phrase beginning with *with*, as in "set about him with a/ an axe, rolling pin, hammer, stick, baton, etc."

**set the world on fire** |set *thu* WURLD ahn FĪR| *v* To accomplish *st* of note.

**settle a/the score** |SET'I u SKAWR / SET'I *thu* SKAWR| *v* To get even with; to seek revenge. ORIGINS: From SE **score** meaning "grievance," a figurative meaning derived from the earlier use of **score** to refer to an accounting kept by tallying score marks on wooden rods.

**settle accounts** |SET'I u KOUNTZ| *v* To get even with; to seek revenge. ORIGINS: From the practices of accounting.

**settle *sb*'s hash** |SET'I *sb*'s HASH| *v* To silence *sb*; to best *sb* in a fight.

**set-to** |SET tū| *n* A physical fight; a riot.

**sewed/sewn up** |SŌD up / SŌN up| *adj* Brought to a satisfactory conclusion; finished; accomplished.

**sex up** |SEK sup| *v* To make more attractive and appealing. ORIGINS: Figurative use of slang sex up meaning "make more sexy." USAGE ALERT: Some people may find the application of the word sex to all manner of things outside the usual realm of the word objectionable, based, for example, on the word being more common in conversations, advertising, etc. that children hear.

**sexy** |SEK sē| *adj* Appealing to consumers, viewers, and other audience members; particularly clever. ORIGINS: Figurative use of SE **sexy** meaning "seductive." USAGE ALERT: Some people may find the application of the word sex to all manner of things outside the usual realm of the word objectionable, based, for example, on the word being more common in conversations, advertising, etc. that children hear.

**Sez you!** |sez YŪ| *excl* I don't believe it/you! ORIGINS: Altered form of "That's what *you* say!"—the implication being that others disagree.

**shabby** |SHA bē| *adj* Worn; badly cared for; dilapidated. USAGE INFO: Used in the negative and with litotes (i.e., ironic understatement) of something outstanding or fabulous, as in, "that party wasn't too shabby."

**shaft** |shaft| *v* To treat unfairly; to be harsh.

**shake a leg** |SHĀK u leg| *v* To hurry. USAGE INFO: Often used as an imperative.

**shake down** |SHĀK doun| *v* To extort money.

**shake in one's shoes** |SHĀK in wunz SHŪZ| *v* To feel extremely frightened or anxious.

**shake the money tree** |SHĀK *thu* MUN ē trē| *v* To earn or come into a great deal of money. ORIGINS: From the fantasy that money could "grow on trees."

**shakes** |shāks| *n* A fit of terror or nervousness. ORIGINS: From slang shakes, first used for delirium tremens. USAGE INFO: Usually used with the.

**shanghai** |SHANG hī| *v* To compel *sb*'s actions through force or fraud. ORIGINS: From the onetime practice of kidnapping sailors in order to make a full crew on ships sailing to China.

**shape up** |SHĀP up| *v* To address one's shortcomings; to improve one's behavior, productivity, or attitude. ORIGINS: Generalized and shortened from shape up or ship out, military slang in WWII, conveying a threat that lack of improvement would result in being sent to a combat zone.

**sharp** |shahrp| *adj* Fashionably attractive; admirable.

**sharpie** |SHAHR pē| *n* A person who is intelligent and perceptive.

**shedload** |SHED lōd| *n* A very large amount. ORIGINS: Extended from slang loads meaning "lots" with SE shed meaning "a small storage building." Originally British; use now spreading. USAGE INFO: Now used as a euphemism for slang **shitload** meaning "a very large amount." USAGE ALERT: Because of the phonetic similarity to **shitload** and the fact that it is used by some people as a euphemism, people may assume that it is in all cases.

**sheesh** |shēsh| *adv* Sentence modifier to convey surprise, relief, annoyance, etc. ORIGINS: Euphemism, oddly, for both **shit** and **Jesus**—a figurative use of SE Jesus whom Christians hold to be the Son of God, but it is milder. USAGE INFO: Used at the beginning of a sentence to modify the sentence as in, "Sheesh, that was a close one!" Many people have no idea of the origins of this phrase and will use it without reference to either of the words it may stand in for. USAGE ALERT: Some people may find this word blasphemous or otherwise objectionable because of its origins.

**Sheesh!** |shēsh| *excl* An interjection used to express surprise, relief, annoyance, etc. ORIGINS: Euphemism, oddly, for both **Shit!** and **Jesus!**—a figurative use of SE Jesus whom Christians hold to be the Son of God, but it is milder. USAGE INFO: Many people have no idea of the origins of this phrase and will use it without reference to either of the words it may stand in for. USAGE ALERT: Some people may find this word blasphemous or otherwise objectionable because of its origins.

**shekels** |SHEK ulz| *n* An unspecified amount of money. ORIGINS: From Hebrew **shekel**, a coin.

**shell out** |SHEL OUT| *v* To hand over money.

**shellac** |shu LAK| *v* To thrash; to defeat.

**shit**[1] |shit| *n* Unspecified "stuff," often, one's possessions. ORIGINS: From slang **shit** meaning "excrement." USAGE INFO: In this particular case, the use of **shit** does not speak to the quality of the items being referred to and is not necessarily drawing a parallel between them and excrement. "I'll get my shit out of the living room in the morning" could refer to "my laptop and DVDs, which I actually treasure." USAGE ALERT: Because it refers to excrement, this term will be objectionable in some situations and to some people.

**shit**[2] |shit| *n* An item or items that are estimated to be of the same value or quality as excrement. ORIGINS: From slang **shit** meaning "excrement." USAGE INFO: In this particular case, the use of **shit** *does* speak to the quality of the items being referred to. Since **shit** can also simply mean "stuff; belongings; possessions; things" it is important to use context to determine which meaning is meant. USAGE ALERT: Because it refers to excrement, this term will be objectionable in some situations and to some people.

**shit** |shit| *v* To fool; to tell untruths; to lie to; to deceive. ORIGINS: From a shortening of **bullshit** meaning "lies; deceptive talk." From the SE name of male cattle (bull) and the slang word for their dung (**shit**). USAGE INFO: Often used to express surprise or disbelief, as in "Are you shitting me?" USAGE ALERT: This word will be objectionable in some contexts and to some people.

**shit** |shit| *adv* Sentence modifier with various meanings. ORIGINS: From slang **shit**, meaning "excrement." USAGE INFO: Used to modify/intensify a whole sentence, as in "Shit, I missed the bus!" USAGE ALERT: This word will be objectionable in some contexts and to some people.

**Shit!** |shit| *excl* An interjection expressing anger, frustration, extreme surprise, shock, realization of a mistake or error, etc. ORIGINS: From slang **shit**, meaning "excrement." USAGE ALERT: This word will be objectionable in some contexts and to some people.

**shit a brick\*** |SHIT u BRIK| *v* To be furious. ORIGINS: From slang **shit** meaning "excrement." May refer to emotionally induced constipation. USAGE ALERT: The inclusion of the word **shit** in the phrase will render it objectionable in some contexts and to some people.
• **shit bricks** |SHIT BRIKS|

**shit-hot** |SHIT HAHT| *a/a* Excellent; first-rate. Extremely; especially. ORIGINS: From slang **shit** meaning "excrement" and hot meaning "attractive." This is a pun, due to the initial temperature of excrement. USAGE INFO: Used as an adjective ("shit-hot videos") or as an adverb ("a shit-hot good plan"). USAGE ALERT: Because it includes **shit**, this word will be objectionable in some contexts and to some people.

**shit on** |SHIT ahn| *v* To denigrate; to verbally abuse. ORIGINS: From slang **shit** meaning "excrement." USAGE ALERT: The inclusion of the word **shit** in the phrase will render it objectionable in some contexts and to some people.

**shit oneself** |SHIT wun self| *v* To be terrified. ORIGINS: Figurative use of slang **shit oneself** meaning "to defecate in one's underwear," since that is a possible physical response to fear. USAGE ALERT: The inclusion of the word **shit** in the phrase will render it objectionable in some contexts and to some people.

**shit out of luck** |SHIT out uv LUK| *phr* Without hope. ORIGINS: From SE out of luck and slang **shit**, meaning "excrement," used here as a modifier to intensify the meaning. USAGE ALERT: The inclusion of the word **shit** will render this phrase objectionable in some contexts and to some people.

**shitbag** |SHIT bag| *n* A contemptible person; a person who is disgusting; a person who isn't trustworthy. ORIGINS: From **shit** meaning "excrement" and the suffix -bag meaning person. USAGE ALERT: Usually used with intent to denigrate or insult and understood as such. Because it includes **shit**, this word will be objectionable in some contexts and to some people.

**shitface** |SHIT fās| *n See* **SHITHEAD**.

**shithead** |SHIT hed| *n* A contemptible person. ORIGINS: From slang **shit** meaning "excrement" and slang suffix -head. USAGE ALERT: Usually used with intent to denigrate or insult and understood as such. Because it includes **shit**, this word will be objectionable in some contexts and to some people.

**shitkicker** |SHIT kik ur| *n* A crude, unsophisticated person. ORIGINS: From the stereotype that *sb* who works on a farm with animals and manure will be of this type. From slang **shit** meaning "excrement." USAGE ALERT: Usually used with intent to denigrate or insult and understood as such. Because it includes **shit**, this word will be objectionable in some contexts and to some people.

**shitload** |SHIT lōd| *n* A very large amount. ORIGINS: From **shit** meaning "excrement" plus SE load. USAGE ALERT: Because it includes **shit**, this word will be objectionable in some contexts and to some people.

**shits, the** |*thu* SHITS| *n* An attack of fear or terror. ORIGINS: From slang the shits meaning "diarrhea," which is sometimes a symptom of great terror or fear. USAGE ALERT: Because it includes **shit**, this word will be objectionable in some contexts and to some people.

**Shitsure!** |SHIT shur| *excl* Positive; absolutely sure. ORIGINS: The idea is that the existence of excrement can be relied on as absolutely certain. Variation on the phrase **sure as shit**. USAGE ALERT: The use of **shit** in this word will make it objectionable in some contexts and to some people.

**shitty** |SHIT ē| *adj* Inferior; despicable; unpleasant; unkind. ORIGINS: Extended from **shit** meaning "excrement." USAGE INFO: Can be applied to a thing or a person. USAGE ALERT: Because it is a form of **shit**, this word will be objectionable in some contexts and to some people.

**shoestring** |SHŪ string| *n* A very small sum of money; a barely adequate amount of money. USAGE INFO: Often occurs in the phrase "on a shoestring" meaning "on a very small budget."

**shoo-in** |SHŪ in| *n* A certainty. ORIGINS: From horse racing jargon for a "guaranteed" winner. USAGE INFO: Often used in the context of political elections.

**Shoot!** |shūt| *excl* An interjection expressing frustration, anger, surprise, etc. ORIGINS: Euphemism for **Shit!**

**shoot off one's mouth** |SHŪT ahf wunz MOUTH| *v* To boast or brag. USAGE INFO: Can also be reordered: shoot one's mouth off.

**shoot one's mouth off** |SHŪT wunz MOUTH awf| *v* To say *st* without due forethought.

**shoot one's wad** |SHŪT wunz WAHD| *v* To make a total commitment to *sb/st*; to wear out (used either of oneself or one's resources). ORIGINS: From shooting jargon meaning "the plug holding the powder."

**shoot oneself in the foot** |SHŪT wun SELF in *thu* FŌOT| *v* To ruin one's own prospects; to blunder in a way that endangers one's future.

**shoot the breeze** |SHŪT *thu* BRĒZ| *v* To talk idly. ORIGINS: From the idea that when one talks into the wind, one's words return with no effect.

**shoot the bull** |SHŪT *thu* BŌOL| *v* To deceive; to lie or exaggerate to the point of untruth. ORIGINS: From **shoot** meaning "to speak" and **bull**, a shortened form of **bullshit**, meaning "lies, deceptive talk."

**shoot the crap/shit** |SHŪT *thu* KRAP / SHŪT *thu* SHIT| *v* To deceive; to lie or exaggerate to the point of untruth. ORIGINS: From **shoot** meaning "to speak" and **crap** or **shit**, literally meaning "excrement" and figuratively meaning "lies, untruths."

**shoot the works** |SHŪT *thu* WURKZ| *v* To make a total commitment of all one's resources.

**shoot-up** |SHŪT up| *n* A gun-fight; an act of property destruction using guns.

**shot** |shaht| *n* An attempt.

**shot** |shaht| *adj* Exhausted; worn out. USAGE INFO: Can be used of people or things.

**shot to hell** |SHAHT tū hell| *adj* Completely exhausted; useless. ORIGINS: Figurative use of SE **hell** meaning "the alternative to heaven; the realm of the devil." USAGE INFO: Can be used of people or things. USAGE ALERT: The inclusion of the word **hell** in the phrase will render it objectionable in some contexts and to some people.

**Shove it!** |SHUV it| *excl* A harsh dismissal. ORIGINS: Shortened, euphemistic form of **Shove it up your ass!** USAGE ALERT: Usually used with intent to be rude and understood as such. The euphemism in this phrase will soften it somewhat, but it may still be objectionable in some contexts and to some people.

**Shove it up your ass!** |SHUV it up yur AS| *excl* A harsh dismissal. ORIGINS: From slang **ass** meaning "rear end or buttocks." USAGE ALERT: Usually used with intent to be rude and understood as such. The inclusion of the word **ass** in the phrase and the graphic image will render it objectionable in some contexts and to some people.

**shove off** |SHUV ahf| *v* To leave; to depart. ORIGINS: From the action of boaters pushing off from the dock. USAGE INFO: Harsher than the similar phrase **push off!**

**Shove off!** |SHUV ahf| *excl* A harsh dismissal. ORIGINS: From the action of boaters pushing off from the dock. USAGE INFO: Harsher than the similar phrase **Push off!**

**shove one's oar in** |SHUV wunz AWR in| *v* To join a discussion to which one hasn't been invited. ORIGINS: From the saying "have an oar in every man's boat" or "put one's oar in every man's boat," the idea being that those with the oars are in charge both of the progress and direction of the vessel. USAGE INFO: Since **shove** is stronger than **put** or **poke**, this particular version of the expression may indicate more forceful intrusion.

**show** *sb* **the door/gate** |SHŌ *sb* thu DAWR / SHŌ *sb* thu GĀT| *v* Dismiss *sb* from employment; send *sb* out of one's presence. USAGE INFO: Note that this is different from show *sb* to the door, which can be a gesture of courtesy, as well as an escort off the premises.

**showboat** |SHŌ bōt| *n* A person who shows off; a boaster.

**shred** |shred| *v* To conquer; to best in an argument; to criticize mercilessly. ORIGINS: By analogy to devices such as a grater or a paper shredder.

**shut out** |SHUT out| *v* To utterly defeat, not only winning but keeping opponents from scoring. ORIGINS: Extended first from baseball jargon to other sports and then to more general use.

**Shut the fuck up!** |SHUT thu FUK up| *excl* Be quiet! ORIGINS: Refers to shutting the mouth. In this phrase **the fuck** is used as an intensifier. USAGE ALERT: Usually used with intent to denigrate or insult and understood as such. In addition, the use of **fuck** in this phrase will make it objectionable in some contexts and to some people.

**Shut up!**[1] |SHUT up| *excl* Be quiet! A strong dismissal of a person's contribution. USAGE ALERT: Usually used with intent to be rude and understood as such.

**Shut up!**[2] |shut UP| *excl* Initial expression of disbelief in what one has been told, but often suggests that the hearer is open to convincing. USAGE INFO: This use of shut up, if said with appropriate tone and body language, will not cause offense.

**Shut your cakehole/piehole!** |shut yŏŏr KĀK hōl / shut yŏŏr PĪ hōl| *excl* Be quiet! ORIGINS: Refers to shutting the mouth using slang cakehole or piehole to refer to the mouth. USAGE ALERT: Usually used with intent to denigrate or insult and understood as such. The use of -hole as a suffix may bring the word **asshole** to mind for some people, and color their perception of this word.

**Shut your face/mouth/head!** |shut yŏŏr FĀS / shut yŏŏr MOUTH / shut yŏŏr HED| *excl* Be quiet! ORIGINS: Refers to shutting the mouth. USAGE ALERT: Usually used with intent to denigrate or insult and understood as such.

**Shut your trap!** |shut yŏŏr TRAP| *excl* Be quiet! ORIGINS: Refers to shutting the mouth. USAGE ALERT: Usually used with intent to denigrate or insult and understood as such.

**sick** |sik| *adj* Excellent; outstanding; good.

**sicko** |SIK ō| *adj* Crazy. ORIGINS: From slang sick and the slang suffix -o used to create adjectives, including some others having to do with mental health, like batso, wacko, and nutso, making them similar to abbreviated schizo and psycho. USAGE ALERT: Often used with intent to denigrate or insult and understood as such. This way of speaking about *sb's* mental health may be considered insensitive and therefore objectionable in some contexts and by some people.

**sidekick** |SĪD kik| *n* A pal; a helper; a dependable back-up.

**sideline** |SĪD līn| *v* To remove *sb* from participation in some event. ORIGIN: From sports such as football in which players who are not actively participating watch the play from a bench at the side of the playing field.

**sign up for** |sīn UP fawr| *v* To leap past the consideration stage and declare oneself all in.

**simmer** |SIM ur| *v* To be filled with unexpressed emotions, often anger.

**simmer down** |SIM ur doun| *v* To become calm (often after being extremely angry or upset). USAGE INFO: Often used as an imperative.

**simp** |simp| *n* A fool. ORIGINS: Shortened from SE **simpleton**. USAGE ALERT: Usually used with intent to denigrate or insult and understood as such.

**sing** |sing| *v* To betray *sb*; to inform against *sb*.

**sing another tune** |SING u nu*th* ur TŪN| *v See* SING A DIFFERENT TUNE.

**sing a different tune** |SING u DIF runt TŪN| *v* To change one's mind; to assume a different stance; to behave differently. USAGE INFO: Often as part of a threat, as in "When I tell him the deal's off, he'll sing a different tune."

**singing the blues** |SING ing *thu* BLŪZ| *v* Feeling upset or depressed. ORIGINS: From the musical genre and its typical content. USAGE INFO: Used very broadly today to refer to businesses that aren't doing as well as expected, defeated sports teams, etc.

**sink** |singk| *v* To defeat in competition.

**sink one's teeth into** |singk wunz TĒTH in tū| *v* To get down to work; to eagerly engage with. ORIGINS: Figurative use of the experience of beginning a meal.

**sissified** |SIS u fīd| *adj* Timid or cowardly; effeminate.

**sissy** |SIS ē| *adj* A fearful or timid person; an effeminate male. USAGE ALERT: Usually used with intent to denigrate or insult and understood as such.

**sit on** |SIT ahn| *v* To reprimand; to quell.

**Sit on it and rotate!** |SIT ahn it and RŌ tāt| *excl* A contemptuous dismissal. USAGE INFO: Often accompanied by the gesture referred to as "giving *sb* the finger." USAGE ALERT: Usually used with intent to be rude and understood as such. In addition, the graphic image will make this expression objectionable in some contexts and to some people.

**sitting pretty** |SIT ing PRIT ē| *adj* Doing well, financially or in general.

**sizzle** |SIZ ul| *v* To be filled with unexpressed emotions, often anger.

**skanky, scanky** |SKANK ē| *adj* Disgustingly filthy. ORIGINS: From slang skank meaning "filth; a prostitute." USAGE ALERT: Also used to mean "sexually promiscuous." Usually used with intent to denigrate or insult and understood as such.

**skedaddle** |ski DAD ul| *v* To leave in haste; to flee.

**skin *sb* (alive)** |SKIN *sb* / SKIN *sb* u LĪV| *v* To destroy, physically or verbally.

**skin-flint** |SKIN flint| *n* A mean, greedy person. ORIGINS: From the concept of a person so greedy they would skin (peel) a flint, if it gained *st*. From the obsolete term skin a flint.

**skip out** |skip OUT| *v* To leave; to depart in a hurry.

**skip out on** |skip OUT ahn| *v* To abandon.

**skip town** |SKIP TOUN| *v* To leave without a trace; to depart without warning.

**skipper** |SKIP ur| *n* A boss. ORIGINS: Generalized from boating jargon skipper meaning "the captain."

**skosh** |skōsh| *adj* A small amount; a little bit. ORIGINS: From Japanese sukoshi, through American servicemen stationed in Japan.

**skunk** |skungk| *n* A contemptible person. ORIGINS: Figurative reference to the characteristic smell of an angered or beleaguered skunk.

S

**slacker** |SLAK ur| *n* A lazy person; a person who avoids work. ORIGINS: From SE slack.

**slam** |slam| *v* To insult; to criticize harshly.

**slam dunk, slam-dunk** |SLAM DUNGK| *n* A certainty; a guaranteed result. ORIGINS: From basketball jargon for a two-handed dunk.

**Slap me five!** |SLAP mē FĪV| *excl* A request for a "high-five," a greeting or celebratory gesture of slapping hands (the five refers to the number of fingers) "high" in the air—often above the head. ORIGINS: From African-American culture. Kept alive by the children's game in which one child invites another to slap him/her five with the hand in different positions, and in the final "round," trying to remove the hand before the other can slap it. The words are, "Slap me five. On the side. Way up high. Down low."—and if s/he succeeds in avoiding the last slap—"You're too slow."

**slathers** |SLA*TH* urz| *n* Large amounts, often of something spreadable. ORIGINS: From SE **slather** meaning "to squander." USAGE INFO: Was primarily British, but spreading, especially in US food writing, where it is most often used to refer to mayonnaise, butter, jam, frosting, as well as to other items in large quantities.

**slaughter[1]** |SLAW tur| *v* To defeat in competition.

**slaughter[2]** |SLAW tur| *v* To cause riotous laughter.

**slay[1]** |slā| *v* To defeat in competition

**slay[2]** |slā| *v* To cause riotous laughter.

**sleaze*** |slēz| *n* A vulgar, contemptible, untrustworthy person; a person involved in immoral or dishonest pursuits, especially those pertaining to sex. ORIGINS: Back-formation from the slang adjective **sleazy** meaning "dirty, vulgar, and dishonest." USAGE ALERT: Usually used with intent to denigrate or insult and understood as such.
• sleazo |SLĒZ ō|

**sleazebag*** |SLĒZ bag| *n* A vulgar, contemptible, untrustworthy person; a person involved in immoral or dishonest pursuits, especially those pertaining to sex. ORIGINS: From the slang noun **sleaze** and slang suffix **-bag, -ball,** or **-bucket** meaning "a person." USAGE ALERT: Usually used with intent to denigrate or insult and understood as such.
• sleazeball |SLĒZ ball|
• sleaze bucket |SLĒZ buk it|

**sleep on *st*** |SLĒP ahn *st*| *v* To postpone consideration of (and therefore action on) *st*.

**slew** |slū| *n* A large number or amount. ORIGINS: From the Irish **sluagh** meaning "crowd."

**slime** |slīm| *n* A repulsive or despicable person. USAGE ALERT: Usually used with intent to denigrate or insult and understood as such.

**slimeball\*** |SLĪM bawl| *n* A repulsive or despicable person. ORIGINS: From slang slime and slang suffix -ball, -bag, or -bucket meaning "a person." Slime bucket made the news in July 2008 when Steve Jobs used it to refer to *NY Times* journalist Joe Nocera in a private phone call, which Nocera reported. USAGE ALERT: Usually used with intent to denigrate or insult and understood as such.
- slimebag |SLĪM bag|
- slime bucket |SLĪM buk it|

**sling it** |SLING it| *v See* SLING THE BULL, **SLING THE CRAP**, **SLING THE SHIT**.

**sling the bull** |sling *thu* BOŌL| *v* To talk nonsense; to boast; to tell untruths; to lie. ORIGINS: From sling meaning "to tell" and bull meaning "lies and flattery." USAGE INFO: Developed prior to **bullshit**, but now used as a euphemism for it.

**sling the crap** |SLING *thu* KRAP| *v* To deceive; to lie or exaggerate to the point of untruth. ORIGINS: From **sling** meaning "to tell" and **crap**, a euphemism for **shit**, literally meaning "excrement" and figuratively meaning "lies, untruths."

**sling the shit** |SLING *thu* SHIT| *v* To deceive; to lie or exaggerate to the point of untruth. ORIGINS: From **sling** meaning "to tell" and **shit**, literally meaning "excrement" and figuratively meaning "lies, untruths."

**slip a cog** |slip u KAHG| *v* To lose one's sanity. ORIGINS: By analogy to a machine that no longer functions because its gears are not turning properly. USAGE ALERT: This way of speaking about *sb*'s mental health may be considered insensitive and therefore objectionable in some contexts and by some people.

**slip-up** |SLIP up| *n* A mistake; an error; an oversight.

**slobby** |SLAHB ē| *adj* Having the characteristics of a slob: untidy, lazy, poorly groomed, crude, and/or obnoxious.

**sloppy** |SLAHP ē| *adj* Messy; imprecise; untidy. ORIGINS: From SE **slop** meaning "to spill."

**slouch** |slouch| *n* An inefficient, lazy, or indifferent person.

**slue** |slū| *n See* SLEW.

**slug** |slug| *n* A disgusting, repulsive person. USAGE INFO: Although slug referring to a person is given dictionary definitions of "lazy," actual usage reveals this alternative meaning, as in the phrase "contemptible slug." USAGE ALERT: Usually used with intent to denigrate or insult and understood as such.

**slug** |slug| *v* To hit hard, usually with the fist. ORIGINS: From slang noun slug meaning "a blow."

**slug it out** |SLUG it out| *v* To seek to settle *st* with a fist fight; to seek to settle *st* with a battle of wits (a verbal fight).

**slugfest** |SLUG fest| *n* A fight or competition in which there is a great deal of scoring—either of blows or of points. ORIGINS: From slang verb slug meaning "to hit hard" and suffix -fest, a shortening of SE **festival**, meaning gathering or event. The meaning is literal for a fight and figurative for most competitions.

**smack** |smak| *v* To slap with an open hand. ORIGINS: Imitative of the sound of a blow.

**small beer** |smawl BER| *n* A small or worthless amount. ORIGINS: From SE **small beer** meaning "weak or inferior beer."

**small fry** |SMAWL frī| *n* People who are unimportant and/or have no influence. ORIGINS: From SE **small fry** meaning "little fish."

**small potatoes** |smawl pu TĀ tōz| *n* An insignificant amount.

**smart-ass** |SMAHRT as| *n* A person with intellectual pretensions; a person who works hard and is academically successful. ORIGINS: From SE **smart** and slang suffix **-ass** meaning "a person." USAGE ALERT: Usually used with intent to denigrate or insult and understood as such.

**smash** |smash| *n* A great success.

**smear** |smir| *v* To beat up; to defeat by a wide margin.

**smidgen** |SMIJ un| *n* A very small quantity.

**smitten with/by, be** |SMIT un with / SMIT un bī| *v* To be infatuated; to be in love. ORIGINS: *Smitten* is the past participle of SE **smite**.

**smoke** |smōk| *v* To kill (with a firearm). ORIGINS: From the smoke that comes out of a gun when it is fired.

**smolder** |SMŌL dur| *v* To be filled with unexpressed anger.

**smooth** |smū*th*| *adj* Superior; well done.

**snag** |snag| *n* A hidden difficulty or obstacle.

**snag** |snag| *v* To take for one's own use; to steal. ORIGINS: By extension of SE **snag** meaning "to catch."

**snap** |snap| *n* A task that is easy to accomplish or resolve.

**snap *sb's* head off** |SNAP *sb's* HED awf| *v* Attack verbally, especially in cases in which the attack is objectively out of proportion to the situation. USAGE INFO: Despite the physical description in the phrase, it is not used for physical altercations.

**snappy** |SNAP ē| *adj* Energetic.

**snarky** |SNAHR kē| *adj* Irritable; liable to anger; sarcastic.

**snarl-up** |SNAHRL up| *n* A difficulty; a state of confusion and disorganization.

**snazzy** |SNAZ ē| *adj* Fashionable.

**sniff *st* out** |snif *st* OUT| *v* To uncover *st*. ORIGINS: From comparison with an animal seeking its prey.

**snit** |snit| *n* A fit of ill temper.

**snitch**[1] |snich| *v* To betray; to reveal *sb's* secret.

**snitch**[2] |snich| *v* To steal.

**snitty** |SNIT ē| *adj* Ill-tempered.

**sniveller** |SNIV ul ur| *n* A person who whines or complains with sniffles and tears.

**snooker** |SNŎŎK ur| *v* To fool *sb*. ORIGINS: From the game of snooker, in which a shot is called a snooker if the cue ball is left in a position that leaves one's opponent no options because the target ball is blocked by another ball.

**snooty** |SNŪT ē| *adj* Snobbish. ORIGINS: From slang snoot meaning "arrogance" from SE **snout** meaning "nose," tied together by the idea of arrogant people looking down their noses at others.

**snooze** |snūz| *v* To nap.

**snot(nose)** |snaht / SNAHT nōz| *n* An arrogant and annoying person. ORIGINS: From slang snot meaning "nasal mucus." USAGE ALERT: Usually used with intent to denigrate or insult and understood as such.

**snot-rag** |SNAHT rag| *n* A disgusting person. ORIGINS: Figurative use of slang snot-rag meaning "a dirty handkerchief." USAGE ALERT: Usually used with intent to denigrate or insult and understood as such.

**snow job** |SNŌ jahb| *n* A convincing, but untrue, story or insincere flattery. ORIGINS: From slang verb snow meaning "insincere talk."

**snowball's chance in hell** |SNŌ bawlz chans in HEL| *v* No chance at all. ORIGINS: From the conception of hell as full of fire. Figurative use of SE **hell** meaning "the alternative to heaven; the realm of the devil." USAGE ALERT: The use of the word **hell** in this phrase will make it objectionable in some contexts and to some people.

**snuff** *sb* **(out)** |snuf *sb* / SNUF *sb* OUT| *v* To murder *sb*. ORIGINS: From slang snuff (it) meaning "to die."

**So don't I!** |SŌ dōnt ī| *excl* Agreement with a negative proposition. USAGE INFO: An example is "I don't like eggplant at all." "So don't I."

**So what!** |sō WHAT| *excl* An interjection of indifference.

**so &lt;word/phrase&gt;** |sō &lt;word/phrase&gt;| *a/a* Utterly; completely. A construction to describe *st* by characterizing it in terms of *st* else. USAGE INFO: Used as an adjective meaning "dated" in constructions with a time period that has passed ("so last year," "so last season," "so last century," "so yesterday"), and as an adverb with other objects with the meaning "completely" ("so not her fault," "so not my favorite subject").

S

**so-and-so** |SŌ und sō| *n* A euphemism for any derogatory phrase. USAGE INFO: Often preceded by one or more modifiers (as in "rotten so-and-so"), which may also be euphemisms, as in "a blinking so-and-so" or "bleeping so-and-so."

**So's your old man!** |SŌZ yŏor ōld man| *excl* A contemptuous dismissive insult. USAGE ALERT: Usually used with intent to be rude and understood as such.

**soak** |sōk| *v* To cheat; to overcharge.

**sock** |sahk| *v* To punch.

**sock it to** *sb* |SAHK it tū *sb*| *v* To deliver a blow, literally or figuratively.

**soft on** |SAWFT ahn| *adj* Attracted to; very fond of.

**soft touch** |SAWFT TUCH| *n* A person who will easily agree to give money or do favors.

**soft-soaper** |SAWFT sōp ur| *n* A flatterer; a person who uses charm to persuade.

**sold on** |SŌLD ahn| *adj* Convinced by; persuaded of *st's* value.

**something awful** |SUM thing AW ful| *adv* To a great degree or extent or with intensive effort. USAGE INFO: Follows the verb it modifies, as in "She loves him something awful."

**something else** |SUM thing ELS| *adj* Wonderful; impressive. USAGE INFO: Often as a predicate adjective after a form of *to be*, as in "She's something else!" Can be used for things that impress negatively as well as positively, as in "The smell from the backed up sewer is something else!"

**something fierce** |SUM thing FIRS| *adv* To a great degree or extent, or with intensive effort. USAGE INFO: Follows the verb it modifies, as in "My ankle hurts something fierce."

**son of a bitch**[1] |sun uv u BICH| *n* Something extremely difficult. ORIGINS: Figurative use of SE **bitch**, meaning "a female dog." USAGE ALERT: The inclusion of the word **bitch** in the phrase will render it objectionable in some contexts and to some people.

**son of a bitch**[2] |sun uv u BICH| *n* A mean or nasty person; an offensive or despicable person. ORIGINS: Figurative use of SE **bitch**, meaning "a female dog." USAGE INFO: Usually used only of males. USAGE ALERT: **Son of a bitch** carries implications not only about the person referred to, but also about his mother. Usually used with intent to denigrate or insult and understood as such. In addition, the phrase will be objectionable in some contexts and to some people.

**Son of a bitch!** |sun uv u BICH| *excl* An interjection of anger and outrage. ORIGINS: Figurative use of SE **bitch**, meaning "a female dog." USAGE ALERT: The inclusion of the word **bitch** in the phrase will render it objectionable in some contexts and to some people.

**son of a whore** |sun uv u HAWR| *n* A contemptible person. ORIGINS: From slang **whore**, meaning "a prostitute" or "*sb* considered sexually promiscuous." USAGE INFO: Usually used only of males. USAGE ALERT: **Son of a whore** carries implications not only about the person referred to, but also about his mother. Usually used with intent to denigrate or insult and understood as such. In addition, the phrase will be objectionable in some contexts and to some people.

**sonic** |SAHN ik| *adj* Extremely fast. ORIGINS: From the actual speed of sound.

**sore** |sōr| *adj* Angry and offended.

**soreheaded** |SŌR hed id| *adj* Bad-tempered, liable to anger.

**sound off** |sound AHF| *v* To boast or brag.

**Sounds like a plan!** |SOUNDZ līk u PLAN| *excl* Agreement with and approval of a proposal.

**soup up** |SŪP up| *v* To modify in order to increase performance or to make more impressive. ORIGINS: From slang **soup** meaning "high performance fuel for customized cars."

**space cadet** |SPĀS ku det| *n* A spacey person; one who has difficulty grasping reality. ORIGINS: A mock military rank. USAGE ALERT: Usually used with intent to denigrate or insult and understood as such.

**spark plug** |SPAHRK plug| *n* An energetic person who facilitates change by setting events in motion.

**spat** |spat| *n* A verbal argument; a quarrel.

**spaz** |spaz| *n* A clumsy or inept person. ORIGINS: Short for SE **spastic** meaning "relating to spastic paralysis" or "hypertonic, with the result that muscle movements become awkward and stiff." Medical spasticity is often associated with cerebral palsy. USAGE ALERT: It is considered objectionable by most people to use this slang to describe *sb* who has a disability such as cerebral palsy. It will also be considered objectionable in some contexts and by some people to apply the term to *sb* who does not have such a medical condition.

**spieler** |SHPĒL ur| *n* A person who can talk people into things, including swindles. ORIGINS: From German **spielen** meaning "to play." USAGE ALERT: Often used with intent to denigrate or insult and understood as such.

**spiff (up)** |spif / SPIF UP| *v* To tidy; to smarten up.

**spiffy** |SPIF ē| *adj* Smart; stylish.

**spill one's guts (out)** |spil wunz GUTS / spil wunz GUTS out| *v* To be completely honest; to confess to whatever has been concealed or untold; to reveal intimate secrets.

**spill the beans** |spil *thu* BĒNZ| *v* To reveal a secret that was meant to be kept.

**spit it out** |SPIT it out| *v* To speak up after being silent or hesitant.

**splendiferous** |splen DIF ur us| *adj* Excellent; outstanding. ORIGINS: From an extension of SE **splendid**.

**split** |split| *v* To leave; to depart in a hurry.

**split a gut** |SPLIT a gut| *v* To laugh very hard. USAGE INFO: This phrase also means "to work very hard; to put in an enormous effort."

**split on** |SPLIT ahn| *v* To betray; to inform against.

**split one's gut** |SPLIT wunz gut| *v* To laugh very hard. USAGE INFO: This phrase also means "to work very hard; to put in an enormous effort."

**split one's sides** |split wunz SĪDZ| *v* To laugh uproariously.

**sponge** |spahnj| *v* To beg, usually from one's friends and usually with no intention of repaying.

**spot** |spaht| *n* A small amount of.

**spot-on** |spaht ahn| *adj* Perfect; accurate; completely correct. USAGE INFO: Often used with nouns like *interpretation, imitation, parody, performance,* and *copy.*

**spout (off)** |spout / SPOUT awf| *v* To talk too much.

**spread it on thick** |SPRĒD it ahn thik| *v* To exaggerate or add elaboration, especially when telling a lie, deceiving, or flattering.

**spunky** |SPUNG kē| *adj* Courageous; spirited. ORIGINS: From slang **spunk** meaning "courage; bravery."

**square off** |skwuar AHF| *v* To assume a fighting stance preparatory to throwing a punch. ORIGINS: From the shape of the ring and the preparation of fighters for the start of a match in boxing.

**squat** |skwaht| *n* Nothing at all. ORIGINS: Shortened form of slang **diddl(e)ysquat** or **doodl(e)ysquat** meaning "nothing at all." USAGE INFO: Often used in a construction with a disguised double negative, as in "I don't have squat." Usually used of money or more generally of possessions.

**squawk** |skwawk| *v* To complain noisily. ORIGINS: From the loud, harsh cry of a bird.

**squawker** |SKWAWK ur| *n* A person who complains noisily or peevishly. ORIGINS: From the loud, harsh cry of a bird.

**squeak by/through** |SKWĒK BĪ / SKWĒK THRŪ| *v* To succeed, win, or pass (an examination), but just barely.

**squeal (on)** |skwēl / SKWĒL ahn| *v* To turn informer; to betray an accomplice or secret.

**squillion** |SKWIL yun| *n* An unspecified, exceedingly large amount. ORIGINS: One of a group of made up numbers ending in *-illion* with pretty indistinguishable meanings; for example, **squillion**, **jillion**, and **zillion**.

**squirrely** |SKWURL ē| *adj* Crazy. ORIGINS: Linked to slang **nutty** through the stereotypical connection of squirrels and nuts. USAGE ALERT: Often used with intent to denigrate or insult and understood as such. This way of speaking about *sb's* mental health may be considered insensitive and therefore objectionable in some contexts and by some people.

**squish** |skwish| *n* A person thought to be weak, often because their stance on some issue(s) is less extreme than the person using the word. USAGE INFO: Used of political moderates, for example.

**stab in the back** |STAB in *thu* BAK| *v* To betray. ORIGINS: From the idea that it is dishonorable to strike *sb* when his/her back is turned.

**stacks** |staks| *n* A large amount.

**stand out** |STAND out| *adj* An outstanding example. ORIGINS: Presumably from the phrasal verb **stand out** meaning "to be distinctive; to be conspicuous."

**steal, a** |u STĒL| *n* An item offered for a price that is judged to be far less than its true value.

**steam** |stēm| *v* To be angry or annoyed.

**steamed** |stēm'd| *adj* Annoyed.

**steamroll** |STĒM RŌL| *v* To force with an application of intense pressure.

**steep** |stēp| *adv* Over-priced; very expensive.

**step on it** |STEP ahn it| *v* To move at very high speed (usually in a vehicle). ORIGINS: "It" refers to the accelerator. From the action of stepping on the accelerator pedal, also called the "gas pedal," to increase a car's speed. USAGE INFO: Also used as an imperative.

**step on one's cock\*** |STEP ahn wunz KAHK| *v* To get oneself into trouble; to make a fool of oneself. ORIGINS: From slang **cock** or **dick** meaning "penis." USAGE INFO: Usually only used by or of males. USAGE ALERT: The inclusion of the word **cock** or **dick** in the phrase will render it objectionable in some contexts and to some people.
• **step on one's dick** |STEP ahn wunz DIK|

**step on the gas** |STEP ahn *thu* GAS| *v* To move at very high speed (usually in a vehicle). ORIGINS: From the action of stepping on the accelerator pedal, also called the "gas pedal," to increase a car's speed. USAGE INFO: Also used as an imperative.

**stew** |stū| *v* To be in a lingering state of sullen anger or feeling offended or insulted, often without expressing it.

**Stick it!** |STIK it| *excl* A rude dismissal. ORIGINS: Shortened form of slang **Stick it up your ass!** or similar phrases. USAGE INFO: Often accompanied by the gesture referred to as "giving *sb* the finger." USAGE ALERT: Usually used with intent to be rude and understood as such. In addition, the euphemistic shortening of this phrase will soften it somewhat, but it may still be objectionable in some contexts and to some people.

**Stick it in your ear!** |STIK it in yŏŏr IR| *excl* A contemptuous dismissal. ORIGINS: Euphemistic form of slang **Stick it up your ass!** from slang **ass** meaning "the rear end or buttocks." USAGE INFO: Often accompanied by the gesture referred to as "giving *sb* the finger." USAGE ALERT: Usually used with intent to be rude and understood as such. Although the euphemistic alteration of this phrase will soften it somewhat, it may still be objectionable in some contexts and to some people.

**stick it to *sb*** |STIK it tū *sb*| *v* To attack *sb* verbally by teasing or maligning; to be harsh or unfair to *sb*.

**Stick it up your ass!** |STIK it up yŏŏr AS| *excl* A contemptuous dismissal. ORIGINS: From slang **ass** meaning "the rear end or buttocks." USAGE INFO: Often accompanied by the gesture referred to as "giving *sb* the finger." USAGE ALERT: Usually used with intent to be rude and understood as such. In addition, the inclusion of **ass** and the graphic image will make this expression objectionable in some contexts and to some people.

**Stick it where the sun doesn't shine!** |STIK it wer *thu* SUN duz 'nt SHĪN| *excl* A contemptuous dismissal. ORIGINS: Euphemistic form of slang **Stick it up your ass!** from slang **ass** meaning "the rear end or buttocks." USAGE INFO: Often accompanied by the gesture referred to as "giving *sb* the finger." USAGE ALERT: Usually used with intent to be rude and understood as such. Although the euphemistic alteration of this phrase will soften it somewhat, the graphic image may still be objectionable in some contexts and to some people.

**stick one's neck out** |stik wunz NEK out| *v* To go beyond one's area of expertise or comfort zone; to interfere in things that aren't one's concern; to take a risk. ORIGINS: From the necessary stretching out of the neck prior to a head being chopped off.

**stick one's nose into *st*** |STIK wunz NŌZ in tū *st*| *v* See POKE ONE'S NOSE INTO *ST*.

**stick up for** |stik UP fawr| *v* To support or defend.

**stiff** |stif| *adj* A very high price, judged to be excessive.

**stiff** |stif| *v* To refuse to pay; to fail to pay without acknowledgment that one is doing so.

**sting** |sting| *v* To swindle in a confidence game; to cheat, defraud, or steal from.

**stinger** |STING ur| *n* A stinging blow.

**stinker(oo)**[1] |STING ker / STING ker ū| *n* An extremely difficult problem. ORIGINS: Figurative use of SE **stink** meaning "to smell." USAGE INFO: When the ending is added, the word may be used playfully.

**stinker(oo)**[2] |STING ker / STING ker ū| *n* A disgusting or loathsome person. ORIGINS: Figurative use of SE **stink** meaning "to smell." USAGE INFO: When the ending is added, the word may be used playfully. USAGE ALERT: Often used with intent to denigrate or insult and understood as such.

**stinking** |STING king| *adj* Adjective that works as a sentence modifier. ORIGINS: Euphemism for **damn(ed)**. From SE **stinking** meaning "having a strong, unpleasant smell." USAGE INFO: Used for negative effect ("I don't have to show you any stinking badges!"—*The Treasure of the Sierra Madre*, 1948) and very often connected with money ("stinking rich"). USAGE ALERT: People who recognize it as a substitute for **damn(ed)** may find stinking objectionable.

**stinking of money** |STINGK uv MUN ē| *adj* Having lots of money.

**stinking with <noun/pronoun>** |STING king with <noun/pronoun>| *adj* Having or owning a large amount. ORIGINS: From SE **stinking** meaning "having a strong, unpleasant smell." USAGE INFO: Often used in connection with money.

**stinko** |STING kō| *adj* Of poor quality.

**stinkpot** |STINGK pot| *n* A despicable or offensive person. ORIGINS: Figurative use of a slang term that once meant "chamberpot." USAGE INFO: Used affectionately for a small child who is still in diapers and is, or is suspected to be, in need of a change or a small child, whether or not in diapers, who is suspected of being, or actually is, involved in some mischief. USAGE ALERT: Sometimes used with intent to denigrate or insult and understood as such.

**stinky** |stingk ē | *adj* Of poor quality; extremely bad or unpleasant. ORIGINS: Figurative use of SE **stink**.

**stir one's stumps** |STIR wunz STUMPS| *v* To get moving; to set off briskly.

**stoked** |stōkt| *adj* Thrilled; intensely excited.

**stomp (all over)** |stahmp / STAHMP awl Ō vur| *v* To deliver a crushing defeat to. ORIGINS: From SE **stomp** meaning "to come down hard on with one's foot."

**stomp on** |STAHMP ahn| *n* To beat up; to defeat; to overcome. ORIGINS: From SE stomp meaning "to come down hard on with one's foot."

**stone-broke/stony-broke** |STŌN BRŌK / STŌN ē BRŌK| *adj* Having no money.

**Stop crowding me!** |stahp kroud ing mē| *excl* Stop pressuring me! Back off! Get out of my personal space! Give me time (to make a decision or accomplish a task) on my own!

**story, the** |*thu* STAWR ē| *n* The essential outline of *st*.

**Stow it!** |STŌ it| *excl* Be quiet! ORIGINS: From SE **stow** meaning "to put baggage or cargo away." USAGE ALERT: Usually used with intent to denigrate or insult and understood as such.

**strapped (for cash)** |strapt / STRAPT fawr KASH| *adj* Broke.

**streak** |strēk| *v* To move with great speed; to move so fast that one's image is blurred to viewers.

**strike it lucky** |STRĪK it LUK ē| *v* To suddenly enjoy great good fortune.

**strike oil** |STRĪK OIL| *v* To prosper; to find (or sometimes do) *st* that insures one's financial future.

**string puller** |STRING PUL ur| *n* A manipulator; a person who secretly influences people or organizations.

**strong-arm** |STRAHNG AHRM| *v* To influence *sb* through threats of violence; to coerce; to use physical force to influence *sb*.

**stuck on** |STUK ahn| *adj* Very attracted to; devoted to.

**stuck-up** |STUK up| *adj* Arrogant; snobbish.

**Stuff and nonsense!** |STUF and NAWN sens| *excl* I don't believe it/you!

**Stuff it!** |STUF it| *excl* Be quiet! ORIGINS: From the idea of stuffing up *sb's* mouth to ensure silence. USAGE ALERT: Usually used with intent to denigrate or insult and understood as such.

**stumblebum** |STUM bul BUM| *n* A loser; an inept, useless person. USAGE ALERT: Usually used with intent to denigrate or insult and understood as such.

**stupe** |stūp| *n* An idiot. ORIGINS: Shortened from SE **stupid**. USAGE ALERT: Usually used with intent to denigrate or insult and understood as such.

**stupidhead** |STŪP id hed| *n* A fool; a person who is clueless. ORIGINS: From SE **stupid** and slang suffix **-head**. USAGE ALERT: Usually used with intent to denigrate or insult and understood as such.

**suck it up** |SUK it UP| *v* To continue in the face of difficulties; to persevere; to endure or cope.

**suck up** |SUK up| *n* A flatterer; a toady.

**suck up (to *sb*)** |suk UP / suk UP tū *sb*| *v* To flatter and otherwise make an attempt to ingratiate oneself; to be obsequious.

**sucker**[1] |SUK ur| *n* A gullible person; a dupe. ORIGINS: From obsolete SE **sucker** meaning "an unweaned baby," whether human or animal, thus, "an innocent." USAGE ALERT: People who know that other words with the letter sequence s-u-c-k come from shortening the phrase **suck dick** or **cocksucker** may mistakenly think that this one does as well. This may result in people finding this word objectionable despite its innocence (pun intended). Nevertheless, it is usually used with intent to denigrate or insult and understood as such.

**sucker**[2] |SUK ur| *n* Any nameless object, or object for which one cannot remember the name. ORIGINS: This noun apparently actually does come from **cocksucker**, though its meaning bears no marks of the relationship. USAGE ALERT: Many people use this word without reference to its origins and, often, without knowing them. This can lead to very different interpretations of proper use, as well as drawing strong objections, especially when children are using the word or within earshot.

**sucker for, be a** |u SUK ur fawr| *v* To be attracted to something indiscriminately. ORIGINS: From obsolete SE **sucker** meaning "an unweaned baby," whether human or animal, thus, "an innocent." USAGE INFO: A sucker is someone who is generally gullible. To be a sucker for (*sh/st*) is to be undiscriminating/gullible in a specific case, specified by the object of the preposition *for*, e.g., "He's a sucker for sentimental movies." USAGE ALERT: People who know that other words with the letter sequence s u c k come from shortening the phrase **suck dick** or **cocksucker** may mistakenly think that this one does as well. This may result in people finding this word objectionable despite the fact that there is no etymological connection.

**sucker punch** |SUK ur punch| *v* To punch without warning or provocation. ORIGINS: From slang **sucker** meaning "a person who is deceived" and SE **punch**.

**sucks to be you. It** |it suks tū bē YŪ| *excl* I don't care; that's too bad. USAGE INFO: The phrase can be used sarcastically. It can also be used to offer commiseration on someone's suffering.

**sucky** |SUK ē| *adj* Awful, unpleasant; causing difficulty. ORIGINS: Apparently another example in which a form of suck is *not* related to **cocksucker**. USAGE ALERT: Anyone who does connect this word to **cocksucker** may find it objectionable.

**Sugar!** |SHŎŎG ur| *excl* An interjection expressing anger, frustration, dismay, surprise, etc. ORIGINS: Euphemism for **shit!**

**sulks** |sulks| *n* A fit of temper; sullen withdrawal. ORIGINS: Back-formation from SE **sulky**.

**Sup?, 'Sup?** |sup / tsup| *phr* How are you? ORIGINS: Abbreviated form of Wassup?—itself an altered form of **What's up?** USAGE INFO: Either pronunciation can be used with either spelling (or other, alternative spellings).

**super(duper)** |SŪ pur / SŪ pur DŪ pur| *adj* Excellent; wonderful. ORIGINS: From slang **super** with reduplication.

**superfly** |SŪ pur FLĪ| *adj* Excellent; superior. ORIGINS: From slang **super** and slang **fly** meaning "sophisticated."

**Sure as hell!** |shur az HEL| *excl* Most certainly. ORIGINS: The idea is that the existence of hell can be relied on as absolutely certain.

**Sure as shit!** |shur az SHIT| *excl* Most certainly. ORIGINS: The idea is that the existence of excrement can be relied on as absolutely certain. USAGE ALERT: The use of **shit** in this phrase will make it objectionable in some contexts and to some people.

S

**Sure as shootin'!** |shur az SHŪT in| *excl* Most certainly. ORIGINS: The idea is that firearms are reliable and so is whatever's being guaranteed.

**Sure as the devil!** |shur az *thu* DEV ul| *excl* Most certainly. ORIGINS: The idea is that the existence of the devil can be relied on as absolutely certain. USAGE ALERT: The use of **devil** in this phrase will make it objectionable in some contexts and to some people.

**sure bet** |SHUR BET| *n* A certainty; a bet that can't be lost.

**Sure enough!** |shur u NUF| *excl* As one would expect.

**Sure-nuff!** |shur NUF| *excl* As one would expect. ORIGINS: Shortened from the phrase Sure enough.

**sure shot** |SHUR SHAHT| *n* A certainty; a shot that is certain to hit its mark.

**sure thing** |SHUR THING| *n* A certainty; a bet that can't be lost.

**Sure thing!** |SHUR thing| *excl* An interjection signaling agreement; Of course! Certainly! Definitely!

**suss (out)** |SUS out| *v* To grasp; to understand; to figure out. ORIGINS: Shortened form of SE suspect.

**swallow** |SWAHL ō| *v* To accept a (false/deceptive) story.

**swallow hook, line, and sinker** |swahl ō HŎŎK LĪN und SINGK ur| *v* To accept in every respect, ignoring every warning sign.

**swank** |swangk| *adj* Pretentious.

**swank(y)** |swangk / SWANG kē| *adj* Elegant; sophisticated; classy. ORIGINS: From slang verb swank, originally meaning "to swagger."

**sweat blood** |SWET BLUD| *v* To endure mental anguish. ORIGINS: An allusion to The New Testament, Luke 22:44 telling of Jesus in the Garden of Gethsemane, which says, "His sweat was, as it were, great drops of blood falling down to the ground." King James Version.

**sweat it out** |SWET it OUT| *v* To persevere; to endure for the sake of results.

**sweep** |swēp| *v* To win a contest or competition by winning at every stage along the way.

**sweep one off one's feet** |SWĒP wun AWF wunz FĒT| *v* To attract *sb*; to cause *sb* to fall in love.

**sweet** |swēt| *adj* Excellent; superb. USAGE INFO: Often used as an exclamation of approval: Sweet!

**sweet on** |SWĒT ahn| *adj* In love with.

**swine** |swīn| *n* A contemptible person.

**swipe** |swīp| *v* To hit; to strike, especially in a glancing blow.

**TAF** That's all folks!

**TAFN, TA4N** That's all for now.

**TAH** Take a hike.

**TARFU** Things are really fucked up.

**TC** Take care.

**TCOY** Take care of yourself.

**TDM** Too damn many.

**TILII** Tell it like it is.

**TLK 2 U L8R** Talk to you later.

**TPTB** The powers that be. USAGE INFO: Source of the parody "the people to blame."

**TS** Tough shit.

**TTFN** Ta ta for now.

**TTMF** Ta ta MOFO! Short for **Ta ta, mother fucker!**

**TTYL** Talk to you later.

**TTYS** Talk to you soon.

**Ta ta! Ta-ta!** |tah tah| *excl* Goodbye. USAGE INFO: Self-conscious, humorous use is what renders this archaic phrase as slang.

**Ta ta, MOFO!** |tah tah MŌ fō| *excl* Goodbye, mother fucker. ORIGINS: From a combination of the archaic farewell **ta-ta** with the current slang **MOFO**, an altered form of **mother fucker**, a general term of extreme abuse, and considered one of the, if not *the,* worst insults one can make to a man, since it suggests that he has an incestuous (i.e., sexual) relationship with his mother. Seems to have experienced an increase in popularity after it was used by Texas Governor Rick Perry in speaking to a reporter on June 21, 2005. A video was posted on YouTube, Governor Perry made several "Quote of the Day" lists, and inspired a tee-shirt with the quotation and his likeness. USAGE ALERT: This word carries implications not only about the person referred to, but also about his mother. The inclusion of **MOFO** will make this phrase objectionable in some contexts and to some people. Usually used with intent to denigrate or insult and understood as such.

**Ta-dah!** |tu DAH| *excl* Pay attention to this remarkable thing/accomplishment! ORIGINS: Imitative of a fanfare, for example, one played when circus performers have achieved a stunt.

T

**-tacular** |TAK yū lur| *sfx* A spectacular example of; an extreme example of. ORIGINS: By extension of SE spectacular. USAGE INFO: The first meaning occurs in punning constructions like **spooktacular**, often used in connection with ghosts and Halloween; the second in constructions like **craptacular**.

**tad** |tad| *n* A very small quantity.

**take a chill pill** |tāk u CHIL pil| *v* To relax; to calm down. ORIGINS: From slang chill pill, an imaginary medicine to calm one down. USAGE INFO: Often used as an imperative.

**take a dig at** |tāk u DIG at| *v* To make a taunting or sarcastic remark to *sb*.

**take a dive** |tāk u DĪV| *v* To purposely lose a fight; to fail. ORIGINS: From boxing, referring to the boxer who "dives" to the floor without actually having been knocked out.

**Take a flying fuck!** |TĀK u FLĪ ing FUK| *v* A contemptuous dismissal. ORIGINS: Figurative use of slang **fuck** meaning "sexual intercourse." USAGE ALERT: Usually used with intent to be rude and understood as such. In addition, the inclusion of the word **fuck** in the phrase will render it objectionable in some contexts and to some people.

**Take a hike!** |TĀK u HĪK| *excl* A contemptuous dismissal. USAGE ALERT: Usually used with intent to be rude and understood as such.

**take a licking/beating** |tāk u LIK ing / tāk u BĒT ing| *v* To be defeated in a fight or competition; to get the worst of an argument; to receive a harsh reprimand or scolding; to lose a lot of money.

**take a powder** |tāk u POU dur| *v* To run away.

**take a shine to** |tāk u SHĪN tū| *v* To discover that one likes *st* very much; to find appealing.

**take a squint at** |tāk u SKWINT at| *v* To examine. ORIGINS: From SE squint meaning "to screw up one's eyes in order to take a careful look."

**take a swipe at** |tāk u SWĪP at| *v* To throw a punch at; to criticize unfairly or unexpectedly.

**take forty winks** |tāk fawr tē WINGKS| *v* To take a short nap during the daytime.

**take it easy** |tāk it Ē zē| *v* To relax.

**take it on the lam** |TĀK it ahn *thu* LAM| *v* To run away, often to escape from the police and a possible jail sentence. ORIGINS: From slang lam meaning "to run away." Re-popularized by, for example, *The Simpsons* episode "Marge on the Lam" (1993).

**Take off!** |TĀK AWF| *excl* Go away!

**take on** |TĀK ahn| *v* To challenge.

**take oneself off** |TĀK wun self AWF| *v* To leave; to depart.

**take *sb* apart** |tāk *sb* u PAHRT| *v* To give *sb* a severe beating; to reprimand strongly.

**take *sb* down** |TĀK *sb* DOUN| *v* To defeat; to humiliate.

**take *sb* down a peg (or two)** |TĀK *sb* DOUN u peg / TĀK *sb* doun u PEG awr tū| *v* To humiliate. ORIGINS: A counterpart to the slang phrase come down a peg (or two).

**take *sb* for a ride** |tāk *sb* fawr u RĪD| *v* To deceive *sb*, usually in order to get money.

**take *sb* out** |tāk *sb* OUT| *v* To kill; murder.

**take *sb* to the cleaners** |TĀK *sb* tū *th*u KLĒN urz| *v* To trick *sb* out of all his/her money.

**take the bait** |TĀK *th*u BĀT| *v* To accept a deceptive story; to fall for a scheme.

**take the cake** |TĀK *th*u KĀK| *v* To achieve top ranking; to win the prize.

**take the mickey out of** |tāk *th*u MIK ē out uv| *v* To tease or mock. ORIGINS: From British English.

**take the piss out of** |tāk *th*u PIS out uv| *v* To tease in an aggressive way.

**Take your finger out (of your ass/butt)!** |tāk yo͞or FIN gur out / tāk yo͞or FIN gur out uv yo͞or AS / tāk yo͞or FIN gur out uv yo͞or BUT| *excl See* TAKE YOUR THUMB OUT (OF YOUR ASS/BUTT)!

**Take your thumb out (of your ass/butt)!** |tāk yo͞or THUM out / tāk yo͞or THUM out uv yo͞or AS / tāk yo͞or THUM out uv yo͞or BUT| *excl* Stop sitting around or messing around and get ready for serious action. ORIGINS: From slang **ass** meaning "the rear end or buttocks" or slang **butt**, a euphemism for **ass**. The suggestion is of someone doing something thoroughly worthless. USAGE ALERT: The crudeness of the image plus the reference to the buttocks or rear end will make this expression objectionable in some contexts and to some people.

**taking it easy** |TĀK ing it Ē zē| *adj* Relaxing.

**talk big** |TAWK BIG| *v* To exaggerate one's accomplishments or prospects.

**talk *sb*'s ear off** |TAWK *sb*'s IR awf| *v* To talk tediously and unrelentingly.

**talk the hind leg off a donkey** |TAWK *th*u HĪND leg ahf u DAWN kē| *v* To characteristically talk to the point of exhausting the audience's interest and patience.

**talk through one's hat** |TAWK thrū wunz HAT| *v* To talk nonsense; to speak untruths; to lie; to boast or exaggerate for effect.

**talk turkey** |tawk TUR kē| *v* To speak openly and without reserve.

**talk up a storm** |TAWK up u STAWRM| *v* To talk loudly or at length. ORIGINS: From comparison of the breath of talkers to the wind in a storm.

**tall order** |TAWL AWR dur| *n* An extremely difficult project or problem; an exceptionally demanding task.

**tan** |tan| *v* To hit repeatedly. ORIGINS: From SE **tan** meaning "the process of turning hides to leather." USAGE INFO: Most often used in the phrase "to tan *sb's* hide."

**tangle** |TANG gul| *n* A fight.

**tank** |tangk| *v* To decline or fail suddenly. ORIGINS: From a play on words, involving SE **tank** meaning "a swimming pool" and the slang expression **take a dive** meaning "to purposely lose."

**tapped out** |TAPT out| *adj* Broke; unable to place any more bets. ORIGINS: From slang **tap out** meaning "to reach the end of one's money."

**-tastic** |TAS tik| *sfx* A fantastic example of; stunningly awful. ORIGINS: By extension of SE **fantastic**. USAGE INFO: The first meaning occurs in constructions like **funtastic**; the second in constructions like **craptastic**, and is generally used ironically.

**tatty** |TAT ē| *adj* Worn; dilapidated; shabby; tattered.

**team up** |TĒM up| *v* To join together spontaneously to form a team.

**tear into** *sb* |ter IN tū *sb*| *v* To make a harsh or violent physical or verbal attack on *sb*, often impetuously.

**tear** *sb* **a new asshole/one** |TER *sb* u NŪ AS hōl / TER *sb* u NŪ wun| *v* To attack *sb* savagely, physically or verbally. ORIGINS: From slang **asshole** meaning "anus." USAGE ALERT: Because of the reference to the human rear end or buttocks, as well as the graphic depiction of violence (even if **asshole** is replaced with euphemistic **one**), this expression will be found objectionable in some contexts and by some people.

**tear** *sb/st* **down** |TER *sb/st* doun| *v* To criticize; to attack verbally.

**tearing one's hair out** |TER ing wunz HER out| *adj* Greatly distressed; extremely upset.

**tee off** |TĒ AWF| *v* To get started. ORIGINS: From the manner of starting a game of golf.

**tee** *sb* **off** |TĒ *sb* AWF| *v* To irritate *sb*; to anger *sb*. ORIGINS: Possibly from the first letter of **tick off**.

**teed off** |TĒD awf| *adj* Irritated; annoyed. ORIGINS: Possibly from the first letter of **ticked off**, in the same way that **peed off** is an alteration of **pissed off**.

**teeny(-weeny)**\* |TĒ nē / TĒ nē WĒ nē| *adj* Very small.
 • teensy(-weensy) |TĒN sē / TĒN sē WĒn sē|

**tell it like it is** |TEL it līk it IZ| *v* To speak openly and honestly.

**Tell it/that to the marines!** |tel it/that tū *thu* mu RĒNZ| *excl* I don't believe it/you! You can't fool me! ORIGINS: A shortened version of the saying, "He may tell that to the marines, but the sailors will not believe him."

**Tell me another (one)!** | tel mē u NU*TH* ur / tel mē u NU*TH* ur wun| *excl* I don't believe it/you!

**tell *sb* off** |TEL *sb* AWF| *v* To reprimand *sb*.

**tell *sb* where to get off\*** |TEL *sb* WER tū get AWF| *v* To express one's anger to *sb*, in no uncertain terms and with little restraint in tone or language. ORIGINS: Euphemism for "tell *sb* to go to hell." **Hell** is where they either get off (like a station on public transportation) or go.
• tell *sb* where to go |TEL *sb* WER tū GŌ|

**Ten-four!** |TEN FAWR| *excl* Message received and understood. ORIGINS: From US Police 10-codes.

**terminally stupid** |TUR mu nul ē STŪ pid| *adj* Extremely stupid. ORIGINS: The word **terminally** is used to refer to medical conditions that are incurable or can lead to death. Appropriated to this slang use, it suggests that the person in question is unbelievably stupid. USAGE ALERT: Usually used with intent to denigrate or insult and understood as such.

**terminate** |TUR mi nāt| *v* To kill; murder.

**testy\*** |TES tē| *adj* Irritated; exasperated; peevish.
• tetchy |TE chē| *adj*

**tetched** |techt| *adj See* TOUCHED.

**tetched in the head** |TECHT in *thu* HED| *adj See* TOUCHED IN THE HEAD.

**That tears it!** |*TH*AT TERZ it| *excl* I am losing my ability to cope! Everything is ruined! Cry of frustration, extreme annoyance, or exasperation. ORIGINS: The idea seems to be that having been "torn," whatever it is is useless or ruined. USAGE INFO: Usually said after a series of events have built up the emotion prompting the exclamation or in response to something cataclysmic.

**That's all folks!** |*that*S AWL fōks| *excl* Casual goodbye, most often to a group. ORIGINS: From the closing line characteristically given at the end of a Looney Tune short, most often (but not exclusively) by Porky Pig.

**That's all for now.** |*that*S AWL fawr nou| *excl* See you later! To be continued... ORIGINS: Of unknown origins, but popularized by Paul McCartney's use as a closing lyric in a song he composed spontaneously in a July 28, 2005 concert at Abbey Road (*Live at Abbey Road*, 2005): "That's all for now! You've got to go home!"

**That's torn it!** |*that*s tawrn it| *excl* An interjection of surprise and dismay when *st* unexpected has upset one's plans. ORIGINS: Primarily British, but spreading in US usage.

**the deuce** |*thu* DŪS| *adv* A sentence modifier. ORIGINS: Euphemism for **the hell**; SE **hell** being the place where the devil resides and **deuce** being a euphemism for **devil**. USAGE INFO: Used following interrogative adverbs (*who, what, where, when, why, how*) to convey surprise, shock, and/or dismay, as in "What the deuce are you doing in Wyoming?" "How the deuce did you get in my house?" "Where the deuce do you think you're going with my barometer?" or "Why the deuce aren't you doing your homework, like I told you?" USAGE ALERT: The inclusion of **deuce** will make this expression objectionable in some contexts and to some people, but usually less so than **devil**.

**the devil** |*thu* DEV ul| *adv* A sentence modifier. ORIGINS: Euphemism for **the hell**; SE **hell** being the place where the devil resides. USAGE INFO: Used following interrogative adverbs (*who, what, where, when, why, how*) to convey surprise, shock, and/or dismay, as in "What the devil is this stain on the floor?" "How the devil am I supposed to read this scrawl?" "Where the devil is my favorite tee-shirt?" or "Who the devil are you?" USAGE ALERT: The inclusion of **devil** will make this expression objectionable in some contexts and to some people.

**the dickens** |*thu* DIK unz| *adv* A sentence modifier. ORIGINS: Euphemism for **the devil**. Slang **dickens** is an altered form of SE **devil**. USAGE INFO: Used following interrogative adverbs (*who, what, where, when, why, how*) to convey surprise, shock, and/or dismay, as in "What the dickens do you want now?" USAGE ALERT: The inclusion of a reference to the devil will make this term objectionable in some contexts and to some people.

**the fuck** |*thu* FUK| *adv* A sentence modifier. ORIGINS: Figurative use of slang **fuck** meaning "sexual intercourse." USAGE INFO: Used following interrogative adverbs (*who, what, where, when, why, how*) to convey surprise, shock, and/or dismay, as in "What the fuck is the matter with you?" Also used in expressions such as **Get the fuck out**. USAGE ALERT: The inclusion of **fuck** will make this expression objectionable in some contexts and to some people.

**the heck** |*thu* HEK| *adv* Sentence modifier. ORIGINS: Euphemism for **the hell**. Heck is an altered form of and euphemism for **hell**. USAGE INFO: Used following interrogative adverbs (*who, what, where, when, why, how*) to express surprise, shock, or dismay, etc., as in "What the heck am I supposed to do now?" USAGE ALERT: The euphemism **heck** in this phrase will soften it somewhat, but it may still be objectionable in some contexts and to some people.

**the hell** |*thu* HEL| *adv* Sentence modifier. ORIGINS: Figurative use of SE **hell** meaning "the alternative to heaven; the realm of the devil." USAGE INFO: Used following interrogative adverbs (*who, what, where, when, why, how*) to convey surprise, shock, and/or dismay, as in "What the hell is going on here?" USAGE ALERT: The inclusion of **hell** will make this expression objectionable in some contexts and to some people.

**thickhead** |THIK hed| *n* A fool; a stupid person. ORIGINS: From SE **thick** and slang suffix **-head**. USAGE ALERT: Usually used with intent to denigrate or insult and understood as such.

**thickie\*** |THIK ē| *n* A stupid person. ORIGINS: From slang **thick** meaning "dull or stupid." USAGE ALERT: Usually used with intent to denigrate or insult and understood as such.
• thicko |THIK ō|

**thingy, thingie\*** |THING ē| *n* A substitute to use when you don't know or can't remember *st's* name or choose not to name *st.*
• thingamabob, thingumabob |THING u mu bahb|
• thingamajig |THING u mu jig|
• thingummy |THING u mē|

**This sucks!** |*th*is SUKS| *excl* To identify something as worthless, contemptible, or maddening. ORIGINS: Figurative use of slang verb **suck**, short for **This sucks dick!** USAGE ALERT: Many people use this word without reference to its origins and, often, without knowing them. This can lead to very different interpretations of proper use, as well as it drawing strong objections, especially when children are using the word or are within earshot.

**thrash** |thrash| *v* To beat soundly.

**throw** |thrō| *v* To deliberately lose a competition. ORIGINS: From professional sports and the SE term **throw away**.

**throw a fit** |THRŌ u FIT| *v* To fly into a rage. USAGE INFO: Compare with **have a fit**.

**throw a hail Mary** |THRŌ u hāl MER ē| *v* To make a last-ditch effort that has little chance, but is the only opportunity for success. ORIGINS: From Catholic prayer called "Hail Mary" used in basketball and football jargon for a long throw in the final seconds of the quarter or game that is only likely to succeed with the aid of divine help, but if it does, may tie or win the game (or at least help assuage the loser's egos).

**throw forty fits** |THRŌ FAWR tē FITS| *v* To fly into a rage. USAGE INFO: Compare with **have forty fits**.

**throw in one's hand** |THRŌ in wunz HAND| *v* To give in; to surrender. ORIGINS: From the gesture of folding in a card game.

**throw in the sponge/towel** |THRŌ in *th*u SPUNJ / THRŌ in *th*u TOU ul| *v* To give in; to capitulate to demands. ORIGINS: From boxing practice, in which either of these items is thrown into the ring as a gesture of accepting defeat.

**throw *sb* out on his/her ass** |THRŌ *sb* out ahn hiz/hur AS| *v* To get rid of *sb* unceremoniously; to dismiss *sb*; to literally throw *sb* off the premises. ORIGINS: From slang **ass** meaning "the rear end or buttocks." USAGE ALERT: The inclusion of the word **ass** in the phrase will render it objectionable in some contexts and to some people.

**throw *sb* out on his/her ear** |THRŌ *sb* out ahn hiz/hur IR| *v* To get rid of *sb* unceremoniously; to dismiss *sb*; to literally throw *sb* off the premises. ORIGINS: The reference to SE **ear** indicates that the person doesn't land on his/her feet, but falls full-length on the ground.

**thrown for a loop** |THRŌN fawr u LŪP| *adj* Surprised and disconcerted. USAGE INFO: Used of people.

**thud** |*th*ud| *v* To strike a blow that makes a dull sound. ORIGINS: Imitative of the sound of a blow.

**thumb down** |THUM DOUN| *v* To vote against; to ostracize. ORIGINS: From the practice of voting using thumbs to signal one's choice. Re-popularized by film critics Roger Ebert and Gene Siskel using the thumbs to signal their critical response to movies.

**thump** |thump| *v* To strike a blow that makes a dull sound; to beat thoroughly. ORIGINS: Imitative of the sound of a blow.

**thunk** |thunk| *v* To strike a blow that makes a dull sound. ORIGINS: Imitative of the sound of a blow.

**thwack** |thwak| *v* To strike or hit with *st* flat. ORIGINS: A variation on **whack**. Imitative of the sound of a blow.

**tick** |tik| *n* An insignificant, but annoying person; an unpleasant, but irritating person, usually male. ORIGINS: From SE **tick** meaning "a parasite."

**tick *sb* off** |TIK *sb* awf| *v* To irritate or annoy *sb*. ORIGINS: Possibly a euphemism for **piss *sb* off**.

**ticked (off)** |tikt / TIKT awf| *adj* Irritated; annoyed. ORIGINS: This seems to be related to military jargon **tick off** meaning "a scolding."

**tidy sum** |TĪ dē SUM| *n* A large amount of money.

**tie into** |TĪ IN tū| *v* To attack *sb* vigorously, either physically or verbally.

**tiff** |tif| *n* A quarrel over *st* trivial.

**tight ass** |TĪT as| *n* A stingy person. ORIGINS: From slang **ass** meaning "the rear end or buttocks." USAGE INFO: Also used for a person who is very strait-laced and proper; an easily offended person. USAGE ALERT: Usually used with intent to denigrate or insult and understood as such. In addition, the inclusion of the word **ass** in the phrase will render it objectionable in some contexts and to some people.

**tight spot** |TĪT SPAHT| *n* A predicament; a difficult situation.

**tight with** |TĪT with| *adj* Very friendly with. ORIGINS: From slang **tight** meaning "very close."

**tightwad** |TĪT wad| *n* A miserly person.

**till one is blue in the face** |TIL wun is BLŪ in *th*u FĀS| *adv* To a great degree or extent, but without notable effect. ORIGINS: One turns blue in the face when experiencing oxygen deprivation through holding one's breath or making an intense effort. USAGE INFO: This expression is used for a determined effort that is frustrated and causes exasperation. It follows the verb it modifies.

**tip one's hand** |TIP wunz HAND| *v* To reveal one's plans, often unintentionally.

**tip** *sb* **off** |tip *sb* AWF| *v* To give insider information (often of illegal activities) to *sb* who wouldn't ordinarily have access to it, for example, law enforcement officers, competitors, or investors.

**to beat the band** |tu BĒT *thu* BAND| *adv* To a great degree or extent as a result of intensive effort. ORIGINS: A band plays loudly, and one makes oneself heard only through great effort. USAGE INFO: Follows the verb it modifies, as in "cheering to beat the band."

**to hell and back** |tu HEL und bak| *adv* To the point of no return; thoroughly. ORIGINS: Hell—the underworld—is conceived as being a great distance away. Figurative use of SE **hell** meaning "the alternative to heaven; the realm of the devil." USAGE INFO: Follows the verb it modifies. USAGE ALERT: The inclusion of the word **hell** will make this expression objectionable in some contexts and to some people.

**to the max** |tū *thu* MAX| *adv* Completely. ORIGINS: Shortened from maximum. USAGE INFO: Follows the verb it modifies.

**to-do** |tū DŪ| *n* A commotion; a quarrel.

**toady** |TŌD ē| *n* A flatterer. USAGE ALERT: Usually used with intent to denigrate or insult and understood as such.

**toe the mark/line** |TŌ *thu* MAHRK / TŌ *thu* LĪN| *v* To behave in a respectable and respectful manner (with the inference that one has not behaved so in the past).

**tommyrot** |TAHM ē raht| *n* Complete nonsense; untruths; lies.

**tons** |tūns| *n* A great deal.

**too much** |TŪ MUCH| *adj* Excellent; unbelievably good.

**Toodle-oo!** |TŪ du LŪ| *excl* Goodbye. ORIGINS: An archaic, originally British, phrase, originating in the magazine *Punch* and connected to the verb **toddle**. USAGE INFO: Self-conscious, humorous use is what renders this archaic phrase as slang.

**toot one's own horn/trumpet** |TŪT wunz ōn HAWRN / TŪT wunz ōn TRUM pit| *v* To boast or brag. ORIGINS: From the practice of announcing important people with a fanfare played on brass instruments.

**top banana** |TAHP bu NA nu| *n* The leader, head, or principal person involved. ORIGINS: From vaudeville acts in which the lead comedian was awarded this title, while the straight man was the "second banana."

**top brass** |TAHP BRAS| *n* High ranking officials or senior officers in business, government, or military settings. ORIGINS: All from **brass hat**, a senior officer in the police, so named for the adornment (gold braid, for example) on their helmets. USAGE INFO: Can be singular, but usually plural.

**top dog** |TAHP DAWG| *n* The leader; in a competition, the winner. ORIGINS: From the "sport" of dog fighting: the winning dog, and the one most worth betting on, is the "top dog."

T

**top gun** |TAHP GUN| *n* The most capable, the most prestigious person; the highest ranking person.

**topnotch** |TAHP NAHCH| *adj* Excellent; highest-rated.

**tops** |tahps| *adj* Excellent.

**torqued** |tawrkt| *adj* Angry.

**toss in one's hand** |TAHS in wunz HAND| *v* To give in; to surrender. ORIGINS: From the gesture of folding in a card game.

**toss in the sponge/towel** |TAHS in *thu* SPUNJ / TAHS in *thu* TOU ul| *v* To give in; to capitulate to demands. ORIGINS: From boxing, in which either of these items is tossed into the ring as a gesture of accepting defeat.

**toss *sb* out** |TAHS *sb* OUT| *v* To get rid of *sb* unceremoniously; to dismiss *sb*; to literally throw *sb* off the premises.

**touch *sb* for** |TOUCH *sb* fawr| *v* To beg for a loan.

**touched** |tucht| *adj* Mentally unbalanced. USAGE ALERT: Often used with intent to denigrate or insult and understood as such. This way of speaking about *sb's* mental health may be considered insensitive and therefore objectionable in some contexts and by some people.

**touched in the head** |TUCHT in *thu* HED| *adj* Mentally unbalanced. USAGE ALERT: Often used with intent to denigrate or insult and understood as such. This way of speaking about *sb's* mental health may be considered insensitive and therefore objectionable in some contexts and by some people.

**touchy** |TUCH ē| *adj* Overly sensitive; easily offended; prone to anger.

**tough it out** |TUF it OUT| *adj* To persevere.

**Tough luck!** |TUF LUK| *excl* The tone of voice greatly influences the meaning of this response to *sb* else's bad fortune: It ranges from "I don't much care (about your bad luck)!" to "I'm sorry to hear (about your bad luck)! and Wish you well!" ORIGINS: From slang tough meaning "unfortunate."

**tough nut** |TUF NUT| *n* A determined or unpleasant person. ORIGINS: By extension from literal difficulty in getting the nut meat out of the shell. USAGE INFO: Sometimes used in a longer form a hard/tough nut to crack, but that generally means "a difficult problem to solve."

**Tough shit!** |TUF SHIT| *excl* I don't care at all (about your bad luck)! ORIGINS: From slang tough meaning "unfortunate" and **shit** meaning "excrement." USAGE ALERT: The inclusion of the word **shit** in the phrase will render it objectionable in some contexts and to some people.

**tough spot** |TUF SPAHT| *n* A difficult situation. USAGE INFO: Used in phrases like "in a tough spot."

**tough stuff** |TUF STUF| *n* Serious problems; difficult circumstances to deal with and/or get through.

**trash¹** |trash| *n* Empty or meaningless words or ideas; untruths; lies.

**trash²** |trash| *n* One or more contemptible or worthless people. USAGE INFO: Trash is not a countable noun, so its reference can be either singular or plural. It takes a singular verb, as in "Wait till the trash goes home, and then we'll have our picnic." USAGE ALERT: Usually used with intent to denigrate or insult and understood as such.

**trash¹** |trash| *v* To attack verbally: to insult, denigrate, or malign.

**trash²** |trash| *v* To destroy property by purposely breaking or damaging it beyond repair; to render into trash.

**trendy** |TREND ē| *adj* In line with the latest fashions.

**trick out** |trik out| *v* To improve the appearance of; to glamorize.

**tripe** |trīp| *n* Nonsense; untruths; lies.

**truck** |truk| *v* To move on steadily; to travel on.

**tsuris, tsouris, tsoris** |TSUR is| *n* Distress; trouble. ORIGINS: From Yiddish tsores.

**tuck in one's tail** |TUK in wunz TĀL| *v* To be ashamed and humiliated. ORIGINS: From the behavior of a dog that has been severely scolded. USAGE INFO: Also, put one's tail between one's legs.

**tuckered out** |TUK urd out| *adj* Worn out; exhausted.

**tumble to** |TUM bul tū| *v* Figure out; discover.

**turd** |turd| *n* A contemptible person. ORIGINS: Figurative use of slang **turd** meaning "a piece of excrement."

**turkey** |TURK ē| *n* An unappealing, worthless person.

**turn chicken** |turn CHIK un| *v* To become afraid; to lose one's nerve.

**turn in** |turn IN| *v* To go to bed.

**turn off** |TURN AWF| *v* To cause disgust, repulsion, boredom, and/or loss of interest.

**turn on** |TURN ahn| *v* To invite interest; to cause pleasure or excitement.

**turn one's stomach** |turn wunz STUM uk| *v* To disgust or repel.

**turn *sb* in** |turn *sb* IN| *v* To hand *sb* over to the relevant authorities.

**turn *sb* out** |TURN *sb* OUT| *v* To dismiss *sb*; to send *sb* away; to have *sb* escorted off the premises.

**turn the trick** |TURN *thu* TRIK| *v* To succeed; to have the desired result. USAGE INFO: Make sure to distinguish this from **turn tricks**, which means "to engage in sexual activity for pay."

**turn up one's toes** |TURN up wunz TŌZ| *v* To die. ORIGINS: Presumably from the position of the body in the casket.

**turn up the heat** |TURN up *thu* HĒT| *v* To increase pressure on *sb* (in order to coerce some desired end).

**turn yellow** |turn YEL Ō| *v* To become afraid; to lose heart.

**turned off** |turnd AWF| *v* Bored; uninterested; unexcited; disgusted.

**turned on by, be** |turnd AHN bī| *v* To be (sexually) attracted to; to be excited about. USAGE INFO: **Be turned on** without the preposition can indicate a general state, unconnected to any particular external stimulus. The inclusion of the preposition *by* indicates a specific person/object of attraction.

**twat** |twaht| *n* A contemptible person, usually a woman. ORIGINS: Figurative use of slang twat meaning "vulva." USAGE ALERT: This term is generally regarded as one of the most objectionable words in English and is most often used with specific intent to give offense.

**twerp, twirp** |twurp| *n* An idiot; a fool. USAGE ALERT: Usually used with intent to denigrate or insult and understood as such.

**twist *sb*'s arm** |TWIST *sb*'s AHRM| *v* To coerce using threats or physical force; to persuade by underhanded means.

**twit** |twit| *n* A fool; a person who is silly and annoying. USAGE ALERT: Usually used with intent to denigrate or insult and understood as such.

**twitchy** |TWICH ē| *adj* Agitated; nervous; ill-at-ease.

**two-bit** |TŪ bit| *adj* An inferior item or trivial sum; insignificant.

**UCWAP** Up [a] creek without a paddle.

**UG2BK** You've got to be kidding!

**Ucky!** |UK ē| *excl* Sound to express disgust.

**Ugh!** |ug| *excl* Sound to express disgust.

**Uh-huh!** |u HU| *excl* Yes. USAGE INFO: A retort to negative rejoinders: **Nu-uh! Uh-uh!**, with which it can be said alternately.

**Uh-oh!** |U Ō| *excl* Sound to express the discovery of an error or mistake or dismay due to some other cause; sound to express concern or alarm.

**Uh-uh!** |U U| *excl* No. USAGE INFO: In a family with negative synonym **Nu-uh!** Both **Uh-uh!** and **Nu-uh!** can be used to respond to **Uh-huh!**

**umpteen** |UMP TĒN| *n* Dozens; i.e., a number of teens. ORIGINS: Said by some to have a military origin in WWI, with the nonspecific **um** replacing a specific number (e.g., four or seven) in order to maintain secrecy in communications.

**unflappable** |un FLAHP u bul| *adj* Enduringly calm; not easily upset.

**Unfuckingbelievable!** |UN FUK ing bu LĒV u bul| *excl* I'm shocked! ORIGINS: SE unbelievable with added emphasis from the infix **fucking**. USAGE ALERT: The use of **fucking** in this phrase will make it objectionable in some contexts and to some people.

**unreal** |un RĒL| *adj* Unbelievably excellent, impressive, etc.

**up** |UP| *adj* Excited and/or hopeful.

**up a creek*** |up u KRĒK| *phr* In serious trouble; facing unpleasant problems. ORIGINS: Euphemism for **up shit creek**.
• up a creek without a paddle |up u KRĒK with out u PAD ul|

**up against it** |UP u GENST it| *adj* In trouble; facing serious problems.

**up shit creek*** |up SHIT krēk| *adj* In serious trouble; facing unpleasant problems. ORIGINS: From SE up and slang **shit** meaning "excrement." USAGE ALERT: The inclusion of the word **shit** in the phrase will render it objectionable in some contexts and to some people.
• **up shit creek without a paddle** |up SHIT KRĒK with out u PAD ul|

**up the ass** |up thē AS| *adj* In excess; in extremely large amounts; many. ORIGINS: From slang **ass** meaning "the rear end or buttocks." USAGE ALERT: The inclusion of the word **ass** in the phrase will render it objectionable in some contexts and to some people.

**up the gazoo** |up thu gu ZŪ| *adj* In excess; in extremely large amounts; many. ORIGINS: Euphemism for **up the ass**, but, oddly, with more specificity, because **gazoo** is a slang term for SE anus. The euphemism **gazoo** in this phrase will soften it somewhat for most people, who don't know it's meaning, but it may still be objectionable in some contexts and to some people.

**up the wall** |up thu WAWL| *adj* Extremely angry, frustrated, or upset.

**up the wazoo** |up thu wah ZŪ| *adj* In excess; in extremely large amounts; many. ORIGINS: Euphemism for **up the ass**, but, oddly, with more specificity, because **wazoo** is a slang term for SE anus. The euphemism **wazoo** in this phrase will soften it somewhat for most people, who don't know it's meaning, but it may still be objectionable in some contexts and to some people.

**up to here with &lt;noun/pronoun&gt;** |up tū HIR with &lt;noun/pronoun&gt;| *adj* Possessing in very large amount; possessing in excess. USAGE INFO: Can be an unemotional statement of quantity, as in "You don't have to rush in to buy it: we're

U

up to here with them." The phrase can also mean "having such a large quantity that I'm fed-up," as in "I'm up to here with this constant bickering."

**up to scratch** |up tū SCRACH| *adj* Of acceptable quality; in good condition. ORIGINS: Figurative use of sports jargon from races in which **scratch** means "the line or marking indicating the starting line." USAGE INFO: *See* NOT UP TO SCRATCH.

**up to snuff** |up tū SNUF| *adj* Of acceptable quality; in good condition. ORIGINS: Either from the quality requirements for tobacco to be used as snuff or from the stimulating effects of snuff usage. USAGE INFO: *See* NOT UP TO SNUFF.

**up to the ass with <noun/pronoun>** |up tū thē AS with <noun/pronoun>| *adj* Possessing in very large amount; possessing in excess. ORIGINS: As an indicator of the height of <whatever it is> stacked around one, this phrase gives a slightly less graphic image than the similar **up the ass** and its euphemistic forms. From slang **ass** to refer to the rear end or buttocks. USAGE ALERT: The inclusion of the word **ass** in the phrase will render it objectionable in some contexts and to some people.

**up to the eyeballs with <noun/pronoun>** |up tū thē Ī bawls with <noun/pronoun>| *adj* Possessing in very large amount; possessing in excess. ORIGINS: As an indicator of the height of <whatever it is> stacked around one, this phrase gives a less graphic image than the very similar **up the ass** and its euphemisms, while suggesting a larger amount than **up to the ass with <noun/pronoun>**.

**Up yours!** |UP YŎORZ| *adj* A rude dismissal. ORIGINS: Shortened and altered form of slang **Stick it up your ass!** or similar phrases. USAGE ALERT: Usually used with intent to be rude and understood as such. In addition, the euphemistic shortening of this phrase will soften it somewhat, but it may still be objectionable in some contexts and to some people.

**upbeat** |UP bēt| *adj* Optimistic, positive.

**upfront, be** |UP FRUNT| *v* To be honest, transparent.

**uptight** |up TĪT| *adj* Annoyed; tense; edgy.

**VIP** |VĒ Ī PĒ| *n* An important or influential person. ORIGINS: Shortened form of Very Important Person.

**Vamoose!** |va MŪS| *excl* Go away! ORIGINS: From Spanish **vamos** meaning "let's go."

**vanilla** |vu NIL lu| *adj* Without adornment or extra trimmings: uninteresting; bland.

**varmint** |VAHR mint| *n* An undesirable person; a person who causes trouble or is obnoxious. ORIGINS: Figurative use of **varmint**, variation of SE **vermin** meaning "animals that are destructive or injurious to people and/or their possessions." USAGE ALERT: Usually used with intent to denigrate or insult and understood as such.

**veg** |vej| *v* To do nothing; to relax. ORIGINS: Shortened form of SE **vegetate**.

**Victory is mine!** |VIK tur ē iz MĪN| *excl* I win! ORIGINS: Popularized as a catchphrase of Stewart Gilligan "Stewie" Griffin on the animated television series *Family Guy* (1999–present), also a video game.

**WAI** What an idiot!

**WDALYIC** Who died and left you in charge?

**WISP** Winning is so pleasurable.

**WITFITS** What in the fuck is this shit?

**WOTAM** Waste of time and money.

**WTF** What the fuck!

**WTFH** What the fucking hell!

**WTH** What the heck/hell!

**WYGIWYPF** What you get is what you pay for.

**WYSIWYG** |WIZ ē wig| What you see is what you get.

**w00t!** |wūt| *excl* Cry of victory or joy. ORIGINS: Wherever it originally came from, now considered an acronym for "We owned the other team" in role-playing games. *See* I OWN YOU. USAGE INFO: Note spelling with zeroes, rather than *o*'s.

**wack** |wak| *adj* Of poor quality; inferior.

**wacko** |WAK ō| *adj* Crazy. ORIGINS: From slang **wacky** meaning "eccentric," and the slang suffix -o used to create adjectives, including some others having to do with mental health, like **batso**, **nutso**, and **sicko**, making them similar to abbreviated **schizo** and **psycho**. USAGE ALERT: Often used with intent to denigrate or insult and understood as such. This way of speaking about *sb's* mental health may be considered insensitive and therefore objectionable in some contexts and by some people.

**wade into** |WĀD IN tū| *v* To commence an assault, either physical or verbal. ORIGINS: A reference to beginning to walk into a large body of water.

**wads** |wads| *n* A large amount.

**waffler** |WAHF lur| *n* A person who is indecisive and changes his/her mind; a person who wavers. ORIGINS: From slang **waffling** meaning "chattering pointlessly."

**Wahoo!** |waw hū| *excl* Cry of victory or delight.

**walk (out on *sb*)** |wawk / WAWK out awn *sb*| *v* To leave; to depart; to forsake; to abandon.

**walkover** |WAWK ō vur| *n* An easily accomplished task.

**wall-to-wall with** |WAWL tū WAWL with| *adj* Present everywhere; all around. ORIGINS: From the description of a carpet installation that covers the whole floor.

**wallop** |WAW lup| *v* To hit hard; to beat up.

**waltz\*** |waltz| *n* An easily resolved problem.
• a waltz in the park |u WALTZ in *thu* PAHRK| *v*

**waltz** |waltz| *v* To move briskly.

**wannabe(e)** |WAH nu bē| *n* One who will never have a particular skill set, but pursues the practice in spite of this. ORIGINS: From the phrase "I want to (wanna) be...." USAGE INFO: Differentiated from **wannabe(e)** as an adjective by standing alone with no reference, as in "Sure, he loves Guitar Hero®, but as for really playing guitar, he's just a wannabe."

**wannabe(e)** |WAH nu bē| *adj* One who aspires to have (but does not yet have and/or may never have) a particular skill set; one who admires *sb* (often a celebrity) inordinately and imitates that person's style. ORIGINS: From the phrase "I want to (wanna) be...." USAGE INFO: Precedes or follows the word or phrase it modifies, as in "a wannabe singer"; "a Madonna wannabe."

**wart** |wawrt| *n* A person who causes ongoing irritation and annoyance. ORIGINS: By analogy to the ongoing annoyance caused by a wart. USAGE ALERT: Usually used with intent to denigrate or insult and understood as such.

**washed out** |WAWSHT out| *adj* Exhausted; worn out.

**washed up** |WAWSHT up| *adj* Ruined; finished.

**washout** |WAWSH out| *n* A person who is a failure or considered a loser.

**Wassup?** |wu SUP / wu TSUP | *phr* What's up? ORIGINS: An altered form of **What's up?** USAGE INFO: Other spellings are also used.

**waste** |wāst| *v* To kill. ORIGINS: From US military jargon.

**waste of space** |WĀST uv SPĀS| *n* A thoroughly worthless individual.

**way** |wā| *adv* Intensifier; very; extremely. USAGE INFO: Precedes the word it modifies, as in "The Medici's pizza is way delicious."

**Way!** |wā| *excl* A rejoinder to No way! USAGE INFO: Way! can only be used to respond to No way! essentially translating an argument in which one person continually says yes and the other says no to a slang equivalent.

**way good** |WĀ gŏŏd| *adj* Extremely good. ORIGINS: From using SE **way** as an intensifier on the model of **way-out**.

**way-in** |WĀ in| *adj* Extremely fashionable. ORIGINS: From slang **in** and intensifier **way** used on the model of **way-out**.

**way-out** |wā OUT| *adj* Exceptional. ORIGINS: Used in jazz contexts.

**weak sister** |WĒK SIS tur| *n* An undependable person; a person who doesn't contribute his/her share. USAGE INFO: Applied to males and things, as well as females.

**wear the pants** |WER *thu* PANTS| *v* To be the supreme authority, often in a home. ORIGINS: Assumes the role of the man (the pants-wearer) in patriarchal society and traditional family and stems from a time at which women wore only skirts or dresses.

**weasel out** |WĒ sul out| *v* To sneakily evade doing *st* one has promised to do; to back out of a commitment in a cowardly way.

**weasel word** |WĒ sul wurd| *n* Language designed to deceive or evade. ORIGINS: Figurative extension of standard image of weasels as sucking out the contents of birds' eggs while leaving the shells intact.

**weeny, weenie** |WĒ nē| *n* An inept or ineffectual person, especially a male. ORIGINS: From slang **weenie** meaning "penis," figuratively based on SE **weiner**, a Vienna sausage. USAGE ALERT: Usually used with intent to denigrate or insult and understood as such. Also, some people may find this euphemism objectionable.

**weird out** |WIRD out| *v* To horrify; to terrify.

**weirded out, be** |WIRD id out| *v* To be scared and confused.

**weirdo** |WIRD ō| *adj* A strange or eccentric person; a non-conformist.

**wet one's pants** |WET wunz pants| *v* To be so terrified that one could (or does) urinate on oneself; to laugh riotously. USAGE INFO: **Pee one's pants** and **piss one's pants** will likely be more objectionable. USAGE ALERT: The figurative reference to urination may make this phrase objectionable in some contexts and to some people.

**W**

**wet oneself** |WET wun self| *v* To be so terrified that one could (or does) urinate on oneself; to laugh riotously. USAGE INFO: **Pee oneself** and **piss oneself** will likely be more objectionable. USAGE ALERT: The figurative reference to urination may make this phrase objectionable in some contexts and to some people.

**whack** |wak| *n* An attempt. USAGE INFO: Often in the phrase "take a whack at."

**whack¹** |wak| *v* To strike with a sharp blow.

**whack²** |wak| *v* To kill; to murder.

**whacked out** |WAKT out| *adj* Crazy. USAGE ALERT: Often used with intent to denigrate or insult and understood as such. This way of speaking about *sb's* mental health may be considered insensitive and therefore objectionable in some contexts and by some people.

**whale (into)** *sb* |WĀL *sb* / WĀL in tū *sb*| *v* To attack, physically or verbally.

**wham** |wham| *v* To punch hard. ORIGINS: Imitative of the sound of a blow.

**whang** |wang| *v* To hit with a lash or a whip. ORIGINS: Imitative of the sound of a blow.

**whangdoodle\*** |WANG dū dul| *n* Any nameless object, or object for which one cannot remember the name; may refer to a gadget. ORIGINS: May derive from people's efforts to recall a forgotten name. USAGE INFO: Exact sound and spelling vary too widely for all variations to be listed.
• whangydoodle |WAN gē dū dul|

**whap** |wap| *v* To strike a quick, sharp blow. ORIGINS: Imitative of the sound of a blow.

**What gives?** |wut GIVZ| *phr* A casual greeting, similar to What's happening?

**What in tarnation!** |wut in tahr NĀ shun| *excl* What in the world! ORIGINS: Euphemism and shortened version of **What in the hell is going on?** Tarnation is a substitution for a figurative use of SE **damnation** meaning "condemnation to hell." USAGE ALERT: The euphemism **blazes** in this phrase will soften it somewhat, but it may still be objectionable in some contexts and to some people.

**What in (the) blazes!** |wut in BLĀ ziz / wut in *thu* BLĀ ziz| *excl* What in the world! ORIGINS: Euphemism and shortened version of **What in the hell is going on?** Blazes is a substitution for a figurative use of SE **hell** meaning "the alternative to heaven; the realm of the devil." **Blazes** is a reference to the fires of hell. USAGE ALERT: The euphemism **blazes** in this phrase will soften it somewhat, but it may still be objectionable in some contexts and to some people.

**What in the fuck is this shit?** |WUT in *thu* FUK iz ths SHIT| *excl* What is this? Why is this stuff that I don't recognize in this place? This is trash! ORIGINS: Figurative use of slang **fuck** meaning "sexual intercourse" and **shit** meaning "excrement." USAGE INFO: Either a phrase requesting an explanation for something that distresses the speaker by its apparent lack of quality, its sudden appearance, or the perception that it is infringing on his or her space, or an interjection of disgust and rejection. USAGE ALERT: The inclusion of **fuck** and **shit** will make this expression objectionable in some contexts and to some people.

**What (in) the hell is going on?** |wut *thu* HEL iz GŌ ing awn / wut in *thu* HEL iz GŌ ing awn| *excl* What in the world! ORIGINS: Figurative use of SE **hell** meaning "the alternative to heaven; the realm of the devil." USAGE ALERT: The inclusion of the word **hell** in this phrase will render it objectionable in some contexts and to some people.

**What (in) the Sam Hill!** |wut *thu* SAM HIL / wut in *thu* SAM HIL| *excl* What in the world! ORIGINS: Euphemism and shortened version of **What in the hell is going on?** Figurative use of SE **hell** meaning "the alternative to heaven; the realm of the devil." USAGE ALERT: The inclusion of the word **hell** in this phrase will render it objectionable in some contexts and to some people.

**What the deuce!** |wut *thu* DŪS| *excl* An interjection signaling surprise, shock, or dismay, annoyance, etc. ORIGINS: Euphemism for **What the hell!**, SE hell being the place where the devil resides and deuce being a euphemism for **devil**. USAGE ALERT: The inclusion of **deuce** will make this expression objectionable in some contexts and to some people, but usually less so than **devil**.

**What the devil!** |wut *thu* DEV ul| *excl* An interjection signaling surprise, shock, dismay, annoyance, etc. ORIGINS: Euphemism for **What the hell!**, SE hell being the place where the devil resides. USAGE ALERT: The inclusion of **devil** will make this expression objectionable in some contexts and to some people.

**What the dickens!** |wut *thu* DIK unz| *excl* An interjection signaling surprise, shock, dismay, annoyance, etc. ORIGINS: Euphemism for **What the devil!** Slang dickens is an altered form of SE **devil**. USAGE ALERT: The inclusion of a reference to the devil will make this term objectionable in some contexts and to some people.

**What the fuck!** |wut *thu* FUK| *excl* An interjection signaling surprise, shock, dismay, annoyance, etc. ORIGINS: Figurative use of slang **fuck** meaning "sexual intercourse." USAGE ALERT: The inclusion of **fuck** will make this expression objectionable in some contexts and to some people.

**What the fuck...?** |wut *thu* FUK| *excl* An interjection signaling incomprehension or befuddlement. ORIGINS: Figurative use of slang **fuck** meaning "to engage in sexual intercourse."

**What the fucking hell?** |wut *thu* FUK ing hel| *excl* An interjection signaling surprise, shock, dismay, annoyance, etc. ORIGINS: Figurative use of SE **hell** meaning "the alternative to heaven; the realm of the devil." From slang **fuck** meaning "to engage in sexual intercourse," used here as a sentence modifier to intensify the whole sentence. USAGE ALERT: The inclusion of the word **hell** and a form of **fuck** in this phrase will render it objectionable in some contexts and to some people.

**What the heck!** |wut *thu* HEK| *excl* An interjection signaling surprise, shock, dismay, annoyance, etc. ORIGINS: Euphemism for **What the hell!** Heck is an altered form of and euphemism for **hell**. USAGE ALERT: The euphemism heck in this phrase will soften it somewhat, but it may still be objectionable in some contexts and to some people.

**What the hell!** |wut *thu* HEL| *excl* An interjection signaling surprise, shock, dismay, annoyance, etc. ORIGINS: Figurative use of SE **hell** meaning "the alternative to heaven; the realm of the devil." USAGE ALERT: The inclusion of **hell** will make this expression objectionable in some contexts and to some people.

**What you see is what you get.** |wut yū SĒ iz wut yū GET| *phr* To be transparent.

**What's happening/happenin'?** |wuts HAP in ing / wuts HAP in in| *phr* A casual greeting, combining the senses of **Hello** and **How are you?**

**whatchamacallit, watchamacallit** |WUCH u mu cahl it| *n* Any nameless object, or object for which one cannot remember the name; may refer to a gadget. ORIGINS: May derive from people's efforts to recall a forgotten name. USAGE INFO: Exact sound and spelling vary too widely for all variations to be listed.

**Whatever!** |wut EV ur| *excl* An exclamation of derisive dismissal and/or lack of interest. USAGE INFO: Often with exaggerated pronunciation.

**whatsit, whatzit, whassit** |WUT sit| *n* Any nameless object, or object for which one cannot remember the name; may refer to a gadget. ORIGINS: May derive from people's efforts to recall a forgotten name. USAGE INFO: Exact sound and spelling vary too widely for all variations to be listed.

**wheel is turning but the hamster's dead, the** |thu WĒL iz TUR ning but thu HAM sturz ded| *phr* Unintelligent. ORIGINS: This slang phrase works in two ways. First, it sets up an expectation and then undercuts it: one would naturally expect the turning wheel to signal the presence of a live and running hamster. Second, it relies on an association between death and the absence of brain function to indicate that the person in question is quite unintelligent. USAGE ALERT: Usually used with intent to denigrate or insult and understood as such.

**wheeler-dealer** |WĒL ur DĒL ur| *n* A manipulative hustler; an unscrupulous opportunist.

**when the chips are down** |when thu CHIPS are doun| *phr* When the situation is really difficult and looks as if it may fail. ORIGINS: Figurative use of gambling jargon **chips**, meaning the counters used to represent money.

**when the going gets tough** |when thu GŌ ing gets TUF| *phr* When the situation becomes challenging. USAGE INFO: Sometimes concluded with "the tough get going."

**when the shit hits the fan** |when thu SHIT hits thu FAN| *phr* When things become really difficult and messy. ORIGINS: From slang **shit** meaning "excrement." USAGE ALERT: The inclusion of the word **shit** in the phrase will render it objectionable in some contexts and to some people.

**where the rubber meets the road** |wer thu RUB bur mēts thu RŌD| *phr* At the most important point; in the most important moment; the essential thing.

**whip** |wip| *v* To beat up; to defeat. ORIGINS: Extended from SE **whip**.

**whip *sb's* ass** |WIP sb's AS| *v* To defeat physically or in an argument; to best intellectually. ORIGINS: From slang **ass** meaning "the rear end or buttocks." USAGE ALERT: The inclusion of the word **ass** in the phrase will render it objectionable in some contexts and to some people.

**whipped** |wipt| *adj* Exhausted.

**white bread** |WĪT bred| *adj* Boring; holding no interest.

**whiz, whizz** |wiz| *n* An extremely skillful or talented person. ORIGINS: Extended from SE **wizard**.

**whiz, whizz** |wiz| *v* To move rapidly.

**whiz-kid, whizz-kid** |WIZ kid| *n* A person, especially a young person, who is exceptionally good at something. ORIGINS: From slang whiz, deriving from SE **wizard**. USAGE INFO: More often used of males than females.

**Who cares?** |hū KERZ| *excl* An interjection signaling indifference.

**Who died and left you in charge?** |hū DĪD and LEFT YŪ in charj| *excl* I'm not taking orders from you!

**Who gives a care?** |hū GIVZ u KER| *excl* An interjection signaling indifference.

**Who gives a damn?** |hū GIVZ u DAM| *excl* An interjection signaling indifference. ORIGINS: By extension from SE **damn**, which literally means "Send (it) to hell." USAGE ALERT: The inclusion of the word **damn** in the phrase will render it objectionable in some contexts and to some people.

**Who gives a fart?** |hū GIVZ u FAHRT| *excl* An interjection signaling indifference. ORIGINS: Euphemism for **Who gives a fuck?** From slang **fart** meaning "to break wind," sometimes used as a euphemism for **fuck** because it is often considered less offensive. USAGE ALERT: The inclusion of the word **fart** in the phrase will render it objectionable in some contexts and to some people.

**Who gives a (flying) fuck?** |hū GIVZ u FUK / hū GIVZ u FLĪ ing FUK| *excl* An interjection signaling indifference. ORIGINS: Figurative use of slang **fuck** meaning "to engage in sexual intercourse." USAGE ALERT: The inclusion of the word **fuck** in the phrase will render it objectionable in some contexts and to some people.

**Who gives a frig?** |hū GIVZ u FRIG| *excl* An interjection signaling indifference. ORIGINS: Euphemism for **Who gives a fuck?** From slang **frig** meaning "masturbate" or "engage in intercourse"—sometimes used as a euphemism for **fuck** by people who think that **frig** is a sanitized version of **fuck** and do not realize that it is a PO word all on its own. USAGE ALERT: The inclusion of the word **frig** in the phrase will render it objectionable in some contexts and to some people.

**Who gives a shit?** |hū GIVZ u SHIT| *excl* An interjection signaling indifference. ORIGINS: From slang **shit** meaning "excrement." USAGE ALERT: The inclusion of the word **shit** in the phrase will render it objectionable in some contexts and to some people.

**whole bag of tricks** |HŌL bag uv TRIKS| *n* Everything. USAGE INFO: Often with *the*.

**whole ball of wax** |HŌL bawl uv WAKS| *n* Everything. USAGE INFO: Often with *the*.

**whole enchilada** |HŌL en chu LAH du| *n* Everything. USAGE INFO: Often with *the*.

**whole hog** |HŌL HAWG| *n* Everything. ORIGINS: From slang go the whole hog meaning "to do *st* thoroughly." USAGE INFO: Often with *the*.

**whole kit and caboodle** |HŌL kit und ku BŪ dul| *n* Everything. ORIGINS: From slang whole kit meaning "the entire lot" and caboodle meaning "a large, unsorted collection." USAGE INFO: Often with *the*.

**whole lot** |HŌL LAHT| *n* With *a*: (a whole lot)—a great many; a large number or amount; with *the*: (the whole lot)—everything.

**whole megillah** |HŌL mu GIL u| *n* Everything. ORIGINS: From slang megillah meaning "a long complicated story," from Hebrew megillah meaning the Old Testament books of Song of Songs, Ruth, Lamentations, Ecclesiastes, and Esther, which have special liturgical significance in celebrating Jewish festivals. USAGE INFO: Often with *the*.

**whole nine yards** |HŌL NĪN YAHRDZ| *n* Everything. USAGE INFO: Often with *the*.

**whole schmeer, schmear** |HŌL SHMIR| *n* Everything. USAGE INFO: Often with *the*.

**whole schmegegge, schmegeggy** |HŌL shma GEG / HŌL shma GEG ē| *n* Everything. ORIGINS: From a Yiddish word that means "nonsense" (and sometimes, "a contemptible or incompetent person"). USAGE INFO: Often with *the*.

**whole shebang** |HŌL shu BANG| *n* Everything. ORIGINS: From US military jargon shebang for tents where a soldier's possessions were stored. USAGE INFO: Often with *the*.

**whole shooting match** |HŌL SHŪT ing mach| *n* Everything. USAGE INFO: Often with *the*.

**whomp** |wawmp| *v* To defeat badly, either in a fight or in a competition.

**whoop** |wūp| *v* To laugh. ORIGINS: From SE whoop meaning "a cry." USAGE INFO: Usually in the phrase "whoop with laughter."

**whoop sb's ass** |WŪP sb's AS| *v See* **WHIP SB'S ASS**.

**Whoops!*** |wūps| *excl* An interjection expressing discovery of an error or mistake and, often, an implicit apology.
• Whoopsie! |WŪP sē|

**whoozis, whoosis*** |HŪ zis| *n* Any nameless object or person, or object or person for which one cannot remember the name; may refer to a gadget. ORIGINS: May derive from people's efforts to recall a forgotten name.
• whosit |HŪ zit|

**whopper** |WAHP pur| *n* A particularly gross untruth or lie.

**whopping** |WAHP ing| *adj* Enormous.

**whump** |wump| *v* To strike a blow that makes a dull sound. ORIGINS: Imitative of the sound of a blow.

**whup *sb's* ass** |WHUP *sb's* AS| *v* See **WHIP *SB'S* ASS**.

**wicked** |WIK id| *adj* Excellent; outstanding. ORIGINS: From SE **wicked** meaning "bad" but modified on the "bad is good" model, probably assisted by the book (1995), musical (2003–), and movie (2010) *Wicked*.

**wicked** |WIK id| *a/a* Very; extremely. ORIGINS: From SE **wicked**. USAGE INFO: Used as an adjective ("a wicked headache") or as an adverb ("a wicked good show").

**widget** |WIJ it| *n* Any nameless small mechanical device, or a small mechanical device for which one cannot remember the name; may refer to a gadget.

**wiggle out of** |WIG ul out uv| *v* To avoid a commitment or responsibility by underhanded means. ORIGINS: Figurative use of SE wriggling to suggest twisting this way and that to extricate oneself.

**wild about** |WĪLD u bout| *adj* Enthusiastically supportive of; in love with.

**willies** |WIL ēz| *n* Feelings of extreme uneasiness. USAGE INFO: Often with *the*.

**wimp** |wimp| *n* A person, usually a male, who is both weak and indecisive. USAGE ALERT: Usually used with intent to denigrate or insult and understood as such.

**wimp out** |wimp OUT| *v* To fail to fulfill a commitment; to renege on a promise out of fear.

**win hands down** |WIN hands DOUN| *v* To achieve a resounding victory.

**win out/through** |win OUT / WIN THRŪ| *v* To succeed through perseverance.

**wind *sb* up** |WĪND *sb* UP| *v* To purposely, even maliciously, annoy or irritate *sb*. ORIGINS: From SE **wind up** and the practice of winding a clock.

**windbag** |WIND bag| *n* A boaster; a person whose talk is empty or devoid of meaning.

**W**

**wipe out** |WĪP OUT| *v* To destroy; to ruin financially.

**wipe *sb* out** |WĪP *sb* OUT| *v* To kill *sb*.

**wipe the floor with** |WĪP *thu* FLAWR with| *v* To thrash; to beat decisively in a physical or verbal fight or a competition. ORIGINS: From the Royal Navy slang wipe the deck with *sb*.

**wiped (out)** |wīpt / WĪPT out| *adj* Completely worn out.

**wiped out** |WĪPT OUT| *adj* Financially ruined; broke.

**wire puller** |WĪR PUL ur| *n* A manipulator; a person who secretly influences people or organizations.

**wired** |wīrd| *adj* Nervous; tense; agitated. ORIGINS: From SE **wired** meaning "carrying electricity."

**wise off** |WĪZ awf| *v* To make jokes at *sb's* expense; to tease.

**with a vengeance** |with u VEN juns| *adv* To an extreme degree.

**with it** |WITH it| *adj* Knowing the latest trends.

**with it, be** |WITH it| *v* To be knowledgeable.

**without a bean** |with OUT u BĒN| *adj* Penniless.

**without a chance/hope in hell** |with OUT u CHANTS in HEL / with OUT u HŌP in HEL| *phr* Having no chance at all. ORIGINS: The concept is of hell as a place where there is no opportunity of any kind. Figurative use of SE **hell** meaning "the alternative to heaven; the realm of the devil." USAGE ALERT: The inclusion of **hell** will make this expression objectionable in some contexts and to some people.

**without a pot to piss in** |with out u pot tū PIS in| *adj* Extremely poor. ORIGINS: From slang **piss**, meaning "urine." USAGE ALERT: The inclusion of the word **piss** in the phrase, plus the overall reference to excretion, will render this phrase objectionable in some contexts and to some people.

**without a prayer** |with OUT u PRER| *phr* Having no chance at all. ORIGINS: Suggests that even praying cannot aid in such a situation.

**without a red cent** |with out u RED SENT| *adj* Broke. ORIGINS: From **red cent** meaning "a trivial amount of money," possibly deriving from the reddish cast of a penny, due to its being made with copper.

**wizard** |WIZ urd| *n* An exceptionally smart person. ORIGINS: Perhaps initially encouraged by the television shows starring "Mr. Wizard" (1951–1990); followed by the popularity of Merlin (*The Once and Future King: The Sword in the Stone*), Gandalf (*The Hobbit* and *The Lord of the Ring*), and, most recently, Albus Dumbledore and others in the Harry Potter books.

**wonk** |wahnk| *n* A person who has exceptional expertise in a particular area.

**Woohoo!** |WŪ HŪ| *excl* An expression of excitement or delight.

**Word (up)!** |wurd / WURD up| *excl* A casual greeting and exclamation of agreement. ORIGINS: Originally from Black English, but popularized by a rhythm and blues album *Word Up!*; a teen magazine for African Americans, *Word Up Magazine*; and by being a catch phrase of WordGirl, the secret pseudonym of superhero Becky Botsford on the PBS series *WordGirl*.

**work like a charm** |WURK līk u CHAHRM| *v* To succeed easily and seamlessly. ORIGINS: From SE **charm** meaning "a magic spell."

**work *sb* over** |WURK *sb* Ō vur| *v* To beat *sb* up.

**worked up** |WURKT UP| *adj* Upset; agitated.

**works (the)** |*thu* WURKZ| *n* Everything; the whole lot. USAGE INFO: This phrase can also mean "a sampling of everything available" as in "a pizza with the works."

**worm** |wurm| *n* A contemptible, disagreeable person. ORIGINS: From typical responses to the animal. USAGE ALERT: Usually used with intent to denigrate or insult and understood as such.

**worm out of** *st* |wurm OUT uv *st*| *v* To avoid a commitment or responsibility by underhanded means. ORIGINS: Figurative reference to the wriggling of worms.

**worm** *st* **out of** *sb* |wurm *st* OUT uv *sb*| *v* To pressure *sb* into a revelation. ORIGINS: Figurative reference to the wriggling of worms.

**worth a bundle** |WURTH u BUN dul| *adj* Having a high value.

**wrap** *st* **up** |RAP *st* UP| *v* To bring to a successful conclusion; to finish.

**wriggle out** |RIG ul out| *v* To avoid a commitment or responsibility by underhanded means. ORIGINS: Figurative use of SE **wriggling** to suggest twisting this way and that to extricate oneself.

**wrinkle** |WRING kul| *n* A problematic (and usually unexpected) development.

**wuss** |wus| *n* A person, usually a male, who is neither dependable nor effective. ORIGINS: From combining the slang words wimp, meaning "an indecisive person" and **pussy**, meaning "a weak, effeminate man"; from slang **pussy** meaning a woman, extended from meaning "the vagina"; from earlier use of **pussy** as affectionate name for a cat. USAGE ALERT: Usually used with intent to denigrate or insult and understood as such.

**YAO** You are owned.

**YGTBK** You've got to be kidding.

**YGWYPF** You get what you pay for.

**YSW, YYSSW** Yeah, sure, whatever. Yeah, yeah; sure, sure; whatever.

**yahoo** |YAH hū| *n* A savage, primitive person. ORIGINS: From the creatures of that name in Jonathan Swift's novel *Gulliver's Travels* (1726).

**Yahoo!** |ya HŪ| *excl* An expression of excitement or delight.

**yak** |yak| *v* To chatter.

**yammer** |YAM ur| *v* To complain peevishly; to whine. ORIGINS: From Middle English **yameren** meaning "to lament."

**yank** |yangk| *v* To remove or expel suddenly.

**yank** *sb's* **chain** |YANGK *sb's* CHĀN| *v* To purposely annoy or harass *sb*; to act in a way that one knows upsets *sb*. ORIGINS: From SE **yank** meaning "to pull sharply." USAGE INFO: See JERK SB'S CHAIN.

**yapper** |YAP ur| *n* A chatterer, especially, a noisy one.

**yawp** |yawp| *v* To talk loudly. ORIGINS: An alternative form of yap.

**Yay!** |yā| *excl* Cry of victory, success, or delight.

**Yechy! Yecchy!** |YEK ē| *adj* Sound indicating disgust or contempt.

**Yeep(s)!** |yēp / yēps| *excl* Sound expressing fear.

**Yeh! Yeah!** |ye| *excl* Sound expressing agreement or approval. ORIGINS: Shortened from SE yes.

**yellow** |YEL ō| *adj* Timid; cowardly.

**yenta** |YEN tu| *n* ORIGINS: A meddler. ORIGINS: From a Yiddish proper name. USAGE ALERT: Usually used with intent to denigrate or insult and understood as such.

**Yeow! Yow!** |you| *excl* A cry of shock and dismay.

**Yep!** |yep| *excl* Sound expressing agreement or approval. ORIGINS: Altered from SE yes.

**Yes sirree (bob)!** |YE SU RĒ / YE SU RĒ BAHB| *excl* An interjection of enthusiastic affirmation.

**Yes-huh!** |YES hu| *excl* It *is* the case, despite what you say. A response to Nu-uh! and similar phrases. USAGE INFO: Synonym of Uh-huh! and antonym of the negative phrases **Nu-uh!** and **Uh-uh!** The phrase **Yes-huh!** can only be used to respond to **Nu-uh!** and its variants.

**yes-man** |YES man| *n* An obsequious person; a person without any gumption; a subservient employee. ORIGINS: From the fact that this person says "yes" to any request made of him/her.

**Yikes!** |yīks| *excl* Sound expressing surprise and mild fear or minor shock.

**Yipes!** |yīps| *excl* Sound expressing surprise, mild fear, or dismay.

**Yo!** |yō| *excl* A greeting or exclamation to attract attention. ORIGINS: Widely used in Black English and the speech of Italian Americans, yo was popularized in the quotation "Yo, Adrian!" spoken by Sylvester Stallone in the character of Rocky Balboa in the 1976 movie *Rocky*; it's number 80 on the American Film Institute's top 100 American cinema quotations.

**You are pwnd, pwned, pwnt!** |yū ar PŌND| *excl* You lose! ORIGINS: There are two theories: one, that pwn is a typo for **own**, sometimes attributed specifically to the game Warcraft 3; two, that pwn is a step above **own**.

**You bet your boots!** |yū BET yŏŏr BŪTS| *excl* You can be absolutely certain! ORIGINS: The idea is that the thing referred to is so certain that you could safely bet your essentials on it.

**You bet your bottom dollar!** |yū BET yŏŏr baht um DAHL ur| *excl* You can be absolutely certain! ORIGINS: The idea is that the thing referred to is so certain that you could safely bet your last dollar on it.

**You bet your life!** |yū BET yŏŏr LĪF| *excl* You can be absolutely certain! ORIGINS: The idea is that the thing referred to is so certain that you could safely bet your life on it.

**You bet your shirt!** |yū BET yŏŏr SHIRT| *excl* You can be absolutely certain! ORIGINS: The idea is that the thing referred to is so certain that you could safely bet your essentials on it.

**You bet your (sweet) ass!** |yū BET yŏŏr (sweet) AS| *excl* You can be absolutely certain! ORIGINS: The idea is that the thing referred to is so certain that you could safely bet body parts on it. USAGE ALERT: The use of **ass** in this phrase will make it objectionable in some contexts and to some people.

**You bet your (sweet) bippy!** |yū BET yŏŏr (sweet) BIP ē| *excl* You can be completely certain! ORIGINS: A euphemism for **You bet your (sweet) ass!** that was invented for and became a catchphrase used on the television show *Rowan & Martin's Laugh-In* (1968–1973) and has never quite gone away.

**You bet(cha)!** |yū BĒT / yū BĒCH u| *excl* An interjection signaling emphatic certainty.

**You can say that again!** |yū kan sā *THAT* u gen| *excl* An interjection signaling emphatic agreement.

**You fail it!** |yū fāil it| *excl* I win: you lose! ORIGINS: From the words said to a loser in the English translation of a Japanese arcade game, *Blazing Star* (1968): "You fail it! Your skill is not enough! See you next time! Bye bye!"

**You have been owned!** |yū hav bin ŌND| *excl* I win; you lose! ORIGINS: Passive form of I own you!

**You just got pwned, pwnd!** |yū just got PŌND| *excl* I win; you lose! ORIGINS: Another variant of the I own you! trope.

**You know what you can do with it?** |yū NŌ wut YŪ can DŪ with IT| *excl* A contemptuous dismissal. ORIGINS: Euphemistic form of slang **Stick it up your ass!** from slang **ass** meaning "the rear end or buttocks." USAGE INFO: Often accompanied by the gesture referred to as "giving *sb* the finger." USAGE ALERT: Usually used with intent to be rude and understood as such. Although the euphemistic alteration of this phrase will soften it somewhat, the graphic image may still be objectionable in some contexts and to some people.

**you know what** |YŪ nō wut| *n* The thing we're talking about, the name of which escapes me; the thing that we're talking about that it is not good or appropriate to name just now.

**You know where you can stick it?** |yū NŌ wer yū can STIK it| *excl* A contemptuous dismissal. ORIGINS: Euphemistic form of slang **Stick it up your ass!** from slang **ass** meaning "the rear end or buttocks." USAGE INFO: Often accompanied by the gesture referred to as "giving *sb* the finger." USAGE ALERT: Usually used with intent to be rude and understood as such. Although the euphemistic alteration of this phrase will soften it somewhat, the graphic image may still be objectionable in some contexts and to some people.

**You said a mouthful/it!** |YŪ sed u MOUTH ful / yū SED it| *excl* An interjection signaling emphatic agreement.

**You think?** |yu THINGK| *excl* Sarcastic agreement to *st* that's obvious (to the speaker).

**You('d) better believe it!** |yū(d) BET ur bi LĒV it| *excl* An interjection signaling emphatic agreement.

**You're damn tootin'!** |yur DAM TŪT'n| *excl* An interjection signaling emphatic agreement. ORIGINS: By extension from SE **damn**, which literally means "Send (it) to hell," used here as an intensifier.

**You're FOS!** |yōŏr ef ō ES| *excl* I don't believe it/you! ORIGINS: Euphemism for **full of shit**, with **shit** meaning "excrement." USAGE ALERT: The inclusion of the word **shit** in this phrase will render it objectionable in some contexts and to some people.

**You're full of shit!** |yōŏr ful uv SHIT| *excl* I don't believe it/you! ORIGINS: From **shit** meaning "excrement." USAGE ALERT: The inclusion of the word **shit** in this phrase will render it objectionable in some contexts and to some people.

**You're telling me!** |YUR tel ing MĒ| *excl* An interjection signaling emphatic agreement. ORIGINS: The implication is that the speaker of the exclamation already knows or approves of whatever is being said.

**yo-yo** |YŌ YŌ| *n* A foolish person.

**Yuck(o)!** |yuk / YUK ō| *excl* Sound to express disgust.

**yucky, yukky** |YUK ē| *adj* Repugnant or disgusting.

**Yucky! Yukky!** |YUK ē| *excl* Sound to express disgust.

**Yum!** |YUM| *excl* Sound expressing delight and/or desire for *st*. ORIGINS: From the sound one makes when smacking one's lips. USAGE INFO: Used to express agreement or approval in contexts such as: "Shall I make scones for breakfast?" "Yum!"

**yummy** |YUM ē| *adj* Delicious; desirable. ORIGINS: Onomatopoeic word from slang **yum**, the sound one makes when smacking one's lips.

**Yup!** |yup| *excl* Sound expressing agreement or approval. ORIGINS: Altered from slang **yep**.

# Z

**zap$^1$** |zap| *v* To destroy or kill *sb* or *st* (e.g., insects) with electricity. ORIGINS: Onomatopoeic in the case of bugs, from the sound of the device referred to as a "bug zapper."

**zap$^2$** |zap| *v* To move swiftly.

**zero** |ZIR ō| *n* A loser; a worthless person; a person considered insignificant.

**zilch** |zilch| *n* Nothing.

**zillion** |ZIL yun| *n* An unspecified, exceedingly large amount. ORIGINS: One of a group of made up numbers ending in *-illion* with pretty indistinguishable meanings, although additional prefixes may be indicating even larger amounts (i.e., a **bazillion** or gadzillion may be larger than a zillion).

**zing along** |ZING u LAWNG| *v* To move really quickly and energetically.

**zingy** |ZING ē| *adj* Energetic; enthusiastic; excited.

**zip** |zip| *n* Nothing.

**zip** |zip| *v* To move really quickly.

**zippy** |ZIP ē| *adj* Speedy; energetic; spirited.

**zonk** |zawnk| *v* To strike, especially a stunning blow. ORIGINS: Imitative of the sound of a blow.

**zonk off/out** |ZAWNK ahf / ZAWNK out| *v* To fall asleep from exhaustion. ORIGINS: By extension from slang **zonk out** meaning "to lose consciousness, especially as a result of using alcohol or drugs."

**zonked** |zawngkt| *adj.* Exhausted. ORIGINS: By extension from slang **zonk out** meaning "to lose consciousness, especially as a result of using alcohol or drugs."

**zoom** |zūm| *v* To move really quickly.

**Zowie!** |ZOU ē| *excl* An exclamation of excitement. ORIGINS: Similar in formation to many words representing speed.

Z

# THESAURUS OF SLANG

## PRONUNCIATION KEY

| | | | | |
|---|---|---|---|---|
| a | bat | h | had |
| ā | bate, bait | j | jade, ridge, giraffe |
| ah | bot, bother | k | cat, kangaroo |
| aw | bought, bawl, for, all, father | l | lad |
| e | bet | 'l | needle |
| ē | beet | m | mad |
| i | bit | n | nap |
| ī | bite | 'n | sudden |
| ō | boat | p | pad |
| u | but | r | rad |
| ōō | put, good | s | sad, cell |
| ū | boot, to, truth | t | tad |
| yū | beaut, you | v | vat |
| oi | boil, boy | w | wag |
| ou | bow, bound | y | yen |
| ahr | bar | z | zen |
| er | bear, bare | ch | chat |
| ir | beer | kh | chutzpah |
| awr | bore, or | sh | shell |
| ur | bur, bird | th | thin |
| b | bad | *th* | the, this |
| d | bad | zh | decision, garage |
| f | fad, fluff, phase | ng | lung |
| g | gad | hw | what |

N.B. The definite article usually shows up as |*thu*| (occasionally |*th*ē|) and the indefinite article as |u| (occasionally |ā|). Since *sb, st,* and *sb/st* are unknowns, the abbreviations, rather than a pronunciation, is used.

### REGISTER STYLING

- **Potentially Offensive Slang**
- Slang
- <u>**Informal Language**</u>
- Non-registered Language
- **Formal Language**

### ALPHABETIZATION

- Words in parentheses are optional.
- In definitions with *be* following, *be* is most often a placeholder for *am*, *is*, *are*, or contractions of those words, and therefore is not included in the pronunciation.

# Communication

This chapter is about various aspects of communication. Slang civilities help set the tone for communication, and Civilities makes up the first section. This is followed by a review of slang words for communicating in different ways. Finally, we'll examine slang intensifiers, which have some interesting and peculiar quirks. The organization of this chapter is as follows:

*Civilities*
  1 Greetings
  2 Partings
  3 Gracious Responses

*Ways to Communicate*
  1 To Boast
  2 To Complain
  3 To Exaggerate Something's Importance
  4 To Flatter
  5 To Inform
  6 To Talk
  7 To Talk Too Much or Indiscreetly
  8 To Tease
  9 To Tell the Truth

*Increasing Intensity—Words and Phrases*
  1 Adjectives
  2 Adverbs
  3 Adjectives/Adverbs
  4 Comparisons
  5 Prefixes and Suffixes

*Increasing Intensity—Whole Sentences*
  1 Introductory Sentence Modifiers
  2 Other Sentence Modifiers

Note that the Intensity sections have some topics for which there are few or no easily identifiable non-slang synonyms.

# CIVILITIES

Although some niceties of communication may be dispensed with in the types of informal settings in which slang is used, often they are still there— just altered to fit the mood and tone of extreme informality.

## 1 Greetings

Perhaps partly because conversations involving slang are often prompted by people coming into visual contact, there is a tendency to plunge into topics of interest or use physical gestures such as high fives, hugs, and handshakes rather than a wide variety of words or phrases to signal the beginning of the conversation. Whatever the causes, there is less variety in greetings than in partings. Here are some of the most common.

**HIG** How's it going?

**Ahoi-hoi! Ahoy-hoy!** |u HOI HOI| *excl* Hello! ORIGINS: Of debatable origins, but commonly used as a nautical greeting and as a general greeting by the eighteenth century. *Ahoy* was Alexander Graham Bell's preferred word for a telephone greeting, but Thomas Edison's preferred word—*hello*—became the actual standard. **Ahoy-hoy** has had a recent surge in popularity due to its use as a telephone greeting by (Charles) Montgomery Burns, a character on the television show *The Simpsons*.

**Aight! Aiight!** |ī ĪT| *excl* A casual greeting; an exclamation of agreement. ORIGINS: From elision of **alright**. USAGE INFO: Usually used in speech, so its spelling is not standardized. There are a number of other spellings in use besides those listed.

**Give me five!** |GI(V) mē FĪV| *excl* A request for a "high-five," a greeting or celebratory gesture of slapping hands (*five* refers to the number of fingers) "high" in the air—often above the head. ORIGINS: From African-American culture. Kept alive by the "Give me 5 for stroke" campaign of the Stroke Collaborative to encourage people to recognize the five most frequent stroke symptoms in order to seek timely assistance. USAGE INFO: May be pronounced as if spelled *gimme*.

**Give me some skin!** |GI(V) mē sum SKIN| *excl* A request for a "high-five," a greeting or celebratory gesture of slapping hands. ORIGINS: Refers to a greeting that involves skin contact (not just words). USAGE INFO: May be pronounced as if spelled *gimme*. See GIVE ME FIVE! and SLAP ME FIVE!

**Hey!** |hā| *excl* A casual greeting; exclamation of delight, surprise, or warning. ORIGINS: Considered both a shortened version of "How are you?" as well as an alternative form of **hi.** At one time enjoyed more widespread use in the South, but is now found throughout the United States.

**Hey, man!** |HĀ man| *excl* Hello. USAGE INFO: Used mainly, but not exclusively, in greeting males. The comma is often omitted in non-formal writing.

**How's tricks?** |houz TRIKS| *excl* How are you? USAGE INFO: Notice that although the subject of the sentence (*tricks*) is plural, the contracted verb (*is*) is singular. This is a hallmark of colloquial usage.

**Howdy!** |HOU dē| *excl* Hello, how are you? ORIGINS: A shortened form of the phrase "How do you do?"

**Iight! Ite!** |ī ĪT| *excl See* AIGHT!

**Long time, no see!** |long tīm nō SĒ| *excl* I haven't seen you for a long time. USAGE INFO: The ellipsis of a standard expression is a hallmark of colloquial language use.

**Slap me five!** |SLAP mē FĪV| *excl* A request for a "high-five," a greeting or celebratory gesture of slapping hands (the five refers to the number of fingers) "high" in the air—often above the head. ORIGINS: From African-American culture. Kept alive by the children's game in which one child invites another to slap him/her five with the hand in different positions, and in the final "round," trying to remove the hand before the other can slap it. The words are, "Slap me five. On the side. Way up high. Down low."—and if s/he succeeds in avoiding the last slap "You're too slow."

**Sup?, 'Sup?** |sup / tsup| *phr* How are you? ORIGINS: Abbreviated form of Wassup?—itself an altered form of **What's up?** USAGE INFO: Either pronunciation can be used with either spelling (or other, alternative spellings).

**Wassup?** |wu SUP / wu TSUP | *phr* What's up? ORIGINS: An altered form of **What's up?** USAGE INFO: Other spellings are also used.

**What gives?** |wut GIVZ| *phr* A casual greeting, similar to What's happening?

**What's happening/happenin'?** |wuts HAP in ing / wuts HAP in in| *phr* A casual greeting, combining the senses of **Hello** and **How are you?**

**Word (up)!** |wurd / WURD up| *excl* A casual greeting and exclamation of agreement. ORIGINS: Originally from Black English, but popularized by a rhythm and blues album *Word Up!*; a teen magazine for African Americans, *Word Up Magazine;* and by being a catch phrase of WordGirl, the secret pseudonym of superhero Becky Botsford on the PBS series *WordGirl*.

**Yo!** |yō| *excl* A greeting or exclamation to attract attention. ORIGINS: Widely used in Black English and the speech of Italian Americans, yo was popularized in the quotation "Yo, Adrian!" spoken by Sylvester Stallone in the character of Rocky Balboa in the 1976 movie *Rocky*; it's number 80 on the American Film Institute's top 100 American cinema quotations.

NON-SLANG SYNONYMS: Hello. How are you? **Hallo. Hey there. Hi. Hiya. Howdy. How's everything? How's it going? Hullo. What's new? What's up? Felicitations. Good afternoon. Good evening. Good morning. Greetings. How do you do? How have you been? Nice to see you. Salutations.**

## 2 Partings

**AMFA** Adios, mother fucker!

**B4N** Bye for now.

**BB4N** Bye-bye for now.

**BBFN** Bye-bye for now.

**BBIAB** Be back in a bit.

**BBIAF** Be back in a few [minutes].

**BBIAS** Be back in a sec[ond].

**BBIAW** Be back in awhile.

**BBL** Be back later.

**BFN** Bye for now.

**BI5** Back in five [minutes].

**BRB** Be right back.

**C4N** Ciao for now!

**CYA** See ya! Also Cover your ass!

**CYL** See you/ya later! Catch you later!

**G2G** Got to go!

**GGN** Gotta go now!

**GTG** Got to go!

**HAGD** Have a good day.

**HAGO** Have a great one!

**HAK** Hugs and kisses.

**HAND** Have a nice day.

**IOH** I'm outta here!

**L8R** [See you] Later.

**MTFBWY** May the Force be with you.

**SYS** See you soon.

**SYT** See you tomorrow/tonight.

**TAF** That's all folks!

**TAFN, TA4N** That's all for now.

**TC** Take care.

**TCOY** Take care of yourself.

**TLK 2 U L8R** Talk to you later.

**TTFN** Ta ta for now.

**TTMF** Ta ta, MOFO! short for **Ta ta, mother fucker!**

**TTYL** Talk to you later.

**TTYS** Talk to you soon.

**Abyssinia!** |ab u SIN ē u| *excl* I'll be seeing you! ORIGINS: Shortened and altered form of "I'll be seeing you," rendered humorous by assuming the form of another word, the former name of the country now known as *Ethiopia*.

**Adios, MOFO!** |ah dē ŌS MŌ fō| *excl* Goodbye, mother fucker. ORIGINS: From Standard Spanish adios meaning "goodbye" and **MOFO**, an abbreviation of **mother fucker**, a general term of extreme abuse. USAGE INFO: **Mother fucker** is considered one of, if not *the*, worst insults one can make to a man, since it suggests that he has an incestuous relationship with his mother. The phrase seems to have experienced an increase in popularity after it was used by Texas Governor Rick Perry in speaking to a reporter on June 21, 2005. A video of the incident was posted on YouTube, Governor Perry made several "Quote of the Day" lists, and he inspired a tee-shirt with the quotation and his likeness. USAGE ALERT: This word carries implications not only about the person referred to, but also about his mother. The inclusion of **MOFO** will make this phrase objectionable in some contexts and to some people. Usually used with intent to denigrate or insult and understood as such.

**Back in a bit/few/sec** |BAK in u BIT/FYŪ/SEK| *phr* I will return shortly. ORIGINS: From SE **bit** meaning "a short period of time": **few**, short for "a few minutes" or "a few moments"; or slang sec, short for "a second."

**Catch you later! Catch ya later! Catcha later! Catchya later!** |KA chū LĀ tur| *excl* See you later! ORIGINS: From slang catch meaning to meet in a casual social encounter.

**Ciao for now!** |CHOU fawr NOU| *excl* Goodbye for now. ORIGINS: From Standard Italian ciao meaning "goodbye." USAGE INFO: The rhyme puts this in the slang category. Ciao by itself is used by people of Italian descent as well as others. However, note that unless one were Italian or there were Italians present, it would be unlikely in formal usage.

**Gotta go!** |GAH tu GŌ| *excl* I have to leave (immediately). ORIGINS: Shortened form of "I've got to go." USAGE INFO: In Instant Messaging (IM), may be used followed by an immediate departure without waiting for a response.

**Hasta la vista, baby!** |AH stu lu VĒS tu BĀ bē| *excl* Casual farewell. ORIGINS: From *Standard* Spanish phrase **hasta la vista** meaning "see you later" and the slang term of address, baby. Initially popularized through the song *Looking for a New Love* by Jody Watley, released in 1987, but gained far more recognition from its use in instructing the Terminator in how to speak, and its subsequent use by the Terminator, played by Arnold Schwarzenegger in the 1991 movie *Terminator 2: Judgment Day*. Schwarzenegger has since become Governor of California and uses the phrase in his political career. It is number 76 on the American Film Institute's top 100 American cinema quotations.

**I'm outta here!** |ĪM OU tu hir| *excl* I'm leaving this place (immediately)! USAGE INFO: In Instant Messaging (IM), may be used followed by an immediate departure without waiting for a response.

**Later, gator!** |LĀ tur GĀ tur| *excl* See you later. ORIGINS: Shortened version of See you later, alligator! *See* SEE YOU LATER, ALLIGATOR!

**May the Force be with you!** |mā *thu* FAWRS bē WITH yū| *excl* Go well! Good luck! ORIGINS: A secular equivalent of "God be with you," the phrase that is the source of the word **goodbye**. Spoken by Harrison Ford as Hans Solo's parting words to Luke Skywalker before the attack on the Death Star battle station in *Star Wars Episode IV: A New Hope* (1977). It is number 8 on the American Film Institute's top 100 American cinema quotations.

**Sayonara!** |sī yu NAH ru| *excl* Casual farewell. ORIGINS: From the casual pronunciation of Japanese **sayonara**, which also has a different formal pronunciation. USAGE INFO: Is likely to be used self-consciously and for humorous effect (because it contrasts with the rest of the English words) by speakers who are not of Japanese descent and do not speak Japanese.

**See you later, alligator!** |sē yu LĀ dur al i GĀ dur| *excl* A casual farewell, often responded to with the rejoinder, **After while, crocodile!** ORIGINS: From a catch phrase that was popularized by Bill Haley and His Comets' 1955 rock-and-roll rendition of the song "See You Later, Alligator," originally by Robert Charles Guidry. USAGE INFO: Though **See you later, alligator!** may be used without the response, the response is never used without **See you later, alligator!** being spoken.

**Ta ta! Ta-ta!** |tah tah| *excl* Goodbye. USAGE INFO: Self-conscious, humorous use is what renders this archaic phrase as slang.

**Ta ta, MOFO!** |tah tah MŌ fō| *excl* Goodbye, mother fucker. ORIGINS: From a combination of the archaic farewell ta-ta with the current slang **MOFO**, an altered form of **mother fucker**, a general term of extreme abuse, and considered one of the, if not *the*, worst insults one can make to a man, since it suggests that he has an incestuous (i.e., sexual) relationship with his mother. Seems to have experienced an increase in popularity after it was used by Texas Governor Rick Perry in speaking to a reporter on June 21, 2005. A video was posted on YouTube, Governor Perry made several "Quote of the Day" lists, and inspired a tee-shirt with the quotation and his likeness. USAGE ALERT: This word carries implications not only about the person referred to, but also about his mother. The inclusion of **MOFO** will make this phrase objectionable in some contexts and to some people. Usually used with intent to denigrate or insult and understood as such.

**That's all folks!** |thatS AWL fōks| *excl* Casual goodbye, most often to a group. ORIGINS: From the closing line characteristically given at the end of a Looney Tune short, most often (but not exclusively) by Porky Pig.

**That's all for now.** |thatS AWL fawr nou| *excl* See you later! To be continued... ORIGINS: Of unknown origins, but popularized by Paul McCartney's use as a closing lyric in a song he composed spontaneously in a July 28, 2005 concert at Abbey Road (*Live at Abbey Road*, 2005): "That's all for now! You've got to go home!"

**Toodle-oo!** |TŪ du LŪ| *excl* Goodbye. ORIGINS: An archaic, originally British, phrase, originating in the magazine *Punch* and connected to the verb toddle. USAGE INFO: Self-conscious, humorous use is what renders this archaic phrase as slang.

NON-SLANG SYNONYMS: Goodbye. <u>Adios. Arrivederci. Auf wiedersehen. Back in a few. Back in awhile. Be back in a bit/few/sec/while. Be back later. Be right back. Bye. Bye bye for now. Bye for now. Catch you later. Ciao. Got to go. Gotta go now. Have a good day. Have a great one. Have a nice day. Hugs and kisses. I'll be seeing you. Later. Namaste. See you. See you around. See you/ya later! See you soon. See you tomorrow/tonight. So long. Ta ta for now. Take care. Take care of yourself. Talk to you later. Talk to you soon. Adieu. Au revoir. Bon voyage. Farewell. God be with you. God bless you.</u> (There are many others.)

Note: Words of parting from other languages may be used informally in a wide range of settings. Those of French origin—**adieu**, **au revoir**, and **bon voyage**—are an exception in that for native speakers of English, these terms are usually used formally, though like much language, a self-conscious or humorous tone can make their use more informal.

# 3 Gracious Responses

Though not all of equal grace, these phrases are all responses to thanks or appreciation and more casual ways of saying "you're welcome." Often, they attempt to assuage concerns that a major debt has been incurred by whatever has led to the other person's offer of thanks.

**NBD** No big deal.

**NP** No problem.

**Don't sweat it.** |dōnt SWET it| *phr* Don't worry about it. ORIGINS: The idea is that the person offering thanks should not get so worked up about the obligation that s/he breaks into a sweat.

**Forget it.** |fur GED it| *phr* You don't need to feel obligated. ORIGINS: The idea is that the person offering thanks does not have to keep track of the obligation and remember to repay it.

**No big deal.** |NŌ big dēl| *phr* It wasn't a major imposition. ORIGINS: The idea is that the person offering thanks has not incurred a major obligation.

No biggie. |nō BIG ē| *phr* It wasn't a major imposition. ORIGINS: Shortened version of No big deal.

No problem. |nō PRAHB lum| *phr* It did not cause me any trouble to help you out. ORIGINS: The idea is that the favor did not cause a major interruption in the helpful person's life.

¡No problemo! |nō prō BLĀM ō| *phr* No problem! ORIGINS: From Spanish meaning "no problem." USAGE INFO: Self-conscious, humorous use by a person who is not a native speaker of Spanish or of Spanish descent is what makes this slang. USAGE INFO: The initial exclamation mark used in Spanish is often omitted in English.

No sweat. |NŌ SWET| *phr* Don't worry about it. ORIGINS: Shortened and altered form of Don't sweat it.

No worries. |nō WUR ēz| *phr* Don't worry about it. ORIGINS: Shortened form of Don't worry about it.

NON-SLANG SYNONYMS: You're welcome. **Any time. Don't give it a second thought. Don't worry about it. It's nothing. It's okay. It's the least I could do. You're more than welcome.**

# WAYS TO COMMUNICATE

In general, slang doesn't trade in subtlety, so slang ways of naming the different ways we communicate tend to be bold, colorful, and often idiomatic.

## 1 To Boast

blow off one's mouth/trap/yap |BLŌ ahf wunz MOUTH/TRAP/YAP| *v* To praise oneself excessively; to reveal what was meant to be secret. ORIGINS: From slang blow meaning "boast or brag."

blow one's bazoo |BLŌ wunz bu ZŪ| *v* To brag or boast. ORIGINS: From slang blow meaning "boast or brag" and slang bazoo meaning "mouth," which comes from Dutch baizu meaning "trumpet." See BLOW ONE'S OWN HORN/TRUMPET and TOOT ONE'S OWN HORN/TRUMPET.

blow one's own horn/trumpet |BLŌ wunz ōn HAWRN/TRUM pit| *v* To boast or brag. ORIGINS: From the practice of announcing important people with a fanfare played on brass instruments.

blow smoke |BLŌ SMŌK| *v* To promote an illusion or fantasy about oneself. ORIGINS: From slang blow meaning "boast or brag" and slang smoke meaning "illusion or fantasy—something beyond the reality."

**brag oneself up** |BRAG wun self UP| *v* To boast about oneself.

**crack one's jaw** |KRAK wunz JAW| *v* To boast or brag. ORIGINS: From SE **crack** meaning "to make a sudden, loud noise."

**mouth off** |mou*th* AWF| *v* To boast or brag.

**pat oneself on the back** |PAT wun SELF ahn *thu* BAK| *v* To speak in a self-congratulatory way. ORIGINS: This slang phrase figuratively appropriates the gesture of patting on the back, usually used to acknowledge and honor *sb* else's accomplishments.

**shoot off one's mouth** |SHUT ahf wunz MOUTH| *v* To boast or brag. USAGE INFO: Can also be reordered: **shoot one's mouth off.**

**sound off** |sound AHF| *v* To boast or brag.

**talk big** |TAWK BIG| *v* To exaggerate one's accomplishments or prospects.

**toot one's own horn/trumpet** |TŪT wunz ōn HAWRN / TŪT wunz ōn TRUM pit| *v* To boast or brag. ORIGINS: From the practice of announcing important people with a fanfare played on brass instruments.

NON-SLANG SYNONYMS: boast; **bluster**, **brag**, **crow**; **tout**, **vaunt**

## 2 To Complain

**beef** |bēf| *v* To complain. ORIGINS: From an old meaning of **beef**: "to raise an alarm."

**bellyache** |BEL lē āk| *v* To complain or moan as if one had a stomachache.

**bitch** |bich| *v* To complain. ORIGINS: By extension from the slang noun **bitch** with the idea that this behavior would be typical of a **bitch**. USAGE ALERT: The reference to **bitch** in this phrase will make it objectionable in some contexts and to some people.

**bitch and moan** |BICH und MŌN| *v* To complain all the time. ORIGINS: By extension from the slang noun **bitch** with the idea that this behavior would be typical of such a person. USAGE ALERT: The reference to **bitch** in this phrase will make it objectionable in some contexts and to some people.

**gripe** |grīp| *v* To complain. ORIGINS: By extension from SE noun **gripes** meaning "the pain of colic," with the idea that this behavior would be a likely result.

**grouch** |grouch| *v* To complain. ORIGINS: By extension from SE noun **grouch** meaning "the pain of colic," with the idea that this behavior would be typical of such a person.

**grouse** |grous| *v* To grumble and complain.

**kick up a fuss** |KIK up u FUS| *v* To respond unfavorably and vocally. ORIGINS: From slang **kick up** meaning "start or increase."

**kvetch** |kvech| *v* To complain or nag. ORIGINS: From Yiddish kvetshn meaning "to complain."

**make a (big) stink** |māk u STINGK / māk u BIG STINGK| *v* To complain in a way that attracts a lot of attention. ORIGINS: By figurative extension of SE stink.

**piss and moan** |PIS und MŌN| *v* To complain repeatedly. ORIGINS: By figurative extension of slang **piss** meaning "to urinate" to mean "to complain." USAGE ALERT: The reference to urine in this phrase will make it objectionable in some contexts and to some people.

**raise a stink** |RĀZ u stingk| *v* To complain in a way that attracts a lot of attention. ORIGINS: By figurative extension of SE stink.

**raise Cain** |RĀZ KĀN| *v* To create as troublesome a complaint as possible. ORIGINS: Euphemism for **raise Hell**. Cain, mentioned in the book of Genesis of the Old Testament, is the eldest son of Adam and Eve and the slayer of his brother Abel. USAGE ALERT: The appropriation of a Biblical reference in this phrase will make it objectionable in some contexts and to some people.

**raise (merry) hell** |RĀZ HEL / RĀZ mer ē HEL| *v* To object as forcefully and disruptively as possible. USAGE ALERT: The reference to **hell** in this phrase will make it objectionable in some contexts and to some people.

**squawk** |skwawk| *v* To complain noisily. ORIGINS: From the loud, harsh cry of a bird.

NON-SLANG SYNONYMS: complain, <u>bleat</u>, <u>carp</u>, <u>cavil</u>, <u>grumble</u>, <u>make a fuss</u>, <u>moan</u>, <u>snivel</u>, dissent, find fault, object

# 3 To Exaggerate Something's Importance

**make a big deal** |MĀK u big DĒL| *v* To exaggerate the importance of. ORIGINS: Treating *st* as if its priority and stature were those of an important business deal.

**make a big production** |MĀK u big pru DUK shun| *v* To exaggerate the importance of. ORIGINS: Treating *st* as if its importance were that of a major performance, a Broadway show, for example.

**make a federal case** |MĀK u FED ur ul KĀS| *v* To exaggerate the importance of. ORIGINS: Treating *st* as if its importance were that of a legal issue that deserved the attention of the highest (federal) courts.

NON-SLANG SYNONYMS: exaggerate, overemphasize, <u>blow out of proportion</u>, <u>make a big thing of</u>, <u>make a mountain out of a molehill</u>, <u>magnify</u>

# 4 To Flatter

**ass-kiss** |AS kis| *v* To seek favor through flattery; to be a sycophant or toady. ORIGINS: From SE **ass** meaning "a donkey," but commonly used as slang to refer to the rear end or buttocks. USAGE ALERT: The use of the word **ass**, the graphic image, and the implied insult will make this phrase objectionable in some contexts and to some people.

**back-slap** |BAK slap| *v* To congratulate effusively, often in order to ingratiate oneself. ORIGINS: From the congratulatory gesture of patting the back of someone who has achieved a notable success.

**butter up** |BUT ur up| *v* To flatter; to curry favor. ORIGINS: From the SE noun **butter**, meaning "flattery." The conception is of smoothly spreading flattery.

**kiss *sb's* ass** |KIS *sb's* AS| *v* To seek favor through flattery; to be a sycophant or toady. ORIGINS: From slang **ass** meaning "the rear end or buttocks." USAGE ALERT: The use of the word **ass**, the graphic image, and the implied insult will make this phrase objectionable in some contexts and to some people.

**lick (*sb's*) ass** | LIK as / LIK *sb's* as| *v* To seek favor through flattery; to be a sycophant or toady. ORIGINS: From slang **ass** meaning "the rear end or buttocks." USAGE ALERT: The use of the word **ass**, the graphic image, and the implied insult will make this phrase objectionable in some contexts and to some people.

**play up to** |plā up tū| *v* To curry favor with; to flatter. ORIGINS: From SE **play** meaning "to act."

**suck up (to *sb*)** |suk UP / suk UP tū *sb*| *v* To flatter and otherwise make an attempt to ingratiate oneself; to be obsequious.

NON-SLANG SYNONYMS: compliment, court, fawn on, flatter, praise, wheedle, **rub the right way**, **sweet talk**, **work on**, **adulate**, **blandish**

# 5 To Inform

**bring *sb* up to speed** |BRING *sb* up tū spēd| *v* To supply *sb* with all information that s/he is lacking. ORIGINS: Treats knowledge and understanding as if they were fuel which, once attained, allow full power to be reached. USAGE INFO: Usually used when *sb* is absent, comes late, or is a recent hire and needs to be made aware of what happened during his/her absence or prior to his/her arrival.

**give *sb* the dope** |giv *sb* thu DŌP| *v* To tell *sb* all the important information they need. ORIGINS: From slang **dope** meaning "essential information."

**give *sb* the low down** |giv *sb* thu LŌ doun| *v* To tell *sb* all the inside information about *st*. ORIGINS: From slang **low down** meaning "the inside facts."

**give *sb* the poop** |giv *sb* thu PŪP| *v* To tell *sb* all the inside information about *st*. ORIGINS: From slang **poop** meaning "the inside information."

**give *sb* the scoop** |giv *sb* thu SCŪP| *v* To tell *sb* all the current and/or exclusively obtained information about *st*. ORIGINS: From slang scoop meaning "exclusive news or the very latest information."

**let *sb* in on** |LET *sb* IN ahn| *v* To share information that was heretofore not shared.

**prep** |prep| *v* To supply with all the necessary information. ORIGINS: Shortened form of SE prepare.

**prime** |prīm| *v* To inform *sb* prior to the information being required.

**put *sb* in the picture** |PŌOT *sb* in thu PIK chur| *v* To provide the scope and depth of information that *sb* needs. ORIGINS: The concept is of stepping into a work of art or a photograph and seeing everything firsthand and up close.

**put *sb* wise to** |pōot *sb* WĪZ tū| *v* To inform *sb* about aspects or elements of *st* that are either not common knowledge and/or reveal potentially dangerous or sensitive attributes.

NON-SLANG SYNONYMS: brief, inform, notify, tell; **clue *sb* in**, **fill *sb* in**, **keep *sb* posted**; **advise**, **apprise**, **enlighten**, **impart to**

# 6 To Talk

**blab** |blab| *v* To talk about trivial things; to reveal information that shouldn't have been shared.

**blat** |blat| *v* To talk shrilly.

**come back** |KUM bak| *v* To respond to *st* previously said.

**flap one's gums/lips** |FLAP wunz GUMZ / FLAP wunz LIPS| *v* To talk about trivial things; to talk, but to no purpose.

**gab** |gab| *v* To chat idly.

**go** |gō| *v* To say. USAGE INFO: Often in present tense as in, "So then she goes, 'Do you want to see a movie?'"

**jabber** |JAB ur| *v* To chatter idly, unrestrainedly, or unintelligibly.

**jaw** |jaw| *v* To chat.

**like, be** |līk| *v* To say. USAGE INFO: Often used in present in reporting conversation ("So he's like, 'I'm much smarter than you,' and I'm like, 'No way!'")

**pipe up** |pīp up| *v* To speak after a long period of silence or when characteristically silent; to interrupt. ORIGINS: By extension of SE pipe.

**shoot the breeze** |SHŪT thu BRĒZ| *v* To talk idly. ORIGINS: From the idea that when one talks into the wind, one's words return with no effect.

**spit it out** |SPIT it out| *v* To speak up after being silent or hesitant.

**talk up a storm** |TAWK up u STAWRM| *v* To talk loudly or at length. ORIGINS: From comparison of the breath of talkers to the wind in a storm.

**yak** |yak| *v* To chatter.

**yammer** |YAM ur| *v* To complain peevishly; to whine. ORIGINS: From Middle English *yameren* meaning "to lament."

**yawp** |yawp| *v* To talk loudly. ORIGINS: An alternative form of yap.

NON-SLANG SYNONYMS: communicate, speak, talk; <u>chat</u>, **<u>chew the fat</u>**, **<u>chew the rag</u>**, **<u>rattle on</u>**; **converse**, **declaim**, **discourse**, **hold forth**, **orate**, **parley**

# 7  To Talk Too Much or Indiscreetly

**beat a dead horse** |bēt u ded hawrs| *v* To refuse to drop a subject that has already been discussed thoroughly and completely.

**bend** *sb's* **ear** |BEND *sb's* IR| *v* To talk tediously.

**blabber** |BLAB ur| *v* To talk indiscreetly; to gossip.

**bore stiff** |BAWR STIF| *v* To be unbearably uninteresting.

**give TMFI** |giv TĒ EM EF Ī| *v* To give T(oo) M(uch) F(ucking) I(nformation). ORIGINS: An intensification of give TMI.

**give TMI** |giv TĒ EM Ī| *v* To give T(oo) M(uch) I(nformation). To talk about topics that the speaker's audience finds too intimate or too detailed for their relationship with the speaker and/or the social context.

**go on (about)** |gō AHN / gō AHN u bout| *v* To talk about a topic beyond the point at which the audience loses interest.

**overshare** |ō vur SHER| *v* To talk about topics that the speaker's audience finds too intimate or too detailed for their relationship with the speaker and/ or the social context.

**run off at the mouth** |run AHF at *thu* MOUTH| *v* To talk excessively; to talk without reference to the occasion or one's audience.

**run one's mouth** |RUN wunz MOUTH| *v* To talk without restraint; to gossip.

**shoot off one's mouth** |SHŪT ahf wunz MOUTH| *v* To boast or brag. USAGE INFO: Can also be reordered: shoot one's mouth off.

**spout (off)** |spout / SPOUT awf| *v* To talk too much.

**talk** *sb's* **ear off** |TAWK *sb's* IR awf| *v* To talk tediously and unrelentingly.

**talk the hind leg off a donkey** |TAWK *thu* HĪND leg ahf u DAWN kē| *v* To characteristically talk to the point of exhausting the audience's interest and patience.

NON-SLANG SYNONYMS: talk indiscreetly, talk too much, **<u>go on (about)</u>**, **<u>ramble</u>**, **<u>rattle</u>**, **<u>run-on</u>**, **be diffuse**, **digress**, **drone**

# 8 To Tease

josh |jawsh| *v* To tease good-naturedly. ORIGINS: From Josh Billings, the pseudonym of US humorist Henry Wheeler Shaw (1818–1885).

pull *sb's* leg |PŎOL *sb's* LEG| *v* To tease *sb*.

rag |rag| *v* To annoy or tease repeatedly.

razz |raz| *v* To tease or deride. ORIGINS: Alteration and shortening of slang raspberry, a derisive spluttering sound made with the tongue and lips.

take the mickey out of |tāk *thu* MIK ē out uv| *v* To tease or mock. ORIGINS: From British English.

**take the piss out of** |tāk *thu* PIS out uv| *v* To tease in an aggressive way.

wise off |WĪZ awf| *v* To make jokes at *sb's* expense; to tease.

NON-SLANG SYNONYMS: mock, tease; **kid**, **make fun of**, **pick on**, **poke fun at**, **rib**, **roast**; **bait**, **deride**, **mock**, **ridicule**, **taunt**

# 9 To Tell the Truth

TILII Tell it like it is.

WYSIWYG |WIZ ē wig| What you see is what you get.

come clean |kum KLĒN| *v* To tell the truth after not having told the truth (or the whole truth) previously.

lay it on the line |LĀ it ahn *thu* LĪN| *v* To speak with complete honesty; to clarify what's at stake.

let it all hang out |let it AWL hang out| *v* To act without regard for (social) restraints; to do whatever one wants. ORIGINS: Originally a musical term. USAGE INFO: This expression can be used to refer to being relaxed and at home; to being completely honest; or to defiantly disregarding constraints, whether or not they are legitimate.

level with |LEV ul with| *v* To tell the truth; to share the full picture after not having done so; to confess.

on the up-and-up, be* |ahn *thu* UP und UP| *v* To be honest, legitimate.
   • on the up and up, be |ahn *thu* UP und UP|

open up |Ō pun up| *v* To speak openly and fully after being less forthcoming (for any reason).

talk turkey |tawk TUR kē| *v* To speak openly and without reserve.

tell it like it is |TEL it līk it IZ| *v* To speak openly and honestly.

**upfront, be** |UP FRUNT| *v* To be honest, transparent.

**What you see is what you get.** |wut yū SĒ iz wut yū GET| *phr* To be transparent.

NON-SLANG SYNONYMS: be candid, be honest, be sincere, tell the truth; **get *st* off one's chest**; **be aboveboard**

For dishonest communication, see Deceit and Treachery > Deception on page 501.

# INCREASING INTENSITY— WORDS AND PHRASES

Slang modifiers can add intensity to individual words and phrases, as adjectives and adverbs generally do, as well as act as sentence modifiers. Note that in some cases, the forms of two different parts of speech (noun and adjective; adjective and adverb) are used interchangeably. As a result, you will find entries with an ending in parentheses, like this **damn(ed)** or this awful(ly). Also, in some cases, a single form is used interchangeably as an adjective or an adverb. I have chosen to treat these together so that you can get a better idea of how they function.

So here's the line-up for this section:

1 Adjectives
2 Adverbs
3 Adjectives/Adverbs
4 Comparisons
5 Prefixes, Suffixes, and Infixes

# 1 Adjectives

**crying** |KRĪ ing| *adj* To an extent that it would be justified to cry about it. USAGE INFO: Commonly found in the phrases "a crying shame," and "a crying need."

**damnedest** |DAM dist| *adj* Most of whatever is being expressed: most amazing, most difficult, etc. ORIGINS: Superlative of **damned**. By extension from SE damn, which literally means "Send (it) to hell." USAGE INFO: Often used in phrases such as "it was the damnedest thing"; "I had the damnedest time (finding the restaurant or whatever)". USAGE ALERT: The use of a form of **damn** will be objectionable in some contexts and to some people.

**darnedest, darndest** |DAHRN dist| *adj* Most of whatever is being expressed: most amazing, most difficult, etc. ORIGINS: Euphemism for **damnedest**. Superlative of darned. USAGE INFO: Often used in phrases such as "It was the darnedest thing"; "I had the darnedest time (getting here)." USAGE ALERT: Euphemisms may still be objectionable in some contexts and to some people.

**durndest, durnedest** |DURN dist| *adj* Most of whatever is being expressed: most amazing, most difficult, etc. ORIGINS: Superlative of **durned**. Euphemism for **damnedest**. USAGE INFO: Often used in phrases such as "he was the durnedest fool." USAGE ALERT: Euphemisms may still be objectionable in some contexts and to some people.

**good and <adjective>** |GŎOD und <adjective>| *adj* A flexible, fill-in-the-blank intensifier to which one can add an adjective. USAGE INFO: Can be used for such expressions as "I'll do it when I'm good and ready" (when I'm completely ready) or "Well, he's good and mad now" (he's extremely mad now), etc.

**gosh-awful** |GAHSH AW ful| *adj* Extremely bad; atrocious. ORIGINS: Euphemism for **god-awful**, with gosh being an alteration of SE god. USAGE INFO: Used as an adjective ("a gosh-awful mess") or an adverb ("gosh-awful bad memories"). Many people do not know the origins of this expression. USAGE ALERT: Some people will consider this substituted use of **god** blasphemous and therefore this phrase will be objectionable in some contexts and to some people; nevertheless, it has become more common and more accepted as time has passed.

**holy** |HŌ lē| *adj* An intensifier. ORIGINS: From the slang intensifier holy from SE **holy** meaning "blessed by God." USAGE INFO: Used as an intensifying adjective, as in the phrases "a holy terror" or "a holy mess." USAGE ALERT: The inclusion of the word **holy** as slang may make it seem blasphemous and objectionable in some contexts and to some people.

**infernal** |in FUR nul| *adj* Extreme; complete. ORIGINS: From SE **infernal** meaning "of hell," used as a euphemism for **damn(ed)**. USAGE INFO: Used as an intensifier in negative contexts, as in "an infernal racket." USAGE ALERT: Euphemisms may still be objectionable in some contexts and to some people.

**kick-ass**\* |KIK ASS| *adj* Excellent; effective. ORIGINS: From slang **ass** meaning "the rear end or buttocks." USAGE INFO: **Kick-ass** can be used equally of negative and positive things: "a kick-ass getaway after the robbery" or "a kick-ass birthday party." USAGE ALERT: The inclusion of the word **ass** in the phrase will render it objectionable in some contexts and to some people.
• **kick-butt** |KIK BUTT|

**royal** |ROI ul| *adj* Extreme. ORIGINS: From SE **royal** meaning "pertaining to the/a royal family." USAGE INFO: Often in phrases like, "a royal mess" or "a royal pain."

**serious** |SIR ē us| *adj* Intensifier. USAGE INFO: Used in phrases such as "he was doing some serious drinking" or "that's some serious money."

NON-SLANG SYNONYMS: extreme, **kind of**, **mighty**, **prize**, **regular**, **thumping**

# 2 Adverbs

This list is of slang adverbs and adverbial modifiers that follow normal placement and modification rules. Adverb sentence modifiers are on page 289.

**<number> ways to/from/'til Sunday** |<number> wāz tū SUN dā / <number> wāz frum SUN dā / <number> wāz til SUN dā| *adv* To an extreme degree; extremely well. ORIGINS: **Six ways for Sunday** comes from as early as 1886, when it appears in the novel *Tracy Park* by US author Mary Jane Holmes. Repopularized by the 1997 film *Six Ways to Sunday* and the song "Six Ways 'Til Sunday" by Rise Against (from their album *The Unraveling*, 2001). USAGE INFO: Though it often appears as **six ways to Sunday**, perhaps influenced by the film, the number, the preposition, and the day of the week can all vary as in, for example, **four ways from Sunday, six ways from Wednesday**, etc. USAGE INFO: Used as an adverb as in "we beat them six ways to Sunday."

**all-fired** |AWL FĪRD| *adv* Extremely. ORIGINS: Either refers to propulsion through the firing of engines or can be a euphemism of **hell-fired**. USAGE INFO: Used as an adverb ("so all-fired smart"). Don't confuse it with the similar looking "all fired up," in which **all** is an adverb modifying the phrasal verb **fired up**.

**awful(ly)** |AW ful / AW flē| *adv* Very. USAGE INFO: Notice that the adjective and adverb forms are both used in an adverbial sense, but using the adjective form (**awful**) in a context where an adverbial modifier (**awfully**) is expected may be considered grammatically incorrect, even in a context in which slang is acceptable. So "I'm awfully sick" may be viewed as more acceptable than "I'm awful sick," though both are used.

**bejesus out of, the** |*thu* bi JĒ zus out uv| *adv* To a great extent. ORIGINS: From SE Jesus Christ, whom Christians hold to be the Son of God. USAGE INFO: Most often used with the verb *scare* and verbs related to fighting, e.g., *beat,* but can also be used with *confuse, bore* and other verbs that indicate someone being put at a disadvantage in some way. *See* **SCARE THE BEJESUS OUT OF** *SB*. USAGE ALERT: The use of the name Jesus in this manner will be considered blasphemous and found objectionable in some contexts and by some people.

**but good** |but GOŌD| *adv* To a great degree or extent. USAGE INFO: Used after the word or phrase it modifies as in "I hope she beats him but good."

**damn(ed) sight, a** |u DAM SĪT / u DAM'D SĪT| *adv* Much; a great degree or extent. ORIGINS: By extension from SE **damn**, which literally means "Send (it) to hell." USAGE ALERT: Even when used in a positive sense, as in "You're a damn(ed) sight smarter than he is," the use of **damned** will be objectionable in some situations and to some people.

**dead** |ded| *adv* Completely, very, extremely. USAGE INFO: Can have negative force, as in "dead broke" or positive, as in "dead right."

**devilishly** |DEV ul ish lē| *adv* Extremely. ORIGINS: From SE **devil** meaning "god's adversary." USAGE INFO: Despite origins, is often used light-heartedly as in, e.g., "devilishly delicious." USAGE ALERT: This use of **devil** will be objectionable in some contexts and to some people.

**dreadfully** |DRED ful ē| *adv* Very much; extremely. ORIGINS: Extended from SE **dreadful** meaning "inspiring dread, awe, or reverence." USAGE INFO: As in "I'm dreadfully sorry."

**drop-dead** |DRAHP DED| *adv* Impressively; enough to knock *sb* out. ORIGINS: From the imagined result of the observer dropping dead from the beauty seen. USAGE INFO: Often in the phrase "drop-dead gorgeous."

**fiendishly** |FĒND ish lē| *adv* Extremely. ORIGINS: Euphemism for **devilishly**. From SE **fiend** meaning "the devil." USAGE INFO: Despite origins, is used light-heartedly as in, e.g., "fiendishly clever."

**fit to burst/bust** |fit tū BURST / fit tū BUST| *adj* To the greatest possible extent. ORIGINS: The concept is of having so much of *st* (emotion, for example) that no more is possible without destruction. USAGE INFO: Often used of displays of emotion, as in "laughing fit to bust."

**fit to kill** |fit tū KIL| *adj* To a great extent; to excess; in a striking manner. USAGE INFO: Often used in the phrases "dressed fit to kill" and "laughing fit to kill."

**frightfully** |FRĪT fu lē| *adj* Very; extremely. ORIGINS: From SE **frightfully**, meaning "horrifyingly." USAGE INFO: Originally British use; in the US, found mostly in puns, especially surrounding Halloween ("have a frightfully spooky Halloween"). The same (origins and beginning to be used in the US in puns) is true of **fearfully**, but it seems a bit less common.

**hellishly** |HEL ish lē| *adv* Extremely. ORIGINS: From SE **hell** meaning "the alternative to heaven; the realm of the devil." USAGE INFO: Unlike related words **devilishly** and **fiendlishly**, **hellishly** is always harsh and negative as in, e.g., "a hellishly difficult examination."

**in spades** |in SPĀDZ| *adv* Intensifier; to a great extent; to the greatest extent possible; extremely. ORIGINS: From the jargon of card games, in some of which, spades is the highest suit. USAGE INFO: Often of competition as in "we beat them in spades."

**infernally** |in FUR nu lē| *adv* Extremely; very. ORIGINS: From SE **infernally** meaning "fiendishly or diabolically," used as a euphemism for **damn(ed)**. USAGE INFO: Used as an intensifier in negative and positive contexts, as in "infernally difficult" or "infernally delicious." USAGE ALERT: Euphemisms may still be objectionable in some contexts and to some people.

**living daylights out of, the** |*thu* LIV ing DĀ lītz out uv| *adv* To a great extent. ORIGINS: From slang **daylights** originally meaning "the eyes" and then "the insides." USAGE INFO: Most often used with verbs denoting fighting (*beat, knock, kick*) and terrifying (*scare*).

**majorly** |MĀ jur lē| *adv* To a very great degree; extremely. ORIGINS: From playful addition of the standard adverb ending *-ly* to a word that doesn't take that a suffix in Standard English. USAGE INFO: As in "He was majorly ticked off by her lateness."

**no end** |NŌ end| *adv* To a great degree or extent; endlessly. USAGE INFO: Used before or after the word or phrase it modifies as in "annoyed him no end."

**one's ass off** |wunz AS awf| *adv* To the best of one's ability; with an intense effort. ORIGINS: From slang **ass** meaning "the rear end or buttocks." USAGE INFO: Follows a verb, as in "work one's ass off." USAGE ALERT: The inclusion of **ass** will make this phrase objectionable in some contexts and to some people.

**one's brains out** |wunz BRĀNZ out| *adv* To such an extent that one's sanity is affected. USAGE INFO: Used after the verb. Be careful to distinguish this adverbial usage from those in which *brains* is the object of the verb, as in **blow one's brains out** ("to shoot oneself in the head") or **beat one's brains out** ("to work hard at understanding something extremely difficult") or **beat** *sb's* **brains out** ("murder by blunt force trauma to the head").

**one's buns off** |wunz BUNZ awf| *adv* To the best of one's ability; with an intense effort. ORIGINS: Euphemism for **one's ass off**. From slang **buns**, a synonym for slang **ass** meaning "the rear end or buttocks." USAGE INFO: Follows a verb. USAGE ALERT: The inclusion of even the less objectionable **buns** will make this phrase objectionable in some contexts and to some people.

**one's damnedest** |wunz DAM dist| *adv* With one's maximum effort; with one's best effort. ORIGINS: Superlative of **damned**. By extension from SE **damn**, which literally means "Send (it) to hell." USAGE INFO: Often used in the phrase "do one's damnedest," as when one tries to ensure that *st* reaches completion, comes to pass, etc. USAGE ALERT: The use of a form of **damn** will be objectionable in some contexts and to some people.

**one's darnedest, darndest** |wunz DAHRN dist| *adv* With one's maximum effort; with one's best effort. ORIGINS: Euphemism for **one's damnedest**. USAGE INFO: Often used in the phrase "do one's darnedest," as when one tries to ensure that *st* reaches completion, comes to pass, etc. USAGE ALERT: Euphemisms may still be objectionable in some contexts and to some people.

**one's head off** |wunz HED awf| *adv* To such an extent that one's sanity is affected. USAGE INFO: Used after the verb. Used after the verb. Be careful to distinguish this adverbial usage from those in which *head* is the object of the verb, as in **blow one's head off** ("to shoot oneself in the head").

**something awful** |SUM thing AW ful| *adv* To a great degree or extent or with intensive effort. USAGE INFO: Follows the verb it modifies, as in "She loves him something awful."

**something fierce** |SUM thing FIRS| *adv* To a great degree or extent, or with intensive effort. USAGE INFO: Follows the verb it modifies, as in "My ankle hurts something fierce."

**till one is blue in the face** |TIL wun is BLŪ in *thu* FĀS| *adv* To a great degree or extent, but without notable effect. ORIGINS: One turns blue in the face when experiencing oxygen deprivation through holding one's breath or making an intense effort. USAGE INFO: This expression is used for a determined effort that is frustrated and causes exasperation. It follows the verb it modifies.

**to beat the band** |tu BĒT *thu* BAND| *adv* To a great degree or extent as a result of intensive effort. ORIGINS: A band plays loudly, and one makes oneself heard only through great effort. USAGE INFO: Follows the verb it modifies, as in "cheering to beat the band."

**to hell and back** |tu HEL und bak| *adv* To the point of no return; thoroughly. ORIGINS: Hell—the underworld—is conceived as being a great distance away. Figurative use of SE **hell** meaning "the alternative to heaven; the realm of the devil." USAGE INFO: Follows the verb it modifies. USAGE ALERT: The inclusion of the word **hell** will make this expression objectionable in some contexts and to some people.

**to the max** |tū *thu* MAX| *adv* Completely. ORIGINS: Shortened from **maximum**. USAGE INFO: Follows the verb it modifies.

**way** |wā| *adv* Intensifier; very; extremely. USAGE INFO: Precedes the word it modifies, as in "The Medici's pizza is way delicious."

**with a vengeance** |with u VEN juns| *adv* To an extreme degree.

NON-SLANG SYNONYMS: extremely, thoroughly, very, **madly**, **precious**, **proper**, **seriously**, **to a great extent**, (note that some of these, like some of those listed above, have very particular uses)

# 3 Adjectives/Adverbs

**big-time** |BIG tīm| *a/a* Important; complete; in a big way; completely. ORIGINS: May draw on the noun **big time**, which means "the highest level of success in a given field." USAGE INFO: Can be used as an adjective ("big-time loser"; "big-time lawyer") or as an adverb ("He's losing it big-time.").

**blame(d)** |blām / blāmd| *a/a* Extreme; extremely; very; blameworthy; etc. ORIGINS: A euphemism for **damn(ed)**. USAGE INFO: Used as an adjective ("a blame(d) idiot") or an adverb ("traffic moving so blame(d) slow"; "a blame(d) fool thing to do"). USAGE ALERT: Euphemisms may still be objectionable in some contexts and to some people.

**blamedest** |BLĀM dist| *a/a* Worst; least; etc. ORIGINS: A euphemism for **damnedest**. USAGE INFO: Used as either an adjective ("the blamedest idea") or an adverb ("the blamedest little thing"). USAGE ALERT: Euphemisms may still be objectionable in some contexts and to some people.

**blanked** |blangkt| *a/a* Extreme; extremely; very; etc. ORIGINS: Euphemism for **damned**. Refers to the blank space sometimes left in a text to replace a PO word. The *-ed* ending is in imitation of the past participles. USAGE INFO: Used as an adjective ("a blanked fool") or an adverb ("so blanked fancy"). USAGE ALERT: Euphemisms may still be objectionable in some contexts and to some people.

**blankety(-blank)** |BLANG ki tē / BLANG ki tē BLANGK| *a/a* Cursed; very; extremely. Also functions as a sentence modifier. ORIGINS: Euphemism for **damned** and other PO words. Refers to the blank space sometimes left in a text to replace a PO word. **Blankety** draws on an adjective suffix used in words like **persnickety, crotchety, fidgety,** etc. Although one might expect blank to replace one-syllable words and blankety or blankety-blank to replace multi-syllable words, this is not always the case. An increased number of syllables may, however, suggest a stronger word. Used as an adjective ("my blankety-blank job") or an adverb ("so blankety-blank often"). USAGE ALERT: Euphemisms may still be objectionable in some contexts and to some people.

**blanking** |BLANG king| *a/a* Extreme; extremely; very; etc. ORIGINS: Euphemism for **fucking** or **damned** or other PO words. Refers to the blank space sometimes left in a text to replace a PO word. The *-ing* ending is in imitation of present participles. Used as an adjective ("a blanking idiot") though blinking idiot is more common, or an adverb ("blanking good news"). USAGE ALERT: Euphemisms may still be objectionable in some contexts and to some people.

**blasted** |BLAS tid| *a/a* Extreme; extremely; very; etc. ORIGINS: A euphemism for **damn(ed)**. USAGE INFO: Used as an adjective ("blasted mosquitoes") or an adverb ("blasted good time"). Note that the *-ed* is not optional for blasted. USAGE ALERT: Euphemisms may still be objectionable in some contexts and to some people.

**bleeped** |blēpt| *a/a* Extreme; extremely; very; etc. ORIGINS: Euphemism for **damn(ed)**. From the sound used to overdub obscenities in broadcasts. The *-ed* ending is in imitation of past participles. USAGE INFO: Used as an adjective ("bleeped fool") or an adverb ("bleeped stupid ass"). Note that the *-ed* is not optional for bleeped. USAGE ALERT: Euphemisms may still be objectionable in some contexts and to some people.

**bleeping** |BLĒP ing| *a/a* Extreme; extremely; very; etc. ORIGINS: Euphemism for **fucking**. From the sound used to overdub obscenities in broadcasts. The *-ing* ending is in imitation of present participles. USAGE INFO: Used as an adjective ("a bleeping fool") or an adverb ("bleeping cool movie"). USAGE ALERT: Euphemisms may still be objectionable in some contexts and to some people.

**blessed** |BLES id| *a/a* Extreme; extremely; very; etc. ORIGINS: Euphemism for **damned**. USAGE INFO: Literally means the opposite of **damned**, so becomes a contronym in this use. Used as an adjective ("not a blessed cent") or an adverb ("a blessed good thing"). USAGE ALERT: Euphemisms may still be objectionable in some contexts and to some people.

**blinking** |BLING king| *a/a* Extreme or extremely. ORIGINS: Originated as a euphemism for the British word **blooming,** itself a euphemism for **bloody**. The use of this term in the US may have been prompted by Shakespeare's phrase "the portrait of a blinking idiot" in II, ix, 57 of *The Merchant of Venice*. USAGE INFO: Used as an adjective ("blinking idiot") or an adverb ("blinking good idea"). USAGE ALERT: Speakers of British English are more likely than speakers of US English to know the actual origins of the word, but it may still be objectionable in some contexts and to some people.

**confounded** |kun FOUN did| *a/a* Extreme; extremely; very; etc. ORIGINS: Euphemism for **damn(ed)**. From SE confound meaning "to bring to perdition." USAGE INFO: Used as an adjective ("confounded idiot") or as an adverb ("confounded good idea"). Note that the *-ed* is not optional for **confounded**. USAGE ALERT: Euphemisms may still be objectionable in some contexts and to some people.

**consarned** |kun SAHRND| *adj* Extreme; extremely; very; etc. ORIGINS: Euphemism for **damn(ed)**. From SE concern. USAGE INFO: Used as an adjective ("now wait a consarned minute") or an adverb ("consarned small thing to care about so much"). Note that the *-ed* is not optional for **consarned**. USAGE ALERT: Euphemisms may still be objectionable in some contexts and to some people.

**cussed** |KUS id| *a/a* Extreme; extremely; very; cursed. ORIGINS: Euphemism for **damn(ed)**. From SE cursed. USAGE INFO: Used as an adjective ("cussed fool") or an adverb ("cussed small serving"). USAGE ALERT: Euphemisms may still be objectionable in some contexts and to some people.

**dad gum(med)/dadgum(med)** |DAD GUM / DAD GUM'D| *a/a* Extreme; extremely; very; blameworthy; etc. ORIGINS: Euphemism for **goddamn(ed)**. Dad is a euphemism used in a number of curses to replace **God** in order to be less objectionable. Gum is a euphemism for **damn(ed)**. USAGE INFO: Used as an adjective ("the dadgum(med) rat") or an adverb ("so dadgum(med) good"). USAGE ALERT: Euphemisms may still be objectionable in some contexts and to some people.

**dadblame(d)** |dad BLĀM / dad BLĀM'd| *a/a* Extreme; extremely; very; blameworthy; etc. ORIGINS: Euphemism for **goddamn(ed)**. Dad is a euphemism used in a number of curses to replace **God** in order to be less objectionable. Blamed is a euphemism for **damn(ed)**. USAGE INFO: Used as an adjective ("dadblame(d) horse") or an adverb ("dadblame(d) awful time"). USAGE ALERT: Euphemisms may still be objectionable in some contexts and to some people.

**dadblasted** |DAD BLAS tid| *a/a* Extreme; extremely; very; blameworthy; etc. ORIGINS: Euphemism for **goddamn(ed)**. Dad is a euphemism used in a number of curses to replace **God** in order to be less objectionable. Blasted is a euphemism for **damn(ed)**. USAGE INFO: Used as an adjective ("the dadblasted thing") or an adverb ("dadblasted stupid person"). USAGE ALERT: Euphemisms may still be objectionable in some contexts and to some people.

**dagnabbed** |DAG NAB'D| *a/a* Goddamn(ed). ORIGINS: **Dag** is an altered form of dad, which is a euphemism used in a number of curses to replace **God** in order to be less objectionable. Nabbed is a euphemism for **damn(ed)**. USAGE INFO: Used as an adjective ("the dagnabbed situation") or an adverb ("dagnabbed stupid person"). USAGE ALERT: Euphemisms may still be objectionable in some contexts and to some people.

**damn(ed)** |dam / dam'd| *a/a* Cursed; very; extremely; extreme. Also functions as a sentence modifier. ORIGINS: By extension from SE **damn**, which literally means "Send (it) to hell." USAGE INFO: Used as an adjective ("damn(ed) fool") or as an adverb ("damn(ed) good meal"). USAGE ALERT: Although these uses of **damn** are often simply equivalent to *very* or *extreme*, and not intended to mean "cursed," nevertheless, people who take issue with cursing are likely to find them objectionable.

**dang(ed)** |dang / dang'd| *a/a* Extreme; extremely; very. ORIGINS: Euphemism for **damn(ed)**. USAGE INFO: Used as an adjective ("dang(ed) idiot") or an adverb ("so dang(ed) stupid"; "dang(ed) good thing"). USAGE ALERT: Euphemisms may still be objectionable in some contexts and to some people.

**darn(ed)** |dahrn / dahrn'd| *a/a* Extreme; extremely; very. ORIGINS: Euphemism for **damn(ed)**. USAGE INFO: Used as an adjective ("darn(ed) cat") or an adverb ("darn(ed) good store"). USAGE ALERT: Euphemisms may still be objectionable in some contexts and to some people.

**dashed** |dasht| *a/a* Extreme; extremely; very. ORIGINS: Euphemism for **damn(ed)**. From the dashes used to replace the middle letters in **damn**, like this: *d--n*, in order to render it less objectionable in print. USAGE INFO: Used as an adjective ("dashed pigeons") or an adverb ("dashed good luck"). USAGE ALERT: Euphemisms may still be objectionable in some contexts and to some people.

**deuced** |dūst| *a/a* Extreme; extremely; very. ORIGINS: Euphemism for **damn(ed)**. Originally a euphemism for the devil, possibly inspired by SE deuce, the lowest, least fortunate throw in games of dice. USAGE INFO: Used as an adjective ("deuced shame") or an adverb ("deuced lucky"; "a deuced good time"). USAGE ALERT: Euphemisms may still be objectionable in some contexts and to some people.

**doggone(d)** |dawg GAWN / dawg GAWN'D| *a/a* Extreme; extremely; very. ORIGINS: Euphemism for **damn(ed)**. USAGE INFO: Used as an adjective ("doggone(d) dog") or an adverb ("doggone(d) good thing"). USAGE ALERT: Euphemisms may still be objectionable in some contexts and to some people.

**dratted** |DRAT id| *a/a* Extreme; extremely; very. Substitute for **damn(ed)**. ORIGINS: From the phrase "God rot it." Subsequently, a euphemism for **damn(ed)**. USAGE INFO: Used as an adjective ("dratted computer") or an adverb ("dratted awful insect"). USAGE ALERT: Euphemisms may still be objectionable in some contexts and to some people.

**durn(ed)** |durn / durn'd| *a/a* Extreme; extremely; very. ORIGINS: Euphemism for **damn(ed)**. USAGE INFO: Used as an adjective ("durn(ed) contraption") or an adverb ("durn(ed) fine day"). USAGE ALERT: Euphemisms may still be objectionable in some contexts and to some people.

**effing** |EF ing| *a/a* Extreme; extremely; very. ORIGINS: Euphemism for **fucking** using the initial letter and suffix. USAGE INFO: Used as an adjective ("effing asshole") or an adverb ("What took you such an effing long time?"). USAGE ALERT: Euphemisms may still be objectionable in some contexts and to some people.

**filthy** |FIL thē| *a/a* A general intensifier: very; extremely. ORIGINS: SE filthy meaning "very dirty." USAGE INFO: Used as an adjective ("filthy temper"), and very often connected with money, as in this adverbial use ("filthy rich").

**flipping** |FLIP ing| *a/a* Extreme; extremely; very. ORIGINS: Euphemism for **fucking**. USAGE INFO: Used as an adjective ("flipping idiot") or an adverb ("flipping good time"). USAGE ALERT: Euphemisms may still be objectionable in some contexts and to some people.

**freaking** |FRĒK ing| *a/a* Extreme; extremely; very. ORIGINS: Euphemism for **fucking**. A slang word that is related to sexuality and sounds very similar to **fucking**. In its denotative use (i.e., when it is not acting as an intensifier), **freaking** means "sexually perverse." USAGE INFO: Used as an adjective ("freaking moron") or an adverb ("freaking good meal"). Note that many users may think that this word is a sanitized version of the word **fucking**, not recognizing it as a real word with an independent existence. USAGE ALERT: People who know the denotative meanings of this word or suspect that it is being used as a euphemism for **fucking** are likely to find the terms objectionable.

**fricking** |FRIK ing| *a/a* Extreme; extremely; very. ORIGINS: Euphemism for **fucking**. A slang word that is related to sexuality and sounds very similar to **fucking**. In its denotative use (i.e., when it is not acting as an intensifier), **frick** (and **frack**) refers to the testicles. USAGE INFO: Used as an adjective ("fricking ass") or an adverb ("fricking beautiful"). Note that many users may think that this word is a sanitized version of the word **fucking**, not recognizing it as a real word with an independent existence. USAGE ALERT: People who know the denotative meanings of this word or suspect that it is being used as a euphemism for **fucking** are likely to find the terms objectionable.

**frigging** |FRIG ing| *a/a* Extreme; extremely; very. ORIGINS: Euphemism for **fucking**. A slang word that is related to sexuality and sounds very similar to **fucking**. In its denotative use (i.e., when it is not acting as an intensifier), **frigging** means either "masturbating" or "intercourse." USAGE INFO: Used as an adjective ("frigging shame") or an adverb ("frigging awful"). Note that many users may think that this word is a sanitized version of the word **fucking**, not recognizing it as a real word with an independent existence. USAGE ALERT: People who know the denotative meanings of this word or suspect that it is being used as a euphemism for **fucking** are likely to find the terms objectionable.

**fucking** |FUK ing| *a/a* Very; complete; total; extremely. ORIGINS: From slang **fuck** meaning "to engage in sexual intercourse." USAGE INFO: Used as an adjective ("fucking asshole") or as an adverb ("fucking good time"). It was this type of use by Bono during the broadcast of the Golden Globe Awards in 2003—reported as "this is really, really fucking brilliant" or "this is fucking great"—that led to an obscenity complaint. However, such use was found *not* to be obscene by the Federal Communications Commission. There are many alternates and euphemisms for this emphatic use of **fucking**. USAGE ALERT: This use of **fucking** will be objectionable in some contexts and to some people.

**god-awful** |GAHD aw ful| *a/a* Extremely bad; atrocious. ORIGINS: This term uses slang **god** as an intensifier. From SE **god** meaning a being conceived as the divine Lord of the universe. USAGE INFO: Used as an adjective ("a god-awful production of a play") or an adverb ("god-awful ugly uniform"). USAGE ALERT: Some people will consider this slang use of god blasphemous and therefore this phrase will be objectionable in some contexts and to some people.

**god dang(ed), goddang(ed), god-dang(ed)** |gahd DANG, gahd DANG'D| *a/a* Extreme; extremely; very. ORIGINS: Euphemism for **goddamn(ed)**. From SE god meaning a being conceived as the divine Lord of the universe and dang, a euphemism for slang **damn**. USAGE INFO: Used as an adjective ("god dang(ed) pain") or an adverb ("god dang(ed) pretty cat"). USAGE ALERT: People who take issue with cursing, or who view this use of god as blasphemy are likely to find this term objectionable.

**goddamn(ed), goddam(ed)** |GAHD dam / gahd DAM'D| *a/a* Cursed; very; extremely; extreme. ORIGINS: By extension from SE **damn**, which literally means "Send (it) to hell," and SE god meaning a being conceived as the divine Lord of the universe. USAGE INFO: Used as an adjective ("goddamn(ed) traffic") or as an adverb ("goddamn(ed) long time"). USAGE ALERT: Although these uses of **goddamn(ed)** are often simply equivalent to *very* or *extreme* and not intended to mean "cursed," nevertheless, people who take issue with cursing or consider this use of god blasphemous are likely to find them objectionable.

**goddarn(ed), god darn(ed)** |gahd DARN'D| *a/a* Extreme; extremely; very. ORIGINS: Euphemism for **goddamn(ed)**. From SE god meaning a being conceived as the divine Lord of the universe and darn, a euphemism for slang **damn**. USAGE INFO: Used as an adjective ("another goddarn(ed) test") or an adverb ("a goddarn(ed) funny joke"). USAGE ALERT: People who take issue with cursing, or who view this use of god as blasphemy are likely to find this term objectionable.

**gol dang(ed), goldang(ed)** |gahl DANG / gahl DANG'D| *a/a* Extreme; extremely; very. ORIGINS: Euphemism for **goddamn(ed)**. USAGE INFO: Used as an adjective ("gol dang(ed) idiot") or an adverb ("a gol dang(ed) great article"). USAGE ALERT: Euphemisms may still be objectionable in some contexts and to some people.

**goldarn(ed), gol darn(ed)*** |gahl DARN / gahl DARN'D| *a/a* Extreme; extremely; very. ORIGINS: Euphemism for **goddamn(ed)**. USAGE INFO: Used as an adjective ("goldarn(ed) mess") or an adverb ("a goldarn(ed) nice guy"). USAGE ALERT: Euphemisms may still be objectionable in some contexts and to some people.
• goldurn(ed) |gahl DURN / gahl DURN'D|

**goshdarn(ed)** |gahsh DARN / gahsh DARN'D| *a/a* Extreme; extremely; very. ORIGINS: Euphemism for **goddamn(ed)**. USAGE INFO: Used as an adjective ("wait a goshdarn(ed) minute") or an adverb ("a goshdarn(ed) bad day"). USAGE ALERT: People who take issue with cursing, or who view the substituted use of god as blasphemy are likely to find this term objectionable; nevertheless, it has become more common and more accepted as time has passed.

**heck of a, heckuva** |HEK uv u| *a/a* Extreme; extremely; very. ORIGINS: An altered form of and euphemism for **hell of a** or **helluva**. USAGE INFO: Used as an adjective ("a heckuva guy") or as an adverb ("one heck of a fine job"). Notice the use of one. USAGE ALERT: Euphemisms may still be objectionable in some contexts and to some people.

**hell of a, helluva** |hel uv u| *a/a* Extreme; extremely; very. ORIGINS: Figurative use of SE **hell** meaning "the alternative to heaven; the realm of the devil." USAGE INFO: Used as an adjective, as in "helluva guy," or as an adverb, as in "hell of a good sandwich." Also prefaced by *one* as in **one hell of a**. USAGE ALERT: Because this phrase includes the word **hell**, it will be objectionable in some contexts and to some people.

**hell-fired** |HEL fīrd| *a/a* Extreme; extremely; very. An intensifier. ORIGINS: From the concept of hell as a place with fire; literally "damned to the fires of hell." Figurative use of SE **hell** meaning "the alternative to heaven; the realm of the devil." USAGE INFO: Notice that **hell-fired** is used both as an adjective ("wrote hell-fired poetry") and as an adverb ("hell-fired mad"). USAGE ALERT: Because this phrase includes the word **hell**, it will be objectionable in some contexts and to some people.

**mondo** |MAHN dō| *a/a* Intensifier: great; greatly; extraordinary; extraordinarily. ORIGINS: From the use of the Italian word **mondo** meaning "large" in the title of the movie *Mondo Cane* meaning *A Dog's World* (1961). USAGE INFO: Used as an adjective, as in "a mondo burger," or as an adverb, as in the oft-used phrase "mondo bizarro" (also spelled "mondo bizzaro" by some).

**perishing** |PER ish ing| *a/a* Extreme; extremely; very. ORIGINS: Euphemism for **damn(ed)**. USAGE INFO: Used as an adjective ("a perishing pity") or an adverb ("perishing cold"). Note that it is never "perishing hot." USAGE ALERT: Euphemisms may still be objectionable in some contexts and to some people.

**pissing** |PIS ing| *a/a* Extreme; extremely; very. ORIGINS: From slang **piss** meaning "to urinate." USAGE INFO: Can be used as an adjective ("such a pissing idiot") or an adverb ("a pissing good joke"). USAGE ALERT: This use of **piss** will be objectionable in some contexts and to some people.

**shit-hot** |SHIT HAHT| *a/a* Excellent; first-rate. Extremely; especially. ORIGINS: From slang **shit** meaning "excrement" and **hot** meaning "attractive." This is a pun, due to the initial temperature of excrement. USAGE INFO: Used as an adjective ("shit-hot videos") or as an adverb ("a shit-hot good plan"). USAGE ALERT: Because it includes **shit**, this word will be objectionable in some contexts and to some people.

**so <word/phrase>** |sō <word/phrase>| *a/a* Utterly; completely. A construction to describe *st* by characterizing it in terms of *st* else. USAGE INFO: Used as an adjective meaning "dated" in constructions with a time period that has passed ("so last year," "so last season," "so last century," "so yesterday"), and as an adverb with other objects with the meaning "completely" ("so not her fault," "so not my favorite subject").

**wicked** |WIK id| *a/a* Very; extremely. ORIGINS: From SE **wicked**. USAGE INFO: Used as an adjective ("a wicked headache") or as an adverb ("a wicked good show").

**NON-SLANG SYNONYMS:** complete, completely, especially, excellent, extreme, extremely, great, greatly, very

# 4 Comparisons

**as <adjective> as a bastard** |az <adjective> az u BAS turd| *adj* Intensifies the named adjective to an extreme degree. ORIGINS: From **bastard** meaning "a mean or nasty person" or "a problematic situation," by extension of SE bastard, meaning "an illegitimate child." USAGE ALERT: The inclusion of the word **bastard** in the phrase will render this phrase objectionable in some contexts and to some people.

**as <adjective> as a bitch** |az <adjective> az a BICH| *adj* Intensifies the named adjective to an extreme degree. ORIGINS: From **bitch** meaning "an unpleasant, offensive, difficult person of either sex" or "extremely difficult," extended from SE bitch, meaning "a female dog." USAGE ALERT: The inclusion of the word **bitch** in the phrase will render it objectionable in some contexts and to some people.

**as <adjective> as all creation** |az <adjective> az awl krē Ā shun| *adj* Intensifies the named adjective to an extreme degree.

**as <adjective> as all get out** |az <adjective> az awl GET out| *adj* Intensifies the named adjective to an extreme degree.

**as <adjective> as anything** |az <adjective> az EN ē thing| *adj* Intensifies the named adjective to an extreme degree.

**as <adjective> as blazes** |az <adjective> az BLĀ zuz| *adj* Intensifies the named adjective to an extreme degree. ORIGINS: Euphemism for **as <adjective> as hell**. Blazes is a euphemism for **hell** from SE hell meaning "the alternative to heaven; the realm of the devil." Blazes to the fires of hell. USAGE ALERT: The euphemism blazes in this phrase will soften it somewhat, but it may still be objectionable in some contexts and to some people.

**as <adjective> as can be** |az <adjective> az kan BĒ| *adj* Intensifies the named adjective to an extreme degree.

**as <adjective> as heck** |az <adjective> az HEK| *adj* Intensifies the named adjective to a moderate degree. ORIGINS: Euphemism for **as <adjective> as hell**. Heck is a euphemism for **hell** from SE hell meaning "the alternative to heaven; the realm of the devil." Heck has a similar-sounding start, but its substitution tends to lessen the intensity of the comparison. USAGE ALERT: The euphemism heck in this phrase will soften it somewhat, but it may still be objectionable in some contexts and to some people.

**as <adjective> as hell** |az <adjective> az HEL| *adj* Intensifies the named adjective to an extreme degree. ORIGINS: Figurative use of SE hell meaning "the alternative to heaven; the realm of the devil." USAGE ALERT: The inclusion of the word **hell** in this phrase will render it objectionable in some contexts and to some people.

**as <adjective> as shit** |az <adjective> az SHIT| *adj* Intensifies the named adjective to an extreme degree. ORIGINS: From **shit** meaning "excrement." USAGE ALERT: The inclusion of the word **shit** in this phrase will render it objectionable in some contexts and to some people.

**as <adjective> as they come** |az <adjective> az *th*ā KUM| *adj* Intensifies the named adjective to an extreme degree.

**like anything** |līk EN ē thing| *adv* To the greatest extent possible; with total commitment.

**like crazy/mad** |līk KRĀ zē / līk MAD| *adv* To the greatest extent possible; with total commitment.

**like hell** |līk HEL| *adv* Very much; to a great extent. ORIGINS: Figurative use of SE **hell** meaning "the alternative to heaven; the realm of the devil." USAGE INFO: This can be an intensifier for something negative, as in "it hurts like hell," or it can be ironic and express disagreement as in: "Deal honestly? Like hell he does!" meaning that he doesn't. USAGE ALERT: The inclusion of **hell** in the phrase will render it objectionable in some contexts and to some people.

**like the devil** |līk *th*u DEV ul| *adv* Very much; to a great extent (of whatever it is). ORIGINS: Euphemism for **like hell**, SE **hell** being the place where the devil resides. USAGE INFO: This phrase can modify a verb as **like hell** can, as in "run like the devil," but it does not share the second type of ironic use. USAGE ALERT: The inclusion of the word **devil** in the phrase will render it objectionable in some contexts and to some people.

NON-SLANG SYNONYMS: as much as possible, -est, the best, the greatest, the maximum, the most, to the greatest degree

# 5 Prefixes and Suffixes

There are actually three kinds of additions that can change words of other registers to slang: prefixes, suffixes, and infixes. Although prefixes and suffixes are well-known, infixes—words placed within other words—are new to many people. Probably best known until recently was the one used by Eliza Dolittle in the musical and movie versions of *My Fair Lady—abso-bloomin'-lutely*. Here, we focus on some of the key slang prefixes and suffixes. See page 594 for more on infixes.

**-ass(ed)** |as / ast| *sfx* The suffix **-ass** can combine with an SE noun (candy) or adjective (sad) to form a noun (**candy-ass**, **sadass**) or an adjective (crazy) to form an adjective (**crazy-ass**). The suffix **-assed** can combine with a noun or adjective (candy, sad) to form an adjective (**candy-assed**, **sadassed**). ORIGINS: From SE **ass** meaning "a donkey," but commonly used as slang to refer to the rear end or buttocks. USAGE INFO: Note that both the noun and the adjective form are used as adjectives. Intensifies the word it follows to an extreme degree, as in: **candy-ass** ("a sissy; not up to expectations"); **crazy-ass** ("an eccentric, a fool, or an out-of-control person"); **hard-ass** ("an uncompromising or mean person"—

beyond <u>hardnose</u>); **raggedyass** ("a disreputable or impoverished person or place"); and **sadass** ("a depressed person"). *See* **BADASS, KICK-ASS,** and **SMART-ASS** for their idiosyncratic meanings. USAGE ALERT: All words containing **ass** will be found objectionable in some contexts and by some people.

**-bag** |bag| *sfx* A person. Combines with a noun (most often) to describe a person who is considered contemptible. ORIGINS: Similar to the idiom **bag of bones** to characterize a person. Terms with **-bag** often depict a person as a bag full of unpleasant or disgusting contents. USAGE INFO: *See* DIRTBAG, **DOUCHEBAG, SCUMBAG,** SCUZZBAG, SLEAZEBAG, and SLIMEBAG, found grouped with SLIMEBALL.

**-ball** |bawl| *sfx See* -BAG.

**-bucket** |BUK it| *sfx See* -BAG.

**-head** |hed| *sfx* A fan, particularly of a music style. ORIGINS: SE head is used to represent the whole person. USAGE INFO: Forms a closed compound with the word it modifies, e.g., a **metalhead** is one who enthusiastically enjoys the music called *heavy metal*. **-head** is also combined with words to indicate foolishness or stupidity, as in blockhead.

**holy** |HŌ lē| *pfx* Combining form to create interjections. ORIGINS: From the slang intensifier **holy** from SE holy meaning "blessed by God." USAGE INFO: Creates an interjection when combined with ordinary words, rhyming words, and PO words, as in holy cow! holy mackerel! holy guacamole! holy moly/moley! holy smoke(s)! and **holy fuck!** The phrases with rhyming words (such as *guacamole*) or oddball word choices (such as *mackerel*) have a touch of humor and are open to being used more light-heartedly. USAGE ALERT: The inclusion of the word **holy** as slang may make it seem blasphemous and objectionable in some contexts and to some people.

**-licious** |LISH us| *sfx* A delicious or enticing example of; an exceptional example of. ORIGINS: By extension of SE **delicious.** USAGE INFO: The first meaning occurs in constructions such as **babelicious** and **bootylicious**, relating to sexual attraction; the second, for example, in nonce situations like movie reviews, as in **grumpilicious**, describing a well-acted portrayal of a grumpy character.

**-o** |ō| *sfx* Used to create adjectives, including some having to do with mental health, like batso, nutso, sicko, and wacko.

**-ola** |Ō la| *sfx* Used as an intensifying suffix. USAGE INFO: As in **crapola.**

**piss-** |pis| *pfx* Used as an intensifying prefix. ORIGINS: From slang **piss** meaning "urine." USAGE INFO: *See* **PISSANT, PISSHEAD, PISS-POOR.** USAGE ALERT: The inclusion of a form of **piss** joined to another word will render it objectionable in some contexts and to some people.

**-tacular** |TAK yū lur| *sfx* A spectacular example of; an extreme example of. ORIGINS: By extension of SE **spectacular.** USAGE INFO: The first meaning occurs in punning constructions like **spooktacular**, often used in connection with ghosts and Halloween; the second in constructions like **craptacular.**

**-tastic** |TAS tik| *sfx* A fantastic example of; stunningly awful. ORIGINS: By extension of SE **fantastic.** USAGE INFO: The first meaning occurs in constructions like **funtastic;** the second in constructions like **craptastic**, and is generally used ironically.

# INCREASING INTENSITY— WHOLE SENTENCES

Some slang forms add intensity to entire sentences. This is a sampling of some of the words most frequently used in this way, but euphemisms for these words can be used similarly. The first section is for interjections that are most often seen added to the beginning of sentences. The second section is for other constructions, such as forms that are placed as we would expect for adjectives and adverbs, but modify the entire sentence rather than the noun, verb, or adjective we would expect.

## 1 Introductory Sentence Modifiers

These adverbs behave as standard sentence modifiers, usually standing at the start of the sentence they modify, separated from the rest of the sentence by a comma. Many of these slang expressions are also used independently as interjections.

**crumbs** |krumz| *adv* Sentence modifier. ORIGINS: Euphemism for **Christ!** An alteration of the name of Jesus Christ by changing letters. USAGE INFO: Often used to express disappointment, as in "Crumbs, what a small serving!" USAGE ALERT: People who recognize it as a replacement for a name of God may find **crumbs** objectionable and/or blasphemous. However, in the twenty-first century, most people will probably not make the connection.

**damn** |DAM it awl| *adv* Sentence modifier with various shades of meaning. ORIGINS: By extension from SE **damn**, which literally means "Send (it) to hell." USAGE INFO: Used to modify/intensify a whole sentence, as in "Damn, that's a gorgeous sunset!" USAGE ALERT: Although this use of **damn** is usually synonymous with a word like *wow* or *well*, nevertheless, people who take issue with cursing are likely to find it objectionable.

**dang** |dang| *adv* Sentence modifier. ORIGINS: Euphemism for **damn**. USAGE INFO: Sentence modifier showing disappointment or frustration, as in "Dang, we missed the bus." USAGE ALERT: Euphemisms may still be objectionable in some contexts and to some people.

**darn** |dahrn| *adv* Sentence modifier. ORIGINS: Euphemism for **damn**. USAGE INFO: Sentence modifier showing disappointment or frustration, as in "Darn, I wish I'd known." USAGE ALERT: Euphemisms may still be objectionable in some contexts and to some people.

**durn** |durn| *adv See* DARN.

**fuck** |FUK| *adv* Sentence modifier with various shades of meaning. ORIGINS: From slang **fuck** meaning "to engage in sexual intercourse." USAGE INFO: Used to modify/intensify a whole sentence, as in "Fuck, that's a lot of money!" USAGE ALERT: This term will be objectionable in some contexts and to some people.

**gee (whiz)** |gē / gē WIZ| *adv* Sentence modifier. ORIGINS: Euphemism for **Jesus** used as a sentence modifier—a figurative use of SE Jesus whom Christians hold to be the Son of God, but it is milder and is more likely to be positive. USAGE INFO: Used as a sentence modifier as in "Gee whiz, what a great movie!" USAGE ALERT: Even euphemized, this phrase will be considered objectionable in some contexts and by some people who may find it blasphemous.

**god dang, goddang, god-dang** |gahd DANG| *adv* Sentence modifier with various shades of meaning. ORIGINS: Euphemism for **goddamn**. From SE god meaning a being conceived as the divine Lord of the universe and dang, a euphemism for slang **damn**. USAGE INFO: Sentence modifier showing frustration, delight, etc., as in "God dang, that was awesome!" USAGE ALERT: People who take issue with cursing, or who view this use of god as blasphemy are likely to find this term objectionable.

**goddamn, goddam** |GAHD dam| *adv* Sentence modifier with various shades of meaning. ORIGINS: By extension from SE **damn**, which literally means "Send (it) to hell," and SE god meaning a being conceived as the divine Lord of the universe. USAGE INFO: Used to modify/intensify a whole sentence, as in "Goddamn, you took a long time!" or "Goddamn, you look good!" USAGE ALERT: Although this use of **damn** is usually synonymous with a word like wow or well, nevertheless, people who take issue with cursing or consider this use of god blasphemous are likely to find it objectionable.

**goddarn, god-darn** |gahd DARN| *adv* Sentence modifier. ORIGINS: Euphemism for **goddamn**. From SE god meaning a being conceived as the divine Lord of the universe and darn, a euphemism for slang **damn**. USAGE INFO: Sentence modifier showing frustration, delight, etc., as in "Goddarn, that was a loud concert." USAGE ALERT: People who take issue with cursing, or who view this use of god as blasphemy are likely to find this term objectionable.

**gol dang, goldang** |gahl DANG| *adv* Sentence modifier. ORIGINS: Euphemism for **goddamn**. USAGE INFO: Sentence modifier showing frustration, delight, etc., as in "Gol dang, that mango was good." USAGE ALERT: Euphemisms may still be objectionable in some contexts and to some people.

**goldarn, gol darn\*** |gahl DARN| *adv* Sentence modifier. ORIGINS: Euphemism for **goddamn**. USAGE INFO: Sentence modifier showing frustration, delight, etc., as in "Goldarn, I wish I'd known sooner." USAGE ALERT: Euphemisms may still be objectionable in some contexts and to some people.
• gol durn |gahl DURN|

**golly** |GAH lē| *adv* Sentence modifier. ORIGINS: Euphemism for slang **god**. From SE god meaning a being conceived as the divine Lord of the universe. USAGE INFO: Sentence modifier showing frustration, delight, etc., as in "Golly, that was a lucky break!" Many people will not know the origins of this expression. USAGE ALERT: Euphemisms may still be objectionable in some contexts and to some people.

**good grief** |GOOD GRĒF| *adv* Sentence modifier with various shades of meaning. ORIGINS: Euphemism for **good god**. From SE god meaning a being conceived as the divine Lord of the universe. USAGE INFO: Used to modify/intensify a whole sentence, as in "Good grief, that was a narrow escape!" Many people will not know the origins of this expression. USAGE ALERT: Although this usage is usually synonymous with a word like *wow* or *well*, nevertheless, people who consider it blasphemy will find this term objectionable. Nevertheless, it has become more common and more accepted as time has passed.

**gosh** |gahsh| *adv* Sentence modifier. ORIGINS: Euphemism for slang **god**. From SE **god** meaning a being conceived as the divine Lord of the universe. USAGE INFO: Sentence modifier showing frustration, delight, etc., as in "Gosh, that was good." Many people do not know the origins of this expression. USAGE ALERT: People who consider this substitution for **god** as blasphemy will find this term objectionable, but it has become more common and more accepted as time has passed.

**heck** |hek| *adv* Sentence modifier. ORIGINS: An altered form of and euphemism for **hell**. USAGE INFO: Sentence modifier showing frustration, delight, etc: "Heck, that was quite a ball game!" USAGE ALERT: Euphemisms may still be objectionable in some contexts and to some people.

**hell** |hel| *adv* Sentence modifier with various shades of meaning. ORIGINS: Figurative use of SE **hell** meaning "the alternative to heaven; the realm of the devil." USAGE INFO: Used to modify/intensify a whole sentence, as in "Hell, I wish I'd known!" USAGE ALERT: Although this use of **hell** is usually synonymous with a word like *wow* or *well*, nevertheless, people who take issue with cursing are likely to find it objectionable.

**Jeepers!** |JĒ purz| *excl* An interjection expressing surprise, shock, dismay, etc. ORIGINS: Euphemism for **Jesus** used as an interjection—a figurative use of SE **Jesus** whom Christians hold to be the Son of God—but it is milder. USAGE INFO: Many people will not know the ORIGINS of this expression. USAGE ALERT: People who consider this substitution for **Jesus** blasphemous are likely to find this term objectionable.

**jeez** |jēz| *adv* Sentence modifier. ORIGINS: Euphemism for **Jesus** used as a sentence modifier—a figurative use of SE **Jesus** whom Christians hold to be the Son of God—but it is milder. USAGE INFO: Used as a sentence modifier to show frustration, relief, and other emotional responses, as in "Jeez, what a day!" Many people will not know the origins of this expression. USAGE ALERT: This saying will be considered objectionable in some contexts and by some people who may find it blasphemous.

**Jesus** |JĒ zus| *adv* Sentence modifier. ORIGINS: From SE **Jesus Christ** whom Christians hold to be the Son of God. USAGE INFO: Used as a sentence modifier to show anger, dismay, frustration, relief, and other emotional responses, as in "Jesus, what happened to my car!?" USAGE ALERT: The use of the word **Jesus** in this way will seem blasphemous and objectionable in some contexts and to some people.

**sheesh** |shēsh| *adv* Sentence modifier to convey surprise, relief, annoyance, etc. ORIGINS: Euphemism, oddly, for both **shit** and **Jesus**—a figurative use of SE **Jesus** whom Christians hold to be the Son of God, but it is milder. USAGE INFO: Used at the beginning of a sentence to modify the sentence as in, "Sheesh, that was a close one!" Many people have no idea of the origins of this phrase and will use it without reference to either of the words it may stand in for. USAGE ALERT: Some people may find this word blasphemous or otherwise objectionable because of its origins.

**shit** |shit| *adv* Sentence modifier with various meanings. ORIGINS: From slang **shit**, meaning "excrement." USAGE INFO: Used to modify/intensify a whole sentence, as in "Shit, I missed the bus!" USAGE ALERT: This word will be objectionable in some contexts and to some people.

# 2 Other Sentence Modifiers

**cotton-picking** |KAHT'n pik ing| *adj* Adjective that works as a sentence modifier. ORIGINS: Euphemism for **damn(ed)**. From the time when people, particularly slaves, picked cotton. USAGE INFO: Like **damn(ed)**, cotton-picking is an all-purpose term that usually intensifies the feeling of a whole sentence rather than specifically the word that it precedes and appears to modify; e.g., "Get your cotton-picking hand out of the cookie jar" is a condemnation of you-taking-a-cookie, not an attack on the quality of your hand. See **DAMN(ED)**. Often heard in the phrases "wait a cotton-picking minute" and "are you out of your cotton-picking mind?" USAGE ALERT: People who identify the reference as racist or who recognize it as a substitute for **damn(ed)** may find cotton-picking objectionable.

**damn(ed)** |dam / dam'd| *adj* Adjective that works as a sentence modifier. ORIGINS: By extension from SE **damn**, which literally means "Send (it) to hell." USAGE INFO: Functions as a sentence modifier while positioned as an adjective ("Get in the damn(ed) house!"; "Why can't I find my damn(ed) wallet?"). USAGE ALERT: People who take issue with cursing are likely to find this use of **damn(ed)** objectionable.

**damn well** |DAM WEL| *adv* Adverb that works as a sentence modifier. ORIGINS: By extension from SE **damn**, which literally means "Send (it) to hell." USAGE INFO: This phrase often modifies the word directly following ("I damn well *will*"; "He damn well *is* going to spend the rest of his life in jail!"). As the italics in the example sentences indicate, the word following the phrase usually receives the most emphasis. See FUCKING WELL. USAGE ALERT: The inclusion of **damn** will make this phrase objectionable in some contexts and to some people.

**fucking** |FUK ing| *a/a* Adjective/adverb that works as a sentence modifier. ORIGINS: From slang **fuck** meaning "to engage in sexual intercourse." USAGE INFO: Used to modify/intensify a whole sentence, as in the phrase "Are you fucking kidding me?" or "Get in the fucking house." USAGE ALERT: This term will be objectionable in some contexts and to some people.

**motherfucking** |MU *thur* FUK ing| *a/a* Adjective/adverb that works as a sentence modifier. ORIGINS: The literal meaning is a male who commits incest with his mother. From slang **fuck** meaning "to engage in sexual intercourse." USAGE INFO: Used nominally as an adjective ("Get your motherfucking ass out of my chair!") or as an adverb ("What a motherfucking stupid idea!"). USAGE ALERT: Forms of **motherfucker** are considered among the most offensive words in English.

**stinking** |STING king| *adj* Adjective that works as a sentence modifier. ORIGINS: Euphemism for **damn(ed)**. From SE <u>stinking</u> meaning "having a strong, unpleasant smell." USAGE INFO: Used for negative effect ("I don't have to show you any stinking badges!"—*The Treasure of the Sierra Madre*, 1948) and very often connected with money ("stinking rich"). USAGE ALERT: People who recognize it as a substitute for **damn(ed)** may find stinking objectionable.

**the deuce** |*thu* DŪS| *adv* A sentence modifier. ORIGINS: Euphemism for **the hell**; SE **hell** being the place where the devil resides and **deuce** being a euphemism for **devil**. USAGE INFO: Used following interrogative adverbs (*who, what, where, when, why, how*) to convey surprise, shock, and/or dismay, as in "What the deuce are you doing in Wyoming?" "How the deuce did you get in my house?" "Where the deuce do you think you're going with my barometer?" or "Why the deuce aren't you doing your homework, like I told you?" USAGE ALERT: The inclusion of **deuce** will make this expression objectionable in some contexts and to some people, but usually less so than **devil**.

**the devil** |*thu* DEV ul| *adv* A sentence modifier. ORIGINS: Euphemism for **the hell**; SE **hell** being the place where the devil resides. USAGE INFO: Used following interrogative adverbs (*who, what, where, when, why, how*) to convey surprise, shock, and/or dismay, as in "What the devil is this stain on the floor?" "How the devil am I supposed to read this scrawl?" "Where the devil is my favorite tee-shirt?" or "Who the devil are you?" USAGE ALERT: The inclusion of **devil** will make this expression objectionable in some contexts and to some people.

**the dickens** |*thu* DIK unz| *adv* A sentence modifier. ORIGINS: Euphemism for **the devil**. Slang dickens is an altered form of SE **devil**. USAGE INFO: Used following interrogative adverbs (*who, what, where, when, why, how*) to convey surprise, shock, and/or dismay, as in "What the dickens do you want now?" USAGE ALERT: The inclusion of a reference to the devil will make this term objectionable in some contexts and to some people.

**the fuck** |*thu* FUK| *adv* A sentence modifier. ORIGINS: Figurative use of slang **fuck** meaning "sexual intercourse." USAGE INFO: Used following interrogative adverbs (*who, what, where, when, why, how*) to convey surprise, shock, and/or dismay, as in "What the fuck is the matter with you?" Also used in expressions such as **Get the fuck out**. USAGE ALERT: The inclusion of **fuck** will make this expression objectionable in some contexts and to some people.

**the heck** |*thu* HEK| *adv* Sentence modifier. ORIGINS: Euphemism for **the hell**. Heck is an altered form of and euphemism for **hell**. USAGE INFO: Used following interrogative adverbs (*who, what, where, when, why, how*) to express surprise, shock, or dismay, etc., as in "What the heck am I supposed to do now?" USAGE ALERT: The euphemism heck in this phrase will soften it somewhat, but it may still be objectionable in some contexts and to some people.

**the hell** |*thu* HEL| *adv* Sentence modifier. ORIGINS: Figurative use of SE **hell** meaning "the alternative to heaven; the realm of the devil." USAGE INFO: Used following interrogative adverbs (*who, what, where, when, why, how*) to convey surprise, shock, and/or dismay, as in "What the hell is going on here?" USAGE ALERT: The inclusion of **hell** will make this expression objectionable in some contexts and to some people.

NON-SLANG SYNONYMS: goodness, my, oh, <u>wow</u>

# Feelings and States

One of the many things we do with slang is add nuance and color to the topic of feelings and states. We use slang to describe the onset of feelings, as well as the feelings and states themselves. This is an area, particularly when speaking of the emotion of anger, in which the subtlety of slang is apparent: slang offers us an enormous array of specificity here. And, as you might expect, since slang deals mainly with passion, caricature, and gusto, it gives a lot more scope to anger than to, say, calm. The organization of this chapter is as follows:

*Anger*
  1 To Cause Mild Anger or Irritation
  2 To Cause Moderate Anger
  3 To Cause Extreme Anger
  4 To Cause Anger and Upset
  5 To Become Angry
  6 To Become Angry or Lose Control
  7 To Feel Angry
  8 To Feel Suppressed Anger
  9 Mildly Angry
  10 Moderately Angry
  11 Extremely Angry
  12 Angry Plus
  13 Liable to Anger
  14 A Fit of Anger

*Arrogance and Conceit*

*Attraction*
  1 To Cause Attraction
  2 To Become Attracted
  3 To Feel Attracted
  4 Attracted
  5 To Feel Mutually Attracted

*Calm*
  1 To Become Calm
  2 To Feel or Maintain Calm
  3 Calm

*Courage*
  1 To Be Brave
  2 Courageous

*Disgust*
  1 To Cause Disgust
  2 Disgusted

*Excitement*
  1 Excited
  2 Agitated

*Fear*
  1 To Cause Fear
  2 To Become Afraid
  3 To Feel Fear
  4 Liable to Fear
  5 A Fit of Fear

*Happiness and Delight*
  1 Happy
  2 To Cause Laughter
  3 To Laugh

*Humiliation*
  1 To Cause Humiliation
  2 To Become Humiliated

*Mental Illness*
  1 Depressed
  2 A Fit of Depression
  3 To Have a Mental Breakdown
  4 Crazy

*Relaxation*
  1 Tired/Out of It
  2 Relaxed
  3 To Sleep

*Stupidity*

# ANGER

## 1 To Cause Mild Anger or Irritation

**bug** |bug| *v* To irritate; to annoy. ORIGINS: To act like an SE **bug** ("an insect").

**get in *sb's* hair** |get in *sb's* HER| *v* To annoy; to irritate. ORIGINS: From the situation of having lice in one's hair.

**get under *sb's* skin** |get un dur *sb's* SKIN| *v* To irritate; to annoy; to pester. ORIGINS: To annoy like a splinter does.

**give *sb* a pain in the neck** |GIV *sb* u PĀN in *th*u NEK| *v* To irritate someone. USAGE INFO: Sometimes purposely substituted for **pain in the ass/butt**, but may also be used in its own right.

**needle** |NĒ dul| *v* To provoke; to tease; to goad.

**nettle** |NE tul| *v* To vex; to annoy; to irritate. ORIGINS: From SE **nettle**, a plant with stinging hairs that cause skin irritation, therefore, "to irritate."

**nudge, noodge, nudzh** |nŏŏj| *v* To irritate; to pester; to nag or complain. ORIGINS: From Yiddish **nudyen** meaning "to pester or bore."

**pick on *sb*** |PIK ahn *sb*| *v* To choose *sb* as the target for annoyance, irritation, insults, etc.

**tee *sb* off** |TĒ *sb* AWF| *v* To irritate *sb*; to anger *sb*. ORIGINS: Possibly from the first letter of tick off.

**tick *sb* off** |TIK *sb* awf| *v* To irritate or annoy *sb*. ORIGINS: Possibly a euphemism for **piss *sb* off**.

NON-SLANG SYNONYMS: annoy, bother, disturb, irk, irritate, pester, **rub *sb* the wrong way**, **peeve**, **provoke**, **ruffle**, **vex**

## 2 To Cause Moderate Anger

**frost *sb*** |FROST *sb*| *v* To cause anger or upset; to cool off a relationship.

**get *sb's* goat** |get *sb's* GŌT| *v* To purposely irritate; to provoke to the point of outburst.

**get in *sb's* face** |get in *sb's* FĀS| *v* To be aggressively irritating. ORIGINS: From the close proximity to one's face of someone who is intruding into one's space.

**get on** *sb's* **nerves** |GET ahn *sb's* NURVZ| *v* To annoy or irritate a lot. USAGE INFO: Note that although you can ask *sb* to "get off my back" or "get off my case," there is no corresponding expression "get off my nerves."

**get up** *sb's* **nose** |get up *sb's* NŌZ| *v* To irritate; to annoy; to bother.

**give** *sb* **a pain in the ass/butt** |GIV *sb* u PĀN in *thu* AS / GIV *sb* u PĀN in *thu* BUT| *v* To irritate someone. ORIGINS: From slang **ass** meaning "the rear end or buttocks." From slang **butt** meaning "the rear end or buttocks" and acting as a euphemism for **ass**. USAGE INFO: Comparison with give *sb* a pain in the neck shows that despite the difference in the body part in which one is pained (and that neck is less likely to be objectionable than **ass** or **butt**), there's not much difference in meaning. USAGE ALERT: The reference to the rear end or buttocks will make both versions of this expression objectionable in some contexts and to some people, though butt might be less objectionable to some than ass.

**gripe** *sb's* **ass** |GRĪP *sb's* AS| *v* To anger *sb*. ORIGINS: By extension of slang gripe, meaning "to complain." From slang **ass** meaning "the rear end or buttocks." USAGE ALERT: The inclusion of the word **ass** will make this phrase objectionable in some contexts and to some people.

**piss** *sb* **off** |PIS *sb* awf| *v* To annoy or irritate. ORIGINS: From slang **piss** meaning "to urinate." USAGE ALERT: The inclusion of the word **piss** in the phrase will render it objectionable in some contexts and to some people.

**rile (up)** |rīl / RĪL up| *v* To make angry; to move to angry action. ORIGINS: From SE roil, meaning "to stir up."

**wind** *sb* **up** |WĪND *sb* UP| *v* To purposely, even maliciously, annoy or irritate *sb*. ORIGINS: From SE **wind up** and the practice of winding a clock.

NON-SLANG SYNONYMS: aggravate, anger, provoke, rile, **madden**, **rankle**

# 3 To Cause Extreme Anger

**burn** *sb* **up** |BURN *sb* up| *v* To cause extreme anger. ORIGINS: A number of slang terms for anger relate to heat.

**drive** *sb* **crazy** |DRĪV *sb* KRĀ zē| *v* To exasperate *sb* to the point of distraction.

**get to** *sb* |GET tū *sb*| *v* To irritate or annoy someone to the point at which they're seriously affected.

**make** *sb's* **blood boil** |māk *sb's* BLUD boil| *v* To infuriate *sb*; to enrage *sb*. ORIGINS: An example of the association of anger and heat.

NON-SLANG SYNONYMS: antagonize, exasperate, **enrage**, **gall**, **incense**, **inflame**, **infuriate**, **outrage**

## 4 To Cause Anger and Upset

**jerk *sb's* chain** |JURK *sb's* CHĀN| *v* To purposely annoy or harass *sb*; to act in a way that one knows upsets *sb*. ORIGINS: From SE **jerk** meaning "to pull sharply." The reference is to using a leash and collar to curb a dog. USAGE INFO: *See* YANK *SB'S* CHAIN. USAGE ALERT: Some people may connect this word to **jerk-off**, although they do not seem to be etymologically linked.

**miff** |mif| *v* To anger and offend; to annoy. ORIGINS: Onomatopoeic from a sniff of disgust.

**pull *sb's* chain** |POŌL *sb's* CHĀN| *v* To purposely annoy or harass *sb*; to act in a way that one knows upsets *sb*.

**pull *sb's* strings** |POŌL *sb's* STRINGZ| *v* To behave in such a way as to gain the desired reaction; to act in a way that one knows will upset, anger, or frustrate *sb*.

**push *sb's* buttons** |POŌSH *sb's* BUT unz| *v* To behave in such a way as to gain the desired reaction; to act in a way that one knows will upset, anger, or frustrate *sb*.

**put *sb's* nose out of joint** |poŏt *sb's* NŌZ out uv joint| *v* To offend and anger *sb*; to upset and annoy *sb*.

**rattle *sb's* cage** |RAT ul *sb's* KĀJ| *v* To annoy or upset *sb* on purpose.

**yank *sb's* chain** |YANGK *sb's* CHĀN| *v* To purposely annoy or harass *sb*; to act in a way that one knows upsets *sb*. ORIGINS: From SE **yank** meaning "to pull sharply." USAGE INFO: *See* JERK *SB'S* CHAIN.

NON-SLANG SYNONYMS: dismay, distress, unnerve, unsettle, upset, **affront**, **faze**, **perturb**, **pique**

## 5 To Become Angry

**boil over** |BOIL Ō vur| *v* To become extremely angry. ORIGINS: From cooking.

**burn², also burn up** |burn / BURN up| *v* To become very angry. ORIGINS: A number of slang terms for anger relate to heat.

**do a slow burn** |dū u SLŌ BURN| *v* To experience a gradually increasing sense or show of anger.

**fly off the handle** |FLĪ ahf *thu* HAN dul| *v* To become extremely angry; to lose control. ORIGINS: From what happens when an axe head becomes detached from the handle.

**get in a wax** |get in u WAKS| *v* To become angry; to be in a rage. ORIGINS: From slang **wax** meaning "anger; temper."

**get into a huff** |get in tū u HUF| *v* To get into a bad temper; to lose one's temper; to become offended.

**get into a lather** |get in tū u LA*TH* ur| *v* To get worked up about something; become anxious. ORIGINS: From the profuse sweating that can accompany anger and anxiety.

**get into a snit** |get in tū u SNIT| *v* To work oneself into a temper; to be so frustrated or angry that one takes it out on others; a state of agitation and irritation.

**get into a stew** |get in tū u STŪ| *v* To get worked up to the point of breaking out in a sweat; to be anxious or agitated.

**get into a sweat** |get in tū u SWET| *v See* GET INTO A LATHER.

**get one's Irish up** |get wunz Ī rish up| *v* To become angry. USAGE ALERT: The association of anger with a particular cultural group will make this expression objectionable in some contexts and to some people.

**get pissed (off)** |get PIST / get PIST awf| *v* To become very annoyed. ORIGINS: From slang **piss**, meaning "urine." USAGE ALERT: The reference to urine will make this expression objectionable in some contexts and to some people.

NON-SLANG SYNONYMS: become angry, become enraged, <u>flare up</u>, <u>get angry</u>, <u>get mad</u>, **burn with a slow blue flame**, **take umbrage at**

# 6 To Become Angry or Lose Control

**blow one's cool** |BLŌ wunz KŪL| *v* To become angry; to lose control. ORIGINS: From extension of slang blow meaning "to squander or waste (money)" along with the conception of cool as a concrete possession that could be spent or lost.

**blow one's cork** |BLŌ wunz KAWRK| *v* To explode with anger; to lose one's temper; to become furious. ORIGINS: By figurative extension of SE **blow** meaning "explode." **Cork** can be replaced with a number of other items that have to do with the topmost part of something: the word **top** itself, the closing mechanism at the top of a bottle (**stopper**), the highest part of a train engine (**stack**), or the item worn on top of the head (**wig**). USAGE INFO: *See* BLOW THE LID OFF (OF) *ST*, which has similar elements, but a quite different meaning.

**blow one's fuse*** |BLŌ wunz FYŪZ| *v* To explode with anger. ORIGINS: A figurative use of the identical phrase from electrical engineering, which refers to the fact that a fuse is a device that protects electrical circuits from overloading. The fuse "blows" to interrupt the circuit and prevent damage. In other technical fields, such as plumbing, a gasket is used to prevent the escape of gas or fluid. If the gasket is "blown," the gas or fluid is released. This is also applied figuratively.
• blow one's gasket |BLŌ wunz GAS kit|

**blow one's stack** |BLŌ wunz STAK| *v See* BLOW ONE'S CORK.

**blow one's stopper** |BLŌ wunz STAH pur| *v See* BLOW ONE'S CORK.

**blow one's top** |BLŌ wunz TAHP| *v See* BLOW ONE'S CORK.

**blow one's wig** |BLŌ wunz WIG| *v See* BLOW ONE'S CORK.

**blow up**[1] |BLŌ up| *v* To lose control; to become enraged. ORIGINS: From SE **blow up** meaning "to explode," used figuratively.

**climb the wall(s)** |KLĪM *thu* WAWL / KLĪM *thu* WAWLZ| *v* To become angry; to lose one's temper; to lose one's mind. ORIGINS: The phrase may be an attempt to create an image of *sb* trying anything and everything to escape the situation s/he is in.

**flip one's lid/wig** |FLIP wunz lid / FLIP wunz wig| *v* To lose one's temper; to fly into a rage; to lose control emotionally; to go crazy. ORIGINS: From slang **lid** meaning "head."

**flip out** |FLIP out| *v* To become angry; to lose control. ORIGINS: By extension of slang **flip** meaning "to lose control."

**go ape** |gō ĀP| *v* To become very angry; to lose one's temper; to lose control. ORIGINS: The conceived behavior of apes. USAGE INFO: Sometimes used to mean "to become happily excited."

**go ape shit** |gō ĀP SHIT| *v* To become very angry; to lose one's temper; to lose control. ORIGINS: From the conceived behavior of apes and slang **shit** meaning "excrement." USAGE ALERT: The inclusion of **shit** will make this expression objectionable in some contexts and to some people.

**go ballistic** |gō bu LIS tik| *v* To lose one's temper; to become violently angry; to become extremely upset. ORIGINS: By extension from SE **ballistic** which refers to firearms, which operate by controlled explosion.

**go bananas** |gō bu NAN uz| *v* To be so angry one loses control. ORIGINS: Possibly extended from SE **bananas** going soft when they're overripe to "going soft in the head."

**go crazy** |gō KRĀ zē| *v* To be so angry that one loses control.

**go off the deep end** |gō ahf *thu* DĒP end| *v* To get out of one's depth, emotionally; to go crazy; to become so angry that one loses control. ORIGINS: Refers to the deep end of the swimming pool (and possibly to being in over one's head). USAGE ALERT: This way of speaking about *sb's* mental health may be considered insensitive and therefore objectionable in some contexts and by some people.

**go out of one's skull** |gō out uv wunz SKUL| *v* To lose control; to go crazy. ORIGINS: The phrases **out of one's skull/mind/head/gourd**, etc. call up a contrast to the idiom **in one's right mind**, meaning "sane and in control."

**go postal** |gō PŌ stul| *v* To become extremely angry; to lose control. ORIGINS: This term refers to historical events of the late twentieth century in which there were several multiple shootings by postal workers of co-workers. USAGE INFO: Some people do not realize the historic background to this term and use it naively. USAGE ALERT: This phrase is offensive to postal workers and may also be to others who know its origins.

**go through the roof** |gō thrū *thu* RŪF| *v* To lose one's temper; to become extremely angry. USAGE INFO: Also used of escalating prices.

**lose it** |lūz it| *v* To lose control; to become extremely angry.

**lose one's cool** |lūz wunz KŪL| *v* To become angry; to lose control. ORIGINS: From extension of SE lose along with the idea of cool being a concrete possession that could be lost.

**lose one's head** |lūz wunz HED| *v* To become angry; to lose control. ORIGINS: From extension of SE lose along with the idea of the head being the seat of rationality and balance.

NON-SLANG SYNONYMS: erupt, lose control, lose one's temper, **fly into a rage**, **go off**

# 7 To Feel Angry

**have a case of the ass** |hav u KĀS uv thē AS| To feel extremely annoyed.

**have a catfit** |hav u KAT fit| *v* To have a tantrum.

**have a conniption fit** |hav u ku NIP shun fit| *v* To become violently angry or panicked.

**have a cow** |hav u KOU| *v* To become angry or upset; to throw a fit. ORIGINS: From the nervousness of an expectant mother animal. USAGE INFO: Often used in the negative imperative, e.g., "Don't have a cow!"

**have a fit** |HAV u FIT| *v* To become very angry; to have an angry outburst. USAGE INFO: Milder than have forty fits. *See also* THROW A FIT, which is stronger on account of the stronger verb.

**have a shitfit** |hav u SHIT fit| *v* To throw a tantrum; to have an (angry) outburst. ORIGINS: From slang **shit** meaning "excrement" and SE fit meaning "a sudden outburst." USAGE ALERT: The reference to excrement will make this phrase objectionable in some contexts and to some people.

**have forty fits** |hav FAWR tē FITS| *v* To become very angry; to have an angry outburst. USAGE INFO: Stronger than have a fit. *See also* THROW FORTY FITS, which is stronger on account of the stronger verb.

**have kittens** |hav KIT 'nz| *v* To become angry or upset; to throw a fit. ORIGINS: From the nervousness of an expectant mother animal. USAGE INFO: Often used in the negative imperative, e.g., "Don't have kittens!"

**have steam coming out of one's ears** |hav STĒM kum ing out uv wunz irz| *v* To be extremely angry or upset. ORIGINS: Related to other phrases that figuratively convey anger with steam. *See* STEAM, STEAMED.

**hit the ceiling** |hit *thu* SĒ ling| *v See* HIT THE ROOF.

**hit the roof** |hit *thu* RŪF| *v* To lose one's temper; to become explosively angry. ORIGINS: From the association of anger with explosions.

**pissed (off), be** |PIST AHF| *v* To feel extremely annoyed. ORIGINS: From slang **piss** meaning "to urinate." USAGE INFO: "He is pissed" and "He is pissed off" can be used interchangeably. USAGE ALERT: The inclusion of a form of the word **piss** in the phrase will render it objectionable in some contexts and to some people.

**pop one's cork** |pahp wunz KAWRK| *v* To lose one's temper; to become extremely angry. ORIGINS: From the association of anger with explosions.

**see red** |SĒ RED| *v* To become extremely angry.

**shit a brick\*** |SHIT u BRIK| *v* To be furious. ORIGINS: From slang **shit** meaning "excrement." May refer to emotionally induced constipation. USAGE ALERT: The inclusion of the word **shit** in the phrase will render it objectionable in some contexts and to some people.
• **shit bricks** |SHIT BRIKS|

**steam** |stēm| *v* To be angry or annoyed.

**throw a fit** |THRŌ u FIT| *v* To fly into a rage. USAGE INFO: Compare with have a fit.

**throw forty fits** |THRŌ FAWR tē FITS| *v* To fly into a rage. USAGE INFO: Compare with have forty fits.

NON-SLANG SYNONYMS: be angry, be cross, be irked, <u>be mad</u>, **be galled**, **be irate**

## 8 To Feel Suppressed Anger

**simmer** |SIM ur| *v* To be filled with unexpressed emotions, often anger.

**sizzle** |SIZ ul| *v* To be filled with unexpressed emotions, often anger.

**smolder** |SMŌL dur| *v* To be filled with unexpressed anger.

**stew** |stū| *v* To be in a lingering state of sullen anger or feeling offended or insulted, often without expressing it.

NON-SLANG SYNONYMS: <u>chomp at the bit</u>, **bristle**, **chafe**, **fume**, **seethe**

## 9 Mildly Angry

**teed off** |TĒD awf| *adj* Irritated; annoyed. ORIGINS: Possibly from the first letter of ticked off, in the same way that **peed off** is an alteration of **pissed off**.

**ticked (off)** |tikt / TIKT awf| *adj* Irritated; annoyed. ORIGINS: This seems to be related to military jargon **tick off** meaning "a scolding."

NON-SLANG SYNONYMS: annoyed, bothered, displeased, irritated

# 10 Moderately Angry

**bent out of shape** |BENT out uv SHĀP| *adj* Very angry. ORIGINS: This phrase is conceived on the analogy of a person to a delicate object that can be damaged in two degrees: 1) bent out of shape; 2) broken. USAGE INFO: The phrase is sometimes abbreviated to bent. The comparable verb form **bend** *sb* **out of shape** is hardly ever used.

**boiled up** |BOILD UP| *adj* To be very angry. ORIGINS: From cooking.

**boiling (mad)** | BOI ling / BOI ling MAD| *adj* To be very angry. ORIGINS: From cooking.

**het up** |HET up| *adj* Agitated; angry; tense. ORIGINS: From SE **heat** and the phrase "heated up."

**hot under the collar** |HAHT UN dur *thu* KAH lur| *adj* Angry.

**huffy** |HUF ē| *adj* Bad-tempered; angry.

**madder than a wet hen** |MAD ur *than* u WET HEN| *adj* Very angry. USAGE INFO: There have been a number of comparisons made to emphasize the extent of *sb's* anger. Mad as a hornet is another. Be careful to distinguish between comparisons in this form that refer to anger and those that refer to loss of sanity, such as mad as a hatter and mad as a march hare—both made popular in Lewis Carroll's (Charles L. Dodgson's) *Alice in Wonderland* (1865).

**pee'd off** |PĒD AWF| *adj* Furious; extremely angry. ORIGINS: Euphemism for **pissed (off)**. From slang **pee**, a euphemism for slang **piss** meaning "to urinate." USAGE INFO: Unlike **pissed (off)** the particle off is rarely dropped from this phrase. USAGE ALERT: The inclusion of a word referring to urine in the phrase will render it objectionable in some contexts and to some people.

**pissed (off)** |pist / PIS tawf| *adj* Furious; extremely angry. ORIGINS: From slang **piss** meaning "to urinate." USAGE INFO: The two forms **pissed** and **pissed off** can be used interchangeably. USAGE ALERT: The inclusion of a form of the word **piss** in the phrase will render it objectionable in some contexts and to some people.

**poed, po'ed, p.o.'d** |PĒ ŌD| *adj* Furious; extremely angry. ORIGINS: Initialized euphemism for **pissed off**. From slang **piss** meaning "to urinate." USAGE ALERT: The reference to a form of the word **piss** in the phrase will render it objectionable in some contexts and to some people.

**steamed** |stēm'd| *adj* Annoyed.

**torqued** |tawrkt| *adj* Angry.

NON-SLANG SYNONYMS: angry, exasperated, mad, riled, **put out**, **irate**, **ireful**

# 11 Extremely Angry

**burning up** |BUR ning up| *adj* Feeling extremely angry. ORIGINS: A number of slang terms for anger relate to heat.

**fit to be tied** |FIT tū bē TĪD| *v* Enraged. ORIGINS: From the situation of someone so angry that s/he needs to be restrained (tied).

**foaming at the mouth** |FŌM ing at *th*u MOUTH| *adj* Furious; enraged. ORIGINS: From the characteristics of a rabid dog.

**hacked (off)** |hakt / HAK tawf| *adj* Extremely angry. ORIGINS: From slang **hack** meaning "to irritate."

**livid** |LIV id| *adj* To be furious; to be filled with rage. ORIGINS: From SE **livid** meaning "ashen," that is white-faced; thus, an interesting contrast to other slang that connects anger with the color red and a red face.

**madder than hell** |MAD ur *than* HEL| *adj* Enraged; furious. ORIGINS: The fires of hell are being referenced. Figurative use of SE **hell** meaning "the alternative to heaven; the realm of the devil." USAGE INFO: This phrase with the comparative form of mad associates anger with heat and fire, as do so many others. **Mad as hell** uses the positive form of the adjective, and so has a bit less force. USAGE ALERT: The inclusion of the word **hell** in the phrase will render it objectionable in some contexts and to some people.

**on the rag** |ahn *th*u RAG| *adj* Irritable; angry and ready for a fight or an argument. ORIGINS: Probably connected to slang **rag** meaning sanitary napkin used during menstruation. USAGE ALERT: This phrase will be objectionable to people who believe that it suggests that women are unable to control their emotions due to hormonal changes, as well as for its graphic image.

**on the warpath** |ahn *th*u WAWR path| *adj* Irritable; angry and ready for a fight or an argument. ORIGINS: From Native American **path to war** meaning "the route traveled to engage in battle." USAGE ALERT: Used today with no reference to its history, but will be objectionable to those who feel it is a racial slur, stereotyping Native Americans.

**rip shit** |RIP shit| *adj* Extremely angry. ORIGINS: From SE **rip** and slang **shit** meaning "excrement."

**up the wall** |up *th*u WAWL| *adj* Extremely angry, frustrated, or upset.

NON-SLANG SYNONYMS: furious, in a rage, outraged, raging, up in arms, <u>ranting and raving</u>, **apoplectic**, **enraged**, **in high dudgeon**, **infuriated**, **wrathful**

## 12  Angry Plus

**miffed** |mift| *adj* Annoyed and insulted; in a petulant bad mood. ORIGINS: Onomatopoeic from a sniff of disgust.

**sore** |sōr| *adj* Angry and offended.

**tearing one's hair out** |TER ing wunz HER out| *adj* Greatly distressed; extremely upset.

NON-SLANG SYNONYMS: <u>sore</u>, <u>sulky</u>, <u>sullen</u>, **aggrieved**, **chagrined**, **disgruntled**, **fuming**, **incensed**, **indignant**, **piqued**, **provoked**

## 13  Liable to Anger

**bitchy** |BICH ē| *adj* Easily roused to anger; difficult to deal with. ORIGINS: From SE bitch, meaning "a female dog." USAGE ALERT: This term will be objectionable in some contexts and to some people. Usually used with intent to denigrate or insult and understood as such.

**crotchety** |KRAHCH i tē| *adj* Irritable; prone to anger; bad-tempered. ORIGINS: The expected behavior of someone with SE **crotchets**, idiosyncratic opinions and/or preference, thus, one who is very particular and easily put-out.

**grouchy** |GROU chē| *adj* Ill-tempered; prone to complaining. ORIGINS: Popularized by the character of Oscar the Grouch on the PBS television program *Sesame Street.*

**grumpy** |GRUM pē| *adj* Out of sorts and surly; ill-tempered and hostile.

**have a short fuse** |hav u SHAWRT FŪZ| *v* To have quick temper; to be liable to anger.

**huffy** |HUF ē| *adj* Bad-tempered; angry.

**miffy** |MI fē| *adj* Easily offended; supersensitive. ORIGINS: Onomatopoeic from a sniff of disgust.

**ornery** |AWR nur ē| *adj* Disagreeble; liable to anger; mean-spirited. ORIGINS: From alteration of SE **ordinary**.

**prickly** |PRIK lē| *adj* Irritable.

**scrappy** |SKRAP ē| *adj* Quarrelsome; prone to fights. ORIGINS: From slang scrap meaning "to fight or box."

**snarky** |SNAHR kē| *adj* Irritable; liable to anger; sarcastic.

**snitty** |SNIT ē| *adj* Ill-tempered.

**soreheaded** |SŌR hed id| *adj* Bad-tempered, liable to anger.

**testy*** |TES tē| *adj* Irritated; exasperated; peevish.
  • tetchy |TE chē| *adj*

**touchy** |TUCH ē| *adj* Overly sensitive; easily offended; prone to anger.

**NON-SLANG SYNONYMS:** cross, hot-tempered, ill-humored, ill-tempered, irritable, quick-tempered, short-tempered, <u>crabby</u>, <u>cranky</u>, <u>snippy</u>, **bilious**, **cantankerous**, **choleric**, **churlish**, **fractious**, **irascible**, **ornery**, **peevish**, **petulant**, **querulous**, **splenetic**, **surly**, **vehement**, **waspish**

# 14  A Fit of Anger

**conniption (fit)** |ku NIP shun / ku NIP shun fit| *n* Fit of anger, panic, or anxiety.

**flare-up** |FLER up| *n* Fit of anger; an eruption of strong feeling.

**hissy fit** |HIS ē fit| *n* A self-indulgent emotional outburst; a tantrum that is partly for show. ORIGINS: Possibly from SE **hysterical** or **hiss** (like a cat). USAGE INFO: More often used of females than males.

**huff** |huf| *n* A fit of ill temper or anger.

**snit** |snit| *n* A fit of ill temper.

**sulks** |sulks| *n* A fit of temper; sullen withdrawal. ORIGINS: Back-formation from SE <u>sulky</u>.

**NON-SLANG SYNONYMS:** fit, mood, outbreak, outburst, tantrum, <u>**bad mood**</u>, **frenzy**, **paroxysm**

## ANGER CAN BE A PAIN

The slang expressions we use to describe causing and feeling anger can make it sound pretty uncomfortable.

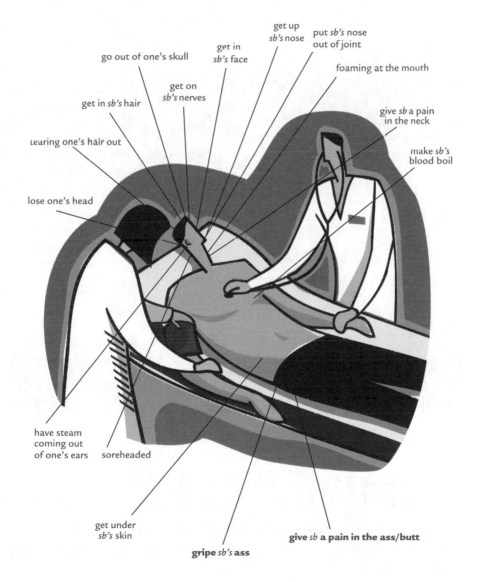

get up
sb's nose

put sb's nose
out of joint

get in
sb's face

foaming at the mouth

go out of one's skull

get on
sb's nerves

get in sb's hair

give sb a pain
in the neck

tearing one's hair out

make sb's
blood boil

lose one's head

have steam
coming out
of one's ears    soreheaded

get under
sb's skin

give sb **a pain in the ass/butt**

**gripe** sb's **ass**

## BEING ANGRY CAN MAKE YOU MAD

It used to be that children were chastised for saying *mad* when they meant *angry*. But slang shows us that the connection between being angry and going crazy runs deep in our language.

## ARROGANCE AND CONCEIT

**big-headed** |BIG hed id| *adj* Arrogant; conceited. ORIGINS: From SE **big** and slang suffix -head.

**high-handed** |HĪ HAN did| *adj* Unnecessarily authoritarian.

**highfalutin', hi falutin'** |HĪ fu LOŌT'n| *adj* Pompous; pretentious.

**hoity-toity** |HOI tē TOI tē| *adj* Pretentiously self-important; arrogant.

**la-di-da, lah-di-dah, la-de-da, lah-de-dah, lah-dee-dah** |lah dē DAH| *adj* Pretentious.

**puffed up** |PUFT up| *adj* Arrogant; conceited.

**snooty** |SNŪT ē| *adj* Snobbish. ORIGINS: From slang **snoot** meaning "arrogance" from SE **snout** meaning "nose," tied together by the idea of arrogant people looking down their noses at others.

stuck-up |STUK up| *adj* Arrogant; snobbish.

swank |swangk| *adj* Pretentious.

NON-SLANG SYNONYMS: arrogant, boastful, conceited, haughty, insolent, scornful, vain, **cocky**, **disdainful**, **imperious**, **narcissistic**, **presumptuous**, **pretentious**, **supercilious**

# ATTRACTION

## 1 To Cause Attraction

send |send| *v* To cause delight.

sweep one off one's feet |SWĒP wun AWF wunz FĒT| *v* To attract *sb*; to cause *sb* to fall in love.

turn on |TURN ahn| *v* To invite interest; to cause pleasure or excitement.

NON-SLANG SYNONYMS: appeal to, arouse, attract, charm, enchant, entrance, fascinate, lure, seduce, tempt, **grab**, **hook**, **rope in**, **suck in**, **allure**, **beckon**, **beguile**, **bewitch**, **captivate**, **enamor**, **entice**, **intrigue**, **inveigle**

## 2 To Become Attracted

fall for *sb* |FAWL fawr *sb*| *v* To fall in love with *sb*. USAGE INFO: The idiom *fall for st* means "to become the victim of."

fall head over heels for |FAWL HED ō vur HĒLS fawr| *v* To grow to be very much in love. ORIGINS: The concept is of someone tumbling over and over.

flip for *sb/st* |FLIP fawr *sb/st*| *v* To become obsessed with *sb/st*; to become infatuated with *sb/st*. ORIGINS: By extension of slang flip meaning "to become overly excited about."

lose one's head over *sb* |lūz wunz HED ō vur *sb*| *v* To become enamored of; to become obsessed with.

take a shine to |tāk u SHĪN tū| *v* To discover that one likes *st* very much; to find appealing.

NON-SLANG SYNONYMS: be charmed by, fall in love, **take a liking to**, **succumb**

## 3 To Feel Attracted

all about that, be |awl u BOUT *THAT*| *v* To accept "that" as crucially important or central to one's being.

**cotton to** |KAHT'n tū| *v* To agree; to get on well together; to become mutually attached; to favor. USAGE INFO: Can also mean "to get to know about, or come to understand."

**dig¹** |dig| *v* To appreciate; to enjoy. ORIGINS: Jazz jargon.

**eat *sb/st* up** |ĒT *sb/st* up| *v* To be obsessed with. ORIGINS: By extension of SE **eat up**, meaning to eat avidly and with delight.

**fancy *sb*** |FAN sē *sb*| *v* To find *sb* attractive and/or desirable.

**get a bang out of** |get u BANG out uv| *v* To enjoy; to get a thrill from. ORIGINS: From slang **bang** meaning "a thrill."

**get a charge out of** |get u CHARJ out uv| *v* To enjoy very much. ORIGINS: From slang **charge** meaning "a feeling of excitement."

**get a kick out of** |get u KIK out uv| *v* To appreciate; to enjoy. ORIGINS: From slang **kick** meaning "a thrill" or "excitement." Popularized by the Cole Porter song, "I Get a Kick Out of You."

**get a lift out of** |get u LIFT out uv| *v* To experience an elevation of spirits. ORIGINS: From SE **lift** meaning "an elevation of one's spirits."

**get off on** |get AWF ahn| *v* To experience pleasure or sexual arousal from. ORIGINS: From slang **get off** meaning "to have or bring to orgasm." USAGE ALERT: Because of the sexual reference, this term will be objectionable in some contexts and to some people.

**go ape for/over** |gō ĀP fawr / gō ĀP ō vur| *v* To become obsessed with; to become very excited about. ORIGINS: From the conceived behavior of apes.

**go for** |gō fawr| *v* To invest oneself in; to feel attracted to.

**go nuts about/over** |gō NUTS u bout / gō NUTS ō vur| *v* To be attracted to; to be obsessed with. ORIGINS: From slang **nuts** meaning "fond of; attracted to."

**go overboard for** |gō Ō vur bawrd FAWR| *v* To become infatuated with; to become obsessed with. ORIGINS: Here, SE **overboard** meaning "over the side of a ship" has been adapted to characterize extreme behavior.

**gobble up** |GAHB ul up| *v* To be strongly drawn to; to seek avidly. ORIGINS: From SE **gobble** meaning "to eat greedily."

**groove on** |GRŪV ahn| *v* To enjoy; to appreciate. ORIGINS: From slang **groove** meaning "to enjoy oneself." USAGE INFO: **Groove on** requires an object.

**have a crush on *sb*** |hav u KRUSH ahn *sb*| *v* To have a (usually temporary) infatuation with someone.

**have a soft spot for** |hav u SAWFT spaht fawr| *v* To be moved by; to have tender feelings for.

**have a thing about/for** *sb* |hav u THING u BOUT *sb* / hav u THING fawr *sb*| *v* To be infatuated with *sb*; to like *sb* very much; to be very interested in *sb*. USAGE INFO: Can also mean the opposite: "to be unable to tolerate *sb*."

**have a yen for** *st* |hav u YEN fawr *st*| *v* To have a strong desire or yearning for; to have a craving for (food).

**have an itch for/to** |hav an ICH fawr / hav an ICH tū| *v* To desire or crave something or some activity.

**lap** *st* **up**[1] |LAP *st* up| *v* To be extremely fond of; to be completely accepting of *st*. ORIGINS: From SE lap meaning "to take in food or liquid by lifting it into the mouth with the tongue" (a description of how a dog or cat drinks, for example.)

**smitten with/by, be** |SMIT un with / SMIT un bī| *v* To be infatuated; to be in love. ORIGINS: *Smitten* is the past participle of SE smite.

**sucker for, be a** |u SUK ur fawr| *v* To be attracted to something indiscriminately. ORIGINS: From obsolete SE sucker meaning "an unweaned baby," whether human or animal, thus, "an innocent." USAGE INFO: A sucker is someone who is generally gullible. To be a sucker for (*sb/st*) is to be undiscriminating/gullible in a specific case, specified by the object of the preposition *for*, e.g., "He's a sucker for sentimental movies." USAGE ALERT: People who know that other words with the letter sequence s-u-c-k come from shortening the phrase **suck dick** or **cocksucker** may mistakenly think that this one does as well. This may result in people finding this word objectionable despite the fact that there is no etymological connection.

**turned on by, be** |turnd AHN bī| *v* To be (sexually) attracted to; to be excited about. USAGE INFO: Be turned on without the preposition can indicate a general state, unconnected to any particular external stimulus. The inclusion of the preposition *by* indicates a specific person/object of attraction.

NON-SLANG SYNONYMS: adore, care for, love, prize, set one's heart on, treasure, <u>hanker after</u>, **be devoted to**, **cherish**, **dote on**, **hold dear**, **yearn for**

# 4 Attracted

**crazy about** |KRĀ zē u BOUT| *adj* Enthusiastic about; keen on; very attracted to; in love with. ORIGINS: Takes the idea of SE <u>crazy</u> and narrows it to apply to a specific slice of life: that having to do with love.

**down with** *st* |DOUN with *st*| *adj* To find something to be cool, enjoyable, or acceptable. ORIGINS: By extension of slang adjective down meaning "to be aware of." USAGE INFO: Not to be confused with "get down with," most of the meanings of which have to do with sexual activity.

**gaga about/for/over** |GAH gah u bout / GAH gah fawr / GAH gah ō vur| *adj* Infatuated with. ORIGINS: From French gaga meaning "a senile person."

**gone on** |GAHN ahn| *adj* Infatuated with. Often used with an adverb such as *totally, completely,* etc.

**hooked** |hŏŏkt| *adj* Captivated or addicted.

**hot for/on** |haht fawr/ HAHT ahn| *adj* Enthusiastic about.

**hung up on** |hung UP ahn| *adj* Obsessing about; preoccupied with; in love with. ORIGINS: By generalization of slang **hung up** meaning "addicted to drugs."

**into** |IN tū| *adj* Attracted to, involved with.

**keen on** |KĒN ahn| *adj* Intensely interested in; attracted to. ORIGINS: From SE **keen** meaning "ardent; eager."

**mad about** |MAD u bout| *adj* Infatuated with; immoderately fond of. ORIGINS: Takes the SE idea of **mad** and narrows it to a particular area of life. USAGE INFO: Also mad for, used by Shakespeare in *All's Well That Ends Well* (1598?) V, iii, 281.

**nuts about** |NUTS u bout| *adj* Wildly attracted to; infatuated with.

**soft on** |SAWFT ahn| *adj* Attracted to; very fond of.

**sold on** |SŌLD ahn| *adj* Convinced by; persuaded of *st's* value.

**stuck on** |STUK ahn| *adj* Very attracted to; devoted to.

**sweet on** |SWĒT ahn| *adj* In love with.

**tight with** |TĪT with| *adj* Very friendly with. ORIGINS: From slang **tight** meaning "very close."

**wild about** |WĪLD u bout| *adj* Enthusiastically supportive of; in love with.

NON-SLANG SYNONYMS: attracted to, enchanted by, fond of, in love with, lovesick for, partial to, <u>moonstruck by</u>, <u>sweet on</u>, **bewitched by**, **captivated by**, **devoted to**

## 5 To Feel Mutually Attracted

**buddy up** |BUD ē YUP| *v* To join together as friends in a pair.

**click**[1] |klik| *v* To become friends; to hit it off. ORIGINS: From the behavior of machinery in good working order, for example, the sound that a metal piece makes when "clicking" into its proper place.

**hit it off** |hit it AWF| *v* To connect with; to be mutually attracted.

**team up** |TĒM up| *v* To join together spontaneously to form a team.

NON-SLANG SYNONYMS: be compatible, <u>be on the same wavelength</u>, <u>take to each other</u>, **feel a rapport**

# CALM

## 1 To Become Calm

**back off** |BAK AHF| *v* To retreat from a position of aggression. USAGE INFO: Also used as an imperative exclamation to request being left in peace.

**chill (out)** |chil / chil OUT| *v* To calm down; to relax; to act cool. ORIGINS: When people get agitated or angry, they often become warm and flushed. So anger is associated with heat, and its opposite, being relaxed, is associated with a cool temperature.

**cool it/out** |KŪL It / kūl OUT| *v* To calm down; to stop what one is doing. ORIGINS: Plays on the concept of anger being hot and relaxation being cool.

**cool one's jets** |KŪL wunz JETS| *v* To calm down; to relax. ORIGINS: Based on the behavior of jet engines, which get hot when they run and require cooling systems to prevent part failure. USAGE INFO: Cool one's heels may seem to be parallel, but it actually means "to be kept waiting."

**give it a rest** |giv it u REST| *v* To calm down; to pull back.

**go easy** |gō Ē zē| *v* To become calm.

**go easy on** *sb* |gō Ē zē ahn *sb*| *v* To limit one's hostility or anger when dealing with *sb*.

**hold one's horses** |hold wunz HAWR siz| *v* To cease activity; to calm down; to restrain oneself. USAGE INFO: Often used as an imperative: "Hold your horses!"

**mellow out** |MEL ō out| *v* To relax; to calm down; to become peaceful and content. ORIGINS: Generalized from slang mellow, which originally meant "drunk" and more recently referred to drugs, including pot (marijuana).

**simmer down** |SIM ur doun| *v* To become calm (often after being extremely angry or upset). USAGE INFO: Often used as an imperative.

**take a chill pill** |tāk u CHIL pil| *v* To relax; to calm down. ORIGINS: From slang chill pill, an imaginary medicine to calm one down. USAGE INFO: Often used as an imperative.

NON-SLANG SYNONYMS: calm down, collect oneself, settle down, unwind, **loosen up**, **quieten**

## 2 To Feel or Maintain Calm

**hang loose** |hang LŪS| *v* To relax; to stay calm.

**keep one's pants/shirt on** |kēp wunz PANTS awn / kēp wunz SHURT awn| *v* To avoid becoming excited; to stay calm.

**mellow, be** |MEL ō| *v* To be calm and relaxed (even in the face of difficulties). ORIGINS: Generalized from slang mellow, which originally meant "drunk" and more recently referred to drugs, including pot (marijuana).

**play it cool** |plā it KŪL| *v* To keep one's temper in check.

**take it easy** |tāk it Ē zē| *v* To relax.

NON-SLANG SYNONYMS: relax, rest, stay calm, **stay loose**, **repose**

## 3 Calm

**chilled out** |child OUT| *adj* Relaxed; calm. ORIGINS: When people get agitated or angry, they often become warm and flushed. Just as anger and being in a temper are associated with heat, being relaxed is associated with a cool temperature.

**mellow** |MEL ō| *adj* Relaxed; calm and in a good mood; to feel peaceful and content. ORIGINS: Generalized from slang mellow, which originally meant "drunk" and more recently referred to drugs, including pot (marijuana).

**unflappable** |un FLAHP u bul| *adj* Enduringly calm; not easily upset.

NON-SLANG SYNONYMS: calm, collected, mild, undisturbed, **laid-back**, **low-key**, **at peace**, **detached**, **dispassionate**, **harmonious**, **imperturbable**, **placid**, **serene**, **tranquil**, **unruffled**

## BLOWING HOT AND COLD

When we make a collection of slang expressions, we can see that anger is allied with heat and calm with cold. Explosions get into the picture, too.

**BLOWING**

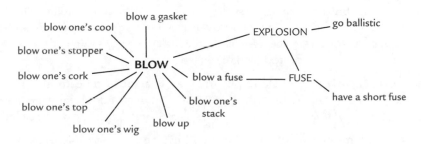

**ANGER**

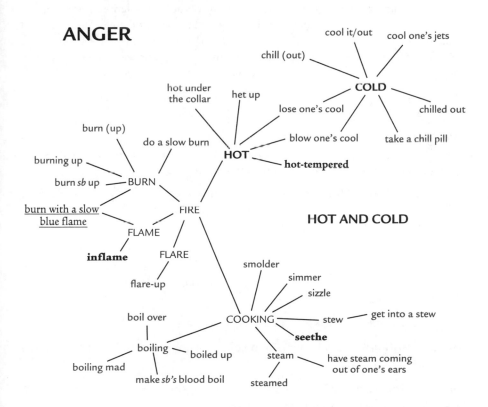

# COURAGE

## 1 To Be Brave

**have balls** |hav BAWLS| v To have courage; to be presumptuous. ORIGINS: From slang **balls**, meaning "testicles," and, by extension, traditionally manly attributes such as courage. USAGE INFO: Usually used exclusively of men, with rare exceptions. USAGE ALERT: The reference to the male sex organs will render this phrase objectionable in some contexts and to some people.

**have chutzpah** |hav KHŌŌT spu| v To be audacious; to be impudent; to be recklessly courageous. ORIGINS: From Hebrew through Yiddish khutspe meaning "to be insolent." USAGE INFO: May be praise or criticism, depending on the situation.

**have cojones** |hav ku HŌ nās| v To have courage. ORIGINS: From Mexican Spanish **cojones**, the equivalent of US slang **balls**, meaning "testicles," and, by extension, traditionally manly attributes such as courage. Popularized first by Ernest Hemingway in his writings and more recently by Stephen Colbert on his television show *The Colbert Report* (2005–). USAGE INFO: Usually used exclusively of men, with rare exceptions. USAGE ALERT: The reference to the male sex organs will render this phrase objectionable in some contexts and to some people.

**have gall** |hav GAWL| v To be outrageously insolent; to be arrogant or impudent. ORIGINS: From SE **gall** meaning "bitterness."

**have guts** |hav GUTS| v To have courage; to be audacious. USAGE INFO: The meaning of this term is similar to **have balls** and **have cojones**, but it is less objectionable because of the part of the body referenced.

**have moxie** |hav MAHK sē| v To have courage, especially in the face of difficulties; to have energy; to be impudent; to have abilities. ORIGINS: From the soft drink Moxie, patented in 1924.

**have nerve** |hav NURV| v To have courage under pressure; to be bold; to be brazen and impudent. ORIGINS: From SE **nerve**. Popularized by the Cowardly Lion in *The Wizard of Oz*, who wished he had, as he pronounces it, "the noive." USAGE INFO: Often in the phrase "have the nerve to."

**have spunk** |hav SPUNGK| v To have courage or spirit.

**man up** |MAN up| v To take steps to display the courage that is considered the hallmark of a mature man.

**NON-SLANG SYNONYMS:** be bold, be brave, be courageous, dare, defy, risk doing *st*, take a risk, **stand up to**, **tough it out**, **venture**

## 2 Courageous

**ballsy** |BAWL zē| *adj* Courageous, masculine. ORIGINS: Masculine traits are connected with the **balls**, meaning "testicles." Usually, but not always, used of males. USAGE ALERT: This form of **balls** will be objectionable in some contexts and to some people.

**feisty** |FĪS tē| *adj* Full of spirit or courage. ORIGINS: From rarely used SE feist meaning "a small dog."

**gutsy** |GUT sē| *adj* Brave; spirited; courageous. ORIGINS: From slang guts meaning "courage; bravery."

**plucky** |PLUK ē| *adj* Spirited; courageous. ORIGINS: From slang pluck meaning "courage."

**spunky** |SPUNG kē| *adj* Courageous; spirited. ORIGINS: From slang spunk meaning "courage; bravery."

**NON-SLANG SYNONYMS:** bold, brash, brave, cocky, confident, courageous, daring, fearless, heroic, overconfident, rash, spirited, unafraid, <u>gritty</u>, <u>nervy</u>, **adventurous**, **audacious**, **cocksure**, **dauntless**, **doughty**, **gallant**, **indomitable**, **intrepid**, **lionhearted**, **mettlesome**, **resolute**, **stalwart**, **stouthearted**, **undaunted**, **valiant**, **valorous**

## DISGUST

## 1 To Cause Disgust

**gross out** |GRŌS out| *v* To cause disgust, repulsion, or strong dislike. ORIGINS: From the slang adjective gross meaning "disgusting" which draws on the SE noun gross meaning "large."

**make one sick** |māk wun SIK| *v* To cause disgust.

**turn off** |TURN AWF| *v* To cause disgust, repulsion, boredom, and/or loss of interest.

**turn one's stomach** |turn wunz STUM uk| *v* To disgust or repel.

**NON-SLANG SYNONYMS:** be repulsive, disgust, nauseate, offend, revolt, sicken, <u>put off</u>, **disenchant**, **fill with loathing**, **repulse**

## 2 Disgusted

**grossed out** |GRŌST out| *adj* Feeling disgust, repulsion, or strong dislike. ORIGINS: From the slang adjective **gross** meaning "disgusting" which draws on the SE noun **gross** meaning "large."

**turned off** |turnd AWF| *v* Bored; uninterested; unexcited; disgusted.

NON-SLANG SYNONYMS: disgusted, nauseated, queasy, repelled, revolted, sickened, **be averse to, repulsed**

# EXCITEMENT

## 1 Excited

**full of beans** |ful uv BĒNZ| *adj* Full of energy. ORIGINS: Said of a spirited horse, possibly because some kind of bean can form part of a horse's diet, providing protein; later applied to people. USAGE INFO: This phrase can also mean "mistaken; full of nonsense; lying" and with that sense is used as a euphemism for **full of shit**. *See* FULL OF BEANS, BE.

**full of pep** |FUL uv pep| *adj* Full of energy. ORIGINS: Pep is short for SE **pepper**.

**full of piss and vinegar** |FUL uv pis und VIN i gur| *adj* Full of energy. ORIGINS: Unknown. Slang **piss** means "urine." First use found in John Steinbeck's novel *The Grapes of Wrath* (1938). USAGE ALERT: The reference to urine will make this expression objectionable in some contexts and to some people.

**gung ho, gung-ho** |GUNG HŌ| *adj* Enthusiastic; exuberant and dedicated. ORIGINS: From the motto of the second Raider Battalion of the US Marine Corps, from the Chinese **kengo ho** (meaning disputed), introduced to them by Lieutenant Co. Evans F. Carlson in 1942.

**hopped up** |HAHPT UP| *adj* Energized; agitated; excited. ORIGINS: By extension of the initial use, which referred to being under the influence of drugs.

**hyped up** |HĪPT up| *adj* Tense and nervous. ORIGINS: By extension from slang **hyped up** meaning "under the influence of stimulants injected with a hypodermic needle."

**jacked (up)** |jakt / jakt UP| *adj* Very excited or agitated; exhilarated. ORIGINS: Figurative version of slang **jack up** meaning "to inject narcotics" or "to drink coffee."

**peppy** |PEP ē| *adj* Energetic; cheerful and enthusiastic. From slang **pep** meaning "energy."

**pumped (up)** |pumpt / PUMPT up| *adj* Excited; enthusiastic; energetic.

**rambunctious** |ram BUNGK shus| *adj* Boisterous; exuberantly unruly; noisily disorderly.

**rarin' to go** |RER in tū GŌ| *adj* Eager to begin; excited; enthusiastic.

**snappy** |SNAP ē| *adj* Energetic.

**stoked** |stōkt| *adj* Thrilled; intensely excited.

**zingy** |ZING ē| *adj* Energetic; enthusiastic; excited.

**zippy** |ZIP ē| *adj* Speedy; energetic; spirited.

**Non-Slang Synonyms:** charged, delighted, electrified, enthusiastic, excited, exhilarated, stimulated, thrilled, **beside oneself**, **fired up**, **in a flurry**, **enlivened**, **enraptured**


# 2 Agitated

**antsy** |ANT sē| *adj* Nervous; fidgety. ORIGINS: Possibly related to the ceaseless movement of ants and the slang phrase **have ants in one's pants**.

**having butterflies in one's stomach** |hav ing BUT ur flīz in wunz STUM uk| *adj* Feeling extremely nervous. ORIGINS: The physical sensation that can accompany nervousness.

**hepped up** |HEPT up| *adj* Agitated; excited.

**hot and bothered** |HAHT und BAH*TH* urd| *adj* In a state of excited expectation; agitated; flustered. ORIGINS: From the physical symptoms of such a state.

**hyper** |HĪ pur| *adj* Over-stimulated; overly emotional; tense. ORIGINS: Shortened from SE **hyperactive**.

**in a dither** |in u DI*TH* ur| *adj* So agitated that one cannot make up one's mind.

**in a doodah** |in u DŪ dah| *adj* In a state of nervous tension. ORIGINS: From the refrain of the Stephen Foster song "Camptown Races" (1850). USAGE INFO: This phrase (as opposed to its synonyms) is often used as an indication that the situation is not too serious.

**in a flutter** |in u FLUT ur| *adj* In a state of nervous excitement. USAGE INFO: May be positive or negative.

**in a lather** |in u LA*TH* ur| *adj* In a state of angry agitation; very anxious. ORIGINS: From the frothy sweat of an upset horse.

**in a state** |in u STĀT| *adj* Feeling extreme excitement or distress.

**in a sweat** |in u SWET| *adj* Agitated and worried or agitated and fearful.

**in a tizzy** |in u TIZ ē| *adj* In a panic; confused and undecided. ORIGINS: From slang *tizzy* meaning "panic."

**itchy** |ICH ē| *adj* Somewhat agitated; slightly anxious. ORIGINS: From the twitchy behavior of someone who has an itch. USAGE INFO: Usually used in a situation where the stakes are not high.

**jittery** |JIT ur ē| *adj* Nervous; tense; feeling uneasy. ORIGINS: Based on slang *jitters* meaning "a state of nervousness or agitation."

**keyed up** |kēd UP| *adj* Agitated; excited; nervous. ORIGINS: From slang *keyed* meaning "drunk or under the influence of a drug."

**on edge** |ahn EJ| *adj* Nervous; worried; agitated. USAGE INFO: The phrase "set one's teeth on edge" can mean both "to make one nervous" or "to be very irritating." In the second sense, it is often used of high pitched screeching noises, like fingernails on a blackboard.

**twitchy** |TWICH ē| *adj* Agitated; nervous; ill-at-ease.

**uptight** |up TĪT| *adj* Annoyed; tense; edgy.

**wired** |wīrd| *adj* Nervous; tense; agitated. ORIGINS: From SE *wired* meaning "carrying electricity."

**worked up** |WURKT UP| *adj* Upset; agitated.

NON-SLANG SYNONYMS: agitated, flustered, nervous, uneasy, **edgy**, **jumpy**, **discomposed**, **disconcerted**, **disquieted**, **unsettled**, **unstrung**

# FEAR

## 1 To Cause Fear

**creep *sb* out** |KRĒP *sb* OUT| *v* To cause fear by exhibiting the qualities of a creep, i.e., unpleasantness, repulsiveness, or some criminal connection. USAGE INFO: About the same as "give *sb* the creeps." USAGE ALERT: Be careful to distinguish creep *sb* out from **creep out**, meaning "to exit or sneak away quietly."

**freak *sb* out** |FRĒK *sb* OUT| *v* To cause *sb* to be afraid.

**freeze *sb*'s blood** |FRĒZ *sb*'s BLUD| *v* To terrify *sb*. To terrify so much as to paralyze.

**frighten the living daylights out of** |FRĪT 'n *thu* LIV ing DĀ līts out uv| *v* To utterly terrify.

**give sb the shivers** |GIV sb thu SHIV urz| v To make sb afraid, nervous, or terrified. ORIGINS: From SE the shivers meaning "an attack of shivering," or figuratively, an attack of fear.

**put the wind up** |po͞ot thu WIND up| v To frighten; to worry.

**scare sb stiff** |sker sb STIF| v To frighten sb to the point that the person is paralyzed with fear.

**scare the bejesus out of sb** |sker thu bi JĒ zus out uv sb| v To terrify sb. ORIGINS: From the slang version of the SE exclamation "By Jesus!" From SE Jesus Christ whom Christians hold to be the Son of God. USAGE ALERT: The inclusion of the word Jesus in the phrase will make it seem blasphemous and objectionable in some contexts and to some people.

**scare the life out of sb** |sker thu LĪF out uv sb| v To terrify.

**scare the living daylights out of sb** |sker thu LIV ing DĀ lītz out uv sb| v To terrify. ORIGINS: From slang daylights originally meaning "the eyes" and then "the insides."

**scare the pants off of sb** |sker thu PANTS awf uv sb| v To terrify.

**scare the shit out of sb** |sker thu SHIT out uv sb| v To terrify. ORIGINS: From slang shit meaning "excrement," and from the fact that extreme fear can make people lose control of their excretory functions. USAGE ALERT: The inclusion of the word shit in the phrase will render it objectionable in some contexts and to some people.

**weird out** |WIRD out| v To horrify; to terrify.

NON-SLANG SYNONYMS: alarm, dismay, frighten, give a fright to, horrify, intimidate, panic, paralyze, scare, startle, terrify, **scare silly**, **scare witless**, **shake up**, **spook**, **affright**, **appall**, **daunt**, **petrify**, **terrorize**, **unnerve**

## 2 To Become Afraid

**chicken out** |CHIK un out| v To be too frightened to act; to back out. ORIGINS: From the association of chickens with fearfulness.

**freeze up** |FRĒ zup| v To become paralyzed by fear; to be so afraid that one cannot move or speak.

**get cold feet** |get kōld FĒT| v To become scared; to back out of a promise.

**lose one's nerve** |lūz wunz NURV| v To lose courage or resolve; to become frightened.

**punk out** |pungk OUT| v To become afraid; to renege on st because of fear.

**turn chicken** |turn CHIK un| v To become afraid; to lose one's nerve.

**turn yellow** |turn YEL Ō| v To become afraid; to lose heart.

**wimp out** |wimp OUT| *v* To fail to fulfill a commitment; to renege on a promise out of fear.

NON-SLANG SYNONYMS: become afraid, become fearful, become hysterical, lose courage, shrink, **break out in a sweat**, **go to pieces**, **falter**, **flinch**, **quaver**

## 3 To Feel Fear

**choke up** |CHŌK UP| *v* To be overcome with such strong emotion that one cannot speak.

**feel weak at the knees** |fēl WĒK at thu NĒZ| *v* Become suddenly overcome with fear or another strong emotion. ORIGINS: From the physical feeling.

**freak out** |FRĒK OUT| *v* To go crazy from fear; to lose control; to become greatly upset; to suffer an emotional breakdown. ORIGINS: From slang freak meaning "drug user"—developed from the volatile emotional state of someone who uses hallucinogenic drugs.

**go weak at the knees** |gō WĒK at thu NĒZ| *v* Become suddenly overcome with fear or another strong emotion. ORIGINS: From the physical feeling.

**have cold feet** |hav kōld FĒT| *v* To suffer from fear or timidity; to be unable to act on account of fear. ORIGINS: The concept is of someone whose feet are frozen in place. USAGE INFO: Often used of someone who has committed to a plan of action and then withdraws.

**have the screaming meemies** |hav thu SKRĒM ing MĒ mēz| *v* To have an attack of nerves; to be extremely frightened. ORIGINS: From slang meemies meaning "hysteria," from WWII US military name screaming meemies for German mortars that were fired from a Nebelwerfer.

**hit the panic button** |HIT thu PAN ik but'n| *v* A hasty or overly emotional response to an emergency situation. ORIGINS: From the button provided in case of emergency, in elevators, for example. Staples' recent "Easy Button" commercials play off the concept of a panic button.

**pee oneself**\* |PĒ wun self| *v* To be so terrified that one could (or does) urinate on oneself; to laugh riotously. ORIGINS: Euphemism for **piss oneself**. From slang **pee**, meaning "urine." USAGE ALERT: The inclusion of the word **pee** in this phrase will render it objectionable in some contexts and to some people. The usage of **pee** rather than **piss** in this phrase will soften it somewhat, but it may still be objectionable in some contexts and to some people. The versions with wet will be even less objectionable: See WET ONESELF; WET ONE'S PANTS.
• **pee (in) one's pants** |PEE wunz pants / PEE in wunz pants|

**piss one's pants**\* |PIS wunz pants| *v* To be so terrified that one could (or does) urinate on oneself; to laugh riotously. ORIGINS: From slang **piss**, meaning "urine." USAGE ALERT: The inclusion of the word **piss** in this phrase will render it

objectionable in some contexts and to some people. *See* bullet under **PEE ONESELF** and the entry **WET ONE'S PANTS** for less offensive alternatives.
• **piss oneself** |PIS wun self|

**push the panic button** |PŎOSH *thu* PAN ik but'n| *v* To make a hasty or overly emotional response to an emergency situation. ORIGINS: From the button provided in case of emergency, in elevators, for example. Staples' recent "Easy Button" commercials play off the concept of a panic button.

**run scared** |run SKERD| *v* To flee in a panic; to harbor fears of failure or defeat.

**scared shitless, be** |skerd SHIT lis| *v* To be completely terrified. ORIGINS: From slang **shit** meaning "excrement," and from the fact that extreme fear can make people lose control of their excretory functions. USAGE ALERT: The inclusion of the word **shit** in the phrase will render it objectionable in some contexts and to some people.

**scared to death, be** |SKERD tū DETH| *v* To be extremely frightened.

**shake in one's shoes** |SHĀK in wunz SHŪZ| *v* To feel extremely frightened or anxious.

**shit oneself** |SHIT wun self| *v* To be terrified. ORIGINS: Figurative use of slang **shit oneself** meaning "to defecate in one's underwear," since that is a possible physical response to fear. USAGE ALERT: The inclusion of the word **shit** in the phrase will render it objectionable in some contexts and to some people.

**sweat blood** |SWET BLUD| *v* To endure mental anguish. ORIGINS: An allusion to The New Testament, Luke 22:44 telling of Jesus in the Garden of Gethsemane, which says, "His sweat was, as it were, great drops of blood falling down to the ground." King James Version.

**weirded out, be** |WIRD id out| *v* To be scared and confused.

**wet one's pants** |WET wunz pants| *v* To be so terrified that one could (or does) urinate on oneself; to laugh riotously. USAGE INFO: **Pee one's pants** and **piss one's pants** will likely be more objectionable. USAGE ALERT: The figurative reference to urination may make this phrase objectionable in some contexts and to some people.

**wet oneself** |WET wun self| *v* To be so terrified that one could (or does) urinate on oneself; to laugh riotously. USAGE INFO: **Pee oneself** and **piss oneself** will likely be more objectionable. USAGE ALERT: The figurative reference to urination may make this phrase objectionable in some contexts and to some people.

**NON-SLANG SYNONYMS:** be afraid, be frightened, be scared, be terrified

# 4 Liable to Fear

**chicken-hearted\*** |CHIK un hahr tid| *adj* Cowardly. ORIGINS: From the association of chickens with fearfulness and the association of the heart and/or the liver as the seats of emotion.
• chicken-livered |CHIK un liv urd|

**lily-livered** |LIL ē liv urd| *adj* Timid; cowardly. ORIGINS: Extends the observation that a person's skin can turn pale with fear to suggest that all his/her organs do as well by using a lily, traditionally white, to convey the comparison. USAGE INFO: Used by Shakespeare in *The Tragedy of Macbeth,* V, iii, 17 (1603) in Macbeth's abuse of the servant.

**mousy** |MOU sē| *adj* Timid and shy; quiet. ORIGINS: From the observed behavior of mice.

**pucker-assed** |PUK ur ast| *adj* Cowardly; timid; fearful. ORIGINS: From SE pucker meaning "wrinkled" and the slang suffix **-ass(ed)**. USAGE ALERT: The inclusion of a form of **ass** in this word will render it objectionable in some contexts and to some people.

**sissified** |SIS u fīd| *adj* Timid or cowardly; effeminate.

**yellow** |YEL ō| *adj* Timid; cowardly.

NON-SLANG SYNONYMS: afraid, cowardly, fearful, spineless, timid, **gutless**, **fainthearted**, **meek**

# 5 A Fit of Fear

**creeps, the** |thu KRĒPS| *n* An attack of fear; a feeling of dread or repulsion. ORIGINS: The feeling of "creeping" in one's flesh when one is scared, horrified, or repulsed.

**heebie-jeebies** |HĒ bē JĒ bēz| *n* A fit of fright; nameless dread; a feeling of uneasiness; a case of the jitters. ORIGINS: Believed to have been coined by cartoonist identified both as Billy Derbeck and Billy DeBeck, in his strip *Barney Google* (1923).

**jim-jams** |JIM jamz| *n* A fit of fear or apprehension; an episode of depression. ORIGINS: Broadened from slang jim-jams meaning "delirium tremens." USAGE INFO: Often used with *the*.

**jitters** |JIT urz| *n* A state of nervousness or agitation; emotional tension; stage fright. ORIGINS: Unlike jim-jams, jitters began with the broader use and was only later applied to delirium tremens. USAGE INFO: Often used with *the*.

**shakes** |shāks| *n* A fit of terror or nervousness. ORIGINS: From slang shakes, first used for delirium tremens. USAGE INFO: Usually used with *the*.

**shits, the** |thu SHITS| *n* An attack of fear or terror. ORIGINS: From slang the shits meaning "diarrhea," which is sometimes a symptom of great terror or fear. USAGE

ALERT: Because it includes **shit**, this word will be objectionable in some contexts and to some people.

**willies** |WIL ēz| *n* Feelings of extreme uneasiness. USAGE INFO: Often with *the*.

**NON-SLANG SYNONYMS:** anxiety, cold feet, dither, nerves, nervousness

# HAPPINESS AND DELIGHT

## 1 Happy

**chipper** |CHIP ur| *adj* Cheerful; in good spirits. ORIGINS: Thought to be from the British dialect term **chipper** meaning a cheerful song.

**happy as a pig in shit** |HAP ē az u PIG in SHIT| *adj* Extremely happy. ORIGINS: From slang **shit** meaning "excrement" and the idea that pigs enjoy rolling around in mud or manure. USAGE ALERT: The inclusion of the word **shit** in the phrase will render it objectionable in some contexts and to some people.

**high** |HĪ| *adj* Filled with joy. ORIGINS: By figurative extension from the positive effect of some drugs on a person's mood.

**high as a kite** |HĪ az u KĪT| *adj* Very happy; stoned; high above the Earth.

**kvelling** |KVEL ing| *adj* Feeling happy. ORIGINS: From Yiddish **kveln** meaning "to be delighted; to be pleased and proud."

**like a pig in shit** |līk u PIG in SHIT| *adj* Extremely happy. ORIGINS: From slang **shit** meaning "excrement" and the idea that pigs enjoy rolling around in mud or manure. This version of the expression, unlike **happy as a pig in shit**, requires the audience to infer that the pig is happy. USAGE ALERT: The inclusion of the word **shit** in the phrase will render it objectionable in some contexts and to some people.

**living it up** |LIV ing it up| *adj* Enjoying oneself greatly; having a good time.

**up** |UP| *adj* Excited and/or hopeful.

**upbeat** |UP bēt| *adj* Optimistic, positive.

**NON-SLANG SYNONYMS:** cheerful, content, contented, delighted, glad, happy, merry, pleased, **blithe**, **elated**, **joyous**, **jubilant**

## 2 To Cause Laughter

**break *sb* up** |BRĀK *sb* up| *v* To make someone laugh heartily. USAGE INFO: **Break *sb* up** is a contronym and can also mean "to make someone extremely upset." **Break up** without an object means "to burst into laughter" or "to stop dating."

**convulse** |kun VULS| *v* To cause overwhelming laughter; to laugh. ORIGINS: By extension from SE **convulse** and the similarity of the bodily effects of laughter to the involuntary muscle contractions of a convulsion.

**crack sb up** |KRAK *sb* UP| *v* To cause *sb* to laugh uproariously. ORIGINS: From SE crack meaning "to break" combined with the idea that one can "break" into laughter.

**fracture** |FRAK chur| *v* To make someone laugh heartily. USAGE INFO: Fracture is a contronym: it can also mean "to beat up."

**have sb in stitches** |HAV *sb* in STICH iz| *v* To cause riotous laughter.

**kill** |kil| *v* To cause to laugh heartily; to delight.

**knock dead** |NAHK DED| *v* To impress to the highest degree: to astonish; to delight; to thrill; to amuse.

**lay them in the aisles** |LĀ *thum* in *thē* ĪLZ| *v* To make people laugh uncontrollably (in a performance); to achieve a great success. ORIGINS: From show business.

**panic** |PA nik| *v* To cause to laugh uproariously.

**put sb in stitches** |PŎŎT *sb* in STICH iz| *v* To cause riotous laughter.

**slaughter²** |SLAW tur| *v* To cause riotous laughter.

**slay²** |slā| *v* To cause riotous laughter.

NON-SLANG SYNONYMS: amuse, cheer, tickle, **tickle sb's funny bone**, **divert**

# 3 To Laugh

**break up** |BRĀK up| *v* To laugh heartily. USAGE INFO: Break up is a contronym and can also mean "to become extremely upset, hysterical," or "to stop dating." Break *sb* up with an object means "to cause to burst into laughter."

**bust a gut** |BUST u gut| *v* To laugh very hard. USAGE INFO: This phrase also means "to work very hard; to put in an enormous effort."

**bust one's gut** |BUST wunz GUT| *v* To laugh very hard. USAGE INFO: This phrase also means "to work very hard; to put in an enormous effort."

**crack up¹** |KRAK UP| *v* To laugh uproariously. ORIGINS: From SE crack meaning "to break" combined with the idea that one can "break" into laughter. USAGE INFO: Be careful to distinguish crack up from crack *sb* up.

**die laughing** |DĪ LAF ing| *v* To laugh uproariously and uncontrollably. ORIGINS: Popularized by being a key plot element in the film *Who Framed Roger Rabbit?* (1988).

**howl** |houl| *v* To laugh uproariously.

**pee oneself*** |PĒ wun self| *v* To be so terrified that one could (or does) urinate on oneself; to laugh riotously. ORIGINS: Euphemism for **piss oneself**. From slang **pee**, meaning "urine." USAGE ALERT: The inclusion of the word **pee** in this phrase will render it objectionable in some contexts and to some people. The usage of **pee** rather than **piss** in this phrase will soften it somewhat, but it may still be objectionable in some contexts and to some people. The versions with wet will be even less objectionable: *See* WET ONESELF; WET ONE'S PANTS.

• **pee (in) one's pants** |PEE wunz pants / PEE in wunz pants|

**piss one's pants**\* |PIS wunz pants| *v* To be so terrified that one could (or does) urinate on oneself; to laugh riotously. ORIGINS: From slang **piss**, meaning "urine." USAGE ALERT: The inclusion of the word **piss** in this phrase will render it objectionable in some contexts and to some people. *See* bullet under **PEE ONESELF** and the entry **WET ONE'S PANTS** for less offensive alternatives.
• **piss oneself** |PIS wun self|

**roar** |rawr| *v* To laugh heartily.

**split a gut** |SPLIT a gut| *v* To laugh very hard. USAGE INFO: This phrase also means "to work very hard; to put in an enormous effort."

**split one's gut** |SPLIT wunz gut| *v* To laugh very hard. USAGE INFO: This phrase also means "to work very hard; to put in an enormous effort."

**split one's sides** |split wunz SĪDZ| *v* To laugh uproariously.

**wet oneself** |WET wun self| *v* To be so terrified that one could (or does) urinate on oneself; to laugh riotously. USAGE INFO: **Pee oneself** and **piss oneself** will likely be more objectionable. USAGE ALERT: The figurative reference to urination may make this phrase objectionable in some contexts and to some people.

**whoop** |wūp| *v* To laugh. ORIGINS: From SE whoop meaning "a cry." USAGE INFO: Usually in the phrase "whoop with laughter."

**NON-SLANG SYNONYMS:** laugh, <u>chortle</u>, <u>chuckle</u>, <u>giggle</u>, <u>guffaw</u>, <u>scream</u>, <u>snicker</u>, <u>snigger</u>, <u>titter</u>

## THE HAZARDS OF LAUGHTER

One wouldn't necessarily connect violence and laughter, but it shows up over and over again in our language.

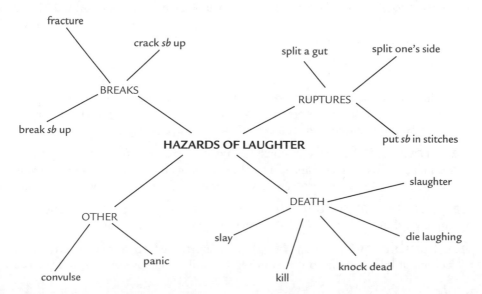

# HUMILIATION

## 1 To Cause Humiliation

**bring *sb* down a peg (or two)** |BRING *sb* DOUN u peg / BRING *sb* doun u PEG awr tū| *v* To humiliate. ORIGINS: A counterpart to the slang phrase come down a peg (or two).

**make a fool of *sb*** |māk u FŪL uv *sb*| *v* To purposely or accidentally do something that makes someone else look foolish or stupid.

**put in the dog house** |PŎOT in *th*u DAWG hous| *v* To shame; to ostracize. ORIGINS: From the practice of confining a dog to a separate doghouse, away from human company, as a punishment.

**run *sb* down** |RUN *sb* DOUN| *v* To insult *sb*; to denigrate *sb*.

**take *sb* down** |TĀK *sb* DOUN| *v* To defeat; to humiliate.

**take *sb* down a peg (or two)** |TĀK *sb* DOUN u peg / TĀK *sb* doun u PEG awr tū| *v* To humiliate. ORIGINS: A counterpart to the slang phrase come down a peg (or two).

**NON-SLANG SYNONYMS:** humble, humiliate, make ashamed, shame, <u>cut down to size</u>, **snub**, **abase**, **abash**, **chagrin**, **chasten**, **debase**, **degrade**, **demean**, **denigrate**, **discomfit**, **mortify**, **put out of countenance**

## 2 To Become Humiliated

**come down a peg (or two)** |kum DOUN u peg / KUM doun u PEG awr tū| *v* To experience humiliation. ORIGINS: The counterpart to the slang phrases take/bring *sb* down a peg (or two).

**eat crap** |ĒT CRAP| *v* To retract an error and accept public humiliation; to undergo humiliation. ORIGINS: Euphemism for **eat shit**. From slang **crap**, a euphemism for **shit**, meaning "excrement." From the imagined suffering of eating excrement. USAGE ALERT: The graphic image along with the use of **crap** will make this phrase objectionable in some contexts and to some people.

**eat crow** |ĒT KRŌ| *v* To publicly admit an error or mistake; to undergo humiliation. ORIGINS: First appeared in the phrase "eat boiled crow," but of uncertain origins. Apparently crow tastes awful, which adds to the imagined unpleasantness.

**eat dirt** |ĒT DIRT| *v* To retract an error and accept public humiliation; to undergo humiliation. ORIGINS: From the imagined suffering of eating dirt.

**eat humble pie** |ĒT hum bul PĪ| *v* To be forced to admit an error and accept public humiliation; to undergo humiliation. ORIGINS: Humble pie is a make-believe food to describe the experience of humiliation, but also a pun on "the umbles," the entrails and organs that the huntsman and servants ate in a pie, while the nobles they served ate the venison.

**eat one's hat** |ĒT wunz HAT| *v* To retract an error; to make a public admission of a mistake.

**eat shit** |ĒT SHIT| *v* To retract an error and accept public humiliation; to undergo humiliation. ORIGINS: From slang **shit** meaning "excrement." From the imagined suffering of eating excrement. USAGE ALERT: The graphic image along with the use of **shit** will make this phrase objectionable in some contexts and to some people.

**get off one's high horse** |GET ahf wunz hī HAWRS| *v* To cease acting superior; to stop being condescending. ORIGINS: The concept is of someone who has been under the impression that s/he is higher (read "better") than everyone else, but is undergoing a change of view.

**pocket one's pride** |PAHK it wunz PRĪD| *v* To accept humiliation; to admit being wrong or having made a mistake.

**pull in one's horns** |PUL in wunz HAWRNS| *v* To retreat from a stance; to give in; to stop arguing and calm down. ORIGINS: From the action of a snail withdrawing into its shell.

**tuck in one's tail** |TUK in wunz TĀL| *v* To be ashamed and humiliated. ORIGINS: From the behavior of a dog that has been severely scolded. USAGE INFO: Also, put one's tail between one's legs.

NON-SLANG SYNONYMS: embarrassed, humiliated, **abashed**, **ashamed**, **chagrined**, **mortified**

# MENTAL ILLNESS

## 1 Depressed

**bummed (out)** |bumd / BUMD OUT| *adj* Depressed; miserable; very unhappy. ORIGINS: Extended from slang adjective **bum** meaning "bad for (you)."

**down** |doun| *adj* Depressed; dejected. ORIGINS: Based on the conceptualization of happy as being equivalent to up and sad being equivalent to down.

**down in the dumps** |doun in *thu* DUMPS| *adj* Miserable; very unhappy or depressed. ORIGINS: An extension from slang **down** meaning "depressed."

**down in the mouth** |doun in *thu* MOUTH| *adj* Miserable; very unhappy or depressed. ORIGINS: The mouth of someone feeling this way has the corners turned down.

**in a funk** |in u FUNGK| *adj* Depressed; in a state of fear. ORIGINS: From Flemish fonck meaning "fear."

**in the dumps** |in *thu* DUMPS| *adj* Miserable or depressed; gloomy. USAGE INFO: Also forms part of the expression down in the dumps.

**singing the blues** |SING ing *thu* BLŪZ| *v* Feeling upset or depressed. ORIGINS: From the musical genre and its typical content. USAGE INFO: Used very broadly today to refer to businesses that aren't doing as well as expected, defeated sports teams, etc.

NON-SLANG SYNONYMS: cheerless, dejected, glum, grim, moody, sad, unhappy, **gloomy**, **crest-fallen**, **depressed**, **despondent**, **disconsolate**, **dispirited**, **downcast**, **downhearted**, **heavy-hearted**, **melancholy**, **morose**, **woebegone**

## 2 A Fit of Depression

**blahs** |blahz| *n* An occurrence of depression. ORIGINS: Extension of blah, which comes from the onomatopoeic sound of meaningless, uninteresting talk. USAGE INFO: Often follows *the*.

**blues** |blūz| *n* A fit of depression or unhappiness. ORIGINS: First recorded use in a letter by British actor David Garrick in 1741, using the spelling *Blews*. Also said to be short for an eighteenth century expression blue devils. USAGE INFO: Often with *the* as in "I've got the blues."

**dumps, the** |*thu* DUMPS| *n* A period of depression. USAGE INFO: Often in the phrase "down in the dumps."

**funk** |fungk| *n* A state of depression; a bad mood. ORIGINS: From the Flemish flonck meaning "fear." USAGE INFO: Used with the indefinite article *a* unlike the blues.

NON-SLANG SYNONYMS: dejection, **black mood**, **doldrums**, **ennui**, **lassitude**, **low spirits**, **melancholia**, **stupor**, **torpor**

## 3 To Have a Mental Breakdown

**blow one's mind** |BLŌ wunz MĪND| *v* To become insane.

**bug out** |bug out| *v* To leave or take off; to run away. ORIGINS: A reference to a flitting insect. USAGE ALERT: Another meaning of bug out, which extends the idea of a bug as irritating or annoying, is "to go insane; to be driven mad."

**come apart at the seams** |kum u PAHRT at *thu* SĒMZ| *v* To lose control. ORIGINS: By analogy between physically and mentally falling apart.

**come unglued** |kum un GLŪD| *v* To lose one's emotional or mental balance. ORIGINS: By analogy between physically and mentally falling apart.

**come unstuck** |kum un STUK| *v* To lose one's emotional or mental balance. ORIGINS: By analogy between physically and mentally falling apart.

**crack** |krak| *v* To suffer an emotional breakdown. ORIGINS: By analogy between physical and mental breakage.

**crack up²** |KRAK UP| *v* To suffer a nervous breakdown. ORIGINS: By analogy between physical and mental breakage. USAGE ALERT: This way of speaking about *sb's* mental health may be considered insensitive and therefore objectionable in some contexts and by some people.

**flip one's lid/wig** |FLIP wunz lid / FLIP wunz wig| *v* To lose one's temper; to fly into a rage; to lose control emotionally; to go crazy. ORIGINS: From slang lid meaning "head."

**freak out** |FRĒK OUT| *v* To go crazy from fear; to lose control; to become greatly upset; to suffer an emotional breakdown. ORIGINS: From slang **freak** meaning "drug user"—developed from the volatile emotional state of someone who uses hallucinogenic drugs.

**go batty** |gō BAT ē| *v* To go insane. ORIGINS: Related to the phrase **have bats in one's belfry**. USAGE ALERT: This way of speaking about *sb's* mental health may be considered insensitive and therefore objectionable in some contexts and by some people.

**go crackers** |gō KRAK urz| *v* To go insane. ORIGINS: By extension of slang **cracked**. USAGE ALERT: This way of speaking about *sb's* mental health may be considered insensitive and therefore objectionable in some contexts and by some people.

**go nuts** |gō NUTS| *v* To lose one's mind. ORIGINS: From slang noun **nut** meaning "an insane person." USAGE ALERT: This way of speaking about *sb's* mental health may be considered insensitive and therefore objectionable in some contexts and by some people.

**go off one's bean** |gō ahf wunz BĒN| *v* To lose one's mind. ORIGINS: From slang **bean** meaning "head." USAGE ALERT: This way of speaking about *sb's* mental health may be considered insensitive and therefore objectionable in some contexts and by some people.

**go off one's chump** |gō ahf wunz CHUMP| *v* To lose one's mind. ORIGINS: From slang **chump** meaning "head or face." USAGE ALERT: This way of speaking about *sb's* mental health may be considered insensitive and therefore objectionable in some contexts and by some people.

**go off one's head** |gō ahf wunz HED| *v* To lose one's mind. USAGE ALERT: This way of speaking about *sb's* mental health may be considered insensitive and therefore objectionable in some contexts and by some people.

**go off one's nut** |gō ahf wunz NUT| *v* To lose one's mind. ORIGINS: From slang **nut** meaning "head or brains." USAGE ALERT: This way of speaking about *sb's* mental health may be considered insensitive and therefore objectionable in some contexts and by some people.

**go off one's rocker** |gō ahf wunz RAH kur| *v* To go crazy. ORIGINS: From SE **rocking chair**; possibly a reference to a person who falls out of his or her rocker. USAGE

ALERT: This way of speaking about *sb's* mental health may be considered insensitive and therefore objectionable in some contexts and by some people.

**go off the deep end** |gō ahf *th*u DĒP end| *v* To get out of one's depth, emotionally; to go crazy; to become so angry that one loses control. ORIGINS: Refers to the deep end of the swimming pool (and possibly to being in over one's head). USAGE ALERT: This way of speaking about *sb's* mental health may be considered insensitive and therefore objectionable in some contexts and by some people.

**go out of one's gourd** |gō out uv wunz GAWRD| *v* To lose one's mind. ORIGINS: From slang **gourd** meaning "head." USAGE ALERT: This way of speaking about *sb's* mental health may be considered insensitive and therefore objectionable in some contexts and by some people.

**go out of one's skull** |gō out uv wunz SKUL| *v* To lose control; to go crazy. ORIGINS: The phrases **out of one's skull/mind/head/gourd**, etc. call up a contrast to the idiom **in one's right mind**, meaning "sane and in control."

**go to pieces** |gō tū PĒ siz| *v* To lose one's emotional or mental balance. ORIGINS: By analogy between physically and mentally falling apart.

**lose one's marbles** |lūz wunz MAR bulz| *v* To go mad. ORIGINS: From slang **marbles** meaning "common sense." USAGE ALERT: This way of speaking about *sb's* mental health may be considered insensitive and therefore objectionable in some contexts and by some people.

**schiz(z) out** |skits OUT| *v* To lose control. ORIGINS: By shortening and alteration of SE **schizophrenia**. USAGE ALERT: This way of speaking about *sb's* mental health may be considered insensitive and therefore objectionable in some contexts and by some people.

**slip a cog** |slip u KAHG| *v* To lose one's sanity. ORIGINS: By analogy to a machine that no longer functions because its gears are not turning properly. USAGE ALERT: This way of speaking about *sb's* mental health may be considered insensitive and therefore objectionable in some contexts and by some people.

**NON-SLANG SYNONYMS:** experience a mental collapse, have a breakdown, suffer a breakdown; **go crazy, go insane**; **go mad, go out of one's mind, lose control**; **become demented, become psychotic, suffer from nervous prostration**

# 4 Crazy

**FINE** Freaked out, insecure, neurotic, emotional. ORIGINS: Popularized in the movie *The Italian Job* (2003). USAGE INFO: *F* is sometimes used to represent other words, such as fucked up, frustrated, or foggy.

**around the bend** |u ROUND *th*u BEND| *adj* Crazy; insane. USAGE ALERT: Often used with intent to denigrate or insult and understood as such. This way of speaking about *sb's* mental health may be considered insensitive and therefore objectionable in some contexts and by some people.

**bananas** |bu NAN uz| *adj* Crazy; insane. ORIGINS: May be referencing go ape in the sense of losing control and the common understanding that apes are extremely fond of bananas. USAGE ALERT: Often used with intent to denigrate or insult and understood as such. This way of speaking about *sb's* mental health may be considered insensitive and therefore objectionable in some contexts and by some people.

**barking mad** |BAHR king MAD| *adj* Crazy; insane. ORIGINS: May be referencing the wild barking of mad dogs. USAGE ALERT: Often used with intent to denigrate or insult and understood as such. This way of speaking about *sb's* mental health may be considered insensitive and therefore objectionable in some contexts and by some people.

**bats** |bats| *adj* Crazy; insane. ORIGINS: Shortened form of bats in the belfry, which describes insanity as if it were an infestation of the brain, drawing an analogy between the belfry at the top of a church tower, and the head at the top of the body. USAGE ALERT: Often used with intent to denigrate or insult and understood as such. This way of speaking about *sb's* mental health may be considered insensitive and therefore objectionable in some contexts and by some people.

**bats in the belfry** |BATS in *thu* BEL frē| *adj* Crazy; insane. ORIGINS: Describes insanity as if it were an infestation of the brain, drawing an analogy between the belfry at the top of a church tower, and the head at the top of the body. USAGE ALERT: Often used with intent to denigrate or insult and understood as such. This way of speaking about *sb's* mental health may be considered insensitive and therefore objectionable in some contexts and by some people.

**batshit crazy** |BAT shit KRĀ zē| *adj* Extremely crazy; recklessly crazy. ORIGINS: From slang bats meaning "insane" and slang **apeshit** meaning "to lose control." USAGE ALERT: The inclusion of the word **shit** will render this phrase objectionable in some contexts and to some people. Often used with intent to denigrate or insult and understood as such. This way of speaking about *sb's* mental health may be considered insensitive and therefore objectionable in some contexts and by some people.

**batso** |BAT sō| *adj* Crazy; insane. ORIGINS: Combines **bats,** which is short for have bats in the belfry and the slang suffix -o used to create adjectives, including some others having to do with mental health, like **nutso, sicko,** and **wacko,** making them similar to abbreviated **schizo** and **psycho.** USAGE ALERT: Often used with intent to denigrate or insult and understood as such. This way of speaking about *sb's* mental health may be considered insensitive and therefore objectionable in some contexts and by some people.

**batty** |BAT ē| *adj* Crazy; insane. ORIGINS: Shortened form of bats in the belfry, which describes insanity as if it were an infestation of the brain, drawing an analogy between the belfry at the top of a church tower, and the head at the top of the body. USAGE ALERT: Often used with intent to denigrate or insult and understood as such. This way of speaking about *sb's* mental health may be considered insensitive and therefore objectionable in some contexts and by some people.

**bonkers** |BAHN kurz| *adj* Crazy; insane. ORIGINS: Madness imagined as the result of a blow (**bonk**) to the head. USAGE ALERT: Often used with intent to denigrate or insult and understood as such. This way of speaking about *sb's* mental health may be considered insensitive and therefore objectionable in some contexts and by some people.

**buggy** |BUG ē| *adj* Crazy. ORIGINS: The idea is that one's mind has become infested with insects. USAGE ALERT: Often used with intent to denigrate or insult and understood as such. This way of speaking about *sb's* mental health may be considered insensitive and therefore objectionable in some contexts and by some people.

**cockeyed** |KAHK īd| *adj* Mildly crazy; outlandish; ludicrous; absurd. ORIGINS: By extension from SE **cock**, meaning "to bend" and SE **eye**, meaning the eyes aren't level and focused. USAGE ALERT: Usually used with intent to denigrate or insult and understood as such. This way of speaking about *sb's* mental health may be considered insensitive and therefore objectionable in some contexts and by some people.

**cracked** |krakt| *adj* Crazy; insane. ORIGINS: From SE **cracked** meaning "broken." USAGE ALERT: Often used with intent to denigrate or insult and understood as such. This way of speaking about *sb's* mental health may be considered insensitive and therefore objectionable in some contexts and by some people.

**crackers** |KRAK urz| *adj* Crazy; insane. ORIGINS: From SE **cracked** meaning "broken." USAGE ALERT: Often used with intent to denigrate or insult and understood as such. This way of speaking about *sb's* mental health may be considered insensitive and therefore objectionable in some contexts and by some people.

**crackpot** |KRAK paht| *adj* Crazy or eccentric; outlandish; absurd; harebrained; foolish; unworkable. ORIGINS: By extension from SE **crack**, meaning "to break" and **pot** meaning "skull," i.e., the kind of suggestions one would expect from someone whose brains were not functioning properly. USAGE INFO: Often used of ideas, as well as of people. USAGE ALERT: When used of people, will usually be used with intent to denigrate or insult and understood as such. This way of speaking about *sb's* mental health may be considered insensitive and therefore objectionable in some contexts and by some people.

**crazy as a bedbug** |KRĀ zē az u BED bug| *adj* Crazy or eccentric. USAGE ALERT: Often used with intent to denigrate or insult and understood as such. This way of speaking about *sb's* mental health may be considered insensitive and therefore objectionable in some contexts and by some people.

**crazy as catshit** |KRĀ zē az KAT shit| *adj* Extremely crazy. USAGE ALERT: The inclusion of a form of the word **shit** will render this phrase objectionable in some contexts and to some people. Often used with intent to denigrate or insult and understood as such. This way of speaking about *sb's* mental health may be considered insensitive and therefore objectionable in some contexts and by some people.

**few beers short of a six-pack, a** |u FYŪ BIRZ shawrt uv u SIKS pak| *adj* Unintelligent; crazy. ORIGINS: One of many synonyms of the term not all there, which indulge in wordplay by representing "all there" in a particular way and designating how the person in question fails to meet the criteria. In this case, "all there" is represented by a **six-pack**, a type of packaging in which beer is typically sold. If you're missing several beers, you do not, in fact, have a six-pack. USAGE ALERT: Usually used with intent to denigrate or insult and understood as such.

## few cents short of a dollar, a |u FYŪ SENS shawrt uv u DAHL ur| adj
Unintelligent; crazy. ORIGINS: One of many synonyms of the term not all there, which indulge in wordplay by representing "all there" in a particular way and designating how the person in question fails to meet the criteria. In this case, "all there" is represented by a **dollar**. If you're missing a few cents, you do not, in fact, have a dollar. USAGE ALERT: Usually used with intent to denigrate or insult and understood as such.

## few fries short of a happy meal, a |u FYŪ FRĪZ shawrt uv u HAP ē mēl| adj Unintelligent; crazy. ORIGINS: One of many synonyms of the term not all there, which indulge in wordplay by representing "all there" in a particular way and designating how the person in question fails to meet the criteria. In this case, "all there" is represented by a **McDonald's Happy Meal**, a child-size meal that includes a main course, a drink, and a side-order, which is—in the stereotypical model—French fries. By a bit of a stretch, if you're missing several fries, you do not have a full-fledged Happy Meal. USAGE ALERT: Usually used with intent to denigrate or insult and understood as such.

## few peas short of a casserole, a |u FYŪ PĒZ shawrt uv u CAS ur ōl| adj
Unintelligent; crazy. ORIGINS: One of many synonyms of the term not all there, which indulge in wordplay by representing "all there" in a particular way and designating how the person in question fails to meet the criteria. In this case, "all there" is represented by a **casserole**, a baked meal-in-one-dish including—in the stereotypical conception—peas. By a bit of a stretch, without the peas, you do not have a full-fledged ideal casserole. USAGE ALERT: Usually used with intent to denigrate or insult and understood as such.

## few pecans short of a fruitcake, a |u FYŪ pē KAHNZ shawrt uv u FRŪT kāk| adj Unintelligent; crazy. ORIGINS: One of many synonyms of the term not all there, which indulge in wordplay by representing "all there" in a particular way and designating how the person in question fails to meet the criteria. In this case, "all there" is represented by a **fruitcake**, a holiday cake made of flour, dried and candied fruit, and nuts (sometimes pecans), which—in the stereotypical model—are de rigeur (required). By a bit of a stretch, if you're missing several pecans, you do not have a full-fledged, authentic fruitcake. The relationship of nuts and fruitcake is also referenced in several slang phrases meaning crazy, such as **nutty as a fruitcake**. USAGE ALERT: Usually used with intent to denigrate or insult and understood as such.

## few sandwiches short of a picnic, a |u FYŪ SAND wich iz shawrt uv u PIK nik| adj Unintelligent; crazy. ORIGINS: One of many synonyms of the term not all there, which indulge in wordplay by representing "all there" in a particular way and designating how the person in question fails to meet the criteria. In this case, "all there" is represented by a **picnic** spread, an outdoor meal including—in the stereotypical conception—sandwiches, side dishes, dessert, and drinks, often designed to be eaten with few or no implements. By a bit of a stretch, without enough sandwiches, you do not have a full-fledged ideal picnic. USAGE ALERT: Usually used with intent to denigrate or insult and understood as such.

**few slices short of a loaf, a** |u FYŪ SLĪ siz shawrt uv u LŌF| *adj* Unintelligent; crazy. ORIGINS: One of many synonyms of the term not all there, which indulge in wordplay by representing "all there" in a particular way and designating how the person in question fails to meet the criteria. In this case, "all there" is represented by a loaf, a typical way of preparing bread and packaging it for sale. If you're missing several slices, you do not, in fact, have a full loaf. USAGE ALERT: Usually used with intent to denigrate or insult and understood as such.

**few spokes short of a wheel, a** |u FYŪ SPŌKS shawrt uv u WĒL| *adj* Unintelligent; crazy. ORIGINS: One of many synonyms of the term not all there, which indulge in wordplay by representing "all there" in a particular way and designating how the person in question fails to meet the criteria. In this case, "all there" is represented by a wheel of the type found on a bicycle, with spokes connecting the outside edge to the hub. By a bit of a stretch, without enough spokes, you do not have a full-fledged ideal wheel. USAGE ALERT: Usually used with intent to denigrate or insult and understood as such.

**flea short of an infestation, a** |u FLĒ shawrt uv an in fes TĀ shun| *adj* Unintelligent; crazy. ORIGINS: One of many synonyms of the term not all there, which indulge in wordplay by representing "all there" in a particular way and designating how the person in question fails to meet the criteria. In this case, "all there" is represented by an infestation, a large group of unwanted animals. By a bit of a stretch, without enough fleas, you do not have a full-fledged infestation. USAGE ALERT: Usually used with intent to denigrate or insult and understood as such.

**food for squirrels** |FŪD fawr SKWURLZ| *adj* Crazy. ORIGINS: A euphemism for nuts. USAGE ALERT: Often used with intent to denigrate or insult and understood as such. This way of speaking about *sb's* mental health may be considered insensitive and therefore objectionable in some contexts and by some people.

**fruitcakey** |FRŪT kāk ē| *adj* Crazy. ORIGINS: Fruitcakes are proverbially full of nuts, a reference to slang nuts meaning "crazy" or a reference to slang fruity, also meaning "nuts." USAGE ALERT: Often used with intent to denigrate or insult and understood as such. This way of speaking about *sb's* mental health may be considered insensitive and therefore objectionable in some contexts and by some people.

**fruity** |FRŪT ē| *adj* Crazy. ORIGINS: Possibly linked to slang bananas, an example of a fruit used to indicate craziness. USAGE ALERT: Often used with intent to denigrate or insult and understood as such. This way of speaking about *sb's* mental health may be considered insensitive and therefore objectionable in some contexts and by some people.

**half sandwich short of a picnic, a** |u HAF SAND wich shawrt uv u PIK nik| *adj* Unintelligent; crazy. ORIGINS: One of many synonyms of the term not all there, which indulge in wordplay by representing "all there" in a particular way and designating how the person in question fails to meet the criteria. In this case, "all there" is represented by a picnic spread, an outdoor meal including—in the stereotypical conception—sandwiches, side dishes, dessert, and drinks, often designed to be eaten with few or no implements. By a bit of a stretch, without enough sandwiches, you do not have a full-fledged ideal picnic. USAGE ALERT: Usually used with intent to denigrate or insult and understood as such.

**having a screw loose** |hav ing u SKRŪ lūs| *adj* Insane. ORIGINS: The idea is that, like a mechanism with a loose screw, things in the brain are not working properly. USAGE ALERT: Often used with intent to denigrate or insult and understood as such. This way of speaking about *sb's* mental health may be considered insensitive and therefore objectionable in some contexts and by some people.

**having bats in one's belfry** |hav ing BATS in wunz BEL frē| *adj* Crazy. ORIGINS: Depicts insanity as an infestation of the brain, which is—like the belfry—the topmost part. USAGE ALERT: Often used with intent to denigrate or insult and understood as such. This way of speaking about *sb's* mental health may be considered insensitive and therefore objectionable in some contexts and by some people.

**lift doesn't go to the top floor, the** |thu LIFT duz 'nt GŌ tū *thu* TAHP FLŌR| *phr* Unintelligent; crazy. ORIGINS: This slang phrase works in two ways. First, it sets up an expectation and then undercuts it: one would naturally expect a lift to go to all floors of a building. Second, it relies on an association between the head, at the top of the body, and the top floor of a building surmounting all the other floors. Thus, the phrase suggests that the person is completely functional, except for his/her brain. USAGE ALERT: Usually used with intent to denigrate or insult and understood as such.

**lights are on, but nobody's home, the** |thu LĪTS ahr AHN but NŌ bahd ēz HŌM| *phr* Unintelligent; crazy. ORIGINS: This slang phrase works in two ways. First, it sets up an expectation and then undercuts it: one would naturally expect a light to signal the presence of a person. Second, it relies on an association between the absence of a person from a physical dwelling, and the failure of a person's intellect or mind, calling to mind an extension of the slang phrase **not all there**. USAGE ALERT: Usually used with intent to denigrate or insult and understood as such.

**loco** |LŌ KŌ| *adj* Crazy. ORIGINS: Borrowed from Spanish **loco** meaning "crazy." USAGE ALERT: Often used with intent to denigrate or insult and understood as such. This way of speaking about *sb's* mental health may be considered insensitive and therefore objectionable in some contexts and by some people.

**loony** |LŪN ē| *adj* Crazy. ORIGINS: Short for SE **lunatic**. USAGE ALERT: Often used with intent to denigrate or insult and understood as such. This way of speaking about *sb's* mental health may be considered insensitive and therefore objectionable in some contexts and by some people.

**loopy** |LŪP ē| *adj* Crazy. USAGE ALERT: Often used with intent to denigrate or insult and understood as such. This way of speaking about *sb's* mental health may be considered insensitive and therefore objectionable in some contexts and by some people.

**meshugah, meshugge, meshuga, meshuggah** |mu SHUG u| *adj* Crazy. ORIGINS: From Yiddish **mushuge** meaning "crazy." USAGE ALERT: Often used with intent to denigrate or insult and understood as such. This way of speaking about *sb's* mental health may be considered insensitive and therefore objectionable in some contexts and by some people.

**not all there**[2] |naht awl THER| *adj* Crazy. ORIGINS: The idea is that the person is lacking all the elements required for sanity. USAGE ALERT: Often used with intent to denigrate or insult and understood as such. This way of speaking about *sb's* mental health may be considered insensitive and therefore objectionable in some contexts and by some people.

**not playing with a full deck** |naht PLĀ ing with u FUL DEK| *adj* Unintelligent; crazy. ORIGINS: One of many synonyms of the term **not all there**, which indulge in wordplay by representing "all there" in a particular way and designating how the person in question fails to meet the criteria. In this case, "all there" is represented by playing cards with a complete set of 52. Anybody who has tried to play a game of cards with less than the required number knows that it doesn't work really well. And herein lies the analogy to the mind or brain of the person who is **not playing with a full deck**. USAGE ALERT: Usually used with intent to denigrate or insult and understood as such.

**nuts** |nuts| *adj* Crazy; insane. USAGE ALERT: Often used with intent to denigrate or insult and understood as such. This way of speaking about *sb's* mental health may be considered insensitive and therefore objectionable in some contexts and by some people.

**nutso** |NUT sō| *adj* Crazy. ORIGINS: From slang **nuts** and the slang suffix -o used to create adjectives, including some others having to do with mental health, like **batso**, **wacko**, and **sicko**, making them similar to abbreviated **schizo** and **psycho**. USAGE ALERT: Often used with intent to denigrate or insult and understood as such. This way of speaking about *sb's* mental health may be considered insensitive and therefore objectionable in some contexts and by some people.

**nutty** |NUT ē| *adj* Crazy; insane. USAGE ALERT: Often used with intent to denigrate or insult and understood as such. This way of speaking about *sb's* mental health may be considered insensitive and therefore objectionable in some contexts and by some people.

**nutty as a fruitcake** |NUT ē az u FRŪT kāk| *adj* Crazy; insane. USAGE ALERT: Often used with intent to denigrate or insult and understood as such. This way of speaking about *sb's* mental health may be considered insensitive and therefore objectionable in some contexts and by some people.

**off one's bean** |ahf wunz BĒN| *adj* Crazy. ORIGINS: From SE **off** and slang **bean** meaning "head." USAGE ALERT: Often used with intent to denigrate or insult and understood as such. This way of speaking about *sb's* mental health may be considered insensitive and therefore objectionable in some contexts and by some people.

**off one's chump** |ahf wunz CHUMP| *adj* Crazy. ORIGINS: From SE **off** and slang **chump** meaning "head or face." USAGE ALERT: Often used with intent to denigrate or insult and understood as such. This way of speaking about *sb's* mental health may be considered insensitive and therefore objectionable in some contexts and by some people.

**off one's head** |ahf wunz HED| *adj* Crazy. ORIGINS: From SE off and head. USAGE ALERT: Often used with intent to denigrate or insult and understood as such. This way of speaking about *sb's* mental health may be considered insensitive and therefore objectionable in some contexts and by some people.

**off one's rocker** |ahf wunz RAHK ur| *adj* Crazy. ORIGINS: From SE off and rocker, meaning "rocking chair"; perhaps the regular motion of the chair represents the smooth workings of sanity. USAGE ALERT: Often used with intent to denigrate or insult and understood as such. This way of speaking about *sb's* mental health may be considered insensitive and therefore objectionable in some contexts and by some people.

**off one's trolley** |ahf wunz TRAHL ē| *adj* Crazy. ORIGINS: From SE off and trolley tracks being used as a metaphor for the "grooves" in which sane people function. USAGE ALERT: Often used with intent to denigrate or insult and understood as such. This way of speaking about *sb's* mental health may be considered insensitive and therefore objectionable in some contexts and by some people.

**out of one's gourd** |out uv wunz GAWRD| *adj* Crazy. ORIGINS: From slang gourd meaning "head." USAGE ALERT: Often used with intent to denigrate or insult and understood as such. This way of speaking about *sb's* mental health may be considered insensitive and therefore objectionable in some contexts and by some people.

**out of one's head/skull** |out uv wunz HED / out uv wunz SKUL| *adj* Crazy. ORIGINS: From SE head or skull. USAGE ALERT: Often used with intent to denigrate or insult and understood as such. This way of speaking about *sb's* mental health may be considered insensitive and therefore objectionable in some contexts and by some people.

**out of one's tree** |out uv wunz TRĒ| *adj* Crazy. ORIGINS: The idea is that the person referred to has fallen out of the tree. USAGE ALERT: Often used with intent to denigrate or insult and understood as such. This way of speaking about *sb's* mental health may be considered insensitive and therefore objectionable in some contexts and by some people.

**out to lunch** |out tū LUNCH| *adj* Crazy. ORIGINS: If one is literally "out to lunch," one is absent from one's place of business. This is interpreted figuratively to play on the idea of being "not all there." USAGE ALERT: Often used with intent to denigrate or insult and understood as such. This way of speaking about *sb's* mental health may be considered insensitive and therefore objectionable in some contexts and by some people.

**pixilated** |PIK sul ā tid| *adj* Insane. ORIGINS: From SE pixie, *sb* whose mind has been taken over by sprites. USAGE ALERT: Often used with intent to denigrate or insult and understood as such. This way of speaking about *sb's* mental health may be considered insensitive and therefore objectionable in some contexts and by some people.

**psycho** |SĪ kō| *adj* Crazy. ORIGINS: Shortened from SE psychotic, rendering it similar to other words having to do with mental health, like batso, nutso, schizo, sicko, and wacko. USAGE ALERT: Often used with intent to denigrate or insult and understood as such. This way of speaking about *sb's* mental health may be considered insensitive and therefore objectionable in some contexts and by some people.

**round the bend** |ROUND *thu* BEND| *adj See* AROUND THE BEND.

**schizo** |SKITS ō| *adj* Crazy. ORIGINS: Shortened from SE **schizophrenic**, rendering it similar to other slang having to do with mental health, like **batso**, **nutso**, **psycho**, **sicko**, and **wacko**. USAGE ALERT: Often used with intent to denigrate or insult and understood as such. This way of speaking about *sb's* mental health may be considered insensitive and therefore objectionable in some contexts and by some people.

**screwy** |SKRŪ ē| *adj* Crazy. ORIGINS: Shortened form of **have a screw loose**. USAGE ALERT: Often used with intent to denigrate or insult and understood as such. This way of speaking about *sb's* mental health may be considered insensitive and therefore objectionable in some contexts and by some people.

**sicko** |SIK ō| *adj* Crazy. ORIGINS: From slang **sick** and the slang suffix -o used to create adjectives, including some others having to do with mental health, like **batso**, **wacko**, and **nutso**, making them similar to abbreviated **schizo** and **psycho**. USAGE ALERT: Often used with intent to denigrate or insult and understood as such. This way of speaking about *sb's* mental health may be considered insensitive and therefore objectionable in some contexts and by some people.

**squirrely** |SKWURL ē| *adj* Crazy. ORIGINS: Linked to slang **nutty** through the stereotypical connection of squirrels and nuts. USAGE ALERT: Often used with intent to denigrate or insult and understood as such. This way of speaking about *sb's* mental health may be considered insensitive and therefore objectionable in some contexts and by some people.

**tetched** |techt| *adj See* TOUCHED.

**tetched in the head** |TECHT in *thu* HED| *adj See* TOUCHED IN THE HEAD.

**touched** |tucht| *adj* Mentally unbalanced. USAGE ALERT: Often used with intent to denigrate or insult and understood as such. This way of speaking about *sb's* mental health may be considered insensitive and therefore objectionable in some contexts and by some people.

**touched in the head** |TUCHT in *thu* HED| *adj* Mentally unbalanced. USAGE ALERT: Often used with intent to denigrate or insult and understood as such. This way of speaking about *sb's* mental health may be considered insensitive and therefore objectionable in some contexts and by some people.

**wacko** |WAK ō| *adj* Crazy. ORIGINS: From slang **wacky** meaning "eccentric," and the slang suffix -o used to create adjectives, including some others having to do with mental health, like **batso**, **nutso**, and **sicko**, making them similar to abbreviated **schizo** and **psycho**. USAGE ALERT: Often used with intent to denigrate or insult and understood as such. This way of speaking about *sb's* mental health may be considered insensitive and therefore objectionable in some contexts and by some people.

**whacked out** |WAKT out| *adj* Crazy. USAGE ALERT: Often used with intent to denigrate or insult and understood as such. This way of speaking about *sb's* mental health may be considered insensitive and therefore objectionable in some contexts and by some people.

**Non-Slang Synonyms:** certifiable, insane, mentally ill, not in one's right mind; <u>crazy</u>, <u>crazy as a loon</u>, <u>cuckoo</u>, <u>daffy</u>, <u>dotty</u>, <u>flakey</u>, <u>kooky</u>, <u>mad</u>, <u>mental</u>, <u>not right in the head</u>, <u>sick in the head</u>, <u>unhinged</u>; **demented, deranged, non compos mentis**

# RELAXATION

## 1 Tired/Out of It

**beat** |bēt| *adj* Worn out, as if from a beating.

**bushed** |bŏŏsht| *adj* Extremely tired; exhausted. ORIGINS: As tired as if one had been wandering for a long time in the woods/bush.

**done for²/in** |DUN fawr / DUN in| *adj* Exhausted; very tired.

**dragging** |DRAG ing| *adj* Feeling ill or lethargic; utterly exhausted. ORIGINS: From the movements of "dragging themselves around" made by people who feel this way.

**fried** |frīd| *adj* Exhausted; worn out; incapable of thought or action. ORIGINS: Figurative use of SE fry.

**pooped** |pūpt| *adj* Worn out; exhausted. ORIGINS: From slang poop meaning "to tire."

**shot** |shaht| *adj* Exhausted; worn out. USAGE INFO: Can be used of people or things.

**shot to hell** |SHAHT tū hel| *adj* Completely exhausted; useless. ORIGINS: Figurative use of SE **hell** meaning "the alternative to heaven; the realm of the devil." USAGE INFO: Can be used of people or things. USAGE ALERT: The inclusion of the word **hell** in the phrase will render it objectionable in some contexts and to some people.

**tuckered out** |TUK urd out| *adj* Worn out; exhausted.

**whipped** |wipt| *adj* Exhausted.

**wiped (out)** |wīpt / WĪPT out| *adj* Completely worn out.

**zonked** |zawngkt| *adj.* Exhausted. ORIGINS: By extension from slang zonk out meaning "to lose consciousness, especially as a result of using alcohol or drugs."

**Non-Slang Synonyms:** drained, drooping, droopy, drowsy, exhausted, fatigued, tired, worn, worn out, <u>burned out</u>, <u>dead on one's feet</u>, <u>dog-tired</u>, <u>out of it</u>, <u>run-down</u>, <u>sleepy</u>, **enervated, flagging, haggard, prostrated, spent**

## 2 Relaxed

hanging loose |HANG ing LŪS| *adj* Staying relaxed or calm.

kicking back |KIK ing bak| *adj* Relaxing.

laid back |LĀD bak| *adj* Relaxed. ORIGINS: From the lounging posture commonly assumed when relaxing.

taking it easy |TĀK ing it Ē zē| *adj* Relaxing.

NON-SLANG SYNONYMS: easing up, loosening up, relaxed, slowing down, unwinding, **de-stressed**, **putting one's feet up**, **unbending**, **reposing**

## 3 To Sleep

bag some z's |BAG sum zēz| *v* To take a nap. ORIGINS: Slang **bag** can mean "take" or "steal." *Z's* are used as an onomatopoeic representation of sleep.

catch some z's |KACH sum zēz| *v* To take a nap. ORIGINS: *Z's* are used as an onomatopoeic representation of sleep.

conk out[1] |KAHNGK OUT| *v* To fall asleep. ORIGINS: By extension from slang verb conk meaning "to knock out."

cop some z's |KAHP sum zēz| *v* To take a nap. ORIGINS: Slang **cop** means "catch" or "steal." *Z's* are used as an onomatopoeic representation of sleep.

crash |krash| *v* To find a place to sleep; to go to sleep; to collapse with tiredness. USAGE INFO: Often refers to a spell of sleep that is not in one's normal routine and sometimes decided upon on the spur of the moment.

drop off |DRAHP AWF| *v* To fall asleep. ORIGINS: A figurative use, perhaps playing on the idea of letting consciousness drop away.

get some shuteye |get sum SHUT ī| *v* To go to sleep.

hit the hay |hit *thu* HĀ| *v* To go to bed; to go to sleep. ORIGINS: From SE **hit** and slang hay meaning "bed."

hit the sack |hit *thu* SAK| *v* To go to bed; to go to sleep. ORIGINS: From SE **hit** and slang sack meaning "bed."

nod off/out |nahd AWF / nahd OUT| *v* To fall asleep. ORIGINS: From the way people's heads nod as they fall asleep in an upright position. USAGE INFO: Most often refers to falling asleep unintentionally when in a sitting position and trying to stay awake for some purpose.

sack out |SAK out| *v* To go to bed; to go to sleep. ORIGINS: From slang sack meaning "bed."

snooze |snūz| *v* To nap.

**take forty winks** |tāk fawr tē WINGKS| *v* To take a short nap during the daytime.

**turn in** |turn IN| *v* To go to bed.

**zonk off/out** |ZAWNK ahf / ZAWNK out| *v* To fall asleep from exhaustion. ORIGINS: By extension from slang **zonk out** meaning "to lose consciousness, especially as a result of using alcohol or drugs."

NON-SLANG SYNONYMS: doze, drift off, fall asleep, go to sleep, nap, rest, take a nap, take a rest, take a siesta, <u>catnap</u>, **drowse**, **slumber**

# STUPIDITY

**BLBBLB** Back like bull, brain like bird.

**LONH** Light on, nobody home.

**PEBCAC** Problem exists between chair and computer.

**PEBCAK** Problem exists between chair and keyboard.

**RCI** Rectal cranial inversion.

**WAI** What an idiot!

**All foam, no beer.** |AWL fōm NŌ bir| *phr* Unintelligent. ORIGINS: Though foam and beer would both be expected when beer is poured into a glass, the proportions are important. Foam is mainly air, while beer is the substance. This phrase then, suggests that the person is an **airbrain**. USAGE ALERT: Usually used with intent to denigrate or insult and understood as such.

**Back like bull, brain like bird.** |BAK līk BŌŌL BRĀN līk BURD| *phr* Unintelligent. ORIGINS: One of a number of synonymous phrases in which the first part sets up an inference, and the second undercuts it. In this case, the first phrase creates the impression that the person being described is extraordinarily gifted, but the second part, drawing on the association of birds with lack of intelligence (*See* **BIRDBRAIN**) belies the initial conclusion. USAGE ALERT: Usually used with intent to denigrate or insult and understood as such.

**few beers short of a six-pack, a** |u FYŪ BIRZ shawrt uv u SIKS pak| *adj* Unintelligent; crazy. ORIGINS: One of many synonyms of the term not all there, which indulge in wordplay by representing "all there" in a particular way and designating how the person in question fails to meet the criteria. In this case, "all there" is represented by a **six-pack**, a type of packaging in which beer is typically sold. If you're missing several beers, you do not, in fact, have a six-pack. USAGE ALERT: Usually used with intent to denigrate or insult and understood as such.

**few cents short of a dollar, a** |u FYŪ SENS shawrt uv u DAHL ur| *adj*
Unintelligent; crazy. ORIGINS: One of many synonyms of the term not all there, which
indulge in wordplay by representing "all there" in a particular way and designating how
the person in question fails to meet the criteria. In this case, "all there" is represented
by a **dollar**. If you're missing a few cents, you do not, in fact, have a dollar. USAGE
ALERT: Usually used with intent to denigrate or insult and understood as such.

**few fries short of a happy meal, a** |u FYŪ FRĪZ shawrt uv u HAP ē
mēl| *adj* Unintelligent; crazy. ORIGINS: One of many synonyms of the term not all
there, which indulge in wordplay by representing "all there" in a particular way and
designating how the person in question fails to meet the criteria. In this case, "all
there" is represented by a **McDonald's Happy Meal**, a child-size meal that includes a
main course, a drink, and a side-order, which is—in the stereotypical model—French
fries. By a bit of a stretch, if you're missing several fries, you do not have a full-
fledged Happy Meal. USAGE ALERT: Usually used with intent to denigrate or insult and
understood as such.

**few peas short of a casserole, a** |u FYŪ PĒZ shawrt uv u CAS ur ōl| *adj*
Unintelligent; crazy. ORIGINS: One of many synonyms of the term not all there, which
indulge in wordplay by representing "all there" in a particular way and designating how
the person in question fails to meet the criteria. In this case, "all there" is represented
by a **casserole**, a baked meal-in-one-dish including—in the stereotypical conception—
peas. By a bit of a stretch, without the peas, you do not have a full-fledged ideal
casserole. USAGE ALERT: Usually used with intent to denigrate or insult and understood
as such.

**few pecans short of a fruitcake, a** |u FYŪ pē KAHNZ shawrt uv u
FRŪT kāk| *adj* Unintelligent; crazy. ORIGINS: One of many synonyms of the term
not all there, which indulge in wordplay by representing "all there" in a particular
way and designating how the person in question fails to meet the criteria. In this
case, "all there" is represented by a **fruitcake**, a holiday cake made of flour, dried and
candied fruit, and nuts (sometimes pecans), which—in the stereotypical model—are
de rigeur (required). By a bit of a stretch, if you're missing several pecans, you do not
have a full-fledged, authentic fruitcake. The relationship of nuts and fruitcake is also
referenced in several slang phrases meaning crazy, such as **nutty as a fruitcake**. USAGE
ALERT: Usually used with intent to denigrate or insult and understood as such.

**few sandwiches short of a picnic, a** |u FYŪ SAND wich iz shawrt uv
u PIK nik| *adj* Unintelligent; crazy. ORIGINS: One of many synonyms of the term
not all there, which indulge in wordplay by representing "all there" in a particular
way and designating how the person in question fails to meet the criteria. In this
case, "all there" is represented by a **picnic** spread, an outdoor meal including—in
the stereotypical conception—sandwiches, side dishes, dessert, and drinks, often
designed to be eaten with few or no implements. By a bit of a stretch, without enough
sandwiches, you do not have a full-fledged ideal picnic. USAGE ALERT: Usually used
with intent to denigrate or insult and understood as such.

**few slices short of a loaf, a** |u FYŪ SLĪ siz shawrt uv u LŌF| *adj* Unintelligent;
crazy. ORIGINS: One of many synonyms of the term not all there, which indulge in

wordplay by representing "all there" in a particular way and designating how the person in question fails to meet the criteria. In this case, "all there" is represented by a **loaf**, a typical way of preparing bread and packaging it for sale. If you're missing several slices, you do not, in fact, have a full loaf. USAGE ALERT: Usually used with intent to denigrate or insult and understood as such.

**few spokes short of a wheel, a** |u FYŪ SPŌKS shawrt uv u WĒL| *adj* Unintelligent; crazy. ORIGINS: One of many synonyms of the term not all there, which indulge in wordplay by representing "all there" in a particular way and designating how the person in question fails to meet the criteria. In this case, "all there" is represented by a **wheel** of the type found on a bicycle, with spokes connecting the outside edge to the hub. By a bit of a stretch, without enough spokes, you do not have a full-fledged ideal wheel. USAGE ALERT: Usually used with intent to denigrate or insult and understood as such.

**flea short of an infestation, a** |u FLĒ shawrt uv an in fes TA shun| *adj* Unintelligent; crazy. ORIGINS: One of many synonyms of the term not all there, which indulge in wordplay by representing "all there" in a particular way and designating how the person in question fails to meet the criteria. In this case, "all there" is represented by an **infestation**, a large group of unwanted animals. By a bit of a stretch, without enough fleas, you do not have a full-fledged infestation. USAGE ALERT: Usually used with intent to denigrate or insult and understood as such.

**half sandwich short of a picnic, a** |u HAF SAND wich shawrt uv u PIK nik| *adj* Unintelligent; crazy. ORIGINS: One of many synonyms of the term not all there, which indulge in wordplay by representing "all there" in a particular way and designating how the person in question fails to meet the criteria. In this case, "all there" is represented by a **picnic** spread, an outdoor meal including—in the stereotypical conception—sandwiches, side dishes, dessert, and drinks, often designed to be eaten with few or no implements. By a bit of a stretch, without enough sandwiches, you do not have a full-fledged ideal picnic. USAGE ALERT: Usually used with intent to denigrate or insult and understood as such.

**half there** |HAF ther| *adj* Somewhat crazy. ORIGINS: A joking allusion to the term not all there, adding a quantification.

**lift doesn't go to the top floor, the** |thu LIFT duz 'nt GŌ tū *thu* TAHP FLŌR| *phr* Unintelligent; crazy. ORIGINS: This slang phrase works in two ways. First, it sets up an expectation and then undercuts it: one would naturally expect a lift to go to all floors of a building. Second, it relies on an association between the head, at the top of the body, and the top floor of a building surmounting all the other floors. Thus, the phrase suggests that the person is completely functional, except for his/her brain. USAGE ALERT: Usually used with intent to denigrate or insult and understood as such.

**lights are on, but nobody's home, the** |thu LĪTS ahr AHN but NŌ bahd ēz HŌM| *phr* Unintelligent; crazy. ORIGINS: This slang phrase works in two ways. First, it sets up an expectation and then undercuts it: one would naturally expect a light to signal the presence of a person. Second, it relies on an association between the absence of a person from a physical dwelling, and the failure of a person's intellect or mind, calling to mind an extension of the slang phrase **not all there**. USAGE ALERT: Usually used with intent to denigrate or insult and understood as such.

## not all there[1] |naht awl THER| *adj* Unintelligent. ORIGINS: The idea is that a portion of the person's brain is missing, resulting in a failure of intelligence. USAGE ALERT: Usually used with intent to denigrate or insult and understood as such.

## not playing with a full deck |naht PLĀ ing with u FUL DEK| *adj* Unintelligent; crazy. ORIGINS: One of many synonyms of the term not all there, which indulge in wordplay by representing "all there" in a particular way and designating how the person in question fails to meet the criteria. In this case, "all there" is represented by playing cards with a complete set of 52. Anybody who has tried to play a game of cards with less than the required number knows that it doesn't work really well. And herein lies the analogy to the mind or brain of the person who is **not playing with a full deck**. USAGE ALERT: Usually used with intent to denigrate or insult and understood as such.

## not the brightest bulb in the chandelier |NAHT *thu* brī tist BULB in *thu* SHAN du lir| *adj* Unintelligent. ORIGINS: One of many synonyms of the term not all there, which indulge in wordplay by representing "all there" in a particular way and designating how the person in question fails to meet the criteria. In this case, "all there" is represented by being a bright lightbulb installed in a chandelier, and the person in question is "dim" by comparison, linking to slang terms such as dimwit. USAGE ALERT: Usually used with intent to denigrate or insult and understood as such.

## not the brightest light in the harbor |NAHT *thu* brī tist LĪT in *thu* HAHR bur| *adj* Unintelligent. ORIGINS: One of many synonyms of the term not all there, which indulge in wordplay by representing "all there" in a particular way and designating how the person in question fails to meet the criteria. In this case, "all there" is represented by being a bright light, like a lighthouse, in a harbor, and the person in question is "dim" by comparison, linking to slang terms such as dimwit. USAGE ALERT: Usually used with intent to denigrate or insult and understood as such.

## not the sharpest knife in the drawer |NAHT *thu* SHAHR pist NĪF in *thu* DRAWR| *adj* Unintelligent. ORIGINS: One of many synonyms of the term not all there, which indulge in wordplay by representing "all there" in a particular way and designating how the person in question fails to meet the criteria. In this case, "all there" is represented by being a well-sharpened knife, and the person in question is "dull" by comparison, linking to descriptions of unintelligent people as being **dull**. USAGE ALERT: Usually used with intent to denigrate or insult and understood as such.

## one brick short of a load |WUN BRIK shawrt uv u LŌD| *adj* Unintelligent; crazy. ORIGINS: One of many synonyms of the term not all there which indulge in wordplay by representing "all there" in a particular way and designating how the person in question fails to meet the criteria.  In this case, "all there" is represented by a **load**, a large group of building materials. By a bit of a stretch, without enough bricks, you do not have a full-fledged load. USAGE ALERT: Usually used with intent to denigrate or insult and understood as such.

**Problem exists between chair and computer.** |PRAHB lum ig ZISTS bu twēn CHER and cum PYŪT ur| *phr* User error. ORIGINS: From the language of technical support people, a humorous description of user error, the point being that the error is in how the user is operating the technology, not a hardware or software error. USAGE ALERT: In the tech support context, usually not said so that the user is aware of it. When said directly to *sb*, often used with intent to denigrate or insult and understood as such.

**Problem exists between chair and keyboard.** |PRAHB lum ig ZISTS bu twēn CHER and KĒ bawrd| *phr* User error. ORIGINS: From the language of technical support people, a humorous description of user error, the point being that the error is in how the user is operating the technology, not a hardware or software error. USAGE ALERT: In the tech support context, usually not said so that the user is aware of it. When said directly to *sb*, often used with intent to denigrate or insult and understood as such.

**rectal cranial inversion** |REK tul CRĀN ē ul in VER zhun| *adj* Unintelligent. ORIGINS: The inversion suggests that the person's brains are in his/her bottom or rear end, while his/her head is full of excrement. USAGE ALERT: Usually used with intent to denigrate or insult and understood as such.

**terminally stupid** |TUR mu nul ē STŪ pid| *adj* Extremely stupid. ORIGINS: The word **terminally** is used to refer to medical conditions that are incurable or can lead to death. Appropriated to this slang use, it suggests that the person in question is unbelievably stupid. USAGE ALERT: Usually used with intent to denigrate or insult and understood as such.

**wheel is turning but the hamster's dead, the** |*thu* WĒL iz TUR ning but *thu* HAM sturz ded| *phr* Unintelligent. ORIGINS: This slang phrase works in two ways. First, it sets up an expectation and then undercuts it: one would naturally expect the turning wheel to signal the presence of a live and running hamster. Second, it relies on an association between death and the absence of brain function to indicate that the person in question is quite unintelligent. USAGE ALERT: Usually used with intent to denigrate or insult and understood as such.

NON-SLANG SYNONYMS: unintelligent; <u>retarded</u>, <u>stupid</u>

## FEELING LIKE AN ANIMAL

Amid the figurative language used in slang we can find a large number of comparisons to animals. Here are examples in the realm of Feelings and States. You can also find a smaller number of examples in entries for Agitated (page 315), Attraction (page 305), and Calm (page 309).

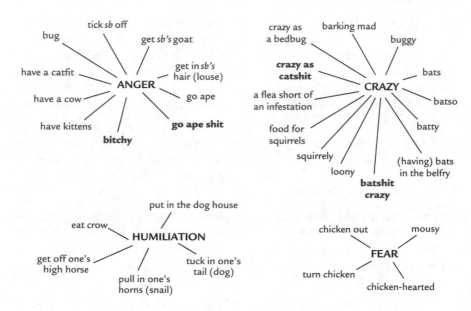

# Expressing Feelings, States, and Attitudes

One of the most interesting areas of slang is the direct expression of feelings and states, when what's going on inside just flies out of our mouths, often in exclamations. In this chapter, we explore this area of slang and the extended and creative use to which certain slang words and phrases are put becomes apparent, as we see the same word—or various forms of it—show up over and over.

We also see that individual slang exclamations can express a wide range of feelings, and this makes categorizing difficult and accounts for some wide-ranging groups.

This section also reveals certain topics for which there aren't a lot of formal, informal, and non-registered synonyms. When you think about this, it's not so surprising: many strong feelings are suppressed in both informal and formal situations, and many are conveyed through a subtle combination of tone, body language, and facial expression, rather than explicitly in words. Because much of what is conveyed in this section of slang is relegated to non-verbal communication—tone of voice, body language, facial expressions—in other registers, this section has a limited selection of non-slang synonyms.

*Agreement and Approval*

*Amusement*

*Anger, Displeasure, Dismay, Disappointment*

*Certainty*

*Desire for Silence*

*Desire for Someone to Stop Doing Something*

*Desire for Understanding*

*Disagreement and Disapproval*

*Disgust*

*Dismissal and Rejection*

*Excitement*

*Failed Understanding*

*Fear*

*Frustration or Exasperation*
  1 With Someone
  2 With Either Someone or Something

*Ignorance*

*Indifference*

*Skepticism or Disbelief*

*Surprise, Shock, Discovery*

*Understanding Achieved*

*Victory*

# AGREEMENT AND APPROVAL

**ITA** I totally agree.

**K** Okay.

**SLAP** Sounds like a plan.

**Aight! Aiight!** |ī ĪT| *excl* A casual greeting; an exclamation of agreement. ORIGINS: From elision of **alright**. USAGE INFO: Usually used in speech, so its spelling is not standardized. There are a number of other spellings in use besides those listed.

**Amen to that!** |ā MEN tū *that*| *excl* Expression of strong agreement. ORIGINS: From standard response to prayer indicating agreement.

**And how!** |AND HOU| *excl* Exclamation of enthusiastic agreement.

**Cool beans!** |kūl BĒNZ| *excl* An exclamation of agreement, approval, or general satisfaction. ORIGINS: Apparently from the 1960s, the phrase was repopularized by the movies *Saving Private Ryan* (1998) and *Hot Rod* (2007).

**Does a bear shit in the woods?** |duz u BER SHIT in *thu* WŎODZ| *excl* Sarcastic rhetorical question in response to a question whose answer is obviously "yes." ORIGINS: From the obvious fact that bears in the wild defecate in the woods. USAGE ALERT: The use of **shit** in this phrase will make it objectionable in some contexts and to some people.

**Don't mind if I do!** |dōnt MĪND if ī DŪ| *excl* A somewhat round-about statement of agreement. ORIGINS: Short for "I don't mind if I do." USAGE INFO: Most phrases starting with *don't* are imperative. In this case, the *I* is dropped, but the sense of a first person indicative expression is retained.

**Fucking ay, aye!** |FUK ing ā| *excl* Yes! Absolutely! Definitely! ORIGINS: From slang **fuck** meaning "to engage in sexual intercourse." USAGE INFO: This term is usually used without any intended provocation. USAGE ALERT: Nevertheless, the inclusion of a form of the word **fuck** will make this expression objectionable in some contexts and to some people.

**Groovy!** |GRŪV ē| *excl* Wonderful! Delightful! Yes, I would enjoy that! Great! ORIGINS: An adjective appropriated to a term of approval. USAGE INFO: **Cool** and other adjectives are used similarly.

**Hot dog!** |haht DAWG| *excl* Delighted agreement. USAGE INFO: Alternate forms are hot diggety dog! and hot diggety!

**I wouldn't/won't say no!** |ī WŎOD unt sā nō / ī WŌNT sā nō| *excl* An interjection offering a somewhat round-about statement of agreement.

ORIGINS: This phrase employing a double negative logically ends up meaning "I would/ will say yes."

**light! Ite!** |ī ĪT| *excl See* AIGHT!

**I'll drink to that!** |ĪL DRINGK tū *that*| *excl* An interjection expressing support for *sb's* idea/plan/decision. ORIGINS: Agreement in the form of a toast. From the niceties of drinking, taken out of context.

**Is the pope Catholic?** |iz *thu* PŌP KATH lik| *excl* Sarcastic, rhetorical question in response to a question whose answer is obviously "Yes." ORIGINS: From the obvious fact that the pope, being the head of the Roman Catholic church is (by definition) Catholic.

**No duh!** |nō DU| *excl* No kidding! Scornful agreement with *st* the speaker thinks should go without saying.

**No fear!** |NŌ FIR| *excl* Agreement with question posed in the negative: "You won't go without me, will you?" "No fear!" (i.e., you should have no fear that I will go without you).

**No shit!** |nō SHIT| *excl* An interjection indicating surprised acceptance of an unexpected truth. ORIGINS: From slang **shit** meaning "excrement." USAGE ALERT: The inclusion of the word **shit** in the phrase will render it objectionable in some contexts and to some people.

**Not much!** |naht MUCH| *excl* Agreement with question posed in the negative: "You don't like television, do you?" "Not much." USAGE INFO: Also used ironically to mean "emphatically yes!" as in "You wouldn't want to go to Tahiti with me, would you?" "Not much!!!"

**Oh, what the heck...!** |Ō wut *thu* HEK| *excl* Interjection signaling more or less reluctant acceptance of *st*. ORIGINS: An altered form of and euphemism for **Oh, what the hell...!** USAGE ALERT: The inclusion of a euphemistic reference to hell will make this term objectionable in some contexts and to some people.

**Oh, what the hell...!** |Ō wut *thu* HEL| *excl* An interjection signaling more or less reluctant acceptance of *st*. ORIGINS: Figurative use of SE **hell** meaning "the alternative to heaven; the realm of the devil." USAGE ALERT: The inclusion of **hell** will make this expression objectionable in some contexts and to some people.

**Right on!** |RĪT ahn| *excl* An interjection expressing strong approval and support.

**Right-o!** |RĪT ō| *excl* An interjection expressing strong agreement.

**So don't I!** |SŌ dōnt ī| *excl* Agreement with a negative proposition. USAGE INFO: An example is "I don't like eggplant at all." "So don't I."

**Sounds like a plan!** |SOUNDZ līk u PLAN| *excl* Agreement with and approval of a proposal.

**Uh-huh!** |u HU| *excl* Yes. USAGE INFO: A retort to negative rejoinders: Nu-uh! Uh-uh!, with which it can be said alternately.

**Yeh! Yeah!** |ye| *excl* Sound expressing agreement or approval. ORIGINS: Shortened from SE yes.

**Yep!** |yep| *excl* Sound expressing agreement or approval. ORIGINS: Altered from SE yes.

**Yes sirree (bob)!** |YE SU RĒ / YE SU RĒ BAHB| *excl* An interjection of enthusiastic affirmation.

**You can say that again!** |yū kan sā THAT u gen| *excl* An interjection signaling emphatic agreement.

**You said a mouthful/it!** |YŪ sed u MOUTH ful / yū SED it| *excl* An interjection signaling emphatic agreement.

**You think?** |yu THINGK| *excl* Sarcastic agreement to st that's obvious (to the speaker).

**You('d) better believe it!** |yū(d) BET ur bi LĒV it| *excl* An interjection signaling emphatic agreement.

**You're damn tootin'!** |yur DAM TŪT'n| *excl* An interjection signaling emphatic agreement. ORIGINS: By extension from SE **damn**, which literally means "Send (it) to hell," used here as an intensifier.

**You're telling me!** |YUR tel ing MĒ| *excl* An interjection signaling emphatic agreement. ORIGINS: The implication is that the speaker of the exclamation already knows or approves of whatever is being said.

**Yum!** |YUM| *excl* Sound expressing delight and/or desire for st. ORIGINS: From the sound one makes when smacking one's lips. USAGE INFO: Used to express agreement or approval in contexts such as: "Shall I make scones for breakfast?" "Yum!"

**Yup!** |yup| *excl* Sound expressing agreement or approval. ORIGINS: Altered from slang yep.

NON-SLANG SYNONYMS: affirmative, agreed, by all means, certainly, definitely, indeed, naturally, of course, yes, **all right**, **amen**, **no kidding**, **okay**, **okey-dokey/ okey-dokie**, **sure**, **sure thing**, **uh-huh**, **assuredly**, **beyond a doubt**, **granted**, **indubitably**, **just so**, **undoubtedly**, **unquestionably**, **willingly**, **without fail**

# AMUSEMENT

**BMGWL** Busting my guts with laughter.

**BWL** Bursting with laughter.

**C&G** Chuckle and grin.

**CSG** Chuckle, snicker, grin.

**CSN** Chuckle, snicker, grin.

**EL** Evil laugh.

**FOFL** Falling on floor, laughing.

**FOMCL** Falling off my chair, laughing.

**LMAO** Laughing my ass off.

**LMFAO** Laughing my fucking ass off.

**PML** Pissing myself laughing.

**ROFL** Rolling on floor, laughing.

**ROTFL** Rolling on the floor, laughing.

**ROTFLMAO** Rolling on the floor, laughing my ass off.

**ROTFLMFAO** Rolling on the floor, laughing my fucking ass off.

**ROTFLOL** Rolling on the floor, laughing out loud.

**SICL** Sitting in chair, laughing.

**Bwa-ha-ha-ha!** |BWAH hah hah hah| *excl* Evil laugh. USAGE INFO: A variety of spellings exist.

**Heh!** |heh| *excl* An ironic or dry laugh.

**Laughing my ass off!** |LAF ing mī AS awf| *excl* A hearty, unrestrained laugh. ORIGINS: From slang **ass** meaning "the rear end or buttocks." USAGE ALERT: The inclusion of **ass** and the graphic image will make this expression objectionable in some contexts and to some people.

**Mwahaha!** |MWAH hah hah| *excl* Evil laugh. USAGE INFO: Many other spellings are used.

**Rolling on the floor laughing!** |RŌL ing ahn *thu* FLAWR LAF ing| *excl* A hearty, unrestrained laugh.

**NON-SLANG SYNONYMS:** Ha ha. Ho ho.

## ANGER, DISPLEASURE, DISMAY, DISAPPOINTMENT

**OMG** Oh my god!

**ONNA** Oh no: not again!

**Blank it!** |BLANGK it| *excl* An interjection expressing anger, frustration, dismay, etc. ORIGINS: Euphemism for several PO exclamations, such as **Damn it!** and **Fuck it!** Refers to the blank space left in a text to replace a PO word. USAGE INFO: People do not ordinarily use blank alone ("blank!"). USAGE ALERT: Euphemisms may still be objectionable in some contexts and to some people.

**Blast (it)!** |blast / BLAST it| *excl* An interjection expressing anger, frustration, dismay, etc. ORIGINS: Euphemism for **Damn! Damn it!** USAGE ALERT: Euphemisms may still be objectionable in some contexts and to some people.

**Bleep (it)!** |blēp / BLĒP it| *excl* An interjection expressing anger, frustration, dismay, etc. ORIGINS: Euphemism for **Damn! Fuck! Shit! Damn it! Fuck it!** or other PO words. From the sound used to overdub obscenities in broadcasts. USAGE ALERT: Euphemisms may still be objectionable in some contexts and to some people.

**Blow (it)!** |blō / BLŌ it| *excl* An interjection expressing anger, frustration, dismay, etc. ORIGINS: Euphemism for **Damn! Fuck! Shit! Damn it!** or other words in the curse formula. USAGE ALERT. Euphemisms may still be objectionable in some contexts and to some people.

**Christ!** |krīst| *excl* An interjection. ORIGINS: SE Christ means "messiah" and is part of the name of **Jesus Christ**, whom Christians hold to be the Son of God. USAGE ALERT: Using the name of **Jesus Christ** in this way will be found objectionable and blasphemous in some contexts and by some people.

**Confound it!** |kun FOUN dit| *excl* An interjection expressing anger, frustration, dismay, etc. ORIGINS: Euphemism for **damn it!** From SE confound meaning "to bring to perdition." USAGE ALERT: Euphemisms may still be objectionable in some contexts and to some people.

**Consarn it!** |kun SAHRN it| *excl* An interjection expressing anger, frustration, dismay, etc. ORIGINS: Euphemism for **Damn it!** From SE concern. USAGE ALERT: Euphemisms may still be objectionable in some contexts and to some people.

**Cripes!** |krīps| *excl* An interjection expressing shock, surprise, dismay, etc. ORIGINS: Euphemism for **Christ!** An alteration of the name of **Jesus Christ** by changing letters. SE **Christ** means "messiah" and is part of the name of Jesus Christ, whom Christians hold to be the Son of God. USAGE ALERT: People who recognize it as a replacement for a name of God may find **Cripes!** objectionable and/or blasphemous. Some people will use it without realizing the connection.

**Crumbs!** |krumz| *excl* Expression of mild to moderate irritation, frustration, dismay, etc. ORIGINS: Euphemism for **Christ!** An alteration of the name of Jesus Christ by changing letters. SE Christ means "messiah" and is part of the name of Jesus Christ, whom Christians hold to be the Son of God. USAGE INFO: Can be used upon discovery of a mistake or problem. USAGE ALERT: People who recognize it as a replacement for a name of God may find Crumbs! objectionable and/or blasphemous. However, in the twenty-first century, most people will probably not make the connection.

**Dad blame it! Dadblame it!** |dad BLĀM it| *excl* An interjection expressing anger, frustration, dismay, etc. ORIGINS: Euphemism for **Goddamn it!** Dad is a euphemism used in a number of curses to replace **God** in order to be less objectionable. Blame is a euphemism for **damn**. USAGE ALERT: Euphemisms may still be objectionable in some contexts and to some people.

**Dad gum it! Dadgum it!** |dad GUM it| *excl* An interjection expressing anger, frustration, dismay, etc. ORIGINS: Euphemism for **Goddamn it!** Dad is a euphemism used in a number of curses to replace **God** in order to be less objectionable. Gum is a euphemism for **damn**. USAGE ALERT: Euphemisms may still be objectionable in some contexts and to some people.

**Dagnab (it)!** |DAG NAB / DAG NAB it| *excl* An interjection expressing anger, frustration, dismay, etc. ORIGINS: Euphemism for **Goddamn!** or **Goddamn it!** Dag is an altered form of dad, which is a euphemism for **God** in a number of replacement curses. Nab is a euphemism for **damn**. USAGE INFO: Used to express displeasure, anger, or frustration. USAGE ALERT: Euphemisms may still be objectionable in some contexts and to some people.

**Damn!** |dam| *excl* An interjection expressing anger, frustration, dismay, etc. ORIGINS: By extension from SE **damn**, which literally means "Send (it) to hell." USAGE ALERT: Usually used to relieve feelings without any intent to curse. Nevertheless, the use of the word **damn** will make it objectionable in some contexts and to some people.

**Damn and blast!** |DAM und BLAST| *excl* An interjection expressing anger, frustration, dismay, etc. ORIGINS: By extension from SE **damn**, which literally means "Send (it) to hell." USAGE ALERT: This term is usually used to relieve feelings without any other purpose. Nevertheless, **damn** and the similar, though euphemistic, blast will make it objectionable in some contexts and to some people.

**Damn it! Dammit! Damnit!** \* |DAM it| *excl* A curse. An interjection expressing anger, frustration, dismay, etc. ORIGINS: By extension from SE **damn**, which literally means "Send (it) to hell" or "May it be sent to hell." USAGE ALERT: Usually used to relieve feelings without any intent to curse. Nevertheless, people who take issue with cursing are likely to find these terms objectionable. • **Damn it all!** |DAM it awl|

**Damn it to hell!** |DAM it tū HEL| *excl* A curse. An interjection expressing anger, frustration, dismay, etc. ORIGINS: By extension from SE **damn**, which literally means "Send (it) to hell," **hell** meaning "the alternative to heaven; the realm of the devil." USAGE ALERT: This term is usually used to relieve feelings without any intent to curse. Nevertheless, people who take issue with cursing are likely to find this term objectionable.

**Dang (it)!** |dang / DANG it| *excl* An interjection expressing anger, frustration, dismay, etc. ORIGINS: Euphemism for **Damn! Damn it!** USAGE ALERT: Euphemisms may still be objectionable in some contexts and to some people.

**Darn (it)!** |dahrn / DAHRN it| *excl* An interjection expressing mild to moderate displeasure, frustration, or irritation, etc. ORIGINS: Euphemism for **Damn! Damn it!** USAGE ALERT: Euphemisms may still be objectionable in some contexts and to some people.

**Dash (it)!** |dash / DASH it| *excl* An interjection expressing mild to moderate displeasure, frustration, or irritation, etc. ORIGINS: Euphemism for **Damn! Damn it!** From the dashes used to replace the middle letters in **damn**, like this: *d--n,* in order to render it less objectionable in print. USAGE INFO: Often in the phrase "dash it all." USAGE ALERT: Euphemisms may still be objectionable in some contexts and to some people.

**Doggone (it)!** |dawg GAWN / dawg GAWN it| *excl* An interjection expressing anger, frustration, dismay, etc. ORIGINS: Euphemism for **Damn! Damn it!** USAGE ALERT: Euphemisms may still be objectionable in some contexts and to some people.

**Drat (it)!** |drat / DRAT it| *excl* An interjection expressing anger, frustration, dismay, etc. ORIGINS: From the phrase "God rot it." Subsequently, a euphemism for **Damn! Damn it!** USAGE ALERT: Euphemisms may still be objectionable in some contexts and to some people.

**Durn (it)!** |durn / DURN it| *excl* An interjection expressing mild to moderate displeasure, frustration, or irritation, etc. ORIGINS: Euphemism for **Damn! Damn it!** USAGE ALERT: Euphemisms may still be objectionable in some contexts and to some people.

**Egad(s)!** |ē GAD / ē GADZ| *excl* An interjection expressing mild anxiety, consternation, frustration, relief, etc. ORIGINS: Euphemism for blasphemous use of **Oh, god!**, i.e., not in prayer. USAGE INFO: Many people will not know the origins of this expression. USAGE ALERT: Euphemisms may still be objectionable in some contexts and to some people.

**Frig!** |frig| *excl* Exclamation of great displeasure. ORIGINS: Euphemism for **Fuck!** A slang word that is related to sexuality and sounds very similar to **fuck**. It means either "masturbating" or "intercourse." USAGE INFO: Note that many users may think that this word is a sanitized version of the word **fuck**, not recognizing it as a real word with an independent existence. USAGE ALERT: People who know the denotative meanings of this word or suspect that it is being used as a euphemism for **Fuck!** are likely to find the terms objectionable.

**Fuck!, also Fuck it!** |FUK / FUK it| *excl* An interjection expressing anger, frustration, extreme surprise, shock, realization of a mistake or error, etc. ORIGINS: From slang **fuck** meaning "to engage in sexual intercourse." USAGE ALERT: This term will be objectionable in some contexts and to some people.

**Fuck it all!** |FUK it awl| *excl* An interjection expressing extreme anger or frustration. ORIGINS: From slang **fuck** meaning "to engage in sexual intercourse." USAGE ALERT: The inclusion of the word **fuck** will make this expression objectionable in some contexts and to some people.

**Fudge(nuts)!** |FUDJ / FUDJ nutz| *excl* Exclamation of moderate displeasure. ORIGINS: Euphemism for **fuck!** From SE fudge meaning "chocolate candy" or slang fudge meaning "excrement." USAGE ALERT: Euphemisms may still be objectionable in some contexts and to some people.

**Gee (whiz)!** |gē / gē WIZ| *excl* An interjection used to express mild surprise, concern, disappointment, approval, etc. ORIGINS: Euphemism for **Jesus** used as a sentence modifier—a figurative use of SE Jesus whom Christians hold to be the Son of God, but it is milder. USAGE INFO: Notice that although it is a euphemism for **Jesus!** it is milder and more likely to be positive. USAGE ALERT: Even euphemized, this saying will be considered objectionable in some contexts and by some people who may find it blasphemous.

**God dang (it)! Goddang (it)! God-dang (it)!** |GAHD dang / gahd DANG it| *excl* An interjection expressing anger, frustration, dismay, etc. ORIGINS: Euphemism for **Goddamn! Goddamn it!** From SE god meaning a being conceived as the divine Lord of the universe and dang, a euphemism for slang **damn**. USAGE ALERT: People who take issue with cursing or consider this use of god blasphemous are likely to find this term objectionable.

**Goddamn! Goddam! God-damn!** |GAHD dam| *excl* An interjection expressing anger, frustration, dismay, etc., interchangeable with **Damn!** ORIGINS: This term uses god as an intensifier. From SE god meaning a being conceived as the divine Lord of the universe, and by extension of SE damn, which literally means "Send (it) to hell." USAGE ALERT: People who take issue with cursing or consider this use of god to be blasphemous will likely find this term objectionable.

**Goddamn it! Goddam it! God-damn it!** |gahd DAM it| *excl* A curse. An interjection expressing anger, frustration, dismay, etc. Interchangeable with **Damn it!** ORIGINS: This term uses slang god as an intensifier. From SE god meaning a being conceived as the divine Lord of the universe and by extension from SE damn, which literally means "Send (it) to hell." USAGE INFO: *All* can be added at the end, as in **Goddamn it all!** USAGE ALERT: People who take issue with cursing or consider this use of god to be blasphemous will likely find this term objectionable.

**Goddarn (it)! God-darn (it)!** |GAHD darn / gahd DARN it| *excl* An interjection expressing displeasure, frustration, or irritation, etc. ORIGINS: Euphemism for **Goddamn! Goddamn it!** From SE god meaning a being conceived as the divine Lord of the universe and darn, a euphemism for slang **damn**. USAGE ALERT: People who take issue with cursing or consider this use of god blasphemous are likely to find this term objectionable.

**Gol dang (it)! Goldang (it)!** |GAHL dang / gahl DANG it| *excl* An interjection expressing displeasure, frustration, or irritation, etc. ORIGINS:

Euphemism for **Goddamn! Goddamn it!** USAGE ALERT: Euphemisms may still be objectionable in some contexts and to some people.

**Goldarn (it)! Gol darn (it)!*** |GAHL darn / gahl DARN it| *excl* An interjection expressing displeasure, frustration, or irritation, etc. ORIGINS: Euphemism for **Goddamn! Goddamn it!** USAGE ALERT: Euphemisms may still be objectionable in some contexts and to some people.
• Gol durn (it)! |GAHL durn / gahl DURN it|

**Golly!** |GAH lē| *excl* An interjection expressing mild to moderate displeasure, frustration, or irritation, etc. ORIGINS: Euphemism for slang **god**. From SE god meaning a being conceived as the divine Lord of the universe. USAGE INFO: Many people will not know the origins of this expression. USAGE ALERT: Euphemisms may still be objectionable in some contexts and to some people.

**Good grief!** |GOŌD GRĒF| *excl* An interjection expressing mild to moderate displeasure, frustration, or irritation, etc. ORIGINS: Euphemism for **Good god!** From SE **god** meaning a being conceived as the divine Lord of the universe. USAGE INFO: Many people will not know the origins of this expression. USAGE ALERT: People who recognize it as a replacement for **god** and who consider it blasphemy will find this term objectionable, but it has become more common and more accepted as time has passed.

**Goshdarn (it)!** |GAHSH darn / gahsh DARN it| *excl* An interjection expressing mild to moderate displeasure, frustration, or irritation, etc. ORIGINS: Euphemism for **Goddamn! Goddamn it!** USAGE ALERT: People who take issue with cursing or consider this substitution for **god** blasphemous are likely to find this term objectionable; nevertheless, it has become more common and more accepted as time has passed.

**Hang it (all)!** |HANG it / HANG it awl| *excl* Exclamation of frustration or dismay. ORIGINS: From SE **hang**.

**Heck!** |hek| *excl* An interjection expressing mild to moderate displeasure, frustration, or irritation, etc. ORIGINS: An altered form of and euphemism for **Hell!** USAGE ALERT: Euphemisms may still be objectionable in some contexts and to some people.

**Hell!** |hel| *excl* An interjection expressing anger, frustration, dismay, etc. ORIGINS: Figurative use of SE **hell** meaning "the alternative to heaven; the realm of the devil." USAGE ALERT: The use of the word **hell** will be objectionable in some contexts and to some people.

**Hell's bells!** |HELZ belz| *excl* An interjection expressing anger, frustration, dismay, etc. ORIGINS: Figurative use of SE **hell** meaning "the alternative to heaven; the realm of the devil." USAGE ALERT: Usually used to relieve feelings without any intent to curse. Nevertheless, the use of the word **hell** will make it objectionable in some contexts and to some people.

**Holy shit!** |HŌ lē SHIT| *excl* An interjection expressing anger, frustration, dismay, etc. ORIGINS: From the slang intensifier **holy** from SE **holy** meaning "blessed by God" and the slang **shit** meaning "excrement." USAGE ALERT: The reference to excrement, especially combined with a word connected to religion, will be objectionable in some contexts and to some people. The inclusion of a slang use of holy in the phrase will make it seem blasphemous and objectionable in some contexts and to some people.

**Jesus!** |JĒ zus| *excl* An interjection expressing anger or dismay, etc. ORIGINS: From SE Jesus Christ whom Christians hold to be the Son of God. USAGE ALERT: The use of the word Jesus in this way will seem blasphemous and objectionable in some contexts and to some people.

**Man!** |man| *excl* An expression of a variety of emotional states, from enjoyment to disappointment.

**Oy!** |oi| *excl* A sound to express sorrow, frustration, weariness, exasperation, dismay, disgust, etc. ORIGINS: Short for Yiddish phrase oy vey/oy veh, which expresses the same range of emotions. USAGE INFO: More frequently used in the shorter form by people who aren't Jewish by heritage.

**Sheesh!** |shēsh| *excl* An interjection used to express surprise, relief, annoyance, etc. ORIGINS: Euphemism, oddly, for both **Shit!** and **Jesus!**—a figurative use of SE Jesus whom Christians hold to be the Son of God, but it is milder. USAGE INFO: Many people have no idea of the origins of this phrase and will use it without reference to either of the words it may stand in for. USAGE ALERT: Some people may find this word blasphemous or otherwise objectionable because of its origins.

**Shit!** |shit| *excl* An interjection expressing anger, frustration, extreme surprise, shock, realization of a mistake or error, etc. ORIGINS: From slang **shit**, meaning "excrement." USAGE ALERT: This word will be objectionable in some contexts and to some people.

**Shoot!** |shūt| *excl* An interjection expressing frustration, anger, surprise, etc. ORIGINS: Euphemism for **Shit!**

**Son of a bitch!** |sun uv u BICH| *excl* An interjection of anger and outrage. ORIGINS: Figurative use of SE **bitch**, meaning "a female dog." USAGE ALERT: The inclusion of the word **bitch** in the phrase will render it objectionable in some contexts and to some people.

**Sugar!** |SHŎŎG ur| *excl* An interjection expressing anger, frustration, dismay, surprise, etc. ORIGINS: Euphemism for **shit!**

**That's torn it!** |*that*s tawrn it| *excl* An interjection of surprise and dismay when *st* unexpected has upset one's plans. ORIGINS: Primarily British, but spreading in US usage.

**This sucks!** |*thi*s SUKS| *excl* To identify something as worthless, contemptible, or maddening. ORIGINS: Figurative use of slang verb suck, short for **This sucks dick!** USAGE ALERT: Many people use this word without reference to its origins and, often, without knowing them. This can lead to very different interpretations of proper use, as well as it drawing strong objections, especially when children are using the word or are within earshot.

NON-SLANG SYNONYMS: Oh my! Oh no! **Oh my Lord! Wow! Goodness!**

# CERTAINTY

**Abso-fucking-lutely!** |ab su FUK ing lūt lē| *excl* Certainly! ORIGINS: SE absolutely with added emphasis from the infix **fucking**. USAGE INFO: Other spellings are also used. USAGE ALERT: The use of **fucking** in this phrase will make it objectionable in some contexts and to some people.

**Abso-goddamn-lutely! Abso-goddam-lutely!** |ab su GAH DAM LŪT lē| *excl* Certainly! ORIGINS: SE **absolutely** with added emphasis from the infix **goddamn**. USAGE INFO: Other spellings are also used. USAGE ALERT: The use of **goddamn** in this phrase will make it objectionable in some contexts and to some people.

**Absotively-posilutely!** |AB su tiv lē PAH zu lūt lē| *excl* Certainly! ORIGINS: An exchange of syllables in the SE words **absolutely** and **positively** to form two portmanteau words.

**Dead sure!** |DED shur| *excl* Absolutely certain. ORIGINS: From slang dead meaning "absolutely."

**For real!** |fawr RĒL| *excl* Honestly; truly.

**For sure!** |fawr SHUR| *excl* Certainly.

**For true!** |fawr TRŪ| *excl* Truly! Honestly!

**fucking well <auxiliary verb>** |FUK ing wel <auxiliary verb>| *excl* A violently emphatic agreement or disagreement. ORIGINS: From slang **fuck** meaning "to engage in sexual intercourse," used as an intensifier. USAGE INFO: This expression picks up or employs an appropriate helping verb to respond emphatically to a statement or question, as in "Should we get some more gas?" "We fucking well should!"; "I'm not going skiing today." "I fucking well am!"; "I know she didn't take my car keys." "She fucking well did!" *See* DAMN WELL. USAGE ALERT: This phrase, which includes a form of **fuck**, will be objectionable in some contexts and to some people.

**Natch!** |nach| *excl* Naturally; of course; certainly. ORIGINS: From shortening of SE **naturally** meaning "of course."

**No buts about it!** |nō BUTS u bout it| *excl* Without a doubt. ORIGINS: Variation on the phrase **no ifs, ands, or buts**, which was originally in the form "ifs and ands" and had the same meaning.

**Shitsure!** |SHIT shur| *excl* Positive; absolutely sure. ORIGINS: The idea is that the existence of excrement can be relied on as absolutely certain. Variation on the phrase **sure as shit**. USAGE ALERT: The use of **shit** in this word will make it objectionable in some contexts and to some people.

**Sure as hell!** |shur az HEL| *excl* Most certainly. ORIGINS: The idea is that the existence of hell can be relied on as absolutely certain.

**Sure as shit!** |shur az SHIT| *excl* Most certainly. ORIGINS: The idea is that the existence of excrement can be relied on as absolutely certain. USAGE ALERT: The use of **shit** in this phrase will make it objectionable in some contexts and to some people.

**Sure as shootin'!** |shur az SHŪT in| *excl* Most certainly. ORIGINS: The idea is that firearms are reliable and so is whatever's being guaranteed.

**Sure as the devil!** |shur az *thu* DEV ul| *excl* Most certainly. ORIGINS: The idea is that the existence of the devil can be relied on as absolutely certain. USAGE ALERT: The use of **devil** in this phrase will make it objectionable in some contexts and to some people.

**Sure enough!** |shur u NUF| *excl* As one would expect.

**Sure-nuff!** |shur NUF| *excl* As one would expect. ORIGINS: Shortened from the phrase Sure enough.

**Sure thing!** |SHUR thing| *excl* An interjection signaling agreement; Of course! Certainly! Definitely!

**You bet your (sweet) ass!** |yū BET yŏor (sweet) AS| *excl* You can be absolutely certain! ORIGINS: The idea is that the thing referred to is so certain that you could safely bet body parts on it. USAGE ALERT: The use of **ass** in this phrase will make it objectionable in some contexts and to some people.

**You bet your (sweet) bippy!** |yū BET yŏor (sweet) BIP ē| *excl* You can be completely certain! ORIGINS: A euphemism for **You bet your (sweet) ass!** that was invented for and became a catchphrase used on the television show *Rowan & Martin's Laugh-In* (1968–1973) and has never quite gone away.

**You bet your boots!** |yū BET yŏor BŪTS| *excl* You can be absolutely certain! ORIGINS: The idea is that the thing referred to is so certain that you could safely bet your essentials on it.

**You bet your bottom dollar!** |yū BET yŏor baht um DAHL ur| *excl* You can be absolutely certain! ORIGINS: The idea is that the thing referred to is so certain that you could safely bet your last dollar on it.

**You bet your life!** |yū BET yŏor LĪF| *excl* You can be absolutely certain! ORIGINS: The idea is that the thing referred to is so certain that you could safely bet your life on it.

**You bet your shirt!** |yū BET yŏor SHIRT| *excl* You can be absolutely certain! ORIGINS: The idea is that the thing referred to is so certain that you could safely bet your essentials on it.

**You bet(cha)!** |yū BĒT / yū BĒCH u| *excl* An interjection signaling emphatic certainty.

**NON-SLANG SYNONYMS:** I know for a fact, I know for certain, I promise; <u>Cross my heart. Definitely. I know for sure. No ifs, ands, or buts. No two ways about it. Sure as I live and breathe</u>. **Beyond (a) doubt. Indubitably. Irrefutably. Undeniably.**

# DESIRE FOR SILENCE

Many of the expressions that people use to demand silence refer to putting something away or shutting or closing something. All of them are more or less offensive with the exception of **Mum's the word! Nuff said!** and—depending on context—**Don't make a peep!** and **Pipe down!** Nevertheless, there may be situations in which even these could be said in an unpleasant or threatening way.

**QYB** Quit your bitching!

**SFTTM** Stop fucking talking to me!

**STFU** Shut the fuck up!

**Bag it!** |BAG it| *excl* Be quiet! ORIGINS: By extension of SE bag meaning "a holder" (used to remove something from active use) or slang bag meaning "to quit or abandon." USAGE ALERT: Often used with intent to denigrate or insult and understood as such.

**Button your lip/face!** |BUT 'n yoŏr LIP/FĀS| *excl* Be quiet! ORIGINS: The idea is that the mouth is sealed shut and no words can escape. USAGE ALERT: Often used with intent to denigrate or insult and understood as such.

**Chuck it!** |CHUK it| *excl* Be quiet! ORIGINS: From slang chuck meaning "to quit or give up." USAGE ALERT: Often used with intent to denigrate or insult and understood as such.

**Clam up!** |KLAM up| *excl* Be quiet! ORIGINS: Based on the tightly shut shell of the bivalve, the idea is that the speaker should seal his or her lips. USAGE ALERT: Often used with intent to denigrate or insult and understood as such.

**Cool it!** |KŪL it| *excl* Be quiet! Relax! ORIGINS: Related to the hot-cold trope for being excited, angry, and vociferous on the one hand or calm and soft-spoken on the other. USAGE ALERT: Sometimes used with intent to denigrate or insult and understood as such.

**Cram it!** |KRAM it| *excl* Be quiet! ORIGINS: By extension of SE <u>cram</u> meaning to force something into a container, thus getting it out of the way. USAGE ALERT: Usually used with intent to denigrate or insult and understood as such.

**Cut the cackle!** |KUT *thu* kak ul| *excl* Be quiet! Get serious! ORIGINS: A shortened form of the expression "Cut the cackle and get to the horses," comparing the more important livestock—horses—to the constant, meaningless noise of chickens. USAGE ALERT: Sometimes used with intent to denigrate or insult and understood as such.

**Don't make a peep!** |DŌNT māk u PĒP| *excl* Be quiet! ORIGINS: SE **peep** was the collective noun for a brood of chickens and is used to mean "the smallest sound" in this phrase as well as in hear a peep out of.

**Dry up!** |DRĪ up| *v* Be quiet! ORIGINS: This expression treats speech as if it were a flow of water, with drying analogous to being quiet. USAGE ALERT: Usually used with intent to denigrate or insult and understood as such.

**Mum's the word!** |MUMZ *thu* WURD| *excl* Be quiet about this! Keep this a secret! ORIGINS: From imitative **mum** representing the kind of soft sound one might make if one was both trying to make a vocal signal and keep one's lips closed.

**Nuff said!** |NUF sed| *excl* Let's close this subject (lest *sb* overhear our discussion). ORIGINS: By shortening of the phrase "Enough said!"

**Pipe down!** |PĪP DOUN| *excl* Be quieter! USAGE INFO: Unlike most of the phrases in this section, Pipe down! can mean to be softer, rather than altogether silent.

**Put a sock in it!** |pŏŏt u SAHK In it| *excl* Be quiet! ORIGINS: The suggestion is that one use a sock to stuff up one's mouth so that no sound can come out. USAGE ALERT: Usually used with intent to denigrate or insult and understood as such.

**Shut the fuck up!** |SHUT *thu* FUK up| *excl* Be quiet! ORIGINS: Refers to shutting the mouth. In this phrase **the fuck** is used as an intensifier. USAGE ALERT: Usually used with intent to denigrate or insult and understood as such. In addition, the use of **fuck** in this phrase will make it objectionable in some contexts and to some people.

**Shut up!**[1] |SHUT up| *excl* Be quiet! A strong dismissal of a person's contribution. USAGE ALERT: Usually used with intent to be rude and understood as such.

**Shut your cakehole/piehole!** |shut yŏŏr KĀK hōl / shut yŏŏr PĪ hōl| *excl* Be quiet! ORIGINS: Refers to shutting the mouth using slang **cakehole** or **piehole** to refer to the mouth. USAGE ALERT: Usually used with intent to denigrate or insult and understood as such. The use of -hole as a suffix may bring the word **asshole** to mind for some people, and color their perception of this word.

**Shut your face/mouth/head!** |shut yŏŏr FĀS / shut yŏŏr MOUTH / shut yŏŏr HED| *excl* Be quiet! ORIGINS: Refers to shutting the mouth. USAGE ALERT: Usually used with intent to denigrate or insult and understood as such.

**Shut your trap!** |shut yŏŏr TRAP| *excl* Be quiet! ORIGINS: Refers to shutting the mouth. USAGE ALERT: Usually used with intent to denigrate or insult and understood as such.

Stow it! |STŌ it| *excl* Be quiet! ORIGINS: From SE **stow** meaning "to put baggage or cargo away." USAGE ALERT: Usually used with intent to denigrate or insult and understood as such.

Stuff it! |STUF it| *excl* Be quiet! ORIGINS: From the idea of stuffing up *sb's* mouth to ensure silence. USAGE ALERT: Usually used with intent to denigrate or insult and understood as such.

NON-SLANG SYNONYMS: Please be quiet. **Enough said**. **Hush**. **Shhh**. **Silence**.

# DESIRE FOR SOMEONE TO STOP DOING SOMETHING

DWB Don't write back.

Get lost! |get LAHST| *excl* Go away! ORIGINS: Ironic reversal of the usual situation of trying to *find* something that is lost. USAGE ALERT: Usually used with intent to be rude and understood as such.

Get off my back! |get AWF mī BAK| *excl* Stop annoying me! Leave me alone! USAGE INFO: This is a response to the action of "getting on *sb's* back." USAGE ALERT: Usually used with intent to create distance and understood as such.

Get off my case! |get AWF mī CĀS| *excl* Stop annoying me! Leave me alone! ORIGINS: From slang **case** meaning "situation." USAGE INFO: This is a response to the action of "getting on *sb's* case." USAGE ALERT: Usually used with intent to be rude and understood as such.

Get out of my face! |get OUT uv mī FĀS| *excl* Leave me alone! Stop annoying me! USAGE INFO: The retort to the experience of having someone **get in one's face**. USAGE ALERT: Usually used with intent to be rude and understood as such.

Get out of my hair! |get OUT uv mī HER| *excl* Leave me alone! Stop annoying me! USAGE INFO: The retort to the experience of having someone **get in one's hair**. USAGE ALERT: Usually used with intent to be rude and understood as such.

Give it a rest! |giv it u REST| *excl* Shut up! Take a break from talking about this topic! Stop nagging me! ORIGINS: Figurative use of **Give** *sb/st* **a rest** by allowing a break. USAGE INFO: Usually refers to spoken language.

Knock it off! |NAHK it AWF| *excl* Stop (whatever you're doing)! ORIGINS: Extended from slang **knock off** meaning "to stop work." USAGE INFO: Often a request for *sb* to stop speaking in a certain way, e.g., nagging, pleading, teasing, etc.

**Lay off!** |LĀ awf| *excl* Stop (whatever you're doing)! ORIGINS: Extended from slang lay off meaning "to take time off from work." USAGE INFO: Often a request for *sb* to stop speaking in a certain way, e.g., nagging, pleading, teasing, etc.

**Leave off!** |lēv awf| *excl* Stop (whatever you're doing)!

**Pack it in!** |PAK it in| *excl* Stop (whatever you're doing)! ORIGINS: From SE **pack** meaning "to put away."

**Stop crowding me!** |stahp kroud ing mē| *excl* Stop pressuring me! Back off! Get out of my personal space! Give me time (to make a decision or accomplish a task) on my own!

NON-SLANG SYNONYMS: Can we stop now? Let's move on. <u>Cut it out</u>! <u>Leave me alone</u>! <u>Quit it</u>! <u>Quit that</u>! <u>Shut up</u>! <u>Stop</u>! <u>Stop it</u>! <u>That's enough</u>! **Cease and desist. Let us move on.**

# DESIRE FOR UNDERSTANDING

One of the hallmarks of polite conversation, whether formal or informal, is checking in to make sure that communication is really occurring, i.e., that everyone understands each other. Note that there is often irony and/or humor in the use of words deriving from other languages to check understanding of English, in which case the usage qualifies as slang. When the same words are used by people who actually speak the other language, their import is quite different and usually not slang.

**KWIM** Know what I mean?

**SWIM** See what I mean?

**SWIS** See what I'm saying?

**Are we on the same sheet of music?** |ahr wē ahn *thu* SĀM SHĒT uv MYŪ zik| *phr* Do we share a common understanding? ORIGINS: From the situation of musicians performing from individual parts and having to pay careful attention to make sure that they are playing in sync with each other.

**Are we on the same wavelength?** |ahr wē ahn *thu* SĀM WĀV lengkth| *phr* Are we understanding things in a similar way? ORIGINS: From radio waves carrying a broadcast. Being on the same wavelength means hearing the same thing, and thus being "in tune" with others.

**Are you tuned in?** |ahr yū tūnd IN| *phr* Are you getting the fine points? ORIGINS: Tuning in a radio is the exercise in achieving the best and clearest reception of a station. So *sb* who is "tuned in" is making a real effort to achieve understanding.

**Capiche? Capisce?** |ku PĒSH| *phr* Do you understand? ORIGINS: Adapted from Italian **capisci** meaning "Do you understand?" USAGE INFO: Numerous other spellings are used as well.

**Comprende?** kōm PREN de *phr* Do you understand? ORIGINS: Adapted from Standard Spanish ¿**Comprende?** meaning "Do you understand?" USAGE INFO: The initial question mark used in Spanish, is often omitted in English.

**Dig (me)?** |dig / DIG mē| *phr* Do you both understand fully and agree with me?

**Do you catch my drift?** |dū yu KACH mī DRIFT| *phr* Do you get the gist of my message? ORIGINS: Not about individual words, but about gist, a meaning of **drift** by the sixteenth century. *See also* DO YOU GET MY DRIFT?

**Do you get my drift?** |dū yu GET mī DRIFT| *phr* Do you understand the point I'm making? ORIGINS: Not about individual words, but about gist, a meaning of **drift** by the sixteenth century. *See also* DO YOU CATCH MY DRIFT?

**Do you read me?** |dū yu RĒD mē| *phr* Have you picked up my transmission? ORIGINS: From the language used in checking on the reception of radio and telephone transmissions, dating from about 1930.

**Dontcha know? Doncha know?** |dōn chu NŌ| *phr* You know this, don't you? ORIGINS: Shortened form of **Don't you know?** USAGE INFO: Often used as a rhetorical tag question—a question tagged onto the end of a statement that may or may not be said with expectation of a response. Other spellings include: Dont ya know? Don't ya know?

**Get it?** |GET it| *phr* Do you understand? ORIGINS: **Get** is used here in the sense of "receive and comprehend."

**Get me?** |GET mē| *phr* Do you understand? ORIGINS: **Get** is used here in the sense of "receive and comprehend the message." USAGE INFO: **Get me** can be used as a verb phrase to mean "has a deep understanding of me as a person" as in "You might be surprised to hear it, but my mom really gets me."

**Get the message?** |get *thu* MES ij| *phr* Do you understand the point I'm making? ORIGINS: Not about individual words, but about gist.

**Get the picture?** |get *thu* PIK chur| *phr* Do you understand the whole scope of what I'm saying? ORIGINS: Not about individual words, but about substance and implications.

**Got it?** |GAH dit| *phr* Do you understand? ORIGINS: The past tense of get is used here in the sense of "receive and comprehend." Compare with **Get it?** USAGE INFO: **Got it?** as opposed to **Got me?** may be used in confirming understanding of something.

**Got me?** |GAHT mē| *phr* Do you understand? ORIGINS: **Get** is used here in the sense of "receive and comprehend." Compare with **Get me?**

**Read me?** |RĒD mē| *phr* Have you picked up my transmission? ORIGINS: Shortened form of **Do you read me?** From the language used in checking on the reception of radio and telephone transmissions, dating from about 1930.

**Savvy?** |SAV ē| *phr* Do you understand? ORIGINS: From Spanish **sabe usted** meaning "you know." Popularized as a catchphrase spoken by Johnny Depp in the character of Captain Jack Sparrow in the *Pirates of the Caribbean* films (2003, 2006, 2007).

NON-SLANG SYNONYMS: Do you know what I mean? Do you see what I'm saying? Is that clear? Is that understood?

# DISAGREEMENT AND DISAPPROVAL

**IBTD** I beg to differ.

**IYD** In your dreams.

**NFW** No fucking way.

**NIMBY** |NIM bē| Not in my backyard.

**NIMJD** [It's] not in my job description.

**NIMY** Never in a million years.

**OMDB** Over my dead body.

**ONID** Oh no I didn't!

**RUNTS** Are you nuts? USAGE INFO: Note that this is not formed in the usual maner of acronyms or initialisms: **are** and **you** are represented by letters that are homophones; **nuts** is abbreviated by leaving out the *u*. This manner of abbreviation forms the plural of an offensive slang term for a short or small person, **runt**.

**WDALYIC** Who died and left you in charge?

**Are you nuts?** |ar yū NUTS| *excl* What you're saying is crazy. ORIGINS: A comment on *sb's* soundness of mind, couched as a question, but not seeking an answer.

**Fuhgeddaboudit! Fuhgedaboudit! Fuggeddaboudit! Fugedaboudit!**
|fu GED u boud it| *excl* Don't even go there! It is not even worth considering. It's not going to happen. ORIGINS: The informal pronunciation of the phrase "Forget about it" captured in written form. There may be other spellings in use. USAGE INFO: Used in exchanges like: "I really wish the boss would give me a raise." "Fuhgeddaboudit!" Can also be used in reference to a further example for *st* already discussed and evaluated, to indicate that the further example is even more extreme— so much so that there's nothing to talk about. For example, "Have you seen the price of their lunch entrees? And dinner for two? Fuhgeddaboudit!"

**Get off your high horse!** |get AHF yŏŏr hī hawrs| *excl* Stop being so pretentious! ORIGINS: From a time when high-ranking people rode tall horses (while commoners walked).

**Get over it!** |get Ō vur it| *excl* Come to terms with whatever is bothering you and stop complaining/moping/etc.

**Get your head out of your ass!** |get yŏŏr HED out uv yŏŏr AS| *excl* Stop being so self-involved! Quit being so wound up in your own little world! USAGE INFO: Tends not to drop the final prepositional phrase as in Get your finger/thumb out!

**In your dreams!** |in yŏŏr DRĒMZ| *excl* No! ORIGINS: The idea is that the content being responded to is completely unrealistic—only possible or valid in fantasy or the imagination.

**Nah!** |na| *excl* A sound expressing a negative response, but not a very strong one. USAGE INFO: Given its meaning, it does not often take an exclamation point.

**Never in a million years!** |NEV ur in u MIL yun YIRZ| *excl* Emphatically no!

**Nix!** |niks| *excl* No.

**No dice!** |nō DĪS| *excl* No! ORIGINS: Refers to an unlucky toss of the dice.

**No fucking way!** |nō FUK ing wā| *excl* Emphatically no! ORIGINS: The slang phrase no way with the intensifier **fucking** added. USAGE ALERT: The use of **fucking** in this phrase, even though it is an intensifier, will make it objectionable in some contexts and to some people.

**No siree (bob)!** |NŌ sur ē / NŌ sur ē BAHB| *excl* Certainly not! ORIGINS: Extension of the phrase No, sir! The extra syllable on siree and the use of bob simply add emphasis.

**No soap!** |nō SŌP| *excl* Certainly not! ORIGINS: Related to the phrase It won't wash, which also references cleaning and refers to disapproval.

**No way (José)!** |nō WĀ / nō WĀ hō ZĀ| *excl* An interjection signaling refusal or denial; interjection signaling surprise at hearing something very unexpected. ORIGINS: Shortened and altered from SE phrase **There is no way.**

**Nope!** |nōp| *excl* An interjection to signal denial or dismissal.

**. . . Not!** |naht| *excl* Rejection of whatever was said previously. USAGE INFO: A proposition is stated and, after a brief pause, the speaker uses this exclamation to reject the proposition, as in "Well I really love to watch watch bowling on television! . . . Not!" The pause is an essential part of the delivery.

**Not in my backyard!** |naht in MĪ bak yahrd| *excl* Opposition based on proximity, by people who may support a project theoretically, but not in their own neighborhood.

**Not in my job description!** |NAHT in mī JAHB du skrip shun| *excl* According to the terms of my contract, I don't have to do this, and I'm not going to. ORIGINS: An excuse/explanation for refusal.

**Not likely!** |NAHT LĪK lē| *adv* A denial or dismissal.

**Not on your life!** |naht ahn your LĪF| *excl* A strong denial or dismissal. USAGE INFO: The *on* construction makes this an oath form—though usually one swears by, for example, the Bible or one's own life.

**Not on your nelly!** |NAHT ahn yōōr NEL ē| *excl* Certainly not! ORIGINS: Shortening of a rhyming slang variant on **Not on your life!** The full phrase is **Not on your Nelly Duff!** which rhymes with **puff** meaning "breath of life." *Nelly* may also be spelled *Nellie*.

**Nothing doing!** |NU thing DŪ ing| *excl* A denial or dismissal.

**Nuh-uh! Nu-huh! Nuh-huh!** |NU U| *excl* USAGE INFO: In a family with negative rejoinder Uh-huh! Both Uh-uh! and Nu-uh! can be used to respond to Uh-huh!

**Over my dead body!** |Ō vur MĪ DED BAHD ē| *excl* Interjection signaling strong refusal or denial. ORIGINS: Suggests that the speaker would die before allowing <whatever it is> to happen.

**Uh-uh!** |U U| *excl* No. USAGE INFO: In a family with negative synonym Nu-uh! Both Uh-uh! and Nu-uh! can be used to respond to Uh-huh!

**Way!** |wā| *excl* A rejoinder to No way! USAGE INFO: Way! can only be used to respond to No way! essentially translating an argument in which one person continually says yes and the other says no to a slang equivalent.

**What in the fuck is this shit?** |WUT in *thu* FUK iz ths SHIT| *excl* What is this? Why is this stuff that I don't recognize in this place? This is trash! ORIGINS: Figurative use of slang **fuck** meaning "sexual intercourse" and **shit** meaning "excrement." USAGE INFO: Either a phrase requesting an explanation for something that distresses the speaker by its apparent lack of quality, its sudden appearance, or the perception that it is infringing on his or her space, or an interjection of disgust and rejection. USAGE ALERT: The inclusion of **fuck** and **shit** will make this expression objectionable in some contexts and to some people.

**Who died and left you in charge?** |hū DĪD and LEFT YŪ in charj| *excl* I'm not taking orders from you!

**Yes-huh!** |YES hu| *excl* It *is* the case, despite what you say. A response to Nu-uh! and similar phrases. USAGE INFO: Synonym of Uh-huh! and antonym of the negative phrases Nu-uh! and Uh-uh! The phrase Yes-huh! can only be used to respond to Nu-uh! and its variants.

NON-SLANG SYNONYMS: I don't think so. Never. No. Not at all. Of course not. Not really. That's a negative. By no means. Most certainly not. Under no circumstances.

## DISGUST

Notice that most slang to express digust takes the form of sounds.

**Ack!** |ak| *excl* A sound to express disgust or dismay.

**Bleah!** |bleh| *excl* A sound to express disgust.

**Blecch!** |blek| *excl* A sound to express disgust.

**Ew! Eww!** |ēū| *excl* Sound expressing disgust.

**Gross!** |grōs| *excl* Disgusting! ORIGINS: From the slang adjective gross meaning "disgusting" which draws on the SE noun **gross** meaning "large." USAGE INFO: Sometimes the pronunciation is elongated into two syllables for effect: |gu RŌS|.

**Ick!** |ik| *excl* A sound to express disgust. ORIGINS: A back-formation from slang icky.

**Ucky!** |UK ē| *excl* Sound to express disgust.

**Ugh!** |ug| *excl* Sound to express disgust.

**Yechy! Yecchy!** |YEK ē| *adj* Sound indicating disgust or contempt.

**Yuck(o)!** |yuk / YUK ō| *excl* Sound to express disgust.

**Yucky! Yukky!** |YUK ē| *excl* Sound to express disgust.

NON-SLANG SYNONYMS: That's disgusting! That's repulsive! **How foul!**

## DISMISSAL AND REJECTION

The suggestion of an extremely unappealing action is one typical form of slang dismissal, as are suggestions of death and damnation.

**BIOYE** Blow it out your ear.

**BMOTA** Bite me on the ass.

**ESAD** Eat shit and die.

**FOAD** Fuck off and die.

**GFY** Go fuck yourself (also, Good for you.)

**GTFO** Get the fuck out.

**GTH** Go to hell.

**KMA** Kiss my ass.

MYOB Mind your own business.

SOIAR Sit on it and rotate.

TAH Take a hike.

**Amscray!** |AM skrā| *excl* Go away! ORIGINS: This is a rendering of slang scram meaning "go away!" in pig Latin, a simple, coded language used primarily by children. USAGE ALERT: Usually used with intent to be rude and understood as such.

**Beat it!** |BĒT it| *excl* To send away without ceremony. ORIGINS: Possibly from a combination of SE beat a path and reference to the sound of rapidly retreating footsteps beating the floor/pavement. USAGE ALERT: Usually used with intent to be rude and understood as such.

**Bite me!** |BĪT mē| *excl* A contemptuous dismissal. ORIGINS: Abbreviated form of slang phrase **Bite my ass!** USAGE ALERT: Usually used with intent to be rude and understood as such. Because **ass** is part of the phrase that is intended, even if it is not spoken, those who know what is meant may be offended by that as well as the graphic image (and the usually offensive tone in which it is said).

**Bite me on the ass!** |BĪT mē ahn *the* AS| *excl* A contemptuous dismissal. ORIGINS: From slang **ass** meaning "the rear end or buttocks." USAGE ALERT: Usually used with intent to be rude and understood as such. In addition, the inclusion of **ass** and the graphic image will make this expression objectionable in some contexts and to some people.

**Bite my ass!** |BĪT mī as| *excl* A contemptuous dismissal. ORIGINS: From slang **ass** meaning "the rear end or buttocks." USAGE ALERT: Usually used with intent to be rude and understood as such. In addition, the inclusion of **ass** and the graphic image will make this expression objectionable in some contexts and to some people.

**Blow it out your ass!** |BLŌ it out yōor AS| *excl* A contemptuous dismissal, often of something that's been said. ORIGINS: From the US military and slang **ass** meaning "the rear end or buttocks." USAGE ALERT: Usually used with intent to be rude and understood as such. In addition, the inclusion of **ass** and the graphic image will make this expression objectionable in some contexts and to some people.

**Blow it out your ear!** |BLŌ it out yōor IR| *excl* A contemptuous dismissal, often of something that's been said. ORIGINS: Euphemism for **blow it out your ass**, which originated with the US military. USAGE ALERT: Usually used with intent to be rude and understood as such.

**Bug off!** |bug AWF| *excl* Go away! ORIGINS: A reference to the experience of having bees or other insects hovering in an annoying way. USAGE ALERT: Often used with intent to be rude and understood as such.

**Buzz off!** |buz AWF| *excl* Go away! ORIGINS: A reference to the experience of having bees or other insects buzzing around annoyingly. USAGE ALERT: Often used with intent to be rude and understood as such.

**Chuck you, Farley!** |CHUK yū fahr lē| *excl* A contemptuous dismissal. ORIGINS: Spoonerism (exchange of first letters of two important words) in order to create a euphemistic version of the phrase **Fuck you, Charley!**, an extension of **Fuck you!** USAGE ALERT: Usually used with intent to be rude and understood as such. In addition, the inclusion of **fuck** will make this expression objectionable in some contexts and to some people.

**Drop dead!** |DRAHP DED| *excl* A contemptuous dismissal. USAGE INFO: Although it may sound like a curse, the phrase is usually not meant literally. USAGE ALERT: Usually used with intent to be rude and understood as such.

**Eat it!** |ĒT it| *excl* A contemptuous dismissal. ORIGINS: Either *it* refers to the penis (in which case the speaker is male) or the phrase is a euphemism for **Eat shit!** (used by both men and women). USAGE ALERT: Usually used with intent to be rude and understood as such.

**Eat shit!** |ēt SHIT| *excl* A contemptuous dismissal. ORIGINS: From slang **shit** meaning "excrement." USAGE ALERT: Usually used with intent to be rude and understood as such. In addition, the inclusion of **shit** and the graphic image will make this expression objectionable in some contexts and to some people.

**Eat shit and die!** |ĒT SHIT and DĪ| *excl* A contemptuous dismissal. ORIGINS: From slang **shit** meaning "excrement." USAGE INFO: Although it may sound like a curse, the phrase is usually not meant literally. USAGE ALERT: Usually used with intent to be rude and understood as such. In addition, the inclusion of **shit** and the graphic image will make this expression objectionable in some contexts and to some people.

**Eff off!** |EFF awf| *excl* Go away! Euphemism for **Fuck off!** ORIGINS: From initial letter of slang **fuck** meaning "to engage in sexual intercourse." USAGE ALERT: The reference to the word **fuck** will make this expression objectionable in some contexts and to some people.

**Fuck off!** |FUK awf| *excl* Go away! ORIGINS: From slang **fuck** meaning "to engage in sexual intercourse." USAGE ALERT: The inclusion of **fuck** will make this expression objectionable in some contexts and to some people.

**Fuck off and die!** |FUK ahf and dī| *excl* A contemptuous dismissal. ORIGINS: From slang **Fuck off!** which is, in turn, from slang **fuck** meaning "to engage in sexual intercourse." USAGE INFO: Although it may sound like a curse, the phrase is usually not meant literally. USAGE ALERT: Usually used with intent to be rude and understood as such. In addition, the inclusion of **shit** and the graphic image will make this expression objectionable in some contexts and to some people.

**Fuck you!** |fuk YŪ| *excl* A contemptuous dismissal. ORIGINS: From slang **fuck** meaning "to engage in sexual intercourse." USAGE INFO: Often accompanied by the gesture referred to as "giving *sb* the finger." USAGE ALERT: Usually used with intent to be rude and understood as such. In addition, the inclusion of **fuck** and the graphic image will make this expression objectionable in some contexts and to some people.

**Get the fuck out!** |get *thu* FUK OUT| *excl* A contemptuous dismissal. ORIGINS: From the sentence modifier **the fuck**, which makes figurative use of slang **fuck** meaning "sexual intercourse" to intensify sentences, and SE <u>Get out!</u> USAGE ALERT: Usually used with intent to be rude and understood as such. In addition, the inclusion of **fuck** will make this expression objectionable in some contexts and to some people.

**Get the hell out!** |get *thu* hel OUT| *excl* An offensive dismissal. ORIGINS: From the sentence modifier **the hell**, which makes figurative use of SE hell meaning "the alternative to heaven; the realm of the devil." USAGE ALERT: The use of **hell** will make this expression objectionable in some contexts and to some people. In addition, this expression is usually used with intent to be rude and understood as such.

**Go fly a kite!** |GŌ flī u KĪT| *excl* Go away! ORIGINS: Popularized in the film *Mary Poppins* (1964) in which, upon being terminated from his employment, Mr. Banks literally goes out to "fly a kite." USAGE ALERT: Usually used with intent to be rude and understood as such.

**Go fuck yourself!** |gō FUK yŏŏr self| *excl* A contemptuous dismissal. ORIGINS: From slang **fuck** meaning "to engage in sexual intercourse." USAGE ALERT: Usually used with intent to be rude and understood as such. In addition, the inclusion of **fuck** and the graphic image will make this expression objectionable in some contexts and to some people.

**Go hang!** |gō HANG| *excl* A contemptuous dismissal. USAGE INFO: Although it may sound like a curse, the phrase is usually not meant literally. USAGE ALERT: Usually used with intent to be rude and understood as such.

**Go piss up a rope!** |gō PIS up u RŌP| *excl* An offensive way to say go away! ORIGINS: The suggestion is for a futile act that will result in a mess for the person addressed. From slang **piss**, meaning "to urinate." USAGE ALERT: This phrase is usually intended to offend, and the graphic image as well as the use of the word **piss** will make it offensive in most contexts and to most people.

**Go soak your head!** |gō SŌK your HED| *excl* Go away! ORIGINS: This phrase suggests that the head in question is swollen (that is, the person is self-important) and soaking it (like soaking a finger or toe swollen by injury or infection) will bring the swelling down (i.e., give the person a more objective view of their own importance). USAGE ALERT: Usually used with intent to be rude and understood as such.

**Go suck eggs!** |gō SUK EGZ| *excl* Go away! ORIGINS: The slang suck eggs is connected with old age ("teach your grandma to suck eggs") and bad manners. It's not clear exactly how go suck eggs fits in. USAGE ALERT: Usually used with intent to be rude and understood as such.

**Go to hell!** |gō tū HEL| *excl* A contemptuous dismissal. ORIGINS: Figurative use of SE hell meaning "the alternative to heaven; the realm of the devil." USAGE INFO: Although it may sound like a curse, the phrase is usually not meant literally. USAGE ALERT: Usually used with intent to be rude and understood as such. In addition, the inclusion of **hell** will make this expression objectionable in some contexts and to some people.

**Kiss my ass!** |KIS mī as| *excl* A contemptuous dismissal. ORIGINS: From slang **ass** meaning "the rear end or buttocks." USAGE ALERT: Usually used with intent to be rude and understood as such. In addition, the inclusion of **ass** and the graphic image will make this expression objectionable in some contexts and to some people.

**Kiss off!** |KIS awf| *excl* A contemptuous dismissal. ORIGINS: From the idea of a parting kiss, but possibly influenced by the similarity of sound to **Piss off!**, for which it may be used as a euphemism.

**Let me breathe!** |let me BRĒTH| *excl* Go away! Stop hanging over me! USAGE ALERT: Usually used with intent to be rude and understood as such.

**Piss off!** |PIS awf| *excl* A contemptuous dismissal. ORIGINS: From slang **piss** meaning "urine." USAGE ALERT: Usually used with intent to be rude and understood as such. In addition, the inclusion of **piss** and the graphic image will make this expression objectionable in some contexts and to some people.

**Piss on you!** |PIS ahn YŪ| *excl* A contemptuous dismissal. ORIGINS: From slang **piss** meaning "urine." USAGE ALERT: Usually used with intent to be rude and understood as such. In addition, the inclusion of **piss** and the graphic image will make this expression objectionable in some contexts and to some people.

**Push off!** |POŌSH awf| *excl* A dismissal. ORIGINS: From the action of boaters pushing off from the dock. USAGE INFO: Not as harsh as its counterpart Shove off!

**Run along!** |RUN u lawng| *excl* An interjection of mild dismissal.

**Scoot!** |skūt| *excl* An interjection signaling gentle dismissal. USAGE INFO: Often used simply as encouragement to get moving, softened by context.

**Scram!** |skram| *excl* A threatening dismissal.

**Screw you!** |SKRŪ yū| *excl* A contemptuous dismissal. ORIGINS: A euphemism for **Fuck you!** From slang **screw**, a euphemism for **fuck**. USAGE ALERT: Usually used with intent to be rude and understood as such. Although the euphemistic alteration of this phrase will soften it somewhat, it may still be objectionable in some contexts and to some people.

**Shove it!** |SHUV it| *excl* A harsh dismissal. ORIGINS: Shortened, euphemistic form of **Shove it up your ass!** USAGE ALERT: Usually used with intent to be rude and understood as such. The euphemism in this phrase will soften it somewhat, but it may still be objectionable in some contexts and to some people.

**Shove it up your ass!** |SHUV it up yur AS| *excl* A harsh dismissal. ORIGINS: From slang **ass** meaning "rear end or buttocks." USAGE ALERT: Usually used with intent to be rude and understood as such. The inclusion of the word **ass** in the phrase and the graphic image will render it objectionable in some contexts and to some people.

**Shove off!** |SHUV ahf| *excl* A harsh dismissal. ORIGINS: From the action of boaters pushing off from the dock. USAGE INFO: Harsher than the similar phrase Push off!

**Shut up!**[1] |SHUT up| *excl* Be quiet! A strong dismissal of a person's contribution. USAGE ALERT: Usually used with intent to be rude and understood as such.

**Sit on it and rotate!** |SIT ahn It and RŌ tāt| *excl* A contemptuous dismissal. USAGE INFO: Often accompanied by the gesture referred to as "giving *sb* the finger." USAGE ALERT: Usually used with intent to be rude and understood as such. In addition, the graphic image will make this expression objectionable in some contexts and to some people.

**So's your old man!** |SŌZ yŏŏr ōld man| *excl* A contemptuous dismissive insult. USAGE ALERT: Usually used with intent to be rude and understood as such.

**Stick it!** |STIK it| *excl* A rude dismissal. ORIGINS: Shortened form of slang **Stick it up your ass!** or similar phrases. USAGE INFO: Often accompanied by the gesture referred to as "giving *sb* the finger." USAGE ALERT: Usually used with intent to be rude and understood as such. In addition, the euphemistic shortening of this phrase will soften it somewhat, but it may still be objectionable in some contexts and to some people.

**Stick it in your ear!** |STIK it in yŏŏr IR| *excl* A contemptuous dismissal. ORIGINS: Euphemistic form of slang **Stick it up your ass!** from slang **ass** meaning "the rear end or buttocks." USAGE INFO: Often accompanied by the gesture referred to as "giving *sb* the finger." USAGE ALERT: Usually used with intent to be rude and understood as such. Although the euphemistic alteration of this phrase will soften it somewhat, it may still be objectionable in some contexts and to some people.

**Stick it up your ass!** |STIK it up yŏŏr AS| *excl* A contemptuous dismissal. ORIGINS: From slang **ass** meaning "the rear end or buttocks." USAGE INFO: Often accompanied by the gesture referred to as "giving *sb* the finger." USAGE ALERT: Usually used with intent to be rude and understood as such. In addition, the inclusion of **ass** and the graphic image will make this expression objectionable in some contexts and to some people.

**Stick it where the sun doesn't shine!** |STIK it wer *thu* SUN duz 'nt SHĪN| *excl* A contemptuous dismissal. ORIGINS: Euphemistic form of slang **Stick it up your ass!** from slang **ass** meaning "the rear end or buttocks." USAGE INFO: Often accompanied by the gesture referred to as "giving *sb* the finger." USAGE ALERT: Usually used with intent to be rude and understood as such. Although the euphemistic alteration of this phrase will soften it somewhat, the graphic image may still be objectionable in some contexts and to some people.

**Take a flying fuck!** |TĀK u FLĪ ing FUK| *v* A contemptuous dismissal. ORIGINS: Figurative use of slang **fuck** meaning "sexual intercourse." USAGE ALERT: Usually used with intent to be rude and understood as such. In addition, the inclusion of the word **fuck** in the phrase will render it objectionable in some contexts and to some people.

**Take a hike!** |TĀK u HĪK| *excl* A contemptuous dismissal. USAGE ALERT: Usually used with intent to be rude and understood as such.

Take off! |TĀK AWF| *excl* Go away!

Up yours! |UP YŎŌRZ| *adj* A rude dismissal. ORIGINS: Shortened and altered form of slang **Stick it up your ass!** or similar phrases. USAGE ALERT: Usually used with intent to be rude and understood as such. In addition, the euphemistic shortening of this phrase will soften it somewhat, but it may still be objectionable in some contexts and to some people.

Vamoose! |va MŪS| *excl* Go away! ORIGINS: From Spanish **vamos** meaning "let's go."

You know what you can do with it? |yū NŌ wut YŪ can DŪ with IT| *excl* A contemptuous dismissal. ORIGINS: Euphemistic form of slang **Stick it up your ass!** from slang **ass** meaning "the rear end or buttocks." USAGE INFO: Often accompanied by the gesture referred to as "giving *sb* the finger." USAGE ALERT: Usually used with intent to be rude and understood as such. Although the euphemistic alteration of this phrase will soften it somewhat, the graphic image may still be objectionable in some contexts and to some people.

You know where you can stick it? |yū NŌ wer yū can STIK it| *excl* A contemptuous dismissal. ORIGINS: Euphemistic form of slang **Stick it up your ass!** from slang **ass** meaning "the rear end or buttocks." USAGE INFO: Often accompanied by the gesture referred to as "giving *sb* the finger." USAGE ALERT: Usually used with intent to be rude and understood as such. Although the euphemistic alteration of this phrase will soften it somewhat, the graphic image may still be objectionable in some contexts and to some people.

NON-SLANG SYNONYMS: I need to be alone now. Please go. You're fired. **Be off! Get going! Go away! Make tracks! Off with you! Take off! class dismissed, Could we have a moment? excuse me, you may go**

# EXCITEMENT

Cowabunga! |kou u BUNG u| *excl* An exclamation of surprise or excitement. ORIGINS: From the exclamation spoken by Chief George "Capps" Thunderthud on the television series, *The Howdy Doody Show*. Used among surfers and repopularized in more recent popular culture, particularly by *The Teenage Mutant Ninja Turtles*, in whose use it is often followed by "Dude."

Woohoo! |WŪ HŪ| *excl* An expression of excitement or delight.

Yahoo! |ya HŪ| *excl* An expression of excitement or delight.

Zowie! |ZOU ē| *excl* An exclamation of excitement. ORIGINS: Similar in formation to many words representing speed.

NON-SLANG SYNONYMS: I'm so excited! This is wonderful!, **How exciting! Wow! Yippee!**

# FAILED UNDERSTANDING

These are phrases to let someone know about a failure of communication, either in response to an inquiry about whether something was understood or simply volunteered by a listener.

**Come again?** |kum u GEN| *phr* Could you repeat that? ORIGINS: In this case come means "speak."

**How do you mean?** |hou dū yū MĒN| *phr* How could this be? What do you mean?

**How's that?** |houz THAT| *phr* What do you mean? Could you explain your logic? ORIGINS: Can be a shortened form of "How is that possible?"

**Huh?** |hu| *phr* I don't have a clue what you're getting at.

**I don't have the foggiest.** |ī DŌNT hav thu FAW gē ist| *phr* I don't have any idea. I don't know the answer to your question. ORIGINS: From shortening of the phrase "I don't have the foggiest idea" and the obscuring property of fog that prevents clear vision.

**It's Greek to me.** |its GRĒK tū MĒ| *phr* It's beyond my knowledge or understanding. ORIGINS: From slang Greek meaning "unintelligible." From a Latin proverb, "Graecum est, non potest legi" (It's Greek, therefore unreadable), but better known through the use in Shakespeare's 1599 play *The Tragedy of Julius Caesar* in which Casca says of Cicero's speech, "for mine own part, it was Greek to me," making a pun (I, ii). May allude to the fact that Greek not only is a different language from Latin, but also has a different alphabet.

**Say what?** |sā WUT| *phr* Could you repeat that? ORIGINS: Alteration of the phrase **What did you say?**

**Search me!** |surch MĒ| *excl* I have no idea. I don't know the answer to your question.

NON-SLANG SYNONYMS: Could you repeat that? I don't understand.; **Could you run that by me again? Eh? I didn't catch that. Let's have that again... What did you say? What? You('ve) lost me.**; **Excuse me? I can't quite make this out. I'm sorry...? Pardon me?**

# FEAR

Eep! |ēp| *excl* Sound to express fear.

Yeep(s)! |yēp / yēps| *excl* Sound expressing fear.

Yikes! |yīks| *excl* Sound expressing surprise and mild fear or minor shock.

Yipes! |yīps| *excl* Sound expressing surprise, mild fear, or dismay.

NON-SLANG SYNONYMS: I'm afraid. This is scary.

# FRUSTRATION OR EXASPERATION

## 1 With Someone

GOI Get over it!

GOYHH Get off your high horse.

**GYHOOYA** Get your head out of your ass.

MITIN More info than I needed.

**Get your finger out (of your ass/butt)!** |get yŏŏr FIN gur out / get yŏŏr FIN gur out uv yŏŏr AS / get yŏŏr FIN gur out uv yŏŏr BUT| *excl See* GET YOUR THUMB OUT (OF YOUR ASS/BUTT)!

**Get your thumb out (of your ass/butt)!** |get yŏŏr THUM out / get yŏŏr THUM out uv yŏŏr AS / get yŏŏr THUM out uv yŏŏr BUT| *excl* Stop sitting around or messing around and get ready for serious action. ORIGINS: From slang **ass** meaning "the rear end or buttocks" or slang **butt**, a euphemism for **ass**. The suggestion is of someone doing something thoroughly worthless. USAGE ALERT: The crudeness of the image plus the reference to the buttocks or rear end will make this expression objectionable in some contexts and to some people.

**Pull your finger out (of your ass/butt)!** |pŏŏl yŏŏr FIN gur out / pŏŏl yŏŏr FIN gur out uv yŏŏr AS / pŏŏl yŏŏr FIN gur out uv yŏŏr BUT| *excl See* PULL YOUR THUMB OUT (OF YOUR ASS/BUTT)!

**Pull your thumb out (of your ass/butt)!** |pŏŏl yŏŏr THUM out / pŏŏl yŏŏr THUM out uv yŏŏr AS / pŏŏl yŏŏr THUM out uv yŏŏr BUT| *excl* Stop sitting around or messing around and get ready for serious action. ORIGINS: From slang **ass** meaning "the rear end or buttocks" or slang **butt**, a euphemism for

**ass**. The suggestion is of someone doing something thoroughly worthless. USAGE ALERT: The crudeness of the image plus the reference to the buttocks or rear end will make this expression objectionable in some contexts and to some people.

**Take your finger out (of your ass/butt)!** |tāk yŏŏr FIN gur out / tāk yŏŏr FIN gur out uv yŏŏr AS / tāk yŏŏr FIN gur out uv yŏŏr BUT| *excl See* TAKE YOUR THUMB OUT (OF YOUR ASS/BUTT)!

**Take your thumb out (of your ass/butt)!** |tāk yŏŏr THUM out / tāk yŏŏr THUM out uv yŏŏr AS / tāk yŏŏr THUM out uv yŏŏr BUT| *excl* Stop sitting around or messing around and get ready for serious action. ORIGINS: From slang **ass** meaning "the rear end or buttocks" or slang **butt**, a euphemism for **ass**. The suggestion is of someone doing something thoroughly worthless. USAGE ALERT: The crudeness of the image plus the reference to the buttocks or rear end will make this expression objectionable in some contexts and to some people.

NON-SLANG SYNONYMS: I'm exasperated. I'm frustrated.

# 2 With Either Someone or Something

**4COL** For crying out loud!

**FTLOG** For the love of God!

**GFF** Go fucking figure.

**GMAB** Give me a break!

**HWGA** Here we go again!

**TARFU** Things are really fucked up.

**WITFITS** What in the fuck is this shit?

**Arrgh!** |ahrg| *excl* Sound to indicate irritation. ORIGINS: Popularized by its use in Talk Like a Pirate Day celebrations and related events and materials. USAGE INFO: Arrgh is spelled in a variety of ways.

**Ay yi yi! Ai yie yie!** |ī yī YĪ| *excl* Oh no! ORIGINS: This is not the same expression used by the Frito Bandito in Frito-Lay® advertisements. USAGE INFO: Always used with either 2 or 4 yi's following the Ay.

**Bother!** |BAH*TH* ur| *excl* An expression of mild irritation or annoyance. ORIGINS: Although more often used in British English, it is notable in fiction that is popular in the US, for example, the stories of Winnie-the-Pooh, which may have encouraged the US use. USAGE INFO: **Bother** is not linked to any particular PO word and is unlikely to offend for that reason. Nevertheless, it can be substituted for virtually any interjection denoting mild anger or frustration.

**Botheration!** |bah*th* u RĀ shun| *excl* An expression of irritation or annoyance. ORIGINS: Extended from SE **bother**. USAGE INFO: Due to length, it may register as a bit stronger than **bother**!

**D'oh!** |dō| *excl* Annoyed grunt of frustration, pain, or realization. ORIGINS: Although people have doubtless grunted throughout history, this particular spelling has been popularized through being the catchphrase of the character Homer Simpson in the television series *The Simpsons* (1989–).

**For Christ's sake!** * |fawr KRĪST sāk| *excl* Oh no! ORIGINS: From SE Jesus Christ whom Christians hold to be the Son of God. USAGE ALERT: The inclusion of the word Jesus in the phrase will make it seem blasphemous and objectionable in some contexts and to some people.
• **For Chrissake!** |fawr KRĪ sāk| *excl*

**For crying out loud!** |fawr KRĪ ing out loud| *excl* Oh no! ORIGINS: Euphemism of phrases **For Christ's sake!**, **Chrissake!** From SE Jesus Christ whom Christians hold to be the Son of God. USAGE ALERT: Most people will not recognize this phrase as a euphemism or know what phrase it comes from.

**For fuck's sake!** |fawr FUK sāk| *excl* Oh no! ORIGINS: From slang **fuck** meaning "to engage in sexual intercourse." USAGE ALERT: The inclusion of **fuck** will make this expression objectionable in some contexts and to some people.

**For God's sake!** |fawr GAHD sāk| *excl* Oh no! ORIGINS: By extension from SE god meaning a being conceived as the divine Lord of the universe. USAGE ALERT: People who consider this use of **god** blasphemous are likely to find it objectionable.

**For Pete's sake!** |fawr PĒT sāk| *excl* Oh no! ORIGINS: Euphemism of phrase **For Christ's sake!**

**For the love of Mike!** |fawr *thu* LUV uv MĪK| *excl* Oh no! ORIGINS: Euphemism of phrase **For the love of God!**

**For the love of Pete!** |fawr *thu* LUV uv PĒT| *excl* Oh no! ORIGINS: Euphemism of phrase **For the love of God!**

**Gawd!** |Gawd| *excl* An exclamation of exasperation. ORIGINS: By alteration from SE god meaning a being conceived as the divine Lord of the universe. USAGE ALERT: People who consider this reference to **god** blasphemous are likely to find it objectionable.

**Give me a break!** |GIV mē u BRĀK| *excl* A plea for help, relief, or patience in the face of *st* annoying or frustrating, especially coming upon other difficult events or situations. ORIGINS: Reworking of the expression give *sb* a break meaning "to ease off, cut *sb* some slack, give another chance to *sb*, help *sb* out."

**I've had it!** |īv HAD it| *excl* I am losing my ability to cope! Cry of frustration, extreme annoyance, or exasperation. ORIGINS: Shortened version of the phrase I've had it with *sb/st* or I've had it up to here. USAGE INFO: Usually said after a series of events have built up the emotion prompting the exclamation.

**That tears it!** |THAT TERZ it| *excl* I am losing my ability to cope! Everything is ruined! Cry of frustration, extreme annoyance, or exasperation. ORIGINS: The idea seems to be that having been "torn," whatever it is is useless or ruined. USAGE

INFO: Usually said after a series of events have built up the emotion prompting the exclamation or in response to something cataclysmic.

**That's torn it!** |*th*ats tawrn it| *excl* An interjection of surprise and dismay when *st* unexpected has upset one's plans. ORIGINS: Primarily British, but spreading in US usage.

Non-Slang Synonyms: I don't care. I need a break. It doesn't matter. It makes no difference to me. It's neither here nor there. It's not important. This is annoying. <u>Enough already! I'm fed up. I'm sick of this! I'm tired of this.</u> <u>So what do you want from me? That's enough! That's it!</u> Thank you, no.

# IGNORANCE

**404** fawr ō fawr No information.

**BHOM** Beats the hell/heck out of me.

**BSOM** Beats the shit out of me.

**BTHOOM** Beats the hell/heck out of me.

**BTSOOM** Beats the shit out of me.

**FIIK** Fucked if I know.

**HSIK** How should I know?

**IDK** I don't know.

**NFI** No fucking idea.

**NHOH** Never heard of him/her.

**Beats me!** |bēts MĒ| *phr* I don't know! ORIGINS: Shortened from phrase "It beats me."

**Beats the hell out of me!** |bēts *thu* HEL out uv MĒ| *phr* I don't know! ORIGINS: Shortened from phrase "It beats the hell out of me." Figurative use of SE **hell** meaning "the alternative to heaven; the realm of the devil." USAGE ALERT: The inclusion of **hell** will make this expression objectionable in some contexts and to some people.

**Beats the shit out of me!** |bēts *thu* SHIT out uv MĒ| *phr* I don't know! ORIGINS: Shortened from phrase "It beats the shit out of me." From slang **shit** meaning "excrement." USAGE ALERT: The inclusion of **shit** will make this expression objectionable in some contexts and to some people.

**Dunno.** |du NŌ| *excl* I don't know. ORIGINS: Shortened and altered from phrase I don't know.

**Fucked if I know!** |FUKT if Ī nō| *excl* I don't know! ORIGINS: Shortened from phrase **I'm fucked if I know!** From slang **fuck** meaning "to engage in sexual intercourse." USAGE ALERT: The inclusion of **fucked** will make this expression objectionable in some contexts and to some people.

**I don't know beans about it.** |Ī dōnt nō BĒNZ u bout it| *excl* I don't know the subject. ORIGINS: From slang beans, which means a minimal amount of something, in this case, knowledge.

**I don't know <pronoun> from Adam.** |Ī dōnt nō <pronoun> frum A dum| *excl* I don't know *sb/st*; I wouldn't recognize *sb/st*. ORIGINS: From slang not know *sb* from, which means "unable to recognize" and **Adam**, the name of the first man reported in Genesis in the Old Testament of the Bible.

**I wouldn't know *sb/st* if I fell over <pronoun>.** |Ī WŎŌD 'nt nō *sb/st* if Ī FEL ō vur <pronoun>| *excl* I don't know *sb/st*; I wouldn't recognize *sb/st*, even up close.

**I wouldn't know *st* if it hit me in the face.** |Ī WŎŌD 'nt nō *st* if it HIT mē in *thu* FĀS| *excl* I don't know *st*; I wouldn't recognize *st* even up close.

**No clue.** |NŌ clū| *excl* I don't know.

**No fucking idea.** |nō FUK ing Ī dē u| *excl* I don't know. ORIGINS: Shortened from phrase **I have no fucking idea.** From slang **fuck** meaning "to engage in sexual intercourse." USAGE ALERT: The inclusion of **fucking** will make this expression objectionable in some contexts and to some people.

**No idea.** |nō Ī DĒ u| *excl* I don't know. ORIGINS: Shortened and altered from phrase I have no idea.

NON-SLANG SYNONYMS: I don't know. I have no idea. **How should I know? I don't know the first thing about it. What do I know? Who knows? I'm at a loss. I'm not familiar with this topic.**

# INDIFFERENCE

**BTDT** Been there, done that.

**CBB** Can't be bothered.

**DILLIGAD** |DIL ē gad| Does it look like I give a damn? Do I look like I give a damn?

**DILLIGAF** |DIL ē gaf| Does it look like I give a fuck? Do I look like I give a fuck?

**DILLIGAS** |DIL ē gas| Does it look like I give a shit? Do I look like I give a shit?

**IDC** I don't care.

**NMP** Not my problem.

**STBY** Sucks to be you.

**TS** Tough shit.

**YSW, YYSSW** Yeah, sure, whatever. Yeah, yeah; sure, sure; whatever.

**And I care because?** |and Ī ker bē CUZ| *phr* I don't care.

**And I care why?** |and Ī ker WĪ| *phr* I don't care.

**Been there, done that.** |BIN ther DUN that| *excl* This is not new or interesting to me.

**Big deal!** |BIG dēl| *excl* I don't care; this is not important or interesting. USAGE INFO: Always said sarcastically with this meaning.

**Does it look like I give a damn?** |duz it LOOK līk Ī giv u dam| *excl* I don't give a damn! *See* I DON'T GIVE A DAMN!

**Does it look like I give a fuck?** |duz it LOOK līk Ī giv u fuk| *excl* I don't give a fuck! *See* I DON'T GIVE A FUCK!

**Does it look like I give a shit?** |duz it LOOK līk Ī giv u shit| *excl* I don't give a shit! *See* I DON'T GIVE A SHIT!

**I could care less!** |Ī kood ker LES| *excl* An interjection expressing complete indifference. ORIGINS: From **I couldn't care less!** with the negative removed. Logically, it means that one does care. Some say that the negative is covered by the phrase being said sarcastically. USAGE INFO: Those who do not believe that the tone covers removing the negative may find this expression to be grammatically incorrect. USAGE ALERT: Usually used with intent to be rude and understood as such.

**I couldn't care less!** |Ī KOOD'nt ker LES| *excl* An interjection expressing complete indifference. USAGE ALERT: Usually used with intent to be rude and understood as such.

**I don't give a care!** |Ī dōnt GIV u ker| *excl* I don't care at all! USAGE INFO: May be used as a euphemism for other, stronger expressions of indifference. USAGE ALERT: Usually used with intent to be rude and understood as such.

**I don't give a crap!** |Ī dōnt GIV u krap| *excl* An interjection expressing complete indifference. ORIGINS: Euphemism for **I don't give a shit!** Slang **crap** is a euphemism for **shit**. USAGE INFO: The intention is to express that the speaker does not even have the most minimal interest. USAGE ALERT: The reference to excrement will make this expression objectionable in some contexts and to some people. Usually used with intent to be rude and understood as such.

**I don't give a damn!** |ī dōnt GIV u dam| *excl* An interjection expressing complete indifference. ORIGINS: By extension from SE **damn**, which literally means "Send (it) to hell." USAGE INFO: The intention is to express that the speaker does not even have the most minimal interest. USAGE ALERT: The use of **damn** will make this expression objectionable in some contexts and to some people. Usually used with intent to be rude and understood as such.

I don't give a darn! |ī dōnt GIV u dahrn| *excl* An interjection expressing complete indifference. ORIGINS: Euphemism for **I don't give a damn!** and similar PO expressions. In this particular case, **darn** is said to serve as a euphemism for not giving a **crap**, **damn**, **fuck**, or **shit**. USAGE INFO: The intention is to express that the speaker does not even have the most minimal interest. USAGE ALERT: Euphemisms may still be objectionable in some contexts and to some people. Usually used with intent to be rude and understood as such.

**I don't give a fuck!** |ī dōnt GIV u fuk| *excl* An interjection expressing complete indifference. ORIGINS: From slang **fuck** meaning "sexual intercourse." USAGE INFO: The intention is to express that the speaker does not even have the most minimal interest. Notice that the use of **fuck** in this expression devalues sex. USAGE ALERT: The use of **fuck** will make this expression objectionable in some contexts and to some people. Usually used with intent to be rude and understood as such.

I don't give a hill of beans! |ī dōnt GIV u hil uv BĒNZ| *excl* An interjection expressing complete indifference. ORIGINS: Euphemism for similar expression with **crap**, **damn**, **fuck**, or **shit**. Beans are conceived to be a minimal item, as in the expression "I don't know beans about it." USAGE INFO: The intention is to express that the speaker does not even have the most minimal interest. USAGE ALERT: Euphemisms may still be objectionable in some contexts and to some people. Usually used with intent to be rude and understood as such.

I don't give a hoot! |ī dōnt GIV u hūt| *excl* An interjection expressing complete indifference. ORIGINS: Euphemism for similar expression with **crap**, **damn**, **fuck**, or **shit**. A hoot, the noise one makes in disgust, is conceived to be something without value. USAGE INFO: The intention is to express that the speaker does not even have the most minimal interest. USAGE ALERT: Euphemisms may still be objectionable in some contexts and to some people. Usually used with intent to be rude and understood as such.

I don't give a rap! |ī dōnt GIV u rap| *excl* An interjection expressing complete indifference. ORIGINS: Slang rap was a nickname in England for a halfpenny, a coin of very little value, the approximate equivalent of the US slang red cent. USAGE INFO: The intention is to express that the speaker does not even have the most minimal interest. USAGE ALERT: Usually used with intent to be rude and understood as such.

**I don't give a rat's ass!** |ī dōnt GIV u RATS AS| *excl* An interjection expressing complete indifference. ORIGINS: From slang **ass** meaning "the rear end or buttocks." USAGE INFO: The intention is to express that the speaker does not even have the most minimal interest. USAGE ALERT: The reference to **ass** will make this expression objectionable in some contexts and to some people. Usually used with intent to be rude and understood as such.

**I don't give a shit!** |ī dōnt GIV u shit| *excl* An interjection expressing complete indifference. ORIGINS: Slang **shit** means "excrement," but is figuratively used to mean "nothing" as in "I don't have shit." USAGE INFO: The intention is to express that the speaker does not even have the most minimal interest. USAGE ALERT: The reference to excrement will make this expression objectionable in some contexts and to some people. Usually used with intent to be rude and understood as such.

**I don't give two fucks!** |ī dōnt GIV tū FUKS| *excl* An interjection expressing complete indifference. ORIGINS: From slang **fuck** meaning "sexual intercourse." USAGE INFO: The intention is to express that the speaker does not even have the most minimal interest. Notice that the use of **fuck** in this expression devalues sex. In this context, oddly, the word *two* acts as an intensifier of worthlessness. USAGE ALERT: The use of **fuck** will make this expression objectionable in some contexts and to some people. Usually used with intent to be rude and understood as such.

**I don't give two hoots!** |ī dōnt GIV tū hūts| *excl* An interjection expressing complete indifference. ORIGINS: Emphatic form of I don't give a hoot! Hoots, noises one makes in disgust, are conceived to be something without value. In this context, oddly, the word *two* acts as an intensifier of worthlessness. USAGE INFO: The intention is to express that the speaker does not even have the most minimal interest. USAGE ALERT: Euphemisms may still be objectionable in some contexts and to some people. Usually used with intent to be rude and understood as such.

**I should worry!** |ī shŏŏd wur ē| *excl* An interjection expressing lack of concern. ORIGINS: From a Yiddish phrase. USAGE INFO: Sometimes said sarcastically.

**Meh!** |meh| *excl* A sound to express reservations, lack of interest, indifference, feeling poorly, etc. USAGE INFO: Given its meaning, it does not often take an exclamation point.

**No skin off my ass/butt!** |nō skin ahf MĪ as / nō skin ahf MĪ BUT| *excl* An interjection signaling complete indifference: No problem! I don't care! It doesn't matter to me! ORIGINS: From slang **ass** meaning "the rear end or buttocks." From slang **butt**, a euphemism for **ass**. USAGE ALERT: The inclusion of the word **ass** or **butt** in the phrase will render it objectionable in some contexts and to some people.

**No skin off my nose!** |nō skin ahf MĪ nōz| *excl* An interjection signaling complete indifference: No problem! I don't care! It doesn't matter to me!

**So what!** |sō WHAT| *excl* An interjection of indifference.

**sucks to be you. It** |it suks tū bē YŪ| *excl* I don't care; that's too bad. USAGE INFO: The phrase can be used sarcastically. It can also be used to offer commiseration on someone's suffering.

**Tough luck!** |TUF LUK| *excl* The tone of voice greatly influences the meaning of this response to *sb* else's bad fortune: It ranges from "I don't much care (about your bad luck)!" to "I'm sorry to hear (about your bad luck)! and Wish you well!" ORIGINS: From slang **tough** meaning "unfortunate."

**Tough shit!** |TUF SHIT| *excl* I don't care at all (about your bad luck)! ORIGINS: From slang **tough** meaning "unfortunate" and **shit** meaning "excrement." USAGE ALERT: The inclusion of the word **shit** in the phrase will render it objectionable in some contexts and to some people.

**Whatever!** |wut EV ur| *excl* An exclamation of derisive dismissal and/or lack of interest. USAGE INFO: Often with exaggerated pronunciation.

**Who cares?** |hū KERZ| *excl* An interjection signaling indifference.

**Who gives a care?** |hū GIVZ u KER| *excl* An interjection signaling indifference.

**Who gives a damn?** |hū GIVZ u DAM| *excl* An interjection signaling indifference. ORIGINS: By extension from SE **damn**, which literally means "Send (it) to hell." USAGE ALERT: The inclusion of the word **damn** in the phrase will render it objectionable in some contexts and to some people.

**Who gives a fart?** |hū GIVZ u FAHRT| *excl* An interjection signaling indifference. ORIGINS: Euphemism for **Who gives a fuck?** From slang **fart** meaning "to break wind," sometimes used as a euphemism for **fuck** because it is often considered less offensive. USAGE ALERT: The inclusion of the word **fart** in the phrase will render it objectionable in some contexts and to some people.

**Who gives a (flying) fuck?** |hū GIVZ u FUK / hū GIVZ u FLĪ ing FUK| *excl* An interjection signaling indifference. ORIGINS: Figurative use of slang **fuck** meaning "to engage in sexual intercourse." USAGE ALERT: The inclusion of the word **fuck** in the phrase will render it objectionable in some contexts and to some people.

**Who gives a frig?** |hū GIVZ u FRIG| *excl* An interjection signaling indifference. ORIGINS: Euphemism for **Who gives a fuck?** From slang **frig** meaning "masturbate" or "engage in intercourse"—sometimes used as a euphemism for **fuck** by people who think that **frig** is a sanitized version of **fuck** and do not realize that it is a PO word all on its own. USAGE ALERT: The inclusion of the word **frig** in the phrase will render it objectionable in some contexts and to some people.

**Who gives a shit?** |hū GIVZ u SHIT| *excl* An interjection signaling indifference. ORIGINS: From slang **shit** meaning "excrement." USAGE ALERT: The inclusion of the word **shit** in the phrase will render it objectionable in some contexts and to some people.

NON-SLANG SYNONYMS: I don't care.

# SKEPTICISM OR DISBELIEF

**DQYDJ** Don't quit your day job.

**IBIWISI** I'll believe it when I see it.

**RUFKM** Are you fucking kidding me?

**UG2BK** You've got to be kidding!

**YGTBK** You've got to be kidding.

**Are you fucking kidding me?** |AR yū FUK ing KID ing mē| *excl* I can hardly believe what you're saying! ORIGINS: From slang **fuck** meaning "to engage in sexual intercourse," used here as a sentence modifier to intensify the whole sentence. USAGE ALERT: This use of a form of **fuck** will be objectionable in some contexts and to some people.

**Balls!** |bawlz| *excl* I don't believe it/you! ORIGINS: From slang **balls**, meaning "testicles." USAGE INFO: Usually used by men, with rare exceptions. USAGE ALERT: The reference to the male sex organs will render this phrase objectionable in some contexts and to some people.

**Come off it!** |kum AHF it| *excl* I don't believe it/you!

**Don't quit your day job!** |DŌNT kwit yōōr DĀ jahb| *excl* I can't believe your prospects are as good as you say: I'd wait and see.

**Get away!** |get u WĀ| *excl* I can hardly believe what you're saying!

**Get out!** |get OUT| *excl* I can hardly believe what you're saying!

**Go on!** |gō AHN| *excl* I can hardly believe what you're saying!

**Guff!** |guf| *excl* I don't believe it/you!

**I don't buy it!** |Ī dōnt BĪ it| *excl* I don't believe it/you!

**It won't wash!** |it WŌNT WAHSH| *excl* I don't believe it/you!

**Like hell (it is)!** |līk HEL / līk HEL it iz| *excl* I don't believe it/you! ORIGINS: Figurative use of SE **hell** meaning "the alternative to heaven; the realm of the devil." USAGE ALERT: The inclusion of the word **hell** in this phrase will render it objectionable in some contexts and to some people.

**My ass!** |mī AS| *excl* I don't believe it/you! ORIGINS: From slang **ass** meaning "the rear end or buttocks." USAGE ALERT: The inclusion of **ass** will make this expression objectionable in some contexts and to some people.

**My eye!** |mī Ī| *excl* I don't believe it/you!

**My foot!** |mī FŌŌT| *excl* I don't believe it/you! ORIGINS: Euphemism for **My ass!**

**Phooey!** |FŪ ē| *excl* I don't believe it/you!

**Piffle!** |PIF ul| *excl* I don't believe it/you! USAGE INFO: Usually used self-consciously.

**Sez you!** |sez YŪ| *excl* I don't believe it/you! ORIGINS: Altered form of "That's what *you* say!"—the implication being that others disagree.

**Shut up!**[2] |shut UP| *excl* Initial expression of disbelief in what one has been told, but often suggests that the hearer is open to convincing. USAGE INFO: This use of shut up, if said with appropriate tone and body language, will not cause offense.

**Stuff and nonsense!** |STUF and NAWN sens| *excl* I don't believe it/you!

**Tell it/that to the marines!** |tel it/*that* tū *thu* mu RĒNZ| *excl* I don't believe it/you! You can't fool me! ORIGINS: A shortened version of the saying, "He may tell that to the marines, but the sailors will not believe him."

**Tell me another (one)!** | tel mē u NU*TH*ur / tel mē u NU*TH*ur wun| *excl* I don't believe it/you!

**You're FOS!** |yōōr ef ō ES| *excl* I don't believe it/you! ORIGINS: Euphemism for **full of shit**, with **shit** meaning "excrement." USAGE ALERT: The inclusion of the word **shit** in this phrase will render it objectionable in some contexts and to some people.

**You're full of shit!** |yōōr ful uv SHIT| *excl* I don't believe it/you! ORIGINS: From **shit** meaning "excrement." USAGE ALERT: The inclusion of the word **shit** in this phrase will render it objectionable in some contexts and to some people.

NON-SLANG SYNONYMS: I don't believe it. That can't be true. That doesn't seem right. That's not true. **I smell a rat. I'll believe it when I see it. Tripe.**

# SURPRISE, SHOCK, DISCOVERY

**FMUTA** Fuck me up the ass!

**WTF** What the fuck!

**WTFH** What the fucking hell!

**WTH** What the heck/hell!

**Crap!** |krap| Oh no! ORIGINS: From slang **crap**, a euphemism for slang **shit** meaning "excrement." USAGE ALERT: The reference to **crap** will make this phrase objectionable in some contexts and to some people, though some people will find **crap** less objectionable than **shit**.

**Erk!** |erk| *excl* Sound to indicate that one is pulled up short by something unexpected and not good.

**Go fucking figure!** |GŌ FUK ing FIG yur| *excl* Who would have thought! ORIGINS: From slang **fuck** meaning "to engage in sexual intercourse." USAGE ALERT: This use of a form of **fuck** will be objectionable in some contexts and to some people.

**Gosh!** |gahsh| *excl* An interjection expressing surprise, slight misgivings, and mild to moderate displeasure, frustration, or irritation, etc. ORIGINS: Euphemism for **God!** From SE god meaning a being conceived as the divine Lord of the universe. USAGE INFO: Many people will not know the origins of this expression. USAGE ALERT: People who consider this substitution for god blasphemous are likely to find this term objectionable, but it has become more common and more accepted as time has passed.

**I'll be jiggered!** |īl bē JIG urd| *excl* I'm shocked! ORIGINS: From jigger meaning "to shake."

**Jeepers!** |JĒ purz| *excl* An interjection expressing surprise, shock, dismay, etc. ORIGINS: Euphemism for **Jesus** used as an interjection—a figurative use of SE Jesus whom Christians hold to be the Son of God—but it is milder. USAGE INFO: Many people will not know the ORIGINS of this expression. USAGE ALERT: People who consider this substitution for Jesus blasphemous are likely to find this term objectionable.

**Jeez!** |jēz| *excl* An interjection expressing surprise, shock, dismay, etc. ORIGINS: Euphemism for **Jesus!** used as an interjection—a figurative use of SE Jesus whom Christians hold to be the Son of God, but it is milder. Many people will not know the origins of this expression. USAGE ALERT: This saying will be considered objectionable in some contexts and by some people who may find it blasphemous.

**Oh my!** |ō MĪ| *excl* An interjection usually signaling mild to moderate surprise, dismay, delight, etc. ORIGINS: Shortened form of SE O, my God, which originally was a direct address to God at the opening of a prayer; later also an imprecation in which the use of God has no actual connection to the speaker's/writer's beliefs or lack thereof. USAGE INFO: This phrase is now unlikely to raise any objection.

**Oh my God!** |Ō mī GAHD| *excl* An interjection signaling strong surprise, dismay, delight, etc. ORIGINS: Secularized use of SE O, my God, which originally was a direct address to God at the opening of a prayer; also a slang imprecation in which the use of god conveys no information whatsoever about the speaker's/ writer's beliefs. Derived from SE god meaning a being conceived as the divine Lord of the universe. USAGE INFO: For some speakers and writers, this formula is prayer and perfectly acceptable, though when that is the case, it is often followed by other words, as in "Oh, my God, help those poor people!" USAGE ALERT: Used without a religious sense, this phrase will be considered objectionable and blasphemous in some contexts and by some people.

Oops!* |ŪPS| *excl* A sound to signal discovery of a minor mistake (as in proofreading and discovering a typo) or the making of a blunder (such as dropping *st*; tripping; bumping into *sb/st*), sometimes conveying an implicit apology as well.
• Oopsie! |ŪP sē|

Rats! |rats| *excl* An interjection signaling an unpleasant surprise, disillusionment, frustration, etc.

Uh-oh! |U Ō| *excl* Sound to express the discovery of an error or mistake or dismay due to some other cause; sound to express concern or alarm.

**Unfuckingbelievable!** |UN FUK ing bu LĒV u bul| *excl* I'm shocked! ORIGINS: SE unbelievable with added emphasis from the infix **fucking**. USAGE ALERT: The use of **fucking** in this phrase will make it objectionable in some contexts and to some people.

What in (the) blazes! |wut in BLĀ ziz / wut in *thu* BLĀ ziz| *excl* What in the world! ORIGINS: Euphemism and shortened version of **What in the hell is going on?** Blazes is a substitution for a figurative use of SE hell meaning "the alternative to heaven; the realm of the devil." Blazes is a reference to the fires of hell. USAGE ALERT: The euphemism blazes in this phrase will soften it somewhat, but it may still be objectionable in some contexts and to some people.

**What (in) the hell is going on?** |wut *thu* HEL iz GŌ ing awn / wut in *thu* HEL iz GŌ ing awn| *excl* What in the world! ORIGINS: Figurative use of SE hell meaning "the alternative to heaven; the realm of the devil." USAGE ALERT: The inclusion of the word **hell** in this phrase will render it objectionable in some contexts and to some people.

What in tarnation! |wut in tahr NĀ shun| *excl* What in the world! ORIGINS: Euphemism and shortened version of **What in the hell is going on?** Tarnation is a substitution for a figurative use of SE **damnation** meaning "condemnation to hell." USAGE ALERT: The euphemism blazes in this phrase will soften it somewhat, but it may still be objectionable in some contexts and to some people.

What (in) the Sam Hill! |wut *thu* SAM HIL / wut in *thu* SAM HIL| *excl* What in the world! ORIGINS: Euphemism and shortened version of **What in the hell is going on?** Figurative use of SE hell meaning "the alternative to heaven; the realm of the devil." USAGE ALERT: The inclusion of the word **hell** in this phrase will render it objectionable in some contexts and to some people.

What the deuce! |wut *thu* DŪS| *excl* An interjection signaling surprise, shock, or dismay, annoyance, etc. ORIGINS: Euphemism for **What the hell!**, SE hell being the place where the devil resides and deuce being a euphemism for **devil**. USAGE ALERT: The inclusion of deuce will make this expression objectionable in some contexts and to some people, but usually less so than **devil**.

**What the devil!** |wut *thu* DEV ul| *excl* An interjection signaling surprise, shock, dismay, annoyance, etc. ORIGINS: Euphemism for **What the hell!**, SE hell being the place where the devil resides. USAGE ALERT: The inclusion of **devil** will make this expression objectionable in some contexts and to some people.

**What the dickens!** |wut *thu* DIK unz| *excl* An interjection signaling surprise, shock, dismay, annoyance, etc. ORIGINS: Euphemism for **What the devil!** Slang dickens is an altered form of SE devil. USAGE ALERT: The inclusion of a reference to the devil will make this term objectionable in some contexts and to some people.

**What the fuck!** |wut *thu* FUK| *excl* An interjection signaling surprise, shock, dismay, annoyance, etc. ORIGINS: Figurative use of slang **fuck** meaning "sexual intercourse." USAGE ALERT: The inclusion of **fuck** will make this expression objectionable in some contexts and to some people.

**What the fuck...?** |wut *thu* FUK| *excl* An interjection signaling incomprehension or befuddlement. ORIGINS: Figurative use of slang **fuck** meaning "to engage in sexual intercourse."

**What the fucking hell?** |wut *thu* FUK ing hel| *excl* An interjection signaling surprise, shock, dismay, annoyance, etc. ORIGINS: Figurative use of SE hell meaning "the alternative to heaven; the realm of the devil." From slang **fuck** meaning "to engage in sexual intercourse," used here as a sentence modifier to intensify the whole sentence. USAGE ALERT: The inclusion of the word **hell** and a form of **fuck** in this phrase will render it objectionable in some contexts and to some people.

**What the heck!** |wut *thu* HEK| *excl* An interjection signaling surprise, shock, dismay, annoyance, etc. ORIGINS: Euphemism for **What the hell!** Heck is an altered form of and euphemism for **hell**. USAGE ALERT: The euphemism heck in this phrase will soften it somewhat, but it may still be objectionable in some contexts and to some people.

**What the hell!** |wut *thu* HEL| *excl* An interjection signaling surprise, shock, dismay, annoyance, etc. ORIGINS: Figurative use of SE hell meaning "the alternative to heaven; the realm of the devil." USAGE ALERT: The inclusion of **hell** will make this expression objectionable in some contexts and to some people.

**Whoops!**\* |wūps| *excl* An interjection expressing discovery of an error or mistake and, often, an implicit apology.
• Whoopsie! |WŪP sē|

**Yeow! Yow!** |you| *excl* A cry of shock and dismay.

NON-SLANG SYNONYMS: Excuse me! My apologies! Oh dear! Oh my! Sorry! <u>Oh dear! Oh no!</u> **Forgive me! Heavens! I beg your pardon! Oh my goodness!**

# UNDERSTANDING ACHIEVED

These phrases range from letting someone know that you heard their words or received their communication to expressions that suggest sympathetic understanding of the message contained in the communication. For simple affirmation, see the section Expressing Feelings, States, and Attitudes > Agreement and Approval, page 346.

**10-4** *excl* Message received and understood. ORIGINS: From US Police 10-codes.

**IKWYM** I know what you mean.

**OIC** Oh, I see.

**Capiche? Capisce?** |ku PĒSH| *phr* Do you understand? ORIGINS: Adapted from Italian **capisci** meaning "Do you understand?" USAGE INFO: Numerous other spellings are used as well.

**Got it!** |GAHT it| *excl* I understand! ORIGINS: A form of **get** is used here in the sense of "receive and comprehend the message." Compare with **Gotcha!** USAGE INFO: **Got it!** is the usual response to **Got it?** or **Get it?** Sometimes used in the sequence—Person A: **Get it?** Person B: **Got it!** Person A: **Good.**—which originated in the 1956 Danny Kaye film, *The Court Jester*.

**Gotcha!** |GAHCH u| *excl* I understand! ORIGINS: Altered form of "Got you!"—an expected response to **Got me?**

**Savvy!** |SAV ē| *excl* I understand! ORIGINS: From Spanish **sabe usted** meaning "you know"—an expected response to **Savvy?**

**Ten-four!** |TEN FAWR| *excl* Message received and understood. ORIGINS: From US Police 10-codes.

**NON-SLANG SYNONYMS:** I know what you mean. I see. I understand. Now it's clear. That makes sense. Understood.; **I get it. Yes, Sir/Ma'am.**

# VICTORY

**AYBABTU** All your base are belong to us.

**<Proper noun> FTW** <Proper noun> for the win. *See* <PROPER NOUN> FOR THE WIN!

**WISP** Winning is so pleasurable.

**YAO** You are owned.

**All your base are belong to us.** |awl yŏŏr BĀS ar bu lawng tū US| *phr* ORIGINS: From the (poorly done) English translation of the Japanese video game "Zero Wing" (1991).

**Booyah!** |BŪ yah| *excl* An exclamation of great success or victory.

**Epic win!** |EP ik win| *excl* I've just won an extremely impressive victory! USAGE INFO: The opposite is not "epic lose," as one might think, but epic fail.

**<Proper noun> for the win!** |<Proper noun> fawr *thu* WIN| *excl* A self-congratulatory announcement of victory in which the winner fills in his or her own name; an acclamation of the value or attractiveness of *sb/st*, e.g., a brand. ORIGINS: Said by the announcer of the winner in *The Hollywood Squares* game show (1966–1981).

**I own you!** |Ī ŌN yū| *excl* I win: you lose! ORIGINS: From the victory cry uttered by players of first-person shooter games.

**Ta-dah!** |tu DAH| *excl* Pay attention to this remarkable thing/accomplishment! ORIGINS: Imitative of a fanfare, for example, one played when circus performers have achieved a stunt.

**Victory is mine!** |VIK tur ē iz MĪN| *excl* I win! ORIGINS: Popularized as a catchphrase of Stewart Gilligan "Stewie" Griffin on the animated television series *Family Guy* (1999–present), also a video game.

**w00t!** |wūt| *excl* Cry of victory or joy. ORIGINS: Wherever it originally came from, now considered an acronym for "We owned the other team" in role-playing games. *See* I OWN YOU. USAGE INFO: Note spelling with zeroes, rather than *o*'s.

**Wahoo!** |waw hū| *excl* Cry of victory or delight.

**Yay!** |yā| *excl* Cry of victory, success, or delight.

**You are pwnd, pwned, pwnt!** |yū ar PŌND| *excl* You lose! ORIGINS: There are two theories: one, that pwn is a typo for **own**, sometimes attributed specifically to the game Warcraft 3; two, that pwn is a step above **own**.

**You fail it!** |yū fāil it| *excl* I win: you lose! ORIGINS: From the words said to a loser in the English translation of a Japanese arcade game, *Blazing Star* (1968): "You fail it! Your skill is not enough! See you next time! Bye bye!"

**You have been owned!** |yū hav bin ŌND| *excl* I win; you lose! ORIGINS: Passive form of I own you!

**You just got pwned, pwnd!** |yū just got PŌND| *excl* I win; you lose! ORIGINS: Another variant of the I own you! trope.

**NON-SLANG SYNONYMS:** Good game. **Hurrah!** **Hurray!** **I win!**

# Qualities of People and Things

The most and the least appealing—that's what this section is devoted to. Since slang springs up rather than being created in measured doses, you will find that the treatment of things and people is uneven. The treatment of people is extended in the chapter Types of People (page 411) and treatment of things in Types of Things (page 456). The divisions are as follows:

*Excellent People and Things*
1 Wonderful, Excellent, Splendid, Fabulous People and Things
2 Fashionable People and Things
3 Successfully Completed Things
4 Excellent People and Things

*Terrible, Unpleasant, Problematic, Irritating People and Things*
1 Broken Things
2 Disgusting People and Things
3 Disorganized or Messy People and Things
4 Ill-conceived Things
5 Incompetent/Inadequate People and Things
6 Inferior Performance or Quality
7 Risky People or Things
8 Uncared-for People or Things
9 Undistinguished People or Things
10 Unpleasant People or Things
11 Worthless People or Things

*People Facing Difficulties*

# EXCELLENT PEOPLE AND THINGS

## 1 Wonderful, Excellent, Splendid, Fabulous People and Things

**<Proper noun> FTW** <Proper noun> for the win. *See* <PROPER NOUN> FOR THE WIN!

**babelicious** |BĀB u LISH us| *adj* Used of a very beautiful or sexually attractive woman. ORIGINS: From the slang word **babe** plus the slang suffix **-licious** by extension of SE **delicious**. *See* **-LICIOUS**. USAGE ALERT: Apt to be considered an objectification of women by some, and therefore objectionable.

**bodylicious, bodilicious, bodelicious** |bahd i LISH us| *adj* Physically attractive. ORIGINS: From SE **body** and slang -licious; possibly a punning reference to bodacious.

**bootylicious** |bū tē LISH us| *adj* Physically attractive; possessing a shapely rear end. ORIGINS: From slang **booty** meaning "rear end or buttocks" and the slang suffix -licious from SE **delicious**. Originally negative and in contrast to **bodylicious**, it is now used as praise as well. USAGE ALERT: The reference to the rear end or buttocks in this term will make it objectionable in some contexts and to some people. Some people will also find it sexist.

**delish** |di LISH| *adj* Delicious; desirable. ORIGINS: Shortened and altered form of SE delicious.

**dishy** |DISH ē| *adj* Attractive (of a thing); physically attractive (of a person). ORIGINS: Based on the concept that the person or thing is "good enough to eat, like a dish of food."

**dreamy** |DRĒM ē| *adj* So outstandingly attractive that one can hardly believe one is seeing it in real life.

**drooly** |DROO lē| *adj* Desirable; sexy. ORIGINS: From the idea that an observer will drool with desire.

**easy on the eyes** |Ē zē ahn *th*ē ĪZ| *adj* Extremely attractive. USAGE INFO: Usually used in ironic understatement (i.e., litotes) of *sb* with extraordinary good looks.

**<Proper noun> for the win!** |<Proper noun> fawr *th*u WIN| *excl* A self-congratulatory announcement of victory in which the winner fills in his or her own name; an acclamation of the value or attractiveness of *sb/st*, e.g., a brand. ORIGINS: Said by the announcer of the winner in *The Hollywood Squares* game show (1966–1981).

**foxy** |FAHK sē| *adj* Sexy; attractive. ORIGINS: Based on a stereotype of behavior of foxes.

**knockout** |NAHK out| *adj* An outstanding or excellent person or thing; a complete success.

**phat** |fat| *adj* Excellent; attractive; admirable. ORIGINS: Altered spelling of slang fat meaning "excellent."

**scrumptious** |SKRUMP shus| *adj* Delicious; desirable.

**sexy** |SEK sē| *adj* Appealing to consumers, viewers, and other audience members; particularly clever. ORIGINS: Figurative use of SE **sexy** meaning "seductive." USAGE ALERT: Some people may find the application of the word sex to all manner of things outside the usual realm of the word objectionable, based, for example, on the word being more common in conversations, advertising, etc. that children hear.

**yummy** |YUM ē| *adj* Delicious; desirable. ORIGINS: Onomatopoeic word from slang yum, the sound one makes when smacking one's lips.

NON-SLANG SYNONYMS: adorable, attractive, charming, enchanting, fascinating, interesting, inviting, magnetic, seductive, tempting, **stunning**, **alluring**, **captivating**, **enthralling**, **enticing**, **luring**, **tantalizing**

# 2 Fashionable People and Things

**CSA** Cool, sweet, awesome. (Context should help distinguish from Confederate States of America.)

**fancy schmancy** |FAN sē SHMAN sē| *adj* A derisive recognition of *st* high class. ORIGINS: From a characteristic Yiddish speech pattern of showing contempt by using reduplication of a word, replacing the initial letters with *shm* or *schm* in the second instance.

**glam** |glam| *adj* Glamorous. ORIGINS: By shortening of SE **glamorous**.

**happenin', happening** |HAP in in(g)| *adj* Fashionable; chic. ORIGINS: Slang usage of the 1960s. USAGE INFO: Today, often used ironically or self-consciously.

**high-toned** |HĪ tōnd| *adj* Pretentiously elegant.

**hip** |hip| *adj* Fashionable or stylish. Sophisticated.

**in** |in| *adj* Fashionable.

**posh** |pahsh| *adj* Fashionable and elegant.

**sharp** |shahrp| *adj* Fashionably attractive; admirable.

**snazzy** |SNAZ ē| *adj* Fashionable.

**spiffy** |SPIF ē| *adj* Smart; stylish.

**trendy** |TREND ē| *adj* In line with the latest fashions.

**way-in** |WĀ in| *adj* Extremely fashionable. ORIGINS: From slang in and intensifier way used on the model of way-out.

**with it** |WITH it| *adj* Knowing the latest trends.

NON-SLANG SYNONYMS: fashionable, well-dressed; **chic**, **dashing**, **natty**, **sharp**; **classy**, **dapper**

# 3 Successfully Completed Things

**in the bag** |in *thu* BAG| *adj* Guaranteed; made certain. USAGE INFO: Often used in forecasting the results of ventures.

**in the can** |in *thu* KAN| *adj* Finished; completed. ORIGINS: From the jargon of filmmaking, in which a completed roll of film is placed into a canister (can).

**nailed down** |NĀLD doun| *adj* Dealt with successfully; completed. ORIGINS: From SE **nail** meaning "to make secure."

**sewed/sewn up** |SŌD up / SŌN up| *adj* Brought to a satisfactory conclusion; finished; accomplished.

**NON-SLANG SYNONYMS:** completed, concluded, finished, settled, **assured**

See Progress and Decline > Succeed, page 523.

# 4 Excellent People and Things

**<Proper noun> FTW** <Proper noun> for the win. *See* <PROPER NOUN> FOR THE WIN!

**<Proper noun> for the win!** |<Proper noun> fawr *thu* WIN| *excl* A self-congratulatory announcement of victory in which the winner fills in his or her own name; an acclamation of the value or attractiveness of *sb/st*, e.g., a brand. ORIGINS: Said by the announcer of the winner in *The Hollywood Squares* game show (1966–1981).

**G8** Great.

**YGWYPF** You get what you pay for.

**WYGIWYPF** What you get is what you pay for.

**A-list** |Ā list| *adj* A highly-regarded celebrity. ORIGINS: From the celebrity ranking system invented by journalist James Ulmer and known as the Ulmer scale. It uses a 100-point system to rank a star's bankability. The most bankable stars are referred to as A-list.

**ace** |ās| *adj* The best. ORIGINS: From the ace's role as the highest-ranked playing card. Recently popularized through an episode of CollegeHumor's video series *Jake and Amir* entitled "Ace," in which Jake pretends that he made up the words **ace** and **gullies**.

**A-OK, A-okay** |Ā ō KĀ| *adj* Fine; well-done. USAGE INFO: Some definitions say "satisfactory," but that suggests a minimal meeting of requirements, and A-OK is actually superior to simply **OK** or **okay**.

**all that** |awl THAT| *adj* Of the highest quality, sophistication, or hotness possible. ORIGINS: Either All that and a bag of chips is a superlative of all that or all that is a shortened form of the longer phrase. Popularized by the movie *She's All That* (1999) based on *Pygmalion* by George Bernard Shaw, a book *All That and a Bag of*

*Chips* (2002) by Darrien Lee, and a rock band of the same name from Oslo, Norway. USAGE INFO: Used in phrases such as "S/he thinks s/he's all that" to suggest that a person has a false sense of being hot and/or sophisticated.

**awesome** |AW sum| *adj* Outstanding, impressive, excellent. ORIGINS: Used in SE to characterize something that inspires or expresses awe, the word lost its spiritual side and gained popularity following its slang use in popular culture, such as the language of the Teenage Mutant Ninja Turtles, beginning with their debut in 1984, and the movie *Bill & Ted's Excellent Adventure* (1989). USAGE INFO: Because of the juvenile associations with its origins, the slang use of **awesome** may be self-mocking, to show that the user is not immature.

**bad** |bad| *adj* Outstandingly good. ORIGINS: Akin to other words, in both English and other languages, that have taken on opposite meanings, i.e., become contronyms. In this case, the reversal has been traced to the origins of this usage in the Black community, which felt that its standards were at odds with the accepted/establishment value system.

**badass(ed)** |BAD as / BAD ast | *adj* First-rate; admirable. ORIGINS: From slang **ass** meaning "the rear end or buttocks." USAGE INFO: **Badass(ed)** is a contronym. It can also mean "aggressive, tough, and frightening." *See* **-ASS(ED)** for more information about the suffix. Note that both the noun and the adjective form are used as adjectives. USAGE ALERT: The inclusion of **ass** will make this term objectionable in some contexts and to some people.

**bardacious** |bahr DĀ shus| *adj See* BODACIOUS, BODASHES.

**bestest** |BES tist| *adj* A superlative superlative. ORIGINS: This word is constructed of two superlatives: best, the superlative of good, and the superlative ending -est. Since only one superlative element is needed and best is already ultimate, the result is humorous.

**bitching, bitchin, bitchen** |BICH ing / BICH un| *adj* Excellent; wonderful. ORIGINS: From SE bitch, meaning "a female dog." USAGE INFO: Note that forms of **bitch** are used with extremely negative as well as extremely positive meanings. The form **bitching** also means "complaining bitterly." USAGE ALERT: Despite their positive meaning, these forms of **bitch** will be objectionable in some contexts and to some people.

**bodacious, bodashes** |bō DĀ shus| *adj* Impressive. ORIGINS: Created by combining the SE words **bold** and **audacious**. Although its origins lie in the nineteenth century, the portmanteau word was popularized in the movie *Bill and Ted's Excellent Adventure* (1989). USAGE INFO: This word has great variety in its spellings, including bowdacious, and bardacious.

**bomb, the** |thu BAHM| *adj* The best; the most outstanding; the coolest.

**boss** |baws| *adj* Outstanding; excellent; wonderful. ORIGINS: From a meaning of the slang noun boss, "an excellent person," which originates from the Dutch **baas**, meaning "master."

**bowdacious** |bō DĀ shus| *adj See* BODACIOUS, BODASHES.

**bully** |BOŎ lē| *adj* Excellent; first-rate; splendid. ORIGINS: Draws on the earliest slang meaning of **bully** as "a good person or companion." USAGE INFO: Used (most often ironically) in the phrase "bully for you."

**cool** |kūl| *adj* Excellent; fine; first-rate. USAGE INFO: Cool is a contronym, with its early uses being negative, e.g., "emotionless," "cold-blooded." Positive uses emerged later.

**copacetic, copasetic** |kō pu SET ik| *adj* Excellent; first-rate. ORIGINS: Bill "Bojangles" Robinson, a US entertainer in the early twentieth century, claims to have coined the word. Although this hasn't been proven, other etymological claims haven't plausibly refuted it.

**crackerjack, crackajack** |KRAK ur jak, KRAK u jak| *adj* Excellent; first-rate. ORIGINS: Likely from SE **crack** meaning "excelling," as in "a crack shot."

**crazy**[1] |KRĀ zē| *adj* Wonderful; amazing. USAGE INFO: Crazy is a contronym.

**cushy** |KOŎSH ē| *adj* Extremely comfortable. ORIGINS: Often traced to the Hindu **khush**, meaning "pleasant," but its etymology isn't certain.

**da bomb** |du BAHM| *adj* The best; the most outstanding; the coolest.

**def** |def| *adj* Excellent; first-rate. ORIGINS: Possibly short for SE **definite** or alteration of **to death** meaning "excessively."

**ducky** |DUK ē| *adj* Excellent; delightful, charming, darling. ORIGINS: Possibly from the charm of ducklings. USAGE INFO: Often used ironically.

**dynamite** |DĪ nu mīt| *adj* Especially fine; excellent; wonderful. ORIGINS: By extension of SE **dynamite** meaning "a powerful explosive."

**evil** |Ē vul| *adj* Excellent; wonderful. ORIGINS: On the "bad is good" model. *See* BAD. USAGE INFO: Used to express admiration for a trait that is so outstanding as to arouse playful jealousy. Evil is a contronym.

**fab** |fab| *adj* Fabulous; wonderful. ORIGINS: Shortened form of SE **fabulous**. Popularized by The Beatles. USAGE INFO: Sometimes used ironically now.

**fantabulous** |fan TAB yu lus| *adj* Both fantastic and fabulous. ORIGINS: A portmanteau word made from two other words, SE **fantastic** and SE **fabulous**.

**fierce** |firs| *adj* Excellent; wonderful. ORIGINS: From SE **fierce** meaning "filled with vehemence," modified on the "bad is good" model. Repopularized in 2008 by Project Runway winner Christian Siriano, who uses **fierce** as a catchphrase.

**fly** |flī| *adj* Fashionable; stylish.

**frabjous** |FRAB jus| *adj* "Probably a blend of fair, fabulous, and joyous." ORIGINS: Definition from Lewis Carroll (Charles L. Dodgson), who coined this portmanteau word for his poem "Jabberwocky" which appeared in *Through the Looking-Glass, and What Alice Found There* (1871).

**gnarly** |NAHR lē| *adj* Wonderful; excellent. ORIGINS: From SE gnarly meaning "covered with knots or lumps," slang gnarly originally meant "disgusting" but on the "bad is good" model, came to have the opposite meaning. Gnarly was popularized in the film *Fast Times at Ridgemont High* (1982). USAGE INFO: Gnarly is a contronym. It is sometimes used self-mockingly to show that the user knows it is dated, although its continued use is attested, including in the phrase rendered either gnarly, dude, or gnarly dude.

**groovy** |GRŪV ē| *adj* Wonderful; delightful. ORIGINS: Originally from jazz jargon, groovy had an initial spate of popularity in the early to mid-twentieth century, but has re-emerged into popular use again in the twenty-first century.

**hellacious** |hu LĀ shus| *adj* Extremely large or impressive. ORIGINS: From slang **hell** and SE **-acious** (as in **audacious**). Figurative use of SE **hell** meaning "the alternative to heaven; the realm of the devil." USAGE ALERT: This form of **hell** will be objectionable in some contexts and to some people.

**hot** |haht| *adj* Fashionable; interesting; exciting; attractive; popular; successful; skillful; on a lucky streak.

**hunky-dory** |HUNG kē DAWR ē| *adj* Fine; wonderful. ORIGINS: Disputed.

**jake** |jāk| *adj* Very satisfactory; fine.

**jamming** |JAM ing| *adj* Excellent; first-rate. ORIGINS: By extension of slang jam meaning "to have a good time."

**jumping** |JUMP Ing| *adj* Filled with excitement. USAGE INFO: Used of a place, not a person.

**key** |kē| *adj* Excellent; worthy of admiration. ORIGINS: By extension of SE **key** meaning "central; important."

**killer** |KIL ur| *adj* Impressive of its kind; terrific; effective.

**mean** |mēn| *adj* Outstanding; excellent. ORIGINS: From slang mean meaning "in poor quality or condition" but turned around on the "bad is good" model. USAGE INFO: Used to praise skills or talents as in "plays a mean bass."

**neat** |nēt| *adj* Great; terrific.

**nifty** |NIF tē| *adj* Capable; appealing; great; clever. USAGE INFO: Often used of small gadgets and technology.

**nitro** |NĪ trō| *adj* Excellent. ORIGINS: From shortening of chemical name nitroglycerine (used in dynamite).

**not too shabby** |NAHT tū SHA bē| *adj* Extremely excellent, lovely, delightful, etc. USAGE INFO: An example of litotes, ironic understatement used to indicate excess.

**out of sight, outasight, outasite** |out uv SĪT / out u SĪT| *adj* Excellent; outstanding; exceptional. ORIGINS: From SE that *st* is "out of visual range," perhaps extended to mean that *st* is "beyond one's everyday, mundane expectations."

**out of this world** |OUT uv this WURLD| *adj* Extraordinary; too good to be true. ORIGINS: From the idea that something is beyond mundane, everyday expectations.

**peachy(-keen)** |PĒ chē / PĒ chē KĒN| *adj* Wonderful; excellent. ORIGINS: From slang peach meaning *"sb or st* especially fine."

**plush** |plush| *adj* Expensive; luxurious. ORIGINS: From SE **plush**, a soft, luxurious-feeling fabric.

**primo** |PRĒ mō| *adj* The best of its kind; excellent. ORIGINS: From Italian or Spanish **primo** meaning "first."

**rad** |rad| *adj* Excellent; the best. ORIGINS: From shortening of slang **radical**, a term of approval, often used as an exclamation.

**radical** |RAD i kul| *adj* Excellent or wonderful.

**ridiculous** |ri DIK yū lus| *adj* Outstanding; excellent.

**righteous** |RĪ chus| *adj* Wonderful; excellent. ORIGINS: Adaptation of SE **righteous** meaning "upright in the sight of God."

**ripper** |RIP ur| *adj* An excellent one of its type.

**rocking** |RAHK ing| *adj* Outstanding; excellent: exciting.

**sick** |sik| *adj* Excellent; outstanding; good.

**smooth** |smūth| *adj* Superior; well done.

**something else** |SUM thing ELS| *adj* Wonderful; impressive. USAGE INFO: Often as a predicate adjective after a form of *to be,* as in "She's something else!" Can be used for things that impress negatively as well as positively, as in "The smell from the backed up sewer is something else!"

**splendiferous** |splen DIF ur us| *adj* Excellent; outstanding. ORIGINS: From an extension of SE **splendid**.

**spot-on** |spaht ahn| *adj* Perfect; accurate; completely correct. USAGE INFO: Often used with nouns like *interpretation, imitation, parody, performance,* and *copy.*

**stand out** |STAND out| *adj* An outstanding example. ORIGINS: Presumably from the phrasal verb **stand out** meaning "to be distinctive; to be conspicuous."

**super(duper)** |SŪ pur / SŪ pur DŪ pur| *adj* Excellent; wonderful. ORIGINS: From slang **super** with reduplication.

**superfly** |SŪ pur FLĪ| *adj* Excellent; superior. ORIGINS: From slang **super** and slang **fly** meaning "sophisticated."

**swank(y)** |swangk / SWANG kē| *adj* Elegant; sophisticated; classy. ORIGINS: From slang verb **swank**, originally meaning "to swagger."

**sweet** |swēt| *adj* Excellent; superb. USAGE INFO: Often used as an exclamation of approval: Sweet!

**too much** |TŪ MUCH| *adj* Excellent; unbelievably good.

**topnotch** |TAHP NAHCH| *adj* Excellent; highest-rated.

**tops** |tahps| *adj* Excellent.

**unreal** |un RĒL| *adj* Unbelievably excellent, impressive, etc.

**way good** |WĀ good| *adj* Extremely good. ORIGINS: From using SE way as an intensifier on the model of way-out.

**way-out** |wā OUT| *adj* Exceptional. ORIGINS: Used in jazz contexts.

**wicked** |WIK id| *a/a* Very; extremely. ORIGINS: From SE wicked. USAGE INFO: Used as an adjective ("a wicked headache") or as an adverb ("a wicked good show").

NON-SLANG SYNONYMS: amazing, astonishing, astounding, awe-inspiring, beautiful, breathtaking, brilliant, excellent, fabulous, fantastic, first-class, glorious, incredible, magnificent, marvelous, phenomenal, remarkable, sensational, spectacular, splendid, superb, terrific, unbelievable, wonderful, **resplendent**, **sumptuous**, **unparalleled**, **unsurpassed**, **wondrous**

# TERRIBLE, UNPLEASANT, PROBLEMATIC, IRRITATING PEOPLE AND THINGS

## 1 Broken Things

**acting up** |AK ting up| *adj* Causing trouble; malfunctioning. USAGE INFO: Used of *sb/st* who or that can or has in the past acted appropriately/functioned well.

**borked** |bawrkt| *adj* Broken; not functioning. ORIGINS: From the rejection of the nomination of Robert Heron Bork to the Supreme Court by the US Senate in 1987. Originally it meant "to savagely attack in order to prevent appointment to public office," but its use has broadened. Its use for **broken** may be particularly attractive because of the letters in common. USAGE INFO: Because this slang is only thirty years old, it may not be universally understood; nevertheless, it is widely used by people who have no idea of the connection to Robert Bork.

**bum** |bum| *adj* Malfunctioning; out-of-order; broken. ORIGINS: Possibly by analogy with slang **bum** meaning "vagrant or tramp" as someone who is not functioning within the standard expectations of society.

**bust(ed)**[2] |bust / BUS tid| *adj* Broken; rendered non-functional. ORIGINS: Equivalent to SE **broken**. Notice the analogous relationship of slang busted and informal **broke**, synonyms for "having no money." In each case, the form of *bust* is the more slangy word.

**conked out** |kahngk'd OUT| *adj* Non-functioning; out-of-order. ORIGINS: The result of slang verb **conk out**.

**done for**[1] |DUN fawr| *adj* Dead. USAGE INFO: Meaning may be literal or figurative.

**kaput, kaputt** |ku POOT| *adj* Incapacitated: broken; non-functioning; out-of-order. ORIGINS: From German **kaputt** and French **être capot**, both of which are names for the situation of a player in the card game piquet who has not won any tricks.

**on the blink** |ahn *thu* BLINGK| *adj* Not functioning properly; out-of-order. ORIGINS: **Blink** is from blinking lights used to signal malfunction.

**on the fritz** |ahn *thu* FRITS| *adj* Not functioning properly; out-of-order. ORIGINS: The origin of **fritz** is not known.

**on the rocks** |ahn *thu* RAHKS| *adj* Likely to fail on account of serious problems; in trouble. ORIGINS: From the experience of a ship running aground and breaking up. USAGE INFO: Also means "on ice," with rocks referring to ice cubes.

**out of whack** |out uv WAK| *adj* Out of order; unbalanced; not functioning properly. ORIGINS: From SE **whack** meaning condition or state. USAGE INFO: *See* IN WHACK.

**NON-SLANG SYNONYMS:** broken, cracked, crushed, damaged, demolished, fractured, in pieces, mutilated, shattered, shredded, split, **mangled**, **smashed**, **defective**, **disintegrated**, **fragmented**, **riven**

## 2 Disgusting People and Things

**cruddy** |KRUD ē| *adj* Dirt-encrusted; worthless; disgusting; inferior. ORIGINS: From slang **crud**, meaning "a coating of filth." USAGE INFO: Because the filth referred to by **cruddy** is not explicitly excrement, it can be substituted for **shitty**, **crappy**, etc. and be considered less objectionable.

**fugly** |FUG lē| *adj* Extraordinarily ugly. ORIGINS: Portmanteau of **fucking** and SE ugly.

**gross** |grōs| *adj* Disgusting; repulsive. ORIGINS: From the slang adjective **gross** meaning "disgusting" which draws on the SE noun **gross** meaning "large."

**icky** |IK ē| *adj* Disgusting; unpleasant; distasteful. USAGE INFO: Can be applied to a semi-solid (gooey) substance, one's health, or something embarrassing.

**ooky** |Ū kē| *adj* Awful: can be applied to a semi-solid (gooey) substance, one's health, or something embarrassing. ORIGINS: From onomatopoeic slang **ook**, a sound signaling disgust.

**putrid** |PŪ trid| *adj* A multi-purpose negative adjective: disgusting; loathsome; awful; repugnant; foul; etc. ORIGINS: From SE **putrid** meaning "the smell of decomposing flesh."

**raunchy** |RAWN chē| *adj* Extremely dirty and uncared for; obscene.

**scummy** |SKUM ē| *adj* Utterly contemptible or disgusting.

**scuzzy** |SKUZ ē | *n* Dirty; disreputable.

**skanky, scanky** |SKANK ē| *adj* Disgustingly filthy. ORIGINS: From slang skank meaning "filth; a prostitute." USAGE ALERT: Also used to mean "sexually promiscuous." Usually used with intent to denigrate or insult and understood as such.

**stinky** |stingk ē | *adj* Of poor quality; extremely bad or unpleasant. ORIGINS: Figurative use of SE **stink**.

**sucky** |SUK ē| *adj* Awful, unpleasant; causing difficulty. ORIGINS: Apparently another example in which a form of suck is *not* related to **cocksucker**. USAGE ALERT: Anyone who does connect this word to **cocksucker** may find it objectionable.

**yucky, yukky** |YUK ē| *adj* Repugnant or disgusting.

See Expressing Feelings, States, and Attitudes > Disgust, page 366.

NON-SLANG SYNONYMS: disgusting, horrid, repulsive, revolting, **detestable**, **distasteful**, **ghastly**, **gruesome**, **loathsome**, **noisome**, **odious**, **offensive**, **repellent**, **repugnant**, **vile**

# 3 Disorganized or Messy People and Things

**FUBAR** |FŪ bahr| *adj* Utterly botched or confused. ORIGINS: Acronym for the phrase f(ucked) u(p) b(eyond) a(ll) r(ecognition), used by the US military. The term is sometimes further euphemized by substituting fouled for **fucked**. Different than foobar, a word used as a placeholder in computer programming. USAGE ALERT: People who recognize that the acronym comes from a phrase that includes the word **fucked** may find it objectionable.

**MUBAR** |MŪ bahr| Messed up beyond all recognition.

**ass backward(s)** |AS BAK wurd / AS BAK wurdz| *adj* Chaotic; in a mess. ORIGINS: From SE **ass** meaning "a donkey," but commonly used as slang to refer to the rear end or buttocks. Thus **assbackward(s)** means "back-to-front," but has the extended figurative meaning of "confused." USAGE ALERT: All words containing **ass** will be found objectionable in some contexts and by some people.

**bassackwards, bass-ackwards** |BAS ak wurdz| *adj* Chaotic; in a mess. ORIGINS: A euphemistic Spoonerism (reversing the initial letters of two major words) of the phrase **assbackwards**, to playfully make meaning in the way that concrete poetry does: by demonstrating its meaning graphically, with the confused letter order paralleling the confused state of affairs it denotes. Developed from slang **ass** meaning "the rear end or buttocks." USAGE ALERT: The use of the word **ass** will make this term objectionable in some contexts and to some people.

**balled-up** |BAWLD up| *adj* Confused; in a mess. ORIGINS: From slang **balls**, euphemism for SE testicles. Entered the language after the verb form **ball up** and before the noun form **balls-up**. USAGE ALERT: The inclusion of **balled** in this phrase will make it objectionable in some contexts and to some people. **Fucked up** will be found more objectionable, messed up less so.

**confuddled** |kun FUD uld| *adj* Extremely confused. ORIGINS: A portmanteau word, from combining confused with either befuddled or muddled. USAGE INFO: Used of people.

**confussed** |kun FUST| *adj* Confused and upset. ORIGINS: A portmanteau word, from combining confused and **fussed** meaning "upset." USAGE INFO: Used of people.

**discombobulated** |dis kum BAHB yū lāt id| *adj* Confused; upset; in disarray. ORIGINS: Possibly by alteration of discompose. USAGE INFO: Used of people and things.

**flummoxed** |FLUM ikst| *adj* Confused or perplexed. USAGE INFO: Used of people.

**fouled up** |FOULD up| *adj* In a mess; chaotic. ORIGINS: Euphemism for **fucked up**. From US military use. *See* **FUBAR** and **SNAFU**. USAGE ALERT: People who suspect euphemistic use may find this objectionable based on the phrase that hasn't been used.

**fucked up** |FUKT up| *adj* Messed up; botched; damaged; incapacitated. ORIGINS: From slang **fuck** meaning "to engage in sexual intercourse." USAGE ALERT: This term with **fucked** will be objectionable in some contexts and to some people.

**futzed up** |FUTST up| *adj* Spoiled; confused. ORIGINS: Euphemism for **fucked up**. From German futz meaning "fart." USAGE ALERT: Euphemisms may still be objectionable in some contexts and to some people.

**galley-west, gally-west** |gal ē WEST| *adj* Confused; scattered. ORIGINS: Considered to likely be from an alteration of Colleyweston, a village in England. USAGE INFO: Often used in the phrases "go galley-west"; "knock galley-west."

**gummed up** |GUMD up| *adj* Messed up; stuck; confused; ruined. ORIGINS: Related to SE chewing gum.

**hairy** |HER ē| *adj* Difficult; hazardous; concerning; scary. USAGE INFO: Carries the implication of st messy or complicated that is not easy to get a handle on.

**helter-skelter** |HEL tur skel tur| *adj* Carelessly scattered; disorderly; haphazard. ORIGINS: From onomatopoeic beginnings, this word gained popularity through The Beatles song "Helter-Skelter" (1968) and murderer Charles Manson's use of the term in 1969 for what he believed to be an impending apocalypse.

**higgledy-piggledy** |HIG ul dē PIG ul dē| *adj* Disordered; jumbled. ORIGINS: Used by US author Nathaniel Hawthorne to describe pigs in his *American Notebooks* (1838): "Pigs, on a march, do not subject themselves to any leader among themselves, but pass on, higgledy-piggledy, without regard to age or sex."

**knocked for a loop** |NAHKT fawr u LŪP| *adj* Surprised and disconcerted. USAGE INFO: Used of people.

**messed up** |MES Tup| *adj* Damaged or ruined: broken; thrown into disarray; beaten up; intoxicated or high; etc.

**sloppy** |SLAHP ē| *adj* Messy; imprecise; untidy. ORIGINS: From SE slop meaning "to spill."

**thrown for a loop** |THRŌN fawr u LŪP| *adj* Surprised and disconcerted. USAGE INFO: Used of people.

NON-SLANG SYNONYMS—DISORGANIZED OR MESSY PEOPLE: confused, disorganized, untidy, **addled**, **befuddled**, **messy**, **muddled**, **a sight**

NON-SLANG SYNONYMS—DISORGANIZED OR MESSY THINGS: chaotic, disordered, disorganized, untidy, **in a mess**, **jumbled**, **messy**, **muddled**, **snarled**, **topsy-turvy**, **anarchic**, **disarranged**, **disorderly**, **in disarray**

# 4 Ill-conceived Things

**birdbrained** |BURD brānd| *adj* Ridiculous or preposterous. USAGE INFO: Often used of an idea that is absurd. USAGE ALERT: Often used with intent to denigrate or insult and understood as such.

**cockeyed** |KAHK īd| *adj* Mildly crazy; outlandish; ludicrous; absurd. ORIGINS: By extension from SE **cock**, meaning "to bend" and SE **eye**, meaning the eyes aren't level and focused. USAGE ALERT: Usually used with intent to denigrate or insult and understood as such. This way of speaking about *sb's* mental health may be considered insensitive and therefore objectionable in some contexts and by some people.

**crackpot** |KRAK paht| *adj* Crazy or eccentric; outlandish; absurd; harebrained; foolish; unworkable. ORIGINS: By extension from SE **crack**, meaning "to break" and **pot** meaning "skull," i.e., the kind of suggestions one would expect from someone whose brains were not functioning properly. USAGE INFO: Often used of ideas, as well as of people. USAGE ALERT: When used of people, will usually be used with intent to denigrate or insult and understood as such. This way of speaking about *sb's* mental health may be considered insensitive and therefore objectionable in some contexts and by some people.

**crazy**[2] |KRĀ zē| *adj* Outlandish; weird; bizarre. USAGE INFO: Crazy is a contronym.

**dopey** |DŌP ē| *adj* Silly; stupid. USAGE INFO: Often of an idea.

**half-baked** |HAF bākt| *adj* Incompletely thought out; ill-conceived. ORIGINS: By analogy to an incompletely cooked item or meal. USAGE INFO: Usually used of an idea, plan, or scheme, but can be applied to a person, in which case it means "having poor judgment; lacking common sense."

**jerky** |JURK ē| *adj* Foolish; idiotic. ORIGINS: From slang jerk meaning "fool." It's not clear that it's tied to other meanings. USAGE ALERT: Some people may connect this word to **jerk-off**, although they do not seem to be etymologically linked.

NON-SLANG SYNONYMS: feeble-minded, ill-conceived, impractical, not well thought out, poorly planned, senseless, short-sighted, **brainless**, **flaky**, **hare-brained**, **insane**, **kooky**, **lunatic**, **eccentric**, **underdeveloped**

Many, but not all, of these words are also applied to foolish people.

## 5 Incompetent/Inadequate People and Things

**bush league** |BŎŎSH lēg| *adj* Amateurish attempt; failure. ORIGINS: From baseball jargon meaning literally, "minor league"; figuratively, "unprofessional."

**D-list** |DĒ list| *adj* A very minor celebrity. ORIGINS: From the celebrity ranking system invented by journalist James Ulmer and known as the Ulmer scale. It considers 100 points in order to rank a star's bankability. The most bankable stars are referred to as A-list. The phrase has been popularized in the twenty-first century by stand-up comedian Kathy Griffin, who has not only proclaimed herself to be on the **D-list**, but also hosts a television series, *My Life on the D-List*. USAGE ALERT: Usually used with intent to denigrate or insult and understood as such.

**half-ass(ed)** |HAF ass / HAF ast| *adj* Incompetent; poorly executed. ORIGINS: From slang **ass** meaning "the rear end or buttocks." *See* **-ASS(ED)** for more information about the suffix. Presumably the standard for competent and well-done is "whole-assed." USAGE INFO: Note that both the noun and the adjective form are used as adjectives: "half-ass approach"; "half-assed job." USAGE ALERT: The inclusion of **ass** will make this term objectionable in some contexts and to some people.

**not making the grade** |naht MĀK ing *thu* GRĀD| *adj* Failing when measured by a set standard.

**not up to scratch** |NAHT up tū SKRACH| *adj* Inadequate; failing to meet requirements or standards; of less than required quality. ORIGINS: Figurative use of sports jargon from races in which **scratch** means "the line or marking indicating the starting line." USAGE INFO: *See* **UP TO SCRATCH.**

**not up to snuff** |NAHT up tū SNUF| *adj* Inadequate; failing to meet requirements or standards; of less than required quality. ORIGINS: Either from the quality requirements for tobacco to be used as snuff or from the stimulating effects of snuff usage. USAGE INFO: Used in constructions like, "He's been practicing, but his performance is not yet up to snuff." *See* **UP TO SNUFF.**

**of sorts** |uv SAWRTS| *adj* Of a very poor sort; a poor example of. USAGE INFO: Used after a noun or noun phrase to undercut it. For example, "Yes, my uncle gave me a computer . . . of sorts" means that the computer was either very old, very inadequate, or was in fact an abacus.

NON-SLANG SYNONYMS: below par, incompetent, low-grade, mediocre, second-class, **bottom-rung**, **second-rate**, **second-string**, **amateurish**, **inadequate**, **second-fiddle**, **substandard**

# 6 Inferior Performance or Quality

**b.s., bs** |BĒ ES| *n* Lies; words or actions meant to be deceptive. ORIGINS: An abbreviation of **bullshit**; from the SE name of male cattle (**bull**) and the slang word for their dung (**shit**). USAGE INFO: Spelled both with and without periods. USAGE ALERT: Despite the attempt to soften by abbreviation, the graphic reference referred to by this phrase makes it objectionable in some contexts and to some people.

**bullshit** |BŎOL shit| *adj* Inferior; worthless; rubbishy. ORIGINS: From SE **bull** (the animal) and slang **shit**, i.e., bull excrement which could be described as "worthless and having a stench"—applied figuratively to things of poor quality. USAGE ALERT: The reference to excrement will make this term objectionable in some contexts and to some people.

**cheapo** |CHĒ pō| *n* A mean or stingy person. ORIGINS: From SE **cheap**. USAGE ALERT: May be used jocularly or as an insult.

**cheesy, cheezy** |CHĒ zē| *adj* Of poor quality; shoddy; cheap and nasty; corny. ORIGINS: Extending the literal meaning of "smelly cheese" to cover things that are figuratively stinky, because of poor quality.

**chintzy** |CHINT sē| *adj* Of poor quality; shoddy; second-rate; inferior. ORIGINS: From the SE **chintz**, a fabric that was commonly used in the nineteenth century and widely disparaged.

**crappy** |KRAP ē| *adj* Inferior; worthless; miserable; contemptible. ORIGINS: Euphemism for **shitty**. From **crap**, a euphemism for **shit**. USAGE ALERT: This term will be objectionable in some situations and to some people.

**crummy, crumby** |KRUM ē| *adj* Shabby; miserable; lousy; inferior. ORIGINS: extension of the original meaning: "louse-infested."

**lame** |lām| *adj* Inadequate; worthless; incompetent; lacking substance. ORIGINS: By extension from SE **lame** meaning "disabled."

**lousy** |LOU zē| *adj* Awful; contemptible; inferior; worthless. ORIGINS: From SE **louse**, referring to the insect.

**no great shakes** |NŌ grāt shāks| *adj* Inadequate; inconsequential.

**piss-poor**[2] |PIS pŏor| *adj* Of unbelievably poor quality; contemptible. ORIGINS: From slang **piss** meaning "urine," used here as an intensifier. USAGE ALERT: The inclusion of the word **piss** in the phrase will render it objectionable in some contexts and to some people.

**ramshackle** |RAM shak ul| *adj* Shoddy; poorly-made; worn out and falling apart. ORIGINS: A back-formation from the rare SE **ransackled** meaning "to ransack." USAGE INFO: Usually used of structures, most often buildings, as in "a ramshackle old shack," but also of other structures, as in "a ramshackle plot" or "ramshackle government."

**ropy, ropey** |RŌP ē| *adj* Inferior; poor; lousy; second-rate.

**schlocky** |SHLAHK ē| *adj* Cheap; inferior; in poor taste. ORIGINS: From Yiddish schlock.

**shitty** |SHIT ē| *adj* Inferior; despicable; unpleasant; unkind. ORIGINS: Extended from **shit** meaning "excrement." USAGE INFO: Can be applied to a thing or a person. USAGE ALERT: Because it is a form of **shit**, this word will be objectionable in some contexts and to some people.

**stinko** |STING kō| *adj* Of poor quality.

**two-bit** |TŪ bit| *adj* An inferior item or trivial sum; insignificant.

**wack** |wak| *adj* Of poor quality; inferior.

NON-SLANG SYNONYMS: poor quality, poor showing, **nothing to brag about**, **nothing to write home about**, **inferior**, **paltry**, **wretched**

## 7 Risky People or Things

**dodgy** |DAHJ ē| *adj* Unreliable; risky; arousing suspicion.

**hinky** |HIN kē| *adj* Unusual, weird, or suspicious. ORIGINS: From law enforcement jargon, popularized by its use on television police procedurals *NCIS* and *CSI Miami*.

NON-SLANG SYNONYMS: delicate, hazardous, risky, uncertain, **chancy**, **dicey**, **iffy**, **fraught with danger**, **perilous**, **precarious**, **speculative**, **treacherous**

## 8 Uncared-for People or Things

**flea-bitten** |FLĒ bit un| *adj* Worn; seedy; dilapidated. ORIGINS: By extension of imagining the kind of place that would have a flea infestation.

**grungy** |GRUN gē| *adj* In poor or dirty, uncared for condition; seedy. ORIGINS: A portmanteau word from SE **grubby** meaning "dirty" and SE **dingy** meaning "darkened with dirt."

**mangy** |MĀN jē| *adj* Filthy; rundown; squalid. ORIGINS: From SE **mange** meaning "a severe, chronic skin disease that causes lesions and hair loss."

**raggedy-ass(ed)** |RA gi dē as / RA gi dē ast| *adj* Over-used; worn-out; pathetic; worthless. ORIGINS: From SE ragged and the slang suffix **-ass(ed)** meaning "a person," extended from slang **ass** meaning "the rear end or buttocks." USAGE INFO: Can be used of both things and people. USAGE ALERT: Usually used with intent to denigrate or insult and understood as such. The inclusion of the word **ass** in the phrase will render it objectionable in some contexts and to some people.

**ratty** |RAT ē| *adj* Run-down; dilapidated; used; worn. ORIGINS: From negative associations with the behavior of rats.

**scruffy** |SCRUF ē| *adj* Uncared for; untidy.

**shabby** |SHA bē| *adj* Worn; badly cared for; dilapidated. USAGE INFO: Used in the negative and with litotes (i.e., ironic understatement) of something outstanding or fabulous, as in, "that party wasn't too shabby."

**slobby** |SLAHB ē| *adj* Having the characteristics of a slob: untidy, lazy, poorly groomed, crude, and/or obnoxious.

**tatty** |TAT ē| *adj* Worn; dilapidated; shabby; tattered.

NON-SLANG SYNONYMS: frayed, mean, miserable, neglected, pitiful, poor, worn-out, **dingy**, **dog-eared**, **gone to seed**, **gone to the dogs**, **moth-eaten**, **ragged**, **rickety**, **run-down**, **seedy**, **bedraggled**, **decrepit**, **desolate**, **dilapidated**, **poverty-stricken**, **squalid**, **uncared for**

# 9 Undistinguished People or Things

**beige** |bāzh| *adj* Bland; uninteresting; boring. ORIGINS: From the perceived insipidity of the color beige.

**blah** |blah| *adj* Without interest; boring. ORIGINS: Onomatopoeic sound of chatter; meaningless, uninteresting talk.

**plain vanilla** |PLĀN vu NIL lu| *adj* Without adornment or extra trimmings: uninteresting; bland.

**vanilla** |vu NIL lu| *adj* Without adornment or extra trimmings: uninteresting; bland.

**white bread** |WĪT bred| *adj* Boring; holding no interest.

NON-SLANG SYNONYMS: boring, dull, everyday, nothing special, plain, routine, usual, **run-of-the-mill**, **so-so**, **bland**, **characterless**, **indifferent**, **pedestrian**, **prosaic**, **undistinguished**, **unexceptional**, **uninspired**, **unremarkable**

# 10 Unpleasant People or Things

**beastly** |BĒST lē| *adj* Awful or extremely unpleasant.

**hellish** |HEL ish| *adj* Awful; reminiscent of hell; horrific. ORIGINS: By extension of descriptions of SE **hell**, "the alternative to heaven; the realm of the devil." USAGE ALERT: Because this word is a form of **hell**, it will be objectionable in some contexts and to some people.

NON-SLANG SYNONYMS: extremely unpleasant, hideous, horrendous, troublesome, unlikable, unpleasant, **dreadful**, **disagreeable**, **harrowing**, **horrific**, **irksome**, **objectionable**, **terribly unpleasant**, **undesirable**

**poopy** |PŪP ē| *adj* Unpleasant; irritating; disagreeable. ORIGINS: Figurative extension of slang **poopy**, a childish word for excrement, which may be onomatopoeic from the sound of defecation or passing wind. USAGE ALERT: The reference to excrement inherent in this word will render it objectionable in some contexts and to some people.

**sucky** |SUK ē| *adj* Awful, unpleasant; causing difficulty. ORIGINS: Apparently another example in which a form of **suck** is *not* related to **cocksucker**. USAGE ALERT: Anyone who does connect this word to **cocksucker** may find it objectionable.

# 11 Worthless People or Things

**<Proper noun> FTL** <Proper noun> for the loss.

**<Proper noun> for the loss!** |<Proper noun> fawr *thu* LOSS| *excl* An alternative cry of victory by naming the other person as the loser; an acclamation of the poor quality of an item. ORIGINS: From computer games. The idea is that choosing/using this item will result in a figurative loss to you. Altered from <Proper noun> for the win!

**WOTAM** Waste of time and money.

**dead** |ded| *adj* Finished; through; over; lost. ORIGINS: By extension from SE **dead**, used of something that was alive.

**dogass(ed)** |DAWG as / DAWG ast| *adj* Worthless; inferior. ORIGINS: The item so described is being compared to a dog's rear end or buttocks, where waste is excreted. From slang **ass** meaning "the rear end or buttocks." *See* **-ASS(ED)** for more information about the suffix. USAGE INFO: Note that both the noun and the adjective form are used as adjectives. USAGE ALERT: The reference to **ass** will make this expression objectionable in some contexts and to some people.

**for the birds** |fawr *thu* BURDZ| *adj* Worthless; absurd; unacceptable. ORIGINS: Conveys the idea of something not appropriate for humans, but possibly acceptable to lesser beings.

**junky** |JUNG kē| *adj* Fitting the category of junk; suitable for discarding; inferior; of poor quality. ORIGINS: From slang **junk** meaning "inferior."

**losingest** |LŪ zing ist| *adj* Less successful or losing more often than any others of its kind.

**Mickey Mouse** |MI kē mous| *adj* Use of *st* that fails to meet standards by a long shot: unimportant, unchallenging; poorly made or designed; silly or trivial. ORIGINS: From Walt Disney's cartoon character Mickey Mouse (1928–).

**no-account** |NŌ u kount| *adj* Worthless; undependable. ORIGINS: From SE **of no account** perhaps meaning "having no history to support a claim to respect, therefore, not worthy."

**piddling** |PID ling| *adj* Worthless; insignificant. ORIGINS: From SE piddle meaning "to be busy with trifles."

**washed up** |WAWSHT up| *adj* Ruined; finished.

**NON-SLANG SYNONYMS:** pointless, useless, worthless, <u>good-for-nothing</u>, <u>no-good</u>, <u>trivial</u>, <u>unessential</u>, <u>unimportant</u>, <u>unusable</u>, <u>valueless</u>, **futile**, **ineffective**, **meaningless**

# PEOPLE FACING DIFFICULTIES

**SOL** Shit out [of] luck.

**UCWAP** Up [a] creek without a paddle.

**behind the eight ball, behind the eightball** |bē HĪND the Ā l bawl| *phr* In trouble; in unfavorable or uncomfortable circumstances. ORIGINS: From a variation of Kelly Pool, in which players are assigned balls by number and those with a number higher than (i.e., "behind") the eight ball, have greatly reduced chances of winning the game.

**down for the count** |doun fawr thu KOUNT| *phr* A hair's breadth from complete failure. ORIGINS: From boxing jargon for the situation in which a boxer who is knocked down has till the end of the count to get up and return to the fight; otherwise the contestant left standing is declared the winner.

**fucked up** |FUKT up| *phr* Messed up; botched; damaged; incapacitated. ORIGINS: From slang **fuck** meaning "to engage in sexual intercourse." USAGE ALERT: This term with **fucked** will be objectionable in some contexts and to some people.

**having one's ass in a sling** |hav ing wunz AS in u sling| *phr* To be in an awkward position and/or in trouble. ORIGINS: From slang **ass** meaning "the rear end or buttocks." USAGE ALERT: The inclusion of **ass** will make this term objectionable in some contexts and to some people.

**having one's work cut out for one** |hav ing wunz wurk kut OUT fawr wun| *phr* To have a challenging job ahead; to have as much as one can handle to do.

**in a hole** |in u HŌL| *phr* In a difficult situation; in debt. USAGE INFO: The same idea is expressed by the phrase in the hole.

**in a pickle** |in u PIK ul| *phr* In a mess; in a difficult situation. ORIGINS: From slang pickle meaning "a predicament."

**in a tight corner/spot** |in u TĪT KAWR nur / in u TĪT SPAHT| *phr* In a very difficult situation; facing a set of circumstances that will prove complicated to deal with. ORIGINS: From slang tight meaning "a tough, difficult to deal with situation."

**in (deep) doo-doo** |in DŪ dū / in DĒP dū dū| *phr* In serious trouble. ORIGINS: Euphemism for **in deep shit**. **Doo-doo** is a childish euphemism for slang

**shit** meaning "excrement." USAGE INFO: Because **doo-doo** is juvenile language, the phrase is often used self-mockingly. USAGE ALERT: The reference to excrement will make the phrase objectionable in some contexts and to some people.

**in deep shit** |in DĒP SHIT| *phr* In a serious situation. ORIGINS: From slang **shit** meaning "excrement." USAGE ALERT: The reference to excrement will make the phrase objectionable in some contexts and to some people.

**in the soup** |in thu SŪP| *phr* In trouble.

**on the ropes** |ahn thu RŌPS| *phr* On the verge of being defeated. ORIGINS: From the situation in boxing in which one of the fighters is held against the ropes and pummelled.

**screwed up** |SKRŪ dup| *phr* In serious trouble of one sort or another. ORIGINS: Euphemism for **fucked-up**. From slang **screw**, a euphemism for **fuck**. USAGE ALERT: The euphemism **screw** in this phrase will soften it somewhat, but it may still be objectionable in some contexts and to some people.

**shit out of luck** |SHIT out uv LUK| *phr* Without hope. ORIGINS: From SE **out of luck** and slang **shit**, meaning "excrement," used here as a modifier to intensify the meaning. USAGE ALERT: The inclusion of the word **shit** will render this phrase objectionable in some contexts and to some people.

**up a creek*** |up u KRĒK| *phr* In serious trouble; facing unpleasant problems. ORIGINS: Euphemism for **up shit creek**.
• up a creek without a paddle |up u KRĒK with out u PAD ul|

**up against it** |UP u GENST it| *phr* In trouble; facing serious problems.

**up shit creek*** |up SHIT krēk| *phr* In serious trouble; facing unpleasant problems. ORIGINS: From SE **up** and slang **shit** meaning "excrement." USAGE ALERT: The inclusion of the word **shit** in the phrase will render it objectionable in some contexts and to some people.
• **up shit creek without a paddle** |up SHIT KRĒK with out u PAD ul|

**without a chance/hope in hell** |with OUT u CHANTS in HEL / with OUT u HŌP in HEL| *phr* Having no chance at all. ORIGINS: The concept is of hell as a place where there is no opportunity of any kind. Figurative use of SE **hell** meaning "the alternative to heaven; the realm of the devil." USAGE ALERT: The inclusion of **hell** will make this expression objectionable in some contexts and to some people.

**without a prayer** |with OUT u PRER| *phr* Having no chance at all. ORIGINS: Suggests that even praying cannot aid in such a situation.

NON-SLANG SYNONYMS: facing a mountain of work, facing an uphill battle/struggle, in difficulties, in trouble, **back to the wall**, **up against it**, **having a Herculean task to perform** (Hercules, also Herakles, is a hero from Greek and Roman mythology, the son of Zeus and Alcmene known for the 12 labors he performed, and repopularized by several television series and mini-series, most recently in 2005, as well as an animated Disney movie in 1997.), **in a predicament**, **in dire straits**

# Types of People

This chapter reviews names for types of people with stand-out traits that are used to characterize them, often negatively. The divisions are as follows:

| | |
|---|---|
| Ambitious | Indecisive and/or Weak |
| Annoying | Inept |
| Aspiring | Influential Through Flattery |
| Attractive | Influential Through Manipulation |
| Complaining | Insignificant or Expendable |
| Contemptible | Intelligent |
| Cowardly | Know-it-All |
| Crude | Lazy |
| Determined | Nasty |
| Enthusiastic | Repulsive |
| Expert | Risk-Taking |
| Expert, but Socially Awkward | Snoopy or Meddlesome |
| Foolish | Stingy or Greedy |
| Generous | Stupid |
| Gullible | Stupid and Clumsy or Socially Inept |
| Helpful | Stupid and Obnoxious |
| Important | Too Talkative |
| Incompetent and Foolish | |

# AMBITIOUS

**ball of fire\*** |BAWL uv FĪR| *n* A person possessed of great energy and drive. USAGE INFO: Notice that the phrase can be formed with the main words in either order. • fireball |FĪR bawl|

**cage rattler** |KĀJ rat lur| *n* A person who stubbornly does something that causes annoyance to others (usually in the process of trying to achieve a higher end). ORIGINS: From imagining a caged animal in a zoo banging into the cage bars while seeking a change in conditions. USAGE INFO: This phrase is a synonym of boat rocker, i.e., someone who figuratively rocks the boat for others while seeking a change in the status quo.

**climber** |KLĪM ur| *n* A person who aspires to be accepted by the upper class. ORIGINS: From the conception of social classes as a hierarchy or ladder. USAGE INFO: Sometimes used in the phrase "a social climber."

**dynamo** |DĪ nu mō| *n* An energetic and aggressive person. ORIGINS: By extension of SE **dynamo** meaning "a power generator."

**eager beaver** |Ē gur BĒ vur| *n* An earnest and hard-working person; an especially industrious person. ORIGINS: From the conventional concept of the SE **beaver** as industrious.

**energizer bunny** |EN ur gī zur BUN ē| *n* Extremely determined, persistent, and industrious. ORIGINS: From the brand symbol of Energizer Batteries, a bunny that "Keeps Going and Going and . . .®" no matter what.

**go-getter** |GO get ur / GO GET ur| *n* An ambitious or enterprising person. ORIGINS: One who "goes and gets" what s/he desires.

**live wire** |LĪV WĪR| *n* A lively, energetic person; a vivacious person. ORIGINS: From slang **live** meaning "alert" and SE **wire**.

**spark plug** |SPAHRK plug| *n* An energetic person who facilitates change by setting events in motion.

NON-SLANG SYNONYMS: bundle of energy, doer, hard worker, mover, **cheater**, **mover and shaker**, **achiever**

# ANNOYING

**PITA** Pain in the ass.

**blister** |BLIS tur| *n* A person who causes ongoing pain and annoyance. ORIGINS: Possibly by analogy to, say, the aggravation of walking with a blister on one's heel. USAGE ALERT: Usually used with intent to denigrate or insult and understood as such.

**fart** |fahrt| *n* An annoying or unpleasant person, usually older than the speaker, thus synonymous with **old fart**. ORIGINS: From slang **fart** meaning "to break wind." USAGE ALERT: This word will be objectionable in some contexts and to some people. In addition, it is usually used with intent to insult, and understood as such.

**headache** |HED āk| *n* A serious or annoying problem or person. ORIGINS: Something capable of giving one a headache.

**nudge, noodge, nudzh** |nŏŏj| *n* A person who is a pest; a persistently annoying person; an irritating person; a nag. ORIGINS: From Yiddish **nudyen** meaning "to pester or bore." USAGE ALERT: Usually used with intent to denigrate or insult and understood as such.

**nudnik, noodnik, nudnick** |NŎŎD nik| *n* A pest; a fool; a bore. ORIGINS: From Yiddish, **nudnik** from **nudyen** meaning "to pester or bore." USAGE ALERT: Usually used with intent to denigrate or insult and understood as such.

**pain** |PĀN| *n* An annoying person; a difficult, complex, and potentially time-consuming problem or development.

**pain in the ass**\* |PĀN in *th*ē AS| *n* An annoying person; a difficult, complex, and potentially time-consuming problem or development. ORIGINS: From slang **ass** meaning "the rear end or buttocks" or slang **butt**, a euphemism for **ass**. USAGE ALERT: A reference to the buttocks or rear end in any form will be objectionable in some contexts and to some people. Usually used with intent to denigrate or insult and understood as such.
• **pain in the butt** |PĀN in *th*u BUT|

**pain in the neck** |PĀN in *th*u NEK| *n* An annoying person; a difficult, complex, and potentially time-consuming problem or development. ORIGINS: A euphemism for **pain in the ass** and synonyms relating to the rear end or buttocks. USAGE ALERT: Often used with intent to denigrate or insult and understood as such.

**pain in the rear (end)**\* |PĀN in *th*u RIR / PĀN in *th*u RIR END| *n* An annoying person; a difficult, complex, and potentially time-consuming problem or development. ORIGINS: Euphemism for **pain in the ass**. Tush(y/ie) and rear (end) are euphemisms for **ass** meaning "the rear end or buttocks." USAGE ALERT: Tush(y/ie) and rear (end) are less in-your-face, but in some contexts and for some people, a reference to the buttocks or rear end in any form will be objectionable. Usually used with intent to denigrate or insult and understood as such.
• pain in the tush(y/ie) |PAN in *th*u TUSH / PĀN in *th*u TU shē|

**pill** |pil| *n* An unpleasant person; a bore; a person who or a thing that is distasteful but not avoidable. ORIGINS: By comparison with unpleasantly-flavored medicine tablets.

**snot(nose)** |snaht / SNAHT nōz| *n* An arrogant and annoying person. ORIGINS: From slang **snot** meaning "nasal mucus." USAGE ALERT: Usually used with intent to denigrate or insult and understood as such.

**tick** |tik| *n* An insignificant, but annoying person; an unpleasant, but irritating person, usually male. ORIGINS: From SE **tick** meaning "a parasite."

**wart** |wawrt| *n* A person who causes ongoing irritation and annoyance. ORIGINS: By analogy to the ongoing annoyance caused by a wart. USAGE ALERT: Usually used with intent to denigrate or insult and understood as such.

NON-SLANG SYNONYMS: aggravation, annoyance, inconvenience, irritation, **pest**, **burden**, **irritant**, **plague**, **vexation**

## ASPIRING

**greenhorn** |GRĒN hawrn| *n* A novice; a beginner at something; a person who is new to a field or subject. ORIGINS: From SE **greenhorn** for a young ox with new horns; expanded by military use to describe new recruits; expanded from there to a beginner at anything.

**newbie** |NŪ bē| *n* A newcomer or novice, particularly in military and online venues. ORIGINS: From SE **new**.

**rookie** |RŎOK ē| *n* A newcomer to a group, team, profession, or project. ORIGINS: Thought to be an alteration of SE **recruit**, which suggests it may come from military or law enforcement. USAGE INFO: Commonly used in sports jargon for athletes just starting their professional careers.

**wannabe(e)** |WAH nu bē| *n* One who will never have a particular skill set, but pursues the practice in spite of this. ORIGINS: From the phrase "I want to (wanna) be...." USAGE INFO: Differentiated from wannabe(e) as an adjective by standing alone with no reference, as in "Sure, he loves Guitar Hero®, but as for really playing guitar, he's just a wannabe."

**wannabe(e)** |WAH nu bē| *adj* One who aspires to have (but does not yet have and/or may never have) a particular skill set; one who admires *sb* (often a celebrity) inordinately and imitates that person's style. ORIGINS: From the phrase "I want to (wanna) be...." USAGE INFO: Precedes or follows the word or phrase it modifies, as in "a wannabe singer"; "a Madonna wannabe."

NON-SLANG SYNONYMS: amateur, apprentice, beginner, newcomer, **new kid on the block**, **abecedarian**, **fledgling**, **neophyte**, **novice**, **trainee**

# ATTRACTIVE

**babe** |bāb| *n* A particularly attractive woman or—in some contexts—man. USAGE INFO: Originally applied only to women, in the late 1980s the term also began to be applied to men.

**bimbette** |bim BET| *n* Vacuous, but notably attractive, person aspiring to be a bimbo. ORIGINS: May derive from the Italian **bimbo** meaning "baby." USAGE INFO: Often applied to a woman seeking to get rich by using her sexuality to gain economic support or who is perceived as doing so. USAGE ALERT: Usually used with intent to denigrate or insult and understood as such. The suggestion of trading sex for money and/or a perception that this word is disparaging to women will make this term objectionable in some contexts and to some people.

**bimbo** |BIM bō| *n* Vacuous, but notably attractive, person. ORIGINS: May derive from the Italian **bimbo** meaning "baby." USAGE INFO: Often applied to a gold-digger, a woman who uses her sexuality in order to gain economic support or who is perceived as doing so. USAGE ALERT: Usually used with intent to denigrate or insult and understood as such. The suggestion of trading sex for money and/or a perception that this word is disparaging to women will make this term objectionable in some contexts and to some people.

**heart-throb** |HAHRT thrahb| *n* A male that many females find attractive. ORIGINS: From the association of the emotion of love with the heart.

**hunk** |hungk| *n* An attractive, well-built man.

**looker** |LŎŎK ur| *n* An extremely attractive person.

**NON-SLANG SYNONYMS:** beauty, <u>dreamboat</u>, <u>knockout</u>, <u>stunner</u>, **belle**, **vision**

# COMPLAINING

**bellyacher** |BEL ē āk ur| *n* A person who complains or moans as if s/he had a stomachache.

**bleater** |blēt ur| *n* A person who often complains feebly or in a whining way. ORIGINS: Imitative of the sound of a sheep or goat.

**griper** |GRĪP ur| *n* A person who complains in a petulant way. ORIGINS: By extension from SE noun <u>gripes</u> meaning "the pain of colic," with the idea that a person with this kind of pain would behave in this way.

kvetch |kvech| *n* A person who complains and whines continually. ORIGINS: From Yiddish **kvetshn** meaning "to complain."

nag |nag| *n* A person who continually whines, complains, scolds, or criticizes.

nitpicker |NIT pik ur| *n* A person who focuses on the micro level, complaining about trivial matters.

quibbler |KWIB lur| *n* A person who raises petty and trivial arguments. ORIGINS: Repopularized as the name of the tabloid newspaper for which Rita Skeeter writes in the Harry Potter books by J.K. Rowling and the movies based on them.

sniveller |SNIV ul ur| *n* A person who whines or complains with sniffles and tears.

squawker |SKWAWK ur| *n* A person who complains noisily or peevishly. ORIGINS: From the loud, harsh cry of a bird.

NON-SLANG SYNONYMS: complainer, **crybaby**, **grumbler**, **moaner**, **whiner**, **fault finder**

# CONTEMPTIBLE

bottom-feeder |BAHT um fē dur| *n* A despicable person. ORIGINS: From SE **bottom-feeder** meaning "a fish that feeds off the ocean floor"—i.e., on the waste created by other ocean life. Figuratively extended to mean "a scavenger; an opportunist who takes advantage of others' misfortune." From there it has been generalized to mean "a contemptible person." USAGE INFO: This phrase has no connection to the human rear end or buttocks. USAGE ALERT: Usually used with intent to denigrate or insult and understood as such.

bum |bum| *n* A contemptible person; a general term of abuse. ORIGINS: Expanded meaning and shortened form from slang **bummer** meaning "vagrant or tramp." **Bum** meaning "vagrant or tramp" now seems to be considered informal. USAGE ALERT: Usually used with intent to denigrate or insult and understood as such.

crumb |krum| *n* A contemptible or mean person. ORIGINS: By extension of the original meaning, "a body louse."

cunt |kunt| *n* A multi-faceted term of abuse for anyone considered contemptible: the foolish, unpleasant, unintelligent, and women. ORIGINS: From slang **cunt**, meaning "vagina." USAGE INFO: At one time, this was an accepted term, used in medical writing. Now, often found in a part-for-the-whole usage to refer to a woman. USAGE ALERT: **Cunt** is considered among the most objectionable terms in the English language. Using **cunt** is nearly always done with specific intent to give offense and will be understood as such.

**dick\*** |dik| *n* A contemptible or stupid person. ORIGINS: From slang **dick** meaning "penis." USAGE ALERT: The inclusion of a reference to sexual organs will make this phrase objectionable in some situations and to some people. In addition, it will be usually used with intent to denigrate or insult and understood as such.
• dickhead |DIK hed|

**dirtbag** |DIRT bag| *n* A contemptible person; a vile person. ORIGINS: From SE **dirt** and the slang suffix -**bag**, which designates a person. USAGE ALERT: Usually used with intent to denigrate or insult and understood as such.

**fuckhead** |FUK hed| *n* A contemptible person. ORIGINS: From slang **fuck** meaning "sexual intercourse" and slang suffix -**head** meaning "person." USAGE ALERT: This form of **fuck** will be objectionable in some contexts and to some people.

**fucker**[2] |FUK ur| *n* A contemptible person; someone who harms others. ORIGINS: From slang **fuck** meaning "to engage in sexual intercourse." USAGE ALERT: This form of **fuck** will be objectionable in some contexts and to some people.

**jerk(-off)** |jurk / JURK awf| *n* A contemptible person; an extremely offensive person. ORIGINS: From slang **jerk-off** meaning "to masturbate." USAGE ALERT: Many people use this word without reference to its origins and, often when using only jerk, without knowing them. This can lead to very different interpretations of acceptable use, especially when children are using the word or within earshot. Usually used with intent to denigrate or insult and understood as such.

**louse** |LOUS| *n* A despicable person; a mean, nasty person. ORIGINS: From SE **louse**, referring to the insect.

**scab** |scab| *n* A contemptible person. ORIGINS: From SE **scab**.

**schmegegge, schmegeggy** |shmu GEG / shmu GEG ē| *n* A contemptible person; an incompetent person. ORIGINS: From a Yiddish word that also means "nonsense." USAGE ALERT: Usually used with intent to denigrate or insult and understood as such.

**scum (of the earth)** |skum / SKUM uv *thu* IRTH| *n* A person or group regarded as worthless. ORIGINS: From SE **scum**, which refers to, for example, the filmy layer that forms in a bathtub and means "refuse." USAGE ALERT: Usually used with intent to denigrate or insult and understood as such.

**scumbag** |SKUM bag| *n* A despicable, contemptible person. ORIGINS: By extension of slang **scumbag** (from slang **scum** meaning "semen" and SE **bag**), meaning "used condom." USAGE ALERT: Many people use this word without knowing its origins, associating it with SE **scum**, which refers to the filmy layer that forms in a bathtub. This can lead to very different interpretations of proper use, especially when children are using the word or are within earshot. Usually used with intent to denigrate or insult and understood as such.

**scuzz, scuz** |SKUZ| *n* A repulsive person. USAGE ALERT: Usually used with intent to denigrate or insult and understood as such.

**scuzzbag\*** |SKUZ bag| *n* A repulsive or contemptible person. ORIGINS: From slang scuzz and slang suffix -bag, -ball, or -bucket meaning "a person." USAGE ALERT: Usually used with intent to denigrate or insult and understood as such.
• scuzzball |SKUZ bawl|
• scuzz bucket |SKUZ buk it|

**shitbag** |SHIT bag| *n* A contemptible person; a person who is disgusting; a person who isn't trustworthy. ORIGINS: From **shit** meaning "excrement" and the suffix -bag meaning person. USAGE ALERT: Usually used with intent to denigrate or insult and understood as such. Because it includes **shit**, this word will be objectionable in some contexts and to some people.

**shitface** |SHIT fās| *n See* **SHITHEAD**.

**shithead** |SHIT hed| *n* A contemptible person. ORIGINS: From slang **shit** meaning "excrement" and slang suffix -head. USAGE ALERT: Usually used with intent to denigrate or insult and understood as such. Because it includes **shit**, this word will be objectionable in some contexts and to some people.

**skunk** |skungk| *n* A contemptible person. ORIGINS: Figurative reference to the characteristic smell of an angered or beleaguered skunk.

**son of a whore** |sun uv u HAWR| *n* A contemptible person. ORIGINS: From slang **whore**, meaning "a prostitute" or "*sb* considered sexually promiscuous." USAGE INFO: Usually used only of males. USAGE ALERT: **Son of a whore** carries implications not only about the person referred to, but also about his mother. Usually used with intent to denigrate or insult and understood as such. In addition, the phrase will be objectionable in some contexts and to some people.

**swine** |swīn| *n* A contemptible person.

**trash**$^2$ |trash| *n* One or more contemptible or worthless people. USAGE INFO: Trash is not a countable noun, so its reference can be either singular or plural. It takes a singular verb, as in "Wait till the trash goes home, and then we'll have our picnic." USAGE ALERT: Usually used with intent to denigrate or insult and understood as such.

**turd** |turd| *n* A contemptible person. ORIGINS: Figurative use of slang **turd** meaning "a piece of excrement."

**twat** |twaht| *n* A contemptible person, usually a woman. ORIGINS: Figurative use of slang twat meaning "vulva." USAGE ALERT: This term is generally regarded as one of the most objectionable words in English and is most often used with specific intent to give offense.

**NON-SLANG SYNONYMS:** brute, dirt, <u>low life</u>, <u>rabble</u>, <u>riffraff</u>, **the dregs of humanity, the lowest of the low**

# COWARDLY

**candy-ass** |KAN dē as| *n* One who is afraid; a sissy. ORIGINS: From slang **candy** meaning "a cowardly, weak person." Note that both the noun and the adjective form are used as adjectives. *See* **-ASS(ED)** for more information about the suffix. USAGE ALERT: Because it contains the word ass, this phrase will be objectionable in some contexts and to some people. Usually used with intent to denigrate or insult and understood as such.

**chicken** |CHIK un| *n* Someone who is afraid; a coward. ORIGINS: Chickens are typically characterized as easily frightened creatures.

**fraidy cat** |FRĀ dē kat| *n* One who's afraid; a coward. ORIGINS: From a childish shortening and alteration of SE **afraid** combined with SE **cat**, perhaps for their sometimes skittish behavior. USAGE INFO: Used in taunts by children; sometimes playfully or in teasing by adults, although it can be used to denigrate and insult.

**gutless (wonder)** |GUT lis / GUT lis WUN dur| *n* A coward. ORIGINS: Draws on the fairly standard connection between guts and courage.

**lily liver** |LIL ē liv ur| *n* A person who's afraid; a coward. ORIGINS: Extends the observation that a person's skin can turn pale with fear to suggest that all his/her organs do as well by using a lily, traditionally white, to convey the comparison. USAGE ALERT: Usually used with intent to denigrate or insult and understood as such.

**marshmallow** |MAHRSH mel ō| *n* Someone who is timid; a fearful, ineffectual person. ORIGINS: From the SE **marshmallow**, a soft, white, not very flavorful confection.

**pussy** |POŌS ē| *n* A cowardly weak man; an effeminate man. ORIGINS: From slang **pussy** meaning a woman, extended from meaning "the vagina"; from earlier affectionate name for a cat. USAGE INFO: Often used in taunting, as in "You pussy!" USAGE ALERT: This term may be found objectionable for the sexual reference, for the stereotyping of women, and for the stereotyping of men. Usually used with intent to denigrate or insult and understood as such.

**scaredy cat** |SKER dē cat| *n* A person who frequently exhibits fear. USAGE ALERT: Usually used with intent to denigrate or insult and understood as such.

**sissy** |SIS ē| *adj* A fearful or timid person; an effeminate male. USAGE ALERT: Usually used with intent to denigrate or insult and understood as such.

**NON-SLANG SYNONYMS:** deserter, quitter, skulker, **alarmist**, **craven** (*craven* is usually seen as an adjective, but it can be used as a noun with this meaning), **malingerer**

# CRUDE

**baboon** |ba BŪN| *n* A crude, boorish person; a brute. ORIGINS: After SE **baboon**, a type of terrestrial monkey found in Africa and Asia, and its (stereotypically) conceived behavior patterns. USAGE ALERT: Usually used with intent to denigrate or insult and understood as such.

**butthead** |BUT hed| *n* An obnoxious, crude, and stupid person. ORIGINS: From slang **butt**, a euphemism for **ass**, meaning "the rear end or buttocks" and slang suffix -head. The concept is of a person who has a rear end or buttocks for a head. Popularized since the 1990s by the MTV television series *Beavis and Butthead*. USAGE ALERT: Because it refers to the human rear end or buttocks, this term will be considered objectionable in some contexts and by some people.

**gorilla** |gu RIL u| *n* A thug; a brutish man. ORIGINS: Stereotype of SE **gorilla** behavior.

**Neanderthal** |nē AN dur thawl| *n* A crude, stupid person; a boorish dolt. ORIGINS: From SE **Homo sapiens neanderthalensis**, an extinct human species that lived during the late Pleistocene Epoch. Popularized by Geico insurance advertisements (2004–). USAGE ALERT: Usually used with intent to denigrate or insult and understood as such.

**roughneck** |RUF nek| *n* A person with no manners; a person who is crude and violent. USAGE ALERT: Usually used with intent to denigrate or insult and understood as such.

**shitkicker** |SHIT kik ur| *n* A crude, unsophisticated person. ORIGINS: From the stereotype that *sb* who works on a farm with animals and manure will be of this type. From slang **shit** meaning "excrement." USAGE ALERT: Usually used with intent to denigrate or insult and understood as such. Because it includes **shit**, this word will be objectionable in some contexts and to some people.

NON-SLANG SYNONYMS: hoodlum, rowdy, tough, **bully**, **punk**, **ruffian**

# DETERMINED

**donkey** |DAHN kē| *n* A person who is obstinate to the point of stupidity. ORIGINS: From conventional characteristics of the SE **donkey**.

**hard-ass** |HAHRD as| *n* A person who is inflexible in following or enforcing rules; a person without kindness. ORIGINS: From slang **ass** meaning "the rear end or buttocks." USAGE ALERT: The inclusion of **ass** will make this term objectionable in some contexts and to some people. In addition, it is usually used with intent to denigrate or insult and understood as such.

**hard case** |HAHRD KĀS| *n* A tough or ruthless person.

**hard nut** |HAHRD NUT| *n* A determined or unpleasant person. ORIGINS: By extension from literal difficulty in getting a nut meat out of the shell. USAGE INFO: Sometimes used in a longer form, a hard nut to crack, but that generally means "a difficult problem to solve."

**hardhead** |HAHRD hed| *n* A stubborn person. ORIGINS: From SE **hard** and slang suffix -head, suggesting that a person's head is impermeable to the advice and ideas of others.

**mule** |MYŪL| *nj* A person who is stubborn or unreasonably obstinate.

**tough nut** |TUF NUT| *n* A determined or unpleasant person. ORIGINS: By extension from literal difficulty in getting the nut meat out of the shell. USAGE INFO: Sometimes used in a longer form a hard/tough nut to crack, but that generally means "a difficult problem to solve."

NON-SLANG SYNONYMS: dictator, realist, tyrant, **tough cookie**, **pragmatist**

# ENTHUSIASTIC

**buff** |buf| *sfx* An amateur enthusiast. ORIGINS: From the uniform color (buff) of volunteer fire fighters in New York City at one time. Follows a noun or gerund, as in a sports buff, skiing buff.

**bum** |bum| *sfx* A fan, usually of a sport. ORIGINS: Extension of informal **bum**, meaning "vagrant or tramp." USAGE INFO: Suggests obsession or unhealthy level of interest, possibly to the detriment of other (necessary) activities, particularly work; e.g., a person who devotes more than what the observer deems as enough time to surfing may be styled a beach bum.

**fiend** |fēnd| *sfx* An avid enthusiast; an addict; one who is obsessed by. ORIGINS: From SE **fiend** meaning "the devil." USAGE INFO: Despite origins, is used light-heartedly, as in, e.g., a tennis fiend.

**freak** |frēk| *sfx* Someone obsessed with or overly fond of something. ORIGINS: From the slang noun **freak**, meaning "someone who's obsessed." USAGE INFO: This word usually has negative connotations, as in "control freak."

**groupie** |GRŪ pē| *n* An avid follower; a fan who is obsessive. Sometimes especially applied to young women. ORIGINS: From SE **group** referring specifically to a rock or pop band.

**-head** |hed| *sfx* A fan, particularly of a music style. ORIGINS: SE head is used to represent the whole person. USAGE INFO: Forms a closed compound with the word it modifies, e.g., a metalhead is one who enthusiastically enjoys the music called *heavy metal*. -head is also combined with words to indicate foolishness or stupidity, as in blockhead.

**junkie, junky** |JUNG kē| *sfx* A person who is obsessively devoted to *st*; a person with a deep interest in *st*. ORIGINS: From generalizing slang junkie meaning "a heroin addict." USAGE INFO: Often spelled as an open compound, as in "sports junkie."

**monster** |MAHN stur| *sfx* A passionate fan of; a person who is devoted to. ORIGINS: From slang monster meaning "an outstanding example of (whatever it is)." Popularized by Cookie Monster, who is both a literal monster as well as the world's most devoted fan of cookies, on the television show, books, and films of *Sesame Street* (1969–).

**nut** |nut| *sfx* An enthusiast, often for a pastime or hobby. ORIGINS: Extended from slang nut "to be crazy" to "to be crazy about *st*." USAGE INFO: Follows the noun or gerund it modifies to form an open compound, as in "health nut."

**rooter** |RŪT ur| *n* A supporter. ORIGINS: From fans who root for their team.

NON-SLANG SYNONYMS: fanatic, **aficionado**, **connoisseur**, **devotee**, **votary**

# EXPERT

**ace** |ās| *n* An outstanding person, noteworthy for qualifications, skills, or character traits. ORIGINS: From the ace's role as the highest-ranked playing card.

**artist** |AHR tist| *sfx* An expert in something (often illegal, unpleasant, or not likely to gain respect). ORIGINS: Extended from SE artist to apply to other fields, sometimes ironically. USAGE INFO: Usually follows a noun, e.g., con artist, **bullshit artist**.

**dab hand** |DAB HAND| *adj* An expert; someone skilled at a particular task. USAGE INFO: Often used with *at* or *with*.

**hired gun** |HĪRD GUN| *n* A highly skilled person, not necessarily an assassin, who is brought in as a consultant to solve a particularly difficult problem. ORIGINS: By extension from hired killers (guns).

**hotshot, hot-shot** |HAHT shaht| *n* A person who is important or influential or expert. USAGE INFO: Used ironically of a self-important person.

**hot stuff** |HAHT stuf| *n* An expert; a particularly intelligent or capable person.

**maven, mavin** |MĀ vun| *n* An expert; a connoisseur. ORIGINS: From Hebrew through Yiddish **meyvn**, meaning "to understand."

**powerhouse** |POU ur hous| *n* An expert; an influential person.

**pro** |prō| *n* A person who has expertise; a professional. ORIGINS: Shortening of SE professional.

**whiz-kid, whizz-kid** |WIZ kid| *n* A person, especially a young person, who is exceptionally good at something. ORIGINS: From slang whiz, deriving from SE wizard. USAGE INFO: More often used of males than females.

**wizard** |WIZ urd| *n* An exceptionally smart person. ORIGINS: Perhaps initially encouraged by the television shows starring "Mr. Wizard" (1951–1990); followed by the popularity of Merlin (*The Once and Future King: The Sword in the Stone*), Gandalf (*The Hobbit* and *The Lord of the Ring*), and, most recently, Albus Dumbledore and others in the Harry Potter books.

**wonk** |wahnk| *n* A person who has exceptional expertise in a particular area.

NON-SLANG SYNONYMS: authority, expert, master, professional, specialist, **virtuoso**

# EXPERT, BUT SOCIALLY AWKWARD

**dweeb** |dwēb| *n* A socially inept person; someone at home in academics to the exclusion of having developed social graces. ORIGINS: Unknown, but popularity possibly influenced by the candy dweebs from the Willy Wonka Candy Company, and the CBS comedy *Dweebs* (1995). USAGE ALERT: May be used teasingly, but usually used with intent to denigrate or insult and understood as such.

**geek** |gēk| *n* A physically or socially inept person, often one who is academically gifted or tech-savvy. ORIGINS: From Low German geck meaning "a fool." USAGE INFO: Used both jokingly and with intent to insult or denigrate.

**nerd, nurd** |nurd| *n* An insignificant and boring person; a studious person who lacks social and athletic skills. ORIGINS: Widely believed to have been influenced by, if not derived from, the imaginary creature called Nerd in *If I Ran the Zoo* (1950) by Theodor Geisel (alias Dr. Seuss). USAGE ALERT: Usually used with intent to denigrate or insult and understood as such.

NON-SLANG SYNONYMS—NOUNS: **techie**, **trekkie** (*Trekkie* refers to a fan of the Star Trek media franchise. It is possibly preferred over *trekker* for this meaning partly because it rhymes with *techie* and possibly because self-identified trekkers think self-identified trekkies are geekier than they themselves are.)

# FOOLISH

**addlebrain\*** |AD 'l brān| *n* A person suffering from confusion; a foolish person. ORIGINS: Addle comes from a Middle English word related to the German **adele**, which means "liquid manure." It can be followed by several synonyms for *head*. USAGE INFO: The current usage is gentler than its etymology suggests: this word is not the equivalent of **shithead**. The etymology of addle is not widely known, so people are not likely to connect the word with excrement. Still, it is usually used with intent to denigrate or insult and understood as such.
• addlehead |AD 'l hed|
• addlepate |AD 'l pāt|

**bubblehead** |BUB ul hed| *n* A silly, careless, unintelligent person. ORIGINS: From SE **bubble** and slang suffix -head. Bubbles are full of air, so a bubblehead has an empty head. USAGE INFO: Similar to **airhead** in meaning. USAGE ALERT: Usually used with intent to denigrate or insult and understood as such.

**cluckhead** |KLUK hed| *n* A silly person; a fool. ORIGINS: From SE **cluck**, the sound a chicken makes, and slang suffix -head, with **cluck** evoking a chicken, which is generally thought of as being unintelligent. USAGE ALERT: Usually used with intent to denigrate or insult and understood as such.

**ding-a-ling** |DING u ling| *n* A scatterbrained or eccentric person; someone who is insane. ORIGINS: From the onomatopoeic sound of a bell tied to the concept of a person who hears bells ringing in his/her head being disturbed in some way. USAGE ALERT: Can be used affectionately, but often used with intent to denigrate or insult and understood as such.

**ding-dong** |DING dahng| *n* A fool; an empty-headed person; an insane person. ORIGINS: From the onomatopoeic sound of a bell tied to the concept of a person who hears bells ringing in his/her head being disturbed in some way. USAGE ALERT: Often used with intent to denigrate or insult and understood as such.

**dingbat** |DING bat| *n* A silly person or fool; an insane person. ORIGINS: Possibly from SE **ding** meaning "the sound of a bell" and slang bats in the belfry meaning "crazy." Popularized by Archie Bunker, who used it frequently of his wife, Edith, on the TV sitcom *All in the Family* (1968–1979, now in reruns). USAGE ALERT: Usually used with intent to denigrate or insult and understood as such.

**ditz** |ditz| *n* A scatterbrained person; a fool. ORIGINS: Altered from SE **dizzy**. USAGE INFO: Most often used of women. USAGE ALERT: Usually used with intent to denigrate or insult and understood as such.

**dope²** |dōp| *n* A fool; a stupid person. USAGE ALERT: Can be used affectionately, but often used with intent to denigrate or insult and understood as such.

**jughead** |JUG hed| *n* A fool. ORIGINS: Possibly from the slang jughead for a mule, from SE **jug** and slang suffix -head. Popularized by the character Jughead Jones in the

Archie Comics (1941). USAGE ALERT: Usually used with intent to denigrate or insult and understood as such.

**lamebrain** |LĀM brān| *n* A foolish person; one who is dull-witted. ORIGINS: Just as slang lame is used in general to describe things that do not work properly or as expected or people who are incompetent, in lamebrain that meaning is applied specifically to a person's intellect. USAGE ALERT: Usually used with intent to denigrate or insult and understood as such.

**mook** |mo͝ok| *n* A fool; an insignificant person.

**nincompoop** |NIN kum po͞op| *n* A silly or foolish person; someone without common sense. USAGE ALERT: Usually used with intent to denigrate or insult and understood as such.

**ninny** |NIN ē| *n* A silly or foolish person; someone without common sense. USAGE ALERT: Usually used with intent to denigrate or insult and understood as such.

**nitwit** |NIT wit| *n* A silly or stupid person. ORIGINS: Different etymologies are offered, one being SE **nit** meaning "louse" and SE **wit**, "brain," thus, "lousebrain." USAGE ALERT: Usually used with intent to denigrate or insult and understood as such.

**poop** |po͞op| *n* A fool; an annoying person. ORIGINS: Thought to be short for nincompoop. USAGE ALERT: People may connect this word with slang **poop** for excrement, in which case they will both understand it differently and possibly find it objectionable.

**putz** |putz| *n* A fool; an idiot. ORIGINS: From Yiddish **putz** meaning "penis." USAGE INFO: People may not know its original meaning. USAGE ALERT: The inclusion of a reference to sexual organs in this phrase will not often raise objections because most people don't make the connection.

**rattlebrain**\* |RAT ul brān| *n* A foolish, chattering person; an empty-headed or scatterbrained person. ORIGINS: Either the person's jaw or brains are rattling around, or both. USAGE ALERT: This word is usually used with intent to denigrate or insult and understood as such.
 • rattlehead |RAT ul hed|

**ringding** |RING ding| *n* A fool. USAGE ALERT: Usually used with intent to denigrate or insult and understood as such.

**saphead** |SAP hed| *n* A fool. ORIGINS: From SE **sap** meaning "the liquid in a tree" and the slang suffix -**head**. USAGE ALERT: Usually used with intent to denigrate or insult and understood as such.

**simp** |simp| *n* A fool. ORIGINS: Shortened from SE **simpleton**. USAGE ALERT: Usually used with intent to denigrate or insult and understood as such.

**twerp, twirp** |twurp| *n* An idiot; a fool. USAGE ALERT: Usually used with intent to denigrate or insult and understood as such.

**twit** |twit| *n* A fool; a person who is silly and annoying. USAGE ALERT: Usually used with intent to denigrate or insult and understood as such.

**yo-yo** |YŌ YŌ| *n* A foolish person.

Note: There are few synonyms because traits like this are frequently either "talked around" or avoided in all registers except slang.

# GENEROUS

**do-gooder** |DŪ gŏŏd ur| *n* A generous person who naively supports change. ORIGINS: From SE **do** and **good**. USAGE INFO: Often used ironically of (possibly) well-intentioned people who assist/interfere in matters and situations that they don't fully understand.

**soft touch** |SAWFT TUCH| *n* A person who will easily agree to give money or do favors.

NON-SLANG SYNONYMS: contributor, donor, sponsor, **benefactor**, **benefactress**, **humanitarian**, **patron**, **philanthropist**

# GULLIBLE

**chump** |chump| *n* A gullible person; someone who is easily taken in. ORIGINS: SE **chump**, meaning "a lump of wood." *See* KLUTZ and BLOCKHEAD. USAGE ALERT: Usually used with intent to denigrate or insult and understood as such.

**doormat** |DAWR mat| *n* A submissive person who gives in to the domination or mistreatment of others. ORIGINS: By extension from the abuse received by an SE **doormat**, a small rug that stands before a door and that is "walked all over."

**easy mark/touch** |Ē zē mahrk / Ē zē tuch| *n* An easily persuadable person; someone gullible. ORIGINS: From SE **easy** and slang **mark** or **touch** meaning "potential victim for a con."

**fall guy** |FAWL gī| *n* A gullible victim of a scheme; a dupe; a scapegoat.

**gudgeon** |GUJ un| *n* An easily-duped person. ORIGINS: From SE **gudgeon** meaning "a small bait fish." Related to its role of being swallowed as bait—similarly, a gullible person will swallow deceptions. USAGE ALERT: Usually used with intent to denigrate or insult and understood as such.

**mark** |mahrk| *n* A person chosen to be the the victim of a swindle; a dupe; someone gullible.

**mug** |mug| *n* A fool or dupe. ORIGINS: From carnival jargon. USAGE ALERT: Often used with intent to denigrate or insult and understood as such.

**patsy** |PAT sē| *n* A gullible person who is easily duped or swindled. ORIGINS: There are suggestions that this word comes from Italian **pazzo** meaning "fool" or the Irish nickname for **Patrick**. USAGE ALERT: If the second etymology is true, or if people think that it is, this term may be viewed as a racial slur and therefore be objectionable.

**pigeon** |PIJ un| *n* A person who is easy to dupe; a person who is gullible and easily taken advantage of. ORIGINS: Possibly shortening of slang clay pigeon—a device used for target practice by hunters—which has the same meaning.

**pushover** |POOSH ō vur| *n* A dupe; a gullible person.

**sap** |sap| *n* An easily manipulated dupe; a gullible person.

**schnook, shnook** |shnook| *n* A gullible person; a dupe; an easy mark. ORIGINS: From Yiddish **shnuk** meaning "nose." USAGE ALERT: Usually used with intent to denigrate or insult and understood as such.

**sucker**[1] |SUK ur| *n* A gullible person; a dupe. ORIGINS: From obsolete SE **sucker** meaning "an unweaned baby," whether human or animal, thus, "an innocent." USAGE ALERT: People who know that other words with the letter sequence s-u-c-k come from shortening the phrase **suck dick** or **cocksucker** may mistakenly think that this one does as well. This may result in people finding this word objectionable despite its innocence (pun intended). Nevertheless, it is usually used with intent to denigrate or insult and understood as such.

NON-SLANG SYNONYMS: casualty, injured party, innocent, prey, sacrifice, target, victim, sitting duck, **martyr**, **pawn**, **quarry**

# HELPFUL

**backup, back-up** |BAK up| *n* A person or item relied on for support. ORIGINS: From SE **back-up** meaning "support or help."

**flunky** |FLUN kē| *n* A menial. ORIGINS: From SE **flunky** meaning "servant."

**gofer** |GŌ fur| *n* An assistant; someone whose role includes going on errands. ORIGINS: From the sending of such a person to "go for such-and-such," with **go for** becoming altered to **gofer**.

**grunt** |grunt| *n* An assistant; one who carries out menial tasks. ORIGINS: Probably onomatopoeic from SE **grunt** meaning "a deep guttural noise or moan." At one time in its history, referred specifically to members of the armed forces, but also has general use.

**sidekick** |SĪD kik| *n* A pal; a helper; a dependable back-up.

NON-SLANG SYNONYMS: backer, supporter, angel, **mentor**, **patron**

# IMPORTANT

**PTB** Powers that be.

**TPTB** The powers that be. USAGE INFO: Source of the parody "the people to blame."

**big boy** |BIG boi| *n* Person with power or influence; in particular, an organized crime boss. USAGE INFO: May be used ironically.

**big cheese** |BIG CHĒZ| *n* Person with power or influence; an important person or "the boss." ORIGINS: Suspected by some to have arisen from a British misapprehension of the Persian or Hindi or Urdu word **chiz**, meaning "thing," during the nineteenth century when many British were in India. USAGE INFO: Often used with *the.*

**big chief** |BIG CHĒF| *n* Person with power or influence; the most important of all the important people. USAGE INFO: Often used with *the.*

**big daddy (of them all)** |big DA dē / big DA dē uv *th*um AWL| *n* Predominant in impact, importance, or other ways; may refer to a person or thing. ORIGINS: From the father as the head of the family in a paternalistic society. USAGE INFO: Often used with *the.*

**big deal** |BIG DĒL| *n* Person with power or influence; an important person. ORIGINS: From SE **big** and slang deal meaning "an individual." USAGE INFO: Often used with *a.*

**big enchilada** |BIG en chu LAH du| *n* Person with power or influence. ORIGINS: Said to be modeled on other slang terms with *big*, such as **big cheese**. Popularized by its appearance in the White House tapes made public on account of the Watergate Scandal. USAGE INFO: Often used with *the.*

**big fellow** |BIG FEL ō| *n* Person with power or influence; in particular, an organized crime boss.

**big fish** |BIG FISH| *n* Person with power or influence. USAGE INFO: Often used with *a* as in the phrase "a big fish in a small pond."

**big gun** |BIG GUN| *n* Person with power or influence. ORIGINS: From military jargon **big gun** meaning "a large-caliber artillery piece." USAGE INFO: Often used in the plural.

**big guy** |BIG gī| *n* Person with power or influence or considered to be powerful or influential.

**big man** |BIG MAN| *n* Person with power or influence; a major drug dealer.

**big shot** |BIG shaht| *n* Person with power or influence, often one who is self-important or perceived as over-reaching. USAGE INFO: Can be used as a back-handed compliment or out of jealousy.

**big spender** |BIG SPEN dur| *n* Person who spends to impress. USAGE INFO: Used ironically of a cheapskate.

**big wheel** |BIG WĒL| *n* Person with power or influence, particularly in the realm of business. ORIGINS: Possibly a reference to wheels and cogs one might imagine in the proverbial "engines of industry."

**big wig** |BIG wig| *n* Person with power or influence. ORIGINS: A reference to the large wigs once worn by influential and important men.

**biggie, biggy** |BIG ē| *n* Anyone or anything large, important, or successful. ORIGINS: By addition of an irreverent ending (one that usually serves to diminish) to SE big.

**boss (man)** |baws / BAWS man| *n* A leader of a company; the manager to whom one reports. ORIGINS: From the Dutch **baas**, meaning "master."

**brass** |bras| *n* High ranking officials or senior officers in business, government, or military settings. ORIGINS: From **brass hat**, a senior officer in the police, so named for the adornment (gold braid, for example) on their helmets. USAGE INFO: Can be singular, but usually plural.

**chief** |chēf| *n* A boss. ORIGINS: From the SE use of chief to designate the head of a Native American or American Indian tribe—therefore, by extension, any head of any organization.

**decider** |du SĪD ur| *n* The person who gets to make the final decisions. ORIGINS: From President George W. Bush's comment in the Rose Garden on April 18, 2006, as he defended his decision to keep Donald Rumsfeld as secretary of defense: "I'm the decider and I decide what's best."

**exec** |ig ZEK| *n* An executive or executive officer. ORIGINS: Shortened form of SE executive.

**fat cat** |FAT KAT| *n* A prosperous or wealthy individual. ORIGINS: From slang fat meaning "wealthy" and slang **cat** meaning "a male person." USAGE INFO: Can be used to imply that the person's wealth was ill-gotten.

**front office** |frunt AW fis| *n* The executive side of an organization; the policy makers; or the people in the organization who interact with customers. ORIGINS: From a frequently used location of the offices of such people.

**head honcho** |hed HAHN chō| *n* An important or influential person; the boss. ORIGINS: From Japanese **han'cho** meaning "group leader." Used by US military stationed in Korea.

**heavy hitter** |HEV ē HIT ur| *n* A person who is important or influential. ORIGINS: From the sport of boxing, someone who has a solid punch.

**heavyweight** |HEV ē wāt| *n* A person who is very important or has a lot of influence. ORIGINS: From the sport of boxing, referring to a weight class or a boxer in that weight class.

**high muck-a-muck*** |HĪ MUK u muk| *n* An important or self-important person. ORIGINS: From Chinook jargon **hiu muckamuck,** meaning "plenty to eat."
• high muckety-muck |HĪ MUK i tē muk|
• high mucky-muck |HĪ MUK ē muk|

**himself** |him SELF| *n* The boss.

**his highness** |hiz HĪ nis| *n* A sarcastic title for a man whose greatness is all in his imagination. ORIGINS: From the title given to royalty.

**his nibs** |hiz NIBZ| *n* The boss. USAGE INFO: May be used sarcastically of someone self-important.

**honcho** |HAHN chō| *n* An important or influential person; the boss. ORIGINS: From Japanese **han'cho** meaning "group leader." Used by US military stationed in Korea.

**kahuna** |ku HŪ nu| *n Sb* or *st* important or large. ORIGINS: Generalized from Hawaiian **kahuna** meaning "wise man or priest." The initial slang meaning was "an expert surfer."

**kingfish** |KING fish| *n* A political leader. ORIGINS: Used by Louisiana Governor and Senator Huey P. Long of himself, as well as being the name of a character in the *Amos and Andy* radio show. More recently popularized by Randy Newman in his song about Long, "Kingfish" (1974).

**kingpin** |KING pin| *n* The central or most important one in a group. ORIGINS: From SE **kingpin,** which refers to either the central pin or the headpin in bowling.

**Man (the)** |man / thu MAN| *n* The boss or person in charge; somebody important or powerful. ORIGINS: From the time when it was pretty inevitable that the boss was a man.

**man in the front office** |man in *thu* frunt AW fis| *n* The executives in an organization. ORIGINS: From the customary location of the executives (as opposed to production, research and development, etc.). USAGE INFO: Today, this term is often noticeable in sports reports on baseball and football, where most of these employees are, in fact, male.

**mastermind** |MAS tur mīnd| *n* A person of exceptional intelligence, able to successfully plan intricate, impressively difficult, and often illegal tasks or projects.

**Mister Big** |MIS tur Big| *n* An important man; the head of a criminal organization. ORIGINS: Recently popularized by the character of Mr. Big in the books, television series, and movies, all called *Sex and the City* (1996–2008).

**muckamuck** |MUK u muk| *n See* HIGH MUCK-A-MUCK.

**nabob** |NĀ bahb| *n* A wealthy or prominent person; someone of importance. ORIGINS: From the title of a governor in India during the Mogul Empire.

**number one** |num bur WUN| *n* Oneself and one's personal interests; the best thing there is; the main person in one's life. ORIGINS: From Spanish **numero uno** or Italian **numero uno**, meaning "number one." USAGE INFO: Often in the phrase "Look out for number one."

**numero uno** |NŪ mu rō Ū nō| *n* Number one, meaning oneself and one's personal interests; the best thing there is; the boss. ORIGINS: From Spanish **numero uno** or Italian **numero uno**, meaning "number one."

**old man** |ŌLD man| *n* A person of importance: one's father, boss, commanding officer, etc.

**panjandrum** |pan JAN drum| *n* An important person; a person with an exaggerated view of his/her own importance. ORIGINS: From the character of the Grand Panjandrum in a nonsensical piece of prose by the dramatist and theatre director Samuel Foote (1754).

**pooh-bah** |PŪ bah| *n* A pompous official; someone in high office. ORIGINS: From the character of Pooh-bah, Lord High Everything Else in the Gilbert and Sullivan opera *Mikado or The Town of Titipu* (1885). Popularized in the twenty-first century by Nike with their Supa Pooh-Bah mountain bike shoes.

**powers that be** |POU urz *that* BĒ| *n* The people in control or who have authority. ORIGINS: From the King James Bible version of Romans 13:1 "For there is no power but of God: the powers that be are ordained of God."

**skipper** |SKIP ur| *n* A boss. ORIGINS: Generalized from boating jargon **skipper** meaning "the captain."

**top banana** |TAHP bu NA nu| *n* The leader, head, or principal person involved. ORIGINS: From vaudeville acts in which the lead comedian was awarded this title, while the straight man was the "second banana."

**top brass** |TAHP BRAS| *n* High ranking officials or senior officers in business, government, or military settings. ORIGINS: All from **brass hat**, a senior officer in the police, so named for the adornment (gold braid, for example) on their helmets. USAGE INFO: Can be singular, but usually plural.

**top dog** |TAHP DAWG| *n* The leader; in a competition, the winner. ORIGINS: From the "sport" of dog fighting: the winning dog, and the one most worth betting on, is the "top dog."

**top gun** |TAHP GUN| *n* The most capable, the most prestigious person; the highest ranking person.

**VIP** |VĒ Ī PĒ| *n* An important or influential person. ORIGINS: Shortened form of Very Important Person.

**NON-SLANG SYNONYMS:** administrator, director, employer, executive, foreperson, leader, manager, overseer, owner, person in charge, superintendent, supervisor

# INCOMPETENT AND FOOLISH

**ass** |as| *n* A foolish, incompetent person. ORIGINS: From SE **ass** meaning "a donkey," but commonly used as slang to refer to the rear end or buttocks. USAGE INFO: Can also, depending on context, mean "an unpleasant, vain, pompous, or offensively stupid person," or—on the other hand—be used affectionately of someone who is silly or characteristically blunders, as in "you silly ass!" USAGE ALERT: All words containing **ass** will be found objectionable in some contexts and by some people. Usually used with intent to denigrate or insult and understood as such.

**bozo** |BŌ zō| *n* A clownish person; a fool; an incompetent person. ORIGINS: Recent US usage most likely influenced by the character of Bozo the Clown, popular in children's television in the last half of the twentieth century. The voice of Krusty the Clown on *The Simpsons* television show is said to be a nod to Bozo. USAGE ALERT: Usually used with intent to denigrate or insult and understood as such.

**doofus, dufus** |DŪ fus| *n* A person who is incompetent, foolish, or stupid. ORIGINS: May be related to slang **goofus** with a similar meaning. Doofus has been popularized by the character of Doofus Drake of Disney's *Duck Tales* (1987–1990) and Daggett Doofus Beaver in Nickelodeon's show *The Angry Beavers* (1997–2001). USAGE ALERT: Usually used with intent to denigrate or insult and understood as such.

**goof¹, also goofball** |gūf / GŪF bawl| *n* A silly or incompetent person. ORIGINS: By several steps, from an obsolete English word **goff** meaning "fool," from an obsolete French word **goffe** meaning "stupid," and the slang suffix -ball meaning "a person not held in high regard." USAGE INFO: Can be used affectionately of, for example, a person who clowns around and makes others laugh.

**goofus** |GŪF us| *n* A stupid, blundering person. ORIGINS: By several steps, from an obsolete English word **goff** meaning "fool," from an obsolete French word **goffe** meaning "stupid." This particular form, however, has been popularized by the long running cartoon feature in *Highlights for Children* magazine, "Goofus and Gallant®" (1948–). USAGE ALERT: Usually used with intent to denigrate or insult and understood as such.

**horse's ass** |HAWR siz AS| *n* A stupid and incompetent person; a contemptible person. ORIGINS: From SE **horse** and slang **ass** meaning "rear end or buttocks." USAGE ALERT: The use of the word **shit** will be objectionable in some contexts and to some people. Can be used affectionately, but often used with intent to be rude and understood as such.

**lunkhead** |LUNGK hed| *n* A stupid person; an incompetent person. ORIGINS: From SE **lump** and slang suffix -head. USAGE ALERT: Usually used with intent to denigrate or insult and understood as such.

**muddlehead** |MU dul hed| *n* A stupid or blundering person. ORIGINS: From SE muddle meaning "a mess; a confused situation" and slang suffix -head. USAGE ALERT: Often used with intent to denigrate or insult and understood as such.

**schlemiel, shlemiel** |shlu MĒL| *n* A fool; an inept person; a bungler. ORIGINS: From Yiddish shlemil. USAGE ALERT: Usually used with intent to denigrate or insult and understood as such.

**schmendrik, shmendrik** |SHMEN drik| *n* A fool; an idiot. ORIGINS: From the name and title character of Abraham Goldfaden's Yiddish operetta *Shmendrik, or the Comical Wedding* (1877). USAGE ALERT: Usually used with intent to denigrate or insult and understood as such.

**schmo, shmo** |shmō| *n* A fool; a loser. ORIGINS: Invented as a euphemism for **schmuck**, from Yiddish **schmok**, meaning "penis." USAGE ALERT: Usually used with intent to denigrate or insult and understood as such.

NON-SLANG SYNONYMS—NOUNS: **buffoon**, **clown**, **goon**

Note: There are few synonyms because traits like this are frequently either "talked around" or avoided in all registers except slang.

# INDECISIVE AND/OR WEAK

**creampuff** |KRĒM puf| *n* A weakling; a person who is out of shape. ORIGINS: From the fragile-shelled pastry. USAGE INFO: Creampuff, which can also mean "an outstanding person," is a contronym. USAGE ALERT: When the negative meaning is the one referenced, usually used with intent to denigrate or insult and understood as such.

**drip** |drip| *n* A weak, spineless, boring person. ORIGINS: From extension of SE **drip**, a weak, inadequate flow of water. USAGE ALERT: Usually used with intent to denigrate or insult and understood as such.

**jellyfish** |JEL ē fish| *n* A person who lacks strength of character; someone with no fortitude. ORIGINS: From perceived characteristics of the animal called a jellyfish.

**lamer** |LĀM ur| *n* An inept or ineffective person. ORIGINS: By extension of SE **lame** meaning "disabled." USAGE ALERT: Usually used with intent to denigrate or insult and understood as such.

**non-starter** |NAHN STAHR tur| *n* An element that proves ineffective. ORIGINS: A person or horse entered in a race, but not participating.

**noodle** |NŪ dul| *n* A fool; someone weak and stupid. USAGE ALERT: Usually used with intent to denigrate or insult and understood as such.

**squish** |skwish| *n* A person thought to be weak, often because their stance on some issue(s) is less extreme than the person using the word. USAGE INFO: Used of political moderates, for example.

**waffler** |WAHF lur| *n* A person who is indecisive and changes his/her mind; a person who wavers. ORIGINS: From slang **waffling** meaning "chattering pointlessly."

**weak sister** |WĒK SIS tur| *n* An undependable person; a person who doesn't contribute his/her share. USAGE INFO: Applied to males and things, as well as females.

**weeny, weenie** |WĒ nē| *n* An inept or ineffectual person, especially a male. ORIGINS: From slang **weenie** meaning "penis," figuratively based on SE **weiner**, a Vienna sausage. USAGE ALERT: Usually used with intent to denigrate or insult and understood as such. Also, some people may find this euphemism objectionable.

**wimp** |wimp| *n* A person, usually a male, who is both weak and indecisive. USAGE ALERT: Usually used with intent to denigrate or insult and understood as such.

**wuss** |wus| *n* A person, usually a male, who is neither dependable nor effective. ORIGINS: From combining the slang words **wimp**, meaning "an indecisive person" and **pussy**, meaning "a weak, effeminate man"; from slang **pussy** meaning a woman, extended from meaning "the vagina"; from earlier use of **pussy** as affectionate name for a cat. USAGE ALERT: Usually used with intent to denigrate or insult and understood as such.

**NON-SLANG SYNONYMS:** pushover, **momma's boy**, **namby-pamby**, **equivocator**

# INEPT

**butterfingers** |BUT ur fin gerz| *n* A person who drops or fails to catch things. ORIGINS: From imagining a person whose fingers are covered with butter, therefore too slippery to maintain a grip. USAGE INFO: May be considered an insult, depending on context.

**duffer** |DUF ur| *n* An incompetent person.

**fuckup** |FUK up| *n* An inept person (one who "fucks things up" for him/herself or others). ORIGINS: From slang **fuck** meaning "sexual intercourse." USAGE ALERT: This form of **fuck** will be objectionable in some contexts and to some people.

**galoot, galloot** |gu LŪT| *n* An awkward, clumsy, or uncouth person. USAGE INFO: Can be used affectionately.

**klutz** |kluts| *n* A clumsy person; a stupid person; a person who is socially inept. ORIGINS: Through Yiddish **klots** from Middle High German **klotz** meaning "a lump of wood." *See* CHUMP and BLOCKHEAD.

**sad-ass** |SAD as| *n* A pathetic person. ORIGINS: From SE **sad** and slang suffix **-ass**. *See* **-ASS(ED)** for more information about the suffix. USAGE ALERT: The inclusion of a form of **ass** in the phrase will render it objectionable in some contexts and to some people.

**screwup, screw-up**[1] |SKRŪ up| *n* A person who characteristically ruins things, either for him- or herself or for others as well; an inept person. ORIGINS: Euphemism for **fuckup, fuck-up**. From slang **screw**, a euphemism for **fuck**. USAGE ALERT: Usually used with intent to denigrate or insult and understood as such. The euphemism **screw** in this phrase will soften it somewhat, but it may still be objectionable in some contexts and to some people.

**spaz** |spaz| *n* A clumsy or inept person. ORIGINS: Short for SE **spastic** meaning "relating to spastic paralysis" or "hypertonic, with the result that muscle movements become awkward and stiff." Medical spasticity is often associated with cerebral palsy. USAGE ALERT: It is considered objectionable by most people to use this slang to describe *sb* who has a disability such as cerebral palsy. It will also be considered objectionable in some contexts and by some people to apply the term to *sb* who does not have such a medical condition.

NON-SLANG SYNONYMS: **bull in a china shop, fumbler, a person with two left feet**

# INFLUENTIAL THROUGH FLATTERY

**apple polisher** |AP ul PAH lish ur| *n* One who seeks favor; a sycophant. ORIGINS: Reference to the practice of a student presenting a shiny apple to a teacher, trying to gain an advantage in grades by being pleasant. USAGE INFO: Despite the positive image, this term is disparaging.

**ass-kisser\*** |AS KIS ur| *n* One who seeks favor; a sycophant. ORIGINS: From SE **ass** meaning "a donkey," but commonly used as slang to refer to the rear end or buttocks. USAGE INFO: **Kiss-ass** is a separate, synonymous word that has the words in the reverse order. USAGE ALERT: The use of the word **ass** and the graphic image will make this phrase objectionable in some contexts and to some people. Usually used with intent to denigrate or insult and understood as such. • **ass-licker** |AS LIK ur|

**bootlicker** |BŪT lik ur| *n* A servile flatterer; a toady or sycophant. ORIGINS: From the posture of groveling at *sb's* feet. USAGE INFO: May be used as a euphemism for **ass licker**. USAGE ALERT: Usually used with intent to denigrate or insult and understood as such.

**brown (nose)\*** |broun / BROUN noz| *n* An obsequious flatterer. ORIGINS: From the imagined behavior of a literal **ass-kisser**: **brown** refers to (the color of) excrement. USAGE ALERT: The reference to excrement and the graphic image will make this term objectionable in some contexts and to some people. In addition, it is usually used with intent to denigrate or insult and understood as such.

• **brown noser** |BROUN nōz ur|

**kiss-ass** |KIS AS| *n* One who seeks favor; a sycophant. ORIGINS: From slang **ass** meaning "the rear end or buttocks." USAGE INFO: **Ass-kisser** is a separate, synonymous word that has the words in the reverse order. USAGE ALERT: The use of the word **ass**, the graphic image, and the implied insult will make this phrase objectionable in some contexts and to some people.

**soft-soaper** |SAWFT sōp ur| *n* A flatterer; a person who uses charm to persuade.

**suck up** |SUK up| *n* A flatterer; a toady.

**toady** |TŌD ē| *n* A flatterer. USAGE ALERT: Usually used with intent to denigrate or insult and understood as such.

**yes-man** |YES man| *n* An obsequious person; a person without any gumption; a subservient employee. ORIGINS: From the fact that this person says "yes" to any request made of him/her.

NON-SLANG SYNONYMS: charmer, sweet talker, teacher's pet, adulator, sycophant

# INFLUENTIAL THROUGH MANIPULATION

**hustler** |HUS lur| *n* An ambitious, hard-working person who inspires others to similar efforts; someone who cheats his or her way through life. USAGE INFO: A word to use carefully because of the very different impressions it might give.

**operator** |AHP u rā tur| *n* An ambitious person who pursues success single-mindedly; a manipulative and ruthless person; a swindler.

**string puller** |STRING PUL ur| *n* A manipulator; a person who secretly influences people or organizations.

**wheeler-dealer** |WĒL ur DĒL ur| *n* A manipulative hustler; an unscrupulous opportunist.

**wire puller** |WĪR PUL ur| *n* A manipulator; a person who secretly influences people or organizations.

NON-SLANG SYNONYMS: planner, strategist, contriver, deviser, maneuverer, opportunist

# INSIGNIFICANT OR EXPENDABLE

**fluffhead** |FLUF hed| *n* A shallow, superficial person. ORIGINS: From SE **fluff** meaning "something with little substance" and the slang suffix -head. USAGE ALERT: Usually used with intent to denigrate or insult, and usually considered an insult.

**lightweight** |LĪT wāt| *n* A person without any strengths; a person who does not "pull his/her weight," i.e., do his or her part or make a significant contribution.

**loser** |LŪZ ur| *n* A failure; a person perceived as worthless; a socially inept person.

**mook** |mo͞ok| *n* A fool; an insignificant person.

**nebbich, nebbish, nebish*** |NE bish| *n* A person who's not worth noticing; a nobody; a pitifully insignificant person; an ineffectual loser. ORIGINS: From Yiddish **nebech** meaning "poor thing." USAGE ALERT: Usually used with intent to denigrate or insult and understood as such.
• nebbishe |NE bish u|
• nebbisher |NE bish ur|

**pipsqueak** |PIP skwēk| *n* An insignificant person. ORIGINS: From SE **pip** and **squeak**, both referring to small, high-pitched noises.

**pissant, piss-ant** |PIS ant| *n* An insignificant person. ORIGINS: From slang **piss** meaning "urine." USAGE ALERT: The use of a form of the word **piss** will be objectionable in some contexts and to some people.

**pleb** |pleb| *n* A plebian; a commoner; an inferior. ORIGINS: Short for SE **plebian** meaning "lower class." USAGE INFO: Don't confuse with **plebe**, the name for first-year students at the US Armed Forces Academies. USAGE ALERT: This word is usually used with intent to denigrate or insult and understood as such.

**roadkill** |RŌD kil| *n* A useless person; a person whose demotion or fall from power is best considered as collateral damage. ORIGINS: From slang **roadkill** for small animals accidentally killed by vehicles on the road (and *st* used for food). USAGE ALERT: Usually used with intent to denigrate or insult and understood as such.

**schlep, shlep** |shlep| *n* An ordinary worker (as opposed to anyone with privilege or entitlement); a person who drearily drags him- or herself and/or things from place to place.

**small fry** |SMAWL frī| *n* People who are unimportant and/or have no influence. ORIGINS: From SE **small fry** meaning "little fish."

**stumblebum** |STUM bul BUM| *n* A loser; an inept, useless person. USAGE ALERT: Usually used with intent to denigrate or insult and understood as such.

**turkey** |TURK ē| *n* An unappealing, worthless person.

**washout** |WAWSH out| *n* A person who is a failure or considered a loser.

**waste of space** |WĀST uv SPĀS| *n* A thoroughly worthless individual.

**weirdo** |WIRD ō| *adj* A strange or eccentric person; a non-conformist.

**zero** |ZIR ō| *n* A loser; a worthless person; a person considered insignificant.

NON-SLANG SYNONYMS: disappointment, failure, **born loser**, **dud**, **flop**, **has-been**, **might-have-been**, **nobody**, **castaway**, **derelict**, **underachiever**

# INTELLIGENT

**brainiac** |BRĀN ē ak| *n* A very intelligent person. ORIGINS: From the D.C. Comics villain, Brainiac, whose name blends SE **brain** and **maniac**. USAGE INFO: The word can be used with no inference of villainy.

**egghead** |EG hed| *n* An intellectual; a very bright, intelligent person. ORIGINS: From SE **egg** and slang suffix **-head**.

**know-it-all** |NŌ it awl| *n* A person with an exaggerated view of his/her own intellectual capabilities; a person who is constantly putting his/her knowledge on display.

**pointy-head** |POIN tē hed| *n* An intellectual. ORIGINS: From SE **pointy** and slang suffix **-head**. USAGE ALERT: Usually used with intent to denigrate or insult and understood as such.

**rocket scientist** |RAHK ut SĪ un tist| *n* An extremely intelligent person. ORIGINS: From admiration given to "real" rocket scientists. USAGE INFO: Also used ironically of *sb* very stupid or of *sb* who always states the obvious; also used for an individual occasion of saying the obvious. USAGE ALERT: The ironic version is usually used with intent to denigrate or insult and understood as such.

**sharpie** |SHAHR pē| *n* A person who is intelligent and perceptive.

**smart-ass** |SMAHRT as| *n* A person with intellectual pretensions; a person who works hard and is academically successful. ORIGINS: From SE **smart** and slang suffix **-ass** meaning "a person." USAGE ALERT: Usually used with intent to denigrate or insult and understood as such.

**whiz, whizz** |wiz| *n* An extremely skillful or talented person. ORIGINS: Extended from SE **wizard**.

NON-SLANG SYNONYMS—NOUNS: doctor, genius, intellectual, **Einstein** (German-born American physicist and Nobel Prize recipient, who postulated the special and general theories of relativity), **highbrow**, **prodigy**, **scholar**

# KNOW-IT-ALL

**armchair general** |AHRM cher GEN ur ul| *n* A person without power or position who pontificates on how the world or a war should be run from the comfort of his/her overstuffed chair at home.

**armchair strategist** |AHRM cher STRAT u jist| *n* A person without power or position who pontificates on how the world or a war should be run from the comfort of his/her overstuffed chair at home.

**backseat driver** |BAK sēt DRĪ vur| *n* A person who persists in offering unwanted advice to the person in charge. ORIGINS: From the practice of motor vehicle passengers who second-guess the driver.

**Monday morning quarterback** |MUN dā MAWRN ing KAWR tur bak| *n* An amateur who feels confident in criticizing a professional's handling of things with the benefit of hindsight. ORIGINS: From the practice of sports fans who dissect the weekend's competitions after they're over.

NON-SLANG SYNONYMS: <u>know-it-all</u>

# LAZY

**G4N** Good for nothing.

**LPOC** Lazy piece of crap.

**LPOS** Lazy piece of shit.

**clock-watcher** |KLAHK wawch ur| *n* A person preoccupied with quitting time rather than work; a lazy, uncommitted worker. ORIGINS: A reference to a worker who is constantly checking the time.

**couch potato** |KOUCH pu tā tō| *n* One who spends inordinate time on the couch watching television; one who lays around and is inactive. ORIGINS: Coined in 1976 from SE **couch** and **potato**, the latter used figuratively.

**gold-brick** |GŌLD brik| *n* A slacker; a lazy person; a loafer; one who avoids working. ORIGINS: This meaning is from US military slang from around WWI. Goldbrick originally referred to the appointment of civilians with no experience to be officers, meaning that they were pretty worthless in their positions, and then—by extension—to refer to a soldier who tries to avoid assignments.

**goof-off** |GŪF awf| *n* A person who squanders time, messes around, and/or avoids work. ORIGINS: By several steps, from an obsolete English word **goff** meaning "fool," from an obsolete French word **goffe** meaning "stupid."

**layabout** |LĀ u BOUT| *n* A person who is lazy or idle; a person who does nothing productive.

**lazy piece of crap/shit** |LĀ zē pēs uv KRAP / LĀ zē pēs uv SHIT| *n* A person judged to be worthless, possibly because s/he doesn't seem to accomplish anything, or just in general. USAGE ALERT: Usually used with intent to denigrate or insult and understood as such.

**lazy-bones** |LĀ zē bōnz| *n* A lazy person. ORIGINS: As in **bone-lazy**, the term suggests that the person is constitutionally lazy. USAGE INFO: Takes a singular verb.

**loafer** |lōf ur| *n* A person who loafs, i.e., one who is idle and accomplishes nothing.

**slacker** |SLAK ur| *n* A lazy person; a person who avoids work. ORIGINS: From SE slack.

**slouch** |slouch| *n* An inefficient, lazy, or indifferent person.

NON-SLANG SYNONYMS: idler, **good-for-nothing**, **lounger**, **shirker**, **sluggard**, **wastrel**

# NASTY

**S.O.B., SOB** |ESS Ō BĒ| *n* Short for son of a bitch; a contemptible, nasty person. USAGE ALERT: **Son of a bitch** and its abbreviations carry implications not only about the person referred to, but also about his or, more rarely, her mother. Usually used with intent to denigrate or insult and understood as such.

**asshole** |AS hōl| *n* A nasty or despicable person. ORIGINS: From SE ass meaning "a donkey," but commonly used as slang to refer to the rear end or buttocks. Thus, with SE **hole**, a reference to the anus. USAGE ALERT: All words containing **ass** will be found objectionable in some contexts and by some people. **Asshole** is stronger than **ass**, and considered more objectionable. Usually used with intent to denigrate or insult and understood as such.

**badass** |BAD as| *n* An aggressive, tough, frightening person. ORIGINS: From slang **ass** meaning "the rear end or buttocks." *See* **-ASS(ED)** for more information about the suffix. USAGE INFO: **Badass** is a contronym. It can also mean "an admirable or formidably talented person." USAGE ALERT: The inclusion of **ass** will make this term objectionable in some contexts and to some people. Usually used with intent to denigrate or insult and understood as such.

**bastard**[1] |BAS turd| *n* A mean or nasty person; an offensive or despicable person. ORIGINS: From SE bastard meaning "an illegitimate child." USAGE ALERT: The SE sense means that this word carries implications not only about the person referred to, but also about his or her mother. The words **SOB** and **son of a bitch** have a similar issue, as does **motherfucker**. In any case, in some contexts and to some people, the term **bastard** with any meaning will be considered objectionable. Usually used with intent to denigrate or insult and understood as such.

**bitch**[1] |bich| *n* An unpleasant, offensive, difficult person of either sex. ORIGINS: From SE **bitch**, meaning "a female dog." It is Marge Dursley's use of the word bitch to describe Lily Potter that leads Harry Potter to make Marge inflate and to run away from the Dursley's home in *Harry Potter and the Prisoner of Azkaban*. USAGE INFO: Original meanings focused on sexuality; current meanings focus on the unpleasantness of a person's disposition. Can also mean an unspecified object or person, as in "Who's the bitch who took my shoes?" USAGE ALERT: This term will be objectionable in some contexts and to some people. Usually used with intent to denigrate or insult and understood as such.

**cocksucker** |KAHK suk ur| *n* A nasty or despicable person. ORIGINS: From slang **cock** meaning "penis" and SE **suck**. USAGE ALERT: This word is considered one of the most offensive in English. Because of the reference to a sex act, and the graphic image, this term will be objectionable in some contexts and to some people. This term is most often used with specific intent to give offense and understood as such.

**hard-on** |HAHRD ahn| *n* A despicable, contemptible person. ORIGINS: By extension of the slang term **hard-on** meaning "an erection of the penis." USAGE INFO: About equivalent to **prick**, **dick**, and similar terms. USAGE ALERT: The reference to sexual activity will make this term objectionable in some contexts and to some people. In addition, it is usually used with intent to denigrate or insult and understood as such.

**heel** |hēl| *n* A contemptible, ill-mannered person; someone (usually a man) who is dishonorable, especially where women are concerned.

**meanie** |MĒ nē| *n* A person who is unkind, nasty, or ill-tempered. ORIGINS: A children's rendering of SE **mean**. USAGE INFO: On account of the association with children, **meanie** may be used self-mockingly, ironically, or in an attempt to gain sympathy.

**MOFO** |MŌ fō| *n* Mother fucker; a general term of extreme abuse. ORIGINS: An abbreviation of **mother fucker**. USAGE INFO: **Mother fucker** is considered one of the, if not *the*, worst insults one can make to a man, since it suggests that he has an incestuous (i.e., sexual) relationship with his mother. Capitalization varies. USAGE ALERT: This word carries implications not only about the person referred to, but also about his mother. The inclusion of **MOFO** will make this phrase objectionable in some contexts and to some people. Usually used with intent to denigrate or insult and understood as such.

**motherfucker** |mu *thur* FUK ur| *n* A person who is completely contemptible or despicable; *st* that is nasty or awful. ORIGINS: The literal meaning is a male who commits incest with his mother. From slang **fuck** meaning "to engage in sexual intercourse." USAGE ALERT: This is considered one of the most offensive words in English. **Motherfucker** carries implications not only about the person referred to, but also about his mother (it is most often used of males, though not exclusively; in any case, it has different overtones when used of a male). Almost always used with intent to denigrate or insult and understood as such.

**muthafucka** |MU *thu* FUK u| *n See* MOTHERFUCKER.

**pisshead** |PIS hed| *n* An unpleasant, obnoxious person; a nasty individual. ORIGINS: From slang **piss** meaning "urine." Essentially the person is being referred to as "urinehead." USAGE ALERT: Use of a term with **piss** will be objectionable in some contexts and to some people. In addition, this word is usually used with intent to denigrate or insult and understood as such.

**prick** |prik| *n* An extremely unpleasant, nasty person, usually male. ORIGINS: From slang **prick** meaning "penis." USAGE ALERT: Usually used with intent to denigrate or insult and understood as such. In addition, the inherent reference to sexual organs will make it objectionable in some contexts and to some people.

**rotten egg** |RAHT'n eg| *n* A villain; a loser; a person who behaves in a nasty way. USAGE ALERT: Usually used with intent to denigrate or insult and understood as such.

**schmuck, shmuck** |shmuk| *n* A nasty, cruel, petty person. ORIGINS: From Yiddish **shmok** meaning "penis." USAGE ALERT: Usually used with intent to denigrate or insult and understood as such. This term will also be objectionable in some contexts and to some people.

**so-and-so** |SŌ und sō| *n* A euphemism for any derogatory phrase. USAGE INFO: Often preceded by one or more modifiers (as in "rotten so-and-so"), which may also be euphemisms, as in "a blinking so-and-so" or "bleeping so-and-so."

**son of a bitch**[2] |sun uv u BICH| *n* A mean or nasty person; an offensive or despicable person. ORIGINS: Figurative use of SE **bitch**, meaning "a female dog." USAGE INFO: Usually used only of males. USAGE ALERT: **Son of a bitch** carries implications not only about the person referred to, but also about his mother. Usually used with intent to denigrate or insult and understood as such. In addition, the phrase will be objectionable in some contexts and to some people.

**varmint** |VAHR mint| *n* An undesirable person; a person who causes trouble or is obnoxious. ORIGINS: Figurative use of **varmint**, variation of SE **vermin** meaning "animals that are destructive or injurious to people and/or their possessions." USAGE ALERT: Usually used with intent to denigrate or insult and understood as such.

**yahoo** |YAH hū| *n* A savage, primitive person. ORIGINS: From the creatures of that name in Jonathan Swift's novel *Gulliver's Travels* (1726).

NON-SLANG SYNONYMS: <u>rascal</u>, <u>rogue</u>, <u>snake</u>, <u>vermin</u>, cad, knave, miscreant, reprobate, scoundrel

# REPULSIVE

**creep** |krēp| *n* An unpleasant or repulsive person, sometimes with intimations of criminal involvement; someone who gives you the creeps. ORIGINS: From figurative extension of SE **creep**. USAGE ALERT: Usually used with intent to denigrate or insult and understood as such.

**douchebag** |DŪSH bag| *n* A disgusting person; a worthless, obnoxious person. ORIGINS: From the SE **douchebag**, a device for cleaning the vaginal cavity and the slang suffix -bag. USAGE ALERT: The implied reference to sex and the sex organs in this term will make it objectionable in some contexts and to some people. Usually used with intent to denigrate or insult and understood as such.

**maggot** |MA gut| *n* A despicable person. ORIGINS: Builds on the common dislike and disgust surrounding SE **maggots**, fly larvae.

**sleaze\*** |slēz| *n* A vulgar, contemptible, untrustworthy person; a person involved in immoral or dishonest pursuits, especially those pertaining to sex. ORIGINS: Back-formation from the slang adjective sleazy meaning "dirty, vulgar, and dishonest." USAGE ALERT: Usually used with intent to denigrate or insult and understood as such.
• sleazo |SLĒZ ō|

**sleazebag\*** |SLĒZ bag| *n* A vulgar, contemptible, untrustworthy person; a person involved in immoral or dishonest pursuits, especially those pertaining to sex. ORIGINS: From the slang noun sleaze and slang suffix -bag, -ball, or -bucket meaning "a person." USAGE ALERT: Usually used with intent to denigrate or insult and understood as such.
• sleazeball |SLĒZ ball|
• sleaze bucket |SLĒZ buk it|

**slime** |slīm| *n* A repulsive or despicable person. USAGE ALERT: Usually used with intent to denigrate or insult and understood as such.

**slimeball\*** |SLĪM bawl| *n* A repulsive or despicable person. ORIGINS: From slang slime and slang suffix -ball, -bag, or -bucket meaning "a person." Slime bucket made the news in July 2008 when Steve Jobs used it to refer to *NY Times* journalist Joe Nocera in a private phone call, which Nocera reported. USAGE ALERT: Usually used with intent to denigrate or insult and understood as such.
• slimebag |SLĪM bag|
• slime bucket |SLĪM buk it|

**slug** |slug| *n* A disgusting, repulsive person. USAGE INFO: Although slug referring to a person is given dictionary definitions of "lazy," actual usage reveals this alternative meaning, as in the phrase "contemptible slug." USAGE ALERT: Usually used with intent to denigrate or insult and understood as such.

**snot-rag** |SNAHT rag| *n* A disgusting person. ORIGINS: Figurative use of slang snot-rag meaning "a dirty handkerchief." USAGE ALERT: Usually used with intent to denigrate or insult and understood as such.

**stinker(oo)**² |STING ker / STING ker ū| *n* A disgusting or loathsome person. ORIGINS: Figurative use of SE **stink** meaning "to smell." USAGE INFO: When the ending is added, the word may be used playfully. USAGE ALERT: Often used with intent to denigrate or insult and understood as such.

**stinkpot** |STINGK pot| *n* A despicable or offensive person. ORIGINS: Figurative use of a slang term that once meant "chamberpot." USAGE INFO: Used affectionately for a small child who is still in diapers and is, or is suspected to be, in need of a change or a small child, whether or not in diapers, who is suspected of being, or actually is, involved in some mischief. USAGE ALERT: Sometimes used with intent to denigrate or insult and understood as such.

**worm** |wurm| *n* A contemptible, disagreeable person. ORIGINS: From typical responses to the animal. USAGE ALERT: Usually used with intent to denigrate or insult and understood as such.

NON-SLANG SYNONYMS: boor, savage, villain, **beast**, **cad**, **churl**, **cur**

# RISK-TAKING

**cowboy** |KOU boi| *n* A reckless man; a reckless showoff. ORIGINS: From SE cowboy. USAGE INFO: This word is a contronym in that it can either condemn or praise adventurous behavior, as it can also mean "an adventurous hero."

**grandstander** |GRAND stan dur| *n* A show-off; one who acts ostentatiously in order to impress. ORIGINS: One who plays to the grandstands—seats at a stadium or racetrack.

**high roller** |HĪ RŌ lur| *n* A person who is extravagant, careless with money, or takes serious risks with money, particularly in gambling.

**hot dog** |HAHT dawg| *n* A person who shows off his or her (sometimes quite expert) skill to get attention; also, a risk-taker.

**showboat** |SHŌ bōt| *n* A person who shows off; a boaster.

NON-SLANG SYNONYMS: crowd pleaser, self-publicist, **hot shot**, **peacock**, **showoff**, **exhibitionist**, **maverick**

# SNOOPY OR MEDDLESOME

**buttinsky, buttinski** |bu TIN skē| *n* A meddler; someone who intrudes or interferes. ORIGINS: From slang butt in meaning "to intrude," from SE **butt** meaning "to push with the head or horns," combined with the **-ski /-sky** ending that is characteristic of many Slavic surnames. USAGE INFO: This use of **butt** is not anatomical, although many people may not know that. USAGE ALERT: Because it singles out a particular ethnic group, this term will be considered objectionable in some contexts and to some people. Usually used with intent to denigrate or insult and understood as such.

**kibitzer** |KI bit sur| *n* A person who meddles in order to offer unsolicited and unwanted advice. ORIGINS: Through Yiddish **kibitsen**, from German **kiebitzen** meaning "to watch a card game without playing," from German **Kiebitz**, the name of a bird noted for being noisy and inquisitive. USAGE INFO: A kibitzer's advice is usually worthless.

**rubberneck** |RUB bur nek| *n* A snoop; a person who pries. USAGE ALERT: Usually used with intent to denigrate or insult and understood as such.

**yenta** |YEN tu| *n* ORIGINS: A meddler. ORIGINS: From a Yiddish proper name. USAGE ALERT: Usually used with intent to denigrate or insult and understood as such.

**NON-SLANG SYNONYMS:** eavesdropper, intruder, meddler, troublemaker, **busybody**, **nosey parker**, **sidewalk superintendent**, **snoop**, **interloper**

# STINGY OR GREEDY

**cheapo** |CHĒ pō| *n* A mean or stingy person. ORIGINS: From SE **cheap**. USAGE ALERT: May be used jocularly or as an insult.

**cheapskate** |CHĒP skāt| *n* A mean, stingy person. ORIGINS: From SE **cheap** and slang skate, meaning "a mean or contemptible person." USAGE ALERT: Usually used with intent to denigrate or insult and understood as such.

**moneygrubber, money-grubber** |MUN ē grub ur| *n* A person whose sole focus is accumulating wealth.

**penny-pincher** |PEN ē pin chur| *n* A miser; a stingy person. ORIGINS: From the idea that someone has carried frugality to an extreme.

**pig** |pig| *n* A person who is piglike: i.e., greedy, fat, dirty, ugly, repulsive. ORIGINS: From the conceived behavior and characteristics of pigs. USAGE ALERT: Usually used with intent to denigrate or insult and understood as such.

skin-flint |SKIN flint| *n* A mean, greedy person. ORIGINS: From the concept of a person so greedy they would skin (peel) a flint, if it gained *st*. From the obsolete term skin a flint.

**tight ass** |TĪT as| *n* A stingy person. ORIGINS: From slang **ass** meaning "the rear end or buttocks." USAGE INFO: Also used for a person who is very strait-laced and proper; an easily offended person. USAGE ALERT: Usually used with intent to denigrate or insult and understood as such. In addition, the inclusion of the word **ass** in the phrase will render it objectionable in some contexts and to some people.

tightwad |TĪT wad| *n* A miserly person.

NON-SLANG SYNONYMS: <u>stiff</u>, **hoarder**, **miser**, **niggard**, **Scrooge** (from the main character in Charles Dickens's novel *A Christmas Carol* from 1843, who begins the novel as a miser and ends as a philanthropist)

# STUPID

airbrain* |ER brān| *n* A stupid person. ORIGINS: Suggests that a person has air—that is, nothing—in his/her head, rather than brains, and so is empty-headed. USAGE ALERT: Usually used with intent to denigrate or insult and understood as such.
• airhead |ER hed|

amoeba-brain |u MĒ bu brān| *n* An extremely stupid person. ORIGINS: An amoeba is a one-celled animal that has no brain. USAGE ALERT: Usually used with intent to denigrate or insult and understood as such.

beetlebrain |BĒT 'I brān| *n* A stupid person. ORIGINS: The implication is that the person's brain is the size of a beetle's. USAGE ALERT: Usually used with intent to denigrate or insult and understood as such.

birdbrain |BURD brān| *n* A person considered to be silly or stupid. ORIGINS: Draws on the perception that birds have low intelligence that one perceives in phrases like running around like a chicken with its head cut off. USAGE ALERT: Usually used with intent to denigrate or insult and understood as such.

blockhead |BLAHK hed| *n* A silly, unintelligent, or foolish person. ORIGINS: From SE **block**, as in a block of wood, and slang suffix -head. USAGE ALERT: Usually used with intent to denigrate or insult and understood as such.

bonehead |BŌN hed| *n* An unintelligent person. ORIGINS: From SE **bone** and slang suffix -head, suggesting a head full of bone rather than brain, so not much thinking going on. USAGE ALERT: Often used with intent to denigrate or insult and understood as such.

boob(y) |būb / BŪ bē| *n* A stupid or foolish person; a dolt. ORIGINS: Possibly from the Spanish **bobo** meaning "a fool." **Boob** is an abbreviated form of **booby**. USAGE ALERT: Often used with intent to denigrate or insult and understood as such.

**chowderhead, chowder-head** |CHOU dur hed| *n* A stupid or foolish person. ORIGINS: Likely a variation on the dialect slang form jolterhead, meaning "blockhead." USAGE ALERT: Usually used with intent to denigrate or insult and understood as such.

**dimwit** |DIM wit| *n* A stupid person. ORIGINS: From dim altered from slang **damn-all** meaning "none" and SE wits; therefore, "a brainless person." USAGE ALERT: Usually used with intent to denigrate or insult and understood as such.

**dodo** |DŌ dō| *n* A stupid person. ORIGINS: By extension from the large clumsy bird dodo that lived in Mauritius, but has become extinct. USAGE INFO: Sometimes used in the phrase "dumb dodo." USAGE ALERT: Often used with intent to denigrate or insult and understood as such.

**dorkus maximus** |DAWRK us MAK si mus| *n* A complete idiot. ORIGINS: Fake Latin construction meaning "the ultimate dork," with dork meaning "a socially inept or stupid person." USAGE ALERT: Usually used with intent to denigrate or insult and understood as such.

**dum-dum** |DUM dum| *n* A stupid person. ORIGINS: Reduplication and alteration of dumb, possibly popularized by the lollipop named the *dum dum,* which may have been named with the British **dummy** meaning "pacifier" in mind. USAGE ALERT: *Dumb* has been used in English to refer to an inability to speak and to stupidity; it is now considered by some to be derogatory in any usage. Moreover, this term, while it may be used affectionately, is often used with intent to denigrate or insult and understood as such.

**dumb bunny** |DUM BUN ē| *n* A person who is both stupid and pathetic. ORIGINS: From slang **dumb,** meaning "lacking in intelligence" and **bunny,** meaning "a fool," based on the convention that bunnies are not too bright. USAGE INFO: *Dumb* has been used in English to refer to an inability to speak and to stupidity; it is now considered by some to be derogatory in any usage.

**dumb dodo** |DUM DŌ dō| *n* A very stupid person. ORIGINS: From slang **dumb,** meaning "lacking in intelligence" and **dodo,** meaning "a fool," based on the convention that the large, clumsy birds that are now extinct were not too bright. USAGE ALERT: *Dumb* has been used in English to refer to an inability to speak and to stupidity; it is now considered by some to be derogatory in any usage.

**dumb ox** |DUM ahks| *n* A very stupid, dull person. ORIGINS: From slang **dumb,** meaning "lacking in intelligence" and **ox,** meaning "slow and stupid," based on the convention that oxen are not too bright. USAGE ALERT: *Dumb* has been used in English to refer to an inability to speak and to stupidity; it is now considered by some to be derogatory in any usage. Moreover, this term is usually used with intent to denigrate or insult and understood as such.

**dumbbell, dumb-bell** |DUM bel| *n* A stupid person. ORIGINS: By extension from the SE **dumbbell,** originally an apparatus to strengthen aspiring bell-ringers employing weights which—not having clappers—functioned as "dumb bells" for the sake of the exercise. USAGE ALERT: *Dumb* has been used in English to refer to an inability to speak and to stupidity; it is now considered by some to be derogatory in any usage. Moreover, this term is usually used with intent to denigrate or insult and understood as such.

**dumbo** |DUM bō| *n* A stupid person; a fool. ORIGINS: By extension of the slang **dumb** meaning stupid; possibly popularized by the taunting treatment of Dumbo in the Disney movie *Dumbo* (1941; but note that re-release in theaters and on VHS and DVD have extended its audience into the twenty-first century). USAGE ALERT: *Dumb* has been used in English to refer to an inability to speak and to stupidity; it is now considered by some to be derogatory in any usage. Moreover, this term is often used with intent to denigrate or insult and understood as such.

**dummkopf, dumkopf** |DUM kupf| *n* A stupid person. ORIGINS: From German **dumm**, meaning "dumb" and **kopf** meaning "head." USAGE ALERT: *Dumb* has been used in English to refer to an inability to speak and to stupidity; it is now considered by some to be derogatory in any usage. Moreover, this term is usually used with intent to denigrate or insult and understood as such.

**dunderhead** |DUN dur hed| *n* A stupid person. ORIGINS: Possibly from Dutch **donder** meaning "thunder" and slang suffix -head. USAGE ALERT: Usually used with intent to denigrate or insult and understood as such.

**fathead** |FAT hed| *n* A stupid person. ORIGINS: From SE **fat** and slang suffix -head. USAGE ALERT: This term is usually used with intent to denigrate or insult and understood as such.

**knucklehead** |NU kul hed| *n* An unintelligent person. ORIGINS: From SE **knuckle** and slang suffix -head, suggesting a head full of bone rather than brain, so not much thinking going on. USAGE ALERT: Often used with intent to denigrate or insult and understood as such.

**lardhead** |LAHRD hed| *n* A stupid person. ORIGINS: From SE **lard** meaning "fat" and slang suffix -head. USAGE ALERT: This term is usually used with intent to denigrate or insult and understood as such.

**musclehead** |MU sul hed| *n* A well-built but stupid person, usually a man. ORIGINS: From SE **muscle** and slang suffix -head, suggesting that the muscle visible in the physique is also present in the head, replacing the brains. USAGE ALERT: Usually used with intent to denigrate or insult and understood as such.

**muttonhead** |MU tun hed| *n* A stupid or foolish person. ORIGINS: From SE **mutton** and slang suffix -head. USAGE ALERT: Usually used with intent to denigrate or insult and understood as such.

**numskull, numbskull** |NUM skul| *n* A dull or stupid person; a fool. ORIGINS: From SE **numb** and **skull** meaning that the person's brains aren't operating at capacity. USAGE ALERT: Usually used with intent to denigrate or insult and understood as such.

**palooka** |pu LOO ku| *n* A large, stupid person; a boxer. ORIGINS: Popularized by the title character of the comic strip *Joe Palooka* (1930–1984), originally by Ham

Fisher. USAGE ALERT: Often used with intent to denigrate or insult and understood as such.

**peabrain** |PĒ brān| *n* A foolish or stupid person. ORIGINS: Often considered to be related to the size of a pea, i.e., denoting a person with a pea-sized brain. USAGE ALERT: Usually used with intent to denigrate or insult and understood as such.

**pinhead** |PIN hed| *n* A foolish or stupid person. ORIGINS: From SE **pinhead** meaning "the head of a pin," suggesting a person with a very small head. USAGE ALERT: Usually used with intent to denigrate or insult and understood as such.

**space cadet** |SPĀS ku det| *n* A spacey person; one who has difficulty grasping reality. ORIGINS: A mock military rank. USAGE ALERT: Usually used with intent to denigrate or insult and understood as such.

**stupe** |stūp| *n* An idiot. ORIGINS: Shortened from SE **stupid**. USAGE ALERT: Usually used with intent to denigrate or insult and understood as such.

**stupidhead** |STŪP id hed| *n* A fool; a person who is clueless. ORIGINS: From SE **stupid** and slang suffix -head. USAGE ALERT: Usually used with intent to denigrate or insult and understood as such.

**thickhead** |THIK hed| *n* A fool; a stupid person. ORIGINS: From SE **thick** and slang suffix head. USAGE ALERT: Usually used with intent to denigrate or insult and understood as such.

**thickie\*** |THIK ē| *n* A stupid person. ORIGINS: From slang thick meaning "dull or stupid." USAGE ALERT: Usually used with intent to denigrate or insult and understood as such.
• thicko |THIK ō|

Note: This is a category for which the non-slang choices are slim because the conceptions and categories are generally so different.

**Non-Slang Synonyms:** a mentally challenged person

## STUPID AND CLUMSY OR SOCIALLY INEPT

**chucklehead** |CHUK ul hed| *n* A stupid, socially tactless person; a blockhead. ORIGINS: Possibly from SE **chuck** meaning "a cut of beef" and slang suffix -head which adds up to the approximate equivalent of meathead. USAGE ALERT: Usually used with intent to denigrate or insult and understood as such.

**clod** |klahd| *n* A dull or stupid person; a rude or socially awkward person. ORIGINS: By figurative extension from SE **clod**, meaning "a lump of earth." USAGE ALERT: Usually used with intent to denigrate or insult and understood as such.

**cretin** |KRĒT'n| *n* An obnoxious or stupid person; an idiot. ORIGINS: By extension from the SE medical term **cretinism**, a disease of the thyroid. USAGE ALERT: Usually used with intent to denigrate or insult and understood as such. In addition, because this term implicitly makes fun of people with a medical disorder, it will be considered objectionable in some contexts and by some people.

**dork** |dawrk| *n* A socially inept or stupid person. ORIGINS: Possibly an alteration from slang **dick**, supported by the fact that another meaning of dork is "penis." USAGE ALERT: Those who know the anatomical use of dork may find its use objectionable on those grounds. May be used in banter, but often used with intent to denigrate or insult and understood as such.

**dumb cluck** |DUM kluk| *n* A person who is both stupid and pathetic. ORIGINS: From slang **dumb**, meaning "lacking in intelligence" and **cluck** meaning "a dull person," based on the convention that chickens are not too bright. USAGE ALERT: *Dumb* has been used in English to refer to an inability to speak and to stupidity; it is now considered by some to be derogatory in any usage. Moreover, this term is usually used with intent to denigrate or insult and understood as such.

**dummy** |DUM ē| *n* A stupid person; one who is socially inept. ORIGINS: By extension from SE **dumb** meaning "without speech." USAGE ALERT: *Dumb* has been used in English to refer to an inability to speak and to stupidity; it is now considered by some to be derogatory in any usage. Moreover, this term is usually used with intent to denigrate or insult and understood as such.

**gomer** |GŌ mur| *n* A fool; a gullible and simple-minded person from a rural area. ORIGINS: From the main character in the television series *Gomer Pyle* (1964–1969), who had these attributes.

**lob** |lob| *n* A clumsy person who is not bright. ORIGINS: From SE **lob** meaning "an awkward and rustic person."

**lummox** |LUM uks| *n* A large and clumsy or ungainly person; a stupid person. USAGE ALERT: Usually used with intent to denigrate or insult and understood as such.

**meatball** |MĒT bawl| *n* A stupid or clumsy person. ORIGINS: From SE **meatball**, a ball of ground meat and seasonings, associated with Italian, Swedish, and other cooking styles. USAGE ALERT: This term has been used in racist remarks directed at Italians and African Americans. Often used with intent to denigrate or insult and understood as such.

**meathead** |MĒT hed| *n* A stupid or clumsy person. ORIGINS: From SE **meat** and slang suffix -head, combined to create the idea that the person has something in his/her head other than brains. USAGE ALERT: Often used with intent to denigrate or insult and understood as such.

**oaf** |ōf| *n* A person who is large, clumsy, and dull. USAGE ALERT: Usually used with intent to denigrate or insult and understood as such.

**retard** |RĒ tahrd| *n* A socially inept person; a stupid person; a person with a disability. ORIGINS: From the formerly acceptable SE **mentally retarded**, the use of which is considerably diminished and is now usually considered objectionable, even when speaking clinically about a disability. USAGE INFO: Often used in phrases like, "What are you: a retard?" USAGE ALERT: Usually used with intent to denigrate or insult and understood as such.

**schloomp, schlump** |shlump| *n* A stupid person; a slob. ORIGINS: From Yiddish **shlump** meaning "sloppy." USAGE ALERT: Usually used with intent to denigrate or insult and understood as such.

**schlub, shlub** |shlub| *n* A coarse, stupid person; a loser. ORIGINS: From Yiddish **schlub**. USAGE ALERT: Usually used with intent to denigrate or insult and understood as such.

Note: This is a category for which the non-slang choices are slim because the conceptions and categories are generally so different.

# STUPID AND OBNOXIOUS

**blithering idiot** |BLI*TH* ur ing ID ē ut| *n* A stupid person who insists on spouting his or her ill-conceived ideas. ORIGINS: A variant of **blethering**, meaning "nonsense." USAGE ALERT: This is a harsher term than most synonyms for **stupid**, many of which could be said with pity or affection; this term is tinged with contempt. Usually used with intent to denigrate or insult and understood as such.

**doo-doo head, do-do head** |DŪ dū hed| *n* A stupid person; an offensive, disgusting, or contemptible person. ORIGINS: From slang **doo-doo**, a childish euphemism for **shit**, and slang suffix -head. Thus, though literally a euphemism for **shithead**, it doesn't have the same impact. USAGE INFO: Because **doo-doo** is a childish word, this term may be used in teasing. USAGE ALERT: The reference to excrement will make this term objectionable in some contexts and to some people.

**dumbass** |DUM as| *n* An idiot; a stupid and obnoxious person. ORIGINS: From slang dumb, meaning "lacking in intelligence" and **ass**, referring to the portion of the anatomy in which the person's brains are estimated to reside. Slang **ass** is an extension of SE **ass** meaning "a donkey," but commonly used as slang to refer to the rear end or buttocks. USAGE ALERT: *Dumb* has been used in English to refer to an inability to speak and to stupidity; it is now considered by some to be derogatory in any usage. In addition, the inclusion of **ass** in this term will make it objectionable in some contexts and to some people. Moreover, this term is usually used with intent to denigrate or insult and understood as such.

**dumb bastard** |DUM BAS turd| *n* An idiot; a person who is both stupid and obnoxious. ORIGINS: From slang dumb, meaning "lacking in intelligence" and **bastard**, meaning "a despicable, nasty person," extended from SE bastard meaning "an illegitimate child." USAGE ALERT: *Dumb* has been used in English to refer to an inability to speak and to stupidity; it is now considered by some to be derogatory in any usage. In addition, the inclusion of **bastard** in this term will make it objectionable in some contexts and to some people. Moreover, this term is usually used with intent to denigrate or insult and understood as such.

**dumb fuck** |DUM fuk| *n* An idiot who is also obnoxious. ORIGINS: From slang dumb, meaning "lacking in intelligence" and **fuck**, meaning "a despicable person," extended from **fuck**, meaning "sexual intercourse." USAGE ALERT: *Dumb* has been used in English to refer to an inability to speak and to stupidity; it is now considered by some to be derogatory in any usage. In addition, the inclusion of **fuck** in this term will make it objectionable in some contexts and to some people. Moreover, this term is usually used with intent to denigrate or insult and understood as such.

**dumb shit** |DUM shit| *n* An idiot who is also obnoxious. ORIGINS: From slang dumb, meaning "lacking in intelligence" and **shit**, meaning "a despicable person," extended from **shit**, meaning "excrement." USAGE ALERT: *Dumb* has been used in English to refer to an inability to speak and to stupidity; it is now considered by some to be derogatory in any usage. In addition, the inclusion of **shit** in this term will make it objectionable in some contexts and to some people. Moreover, this term is usually used with intent to denigrate or insult and understood as such.

**dumbbutt, dumbutt** |DUM but| *n* An idiot; a stupid and obnoxious person. ORIGINS: A euphemism for **dumbass**. From slang dumb, meaning "lacking in intelligence" and **butt**, referring to the portion of the anatomy in which the person's brains are estimated to reside. Slang **butt** is a euphemism for **ass**, an extension of SE ass meaning "a donkey," but commonly used as slang to refer to the rear end or buttocks. USAGE ALERT: *Dumb* has been used in English to refer to an inability to speak and to stupidity; it is now considered by some to be derogatory in any usage. In addition, the inclusion of **butt** in this term will make it objectionable in some contexts and to some people. Moreover, this term is usually used with intent to denigrate or insult and understood as such.

**dumbhead** |DUM hed| *n* An idiot; a stupid and obnoxious person. ORIGINS: From slang dumb, meaning "lacking in intelligence" and slang suffix -head. USAGE ALERT: *Dumb* has been used in English to refer to an inability to speak and to stupidity; it is now considered by some to be derogatory in any usage. Moreover, this term is usually used with intent to denigrate or insult and understood as such.

**jackass** |JAK as| *n* A foolish or stupid person who is loud, incompetent, and crude. ORIGINS: From SE jackass.

**NON-SLANG SYNONYMS: beast, lout, barbarian, philistine** (a term for one's enemies with origins in the Biblical stories of Samson, Saul, and David), **vulgarian**

# TOO TALKATIVE

**babbler** |BA blur| *n* A person whose conversation is trivial, foolish, or revealing of things better left undisclosed. ORIGINS: It may be that the association of the SE word **babble** with the unceasing sound of flowing water, particularly a brook, adds to the denotation a suggestion of excess.

**bag of wind** |bag uv WIND| *n* A person who talks too much and says little of value. ORIGINS: From the slang suffix **-bag**, here in a different position, but still functioning as a derogatory reference to a person. Wind here is similar to hot air: all breath and no substance. USAGE ALERT: Usually used with intent to denigrate or insult and understood as such.

**bigmouth, big mouth** |BIG mouth| *n* A boaster; a gossip; a person who is indiscreet. ORIGINS: From drawing a connection between mouth size and the amount that a person says. USAGE ALERT: Usually used with intent to denigrate or insult and understood as such.

**blabbermouth** |BLA bur mouth| *n* An indiscreet or gossiping person. ORIGINS: From slang blab, meaning "to reveal information that shouldn't have been shared." USAGE ALERT: Often used with intent to denigrate or insult and understood as such.

**blah-blaher** |blah BLAH ur| *n* A person who chatters continually and meaninglessly. ORIGINS: Onomatopoeic sound of meaningless, uninteresting talk. The *-er* suffix is applied to show that the word is naming the person who is chattering. USAGE ALERT: Often used with intent to denigrate or insult and understood as such.

**chatterbox** |CHAT ur bahks| *n* A person who doesn't know when to be quiet. USAGE ALERT: Usually used with intent to denigrate or insult and understood as such.

**chinwagger** |CHIN wag ur| *n* An avid talker. ORIGINS: By extension from slang chinwag, meaning "a chat," from the motion of the jaw, chin when talking.

**fat mouth** |FAT mouth| *n* A boaster or braggart. USAGE ALERT: Usually used with intent to denigrate or insult and understood as such.

**gabber** |GAB ur| *n* A gossip; a person who speaks indiscreetly; someone who chatters. ORIGINS: From slang **gab** meaning "to talk a lot."

**gasbag** |GAS bag| *n* A person who engages in excessive idle talk. ORIGINS: From slang gas meaning "idle talk" and slang suffix -bag meaning "a person."

**gasser** |GAS ur| *n* A talkative, chatty person. ORIGINS: From slang gas meaning "idle talk" and SE suffix **-er** meaning "one who."

**hot-air artist** |HAHT ER ahr tist| *n* A person who talks a lot of nonsense.

**loudmouth** |LOUD mouth| *n* A person who is noisy and tactless; a boaster; an indiscreet person. USAGE ALERT: Usually used with intent to denigrate or insult and understood as such.

**motormouth** |MŌ tur mouth| *n* A person who talks continuously. USAGE ALERT: Usually used with intent to denigrate or insult and understood as such.

**spieler** |SHPĒL ur| *n* A person who can talk people into things, including swindles. ORIGINS: From German **spielen** meaning "to play." USAGE ALERT: Often used with intent to denigrate or insult and understood as such.

**windbag** |WIND bag| *n* A boaster; a person whose talk is empty or devoid of meaning.

**yapper** |YAP ur| *n* A chatterer, especially, a noisy one.

NON-SLANG SYNONYMS: gossip, informer, **busybody**, **prattler**, **scandalmonger**, **tattler**, **telltale**

## FORELEGS BAD—ANIMAL NAME CALLING

There's a great deal of slang available to let other people know about their failings, and a lot of it is ... well, the opposite of personification—animalification? Name calling using animals is pretty unfailingly critical, with notable exceptions for ambitious and important types.

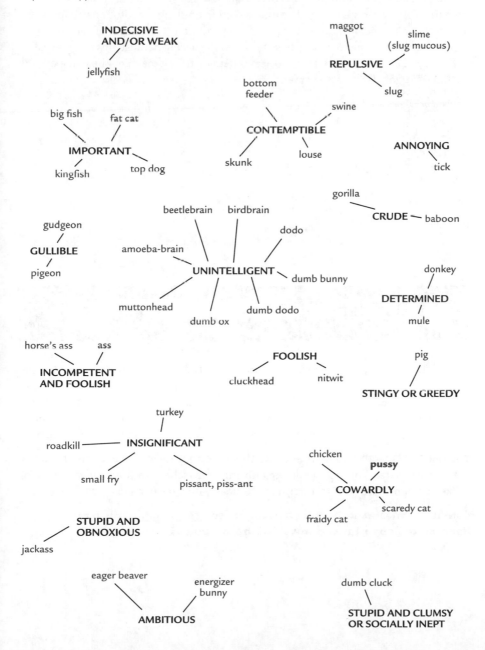

# Types of Things

We use the all-purpose word *thing* to cover a whole lot of ground, but sometimes an alternative generic term is handy. The fourth section on slang substitutions people use when they can't remember, don't know, or don't wish to use the name of something makes no attempt to include every possible word or spelling because this category is continually expanding as people improvise something to call the thing the name of which they forgot. This chapter covers:

*Confused or Disorderly Things*

*Essential Things*

*Hopeless Things*

*Names for Things You Can't Remember the Names of*

*Viscous Things*

*Worthless Things*

## CONFUSED OR DISORDERLY THINGS

**SNAFU** |sna FŪ| *n* An institutional mess; a situation of chaos and confusion. ORIGINS: From the military jargon acronym **Situation Normal All Fucked Up**. Fouled is sometimes substituted for **fucked** to create a euphemism. USAGE ALERT: The fact that the word **fucked** gets concealed within this acronym will soften the phrase somewhat, but it may still be objectionable in some contexts and to some people.

**mish-mash** |MISH mash| *n* A confused or jumbled collection of things. ORIGINS: Related both to Middle English **misse-masche** with a meaning something like "a soft mixture" and to Yiddish **mish-mash** with a meaning related to "to mix."

**NON-SLANG SYNONYMS:** chaos, clutter, confusion, <u>mess</u>, <u>muddle</u>, **disarray**, **disorder**, **mélange**, **miscellany**, **pastiche**, **potpourri**

# ESSENTIAL THINGS

**bottom line** |BAHT um LĪN| *n* A succinct summary of what's at stake; the essentials. ORIGINS: From SE **bottom line**, meaning "the profit/loss figure for an account."

**business end** |BIZ nis end| *n* The functional part; the part that really matters. ORIGINS: The part that does the business.

**clincher** |KLIN chur| *n* The decisive factor; the factor that seals the deal. ORIGINS: From SE **clinch**, a variation on SE **clench**.

**dope**[1] |dōp| *n* Reliable information; essential, important information. USAGE INFO: Often in the phrases "the inside dope" or "get the dope on . . . ."

**guts** |guts| *n* The essence of something. ORIGINS: By extension from slang **guts** meaning "stomach; a person's insides."

**lowdown, low-down, the** |*thu* LŌ doun| *n* Inside information.

**meat and potatoes** |MĒT und pu TĀ tōz| *n* The essence; the fundamentals. ORIGINS: From the conception of these two foods forming the essentials of a good sit-down meal.

**name of the game** |NĀM uv *thu* GĀM| *n* The essential part or quality.

**nitty-gritty** |NIT ē GRIT ē| *n* The most crucial or basic element.

**nuts and bolts** |NUTS und BŌLTS| *n* The working parts of *st* (as opposed to cosmetic elements); the practical or essential parts of. ORIGINS: From the make-up of many machines, which are held together with nuts and bolts.

**payoff** |PĀ ahf| *n* The end result; the outcome of a project or plan.

**poop, the** |*thu* PŪP| *n* Inside information; news; gossip.

**scoop, the** |the SKŪP| *n* The latest information. ORIGINS: From journalism, in which it refers to an exclusive news story published before the information is reported by anyone else.

**score, the** |*thu* SKAWR| *n* The essential element(s); the important part. USAGE INFO: Often used in the phrase "to know the score."

**story, the** |*thu* STAWR ē| *n* The essential outline of *st*.

**where the rubber meets the road** |wer *thu* RUB bur mēts *thu* RŌD| *phr* At the most important point; in the most important moment; the essential thing.

**NON-SLANG SYNONYMS:** cases, core, foundation, key point, last word, main idea, main thing, what it's all about (this expression may be undercut by the fact that it will remind people of the dance "The Hokey-Pokey," the verses of which end with these words), whole story, **brass tacks**, **the goods**, **crux**, **essence**, **fundamentals**, **sum and substance**

# HOPELESS THINGS

**cat's chance in hell** |KATS chans in hel| *n* No chance of achieving one's goal. ORIGINS: Figurative use of SE **hell** meaning "the alternative to heaven; the realm of the devil." USAGE INFO: Usually after the verb *have,* as in "He doesn't have a cat's chance in hell of winning *American Idol*." USAGE ALERT: The inclusion of the word **hell** in the phrase will render it objectionable in some contexts and to some people.

**Chinaman's chance in hell** |CHĪ nu munz CHANS in HEL| *v* No chance. ORIGINS: Said to be from the time of the US Gold Rush, during which Chinese prospectors, who were late to the scene, ended up having to work other people's abandoned mines, with little chance of finding anything of value. Figurative use of SE **hell** meaning "the alternative to heaven; the realm of the devil." USAGE ALERT: Today, this expression may be considered racist. The reference to **hell** will make it objectionable in some contexts and to some people, as well.

**dog's chance** |DOGZ chans| *n* A very small chance. ORIGINS: From the perception of a dog's limited opportunities. USAGE INFO: Most often used in the negative, as in "doesn't have a dog's chance."

**fat chance** |FAT CHANS| *n* Used sarcastically to mean "no chance."

**snowball's chance in hell** |SNŌ bawlz chans in HEL| *v* No chance at all. ORIGINS: From the conception of hell as full of fire. Figurative use of SE **hell** meaning "the alternative to heaven; the realm of the devil." USAGE ALERT: The use of the word **hell** in this phrase will make it objectionable in some contexts and to some people.

NON-SLANG SYNONYMS: impossibility, no chance, poor outlook, **chance in a million**, **no way**, **not a ghost of a chance**, **poor prospect**

# NAMES FOR THINGS YOU CAN'T REMEMBER THE NAMES OF

**blivit, blivet** |BLIV it| *n* Something that is useless, annoying, or nameless. ORIGINS: A meaningless word used to set up a joke by inducing one's audience to ask, "what's a blivit?" The answer was/is a variant on "ten pounds of shit in a five pound bag."

**contraption** |kun TRAP shun| *n* An unspecified mechanical device; a gadget. ORIGINS: Possibly a portmanteau word from a combination of two or more of the SE words **contrivance, trap,** and **invention.**

**crap[3], also crapola** |krap / kra PŌ lu| *n* Unspecified "stuff." ORIGINS: Euphemism for **shit**. From **crap**, a euphemism for **shit** meaning "things" and **-ola**, a slang intensifying suffix. USAGE INFO: The use of **crap(ola)** to refer to items does not necessarily speak to the quality of the items being referred to nor the speaker's attitude. "I'll get my crap out of the living room in the morning" could refer to the speaker's laptop and DVDs, which s/he treasures. USAGE ALERT: This term will be objectionable in some situations and to some people.

**dingus** |DING us| *n* Any item the name of which can't be recalled. ORIGINS: From Dutch **ding** meaning "thing." USAGE INFO: Dingus is also used as a slang euphemism for SE **penis**, so there is the possibility for misinterpretation.

**doobob** |DŪ bahb| *n See* DOODAD.

**doodad, doodah, dooda, do-da** |DŪ dah| *n* Any nameless small object, or small object for which one cannot remember the name; often refers to a gadget. ORIGINS: May derive from people's efforts to recall a forgotten name. USAGE INFO: Exact sound and spelling vary too widely for all variations to be listed.

**doohickey, dohickey, doohicky\*** |DŪ hi kē| *n* Any nameless small object, or small object for which one cannot remember the name; often refers to a gadget. ORIGINS: May derive from people's efforts to recall a forgotten name. USAGE INFO: Exact sound and spelling vary too widely for all variations to be listed.
• doohinky |DŪ hing kē|

**doojigger, dojigger** |DŪ jig ur| *n* Any nameless small object, or small object for which one cannot remember the name; often refers to a gadget. ORIGINS: May derive from people's efforts to recall a forgotten name. USAGE INFO: Exact sound and spelling vary too widely for all variations to be listed.

**fucker**[1] |FUK ur| *n* An unspecified object, animal, or person. ORIGINS: From slang **fuck** meaning "to engage in sexual intercourse." USAGE INFO: This term can be used with no opprobrium or criticism attached or it can be used to provoke. USAGE ALERT: This form of **fuck** will be objectionable in some contexts and to some people.

**gizmo, gismo** |GIZ mō| *n* A gadget or device with an unknown or forgotten name.

**hooha, hoo-ha\*** |HŪ hah| *n* Any nameless object, or object for which one cannot remember the name. ORIGINS: May derive from people's efforts to recall a forgotten name.
• hoo-hoo |HŪ hū|

**jigger** |JIG ur| *n* Any nameless object, or object for which one cannot remember the name; often refers to a gadget. ORIGINS: Possibly short for watchamajigger or whatchamajigger or thingamajig or any of the very many other synonyms.

**oojah, oojar** |Ū ju / Ū jahr| *n* Any nameless small object, or small object for which one cannot remember the name; often refers to a gadget. ORIGINS: May derive from people's efforts to recall a forgotten name. USAGE INFO: Exact sound and spelling vary too widely for all variations to be listed.

**shit**[1] |shit| *n* Unspecified "stuff," often, one's possessions. ORIGINS: From slang **shit** meaning "excrement." USAGE INFO: In this particular case, the use of **shit** does not speak to the quality of the items being referred to and is not necessarily drawing a parallel between them and excrement. "I'll get my shit out of the living room in the morning" could refer to "my laptop and DVDs, which I actually treasure." USAGE ALERT: Because it refers to excrement, this term will be objectionable in some situations and to some people.

**sucker**[2] |SUK ur| *n* Any nameless object, or object for which one cannot remember the name. ORIGINS: This noun apparently actually does come from **cocksucker**, though its meaning bears no marks of the relationship. USAGE ALERT: Many people use this word without reference to its origins and, often, without knowing them. This can lead to very different interpretations of proper use, as well as drawing strong objections, especially when children are using the word or within earshot.

**thingy, thingie**\* |THING ē| *n* A substitute to use when you don't know or can't remember *st*'s name or choose not to name *st*.
• thingamabob, thingumabob |THING u mu bahb|
• thingamajig |THING u mu jig|
• thingummy |THING u mē|

**whangdoodle**\* |WANG dū dul| *n* Any nameless object, or object for which one cannot remember the name; may refer to a gadget. ORIGINS: May derive from people's efforts to recall a forgotten name. USAGE INFO: Exact sound and spelling vary too widely for all variations to be listed.
• whangydoodle |WAN gē dū dul|

**whatchamacallit, watchamacallit** |WUCH u mu cahl it| *n* Any nameless object, or object for which one cannot remember the name; may refer to a gadget. ORIGINS: May derive from people's efforts to recall a forgotten name. USAGE INFO: Exact sound and spelling vary too widely for all variations to be listed.

**whatsit, whatzit, whassit** |WUT sit| *n* Any nameless object, or object for which one cannot remember the name; may refer to a gadget. ORIGINS: May derive from people's efforts to recall a forgotten name. USAGE INFO: Exact sound and spelling vary too widely for all variations to be listed.

**whoozis, whoosis**\* |HŪ zis| *n* Any nameless object or person, or object or person for which one cannot remember the name; may refer to a gadget. ORIGINS: May derive from people's efforts to recall a forgotten name.
• whosit |HŪ zit|

**widget** |WIJ it| *n* Any nameless small mechanical device, or a small mechanical device for which one cannot remember the name; may refer to a gadget.

**you know what** |YŪ nō wut| *n* The thing we're talking about, the name of which escapes me; the thing that we're talking about that it is not good or appropriate to name just now.

NON-SLANG SYNONYMS: appliance, contraption, invention, thing, utensil, **apparatus, contrivance**

## VISCOUS THINGS

**glop** |glahp| *n* A semi-solid, squishy substance; unappetizing (and unidentifiable) mushy mix of food. ORIGINS: Coined by Elzie Segar for use in the cartoon strip *Popeye the Sailor* from the onomatopoeic sound of mushy food being served, this word served initially as baby Swee'pea's entire vocabulary.

**goo** |gū| *n* Sticky, semi-solid material.

**goop** |gūp| *n* A sticky, but slippery, semi-solid substance. ORIGINS: Possibly an alternate form of goo.

**guck** |guk| *n* Thick, messy, semi-solid stuff, usually a waste product or something perceived as dirty.

**gunk** |gungk| *n* A thick or viscous substance. ORIGINS: From a proprietary name for cleansers used in 1932 by the A. F. Curran Company.

**NON-SLANG SYNONYMS:** mass, **blob**, **clump**, **hunk**, **wad**

## WORTHLESS THINGS

**<Proper noun> FTL** <Proper noun> for the loss.

**<Proper noun> for the loss!** |<Proper noun> fawr *thu* LOSS| *excl* An alternative cry of victory by naming the other person as the loser; an acclamation of the poor quality of an item. ORIGINS: From computer games. The idea is that choosing/using this item will result in a figurative loss to you. Altered from <Proper noun> for the win!

**chazzerei, chazerei** |KHAHZ ur ī| *n* See CHOZZERAI, CHOZERAI.

**chozzerai, chozerai** |KHAHZ ur ī| *n* Junk; trashy stuff; inferior or worthless goods. ORIGINS: From Yiddish **chozzer** meaning "pig," hence **chozzerai** meaning "pig food; swill."

**crap**[1] |krap| *n* An item or items that are estimated to be of the same value or quality as excrement. ORIGINS: From **crap**, a euphemism for slang **shit** meaning "excrement." USAGE ALERT: Because it refers to excrement, this term will be objectionable in some situations and to some people.

**dogshit** |DAWG shit| *n* An item or items that are estimated to be of the same value or quality as excrement. ORIGINS: From slang **shit** meaning "excrement." USAGE INFO: Whereas **bullshit** usually refers to lies, doublespeak, and other examples of false or untruthful communications, **dogshit** generally refers to physical items of extremely poor quality or extremely low value. USAGE ALERT: Because it refers to excrement, this term will be objectionable in some situations and to some people.

**dreck** |drek| *n* An item or items that are estimated to be of the same value or quality as excrement. ORIGINS: From Yiddish **drek** and German **dreck** meaning "excrement" and "trash" respectively.

**piece of crap/shit** |pēs uv KRAP / pēs uv SHIT| *n* A person or thing judged to be of inferior quality or worthless. USAGE ALERT: When used of a person, usually used with intent to denigrate or insult and understood as such.

**schlock** |schlahk| *n* Items of inferior quality; worthless goods. ORIGINS: Possibly from Yiddish **shlak** meaning "evil."

**shit**² |shit| *n* An item or items that are estimated to be of the same value or quality as excrement. ORIGINS: From slang **shit** meaning "excrement." USAGE INFO: In this particular case, the use of **shit** *does* speak to the quality of the items being referred to. Since **shit** can also simply mean "stuff; belongings; possessions; things" it is important to use context to determine which meaning is meant. USAGE ALERT: Because it refers to excrement, this term will be objectionable in some situations and to some people.

NON-SLANG SYNONYMS: garbage, waste, waste of time and money, <u>junk</u>, <u>lemon</u>, <u>rubbish</u>, <u>shoddy goods</u>, <u>trash</u>, <u>turkey</u>, **refuse**, **waste matter**, **waste product**

# The Use and Abuse of Power

The use and abuse of power is at the core of human relationships, and since speech is one power the have-nots can use and slang provides useful language for describing a variety of types of struggle, a great deal of slang focuses on power. The subgroups for this chapter deal with very different kinds of power, and they are:

*To Lead*

*To Support*

*To Dismiss, Fire, Eject, or Send Away*

*To Ostracize*

*To Coerce or Intimidate*

*To Make Someone's Life Difficult*

*To Interfere or Intrude*

*To Kill*

*To Die*

## TO LEAD

**at the helm, be** |at *thu* HELM| *v* To lead; to set the direction. ORIGINS: From the sphere of the navy in which the **helm** is the mechanism for steering a boat or ship.

**call the shots** |kawl *thu* SHAHTS| *v* To lead; to dictate the strategy to be adopted. ORIGINS: From the sphere of gambling with dice.

**carry the ball** |KER ē *thu* BAWL| *v* To lead; to take charge; to take responsibility for the course of action. ORIGINS: From the sphere of football, rugby, and other sports in which players run with the ball to advance it toward a goal.

**crack the whip** |KRAK *thu* WHIP| *v* To lead in a domineering way; to be a demanding taskmaster. ORIGINS: From the era of horse-drawn carriages, when the drivers would exercise control over the horses with loud cracks of their whips.

**have the final say** |hav *thu* FĪN ul SĀ| *v* To be the ultimate decision-maker.

**have the last word** |hav *thu* LAST WURD| *v* To be the ultimate decision-maker.

**head up** |hed UP| *v* To be the head of.

**hold the reins** |hōld *thu* RĀNZ| *v* To guide the direction forward. ORIGINS: A reference to the way one controls a horse.

**mastermind** |MAS tur mīnd| *v* To direct or supervise. ORIGINS: By extension from the noun form mastermind.

**rule the roost** |RŪL *thu* rūst| *v* To be the leader. ORIGINS: From the role of a rooster controlling which hens roost near him or the role of the cook who "rules the roast," an alternate spelling for some time.

**wear the pants** |WER *thu* PANTS| *v* To be the supreme authority, often in a home. ORIGINS: Assumes the role of the man (the pants-wearer) in patriarchal society and traditional family and stems from a time at which women wore only skirts or dresses.

NON-SLANG SYNONYMS: chair, direct, head, lead, spearhead, take charge, take control; **be in the driver's seat**, **boss**

# TO SUPPORT

**be in *sb*'s corner** |BĒ in *sb*'s KAWR nur| *v* To supply *sb* with whatever assistance they need. ORIGINS: From the role of a boxer's support staff in boxing matches.

**go to bat for** |gō tū BAT fawr| *v* To take *sb*'s side. ORIGINS: From the practice of pinch hitting in baseball, where one player stands in for another.

**go to the mat for** |gō tū *thu* MAT fawr| *v* To do one's utmost on behalf of something. ORIGINS: From the sport of wrestling, referring to a dispute that lasts until one side is victorious, i.e., pinned to the mat.

**put one's money on** |pŏŏt wunz MUN ē ahn| *v* To believe in. ORIGINS: From sports and games in which it refers to placing a bet.

**stick up for** |stik UP fawr| *v* To support or defend.

NON-SLANG SYNONYMS: back, defend, sponsor, stand behind, support; **bet on**, **buck up**, **champion**, **promote**, **prop up**, **shore up**, **throw support behind**; **advocate for**, **endorse**, **stand behind**, **subsidize**

# TO DISMISS, FIRE, EJECT, OR SEND AWAY

**axe** |aks| *v* To fire or terminate unceremoniously. ORIGINS: From the hand tool. The sharp edge and violent potential of the axe lend this particular term a sense of cruelty.

**bag *sb*/*st*** |bag *sb*/*st*| *v* To abandon, get rid of, dismiss *sb* or *st*. USAGE INFO: Bag is a contronym: it can also mean "to capture or secure *st* for oneself."

**bench** |bench| *v* To remove *sb* from participation in some event. ORIGINS: From sports such as baseball and football in which players who are not actively participating watch the play from a bench at the side of the playing field

**boot (out)** |būt / BŪT out| *v* To fire; get rid of; throw out. ORIGINS: A reference to kicking someone out with a booted foot.

**bounce** |bouns| *v* To fire; to expel by force. ORIGINS: Perhaps the force is so strong that the person who is expelled is imagined to bounce on the pavement.

**brush off** |BRUSH awf| *v* To dismiss; to ignore; to treat with contempt. ORIGINS: From the SE **brush off** as in using the hand to flick a small piece of lint off of one's clothing.

**bump²** |bump| *v* To dismiss someone from employment or a group. ORIGINS: Possibly by extension of SE **bump** meaning "to knock into; to shift to a new position; to push (out of the way)." USAGE ALERT: **Bump** is a contronym and can also mean "to promote."

**can** |kan| *v* To fire, abandon, or dismiss. ORIGINS: From the slang meaning of can—a euphemism for **ass** meaning "the rear end or buttocks"—in the phrase: to **toss out on one's can**. USAGE INFO: Sufficiently disconnected from its origins that it is unlikely to be objectionable.

**chuck out** |CHUK out| *v* To throw out a person; to discard an object. ORIGINS: From the slang **chuck**, meaning "to throw away."

**dehire** |dē HĪR| *v* To lay off or terminate. ORIGINS: Prefix de- meaning "undo" and the SE verb **hire**, meaning "to employ."

**dump** |dump| *v* To get rid of; to abruptly end a relationship with.

**get shut/shot of** |get SHUT uv / get SHAHT uv| *v* To get rid of.

**give *sb* his/her marching orders** |GIV *sb* hiz/her MAR ching awr durz| *v* To dismiss someone from employment. ORIGINS: From military jargon, in which **marching orders** means "military orders to depart or move on."

**give *sb* his/her walking papers** |GIV *sb* hiz/her WAWK ing pā purz| *v* To dismiss someone from employment. ORIGINS: From slang **walking papers** meaning "a notice of dismissal."

**give *sb* the axe** |GIV *sb* thu AKS| *v* To fire or terminate unceremoniously; to discharge abruptly. ORIGINS: From SE **axe**, the hand tool. The sharp edge and violent potential of the axe lend this particular term a sense of cruelty. USAGE INFO: It is possible to both **give the axe** and **get the axe**, as well as **get axed**.

**give *sb* the boot** |GIV *sb* thu BŪT| *v* To dismiss from employment; to end a romantic relationship. ORIGINS: From the mechanics of kicking someone with the toe of one's boot. USAGE INFO: It is possible to both **give the boot** and **get the boot**, as well as **get booted**.

**give *sb* the bum's rush** |GIV *sb* thu BUMZ rush| *v* To get rid of an unwanted person. ORIGINS: From slang **bum** meaning "a tramp or vagrant" and SE **rush** meaning "a sudden attack." Originated in the efforts of taverns who offered "free lunch" to paying customers to prevent non-paying "bums" from taking the food by expelling them from the premises. USAGE INFO: It is possible to both give the bum's rush and get the bum's rush.

**give *sb* the chop** |GIV *sb* thu CHAHP| *v* To dismiss from employment. ORIGINS: By extension of SE **chop** meaning "to sever with a blow." USAGE INFO: It is possible to both give the chop and get the chop, as well as get chopped.

**give *sb* the chuck** |GIV *sb* thu CHUK| *v* To terminate employment; to end a relationship. ORIGINS: From slang **the chuck** meaning "an act of rejection." USAGE INFO: It is possible to both give the chuck and get the chuck, as well as get chucked (out).

**give *sb* the gate** |GIV *sb* thu GĀT| *v* To abruptly end a relationship. ORIGINS: The reference is to being shown the exit. USAGE INFO: It is possible to both give the gate and get the gate.

**give *sb* the (old) heave-ho** |GIV *sb* thu HĒV HŌ / GIV *sb* thu OLD HĒV HŌ| *v* To dismiss *sb* from employment; to end a relationship. ORIGINS: From slang **heave-ho** or **old heave-ho** meaning "rejection; ejection"; from nautical jargon **heave-ho**, a cry used to time the joint efforts when hauling the anchor cable, for example. Here, the work cry has been appropriated to the saloon bouncer's work of throwing an offending person out the door. USAGE INFO: It is possible to both give the heave-ho and get the heave-ho.

**give *sb* the push** |GIV *sb* thu POOSH| *v* To dismiss *sb* from a job; to end a relationship with *sb*; to eject *sb* (from a place of business). ORIGINS: From slang **the push** meaning "dismissal or ejection" by extension from SE **push** meaning "to shove." USAGE INFO: It is possible to both give the push and get the push.

**give *sb* the sack(eroo)** |GIV *sb* thu SAK / GIV *sb* thu SAK u rū| *v* To dismiss *sb* from a job; to reject a romantic partner. ORIGINS: From the situation of being handed one's possessions in a sack while being sent away. USAGE INFO: It is possible to both give the sack and get the sack, as well as get sacked.

**give *sb* the shaft** |GIV *sb* thu SHAFT| *v* To reject; to treat unfairly; to cheat or deceive. ORIGINS: From slang **shaft** meaning "unfair treatment" by extension from SE **shaft** meaning "a projectile used to inflict injury, such as an arrow or spear." USAGE INFO: It is possible to both give the shaft and get the shaft, as well as get shafted.

**give *sb* the shove** |GIV *sb* thu SHUV| *v* To dismiss *sb* from a job; to end a romance. ORIGINS: From slang **the shove** meaning "dismissal" by extension from SE **shove** meaning "to push." USAGE INFO: It is possible to both give the shove and get the shove.

**kick *sb* out** |kik *sb* OUT| *v* To force *sb* to leave; to eject *sb*.

**kiss goodbye** |KIS good bī| *v* To end *st*.

**kiss off** |KIS awf| *v* To dismiss or terminate *sb* from employment; to reject *sb*. ORIGINS: From the idea of a parting kiss.

**pink slip** |PINK slip| *v* To fire or dismiss *sb* from employment. ORIGINS: The slang noun pink slip meaning "a notice of termination" (because that is the color paper they were printed on) has been turned into a verb.

**sack** |sak| *v* To fire; to terminate from a job. ORIGINS: From slang the sack meaning "loss of employment" so that the ironic phrasing "give the sack" is actually not giving at all, but taking away.

**send *sb* packing** |SEND *sb* PAK ing| *v* To dismiss *sb* either in a business or personal setting.

**send *sb* to the showers** |SEND *sb* tū thu SHOU urz| *v* To dismiss; to remove from the action. ORIGINS: From sports jargon.

**show *sb* the door/gate** |SHŌ *sb* thu DAWR / SHŌ *sb* thu GĀT| *v* Dismiss *sb* from employment; send *sb* out of one's presence. USAGE INFO: Note that this is different from show *sb* to the door, which can be a gesture of courtesy, as well as an escort off the premises.

**sideline** |SĪD līn| *v* To remove *sb* from participation in some event. ORIGIN: From sports such as football in which players who are not actively participating watch the play from a bench at the side of the playing field.

**throw *sb* out on his/her ass** |THRŌ *sb* out ahn hiz/hur AS| *v* To get rid of *sb* unceremoniously; to dismiss *sb*; to literally throw *sb* off the premises. ORIGINS: From slang **ass** meaning "the rear end or buttocks." USAGE ALERT: The inclusion of the word **ass** in the phrase will render it objectionable in some contexts and to some people.

**throw *sb* out on his/her ear** |THRŌ *sb* out ahn hiz/hur IR| *v* To get rid of *sb* unceremoniously; to dismiss *sb*; to literally throw *sb* off the premises. ORIGINS: The reference to SE **ear** indicates that the person doesn't land on his/her feet, but falls full-length on the ground.

**toss *sb* out** |TAHS *sb* OUT| *v* To get rid of *sb* unceremoniously; to dismiss *sb*; to literally throw *sb* off the premises.

**turn *sb* out** |TURN *sb* OUT| *v* To dismiss *sb*; to send *sb* away; to have *sb* escorted off the premises.

**yank** |yangk| *v* To remove or expel suddenly.

NON-SLANG SYNONYMS—GENERAL: cast out, dismiss, drop, eject, expel, fire, force out, have done with, let *sb* go, reject, release, send away, turn out, **get rid of**, **lay off**, **discharge**, **give notice to**, **oust**, **pension off**, **repudiate**, **terminate**

NON-SLANG SYNONYMS—RELATIONSHIP: divorce, **dump**, **jilt**, **forsake for another**, **leave at the altar**

# TO OSTRACIZE

**freeze** *sb* **out** |frēz *sb* OUT| *v* To snub *sb*; to exclude *sb* from participation.

**give** *sb* **the cold shoulder** |GIV *sb* *thu* KŌLD SHŌL dur| *v* To ignore, avoid, or ostracize *sb*, intentionally and often without explanation. ORIGINS: From Sir Walter Scott's novel *The Antiquary* (1816) in which a countess uses body language (turning her back on someone) as an act of dismissal.

**put in the dog house** |POOT in *thu* DAWG hous| *v* To shame; to ostracize. ORIGINS: From the practice of confining a dog to a separate doghouse, away from human company, as a punishment.

**put on the crap/shit list** |poot ahn *thu* KRAP list / poot ahn *thu* SHIT list| *v* To ostracize; to add to the list of people with whom one is greatly annoyed or displeased; to consider *sb* untrustworthy. ORIGINS: From slang **crap** or **shit** meaning "excrement," with *crap* usually considered less objectionable, and SE **list**. Possibly influenced by slang hit list, a list of potential targets for swindling or murder. USAGE ALERT: The inclusion of the word **crap** or **shit** in the phrase will render it objectionable in some contexts and to some people.

**thumb down** |THUM DOUN| *v* To vote against; to ostracize. ORIGINS: From the practice of voting using thumbs to signal one's choice. Re-popularized by film critics Roger Ebert and Gene Siskel using the thumbs to signal their critical response to movies.

NON-SLANG SYNONYMS: avoid, banish, blackball, blacklist, boycott, exclude, exile, expel, reject, shut out, <u>snub</u>, **deport**, **excommunicate**, **ostracize**, **oust**, **shun**

# TO COERCE OR INTIMIDATE

**bang heads together** |BANG HEDS tū ge*th* ur| *v See* KNOCK HEADS TOGETHER.

**buffalo** |BUF u lō| *v* To pressure; to intimidate. ORIGINS: From the size and power of the SE buffalo.

**build a fire under** *sb* |bild u FĪR un dur *sb*| *v* To urge or goad into action. ORIGINS: Based on the idea that a fire burning very close nearby would make even the laziest person anxious to get moving.

**bulldoze** |BOOL dōz| *v* To intimidate; to coerce; to force by using violence. ORIGINS: From the size and power of the SE bulldozer.

**crowd** |kroud| v To pressure someone; to try to force someone's hand. ORIGINS: Extension of SE **crowd**, in which one is jostled into a limited space.

**do a number on**[1] |dū u NUM bur ahn| v To subject to pressure, whether emotional blackmail or moral pressure. ORIGINS: From SE **number** meaning "a performance" extended to mean "an emotional outburst intended to manipulate."

**get the goods on** |get thu GŌODZ ahn| v To come into possession of previously secret or concealed information that is incriminating or otherwise damaging, with the intent of using it to one's advantage.

**get tough with** |get TUF with| v To intimidate; to act aggressively tough with.

**have** sb **by the balls*** |hav sb bī thu BAWLS| v To have sb at one's mercy. ORIGINS: From slang **balls**, meaning "testicles." **Short hairs** and **short and curlies** both refer to pubic hair. USAGE INFO: Also **have the world by the balls** (and similarly for the others listed on the next page). Usually used of males. USAGE ALERT: The inclusion of the word **balls** in the phrase will render it objectionable in some contexts and to some people.
• **have** sb **by the short and curlies** |hav sb bī thu SHAWRT und KUR lēz|
• **have** sb **by the short hair(s)** |hav sb bī thu SHAWRT HER(Z)|
• have sb by the tail |hav sb bī thu TĀL|

**have** sb **over a barrel** |hav sb ō vur u BER ul| v To have someone in a weak position; to have someone at a disadvantage. ORIGINS: Reportedly from a practice for treating of victims of drowning.

**have** st **on** sb |hav st AHN sb| v To be in possession of information or evidence that puts someone in one's power. USAGE INFO: Can be used of information that is incriminating, scandalous, etc.

**have the goods on** |hav thu GŌODZ ahn| v To be in possession of previously secret or concealed information that is incriminating or otherwise damaging with the intent of using it to one's advantage.

**hold** sb's **feet to the fire** |hōld sb's FĒT tū thu FĪR| v To try to influence sb's actions with pressure or by putting him/her under stress.

**knock heads together** |NAHK HEDS tu geth ur| v To use whatever means necessary to get people to stop quarreling or to stop working at cross purposes. USAGE INFO: Usually used as a threat, rather than as a description of an actual action, as in: "The new boss will knock heads together if she has to, to get the company out of this slump."

**lean on** |LĒN ahn| v To pressure sb for a desired outcome; to attempt to influence sb through threats.

**light a fire under** |līt u FĪR un dur| v To urge or goad into action. ORIGINS: Based on the idea that a fire burning very close nearby would make even the laziest person anxious to get moving.

**play hardball** |plā HAHRD bawl| v To use any means to reach one's end; to seek one's self interest without concern for others. ORIGINS: From sports: refers to the choice to play baseball (with its smaller, harder ball) rather than softball (with a larger, softer ball).

**press** *sb's* **buttons** |PRES *sb's* BUT'nz| *v* To behave in such a way as to gain the desired reaction; to act in a way that one knows will upset, anger, or frustrate *sb*.

**press-gang** |PRES gang| *v* To force or coerce into service, especially military or naval service.

**pull** *sb's* **strings** |PŌOL *sb's* STRINGZ| *v* To behave in such a way as to gain the desired reaction; to act in a way that one knows will upset, anger, or frustrate *sb*.

**put the heat on** |pŏot *thu* HĒT ahn| *v* To pressure or threaten. ORIGINS: From slang heat meaning "pressure."

**put the screws on** |pŏot *thu* SKREWZ ahn| *v* To pressure or threaten. ORIGINS: From SE **thumbscrew**, a torture device.

**put the squeeze on** |pŏot *thu* SKWĒZ ahn| *v* To attempt to influence through undue pressure.

**railroad** |RĀL rōd| *v* To pressure; to threaten; to rush through *st* in the attempt to prevent dissent. ORIGINS: From the idea of going straight to some goal with no side trips.

**ride** |rīd| *v* To keep under constant pressure; to keep constant watch and pressure on. ORIGINS: From the rider's control over a horse when riding.

**rough** *sb* **up** |RUF *sb* up| *v* To beat up; to use physical force to intimidate *sb*.

**shanghai** |SHANG hī| *v* To compel *sb's* actions through force or fraud. ORIGINS: From the onetime practice of kidnapping sailors in order to make a full crew on ships sailing to China.

**steamroll** |STĒM RŌL| *v* To force with an application of intense pressure.

**strong-arm** |STRAHNG AHRM| *v* To influence *sb* through threats of violence; to coerce; to use physical force to influence *sb*.

**turn up the heat** |TURN up *thu* HĒT| *v* To increase pressure on *sb* (in order to coerce some desired end).

**twist** *sb's* **arm** |TWIST *sb's* AHRM| *v* To coerce using threats or physical force; to persuade by underhanded means.

**worm** *st* **out of** *sb* |wurm *st* OUT uv *sb*| *v* To pressure *sb* into a revelation. ORIGINS: Figurative reference to the wriggling of worms.

**NON-SLANG SYNONYMS:** bully, force, make *sb* an offer s/he can't refuse, scare into, threaten, **hassle**, **hit below the belt**, **push around**, **put the squeeze on**, **strong-arm**, **take off the gloves**, **browbeat**, **coerce**, **compel**, **constrain**, **cow**, **intimidate**, **oblige**, **terrorize**, **urge**

# TO MAKE SOMEONE'S LIFE DIFFICULT

**bust *sb*'s ass** |BUST *sb*'s AS| *v* To beat up; to harass or annoy. ORIGINS: From slang **ass** meaning "rear end or buttocks." USAGE INFO: Don't confuse this form with **break** or **bust one's ass** (that is, one's own **ass**), which means "to make a great effort; to work very hard." USAGE ALERT: The inclusion of **ass** will make this phrase objectionable in some contexts and to some people.

**bust *sb*'s balls** |BUST *sb*'s BAWLZ| *v* To beat up; to harass or annoy. ORIGINS: From slang **balls** meaning "testicles." USAGE INFO: Don't confuse this form with **break** or **bust one's balls** (that is, one's own **balls**),which means "to make a great effort; to work very hard." **Balls** is usually only used to refer to, or used self-referentially by, males. USAGE ALERT: The inclusion of **balls** will make this phrase objectionable in some contexts and to some people.

**bust *sb*'s buns** | BUST *sb*'s BUNZ | *v* To beat up; to harass or annoy. ORIGINS: Euphemism for **beat *sb*'s ass**. From slang **buns**, a euphemism for slang **ass**, meaning "the rear end or buttocks." USAGE INFO: Since spanking has been a standard punishment for some time, this expression does not seem as violating as **bust *sb*'s balls**, for example. USAGE ALERT: The reference to the human rear end or buttocks will render this phrase objectionable in some contexts and to some people. Some people will find **buns** less offensive than **butt**, which is, in turn, often considered less objectionable than **ass**.

**bust *sb*'s butt** |BUST *sb*'s BUT| *v* To beat up; to harass or annoy. ORIGINS: Euphemism for **bust *sb*'s ass**. From slang **butt**, a euphemism for slang **ass** meaning "the rear end or buttocks." USAGE INFO: Don't confuse this form with **break** or **bust one's butt** (that is, one's own **butt**), which means "to make a great effort; to work very hard." USAGE ALERT: The reference to the human rear end or buttocks will render this phrase objectionable in some contexts and to some people. Some people will find **butt** less offensive than **ass**.

**crack down on** |krak DOUN awn| *v* To act with more force, usually in pressuring people or finding and punishing infringements.

**fuck *sb* over** |FUK *sb* ō vur| *v* To cause huge problems for *sb*, often by deception. ORIGINS: From slang **fuck** meaning "to engage in sexual intercourse." USAGE ALERT: The inclusion of **fuck** will make this expression objectionable in some contexts and to some people.

**get down on *sb*** |get DOUN ahn *sb*| *v* To develop a grudge against *sb*; to be abusive or hostile to *sb*.

**get on *sb*'s back** |GET ahn *sb*'s BAK| *v* To micromanage; to annoy with too much oversight.

**get on *sb*'s case** |GET ahn *sb*'s CĀS| *v* To criticize someone extensively; to persecute. ORIGINS: From slang case meaning "situation." USAGE INFO: Note how this differs from be on the case, which means "attending to what's needed in a particular situation."

**give *sb* a bad/hard time** |GIV *sb* u BAD TĪM / GIV *sb* u HAHRD TĪM| *v* To harrass *sb*; to make life difficult for *sb*.

**hassle *sb*** |HAS ul *sb*| *v* To irritate or bother *sb*; to give *sb* a hard time.

**make it hot for** |māk it HAHT fawr| *v* To reprimand; to punish; to make life unpleasant for someone.

**piss on *sb/st*** |PIS ahn *sb/st*| *v* To denigrate; to treat with contempt. ORIGINS: Figurative interpretation of slang **piss on** meaning "the act of urinating." USAGE ALERT: The inclusion of the word **piss** in the phrase will render it objectionable in some contexts and to some people.

**put *sb* through the wringer\*** |poͦot *sb* thrū *thu* RING ur| *v* To make things very difficult or unpleasant for *sb*. ORIGINS: Refers to the wringer used to help squeeze water out of clothes before laundry was mainly done by machine. USAGE INFO: The agent can be personal, as in "Her boss is putting her through the wringer" or impersonal as "This lengthy divorce has really put him through the wringer."
• put *sb* through it |poͦot *sb* THRŪ it|

**rub *sb*'s nose in it** |rub *sb*'s NŌZ in it| *v* To repeatedly force *sb* to review his/her error; to not let a failure or mistake pass out of memory. ORIGINS: From a training technique used for housebreaking puppies.

**shaft** |shaft| *v* To treat unfairly; to be harsh.

NON-SLANG SYNONYMS: cause concern to, harass, torment, worry, **badger**, **hound**, **bedevil**, **beleaguer**, **importune**, **persecute**, **plague**, **vex**

# TO INTERFERE OR INTRUDE

**butt in** |BUD IN| *v* To get in the way; to interfere. ORIGINS: From SE **butt** meaning "to push with the head or horns." USAGE INFO: This use of **butt** is not anatomical, although many people may not know that.

**hack into** |HAK IN tū| *v* To use computer skills to gain unauthorized access to files or networks.

**muscle in** |MUS ul IN| *v* To enter by force, often taking *sb* else's place.

**poke one's nose into *st*** |PŌK wunz NŌZ in tū *st*| *v* To interfere in; to demonstrate nosy interest in; to snoop; to investigate what is not one's business.

**poke one's oar in** |PŌK wunz AWR in| *v* To join a discussion to which one hasn't been invited. ORIGINS: From the sayings "have an oar in every man's boat" and "put one's oar in every man's boat," the idea being that those with the oars are in charge both of the progress and direction of the vessel.

**put one's oar in** |POŌT wunz AWR in| *v* To join a discussion to which one hasn't been invited. ORIGINS: From the saying "have an oar in every man's boat" or "put one's oar in every man's boat," the idea being that those with the oars are in charge both of the progress and direction of the vessel.

**put one's two cents in** |POŌT wunz TŪ SENS IN| *v* To join a discussion to which one hasn't been invited.

**shove one's oar in** |SHUV wunz AWR in| *v* To join a discussion to which one hasn't been invited. ORIGINS: From the saying "have an oar in every man's boat" or "put one's oar in every man's boat," the idea being that those with the oars are in charge both of the progress and direction of the vessel. USAGE INFO: Since **shove** is stronger than **put** or **poke**, this particular version of the expression may indicate more forceful intrusion.

**stick one's nose into** *st* |STIK wunz NŌZ in tū *st*| *v See* POKE ONE'S NOSE INTO *ST*.

NON-SLANG SYNONYMS: interfere, intrude; **barge in**, **burst in**, **bust in**, **get in the way**, **get into the act**, **horn in**, **pry**; **encroach**, **impede**, **interlope**, **interpose**, **intervene**

# TO KILL

There are a fair number of words that mean both "to kill" and "to die."

**blow** *sb* **away** |BLŌ *sb* u WĀ| *v* To kill by shooting with a firearm. ORIGINS: Possibly a reference to the projectile (bullet) being blown out of the gun due to the controlled explosion that is caused by firing.

**bump³, also bump off** |bump / BUMP AWF| *v* To kill; to murder; to shoot to death. ORIGINS: Expanded from SE **bump** meaning "to knock into; to shift to a new position; to push (out of the way)." USAGE INFO: By extension, **bump oneself off** means "to commit suicide."

**cook** *sb's* **goose** |KOŌK *sb's* GŪS| *v* To kill *sb*; to ruin *sb*; to spoil *sb's* chances. USAGE INFO: Can be used reflexively for *sb* who has ruined his/her own chances. Though it has a similar construction, it is different from **settle** *sb's* hash, which suggests getting revenge.

**croak** |krōk| *v* To kill; to die. ORIGINS: Possibly onomatopoeic use of SE **croak** to invoke the sound of the death rattle.

**do away with** *sb* |dū u WĀ with *sb*| *v* To murder *sb*. USAGE INFO: By extension, "do away with oneself" means "to commit suicide."

**do for** *sb* |DŪ fawr *sb*| *v* To murder *sb*.

**do** *sb* **in** |dū *sb* IN| *v* To murder *sb*. USAGE INFO: By extension, "do oneself in" means "to commit suicide."

**frag** |frag| *v* To wound or kill a fellow soldier or ally with an explosive, such as a fragmentation grenade. ORIGINS: Shortened from SE **fragmentation**.

**gun** *sb* **down** |GUN *sb* DOUN| *v* To shoot *sb*, often killing the person.

**hose** |hōz| *v* To kill with a firearm. ORIGINS: First used of a machine gun, perhaps because of the similarity of the motion of firing to that of using a hose to spray water from side to side on plants, for example.

**ice** |īs| *v* To defeat or kill; to murder.

**knock off** |NAHK AWF| *v* To kill; to murder.

**liquidate** |LIK wi dāt| *v* To kill. ORIGINS: From Russian **likvidirovat**, a euphemism for killing used during Stalin's leadership in the USSR. A famous, popular, and punning use of the word occurs in the movie *The Wizard of Oz* (1939), released during the Stalinist era, in which the Wizard says to Dorothy after the inadvertent death of the Wicked Witch of the West by water, "Ohhh! You liquidated her, eh? Very resourceful."

**mow down** |MŌ DOUN| *v* To kill a large number (of people), most often using gunfire; to do violence to a number of things that were arrayed more or less in a row. ORIGINS: From SE **mow** meaning "to cut down large swaths of grass, leaving it to fall where it once stood."

**neutralize** |NŪ tru līz| *v* To render harmless, especially by killing. ORIGINS: A euphemism for killing.

**off** |ahf| *v* To kill; to murder. ORIGINS: Shortened from slang knock off meaning "to kill; to murder."

**rub out** |RUB OUT| *v* To kill; murder.

**smoke** |smōk| *v* To kill (with a firearm). ORIGINS: From the smoke that comes out of a gun when it is fired.

**snuff** *sb* **(out)** |snuf *sb* / SNUF *sb* OUT| *v* To murder *sb*. ORIGINS: From slang snuff (it) meaning "to die."

**take** *sb* **out** |tāk *sb* OUT| *v* To kill; murder.

**terminate** |TUR mi nāt| *v* To kill; murder.

**waste** |wāst| *v* To kill. ORIGINS: From US military jargon.

**whack**[2] |wak| *v* To kill; to murder.

**wipe** *sb* **out** |WĪP *sb* OUT| *v* To kill *sb*.

zap¹ |zap| v To destroy or kill *sb* or *st* (e.g., insects) with electricity. ORIGINS: Onomatopoeic in the case of bugs, from the sound of the device referred to as a "bug zapper."

NON-SLANG SYNONYMS: destroy, execute, finish, kill, murder, put to death, put to sleep, **hit**, **annihilate**, **assassinate**, **deprive of life**, **dispatch**, **eradicate**, **euthanize**, **exterminate**, **extirpate**, **slaughter**, **slay** (Note that while *slaughter* and *slay* are formal for "to kill," they are slang for "to defeat" and "to make *sb* laugh riotously.")

# TO DIE

bite the dust |BĪT thu dust| v To die; to be utterly defeated. ORIGINS: Although associated in many people's minds with US Westerns, the concept of dying in battle with one's face in the dirt goes back at least to Homer's *Iliad* (Book II, line 418, for example), and the phrase *bite the dust* was used in Samuel Butler's translation of *The Iliad* into English in 1898, at which time, it was not slang.

buy the farm* |BĪ thu fahrm| v To die, especially suddenly, or by violence. ORIGINS: From US Air Force slang referring to a scenario in which a jet pilot dies crashing into a farm and the farmer is awarded enough in damages to pay off the mortgage, with the result that the pilot has, in effect, bought the farm. USAGE INFO: It can replace either *farm* or *ranch*.
• buy the ranch |BĪ thu ranch|
• buy it |BĪ it|

cash in², also cash in one's chips |KASH in / KASH in wunz CHIPS| v To die. ORIGINS: From the world of gambling: when one is withdrawing from a game, one exchanges one's chips for cash as one's final act before departing.

check out |CHEK OUT| v To die. ORIGINS: From the practice of signing out just prior to leaving a hotel or other temporary residence.

conk out² |KAHNGK OUT| v To die; to come to an end or give out. ORIGINS: Initially used of a machine giving out, and then by figurative extension from that to people.

cop it |KAHP it| v To die; to get into trouble. ORIGINS: From slang cop meaning "a beating" and SE **it** referring to trouble.

croak |krōk| v To kill; to die. ORIGINS: Possibly onomatopoeic use of SE **croak** to invoke the sound of the death rattle.

exit |EG zit| v To die. ORIGINS: Possibly from an actor's exit in the theatre.

get his/hers/theirs |get HIZ/HURZ/*THERZ*| v To get what one deserves; to die. ORIGINS: Possibly abbreviation of the phrase "get what's coming to one" or "to get what one deserves." USAGE INFO: Since "what one deserves" can be very good or very bad, this expression is a contronym.

**give up the ghost** |GIV up *thu* GŌST| *v* To die; to stop working or cease functioning (of a machine). ORIGINS: From the concept of the ghost/soul/spirit leaving the body upon death.

**go belly up** |gō BEL lē up| *v* To die; to be ruined financially. ORIGINS: From the floating position of a dead fish. USAGE INFO: When speaking of finances, used more often of a business than of a personal financial failure.

**go home feet first** |gō HŌM fēt FIRST| *v* To die. ORIGINS: From the practice of being carried out of a place (because, being dead, one cannot leave under one's own power).

**go home in a box** |gō HŌM in u BAHKS| *v* To die. ORIGINS: The box is a coffin.

**go to glory** |gō tū GLAW rē| *v* To die. ORIGINS: SE **glory** means "heaven," so this is a euphemism for dying and going to heaven.

**hand in one's chips** |HAND in wunz CHIPS| *v* To die. ORIGINS: From the world of gambling: when one is withdrawing from a game, one exchanges one's chips for cash as one's final act before departing.

**kick off** |KIK AWF| *v* To die. ORIGINS: Possibly related to other slang terms for die with kick, like kick the bucket, kick the wind, and kick the clouds, the latter two of which are outdated terms referring to death by hanging.

**kick the bucket** |kik *thu* BU kit| *v* To die.

**pass in one's chips** |PAS in wunz CHIPS| *v* To die. ORIGINS: From the world of gambling: when one is withdrawing from a game, one exchanges one's chips for cash as one's final act upon leaving.

**peg out** |PEG OUT| *v* To die.

**pop off** |PAHP AWF| *v* To die.

**push up daisies** |POŌSH up DĀ zēz| *v* To die. ORIGINS: A reference to flowers growing on a grave.

**turn up one's toes** |TURN up wunz TŌZ| *v* To die. ORIGINS: Presumably from the position of the body in the casket.

NON-SLANG SYNONYMS: die, expire, pass away, perish, rest in peace, **be no more**, **be taken up to heaven**, **be with the angels**, **be with God**, **breathe one's last**, **cease to be**, **cease to exist**, **decease**, **depart this life**, **give up the ghost**, **go the way of all flesh**, **go to meet one's maker**, **join the choir invisible** (be careful with this, because, while originating in a poem by George Eliot in 1867, it was used in the Monty Python "Dead Parrot" sketch in 1969—"joined the bleedin' choir invisible"— and some people will find it funny), **shuffle off this mortal coil** (this is a slight paraphrase from William Shakespeare's play *Hamlet, Prince of Denmark* III, i, 77)

# Confrontation and Competition

Fights, altercations, quarrels, and arguments bring out lots of slang. Some slang vocabulary refers to a particular type of altercation—verbal, physical, or competition—while other slang is used more broadly. This means that the categories in this section may not exactly match your expectations if a word has a context that you haven't run into. So if you don't find exactly what you're looking for where you expect it, you may want to browse other categories of this chapter.

| | |
|---|---|
| A Fight, Quarrel, or Argument | To Knock Unconscious |
| To Seek a Confrontation | To Defeat Physically |
| To Start a Fight | To Defeat Physically or Verbally |
| To (Settle With a) Fight | To Defeat in Competition |
| To Strike a Blow | To Defeat in a Fight or Competition |
| To Attack Verbally | To Defeat in Any Realm |
| To Attack Physically or Verbally | To Be Defeated —To Surrender |
| To Attack Unexpectedly | To Seek Revenge |
| To Knock Down | |

# A FIGHT, QUARREL, OR ARGUMENT

**bust-up²** |BUST up| *n* A serious argument or quarrel, especially a relationship-ending one. ORIGINS: An incident of "breaking," in this case, applied to a relationship. *See* BUST-UP.

**dusting** |DUS ting| *n* A beating. ORIGINS: From the practice of beating the dust out of a carpet.

**dustup** |DUS tup| *n* A fight. ORIGINS: From military operations in which the interaction of men on horseback with each other raised a lot of dust.

**face-off** |FĀS awf| *n* A confrontation. ORIGINS: From sports jargon in, e.g., hockey, in which two opponents face each other (face off) and attempt to gain control of the puck that is dropped in between them.

**rhubarb** |RŪ bahrb| *n* A heated debate; a quarrel; an argument with an umpire (in baseball). ORIGINS: From SE **rhubarb**, the plant.

**riot** |RĪ ut| *n* An unrestrained physical fight.

**row** |rō| *n* A fight.

**ruckus** |RUK us| *n* A disturbance; a fight.

**rumble** |RUM bul| *n* A gang fight; a large-scale brawl.

**rumpus** |RUM pus| *n* A commotion; a riot.

**run-in** |RUN in| *n* An argument; a fight, whether physical or verbal.

**scrap** |skrap| *n* A fight. ORIGINS: From boxing jargon.

**set-to** |SET tū| *n* A physical fight; a riot.

**shoot-up** |SHŪT up| *n* A gun-fight; an act of property destruction using guns.

**slugfest** |SLUG fest| *n* A fight or competition in which there is a great deal of scoring—either of blows or of points. ORIGINS: From slang verb slug meaning "to hit hard" and suffix -fest, a shortening of SE **festival**, meaning gathering or event. The meaning is literal for a fight and figurative for most competitions.

**spat** |spat| *n* A verbal argument; a quarrel.

**tangle** |TANG gul| *n* A fight.

**tiff** |tif| *n* A quarrel over *st* trivial.

**to-do** |tū DŪ| *n* A commotion; a quarrel.

NON-SLANG SYNONYMS: argument, battle, brawl, clash, combat, conflict, controversy, debate, difference of opinion, disagreement, dispute, duel, feud, quarrel, skirmish, struggle, war, **bicker**, **free-for-all**, **scuffle**, **squabble**, **altercation**, **confrontation**, **contention**, **fracas**, **fray**, **melee**

## TO SEEK A CONFRONTATION

**gun for *sb*** |GUN fawr *sb*| *v* To seek *sb* for a showdown confrontation; to pursue with the aim of destroying; to seek determinedly.

**take on** |TĀK ahn| *v* To challenge.

NON-SLANG SYNONYMS: hunt, look for, pursue, track, trail, **seek**

# TO START A FIGHT

**come out swinging** |kum out SWING ing| *v* To go on the offensive from the very start. ORIGINS: SE **swinging** refers to the arm movement of a fighter who is throwing punches.

**get physical** |get PHIZ i kul| *v* To move from a verbal interaction to a physical one, either for the sake of violence or of seeking physical intimacy.

**go at it** |gō AT it| *v* To engage fully, either physically in a fight or love-making, verbally in a fight, or by engaging in some other activity with all one's energy.

**set about** |set u BOUT| *v* To attack. USAGE INFO: The weapon used is often named in a following prepositional phrase beginning with *with*, as in "set about him with a/ an axe, rolling pin, hammer, stick, baton, etc."

**square off** |skwuar AHF| *v* To assume a fighting stance preparatory to throwing a punch. ORIGINS: From the shape of the ring and the preparation of fighters for the start of a match in boxing.

NON-SLANG SYNONYMS: assault, attack, challenge, fight, **commit an act of aggression**, **cross swords**, **take the field**

# TO (SETTLE WITH A) FIGHT

**mix it up** |MIKS it up| *v* To engage in a physical fight or competition; to launch an argument or other verbal attack; to cause trouble. ORIGINS: From slang mix meaning "to fight."

**roughhouse** |RUF hous| *v* To fight. USAGE INFO: Often used for the boisterous play-fighting of children as well.

**slug it out** |SLUG it out| *v* To seek to settle *st* with a fist fight; to seek to settle *st* with a battle of wits (a verbal fight).

NON-SLANG SYNONYMS: duel, spar, **duke it out**, **have a shootout**, **engage in single combat**

# TO STRIKE A BLOW

Many onomatopoeic words are used both as verbs and to name the sound of a blow.

**bam** |bam| *v* To punch. ORIGINS: Imitative of the sound of a blow.

**belt** |belt| *v* To strike a strong blow with a belt or one's fist.

**biff** |bif| *v* To punch lightly. ORIGINS: Imitative of the sound of a blow.

**blam** |blam| *v* To punch hard. ORIGINS: Imitative of the sound of a blow.

**bonk** |bahnk| *v* To hit, especially on the head. ORIGINS: From WWI military expression bonk meaning "to shell." Has an onomatopoeic element. USAGE INFO: Possibly because of the onomatopoeia, it is often used in jest or teasing.

**bop** |bahp| *v* To hit, strike. ORIGINS: An onomatopoeic word. USAGE INFO: Possibly due to the onomatopoeia, often used in jest.

**brain** |brān| *v* To hit on the head; to knock out. ORIGINS: Like bean, a slang verb that refers to the object of the action.

**clip** |klip| *n* An attempt; a try; a time; an occasion. USAGE INFO: Especially in the phrases "at one clip" or "at a clip."

**clobber**[1] |KLAH bur| *v* To strike violently.

**clock** |klahk| *v* To hit (in the face). ORIGINS: By extension of slang clock meaning "a person's face or head," from SE **clock**.

**clonk** |klahngk| *v* To hit. ORIGINS: By extension of onomatopoeic SE **clonk** meaning "to make a dull thud or metallic thud."

**clout** |klout| *v* To strike a heavy blow.

**clunk** |klungk| *v* To strike or collide with. ORIGINS: Imitative of the sound of a blow.

**conk** |kahngk| *v* To hit, particularly on the nose or in the head. ORIGINS: Onomatopoeic, from the sound of a blow and slang conk, meaning "the nose."

**crown** |kroun| *v* To hit over the head. ORIGINS: By extension of SE **crown**, meaning "the top of the head." Like bean and brain, crown names the part of the body that receives the blow.

**give *sb* a knuckle sandwich** |GIV *sb* u NU kul SAND wich| *v* To punch *sb* in the mouth. ORIGINS: The fist going into the opponent's mouth is being compared to a sandwich with the main ingredient being knuckles.

**hit *sb* where it counts** |HIT *sb* wer it KOUNTZ| *v* To strike a blow at a man's groin. ORIGINS: Where it counts is a euphemism for a male's groin. USAGE INFO: This phrase is commonly used in talking about self-defense for women. USAGE ALERT:

Despite the anatomical reference, when speaking of self-defense, this term is not likely to be found objectionable.

**kabam** |ku BAM| *v* To punch. ORIGINS: Imitative of the sound of a blow.

**kapow** |ku POU| *v* To punch. ORIGINS: Imitative of the sound of a blow.

**kick *sb* where it counts** |KIK *sb* wer it KOUNTZ| *v* To strike a blow at a man's groin using the foot. ORIGINS: Where it counts is a euphemism for a male's groin. USAGE INFO: This phrase is commonly used in talking about self-defense for women. USAGE ALERT: Despite the anatomical reference, when speaking of self-defense, this term is not likely to be found objectionable.

**knock *sb's* block off** |NAHK *sb's* BLAHK awf| *v* To deliver a strong blow. ORIGINS: From slang block meaning "head." USAGE INFO: Used as a threat, rather than as a description of a particular action, as in, "If you say that again, I'm going to knock your block off."

**paste** |pāst| *v* To hit hard. ORIGINS: Alteration of baste as in lambaste.

**plug** |plug| *v* To punch; to shoot with a gun. ORIGINS: From slang plug meaning "a blow."

**pop** |pahp| *v* To hit or punch.

**pow** |pou| *v* To deliver a solid punch. ORIGINS: Imitative of the sound of a blow.

**sandbag** |SAND bag| *v* To hit a strong blow, as if with a sandbag. ORIGINS: From SE **sandbag**, a bag filled with sand used in fortification or as a weapon.

**slug** |slug| *v* To hit hard, usually with the fist. ORIGINS: From slang noun slug meaning "a blow."

**smack** |smak| *v* To slap with an open hand. ORIGINS: Imitative of the sound of a blow.

**sock** |sahk| *v* To punch.

**sock it to *sb*** |SAHK it tū *sb*| *v* To deliver a blow, literally or figuratively.

**swipe** |swīp| *v* To hit; to strike, especially in a glancing blow.

**tan** |tan| *v* To hit repeatedly. ORIGINS: From SE **tan** meaning "the process of turning hides to leather." USAGE INFO: Most often used in the phrase "to tan *sb's* hide."

**thud** |*thud*| *v* To strike a blow that makes a dull sound. ORIGINS: Imitative of the sound of a blow.

**thump** |thump| *v* To strike a blow that makes a dull sound; to beat thoroughly. ORIGINS: Imitative of the sound of a blow.

**thunk** |thunk| *v* To strike a blow that makes a dull sound. ORIGINS: Imitative of the sound of a blow.

**thwack** |thwak| *v* To strike or hit with *st* flat. ORIGINS: A variation on whack. Imitative of the sound of a blow.

**wallop** |WAW lup| *v* To hit hard; to beat up.

**whack¹** |wak| *v* To strike with a sharp blow.

**wham** |wham| *v* To punch hard. ORIGINS: Imitative of the sound of a blow.

**whang** |wang| *v* To hit with a lash or a whip. ORIGINS: Imitative of the sound of a blow.

**whap** |wap| *v* To strike a quick, sharp blow. ORIGINS: Imitative of the sound of a blow.

**whump** |wump| *v* To strike a blow that makes a dull sound. ORIGINS: Imitative of the sound of a blow.

**zonk** |zawnk| *v* To strike, especially a stunning blow. ORIGINS: Imitative of the sound of a blow.

NON-SLANG SYNONYMS: hit, punch, slap, strike, <u>cuff</u>, <u>smack</u>, <u>swat</u>, <u>thump</u>, **smite**

# TO ATTACK VERBALLY

**bad mouth, bad-mouth** |BAD mouth| *v* To attack verbally; to criticize unfairly.

**bawl *sb* out** |bawl *sb* OUT| *v* To reprimand *sb* harshly. ORIGINS: From SE **bawl** meaning "to cry loudly."

**bite *sb's* head off** |BĪT *sb's* HED awf| *v* Attack verbally, used especially in cases in which the attack is objectively out of proportion to the situation. USAGE INFO: Despite the physical description in the phrase, it is not used for physical altercations.

**break *sb's* chops** |brāk *sb's* CHAHPS| *v* To nag *sb*; to criticize *sb* harshly. ORIGINS: From SE **break** and chops, which refers to the mouth. USAGE INFO: Don't confuse this form with break one's chops (that is, one's own chops), which means "to make a great effort; to work very hard."

**bust *sb's* chops** |BUST *sb's* CHAHPS| *v* To nag *sb*; to criticize *sb* harshly. ORIGINS: Slang **bust** meaning "to break" and chops, which refers to the mouth. USAGE INFO: Don't confuse this form with bust one's chops (that is, one's own chops), which means "to make a great effort; to work very hard."

**call down** |kawl DOUN| *v* To scold or reprimand. ORIGINS: Perhaps referring to the SE meaning of **down**, "from a higher to a lower place or position," since being called down damages one's status.

**call on the carpet** |KAWL ahn *thu* KAR pit| *v* To scold or reprimand. ORIGINS: Refers to a carpet that is placed in front of the boss's desk, so the suggestion is that one is called into the boss's office to be scolded or dressed down.

**chew *sb* out** |CHŪ *sb* out| *v* To reprimand, scold. ORIGINS: From the figurative extension of SE **chew** to compare the scolding to being gnawed.

**chew *sb's* ass (off)** |CHŪ *sb's* AS / CHŪ *sb's* AS awf| *v* To reprimand; to berate; to criticize severely. ORIGINS: From the figurative extension of SE **chew** to compare the scolding to being gnawed and SE **ass** meaning "a donkey," but commonly used as slang to refer to the rear end or buttocks. USAGE ALERT: The reference to **ass** and the graphic image evoked will make this phrase objectionable in some contexts and to some people.

**come down hard (on)** |KUM doun HAHRD / kum doun HAHRD ahn| *v* To reprimand; to assault verbally.

**cuss out** |KUS OUT| *v* To verbally abuse; to reprimand with swearing. ORIGINS: The word **cuss**, slang for "swearing" comes from SE **curse**.

**cut *sb* down (to size)** |KUT *sb* DOUN / kut *sb* DOUN tū sīz| *v* To insult. ORIGINS: The concept is of trimming an oversized ego. USAGE INFO: The emphasis in this construction can vary quite a bit: THAT'LL cut him down to size. That'll cut HIM down to size. That'll cut him down to SIZE.

**dis, diss** |dis| *v* To disrespect; to disparage; to denigrate. ORIGINS: Shortening of SE **disrespect** or **disparagement**. USAGE INFO: Often refers to public humiliation.

**do a hatchet job on** |dū u HACH ut jahb ahn| *v* To destroy by means of a false or malicious verbal attack. ORIGINS: By analogy to SE **hatchet** meaning a chopping tool that is meant for hacking *st* to pieces.

**give *sb* a piece of one's mind** |GIV *sb* u PĒS uv wunz MĪND| *v* To reprimand forcefully; to tell off; to scold.

**give *sb* an earful** |GIV *sb* an IR fōōl| *v* To scold or reprimand *sb*.

**give *sb* flak** |GIV *sb* FLAK| *v* To berate with excessive or abusive criticism. ORIGINS: From an acronym for German Fl(ieger)a(bwehr)k(anone) meaning "aircraft defense gun."

**give *sb* grief** |GIV *sb* GRĒF| *v* To criticize *sb* in an angry way.

**give *sb* the business** |GIV *sb* thu BIZ nis| *v* To reprimand; to criticize. ORIGINS: From slang **business** meaning "complaints." USAGE INFO: It is possible to both **give the business** and **get the business.**

**give *sb* the dickens** |GIV *sb* thu DIK uns| *v* To reprimand *sb* severely. ORIGINS: Slang **dickens** is an altered form of SE **devil**. USAGE ALERT: The inclusion of a reference to the devil will make this term objectionable in some contexts and to some people.

**give the gaff** |GIV thu GAF| *n* To criticize; abuse; treat harshly.

**go for the jugular** |gō fawr thu JUG yū lur| *v* To criticize in the way that seems most likely to do damage. ORIGINS: From SE **jugular** meaning the large vein in the neck that carries blood to the heart and which, when severed, leads to a quick death.

**haul** *sb* **over the coals** |HAWL *sb* Ō vur *thu* KŌLZ| *v* To reprimand angrily. ORIGINS: Related to other phrases that link verbal attacks with heat, such as **make it hot for.** USAGE INFO: Sometimes seen as **drag over the coals.** *Also see* RAKE OVER THE COALS. *Drag* and *haul* just mean "pull," while *rake* means "scrape or scratch" and suggests more malice in the attack.

**jump all over** *sb* |jump awl Ō vur *sb*| *v* To launch a verbal attack against *sb*; to berate *sb*.

**jump on** *sb* |JUMP ahn *sb*| *v* To launch a verbal attack against *sb*; to berate *sb*.

**knock** |nahk| *v* To criticize; to find fault with. ORIGINS: Figurative extension of SE knock meaning "to hit."

**put down** |POŌT DOUN| *v* To insult; to denigrate. ORIGINS: From the general conception of down as bad and up as good.

**rake** *sb* **over the coals** |RĀK *sb* ō vur *thu* KŌLZ| *v* To reprimand angrily. ORIGINS: Related to other phrases that link verbal attacks with heat, such as make it hot for. USAGE INFO: Sometimes seen as **drag over the coals.** *See also* HAUL OVER THE COALS. *Drag* and *haul* just mean "pull," while *rake* means "scrape or scratch" and suggests more malice in the attack.

**rap** *sb's* **knuckles** |RAP *sb's* NU kuls| *v* To scold or reprimand *sb*. ORIGINS: From the traditional use of a ruler slap to the knuckles as a disciplinary tool in classrooms. USAGE INFO: Often used to refer to a minimal punishment (often when the speaker feels that a more substantial punishment is deserved), as in the phrase "let off with a rap on the knuckles."

**read the riot act to** |rēd *thu* RĪ ut akt tū| *v* To reprimand severely. ORIGINS: From the historical practice of British law enforcement reading the legislation (the Riot Act, 1715) by the authority of which they acted to disorderly crowds before acting on it if the crowd failed to cooperate.

**rip (into)** |rip / rip IN tū| *v* To verbally attack.

**scorch**[1] |skawrch| *v* To reprimand severely; to criticize harshly.

**sit on** |SIT ahn| *v* To reprimand; to quell.

**shit on** |SHIT ahn| *v* To denigrate; to verbally abuse. ORIGINS: From slang **shit** meaning "excrement." USAGE ALERT: The inclusion of the word **shit** in the phrase will render it objectionable in some contexts and to some people.

**slam** |slam| *v* To insult; to criticize harshly.

**snap** *sb's* **head off** |SNAP *sb's* HED awf| *v* Attack verbally, especially in cases in which the attack is objectively out of proportion to the situation. USAGE INFO: Despite the physical description in the phrase, it is not used for physical altercations.

**stick it to** *sb* |STIK it tū *sb*| *v* To attack *sb* verbally by teasing or maligning; to be harsh or unfair to *sb*.

**take a dig at** |tāk u DIG at| *v* To make a taunting or sarcastic remark to *sb*.

**tear** *sb/st* **down** |TER *sb/st* doun| *v* To criticize; to attack verbally.

**tell** *sb* **off** |TEL *sb* AWF| *v* To reprimand *sb*.

**tell** *sb* **where to get off**\* |TEL *sb* WER tū get AWF| *v* To express one's anger to *sb*, in no uncertain terms and with little restraint in tone or language. ORIGINS: Euphemism for "tell *sb* to go to hell." **Hell** is where they either get off (like a station on public transportation) or go.
• tell *sb* where to go |TEL *sb* WER tū GŌ|

**trash**[1] |trash| *v* To attack verbally: to insult, denigrate, or malign.

NON-SLANG SYNONYMS: abuse, blame, criticize, cross swords with, libel, lock horns with *sb*, shout, slander, yell at, <u>dress down</u>, **give** *sb* **a good talking to**, **berate**, **censure**, **denigrate**, **impugn**, **malign**, **reprove**, **revile**, **vilify**

# TO ATTACK PHYSICALLY OR VERBALLY

**bash** *sb* |BASH *sb*| *v* To hit *sb* a solid blow; to criticize harshly and with accusations and threats. ORIGINS: The meaning of verbal attack is a figurative extension of the physical attack.

**blast** |blast| *v* To attack violently with a gun; to attack verbally with strong criticism or accusations.

**blast** *sb/st* **out of the water** |BLAST *sb/st* OUT uv *th*u WAH tur| *v* To launch an attack of devastating proportions; to destroy. ORIGINS: The imagery comes from a naval battle.

**cut** *sb* **a new asshole/one** |KUT *sb* u NŪ AS hōl / KUT *sb* u NŪ wun| *v* To attack *sb* savagely, physically or verbally. ORIGINS: The graphic image speaks to the violence of the attack. From slang **asshole** meaning "anus." USAGE ALERT: Because of the reference to the human rear end or buttocks, as well as the graphic depiction of violence (even if **asshole** is replaced with euphemistic **one**), this expression will be found objectionable in some contexts and by some people.

**give it to** *sb* |GIV it tū *sb*| *v* To hit, beat, or stab; to admonish severely.

**give** *sb* **(holy/merry) hell** |GIV *sb* HEL / GIV *sb* HŌ lē HEL / GIV *sb* ME rē HEL| *v* To injure seriously; to scold. ORIGINS: The concept is of making someone's life hellish, and from the slang intensifier holy from SE **holy** meaning "blessed by God." Figurative use of SE **hell** meaning "the alternative to heaven; the realm of the devil." USAGE INFO: Strangely, in this context holy and merry become intensifiers for the injurious behavior. USAGE ALERT: The inclusion of the word **hell** in this expression will make it objectionable in some contexts and to some people. The inclusion of the word holy in the phrase will make it seem blasphemous and objectionable in some contexts and to some people.

**give** *sb* **the works** |GIV *sb* th*u* WURKZ| *v* To hurt physically, ranging from a beating to murder; to attack verbally; to fill someone in on the whole picture, with both words and experiences; to put on one's best show for *sb*; to provide all the embellishments available. ORIGINS: From slang **the works** meaning "everything associated with a particular thing."

**lay into** |lā IN tū| *v* To attack physically; to attack verbally.

**let fly at** *sb* ||let FLĪ at *sb*| *v* To attack *sb* physically by throwing something; to attack *sb* verbally. ORIGINS: From loosing an arrow.

**let loose on/at** ||let LŪS ahn / let LŪS at| *v* To attack physically; to attack verbally.

**light into** *sb* |LĪT IN tū *sb*| *v* To attack physically; to attack verbally. ORIGINS: From SE **alight** meaning "to descend."

**mill** |mil| *v* To fight with ones fists. ORIGINS: From the jargon of boxing.

**pile into** |pīl IN tū| *v* To attack physically; to attack verbally.

**pitch into** |pich IN tū| *v* To attack physically; to attack verbally.

**plow into** |plou IN tū| *v* To attack forcefully, either physically or verbally. ORIGINS: From SE **plow**. USAGE INFO: Distinct from **plow through** meaning "to work diligently to get through a difficult, long, or complicated task."

**rip** *sb* **a new asshole/one** |RIP *sb* u NŪ AS hōl / RIP *sb* u NŪ wun| *v* To attack *sb* savagely, physically or verbally. ORIGINS: From slang **asshole** meaning "anus." USAGE ALERT: Because of the reference to the human rear end or buttocks, as well as the graphic depiction of violence (even if **asshole** is replaced with euphemistic **one**), this expression will be found objectionable in some contexts and by some people.

**tear into** *sb* |ter IN tū *sb*| *v* To make a harsh or violent physical or verbal attack on *sb*, often impetuously.

**tear** *sb* **a new asshole/one** |TER *sb* u NŪ AS hōl / TER *sb* u NŪ wun| *v* To attack *sb* savagely, physically or verbally. ORIGINS: From slang **asshole** meaning "anus." USAGE ALERT: Because of the reference to the human rear end or buttocks, as well as the graphic depiction of violence (even if **asshole** is replaced with euphemistic **one**), this expression will be found objectionable in some contexts and by some people.

**tie into** |TĪ IN tū| *v* To attack *sb* vigorously, either physically or verbally.

**wade into** |WĀD IN tū| *v* To commence an assault, either physical or verbal. ORIGINS: A reference to beginning to walk into a large body of water.

**whale (into)** *sb* |WĀL *sb* / WĀL in tū *sb*| *v* To attack, physically or verbally.

NON-SLANG SYNONYMS: assail, assault, attack, take the offensive, **pounce upon**, **beset**, **set upon**

# TO ATTACK UNEXPECTEDLY

**blindside** |BLĪND sīd| *v* Attack unexpectedly or by surprise. ORIGINS: From the football term meaning "to attack an opponent from a point where his vision is obscured."

**blow** *sb/st* **out of the water** |BLŌ *sb/st* OUT uv *th*u WAH tur| *v* To launch a surprise attack of devastating proportions; to destroy. ORIGINS: Imagery comes from a naval battle. USAGE INFO: Can also mean to surprise pleasantly but utterly.

**bowl** *sb* **over**[1] |bōl *sb* Ō vur| *v* To take by surprise. ORIGINS: From the sport of cricket, in which the term means to retire a batsman by bowling in such a way that both bails are knocked off the wicket.

**bushwhack** |BŌOSH hwak| *v* Attack unexpectedly; ambush. ORIGINS: From SE bushwhack, meaning "to travel through a thickly wooded area by clearing away branches and bushes as one goes." Because an attack on *sb* emerging from thick woods is a technique of guerilla warfare, the word became connected with such an ambush.

**dump on** |DUMP ahn| *v* To criticize unfairly or unexpectedly; to let loose one's emotional baggage on someone. ORIGINS: By extension of SE dump.

**jump down** *sb's* **throat** |jump doun *sb's* THRŌT| *v* To launch a verbal attack—which could consist of an accusation, reprimand, criticism, or disagreement—against *sb*, often without any warning.

**sucker punch** |SUK ur punch| *v* To punch without warning or provocation. ORIGINS: From slang sucker meaning "a person who is deceived" and SE punch.

**take a swipe at** |tāk u SWĪP at| *v* To throw a punch at; to criticize unfairly or unexpectedly.

NON-SLANG SYNONYMS: ambush, launch a surprise attack, lie in wait, **sucker-punch**, **catch unawares**, **launch a preemptive strike**, **waylay**

## I'M INTO YOU

The first thought that probably comes to mind with this title is attraction, two becoming one, and intermingling of two people's minds, hearts, and souls. But we put the preposition *into* to use for violating attacks as well.

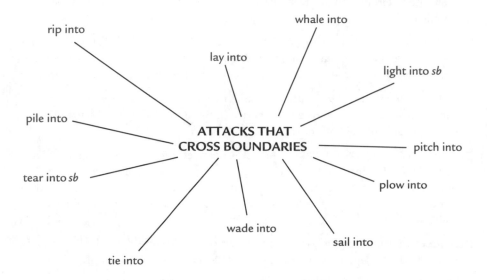

# TO KNOCK DOWN

**deck** |dek| *v* To knock *sb* down. ORIGINS: Extended from SE **deck**, meaning "the floor or ground"—the end location of someone who is "decked."

**drop** |drahp| *v* To knock *sb* down. ORIGINS: From SE **drop** meaning "to fall down," which is what the recipient of a **drop** does.

**flatten** |FLAT un| *v* To knock *sb* down. ORIGINS: The word suggests the person who has been hit lying flat on the floor.

**floor** |flawr| *v* To knock *sb* down. ORIGINS: The concept is of the person who has been hit falling to the floor as a result.

**lay *sb* (out) flat** |lā *sb* FLAT / lā *sb* out FLAT| *v* To knock *sb* down.

NON-SLANG SYNONYMS: bring down, knock down, level, throw, **fell**, **lay low**, **prostrate**, **strike down**

# TO KNOCK UNCONSCIOUS

**coldcock** |KŌLD kahk| *v* To knock *sb* unconscious. ORIGINS: From SE **out cold** meaning "unconscious" and SE **knock cold**, meaning "to knock out." USAGE ALERT: Although this word has nothing to do with slang **cock** meaning "penis," some people may assume that it does.

**kayo** |KĀ Ō| *v* To incapacitate; to put out of commission. ORIGINS: Pronunciation of KO, the slang abbreviation for boxing jargon **knock out**, meaning "knock unconscious."

**knock *sb*'s lights out** |NAHK *sb*'s LĪT zout| *v* To knock *sb* unconscious by any means (e.g., with a blow of the fist, by conking on the head with a pistol butt, etc.). ORIGINS: From slang **lights** meaning "eyes."

**knock *sb* out** |NAHK *sb* OUT| *v* To knock *sb* unconscious; to kill *sb*; to best in a competition. USAGE INFO: Also used to mean "to amaze or impress."

**punch *sb*'s lights out** |PUNCH *sb*'s LĪTZ out| *v* To knock *sb* unconscious with one or more punches. ORIGINS: From slang **lights** meaning "eyes."

**put *sb* away** |pŏŏt *sb* u WĀ| *v* To knock out; to defeat in a physical fight.

NON-SLANG SYNONYMS: knock senseless, knock unconscious

# TO DEFEAT PHYSICALLY

**bash *sb* up** |BASH *sb* up| *v* To beat thoroughly using repeated strikes and/or kicks. ORIGINS: By extension of slang **bash *sb***.

**beat the crap out of *sb*** |BĒT *thu* KRAP out uv *sb*| *v* To beat severely. ORIGINS: Euphemism for **beat the shit out of *sb***. From slang **crap**, a euphemism for slang **shit**, meaning "excrement." USAGE ALERT: The reference to **crap** will make this phrase objectionable in some contexts and to some people, though some people will find **crap** less objectionable than **shit**.

**beat the (living) daylights out of *sb*** |BĒT *thu* (LIV ing) DĀ līts out uv *sb*| *v* To beat severely. ORIGINS: From SE **beat** and slang **daylights** originally meaning "the eyes" and then "the insides."

**beat the shit out of *sb*** |BĒT *thu* SHIT out uv *sb*| *v* To beat severely. ORIGINS: From slang **shit** meaning "excrement." USAGE ALERT: The reference to **shit** will make this phrase objectionable in some contexts and to some people.

**beat the stuffing out of** *sb* |BĒT *thu* STUF ing out uv *sb*| *v* To beat severely; to undermine someone's confidence. ORIGINS: **Stuffing** is conceived as in a ragdoll: if it were to be taken out, there would just be a saggy cloth bag left.

**beat the tar out of** *sb* |BĒT *thu* TAR out uv *sb*| *v* To beat severely. ORIGINS: Perhaps because organic substances break down into tar eventually, in this expression tar is conceived of as the essence of a person.

**beat** *sb* **to a pulp** |BĒT *sb* tū u pulp| *v* To beat *sb* until s/he is seriously injured. ORIGINS: Pulp is a shapeless, wet mass of material, and the slang term draws a comparison between that and the damage that is sustained by a severely beaten person.

**break** *sb's* **head** |BRĀK *sb's* HED| *v* To deliver a violent blow to *sb's* skull (such that they are overcome); to defeat in a physical fight.

**drub** |drub| *v* To hit with repeated, heavy blows, often with a stick.

**dust** |dust| *v* To beat up; to thrash. ORIGINS: From the practice of beating the dust out of a carpet.

**fuck** *sb* **up** |FUK *sb* up| *v* To hurt or injure severely. ORIGINS: From slang **fuck** meaning "to engage in sexual intercourse." USAGE ALERT: The inclusion of **fuck** will make this expression objectionable in some contexts and to some people.

**kick the crap out of** *sb/st* |KIK *thu* KRAP out uv *sb/st*| *v* To beat up severely (with or without literal kicking). ORIGINS: Euphemism for **kick the shit out of** *sb/st*. Slang **crap** is a euphemism for **shit**. USAGE ALERT: The reference to excrement will make this phrase objectionable in some contexts and to some people, though some people will find **crap** less objectionable.

**kick the shit out of** *sb/st* |KIK *thu* SHIT out uv *sb/st*| *v* To beat up severely (with or without literal kicking). ORIGINS: From SE **kick** and slang **shit** meaning "excrement." USAGE ALERT: The reference to excrement will make this phrase objectionable in some contexts and to some people.

**knock the crap out of** *sb/st* |NAHK *thu* KRAP out uv *sb/st*| *v* To beat severely. ORIGINS: Euphemism for **knock the shit out of** *sb/st*. Slang **crap** is a euphemism for **shit**. USAGE ALERT: The reference to **crap** will make this phrase objectionable in some contexts and to some people, though some people will find **crap** less objectionable.

**knock the (living) daylights out of** *sb* |NAHK *thu* (LIV ing) DĀ lītz out uv *sb*| *v* To beat severely. ORIGINS: From SE **knock** and slang **daylights** originally meaning "the eyes" and then "the insides."

**knock the shit out of** *sb/st* |NAHK *thu* SHIT out uv *sb/st*| *v* To beat severely. ORIGINS: From SE **knock** and slang **shit** meaning "excrement." USAGE ALERT: The reference to **shit** will make this phrase objectionable in some contexts and to some people.

**knock the tar out of** *sb* |NAHK *thu* tar out uv *sb*| *v* To beat severely. ORIGINS: Perhaps because organic substances break down into tar eventually, in this expression tar is conceived of as the essence of a person.

**lam(baste), lambast** |lam BAST/ lam BĀST| *v* To beat or thrash; to attack verbally: to scold or berate; to defeat in competition. ORIGINS: Related to Old Norse **lemja** meaning "to lame by beating."

**rough** *sb* **up** |RUF *sb* up| *v* To beat up; to use physical force to intimidate *sb*.

**wallop** |WAW lup| *v* To hit hard; to beat up.

**work** *sb* **over** |WURK *sb* Ō vur| *v* To beat *sb* up.

NON-SLANG SYNONYMS: defeat, work over, <u>beat up</u>, <u>knock around</u>, **buffet**, **trounce**

## TO DEFEAT PHYSICALLY OR VERBALLY

**beat** *sb's* **ass** |BĒT *sb's* AS| *v* To beat *sb* up; to harass or annoy *sb*. ORIGINS: From slang **ass** meaning "the rear end or buttocks." USAGE INFO: Since spanking has been a standard punishment for some time, this expression does not seem as violating as **beat** *sb's* **balls**, for example. USAGE ALERT: The inclusion of **ass** will make this phrase objectionable in some contexts and to some people.

**beat** *sb's* **balls** |BĒT *sb's* BAWLZ| *v* To beat *sb* up; to harass or annoy *sb*. ORIGINS: From slang **balls** meaning "testicles." USAGE INFO: **Beat** *sb's* **balls** is usually only used to refer to, or used self-referentially by, males. **Beat** *sb's* **balls** may suggest a more personal and more violent attack than **beat** *sb's* **ass**. USAGE ALERT: The inclusion of **balls** will make this phrase objectionable in some contexts and to some people.

**beat** *sb's* **buns** |BĒT *sb's* BUNZ| *v* To beat *sb* up; to harass or annoy *sb*. ORIGINS: Euphemism for **beat** *sb's* **ass**. From slang **buns**, a euphemism for slang **ass**, meaning "the rear end or buttocks." USAGE INFO: Since spanking has been a standard punishment for some time, this expression does not seem as violating as **beat** *sb's* **balls**, for example. USAGE ALERT: The reference to the human rear end or buttocks will render this phrase objectionable in some contexts and to some people. Some people will find **buns** less offensive than **butt**, which is, in turn, often considered less objectionable than **ass**.

**beat** *sb's* **butt** |BĒT *sb's* BUT| *v* To beat *sb* up; to harass or annoy *sb*. ORIGINS: Euphemism for **beat** *sb's* **ass**. From slang **butt**, a euphemism for slang **ass**, meaning "the rear end or buttocks." USAGE INFO: Since spanking has been a standard punishment for some time, this expression does not seem as violating as **beat** *sb's* **balls**, for example. USAGE ALERT: Although it is a euphemism, the inclusion of **butt** will make this phrase objectionable in some contexts and to some people.

**break *sb's* ass** |BRĀK *sb's* AS| *v* To beat up; to harass or annoy. ORIGINS: From slang **ass** meaning "the rear end or buttocks." USAGE INFO: Don't confuse this form with **break one's ass** (that is, one's own **ass**), which means "to make a great effort; to work very hard." USAGE ALERT: The inclusion of **ass** will make this phrase objectionable in some contexts and to some people.

**break *sb's* balls** |BRĀK *sb's* BAWLZ| *v* To beat up; to harass or annoy. ORIGINS: From slang **balls** meaning "testicles." USAGE INFO: Don't confuse this form with **break one's balls** (that is, one's own **balls**), which means "to make a great effort; to work very hard." **Break *sb's* balls** is usually only used to refer to males. **Break *sb's* balls** may suggest a more personal and more violent attack than **break *sb's* ass**. USAGE ALERT: The inclusion of **balls** will make this phrase objectionable in some contexts and to some people.

**break *sb's* buns** | BRĀK *sb's* BUNZ | *v* To beat up; to harass or annoy. ORIGINS: Euphemism for **break *sb's* ass**. From slang **buns**, a euphemism for slang **ass**, meaning "the rear end or buttocks." USAGE INFO: Since spanking has been a standard punishment for some time, this expression does not seem as violating as **break *sb's* balls**, for example. USAGE ALERT: The reference to the human rear end or buttocks will render this phrase objectionable in some contexts and to some people. Some people will find **buns** less offensive than **butt**, which is, in turn, often considered less objectionable than **ass**.

**break *sb's* butt** |BRĀK *sb's* BUT| *v* To beat up; to harass or annoy. ORIGINS: Euphemism for **break *sb's* ass**. From slang **butt**, a euphemism for slang **ass**, meaning "the rear end or buttocks." USAGE INFO: Don't confuse this form with **break one's butt** (that is, one's own **butt**), which means "to make a great effort; to work very hard." USAGE ALERT: Although it is a euphemism, the inclusion of **butt** will make this phrase objectionable in some contexts and to some people.

**bust *sb's* ass** |BUST *sb's* AS| *v* To beat up; to harass or annoy. ORIGINS: From slang **ass** meaning "rear end or buttocks." USAGE INFO: Don't confuse this form with **break** or **bust one's ass** (that is, one's own **ass**), which means "to make a great effort; to work very hard." USAGE ALERT: The inclusion of **ass** will make this phrase objectionable in some contexts and to some people.

**bust *sb's* balls** |BUST *sb's* BAWLZ| *v* To beat up; to harass or annoy. ORIGINS: From slang **balls** meaning "testicles." USAGE INFO: Don't confuse this form with **break** or **bust one's balls** (that is, one's own **balls**),which means "to make a great effort; to work very hard." **Balls** is usually only used to refer to, or used self-referentially by, males. USAGE ALERT: The inclusion of **balls** will make this phrase objectionable in some contexts and to some people.

**bust *sb's* butt** |BUST *sb's* BUT| *v* To beat up; to harass or annoy. ORIGINS: Euphemism for **bust *sb's* ass**. From slang **butt**, a euphemism for slang **ass** meaning "the rear end or buttocks." USAGE INFO: Don't confuse this form with **break** or **bust one's butt** (that is, one's own **butt**), which means "to make a great effort; to work very hard." USAGE ALERT: The reference to the human rear end or buttocks will render this phrase objectionable in some contexts and to some people. Some people will find **butt** less offensive than **ass**.

**do a job on** |dū u JAHB ahn| *v* To beat up; to harass or pressure; to cause trouble for.

**give** *sb* **what-for, what for** |GIV *sb* what FAWR| *v* To beat up; to inflict serious pain; to let one's anger loose on *sb* verbally. ORIGINS: From slang what-for meaning "a punishment."

**hand** *sb* **his/her head on a plate\*** |HAND *sb* hiz / hur HED ahn u PLĀT| *v* Destroy someone, physically or verbally. ORIGINS: From the New Testament story of King Herod's birthday celebration at which he promised Herodias's daughter anything she asked for after she danced, and at her mother's prompting she asked for the head of John the Baptist on a platter (Mark 6).
  • hand *sb* his/her head on a platter |HAND *sb* hiz/hur HED ahn u PLA tur|

**let** *sb* **have it** |let *sb* HAV it| *v* To administer a beating to *sb*; to scold *sb*; to punish *sb*.

**settle** *sb's* **hash** |SET'l *sb's* HASH| *v* To silence *sb*; to best *sb* in a fight.

**skin** *sb* **(alive)** |SKIN *sb* / SKIN *sb* u LĪV| *v* To destroy, physically or verbally.

**take** *sb* **apart** |tāk *sb* u PAHRT| *v* To give *sb* a severe beating; to reprimand strongly.

NON-SLANG SYNONYMS: See To Defeat in Any Realm, page 495, for non-slang synonyms.

# TO DEFEAT IN COMPETITION

**massacre** |MAS u kur| *v* To defeat convincingly; to spoil or ruin; to botch. ORIGINS: From SE **massacre** meaning "to kill."

**run circles/rings around** |run SUR kulz u round / run RINGZ u round| *v* To surpass in a contest of some kind by a greater display of skill.

**scalp** |skalp| *v* To win a competition. ORIGINS: From SE **scalp** meaning "to remove an enemy's scalp as a war trophy." USAGE INFO: Often used in sports journalism when the winning team's name bears reference to Native Americans or American Indians, e.g., baseball: Atlanta Braves and Cleveland Indians; football: Kansas City Chiefs and Washington Redskins.

**shut out** |SHUT out| *v* To utterly defeat, not only winning but keeping opponents from scoring. ORIGINS: Extended first from baseball jargon to other sports and then to more general use.

**sink** |singk| *v* To defeat in competition.

**slaughter**[1] |SLAW tur| *v* To defeat in competition.

**slay**[1] |slā| *v* To defeat in competition

**sweep** |swēp| v To win a contest or competition by winning at every stage along the way.

**take the cake** |TĀK *thu* KĀK| v To achieve top ranking; to win the prize.

**Non-Slang Synonyms:** See To Defeat in Any Realm, page 495, for non-slang synonyms.

## TO DEFEAT IN A FIGHT OR COMPETITION

**cream** |krēm| v To beat up; to beat decisively in a sporting event or other competition. ORIGINS: The idea is that cream, being superior to milk, rises to the top.

**lick** |lik| n A small amount. USAGE INFO: Used with *a* as in, "he hasn't got a lick of sense."

**make hamburger of** |māk HAM bur gur uv| v To beat up; to destroy. ORIGINS: From the comparison of the appearance of the beat up person to chopped meat.

**make mincemeat of** |māk MINS mēt uv| v To beat up; to destroy. ORIGINS: From the comparison of the appearance of the beat up person to chopped meat.

**maul** |mawl| v To defeat resoundingly. ORIGINS: From SE **maul** meaning "to injure by beating." USAGE INFO: Often used in sports headlines with large score differentials.

**mop the floor with** *sb* |MAHP *thu* FLAWR with *sb*| v To thrash; to beat convincingly. ORIGINS: Related to the Royal Navy slang **wipe the deck with** *sb*.

**polish off** |PAH lish ahf| v To defeat in a physical fight or a sports competition.

**powder** |POU dur| v To defeat easily or notably. ORIGINS: From SE **powder** meaning "to reduce to powder."

**shellac** |shu LAK| v To thrash; to defeat.

**smear** |smir| v To beat up; to defeat by a wide margin.

**stomp (all over)** |stahmp / STAHMP awl Ō vur| v To deliver a crushing defeat to. ORIGINS: From SE **stomp** meaning "to come down hard on with one's foot."

**stomp on** |STAHMP ahn| n To beat up; to defeat; to overcome. ORIGINS: From SE **stomp** meaning "to come down hard on with one's foot."

**thrash** |thrash| v To beat soundly.

**whip** |wip| v To beat up; to defeat. ORIGINS: Extended from SE **whip**.

**whomp** |wawmp| v To defeat badly, either in a fight or in a competition.

**Non-Slang Synonyms:** See To Defeat in Any Realm, page 495, for non-slang synonyms.

# TO DEFEAT IN ANY REALM

**blitz** |blitz| *v* To defeat utterly; to destroy; to overcome in a sudden and comprehensive attack. ORIGINS: From the German **blitzkrieg**, meaning "a violent surprise attack" (literally, "lightning war"), a strategy the Germans used in WWII. USAGE INFO: Blitz is used figuratively for performing outstandingly on an examination, in which sense it is synonymous with **ace**, or the recent **pwn**.

**bowl *sb* over**[2] |BŌL *sb* ō vur| *v* To overwhelm. ORIGINS: From the sport of cricket, in which the term means to retire a batsman by bowling in such a way that both bails are knocked off the wicket.

**clobber**[2] |KLAH bur| *v* To beat up or batter; to criticize harshly; to defeat soundly.

**come out on top** |kum out ahn TAHP| *v* To surpass in a contest of some kind; to overcome difficulties. ORIGINS: Draws on the concept of the highest being the best.

**do a number on**[2] |dū u NUM bur ahn| *v* To thoroughly defeat; to purposefully humiliate. ORIGINS: From SE **number** meaning "a display."

**eat for breakfast** |ĒT fawr BREK fust| *v* To criticize harshly; to deal with or defeat handily or easily.

**have for breakfast** |HAV fawr BREK fust| *v* To criticize harshly; to deal with or defeat handily or easily.

**have it all over *sb/st*** |hav it AWL ō vur *sb/st*| *v* To surpass in a contest of some kind; to have *sb* at a disadvantage.

**have *sb* on toast** |hav *sb* ahn TŌST| *v* To have in one's power or at one's mercy. ORIGINS: Along the lines of eat/have *sb* for breakfast, the meal at which toast is most often consumed.

**kick *sb*'s ass/butt** |kik *sb*'s AS / kik *sb*'s BUT| *v* To beat *sb* in a fight; to achieve a success; to win a competition (such as a sports event) decidedly; to best *sb* in an argument. ORIGINS: From slang **ass** meaning "the rear end or buttocks." **Butt** is a euphemism for **ass**. USAGE ALERT: The reference to the rear end or buttocks will make this phrase objectionable in some contexts and to some people, though some people will find **butt** less objectionable.

**knock for a loop** |NAHK fawr u LŪP| *v* To overcome. USAGE INFO: Don't confuse with throw for a loop meaning "to confuse."

**knock the socks off *sb*\*** |NAHK *thu* SAHKS awf *sb*| *v* To overwhelm or defeat utterly. ORIGINS: Possibly a reference to cartoons in which someone hit by an uppercut flies out of his/her shoes and socks. USAGE INFO: Can also mean "to amaze or impress."
• knock *sb*'s socks off |NAHK *sb*'s SAHKS awf|

**knock the stuffing out of** *sb* |NAHK *thu* STUF ing out uv *sb*| *v* To beat severely; to undermine someone's confidence. ORIGINS: **Stuffing** is conceived as in a rag-doll: if it were to be taken out, there would just be a saggy cloth bag left.

**outfox** |out FAHKS| *v* To win a battle of wits. ORIGINS: From the common conception of the fox as a sly, clever creature.

**pulverize** |PUL vur īz| *v* To demolish or annihilate in a physical fight, verbal battle, or competition.

**shred** |shred| *v* To conquer; to best in an argument; to criticize mercilessly. ORIGINS: By analogy to devices such as a grater or a paper shredder.

**take** *sb* **down** |TĀK *sb* DOUN| *v* To defeat; to humiliate.

**whip** *sb's* **ass** |WIP *sb's* AS| *v* To defeat physically or in an argument; to best intellectually. ORIGINS: From slang **ass** meaning "the rear end or buttocks." USAGE ALERT: The inclusion of the word **ass** in the phrase will render it objectionable in some contexts and to some people.

**whoop** *sb's* **ass** |WŪP *sb's* AS| *v* See **WHIP** *SB's* **ASS**.

**whup** *sb's* **ass** |WHUP *sb's* AS| *v* See **WHIP** *SB's* **ASS**.

**win hands down** |WIN hands DOUN| *v* To achieve a resounding victory.

**wipe the floor with** |WĪP *thu* FLAWR with| *v* To thrash; to beat decisively in a physical or verbal fight or a competition. ORIGINS: From the Royal Navy slang wipe the deck with *sb*.

**NON-SLANG SYNONYMS:** beat, best, defeat, overthrow, <u>crush</u>, <u>demolish</u>, <u>finish off</u>, <u>lick</u>, <u>obliterate</u>, <u>rout</u>, <u>upset</u>, <u>wipe out</u>, **annihilate**, **decimate**, **prevail over**, **vanquish**

# TO BE DEFEATED—TO SURRENDER

**bend over (for** *sb***)** |bend Ō vur / bend Ō vur fur *sb*| *v* To submit. ORIGINS: A reference to a posture assumed for sex. USAGE INFO: Some people may not know the origins and may use this phrase innocently. USAGE ALERT: This phrase is not related to bend over backwards, which has inoffensive ORIGINS and a different meaning. The origins of and graphic image presented by this phrase will make its use objectionable in some contexts and to some people.

**buckle under** |BUK ul UN dur| *v* To give in; to consent reluctantly. ORIGINS: Related to SE **buckle** meaning "bending or warping under pressure." USAGE INFO: See KNUCKLE UNDER.

**catch it in the neck** |KACH it in *thu* NEK| *v* To be verbally attacked; to be punished or criticized severely. ORIGINS: A figurative interpretation of a phrase that was originally used literally and meant "to be killed or severely wounded." USAGE INFO: The location of the wound makes the attack seem particularly blameworthy and unjustified.

**cave in** |CĀV in| v To yield to pressure. ORIGINS: The reference is to a cave roof collapsing. USAGE INFO: Often in the phrase "cave in to *sb/st.*"

**cry uncle** |KRĪ UNG kul| v To surrender. ORIGINS: Said to be from the Old Irish word *anacol*, meaning "safety; deliverance."

**down for the count, be** |doun fawr *thu* KOUNT| v To be defeated. ORIGINS: From boxing, for the situation in which a boxer who is knocked down has a count of 10 to arise and resume fighting; otherwise s/he loses.

**get it**[2] |GET it| v To suffer the consequences; to be punished. USAGE INFO: Often in phrases like "You're really going to get it!"

**get it in the neck** |GET it in *thu* NEK| v To be verbally attacked; to be punished or criticized severely. ORIGINS: A figurative interpretation of a phrase that was originally taken literally and meant "to be killed or severely wounded." USAGE INFO: The location of the wound makes the attack seem particularly blameworthy and unjustified.

**give over** |giv Ō vur| v To submit; to admit defeat.

**holler uncle** |HAHL ur UN kul| v See CRY UNCLE.

**knuckle under** |NU kul UN dur| v To give in; to consent reluctantly. ORIGINS: From the position of the knuckles coming close to the ground when a person stoops or kneels in submission. USAGE INFO: See BUCKLE UNDER.

**say uncle** |sā UN kul| v See CRY UNCLE.

**take a licking/beating** |tāk u LIK ing / tāk u BET ing| v To be defeated in a fight or competition; to get the worst of an argument; to receive a harsh reprimand or scolding; to lose a lot of money.

**throw in one's hand** |THRŌ in wunz HAND| v To give in; to surrender. ORIGINS: From the gesture of folding in a card game.

**throw in the sponge/towel** |THRŌ in *thu* SPUNJ / THRŌ in *thu* TOU ul| v To give in; to capitulate to demands. ORIGINS: From boxing practice, in which either of these items is thrown into the ring as a gesture of accepting defeat.

**NON-SLANG SYNONYMS:** be beaten, be defeated, fold, give in, lose, surrender, **give up, be bested, be vanquished, capitulate, concede, submit, succumb, suffer defeat, yield**

# TO SEEK REVENGE

**even the score** |Ē vun *thu* SKAWR| *v* To do something that one believes makes things even; to get revenge. ORIGINS: From sports jargon.

**fix *sb's* wagon** |FIKS *sb's* WAG un| *v* To get revenge; to thwart another's plans. USAGE INFO: A negative use of *fix*, which usually means to repair rather than to disable, making *fix* a contronym.

**get even** |get Ē vun| *v* To get revenge; to punish a (perceived) wrong; to get back at someone.

**get one's own back** |get wunz ŌN bak| *v* To retaliate; to get revenge. ORIGINS: The concept is of someone taking back something that was taken from one.

**get square** |get SKWER| *v* To get even; to get revenge; to retaliate.

**settle a/the score** |SET'l u SKAWR / SET'l *thu* SKAWR| *v* To get even with; to seek revenge. ORIGINS: From SE **score** meaning "grievance," a figurative meaning derived from the earlier use of **score** to refer to an accounting kept by tallying score marks on wooden rods.

**settle accounts** |SET'l u KOUNTZ| *v* To get even with; to seek revenge. ORIGINS: From the practices of accounting.

**NON-SLANG SYNONYMS:** give just desserts, seek revenge, take an eye for an eye, **pay back**, **settle with**, **square**, **turn the tables on**, **avenge**, **give** *sb* **a comeuppance**, **reciprocate**, **redress**, **retaliate**, **vindicate**

# FOOD FIGHT

Children are told not to play with their food, but in our language, we often fight with it.

whip

cream

rhubarb

knock the stuffing out of *sb*

take a licking

chew *sb* out

hand *sb* his/her head on a plate/platter

make hamburger of

eat/have for breakfast

give *sb* a knuckle sandwich

have *sb* on toast

settle *sb*'s hash

cook *sb*'s goose

make mincemeat of

# Deceit and Treachery

I have evidence to show that *bullshit* is often, though not always, used to mean "lie." But "lie" or even "falsehood" does not show up in the definition of the noun *bullshit* in *Merriam Webster's Collegiate Dictionary, 11th Edition, Webster's New World College Dictionary, Fourth Edition,* or *The American Heritage Dictionary of the English Language, Fourth Edition.* The definitions seem to uniformly beat around the bush and talk about *bullshit* and its synonyms as having meanings like "nonsense." Is that a gentile word for *lie?* Are our reference books suffering from truthiness with regard to lies? Does Stephen Colbert know about this?

I have never before sought to bolster an argument with information from Urban Dictionary, but I'll use it as backing for this one: Although notably lacking in authority and full of actual nonsense, not to mention typos, the Urban Dictionary at least acknowledges the truth about *bullshit* in its number 1 definition: "a blatant lie, a fragrant [sic*] untruth, an obvious falicy [sic]." If you want the truth about bullshit, you've come to the right place. Here are the subgroups for this chapter:

*Deception*
1 Lies
2 Words Intended to Confuse
3 To Be Dishonest
4 To Falsify
5 To Defraud/Cheat
6 To Deceive
7 To Make Exaggerated Claims
8 To Steal

*Betrayal*
1 To Betray a Secret or Expose Betrayal
2 To Discover Betrayal
3 To Betray by Reneging or Abandoning
4 To Betray by Shifting Blame

*If it weren't for the misspelling of *fallacy,* I'd think that *fragrant* was an extremely clever typo.... Data collected January 2009.

# DECEPTION

## 1 Lies

NBIF no basis in fact

**bafflegab** |BA ful gab| n Words intended to deceive and baffle. ORIGINS: A rare coined bit of slang originating in May 1952, **bafflegab** was invented by Milton Smith, assistant general counsel of the US Chamber of Commerce, to describe the baffling language commonly found in government regulations.

**bilge (water)** |BILJ / BILJ WAH tur| n Rubbish; untruths; lies. ORIGINS: By analogy to the foul water that collects in the bilge of a ship; along the same lines as calling a lie **shit** or **crap**. USAGE INFO: Despite the analogy, this term does not cause the type of offense that a term including the word **shit** or **crap** does.

**bosh** |bahsh| n Worthless or untrue words. ORIGINS: Influenced by the slang noun bosh from the Turkish **bosh**, meaning "empty or worthless" and possibly reinforced by **bosh**, an artificial substitute for butter, some of which was manufactured at Hertogenbosch in Holland.

**b.s., bs** |BĒ ES| n Lies; words or actions meant to be deceptive. ORIGINS: An abbreviation of **bullshit**; from the SE name of male cattle (**bull**) and the slang word for their dung (**shit**). USAGE INFO: Spelled both with and without periods. USAGE ALERT: Despite the attempt to soften by abbreviation, the graphic reference referred to by this phrase makes it objectionable in some contexts and to some people.

**bucket of shit** |BUK it uv SHIT| n Falsehoods; untruths; lies. ORIGINS: From SE bucket, a container, and slang **shit** meaning "excrement." USAGE ALERT: Because this term includes the word **shit**, it will be considered objectionable in some contexts and by some people.

**bullshit** |BŌOL shit| n Nonsense; untruths; lies. ORIGINS: From SE bull (the animal) and slang **shit**, i.e., bull excrement which could be described as "worthless and having a stench"—applied figuratively to worthless or deceptive statements. USAGE ALERT: The reference to excrement will make this term objectionable in some contexts and to some people.

**bunk** |bungk| n Nonsense; worthless talk; untruths, lies. ORIGINS: Shortened from bunkum meaning "insincere or empty talk" from the characterization of a speech made by a congressman from Buncombe County, North Carolina.

**claptrap** |KLAP trap| n Meaningless talk; incorrect or misinformed comments; untruths; lies. ORIGINS: By extension from theatre jargon **claptrap**, meaning "a theatrical trick (trap) to win audience applause (clapping)."

**codswallop** |KAHDZ wawl up| n Nonsense; lies.

**crap**$^2$, **also crapola** |krap / kra PŌ lu| *n* Lies; untruths; nonsense; boasts. ORIGINS: From **crap**, a euphemism for **shit** meaning "excrement" and -ola, a slang intensifying suffix. USAGE ALERT: This term will be objectionable in some situations and to some people.

**crock, a** |u KRAHK| *n* Falsehoods; untruths; lies. ORIGINS: Euphemism for **crock of shit**. From SE crock meaning "a large pottery container." USAGE INFO: Often occurs in the phrase "that's a crock." When crock is used by itself, the usage is the figure of speech called metonymy, specifically, using the name of the container to signify the thing contained. USAGE ALERT: Euphemisms may still be objectionable in some contexts and to some people.

**crock of shit** |KRAHK uv SHIT| *n* Falsehoods; untruths; lies. ORIGINS: From SE crock meaning "a large pottery container" and slang **shit** meaning "excrement." USAGE ALERT: Because this term includes the word **shit**, it will be considered objectionable in some contexts and by some people.

**fiddle-faddle** |FID ul fad ul| *n* Nonsense or untrue words. ORIGINS: Reduplication of fiddle.

**flapdoodle** |FLAP dū dul| *n* Foolish or nonsensical talk.

**guff** |guf| *n* Lies; untruths; nonsense; sass.

**hooey** |HŪ ē| *n* Nonsense; untruths; lies.

**horsefeathers** |HAWRS fe *th*urz| *n* Nonsense; untruths; lies. ORIGINS: Euphemism for **horseshit**, coined by Billy DeBeck in his comic strip *Barney Google* (1928) and popularized by the Marx Brothers in their film *Horse Feathers* (1932). USAGE ALERT: Euphemisms may still be objectionable in some contexts and to some people.

**horseshit** |HAWRS SHIT| *n* Rubbish; untruths; lies. ORIGINS: From SE horse and slang **shit** meaning "excrement." Extended from the original meaning of "horse dung." USAGE ALERT: The use of the word **shit** will be objectionable in some contexts and to some people.

**jive** |JĪV| *n* Deceptive talk; untruths; lies; nonsense. USAGE INFO: Jive is also the name of a type of slang.

**load of shit** |LŌD uv SHIT| *n* Falsehoods; untruths; lies. ORIGINS: From SE load, meaning a large amount and slang **shit** meaning "excrement." USAGE ALERT: Because this term includes the word **shit**, it will be considered objectionable in some contexts and by some people.

**meshugaas, mishegaas, mishegoss** |mish u GAWS| *n* Nonsense; idiocy; crazy or senseless actions. ORIGINS: Through Yiddish **meshegas** from Hebrew.

**phon(e)y-baloney** |FŌ nē bu LŌ nē| *n* Nonsense; insincere talk; fake presentation or emotions. ORIGINS: From slang **phon(e)y** meaning "fake" and baloney meaning "nonsense." USAGE INFO: Other spellings are also used.

**piffle** |PIF ul| *n* Nonsense; shallow and insignificant talk.

**pile of crap** |PĪL uv KRAP| *n* Falsehoods; untruths; lies. ORIGINS: From SE pile meaning "a large amount" and slang **crap** meaning "excrement." USAGE ALERT: Because this term refers to excrement, it will be considered objectionable in some contexts and by some people. Unlike *crock, bucket,* and *load,* which are also combined with **shit** to denote lies, *pile* is more often heard with **crap**.

**pile of shit** |PĪL uv SHIT| *n* Falsehoods; untruths; lies. ORIGINS: From SE pile, meaning "a large amount" and slang **shit** meaning "excrement." USAGE ALERT: Because this term includes the word **shit**, it will be considered objectionable in some contexts and by some people.

**snow job** |SNŌ jahb| *n* A convincing, but untrue, story or insincere flattery. ORIGINS: From slang verb snow meaning "insincere talk."

**tommyrot** |TAHM ē raht| *n* Complete nonsense; untruths; lies.

**trash**[1] |trash| *n* Empty or meaningless words or ideas; untruths; lies.

**tripe** |trīp| *n* Nonsense; untruths; lies.

**weasel word** |WĒ sul wurd| *n* Language designed to deceive or evade. ORIGINS: Figurative extension of standard image of weasels as sucking out the contents of birds' eggs while leaving the shells intact.

**whopper** |WAHP pur| *n* A particularly gross untruth or lie.

NON-SLANG SYNONYMS—LIE: deceit, deception, dishonesty, falsehood, inaccuracy, invention, lie, slander, white lie, **aspersion**, **calumny**, **equivocation**, **fabrication**, **hyperbole**, **mendacity**, **misrepresentation**, **misstatement**, **perjury**, **prevarication**, **untruth**, **vilification**

NON-SLANG SYNONYMS—UNTRUTH: applesauce, blather, fib, garbage, hogwash, hokum, hot air, hype, moonshine, poppycock, puffery, rot, rubbish, whopper

# 2 Words Intended to Confuse

**eyewash** |Ī wahsh| *n* Words or actions meant to conceal reality rather than reveal it; lies or untruths. ORIGINS: Extending the original meaning of "a treatment of the eyes."

**gobbledygook** |GAHB ul dē gŏŏk| *n* Unclear, incomprehensible language. ORIGINS: Imitative from the sound a turkey makes, written in English as **gobble**.

**mumbo jumbo** |MUM bō JUM bō| *n* Incomprehensible language; language that is meant to confuse or the meaning of which is purposefully left unclear.

NON-SLANG SYNONYMS: double-speak, double-talk, nonsense; **babble**, **double-speak**, **double talk**, **gibberish**; **equivocation**, **intentional ambiguity**
(Note: Some people use *jargon* for this meaning, but *jargon* can also mean "the technical language of a trade, profession, or other area," and using it for both purposes is confusing.)

# 3 To Be Dishonest

**full of baloney, be** |FUL uv bu LŌ nē| *v* To speak nonsense or untruths; to lie. ORIGINS: Euphemism for **full of bullshit**, possibly because of the nearly identical sound of the first syllables. USAGE ALERT: People who recognize it as a replacement for **bullshit** may find the expression objectionable.

**full of beans, be** |ful uv BĒNZ| *v* To speak nonsense or untruths; to lie. ORIGINS: Euphemism for **full of shit**. Beans, being laxatives, are connected to excrement, and so are used to create an approximately synonymous euphemism for **full of shit**. USAGE ALERT: Euphemisms may still be objectionable in some contexts and to some people.

**full of boloney, be** |FUL uv bu LŌ nē| *v See* FULL OF BALONEY, BE.

**full of (bull)shit, be** |ful uv SHIT / ful uv BOŌL SHIT| *v* To speak nonsense or untruths; to lie. ORIGINS: From slang **bullshit** meaning "excrement." USAGE ALERT: The inclusion of the word **bullshit** or the shortened form **shit** will make this phrase objectionable in some contexts and to some people.

**full of crap, be** |ful uv KRAP| *v* To speak nonsense or untruths; to lie. ORIGINS: Euphemism for **full of shit**. From slang **crap**, a euphemism for slang **shit** meaning "excrement." USAGE ALERT: Euphemisms may still be objectionable in some contexts and to some people.

**full of it, be** |FUL uv it| *v* To speak nonsense or untruths; to lie. ORIGINS: Euphemism for **full of shit**. While *it* is often used as a replacement for a word that's considered offensive in order to create a euphemism, in this case, the fact that **it** and **shit** rhyme may make it even more satisfactory as a substitute. USAGE ALERT: Euphemisms may still be objectionable in some contexts and to some people.

**full of prunes, be** |ful uv PRŪNZ| *v* To speak nonsense or untruths; to lie. ORIGINS: Euphemism for **full of shit**. Prunes, being laxatives, are connected to excrement, and so are used to create an approximately synonymous euphemism for **full of shit**. USAGE ALERT: Euphemisms may still be objectionable in some contexts and to some people.

**hustle** |HUS ul| *v* To sell by using pressure, aggressive techniques, or deceit, especially misrepresentation of oneself.

**jerk *sb* around** |JERK *sb* u ROUND| *v* To take advantage of *sb*; to manipulate *sb*; to deceive *sb*; to treat *sb* badly. ORIGINS: Possibly related to the slang verb jerk meaning "to harass or deliberately annoy *sb*" or to jerk *sb's* chain (see the following entry). USAGE ALERT: Some people may connect this word to **jerk-off**, although they do not seem to be etymologically linked.

**lay it on (with a trowel)** |lā it AHN / lā it AHN with u TROU ul| *v* To exaggerate; to concoct an elaborate deception or lie with far more detail than needed; to flatter shamelessly. ORIGINS: Presumably from the trades in which mortar or plaster is applied with a trowel.

**pile it on** |PĪL it ahn| *v* To concoct an elaborate deception or lie with far more detail than needed; to flatter shamelessly.

**put *sb* on** |poŏt *sb* AHN| *v* To deceive *sb*; to say things that aren't truth; to lie to *sb*; to convince *sb* of *st* untrue as a joke. USAGE INFO: When one puts *sb* on for fun, one reveals the deception afterwards.

**shit** |shit| *v* To fool; to tell untruths; to lie to; to deceive. ORIGINS: From a shortening of **bullshit** meaning "lies; deceptive talk." From the SE name of male cattle (bull) and the slang word for their dung (**shit**). USAGE INFO: Often used to express surprise or disbelief, as in "Are you shitting me?" USAGE ALERT: This word will be objectionable in some contexts and to some people.

**shoot the bull** |SHŪT *thu* BOŎL| *v* To deceive; to lie or exaggerate to the point of untruth. ORIGINS: From shoot meaning "to speak" and **bull**, a shortened form of **bullshit**, meaning "lies, deceptive talk."

**shoot the crap/shit** |SHŪT *thu* KRAP / SHŪT *thu* SHIT| *v* To deceive; to lie or exaggerate to the point of untruth. ORIGINS: From shoot meaning "to speak" and **crap** or **shit**, literally meaning "excrement" and figuratively meaning "lies, untruths."

**sling the bull** |sling *thu* BOŎL| *v* To talk nonsense; to boast; to tell untruths; to lie. ORIGINS: From sling meaning "to tell" and bull meaning "lies and flattery." USAGE INFO: Developed prior to **bullshit**, but now used as a euphemism for it.

**sling the crap** |SLING *thu* KRAP| *v* To deceive; to lie or exaggerate to the point of untruth. ORIGINS: From sling meaning "to tell" and **crap**, a euphemism for **shit**, literally meaning "excrement" and figuratively meaning "lies, untruths."

**sling the shit** |SLING *thu* SHIT| *v* To deceive; to lie or exaggerate to the point of untruth. ORIGINS: From sling meaning "to tell" and **shit**, literally meaning "excrement" and figuratively meaning "lies, untruths."

NON-SLANG SYNONYMS: be dishonest, be untruthful, commit perjury, deceive, lie, misinform, mislead, <u>con, fib, stretch the truth, string along, bear false witness,</u> delude, dissemble, dissimulate, equivocate, falsify, forswear oneself, perjure oneself, prevaricate

# 4 To Falsify

**cook the books** |KOŎK *thu* BOŎKS| *v* To falsify or manipulate records or documentation of financial transactions for the purpose of deceiving.

**doctor** |DAHK tur| *v* To modify or alter for the sake of deception or for other purposes.

**fudge** |FUJ| *v* To stretch the truth; to fabricate.

NON-SLANG SYNONYMS: alter, tamper, <u>fake, juggle,</u> fabricate, falsify, misrepresent

# 5 To Defraud/Cheat

**burn**[1] |burn| *v* To cheat or swindle.

**con** |kahn| *v* To deceive *sb* with a confidence trick or game, a type of swindle.

**finagle** |fin Ā gul| *v* To cheat; to obtain deceitfully.

**fleece** |flēz| *v* To defraud; to swindle. ORIGINS: The concept is of peeling off money as easily as the fleece is peeled off a sheep by an expert shearer.

**hornswoggle** |HAWRN swahg ul| *v* To cheat or swindle.

**on the take, be** |ahn *thu* TĀK| *v* To accept bribes.

**rip off** |RIP awf| *v* To defraud; to swindle; to cheat; to steal from, often by charging an excessive amount.

**scam** |skam| *v* To defraud or swindle.

**screw (over)** |skrū / skrū Ō vur| *v* To mistreat; to cheat. ORIGINS: Euphemism for **fuck (over)**. From slang screw, a euphemism for **fuck**. USAGE ALERT: The euphemism screw in this phrase will soften it somewhat, but it may still be objectionable in some contexts and to some people.

**sell *sb* a bill of goods** |SEL *sb* u BIL uv GŎODZ| *v* To deceive *sb*; to cheat *sb*; to lie to *sb*. ORIGINS: From slang bill of goods meaning "false promises" from SE **bill of goods** meaning "a consignment of items being sold."

**send *sb* to the cleaners** |SEND *sb* tū *thu* KLĒN urz| *v* To trick *sb* out of all his/her money.

**shake down** |SHĀK doun| *v* To extort money.

**sting** |sting| *v* To swindle in a confidence game; to cheat, defraud, or steal from.

**take *sb* for a ride** |tāk *sb* fawr u RĪD| *v* To deceive *sb*, usually in order to get money.

**take *sb* to the cleaners** |TĀK *sb* tū *thu* KLĒN urz| *v* To trick *sb* out of all his/her money.

NON-SLANG SYNONYMS: deceive, pull the wool over *sb's* eyes, <u>bamboozle</u>, <u>cheat</u>, <u>do a number on</u>, <u>dupe</u>, <u>pull a fast one</u>, <u>rook</u>, **abscond**, **defraud**, **embezzle**

# 6 To Deceive

**fake out** |FĀK out| *v* To trick, deceive, or fool.

**feed *sb* a line** |FĒD *sb* u LĪN| *v* To say *st* untrue, often to appease *sb*.

**fox** |fahks| *v* To outwit; to deceive with cunning. ORIGINS: From the common conception of the fox as a sly, clever creature.

**give *sb* a line** |GIV *sb* u LĪN| *v* To say *st* untrue, often to appease.

**pull a fast one** |pŏŏl u FAST wun| *v* To successfully deceive *sb*.

**snooker** |SNŎŎK ur| *v* To fool *sb*. ORIGINS: From the game of snooker, in which a shot is called a snooker if the cue ball is left in a position that leaves one's opponent no options because the target ball is blocked by another ball.

NON-SLANG SYNONYMS: deceive, mislead; <u>double-cross</u>, <u>fool</u>, <u>gull</u>, <u>hoodwink</u>, <u>lead on</u>, <u>outwit</u>, <u>pull *st* over on *sb*</u>, <u>take in</u>, <u>trick</u>, <u>two-time</u>; **delude**, **inveigle**, **misrepresent**

# 7 To Make Exaggerated Claims

**ballyhoo** |BAL ē hū| *v* To publicize in a sensationalist way.

**blow up²** |blō UP| *v* To make exaggerated claims. ORIGINS: From SE **blow up** meaning "to increase the size of by filling with air," used figuratively.

**hype** |hīp| *v* To make exaggerated claims for the sake of promotion.

**lay it on thick** |LĀ it ahn THIK| *v* To exaggerate; to concoct an elaborate deception or lie with far more detail than needed; to flatter shamelessly.

**pump up** |PUMP up| *v* To exaggerate the qualities of *sb* or *st* for the sake of promotion.

**spread it on thick** |SPRĒD it ahn thik| *v* To exaggerate or add elaboration, especially when telling a lie, deceiving, or flattering.

NON-SLANG SYNONYMS: exaggerate, overestimate, promote, publicize; <u>pitch</u>, <u>plug</u>; **aggrandize**, **amplify**, **hyperbolize**, **inflate**

# 8 To Steal

**bag** |bag| *v* To gain possession of; to steal.

**clean *sb* out** |KLĒN *sb* OUT| *v* To steal; to take all of an opponent's money (in gambling); to ruin financially. ORIGINS: Figurative use of SE **clean**. USAGE INFO: Don't confuse with **clean *st* out** meaning "to empty of contents."

**cop** |kahp| *v* To get possession of for oneself; to steal. ORIGINS: From Old French **caper** meaning "to seize."

**filch** |filch| *v* To furtively take *st*; to steal. ORIGINS: Popularized by the name of the character Argus Filch, Hogwarts' caretaker known for taking away students' possessions in the Harry Potter series.

**glom onto** |glom AHN tū| *v* To take over possession of; to steal.

**heist** |hīst| *v* To steal. ORIGINS: By variation of hoist, meaning "to shoplift, to rob."

**hoist** |hoist| *v* To shoplift or rob.

hook |ho͞ok| v To steal. ORIGINS: By extension of SE **hook** meaning "to snare *st* with a hook."

liberate |LIB u rāt| v To steal. ORIGINS: Liberation applied to goods has roots in the actions of the WWII liberating forces as well as in anarchist thinking about property.

lift |lift| v To steal. ORIGINS: By extension of SE **lift** meaning "to alter *st's* position by moving it upwards."

nick |nik| v To cheat by overcharging; to steal.

pinch |pinch| v To take what isn't one's own; to steal. ORIGINS: By extension of SE **pinch** meaning "to grasp and squeeze between the thumb and finger."

rip off |RIP awf| v To defraud; to swindle; to cheat; to steal from, often by charging an excessive amount.

snag |snag| v To take for one's own use; to steal. ORIGINS: By extension of SE **snag** meaning "to catch."

snitch² |snich| v To steal.

NON-SLANG SYNONYMS: steal, take; <u>do out of</u>, <u>grab</u>, <u>latch onto</u>, <u>lift</u>, <u>make off with</u>, <u>nab</u>, <u>net</u>, <u>pinch</u>, <u>sneak</u>, <u>swipe</u>, <u>walk off with</u>, **misappropriate**, **pilfer**, **purloin**

# BETRAYAL

## 1 To Betray a Secret or Expose Betrayal

blow¹ |blō| v To expose; to betray a secret. ORIGINS: Possibly shortened from longer slang phrases like blow the lid off (of) *st*. USAGE INFO: Can be a positive or a negative act, depending on the morality of keeping the secret.

blow *st* sky-high |BLŌ *st* SKĪ HĪ| v To destroy or ruin, often through a revelation of something that had been secret or concealed. USAGE INFO: This action can either be destructive or good (e.g., when done by a whistle-blower to expose illegal activity).

blow *st* wide open |BLŌ *st* WĪD Ō pun| v To make public something that had been secret. USAGE INFO: This action can either be destructive or good (e.g., when someone exposes a scandal).

blow the lid off (of) *st* |BLŌ *thu* LID awf (uv) *st*| v To make public something that had been unknown or concealed. USAGE INFO: This action can either be destructive or good (e.g., when an expert makes great advances in a field of study, significantly changing its nature, or when someone exposes a scandal).

blow the whistle on *st* |BLŌ *thu* WIS ul ahn *st*| v To bring something to an end; to inform authorities about wrongdoing in order to stop it. ORIGINS:

From the practice of a referee for a sporting event blowing a whistle to stop play when a rule is being violated.

**finger** |FIN gur| *v* To inform on; to tip off about. ORIGINS: From the practice of pointing an accusing finger at someone.

**fink** |FINGK| *v* To inform against.

**give away** |GIV u wā| *v* To reveal; to betray.

**let on** |let AHN| *v* To allow *st* to be known or come to light. USAGE INFO: Most often in the negative, as in "Don't let on!"

**point the/one's finger at** |POINT *thu* FIN gur at / POINT wunz FIN gur at| *v* To identify the guilty party; to accuse *sb* of responsibility for <whatever>.

**pull the rug out from under** |POOL *thu* RUG out frum UN dur| *v* To suddenly withdraw support from *sb*.

**put the finger on** |poot *thu* FIN gur ahn| *v* To inform on; to identify as the perpetrator; to betray.

**sell down the river** |SEL doun *thu* RIV ur| *v* To betray. ORIGINS: From the historical practice of selling recalcitrant slaves to a harsher master whose plantation happened to be down river.

**sell out** |sel OUT| *v* To betray one's principles, beliefs, or commitments.

**sing** |sing| *v* To betray *sb*; to inform against *sb*.

**snitch**[1] |snich| *v* To betray; to reveal *sb's* secret.

**spill one's guts (out)** |spil wunz GUTS / spil wunz GUTS out| *v* To be completely honest; to confess to whatever has been concealed or untold; to reveal intimate secrets.

**spill the beans** |spil *thu* BĒNZ| *v* To reveal a secret that was meant to be kept.

**split on** |SPLIT ahn| *v* To betray; to inform against.

**squeal (on)** |skwēl / SKWĒL ahn| *v* To turn informer; to betray an accomplice or secret.

**stab in the back** |STAB in *thu* BAK| *v* To betray. ORIGINS: From the idea that it is dishonorable to strike *sb* when his/her back is turned.

**tip one's hand** |TIP wunz HAND| *v* To reveal one's plans, often unintentionally.

**tip *sb* off** |tip *sb* AWF| *v* To give insider information (often of illegal activities) to *sb* who wouldn't ordinarily have access to it, for example, law enforcement officers, competitors, or investors.

**turn *sb* in** |turn *sb* IN| *v* To hand *sb* over to the relevant authorities.

NON-SLANG SYNONYMS: betray, inform, uncover, unmask, **blurt out**, **double-cross**, let slip, rat on, tattle, tell, tell on *sb*, turn in, **break faith**, **commit treason**, **disclose**, **lay bare**, **make known**

# 2 To Discover Betrayal

**catch red-handed** |KACH red HAN did| *v* To catch in the act of doing something morally wrong or illegal. ORIGINS: The image of red hands comes from the Scottish law stating that blood-stained hands were required for the sheriff to act against a suspected murderer.

**catch *sb* with his/her pants down** |KACH *sb* with hiz/hur PANTS doun| *v* To catch *sb* in the act of doing something morally wrong or illegal. ORIGINS: The idea is of seeing *sb* commit the crime (the suggestion is adultery, rape, or something similar or—taken figuratively—of catching *sb* in an embarrassing and defenseless position), incontrovertible proof of guilt. USAGE INFO: Despite the image, this phrase can be used of any embarrassing, illegal, or immoral act, not just sex crimes.

**catch with a hand in the cookie jar/till** |KACH with u HAND in *th*u KOOK ē jar / KACH with u HAND in *th*u TIL| *v* To catch in the act of doing something morally wrong or illegal, especially theft or embezzlement. ORIGINS: The **cookie jar** is a place for storing goodies. The **till** is a place to store money. The idea is of seeing *sb* commit the crime, incontrovertible proof of guilt.

**catch with a smoking gun** |KACH with u smōk ing gun| *v* To catch in the act of doing something morally wrong or illegal. ORIGINS: The idea is of catching *sb* holding a firearm used in a crime, still giving off evidence of having been just fired (smoking).

**catch with the goods/merchandise** |KACH with *th*u GOODZ / KACH with *th*u MUR chun dīz| *v* To catch in the act of doing something morally wrong or illegal. ORIGINS: The idea is of catching a thief or robber still in possession of the stolen items.

**have *sb* cold** |HAV *sb* KŌLD| *v* To have *sb* at one's mercy; to have caught *sb* doing something illegal or immoral. ORIGINS: From slang cold meaning "completely; absolutely."

**nail²** |nāl| *v* To catch in the act. ORIGINS: From SE **nail** meaning "to make secure."

NON-SLANG SYNONYMS: **catch in the act**, **catch in flagrante delicto**

# 3 To Betray by Reneging or Abandoning

**blow off** |BLŌ awf| *v* To purposely miss an engagement; to skip out on something after committing. USAGE INFO: The object can be placed between the main verb and the particle as in "blow the meeting off," but is most often placed after the entire phrasal verb as in "blow off the meeting."

**bow out** |BOU OUT| *v* To leave, resign, withdraw. ORIGINS: From the graceful gesture at the end of a performance, acknowledging the audience before the final curtain. USAGE INFO: Can indicate a gracious withdrawal or avoidance of an obligation. Can be used euphemistically to cover a more complicated/fraught situation.

**cop out** |KAHP out| *v* To fail to fulfill what's promised; to give up; to renege. ORIGINS: Related to cop a plea, in which one takes less responsibility than one is actually accountable for.

**cut (and run)** |kut / KUT und RUN| *v* To escape; to run away; to avoid a difficult situation by fleeing. ORIGINS: From nautical jargon **cut and run**, meaning "to cut the anchor cable and run before the wind."

**ditch** |DICH| *v* To leave *sb* in the lurch; to discard. ORIGINS: Possibly by extension of jargon **ditch**, originating with the Royal Air Force and meaning "to land one's plane in the sea," usually in a body of water referred to as "the big ditch"—either the English Channel or the North Sea.

**fink out** |FINGk out| *v* To withdraw support; to renege.

**give *st* a miss** |giv *st* u MIS| *v* To skip an event or occasion.

**go AWOL** |gō Ā wahl| *v* To leave one's assigned position; to abandon one's duties. ORIGINS: From military slang acronym AWOL meaning "absent without leave," but carrying the implication that there is an intention to return, differentiating it from desertion.

**leave *sb* in the lurch** |LĒV *sb* in thu LURCH| *v* To abandon *sb* in a difficult situation; to desert a person in distress. ORIGINS: From the French **lourche**, a parlor game in which a player often lost with a score of nothing or next to nothing.

**opt out** |AHPT out| *v* To cancel a previous decision; to indicate unwillingness to participate. ORIGINS: Shortened from SE **option**.

**run out on *sb/st*** |run OUT ahn *sb/st*| *v* To renege on a commitment, whether business or personal.

**skip out on** |skip OUT ahn| *v* To abandon.

**walk (out on *sb*)** |wawk / WAWK out awn *sb*| *v* To leave; to depart; to forsake; to abandon.

**weasel out** |WĒ sul out| *v* To sneakily evade doing *st* one has promised to do; to back out of a commitment in a cowardly way.

**wiggle out of** |WIG ul out uv| *v* To avoid a commitment or responsibility by underhanded means. ORIGINS: Figurative use of SE **wriggling** to suggest twisting this way and that to extricate oneself.

**worm out of** *st* |wurm OUT uv *st*| *v* To avoid a commitment or responsibility by underhanded means. ORIGINS: Figurative use of the wriggling of worms.

**wriggle out** |RIG ul out| *v* To avoid a commitment or responsibility by underhanded means. ORIGINS: Figurative use of SE **wriggling** to suggest twisting this way and that to extricate oneself.

NON-SLANG SYNONYMS: abandon, be a Judas (Judas is the betrayer of Jesus Christ in the Gospels of the New Testament), be unfaithful, bite the hand that feeds one, desert, go back on one's word, knife in the back, leave, stab in the back, trick, walk out on, **bail**, **dump**, **jilt**, **leave high and dry**, **let down**, **sell out**, **throw over**, **abdicate**, **forsake**

# 4 To Betray by Shifting Blame

**drop** *sb* **in it** |DRAHP *sb* IN it| *v* To do or say something that gets another person in trouble; to deliberately pass the responsibility. ORIGINS: As in other expressions, *it* can refer to trouble, but a parallel expression **drop** *sb* **in the shit** suggests that in some people's minds, **shit** might be the reference for it. USAGE ALERT: If the reference of *it* is **shit**, or if people think it is, this saying could be objectionable in some contexts and to some people.

**leave** *sb* **holding the baby** |LĒV *sb* HŌL ding *thu* BĀ bē| *v* To leave *sb* else to solve or deal with a difficult situation; to shift responsibility and/or blame to *sb* else. USAGE INFO: The person who is the indirect object of the verb is then "left holding the baby."

**make a patsy of** |māk u PAT sē uv| *v* A gullible person who is easily duped or swindled. ORIGINS: From slang **patsy** meaning "a gullible person; a person easily taken advantage of." There are suggestions that this word comes from Italian **pazzo** meaning "fool" or the Irish nickname for *Patrick*. USAGE ALERT: If the second etymology is true, or if people think that it is, this term may be viewed as a racial slur and therefore objectionable.

**offload** |AHF lōd| *v* To get rid of; to (unfairly) pass on to *sb* else. ORIGINS: Extension of the concept in shipping or computer science of removing *st* from one locale to another.

NON-SLANG SYNONYMS: scapegoat, **make a fall guy**, **use as a whipping boy**, **victimize**

# Progress and Decline

Progress is part of the American way of life, and there are a lot of slang words to help convey how we're moving ahead ... or falling behind. The subsections for this chapter are:

*Begin*
1 An Attempt
2 To Start
3 To Exert Effort

*Improve*
1 To Get Back on Track
2 To Enhance
3 To Make Good Progress

*Succeed*
1 To Succeed
2 To Succeed Through Perseverance
3 In a Promising Situation
4 A Certainty
5 A Success

*Stall*
1 To Make Minimal Progress
2 To Postpone
3 To Waste Time

*Deteriorate*
1 To Mishandle or Meddle With
2 To Backtrack or Worsen
3 To Ruin

*Hit Obstacles*
1 To Blunder or Make a Mistake
2 To Malfunction
3 To Cause Problems for Oneself
4 Moderate to Difficult Problems
5 Easily Resolved Problems
6 Errors
7 Malfunctions
8 Unexpected Difficulties
9 Unfair Situations
10 Problematic Situations
11 Risky Situations
12 To Take a Risk

*Fail*
1 To Fall Short
2 To Fail
3 To Fail Utterly and Completely
4 To Cause to End
5 A Failure

# BEGIN

## 1 An Attempt

**clip** |klip| *n* An attempt; a try; a time; an occasion. USAGE INFO: Especially in the phrases "at one clip" or "at a clip."

**crack (at)** |krak / KRAK at| *n* An attempt. USAGE INFO: Often found in the phrase "take a crack at."

**go** |gō| *n* An opportunity; a turn in a game; a try. USAGE INFO: Used in the phrases "all in one go" and "have a go at...."

**lick at** |LIK at| *n* An attempt.

**pop** |pahp| *n* An attempt; a turn. USAGE INFO: Sometimes in a phrase that gives a price per try, as in "Bumper car rides are a dollar a pop."

**shot** |shaht| *n* An attempt.

**whack** |wak| *n* An attempt. USAGE INFO: Often in the phrase "take a whack at."

NON-SLANG SYNONYMS: attack, attempt, trial, try, <u>fling</u>, <u>stab</u>, **endeavor**, **venture**

## 2 To Start

**buckle down** |BUK ul doun| *v* To get to work; to apply oneself diligently to a task. ORIGINS: Possibly from the practice of fastening one's buckles (on armor or a sandal) preparatory to engaging in a task. USAGE INFO: *See* KNUCKLE DOWN.

**get a move on** |get u MŪV ahn| *v* To hurry; to begin moving. USAGE INFO: Can be used as an imperative.

**get cracking** |get KRAK ing| *v* To start work on; to turn to with more zeal; to work quickly and efficiently; to hurry. USAGE INFO: Can be used as an imperative.

**get going** |get GŌ ing| *v* To get started; to make a beginning.

**get in on the ground floor** |get in ahn *thu* GROUND FLAWR| *v* To be involved from the very beginning; to be in an advantageous position.

**get moving** |get MŪ ving| *v* To hurry; to begin moving. USAGE INFO: Can be used as an imperative.

**get on the stick** |GET ahn *thu* STIK| *v* To get down to work. ORIGINS: From the gear shift in a car, also called "the stick," or the joystick of an airplane.

**get one's foot in the door** |get wunz FOŌT in *thu* door| *v* To reach the initial stage in accomplishing something. ORIGINS: From the experience of crossing a threshold to enter a building.

**get one's teeth into** |get wunz TĒTH in tū| *v* To get down to work; to eagerly engage with. ORIGINS: Figurative use of the experience of beginning a meal.

**get the show on the road** |get *thu* SHŌ ahn *thu* RŌD| *v* To start; to set an operation in motion. ORIGINS: From show business tours.

**go off with a bang** |gō ahf with u BANG| *v* To get off to a good start. ORIGINS: Perhaps referring to a firecracker successfully exploding.

**have a/one's foot in the door** |hav u FOŌT in *thu* door / hav wunz FOŌT in *thu* door| *v* To reach the initial stage in accomplishing something. ORIGINS: From the experience of entering a building.

**have a go at** *st* |hav u GŌ at *st*| *v* To give something a try; to make an attempt.

**hop to it** |hahp TŪ it| *v* To hurry; to make an energetic start on *st*; to get to work.

**knuckle down** |NU kul doun| *v* To get to work; to apply oneself diligently to a task. ORIGINS: From the position of the hand in the game of marbles. USAGE INFO: *See* BUCKLE DOWN.

**pull up one's socks** |POŌL up wunz SAHKS| *v* To get ready for serious action.

**sink one's teeth into** |singk wunz TĒTH in tū| *v* To get down to work; to eagerly engage with. ORIGINS: Figurative use of the experience of beginning a meal.

**tee off** |TĒ AWF| *v* To get started. ORIGINS: From the manner of starting a game of golf.

NON-SLANG SYNONYMS: begin, establish, get underway, launch, open, set in motion, start, take off, take the first steps in, **get the ball rolling**, **jump off**, **kick off**, **take the plunge**, **commence**, **embark**, **enter upon**, **found**, **inaugurate**, **initiate**, **lay the foundation for**, **make a beginning on**, **set about**

# 3  To Exert Effort

**bend over backwards** |BEND ō vur BAK wurdz| *v* To make a great effort. ORIGINS: From the difficulty of bending backwards in, for example, the game of limbo. USAGE ALERT: This phrase is completely distinct from **bend over (for)**.

**break one's ass** |BRĀK wunz AS| *v* To work very hard; to put in an enormous effort. ORIGINS: From slang **ass** meaning "the rear end or buttocks." USAGE INFO: Compare with **break sb's ass**. USAGE ALERT: The reference to the human rear end or buttocks will render this phrase objectionable in some contexts and to some people.

**break one's balls** | BRĀK wunz BAWLZ | *v* To work very hard; to put in an enormous effort. ORIGINS: From slang **balls** meaning "testicles." USAGE INFO: Don't confuse this form with **break *sb's* balls** (that is, someone else's **balls**), which means "to beat up; to harass or annoy." **Break one's balls** is usually only used to refer to, or used self-referentially by, males. USAGE ALERT: The inclusion of **balls** will make this phrase objectionable in some contexts and to some people.

**break one's buns** | BRĀK wunz BUNZ | *v* To work very hard; to put in an enormous effort. ORIGINS: Euphemism for **break one's ass**. From slang **buns**, a euphemism for slang **ass**, meaning "the rear end or buttocks." USAGE INFO: Compare with **break *sb's* buns** meaning "to beat up; to harass or annoy." USAGE ALERT: The reference to the human rear end or buttocks will render this phrase objectionable in some contexts and to some people. Some people will find **buns** less offensive than **butt**, which is, in turn, often considered less objectionable than **ass**.

**break one's butt** | BRĀK wunz BUT| *v* To work very hard; to put in an enormous effort. ORIGINS: Euphemism for **break one's ass**. From slang **butt**, a euphemism for slang **ass**, meaning "the rear end or buttocks." USAGE INFO: Compare with **break *sb's* butt**, meaning "to beat up; to harass or annoy." USAGE ALERT: The reference to the human rear end or buttocks will render this phrase objectionable in some contexts and to some people.

**break one's chops** |BRĀK wunz CHAHPS| *v* To work hard; to talk ceaselessly. ORIGINS: From SE **break** and slang **chops**, which refers to the mouth. USAGE ALERT: In its first meaning, this phrase is synonymous with **break one's ass**, **buns**, or **butt**, but is less offensive because of the particular part of the body referenced. But also, unlike those phrases, it has a second meaning that ties explicitly to the mouth.

**bust a gut** |BUST u gut| *v* To laugh very hard. USAGE INFO: This phrase also means "to work very hard; to put in an enormous effort."

**bust one's ass** |BUST wunz AS| *v* To work very hard; to put in an enormous effort. ORIGINS: From slang **ass** meaning "the rear end or buttocks." USAGE INFO: Compare with **bust *sb's* ass**. USAGE ALERT: The reference to the human rear end or buttocks will render this phrase objectionable in some contexts and to some people. Some people will find **buns** or **butt** less offensive than **ass**.

**bust one's balls** |BUST wunz BAWLS| *v* To work very hard; to put in an enormous effort. ORIGINS: From slang **balls**, euphemism for SE **testicles**. USAGE INFO: This phrase is usually only used self-referentially by males. USAGE ALERT: The reference to the male sex organs will render this phrase objectionable in some contexts and to some people.

**bust one's buns** |BUST wunz BUNZ| *v* To work very hard; to put in an enormous effort. ORIGINS: Euphemism for **bust one's ass**. From slang **buns**, a euphemism for slang **ass**, meaning "the rear end or buttocks." USAGE INFO: **Buns** is more apt than **butt** to be used coyly, with a wink and a nod, so to speak. USAGE ALERT:

The reference to the human rear end or buttocks will render this phrase objectionable in some contexts and to some people. Some people will find **buns** less offensive than **butt**, which is, in turn, often considered less objectionable than **ass**.

**bust one's butt** |BUST wunz BUT| *v* To work very hard; to put in an enormous effort. ORIGINS: Euphemism for **bust one's ass**. From slang **butt**, a euphemism for slang **ass** meaning "the rear end or buttocks." USAGE INFO: Compare with **bust sb's butt**. USAGE ALERT: The reference to the human rear end or buttocks will render this phrase objectionable in some contexts and to some people. Some people will find **butt** less offensive than **ass**, but possibly more offensive than **buns**.

**bust one's chops** |BUST wunz CHAHPS| *v* To work hard; to talk ceaselessly. ORIGINS: Slang bust meaning "to break" and chops, which refers to the mouth. USAGE ALERT: In its first meaning, this phrase is synonymous with **bust one's ass**, **bust one's butt**, **bust one's buns**, and **bust one's balls**, but is less offensive because of the particular part of the body referenced. But also, unlike those phrases, it has a second meaning that ties explicitly to the mouth.

**bust one's gut** |BUST wunz GUT| *v* To laugh very hard. USAGE INFO: This phrase also means "to work very hard; to put in an enormous effort."

**bust one's hump** |BUST wunz HUMP| *v* To work very hard; to put in an enormous effort. ORIGINS: Generalized from SE hump meaning "a back deformity" to mean "the back." It has no relationship to the slang verb **hump** meaning "to engage in sex." USAGE INFO: The phrase is, roughly, a slang version of "doing back-breaking labor." USAGE ALERT: Because **hump** referring to the back is not in common use, this term may send people's minds toward the other slang meaning.

**do one's damnedest\*** |dū wunz DAM dist| *v* To do everything in one's power; to give one's utmost. ORIGINS: By extension from SE **damn**, which literally means "Send (it) to hell." USAGE ALERT: The use of **damnedest** will make this expression objectionable in some contexts and to some people.
• do one's darnedest |dū wunz DAHRN dist|

**do the heavy lifting** |DŪ thu hev ē LIF ting| *v* To take on tasks that require serious and devoted work.

**give it all one's got** |GIV it awl wunz GAHT| *v* To exert maximum effort; to put forth one's best effort.

**give it one's all** |GIV it wunz awl| *v* To exert maximum effort; to put forth one's best effort.

**give it one's best (shot)** |GIV it wunz BEST / GIV it wunz BEST SHAHT| *v* To exert maximum effort; to put forth one's best effort.

**go all the way** |GŌ awl thu WĀ| *v* To see something through; to give one's best effort; in competition, to get to the finals, to win. USAGE ALERT: Also means "to have sexual intercourse."

**go the distance** |gō *thu* DIS tuns| *v* To continue until a successful conclusion is reached. ORIGINS: From sports jargon in boxing and horse racing. USAGE INFO: Also used of having sexual intercourse.

**go the extra mile** |gō *thu* ek stru MĪL| *v* To make a greater effort than is expected or required.

**go the limit** |gō *thu* LI mit| *v* To give maximum effort. USAGE INFO: Also used of having sexual intercourse.

**go the whole hog** |gō *thu* HŌL HAWG| *v* To do something unreservedly; to do thoroughly; to do to the fullest extent possible.

**go the whole nine yards** |gō *thu* HŌL NĪN YAHRDZ| *v* To do something unreservedly; to do thoroughly; to do to the fullest extent possible.

**hang in** |HANG IN| *v* To stick with something, overcoming fear or adversity.

**haul ass** |HAWL AS| *v* To move really quickly; to rush; to work really hard. ORIGINS: From SE **haul** and slang **ass** referring to the whole person as in the phrase "get your ass over here." Extended from slang **ass** to refer to the rear end or buttocks. USAGE ALERT: The inclusion of the word **ass** in the phrase will render it objectionable in some contexts and to some people.

**keep on trucking** |kēp ahn TRUK ing| *v* To continue on with the (good) job or action one is doing; to keep moving. USAGE INFO: A phrase of encouragement when said to someone else. A statement of one's intent to continue in the same lines, when used of oneself.

**knock oneself out** |NAHK wun self OUT| *v* To put in a great effort; to work very hard. ORIGINS: By extension of slang **knock out** meaning "to knock unconscious." The idea is that one expends effort until one is in a similar state. USAGE INFO: Said to another person, as in "knock yourself out" either to give approval to the person doing something that is thought to be unnecessary or overkill or to sarcastically pass off a task to someone who has criticized the speaker's efforts. Also used as an exclamation to mean "have a good time."

**make a full-court press** |māk u FUL kawrt pres| *v* To make a vigorous response; to go on the offensive. ORIGINS: From basketball jargon, **full-court press** is a style of defense that engages the offense man-to-man from the moment of the inbound pass rather than picking up the defense at half court.

**pour it on** |PAWR it ahn| *v* To move at maximum speed; to exert maximum effort.

**split a gut** |SPLIT a gut| *v* To laugh very hard. USAGE INFO: This phrase also means "to work very hard; to put in an enormous effort."

**split one's gut** |SPLIT wunz gut| *v* To laugh very hard. USAGE INFO: This phrase also means "to work very hard; to put in an enormous effort."

**suck it up** |SUK it UP| *v* To continue in the face of difficulties; to persevere; to endure or cope.

sweat it out |SWET it OUT| *v* To persevere; to endure for the sake of results.

tough it out |TUF it OUT| *adj* To persevere.

NON-SLANG SYNONYMS: attempt, do one's best, exert oneself, make an effort, press on, stay the course (this phrase is associated with continuing a policy of war, and is connected with Republican presidents Ronald Reagan, George H.W. Bush, and George W. Bush), stick with it, try, work hard, <u>drive on</u>, <u>go all out</u>, <u>plug away</u>, <u>put one's back into it</u>, <u>put oneself out</u>, <u>see *st* through</u>, <u>tackle</u>, **labor**, **leave no stone unturned**, **persevere**, **persist**, **undertake**

# IMPROVE

## 1 To Get Back on Track

clean up one's act |KLĒN up wunz AKT| *v* To improve one's behavior or performance. ORIGINS: Figurative use of SE **clean up**.

**clean up one's shit** |KLĒN up wunz SHIT| *v* To improve one's behavior or performance; to organize one's possessions. ORIGINS: Figurative use of SE **clean up**. Extended from slang **shit** meaning "possessions." USAGE ALERT: The inclusion of **shit** will make this phrase objectionable in some contexts and to some people.

**cut the crap** |KUT *thu* KRAP| *v* To stop goofing around; to stop talking nonsense or telling lies; to get serious. ORIGINS: Euphemism for **cut the shit**. From **crap**, a euphemism for **shit**, meaning "excrement." USAGE ALERT: The reference to excrement will make this phrase objectionable in some situations and to some people. People may find **crap** less objectionable than **shit**. Usually used with intent to be rude and understood as such.

cut the funny business |KUT *thu* FUN ē biz nis| *v* To get focused; to get serious; to stop dishonest practices.

**cut the shit** |KUT *thu* SHIT| *v* To stop goofing around; to stop talking nonsense or telling lies; to get serious. ORIGINS: From **shit** meaning "excrement." USAGE ALERT: The reference to excrement will make this phrase objectionable in some situations and to some people. People may find **crap** less objectionable than **shit**. Usually used with intent to be rude and understood as such.

do a 180 |DŪ u wun Ā tē| *v* To turn one's life around. ORIGINS: From the mathematical fact that turning 180° results in facing the opposite direction: by extension, a radical, complete change.

get it together |get it tū GE*TH* ur| *v* To get focused; to get organized; to come to a decision; to pull oneself together.

**get off one's ass**\* |get awf wunz AS| *v* To get to work; to get moving; to stop sitting around, wasting time. ORIGINS: The idea is of a worker sitting around rather than working. From slang **ass** meaning "the rear end or buttocks." Slang **butt** is a euphemism for **ass**. Duff is either "even more euphemistic" or "generally less objectionable," depending on how you look at it. USAGE ALERT: The use of a reference to the rear end or buttocks will be objectionable in some contexts and to some people. When used as an imperative "get off your ass," the phrase is usually used with intent to be rude and understood as such.

- **get off one's butt** |get awf wunz BUT|
- get off one's duff |get awf wunz DUF|

**get on the ball** |GET ahn *thu* BAWL| *v* To become focused; to become active and aware of the needs of the situation. ORIGINS: From baseball jargon.

**get one's act together** |get wunz AKT tu ge*th* ur| *v* To get organized in working toward a goal; to get focused.

**get one's ass in gear** |get wunz AS in GIR| *v* To stop wasting time; to start operating with more drive and efficiency; to begin applying oneself in a useful way. ORIGINS: The reference is to one's body as a vehicle that is in neutral or park. From slang **ass** meaning "the rear end or buttocks." USAGE ALERT: Usually used with intent to denigrate or insult and understood as such.

**get one's ducks in a row** |get wunz DUKS in u RŌ| *v* To reach a satisfactory level of organization. ORIGINS: From the practice of lining like things up neatly. USAGE INFO: Also used in the negative to speak of disorganization or inability to organize.

**get one's finger out (of one's ass/butt)** | get wunz FIN gur out / get wunz FIN gur out uv wunz AS / get wunz FIN gur out uv wunz BUT| *v See* GET ONE'S THUMB OUT (OF ONE'S ASS/BUTT).

**get one's head on straight** |get wunz HED ahn strāt| *v* To figure things out for oneself; to see one's situation clearly.

**get one's head out of one's ass/butt** |get wunz HED out uv wunz AS / get wunz HED out uv wunz BUT| *v* To stop acting stupidly. ORIGINS: The suggestion is of someone doing something thoroughly stupid. From slang **ass** meaning "the rear end or buttocks." From slang **butt** meaning "the rear end or buttocks" and acting as a euphemism for **ass**. USAGE ALERT: The crudeness of the image plus the reference to the buttocks or rear end will make this expression objectionable in some contexts and to some people.

**get one's head together** |get wunz HED tu ge*th* ur| *v* To become focused and centered after being scattered.

**get one's shit together** |get wunz SHIT tu ge*th* ur| *v* To get focused and organized; to develop and carry out a plan for one's life. ORIGINS: From slang **shit** meaning "possessions" extended from slang **shit** meaning "excrement." USAGE ALERT: The inclusion of the word **shit** will make this expression objectionable in some contexts and to some people.

**get one's stuff together** |get wunz STUF tu ge*th* ur| *v* To get focused and organized; to develop and carry out a plan for one's life. ORIGINS: Euphemism for **get one's shit together**.

**get one's thumb out (of one's ass/butt)** |get wunz THUM out / get wunz THUM out uv wunz AS / get wunz THUM out uv wunz BUT| *v* To stop sitting around or messing around and get ready for serious action. ORIGINS: From slang **ass** meaning "the rear end or buttocks" or slang **butt**, a euphemism for **ass**. The suggestion is of someone doing something thoroughly worthless. USAGE ALERT: The crudeness of the image plus the reference to the buttocks or rear end will make this expression objectionable in some contexts and to some people.

**get with it** |get WITH it| *v* To get ready for serious action; to accept the established conventions and act accordingly.

**get with the program** |GET with thu PRŌ gram| *v* To get ready for serious action; to accept the established conventions and act accordingly.

**shape up** |SHĀP up| *v* To address one's shortcomings; to improve one's behavior, productivity, or attitude. ORIGINS: Generalized and shortened from shape up or ship out, military slang in WWII, conveying a threat that lack of improvement would result in being sent to a combat zone.

**sing another tune** |SING u nu*th* ur TŪN| *v See* SING A DIFFERENT TUNE.

**sing a different tune** |SING u DIF runt TŪN| *v* To change one's mind; to assume a different stance; to behave differently. USAGE INFO: Often as part of a threat, as in "When I tell him the deal's off, he'll sing a different tune."

**toe the mark/line** |TŌ thu MAHRK / TŌ thu LĪN| *v* To behave in a respectable and respectful manner (with the inference that one has not behaved so in the past).

NON-SLANG SYNONYMS: change, come around, fall in line, improve, make strides, mend, overhaul, revamp, straighten out, turn the corner, **come to heel**, **get back on track**, **pick oneself up**, **snap out of it**, **straighten up and fly right**, **amend**, **conform**, **self-correct**, **transform**

# 2 To Enhance

**bump**[1] |bump| *v* To glamorize; to adorn so as to increase value.

**glam (up)** |glam / glam UP| *v* To glamorize; to take special care in preparing. ORIGINS: Shortened form of SE **glamorize**.

**jack (up)** |jak / Jak UP| *v* To increase the price; to enhance. ORIGINS: Akin to SE jack meaning "a device to raise a car."

**pimp (out/up)** |pimp / PIMP OUT / PIMP UP| *v* To improve the appearance and impressiveness of *st*; to improve the quality or functionality of *st* through modification or adding elements, like aftermarket accessories, in the case of a vehicle. ORIGINS: From slang **pimp** meaning "a procurer of customers for one or more prostitutes." USAGE ALERT: Some people will find the use of **pimp** in this phrase objectionable, possibly on the grounds that it may seem to be a glorification of pimping.

**posh up** |PAHSH up| *v* To make attractive and inviting; to accessorize; to glamorize.

**sex up** |SEK sup| *v* To make more attractive and appealing. ORIGINS: Figurative use of slang **sex up** meaning "make more sexy." USAGE ALERT: Some people may find the application of the word **sex** to all manner of things outside the usual realm of the word objectionable, based, for example, on the word being more common in conversations, advertising, etc. that children hear.

**soup up** |SŪP up| *v* To modify in order to increase performance or to make more impressive. ORIGINS: From slang **soup** meaning "high performance fuel for customized cars."

**spiff (up)** |spif / SPIF UP| *v* To tidy; to smarten up.

**trick out** |trik out| *v* To improve the appearance of; to glamorize.

**NON-SLANG SYNONYMS:** add bells and whistles, enrich, optimize, refine, upgrade (*optimize* and *upgrade* both are applied to improving systems based on technology), **gussy up**, **augment**, **beautify**, **elevate**, **embellish**, **embroider**, **enhance**, **garnish**, **gild**, **refurbish**, **renovate**, **transfigure**, **transform**

# 3 To Make Good Progress

**churn (st) out** |CHURN out / CHURN st out| *v* To produce large quantities on a regular schedule. ORIGINS: A reference to production with a butter churn. USAGE INFO: May imply efficiency or automatic and thoughtless production of a product that suffers from such an approach.

**come up roses** |KUM up RŌ zis| *v* To have an auspicious or favorable result; to succeed. ORIGINS: Similar to "come up smelling of violets," the phrase suggests an attractive ending (even if the process was rocky). The "rose" version has been popularized by the song "Everything's Coming Up Roses," from the musical *Gypsy: A Musical Fable.*

**go great guns** |GŌ grāt GUNZ| *v* To progress well; to advance with great speed.

**go like gangbusters** |GŌ līk GANG bus turz| *v* To achieve great success; forging ahead easily and without problems. ORIGINS: From a radio drama *Gangbusters* (1936–1957) featuring officers of the law who "busted" criminal gangs.

**go places** |GŌ plā siz| *v* To make good progress; to advance toward the desired goals.

**make short work of** |māk SHAWRT wurk uv| *v* To complete quickly through expedience and skill; to consume quickly, often from greed.

NON-SLANG SYNONYMS: advance, cover ground, forge ahead, gain ground, get on, go forward, make headway, make progress, make strides, pick up speed, push on, **press forward**, **press on**

# SUCCEED

## 1 To Succeed

**ace (it)** |ās / ĀS it| *v* To perform superbly, especially on an examination. ORIGINS: From the ace's role as the highest-ranked playing card.

**arrive** |u RĪV| *v* To attain success.

**bring off** |BRING awf| *v* To succeed, accomplish.

**cinch** |SINCH| *v* To make conclusive. ORIGINS: By extension from SE cinch meaning "to grasp tightly" and derived from Spanish **cincha**, meaning "a saddle girth" in a figurative sense: something that has been obtained. USAGE INFO: Often in the phrase "cinch the deal." Compare with the very similarly spelled and sounding SE **clinch the deal**, with a virtually identical meaning.

**deliver (the goods)** |di LIV ur / di LIV ur thu GOŌDZ| *v* To complete *st.*; to fulfill a promise. ORIGINS: Extended from the literal notion of SE **delivery**.

**do the trick** |dū *thu* TRIK| *v* To do the thing that solves a problem, fixes what's broken, or puts things right; to succeed.

**get somewhere** |GET sum wer| *v* To succeed; to fulfill one's own dreams.

**have (got) it made** |HAV it mād / GAHT it mād| *v* To be in a situation in which success is guaranteed; to have acquired wealth and success. USAGE INFO: Note that this can refer to either (assured) potential for success or success that has been achieved already.

**hit the jackpot** |hit *thu* JAK paht| *v* To have an important success; to have great (unexpected) luck; to win a lot of money. ORIGINS: Possibly from the procedure in the game of draw poker.

**make it** |MĀK it| *v* To succeed.

**make the grade** |MĀK *thu* GRĀD| *v* To succeed; to qualify or meet the requirements of; to do really well. ORIGINS: From the concept of a system of standards in which one must reach a certain level in order to be judged acceptable.

**nail**[1] |nāl| *v* To do something perfectly, often something practiced and for which there is a standard, like a dive, a stage performance, a presentation, etc. ORIGINS: From SE **nail** meaning "to drive a nail with a hammer."

**on a roll, be** |bē ahn u RŌL| *v* To experience a winning streak or a period of repeated successes. ORIGINS: From the action of rolling the dice in gambling.

**score** |skawr| *v* To succeed.

**set the world on fire** |set *thu* WURLD ahn FĪR| *v* To accomplish *st* of note.

**strike it lucky** |STRĪK it LUK ē| *v* To suddenly enjoy great good fortune.

**strike oil** |STRĪK OIL| *v* To prosper; to find (or sometimes do) *st* that insures one's financial future.

**turn the trick** |TURN *thu* TRIK| *v* To succeed; to have the desired result. USAGE INFO: Make sure to distinguish this from **turn tricks**, which means "to engage in sexual activity for pay."

**work like a charm** |WURK līk u CHAHRM| *v* To succeed easily and seamlessly. ORIGINS: From SE **charm** meaning "a magic spell."

**wrap *st* up** |RAP *st* UP| *v* To bring to a successful conclusion; to finish.

**NON-SLANG SYNONYMS:** be successful, become rich, carry off, do well, make good, profit, prosper, succeed, turn out well, win, <u>sew up</u>, <u>win by a nose</u>, **bear fruit**, **conquer**, **flourish**, **prevail**, **thrive**, **triumph**

## 2 To Succeed Through Perseverance

**bounce back** |bouns BAK| *v* To recover quickly from adversity; to rebound. ORIGINS: From the concept of a ball or spring returning to its original position after a bounce.

**make a go of it** |māk u GŌ uv it| *v* To succeed in spite of difficulties or poor odds.

**pull off** |PUL ahf| *v* To accomplish (despite the odds being against it); to succeed.

**win out/through** |win OUT / WIN THRŪ| *v* To succeed through perseverance.

**NON-SLANG SYNONYMS:** bring about, bring off, get there, overcome, rebound, recover, turn the corner, **bring to pass**, **persevere**, **recuperate**, **renew one's strength**

## 3 In a Promising Situation

**catbird seat, in the** |in *thu* KAT burd SĒT| *adj* In a privileged position; in a position of power or prominence. ORIGINS: Likely from the catbird's choice of the highest perch in a tree from which to sing. The phrase was popularized by US sports announcer Red Barber in his career from 1934–1966, and by author James Thurber who quoted Red Barber in the short story "The Catbird Seat" (1942), but has remained popular.

**cooking (with gas)** |KOOK ing / KOOK ing with GAS| *adj* Doing very well; performing wonderfully; making progress. ORIGINS: From an advertisement by the gas industry—"Now you're cooking with gas!"—to counteract the popularity of the electric range during the 1930s. Also used by jazz musicians to praise an exceptional performance. USAGE INFO: Sometimes appears as cooking on gas.

**in great shape** |in GRET SHĀP| *adj* In excellent condition in terms of physical health, emotional well-being, financial outlook, or overall. USAGE INFO: Also used more specifically of athletes and others of being in prime physical condition.

**in whack** |in WAK| *adj* In good condition. ORIGINS: From SE **whack** meaning condition or state. USAGE INFO: *See* OUT OF WHACK.

**looking up** |LOOK ing UP| *adj* Improving; becoming better. USAGE INFO: Often used of finances or prospects.

**no-lose** |NŌ LŪZ| *adj* Certain to end happily or successfully for all participants.

**rosy** |RŌ zē| *adj* Promising; indicative of success.

**up to scratch** |up tū SCRACH| *adj* Of acceptable quality; in good condition. ORIGINS: Figurative use of sports jargon from races in which **scratch** means "the line or marking indicating the starting line." USAGE INFO: *See* NOT UP TO SCRATCH.

**up to snuff** |up tū SNUF| *adj* Of acceptable quality; in good condition. ORIGINS: Either from the quality requirements for tobacco to be used as snuff or from the stimulating effects of snuff usage. USAGE INFO: *See* NOT UP TO SNUFF.

NON-SLANG SYNONYMS: having complete control, successful, **on top of the heap**, **sitting pretty**, **flourishing**, **in an enviable position**, **in a position of power**, **prospering**

# 4 A Certainty

**ace in the hole** |ĀS in *thu* HŌL| *n* A concealed asset that insures a win. ORIGINS: From the ace's role as the highest-ranked playing card and the role in poker of the "hole card," kept face-down until the showdown.

**cert** |surt| *n* A certainty. ORIGINS: Shortened from SE **certainty**.

**cinch²** |SINCH| *n* A certainty; a sure thing. ORIGINS: By extension from SE cinch meaning "to grasp tightly" and derived from Spanish **cincha**, meaning "a saddle girth"—something that can be easily grasped. USAGE INFO: Always with the indefinite article and often followed by a clause, with or without an introductory *that* as in: "It's a cinch that Wobbly Legs will win the third race."

**open-and-shut case** |Ō pun und SHUT CĀS| *n* An issue with a foregone conclusion; a problem to which the solution is obvious. ORIGINS: The idea is that you do not have to keep the case file open very long, but can shut it virtually as soon as you open it, signaling that a solution or conclusion is at hand.

**shoo-in** |SHŪ in| *n* A certainty. ORIGINS: From horse racing jargon for a "guaranteed" winner. USAGE INFO: Often used in the context of political elections.

**slam dunk, slam-dunk** |SLAM DUNGK| *n* A certainty; a guaranteed result. ORIGINS: From basketball jargon for a two-handed dunk.

**sure bet** |SHUR BET| *n* A certainty; a bet that can't be lost.

**sure shot** |SHUR SHAHT| *n* A certainty; a shot that is certain to hit its mark.

**sure thing** |SHUR THING| *n* A certainty; a bet that can't be lost.

NON-SLANG SYNONYMS: certainty, **certitude**, **surety**

## 5 A Success

**killing** |KIL ing| *n* An impressive (financial) success. USAGE INFO: Often in the phrase "make a killing."

**knockout** |NAHK out| *adj* An outstanding or excellent person or thing; a complete success.

**smash** |smash| *n* A great success.

NON-SLANG SYNONYMS: accomplishment, achievement, success, victory, win, **big hit**, **grand slam**, **attainment**, **consummation**, **triumph**

# STALL

## 1 To Make Minimal Progress

**get along** |get u LAWNG| *v* To make reasonable progress; to achieve minimum satisfaction.

**get by** |get BĪ| *v* To achieve minimum satisfaction; to manage; to do acceptably well, but no better.

**get on** |get AHN| *v* To do well enough to be satisfied; to achieve minimum satisfaction; to keep on keeping on.

**hack it** |HACK it| *v* To succeed or manage; to handle whatever one is facing; to accomplish. ORIGINS: From SE **hack** meaning "to cut through." USAGE INFO: Used both positively and negatively.

**manage** |MA nij| *v* To achieve (at least) minimum satisfaction.

**muddle through** |MU dul thrū| *v* To achieve something or get through something, despite confusion and/or difficulties.

**scrape along/by** |SKRĀP u lawng / SKRĀP BĪ| *v* To get by; to just manage what is needed.

**squeak by/through** |SKWĒK BĪ / SKWĒK THRŪ| *v* To succeed, win, or pass (an examination), but just barely.

NON-SLANG SYNONYMS: struggle, <u>cut it close</u>, <u>make do</u>

## 2 To Postpone

**let** *st* **ride** |LET *st* RĪD| *v* To hold off from taking expected action, such as punishment; to forgive or excuse *st*.

**put** *st* **on hold** |PŎŎT *st* ahn HŌLD| *v* To postpone; to delay. ORIGINS: From the practice of putting one telephone call "on hold" in order to take another.

**put** *st* **on ice** |PŎŎT *st* ahn ĪS| *v* To set aside a project idea for later use. ORIGINS: From slang **on ice** meaning "in reserve," possibly from the practice of using trays of ice to hold food for later, while maintaining its quality.

**put** *st* **on the back burner** |PŎŎT *st* ahn *thu* BAK BURN ur| *v* To temporarily devote less attention to *st*; to deactivate *st* with the plan of starting it up again later; to lessen the priority of *st*.

**sleep on** *st* |SLĒP ahn *st*| *v* To postpone consideration of (and therefore action on) *st*.

NON-SLANG SYNONYMS: delay, hold over, postpone, put back, put on hold, put off, <u>hang fire</u>, <u>hold off</u>, <u>hold up</u>, <u>mothball</u>, **defer**, **shelve**, **suspend**, **table**

## 3 To Waste Time

**crap around** |krap u ROUND| *v* To fool around; to waste time. ORIGINS: From **crap**, a euphemism for **shit**, meaning "excrement." USAGE INFO: Along the lines of **fuck around**, **futz around**, **fart around**, etc. USAGE ALERT: This term will be objectionable in some situations and to some people.

**dick around** |DIK u ROUND| *v* To waste time; to mess around. ORIGINS: From slang **dick** meaning "penis." USAGE ALERT: The inclusion of a reference to sexual organs will make this phrase objectionable in some situations and to some people.

**dog it** |DAWG it| *v* To waste time; to shirk one's work. ORIGINS: Comparing human behavior to a stereotype of dog behavior.

**fart around/about** |FAHRT u round / FAHRT u bout| *v* To waste time; to mess around. ORIGINS: Euphemism for **fuck around/about**. From slang **fart** meaning "to break wind." USAGE ALERT: Euphemisms may still be objectionable in some contexts and to some people.

**fiddle around** |FID ul u ROUND| *v* To fool around; to waste time. ORIGINS: From slang fiddle meaning "to shirk one's duty."

**fool around** |FŪL u ROUND| *v* To act without aim or accomplishment; to waste time. USAGE INFO: Can also refer to sexual activity especially with someone who is not one's spouse or partner.

**fuck around** |FUK u ROUND| *v* To waste time; to mess around. ORIGINS: From slang **fuck** meaning "to engage in sexual intercourse." USAGE INFO: Can also refer to sexual activity. USAGE ALERT: The inclusion of **fuck** will make this expression objectionable in some contexts and to some people.

**futz around/about** |FUTZ u round / FUTZ u bout| *v* To waste time; to mess around. ORIGINS: Euphemism for **fuck around/about**. From German futz meaning "fart." USAGE ALERT: Euphemisms may still be objectionable in some contexts and to some people.

**goof around** |GŪF u ROUND| *v* To squander one's time; to mess around; to avoid work. ORIGINS: By several steps, from an obsolete English word goff meaning "fool," from an obsolete French word goffe meaning "stupid."

**goof off** |GŪF AWF| *v* To squander one's time; to mess around; to avoid work. ORIGINS: By several steps, from an obsolete English word goff meaning "fool," from an obsolete French word goffe meaning "stupid."

**jack around** |JAK u ROUND| *v* To mess around; to engage in useless/time-wasting activities. ORIGINS: By extension of slang jack, meaning fool and shortened from SE jackass.

**lollygag, lallygag** |LAH lē gag| *v* To waste time; to putter around; to linger or lag behind.

**loaf (around)** |lōf / LŌF u ROUND| *v* To hang around without accomplishing anything; to be idle.

**mess around/about** |mes u ROUND / MES u BOUT| *v* To act without aim or accomplishment; to waste time.

**monkey around/about** |MUN kē u ROUND / MUN kē u BOUT| *v* To act without aim or accomplishment; to waste time. ORIGINS: From ideas about the behavior of monkeys. USAGE INFO: Unlike some other phrases about wasting time, this one can be playful.

**moon (about)** |mūn / MŪN u BOUT| *v* To wander about aimlessly while lamenting to oneself about love, often unrequited.

muck about/around |MUK u BOUT / MUK u ROUND| *v* To act without aim or accomplishment; to waste time.

piddle about/around |PID'l u BOUT / PID'l u ROUND| *v* To waste time; to mess around. ORIGINS: From SE piddle meaning "to be busy with trifles." USAGE ALERT: Although this expression is unrelated to slang piddle meaning "to urinate," people may believe that it is a euphemism for **piss about/around**.

**piss about/around** |PIS u bout / PIS u round| *v* To fool around; to waste time. ORIGINS: From slang **piss** meaning "to urinate." USAGE INFO: Along the lines of **fuck around**, **futz around**, **fart around**. USAGE ALERT: The inclusion of the word **piss** in the phrase will render it objectionable in some contexts and to some people.

putz around |PUTZ u ROUND| *v* To waste time; to mess around. ORIGINS: From Yiddish **putz** meaning "penis." USAGE INFO: Putz is also used to mean "fool," so people may not know its original meaning. In addition, the similarity of sound, spelling, and meaning to **putter** are likely to create associations with that word. USAGE ALERT: The somewhat distant reference to sexual organs in this phrase will not often raise objections because most people don't make the connection.

screw around |SKREW u round| *v* To waste time; to mess around. ORIGINS: Euphemism for **fuck around**. From slang screw, a euphemism for **fuck**. USAGE INFO: Can also refer to sexual activity. USAGE ALERT: The euphemism screw in this phrase will soften it somewhat, but it may still be objectionable in some contexts and to some people.

veg |vej| *v* To do nothing; to relax. ORIGINS: Shortened form of SE vegetate.

NON-SLANG SYNONYMS: be idle, dawdle, delay, drag one's feet, loiter, shirk, slack, take one's sweet time, take one's time, waste time, dillydally, fritter time away, horse around, kill time, dally, linger, procrastinate, tarry

# DETERIORATE

## 1 To Mishandle or Meddle With

**dick (around) with** *st* |DIK with *st* / DIK u ROUND with *st*| *v* To mess or fool around with *st*; to handle irresponsibly or without understanding. ORIGINS: From slang **dick** meaning "penis." USAGE ALERT: The inclusion of a reference to sexual organs will make this phrase objectionable in some situations and to some people.

diddle (around) with *st* |DID 'l with *st*/ DID 'l u ROUND with *st*| *v* To mess or fool around with; to handle irresponsibly or without understanding.

**fart (around) with** *st* |FAHRT u round with *st*| *v* To use something irresponsibly or without understanding; to mess around with. ORIGINS:

Euphemism for **fuck (around) with** *st*. From slang **fart** meaning "to break wind." USAGE ALERT: Euphemisms may still be objectionable in some contexts and to some people.

**fiddle (around) with** *st* |FID ul with *st*/ FID ul u ROUND with *st*| *v* To use something irresponsibly or without understanding; to mess around with. ORIGINS: From slang fiddle meaning "to shirk one's duty."

**fool (around) with** *st* |FŪL with *st* / FŪL u ROUND with *st*| *v* To use something irresponsibly or without understanding; to mess around with. USAGE INFO: Distinct from fool around with *sb*, which can refer to joint goofing off or to sexual activity.

**fuck (around) with** *st* |FUK with *st* / FUK u ROUND with *st*| *v* To use something irresponsibly or without understanding; to mess around with. ORIGINS: From slang **fuck** meaning "to engage in sexual intercourse." USAGE INFO: Distinct from **fuck around with** *sb*, which can either mean to goof around together, or refer to sexual activity. USAGE ALERT: The inclusion of **fuck** will make this expression objectionable in some contexts and to some people.

**futz (around) with** *st* |FUTZ with *st* / FUTZ u round with *st*| *v* To use something irresponsibly or without understanding; to mess around with. ORIGINS: Euphemism for **fuck around with** *st*. From German futz meaning "fart." USAGE ALERT: Euphemisms may still be objectionable in some contexts and to some people.

**goof around with** *st* |gūf u ROUND with *st*| *v* To use something irresponsibly or without understanding; to mess around with. ORIGINS: By several steps, from an obsolete English word goff meaning "fool," from an obsolete French word goffe meaning "stupid."

**jack (around) with** *st* |jak with *st* / jak u ROUND with *st*| *v* To use something irresponsibly or without understanding; to mess around with. ORIGINS: Possibly from slang jack meaning "fool," a shortening of SE jackass, therefore a synonym for fool (around) with. USAGE ALERT: Because jack is used in phrases such as **jack off**, a euphemism for **jerk-off** meaning "to masturbate," and **jackshit** (see above), it's difficult to tell how this phrase may be received: as perfectly ordinary or as euphemistic and objectionable.

**mess (around) with** *st* |MES with *st* / mes u ROUND with *st*| *v* To use something irresponsibly or without understanding. USAGE INFO: Mess with can also mean "to tease," as in "I'm just messing with you," or "to harass or interfere with," as in "You mess with the bull, you get the horns."

**monkey around with** *st*\* |MUN kē u ROUND with *st*| *v* To use something irresponsibly or without understanding; to mess around with. ORIGINS: From (incorrect) ideas about the intelligence of SE monkeys.
• monkey with *st* |MUN kē with *st*|

**muck (around) with** *st* |MUK with *st* / muk u ROUND with *st*| *v* To use something irresponsibly or without understanding.

**potchky, potchkie (around) with** *st* |PAHCH kē with *st* / PAHCH kē u ROUND with *st* | *v* To use something irresponsibly or without understanding; to mess around with. ORIGINS: From Yiddish patsch meaning "a slap."

**putz (around) with** *st* |PUTZ with *st* / PUTZ u ROUND with *st*| *v* To mess or fool around with *st*; to handle irresponsibly or without understanding. ORIGINS: From Yiddish **putz**, meaning "penis." In addition, the similarity of sound, spelling, and meaning to **putter** are likely to create associations with that word. USAGE INFO: Putz is also used to mean "fool," so people may not know its original meaning. USAGE ALERT: The somewhat distant reference to sexual organs in this phrase will not often raise objections because most people don't make the connection.

**screw (around) with** *st* |SKREW with *st* / SKREW u round with *st* | *v* To use something irresponsibly or without understanding; to mess around with. ORIGINS: Euphemism for **fuck (around) with** *st*. From slang screw, a euphemism for **fuck**. USAGE INFO: Distinct from screw around with *sb*, which can either mean "to goof around together," or refer to sexual activity. USAGE ALERT: The euphemism screw in this phrase will soften it somewhat, but it may still be objectionable in some contexts and to some people.

NON-SLANG SYNONYMS: abuse, harm, meddle, mistreat, misuse, **fumble**, **gum up**, **rummage through**, **misemploy**, **mishandle**

## 2 To Backtrack or Worsen

**go back to square one** |gō BAK tū skwer WUN| *v* To restart; to resume from the beginning, often because of encountering problems or some kind of failure. ORIGINS: Possibly from the practice of a player being sent back in a board game in which the game path is drawn as a series of squares.

**go back to the drawing board** |gō BAK tū thu DRAW ing bawrd| *v* To restart; to return to the planning stage. ORIGINS: From SE drawing board, the desk used for drafting, as in drawing up architectural blueprints, etc.

**go south** |gō SOUTH| *v* To become less successful; to lose value; to stop functioning; to be defeated. ORIGINS: Possibly from the practice of heading south of the southern US border to escape from accountability or from the law. *See* GO WEST.

**go to the dogs** |gō tū thu DAWGZ| *v* To become less successful; to go downhill; to be ruined; to decline in social status. ORIGINS: From the practice of once-famous race horses becoming dog food after death.

**hit the skids** |hit thu SKIDZ| *v* To experience a decline in value; to run into difficulties that forecast a demise.

NON-SLANG SYNONYMS—BACKTRACK: backtrack, fall back, restart, **backpedal**, **retreat**

NON-SLANG SYNONYMS—WORSEN: fall off, **get worse**, **go downhill**, **go to pot**, **sink**, **decline**, **deteriorate**, **disintegrate**,

## 3 To Ruin

**blow it** |BLŌ it| *v* To botch, destroy, or ruin through ineptitude.

**bust** |bust| *v* To smash or break, especially using force; to render useless or inoperable.

**fry** |frī| *v* To destroy an electronic device with heat or electrical current.

**fuck *st* up** |FUK *st* up| *v* To ruin or destroy *st*; to make a complete mess of; to blunder; to make a mistake. ORIGINS: From slang **fuck** meaning "to engage in sexual intercourse." USAGE ALERT: The inclusion of **fuck** will make this expression objectionable in some contexts and to some people.

**muck *st* up** |muk *st* UP| *v* To spoil *st*; to ruin *st*.

**trash²** |trash| *v* To destroy property by purposely breaking or damaging it beyond repair; to render into trash.

**wipe out** |WĪP OUT| *v* To destroy; to ruin financially.

NON-SLANG SYNONYMS: bring down, ruin, waste, <u>wreck</u>, **decimate**, **wreak havoc on**

# HIT OBSTACLES

## 1 To Blunder or Make a Mistake

**ball up** |BAWL up| *v* To make a mistake; to ruin; to make a mess of. ORIGINS: Euphemism for **fuck up**. **Ball** means "testicle." USAGE INFO: Used of messes made by females as well as males. USAGE ALERT: This slang phrase is often somewhat less objectionable than **fuck up**, because a) it refers to sex organs, but not sexual activity, and b) **ball** has alternate SE meanings that are unrelated to sexuality.

**cock up** |KAHK up| *v* To make a mistake; to ruin; to make a mess of. ORIGINS: Euphemism for **fuck up**. **Cock** means "penis." USAGE INFO: Used of messes made by females as well as males. USAGE ALERT: This slang phrase is often somewhat less objectionable than **fuck up**, because a) it refers to sex organs, but not sexual activity, and likely because b) on its own, SE **cock** has alternate meanings that are unrelated to sexuality.

**drop the ball** |DRAHP *thu* bawl| *v* To make a mistake at a telling moment. ORIGINS: From sports imagery that could apply to several sports, including baseball and football, in which it is legal to catch or carry the ball and losing hold of it can result in a penalty.

**excessorize** |ek SES awr īz| *v* To add an excessive number of accessories, destroying the effect. ORIGINS: A punning portmanteau of SE **excess** and **accessorize**.

**flub** |flub| *v* To make a mess of; to bungle; to botch.

**fluff** |fluf| *v* To make a mistake; to bungle; to fail because of memory lapse. ORIGINS: From theatre jargon for actors who forget or confuse their lines.

**fuck up** |FUK up| *v* To make a mistake; to ruin; to make a mess of; to blunder. ORIGINS: From slang **fuck** meaning "to engage in sexual intercourse." USAGE INFO: Unlike **fuck *sb* up** and **fuck *st* up**, **fuck up** does not take an object, as in "You know, you really fucked up!" USAGE ALERT: The inclusion of **fuck** will make this expression objectionable in some contexts and to some people.

**lay an egg** |lā an EG| *v* To commit a social error; to make a mistake in public, such as in a performance. ORIGINS: From vaudeville slang.

**louse up** |LOUS up| *v* To ruin; to make a mess of; to spoil. ORIGINS: From WWI military slang: the trenches were filled with lice (the plural of **louse**), who "loused up" things for the soldiers.

**make a balls of** |māk u BAWL zuv| *v* To spoil; to ruin; to make a mistake. ORIGINS: From slang **balls** meaning "testicles." USAGE ALERT: The inclusion of the word **balls** in the phrase will render it objectionable in some contexts and to some people.

**make a muck of** |māk u MUK uv| *v* To add confusion or difficulty to a situation; to make a mess of *st*.

**make a pig's ear of** |māk u PIGZ IR uv| *v* To ruin or spoil *st*. ORIGINS: From slang pig's ear meaning "a mess."

**make hash of** |māk HASH uv| *v* To confuse things; to make a muddle of things. ORIGINS: From SE **hash** meaning "a jumble."

**mess up** |MES UP| *v* To make a mistake, as on a test or in a presentation; to ruin *st*. ORIGINS: From SE **mess**.

**miss the boat** |MIS *thu* BŌT| *v* To misunderstand; to miss an opportunity. ORIGINS: From the experience of being too late and arriving at the dock to find that the boat has departed.

**muck up** |muk UP| *v* To damage or ruin. ORIGINS: Euphemism for **fuck up**.

**muff** |muf| *v* To fail because of memory lapse; to make a blunder; to make a mess.

**put a crimp in** |pŏŏt u CRIMP in| *v* To thwart, limit, or interfere with, whether purposely or unintentionally. ORIGINS: From SE **crimp** meaning "to compress." USAGE INFO: Can be used with a personal subject as in, "His attitude put a crimp in my enjoyment of the evening" or an impersonal subject, as in "Well, the weather sure puts a crimp in our plans, doesn't it?"

**screw (*sb/st*) up** |SKRŪ UP / SKRŪ *sb/st* UP | *v* To spoil; to ruin; to cause another person severe psychological distress. ORIGINS: Euphemism for **fuck (*sb/st*) up**. From slang screw, a euphemism for **fuck**. USAGE INFO: Can be used with or without an object. USAGE ALERT: The euphemism screw in this phrase will soften it somewhat, but it may still be objectionable in some contexts and to some people.

**NON-SLANG SYNONYMS:** be wrong, err, make a mistake, miss, stumble, <u>blunder</u>, <u>drop the ball</u>, <u>put one's foot in it</u>, **commit an error**, **miscalculate**, **misjudge**

## 2  To Malfunction

act up |AK tup| *v* To cause trouble; to malfunction. USAGE INFO: Used of *sb/st* who or that can or has in the past acted appropriately/functioned well.

crap out |krap OUT| *v* To stop working properly or at all. ORIGINS: By extension of the gambling jargon **crap out**, meaning "make a losing throw in the game of craps." USAGE ALERT: Some people may misconstrue this term as being related to excrement.

go haywire |gō HĀ wīr| *v* To malfunction; to fail to work properly.

**NON-SLANG SYNONYMS:** work improperly, <u>misbehave</u>, **malfunction**

## 3  To Cause Problems for Oneself

cut one's own throat |KUT wunz ōn THRŌT| *v* To ruin one's own prospects. ORIGINS: Figurative interpretation of the words describing suicide.

cut oneself off at the knees |KUT wun self AWF at *th*u NĒZ| *v* To ruin one's own prospects. ORIGINS: Figurative interpretation of the words describing incapacitating oneself.

shoot oneself in the foot |SHŪT wun SELF in *th*u FŎOT| *v* To ruin one's own prospects; to blunder in a way that endangers one's future.

**step on one's cock*** |STEP ahn wunz KAHK| *v* To get oneself into trouble; to make a fool of oneself. ORIGINS: From slang **cock** or **dick** meaning "penis." USAGE INFO: Usually only used by or of males. USAGE ALERT: The inclusion of the word **cock** or **dick** in the phrase will render it objectionable in some contexts and to some people.
• **step on one's dick** |STEP ahn wunz DIK|

**NON-SLANG SYNONYMS:** destroy one's own future, embarrass oneself, make a mistake, <u>ruin one's prospects</u>

## 4  Moderate to Difficult Problems

bad job |BAD JAHB| *n* A difficulty with no reasonable resolution. USAGE INFO: Often used in the phrase "give *st* up as a bad job."

bad news |BAD NŪZ| *n* Difficulties or trouble. USAGE INFO: Used of a person who is perpetually in trouble or who drags acquaintances into bad situations.

**bad shit** |BAD SHIT| *n* Serious problems. ORIGINS: From slang **shit** meaning "excrement." USAGE ALERT: The use of the word **shit** will make this phrase objectionable in some contexts and to some people.

**ball-buster** |BAWL bus tur| *n* Extremely demanding and difficult problem. ORIGINS: From slang **balls** meaning "testicles," and SE buster, "someone or something that breaks things." USAGE INFO: Most often used by males. Can also be used of a person who is extremely demanding, in which case it can refer to a male or a female. USAGE ALERT: The use of **ball** in this phrase will make it objectionable in some contexts and to some people. Usually used with intent to denigrate or insult and understood as such.

**bastard**[2] |BAS turd| *n* A very difficult problem. ORIGINS: From SE bastard meaning "an illegitimate child." USAGE ALERT: The term **bastard** will be considered objectionable in some contexts and by some people.

**bear** |ber| *n* A difficult or unpleasant thing or situation. ORIGINS: Based on SE bear, the large, omnivorous, and sometimes aggressive mammals that can be dangerous to humans.

**bind** |bīnd| *n* Predicament or difficult situation.

**bitch**[2] |bich| *n* An extremely difficult or unpleasant problem. ORIGINS: From SE bitch, meaning "a female dog." USAGE ALERT: **Bitch** will be objectionable in some contexts and to some people.

**bone-breaker** |BŌN brā kur| *n* An extremely difficult problem. ORIGINS: Implying that the difficulty will literally break one's bones.

**brute** |brūt| *n* An extremely large or difficult problem. ORIGINS: From SE brute. USAGE INFO: Often in the phrase "a brute of a...."

**bun-buster** |BUN bus tur| *n* Extremely difficult, overwhelming, arduous, or punishing problem. ORIGINS: From SE bust meaning "to break" combined with slang for a core body part: **bun**, a euphemism for slang **ass** meaning "the rear end or buttocks." USAGE ALERT: Although **bun** is generally considered less objectionable than **ass** or **butt**, it will still be objectionable in some contexts and to some people. A less objectionable choice would be gut-buster.

**butt-buster** |BUT bus tur| *n* Extremely difficult, overwhelming, arduous, or punishing problem. ORIGINS: From SE bust meaning "to break" combined with slang for a core body part: **butt**, a euphemism for slang **ass** meaning "the rear end or buttocks." USAGE ALERT: Although **butt** is generally considered less objectionable than **ass**, it will still be objectionable in some contexts and to some people. A less objectionable choice would be gut-buster.

**can of worms** |kan uv WURMZ| *n* A complex or serious problem. ORIGINS: The unappealing scenario of discovering a difficult problem is compared in the phrase to the sensation upon opening a can and unexpectedly finding it full of worms.

**fly in the ointment** |FLĪ in *thu* OINT munt| *n* Something small that nevertheless spoils an entire plan or project; a small setback; a detraction. From SE **fly** meaning "a flying insect" and SE **ointment** meaning "salve."

**grind** |grīnd| *n* Difficult or demanding work, especially when it is unrelenting and academic. ORIGINS: By extension from SE **grind** meaning "to oppress continually." USAGE INFO: A **grind** is also a person who engages in such work. USAGE ALERT: Grind also refers to sexually provocative dance moves.

**gut-buster** |GUT bus tur| *n* Extremely difficult, overwhelming, arduous, or punishing problem. ORIGINS: From SE **bust** meaning "to break" combined with **gut**, which represents a person's essence (as in "I hate your guts").

**hard row to hoe** |HAHRD rō tū HŌ| *n* An extremely difficult task. ORIGINS: By analogy to farming.

**headache** |HED āk| *n* A serious or annoying problem or person. ORIGINS: Something capable of giving one a headache.

**heavy sledding** |HEV ē SLED ing| *n* A challenging problem. ORIGINS: In contrast to the usual smooth, quick movement of a sled over the snow.

**hot potato** |haht pu TĀ tō| *n* A problem that is felt to be "too hot to handle"; a sensitive or politicized issue that people wish would go away. ORIGINS: From the earlier expression **drop like a hot potato**, which alludes to the heat-retaining properties of a baked potato. Popularized by the children's game Hot Potato.

**large order** |LAHRJ AWR dur| *n* An extremely difficult project or problem; an exceptionally demanding task.

**mare's nest** |MERZ nest| *n* A serious problem; a very complex situation; a hoax. ORIGINS: Extended from slang **mare's nest** meaning "something imaginary" (i.e., mares don't build nests).

**mind-fucker** |MĪND FUK ur| *n* A serious problem that tests one's mental abilities; a trick meant to deceive, confound, or disturb *sb*. ORIGINS: From slang **fuck** meaning "to engage in sexual intercourse." USAGE ALERT: The inclusion of a form of the word **fuck** in the phrase will render it objectionable in some contexts and to some people.

**no joke** |nō JŌK| *n* A serious, consequential, or important problem. USAGE INFO: Usually used in ironic understatement (i.e., litotes) of something extremely difficult; horrendously problematic; etc.

**no picnic** |nō PIK nik| *n* A difficult, unpleasant problem that will allow neither enjoyment nor relaxation. ORIGINS: From standard conception of an SE **picnic** as relaxing, enjoyable, etc. USAGE INFO: Usually used in ironic understatement (i.e., litotes) of something extremely difficult; horrendously problematic; etc.

**no tea party** |nō TĒ pahr tē| *n* A difficult, unpleasant problem that will allow neither enjoyment nor relaxation. ORIGINS: From standard conception of an SE **tea party** as relaxing, enjoyable, cultivated, etc. USAGE INFO: Usually used in ironic understatement (i.e., litotes) of something extremely difficult; horrendously problematic; etc.

**pain** |PĀN| *n* An annoying person; a difficult, complex, and potentially time-consuming problem or development.

**pain in the ass**\* |PĀN in *th*ē AS| *n* An annoying person; a difficult, complex, and potentially time-consuming problem or development. ORIGINS: From slang **ass** meaning "the rear end or buttocks" or slang **butt**, a euphemism for **ass**. USAGE ALERT: A reference to the buttocks or rear end in any form will be objectionable in some contexts and to some people. Usually used with intent to denigrate or insult and understood as such.
• **pain in the butt** |PĀN in *th*u BUT|

**pain in the neck** |PĀN in *th*u NEK| *n* An annoying person; a difficult, complex, and potentially time-consuming problem or development. ORIGINS: A euphemism for **pain in the ass** and synonyms relating to the rear end or buttocks. USAGE ALERT: Often used with intent to denigrate or insult and understood as such.

**pain in the rear (end)**\* |PĀN in *th*u RIR / PĀN in *th*u RIR END| *n* An annoying person; a difficult, complex, and potentially time-consuming problem or development. ORIGINS: Euphemism for **pain in the ass**. Tush(y/ie) and rear (end) are euphemisms for **ass** meaning "the rear end or buttocks." USAGE ALERT: Tush(y/ie) and rear (end) are less in-your-face, but in some contexts and for some people, a reference to the buttocks or rear end in any form will be objectionable. Usually used with intent to denigrate or insult and understood as such.
• pain in the tush(y/ie) |PĀN in *th*u TUSH / PĀN in *th*u TU shē|

**pisser** |PIS ur| *n* A difficult task. ORIGINS: From slang **piss** meaning "to urinate," so *st* that makes one piss or perhaps that makes one pissed. USAGE ALERT: Use of a form of **piss** will be objectionable in some contexts and to some people.

**poison** |POI zun| *n* A serious problem; name for *sb/st* that should be avoided.

**son of a bitch**[1] |sun uv u BICH| *n* Something extremely difficult. ORIGINS: Figurative use of SE **bitch**, meaning "a female dog." USAGE ALERT: The inclusion of the word **bitch** in the phrase will render it objectionable in some contexts and to some people.

**stinker(oo)**[1] |STING ker / STING ker ū| *n* An extremely difficult problem. ORIGINS: Figurative use of SE **stink** meaning "to smell." USAGE INFO: When the ending is added, the word may be used playfully.

**tall order** |TAWL AWR dur| *n* An extremely difficult project or problem; an exceptionally demanding task.

**tough stuff** |TUF STUF| *n* Serious problems; difficult circumstances to deal with and/or get through.

NON-SLANG SYNONYMS: brain twister, issue, obstacle, problem, teaser, **stumper**, **complication**, **dilemma**, **predicament**, **quandary**

# 5 Easily Resolved Problems

blip |blip| *n* A small, easily amended problem; a temporary hiatus. ORIGINS: From technology jargon **blip**, which refers to the transient appearance of a small spot on a radar screen.

breeze |brēz| *n* Simple, easy to resolve or complete. ORIGINS: From analogy to wind in being able to "blow" through something. USAGE INFO: Often used in the phrase "It's a breeze."

cinch[1] |SINCH| *n* An easy to resolve problem. ORIGINS: By extension from SE **cinch** meaning "to grasp tightly" and derived from Spanish **cincha**, meaning "a saddle girth"—something that can be easily grasped. USAGE INFO: Always with the indefinite article, as in: "It'll be a cinch to fix."

duck soup |DUK sūp| *n* Easily resolved; simple. ORIGINS: Popularity boosted by the (still popular) 1933 Marx Brothers' film *Duck Soup*.

hiccup |HIK up| *n* A minor difficulty or interruption. ORIGINS: SE **hiccup**.

no problem |nō PRAHB lum| *n* A problem that is easy to resolve. USAGE INFO: Also used as a twenty-first century substitute for "you're welcome," although some people find this problematic on the grounds that the response suggests that whatever it is was only done because it wasn't a major inconvenience, not out of some true desire to assist, help, support, etc.

no sweat |NŌ SWET| *n* A problem that is capable of being dealt with without hard work. ORIGINS: The expectation is that there is no need to break a sweat in order to fix <whatever it is>.

picnic |PIK nik| *adj* An easily dealt with issue; a straightforward and simple project. ORIGINS: From standard conception of an SE **picnic** as relaxing, enjoyable, etc. USAGE INFO: Usually used in the negative with ironic understatement (i.e., litotes) of something extremely difficult; horrendously problematic; etc. *See* NO PICNIC.

pie |pī| *n* An issue that is (apparently problematic but) easily dealt with; *st* that can be easily and efficiently handled. ORIGINS: Has to do with the ease of eating pie, rather than making it. USAGE INFO: Often, but not always, in the phrase "as easy as pie." **Pie in the sky** is something different—an empty promise.

piece of cake |PĒS uv CĀK| *n* An issue that is (apparently problematic but) easily dealt with; something that can be easily and efficiently handled. USAGE INFO: Often, but not always, used in "It's a piece of cake."

romp |rahmp| *n* An easily accomplished task.

snap |snap| *n* A task that is easy to accomplish or resolve.

walkover |WAWK ō vur| *n* An easily accomplished task.

waltz* |waltz| *n* An easily resolved problem.
  • a waltz in the park |u WALTZ in *thu* PAHRK| *v*

NON-SLANG SYNONYMS: child's play, easy task, **kid-stuff**, **no-brainer**

# 6 Errors

**balls-up** |BAWLZ up| *n* An error or blunder. ORIGINS: From slang **balls** meaning "testicles." Originally a military usage. *See* **FUBAR** and **SNAFU**. USAGE ALERT: The inclusion of **balls** in this phrase will make it objectionable in some contexts and to some people.

**bloomer** |BLŪ mur| *n* A blunder. ORIGINS: Blooming is a British English substitute for **bloody**. Bloomer is said to combine slang blooming and SE **error**. USAGE ALERT: Speakers of British English are more likely than speakers of US English to know the actual ORIGINS of the word, and some of them may find it objectionable.

**blooper** |BLŪ pur| *n* An embarrassing verbal faux pas or other public mistake. ORIGINS: Possibly from extension of oops or from baseball jargon for a fly ball that goes over the infield but is too close in for the outfielders to catch.

**bobble** |BAHB ul| *n* A mistake or blunder. ORIGINS: A generalization of the jargon of baseball and football for the mishandling or fumbled catch of the ball.

**boner** |BŌN ur| *n* A mistake; a blunder. ORIGINS: The action of a bonehead. USAGE INFO: A boner may be mild or serious.

**boo-boo** |BŪ bū| *n* A mistake or blunder, often embarrassing. ORIGINS: Extended from boob meaning an error or blunder. USAGE INFO: The reduplication makes the word seem childish, thus it is often used self-consciously, employed when someone is acknowledging an embarrassing mistake, or used in an attempt to diminish the importance of another's misstep. Boo-boo is also a child's word for a minor injury.

**clinker** |KLINK ur| *n* A blunder; a muffed performance. ORIGINS: From baseball jargon for an error.

**foul up** |FOUL up| *n* To make a mistake; to commit a blunder. ORIGINS: Euphemism for **fuck up**. From US military use. *See* **FUBAR** and **SNAFU**. USAGE ALERT: People who suspect euphemistic use may find this objectionable based on the phrase that hasn't been used.

**goof², also goof up** |gūf / GŪF up| *n* A silly or stupid mistake; a bungle. ORIGINS: By several steps, from an obsolete English word goff meaning "fool," from an obsolete French word goffe meaning "stupid."

**howler** |houl ur| *n* A laughable mistake; a serious error. USAGE INFO: Two very different meanings, the first one a howl of laughter, the second, a howl of pain.

**screwup, screw-up²** |SKRŪ up| *n* An error. ORIGINS: Euphemism for **fuckup**, **fuck-up**. From slang screw, a euphemism for **fuck**. USAGE ALERT: The euphemism screw in this phrase will soften it somewhat, but it may still be objectionable in some contexts and to some people.

**slip-up** |SLIP up| *n* A mistake; an error; an oversight.

NON-SLANG SYNONYMS: error, inaccuracy, mistake, omission, oversight, <u>slip</u>, **faux pas**, **flaw**, **lapse**, **miscalculation**, **misstep**

# 7 Malfunctions

bug |bug| *n* A malfunction, defect, or problem. ORIGINS: By extension from the annoyance of an SE **bug** ("an insect"). USAGE INFO: Frequently used of problems arising in computer software.

glitch |glich| *n* A minor malfunction; a small mishap or problem. ORIGINS: From Yiddish **glitsch** meaning "a lapse," from German **glitschen** meaning "to slip." Initially computer jargon and first used in writing by astronaut John Glenn (1962), it moved from technical meanings related to power supply (loss of or spike in power) to more general meanings.

hitch |hich| *n* A malfunction; an impediment to progress; a delay.

kink |kingk| *n* A malfunction; a difficulty; a flaw. ORIGINS: From SE **kink** meaning a bend in some material otherwise straight and meant to be straight. USAGE INFO: Kink can also mean a personal peculiarity of some kind.

NON-SLANG SYNONYMS: defect, fault, malfunction, problem, **flaw**, **impairment**

See also Qualities of People and Things > Terrible, Unpleasant, Problematic, Irritating People and Things > 1 Broken Things, page 399.

## ANIMAL WRONGS

Sure, animals can cause problems for people, but sometimes we get them involved even when it's a clear case of human error.

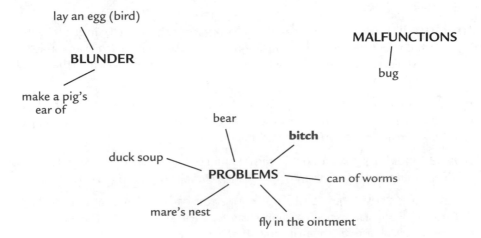

# 8 Unexpected Difficulties

**kicker** |KIK ur| *n* A pitfall; a previously hidden or concealed difficulty or problem. ORIGINS: Seems logically (if not historically) connected to the effect of a poker player revealing his/her **kicker(s)**—an unmatched card or cards that can, nevertheless, play a role in winning a hand.

**snag** |snag| *n* A hidden difficulty or obstacle.

**wrinkle** |WRING kul| *n* A problematic (and usually unexpected) development.

**NON-SLANG SYNONYMS:** brake, catch, Catch-22 (from Joseph Heller's novel *Catch-22* of 1961, in which unexpected pitfalls of trying to deal with bureaucracy are parodied), trap, twist, **hazard**, **pitfall**, **snare**, **stumbling block**

# 9 Unfair Situations

**bad rap** |BAD RAP| *n* False accusation; unjust condemnation; unfair punishment. ORIGINS: Extended from the earlier slang meaning of "a (serious) criminal charge." From SE **rap** meaning "a tap on the shoulder."

**bum deal** |BUM DĒL| *n* A bad bargain; an agreement that falls through. ORIGINS: Slang **bum** meaning "broken" and SE **deal**.

**bum rap** |BUM RAP| *n* A false accusation; an unfair sentence. ORIGINS: From slang **bum** meaning "unfair" and slang **rap** meaning "a criminal charge or jail sentence."

**raw deal** |RAW DĒL| *n* Unfair or unjust treatment; extremely bad luck. ORIGINS: From slang **raw** meaning "unfair" and SE **deal**.

**NON-SLANG SYNONYMS:** bias, bigotry, broken promise, dishonesty, false accusation, illegality, injustice, unfair sentence, unlawfulness, **bad bargain**, **cheating**, **discrimination**, **immorality**, **inequity**

# 10 Problematic Situations

**bad scene** |BAD SĒN| *n* An unpleasant situation or one in which trouble is likely to befall.

**deep doo-doo** |dēp DŪ dū| *n* Serious trouble. ORIGINS: Euphemism for **deep shit**. From SE **deep** and slang **doo-doo**, a childish euphemism for **shit**. USAGE ALERT: The euphemism **doo-doo** in this phrase will soften it somewhat, but it may still be objectionable in some contexts and to some people.

**deep shit** |DĒP SHIT| *n* A serious situation. ORIGINS: From slang **shit** meaning "excrement." USAGE ALERT: The word **shit** may make this phrase objectionable in some contexts and to some people.

**downer** |DOUN ur| *n* A bad situation; a situation that is worrisome or depressing. ORIGINS: By extension of slang **down** meaning "a state of depression."

**fix** |fiks| *n* A predicament; a problematic situation. ORIGINS: The situation in which one is stuck or "fixed."

**hole** |hōl| *n* A predicament; a difficult situation; a mess. USAGE INFO: Often appears in phrases such as in a hole meaning "in a fix" or in the hole, which can mean "at a disadvantage" or "short of money."

**hot spot** |HAHT spaht| *n* An area of trouble; a difficult or dangerous situation.

**hot water** |HAHT WAH tur| *n* A predicament; difficulties. USAGE INFO: Often in the phrases "in hot water" or "landed in hot water."

**mell of a hess** |MEL uv a hes| *n* A major predicament; a very bad situation. ORIGINS: A euphemistic Spoonerism (reversing the initial letters of two major words) of the phrase **hell of a mess**. USAGE ALERT: The underlying reference to **hell** may make this phrase objectionable in some contexts and to some people.

**pickle** |PIK ul| *n* A predicament; a problematic set of circumstances.

**pinch** |pinch| *n* A predicament; a problematic situation.

**scrape** |skrāp| *n* An embarrassing situation; trouble.

**snarl-up** |SNAHRL up| *n* A difficulty; a state of confusion and disorganization.

**tight spot** |TĪT SPAHT| *n* A predicament; a difficult situation.

**tough spot** |TUF SPAHT| *n* A difficult situation. USAGE INFO: Used in phrases like "in a tough spot."

**tsuris, tsouris, tsoris** |TSUR is| *n* Distress; trouble. ORIGINS: From Yiddish tsores.

NON-SLANG SYNONYMS: corner, dilemma, jam, **plight**, **predicament**, **quandary**

# 11  Risky Situations

**close call/shave** |KLŌS KAWL / KLŌS SHĀV| *n* A very near thing (either positive or negative). ORIGINS: From the referee's call of, for example, a shot being in or out of bounds. USAGE INFO: Always perceived in retrospect.

**clutch** |kluch| *n* A difficult or tense situation. ORIGINS: Popularized by, if not originating in, sports broadcasting, particularly the baseball term **clutch hitter**. USAGE INFO: Often in the phrase "in the clutch."

**crapshoot** |KRAP shūt| *n* A situation in which luck matters more than intelligence; a risky enterprise. ORIGINS: From gambling jargon **shooting craps**, a game of dice in which luck is the deciding factor. USAGE ALERT: Some people may misconstrue this term as being related to excrement.

**crunch-time** |KRUNCH tīm| *n* A critical moment calling for decisive action. ORIGINS: From SE **the crunch**.

**dicey proposition** |DĪ sē prahp u ZISH un| *n* An untrustworthy or unreliable plan or proposal. ORIGINS: Based on imagery from gambling games in which dice are rolled.

**gamble** |GAM bul| *n* A risky situation. ORIGINS: From SE gamble. USAGE INFO: Often in the phrase "It's a gamble."

**high-wire act** |HĪ wīr akt| *n* A risky endeavor. ORIGINS: Generalized from the dangers of the tightrope act performed by an aerialist, in the context of a circus, for example.

**hot seat** |HAHT SĒT| *n* A difficult position, subject to scrutiny; a situation in which one is subject to harsh criticism. ORIGINS: By generalization of the slang hot seat meaning "the electric chair." USAGE INFO: Often in the phrase "in the hot seat."

**iffy proposition** |IF ē prahp u ZISH un| *n* A risky undertaking; a situation with an uncertain outcome. ORIGINS: From SE if plus the suffix -y.

**narrow shave/squeak** |ner ō SHĀV / ner ō SKWĒK| *n* A very near thing (either positive or negative). USAGE INFO: Always perceived in retrospect.

**near miss/thing** |NIR MIS / NIR THING| *n* A near miss (whether negative or positive); a brush with disaster. USAGE INFO: Always perceived in retrospect.

**risky business** |RIS kē BIZ nis| *n* A dangerous venture.

**when the chips are down** |when *thu* CHIPS are doun| *phr* When the situation is really difficult and looks as if it may fail. ORIGINS: Figurative use of gambling jargon chips, meaning the counters used to represent money.

**when the going gets tough** |when *thu* GŌ ing gets TUF| *phr* When the situation becomes challenging. USAGE INFO: Sometimes concluded with "the tough get going."

**when the shit hits the fan** |when *thu* SHIT hits *thu* FAN| *phr* When things become really difficult and messy. ORIGINS: From slang **shit** meaning "excrement." USAGE ALERT: The inclusion of the word **shit** in the phrase will render it objectionable in some contexts and to some people.

NON-SLANG SYNONYMS: long shot, risk, <u>shot in the dark</u>, <u>spin of the roulette wheel</u>, **uncertainty**, **venture**

See also Qualities of People and Things > Terrible, Unpleasant, Problematic, Irritating People and Things > 7 Risky People or Things, page 406.

## 12 To Take a Risk

**ask for trouble/it** |ASK fawr TRU bul / ASK fawr it| *v* Take an unnecessary risk; do something despite knowing the (unpleasant) consequences. USAGE INFO: *Trouble* can be substituted by *it* as in "You asked for it."

**bet the farm\*** |BET *thu* FAHRM| *v* To risk everything. ORIGINS: Depending on which property is chosen—farm, house, or ranch—one is risking one's livelihood or one's residence—in any case, taking an enormous risk.
• bet the house |BET *thu* HOUS|
• bet the ranch |BET *thu* RANCH|

**chance it** |CHANS it| *v* To take a risk. ORIGINS: Extension of SE chance.

**fly by the seat-of-one's-pants** |FLĪ bī *thu* SĒT uv wunz PANTS| *v* To act based on intuition rather than a concrete plan; to improvise; to indulge in extremely risky behavior by choice. ORIGINS: From WWII aviators describing the experience of flying when instruments were not functioning or visibility was poor. USAGE INFO: The phrase can be merely a description of how someone behaves by necessity (when they run out of time, for example) or a condemnation of reckless behavior.

**go for broke/it** |GŌ fawr BRŌK / GŌ fawr it| *v* To take a risk in order to accomplish something; to commit all of one's resources to a project or task. ORIGINS: By extension from slang **broke** meaning "bankrupt" to convey the idea that one risks losing everything.

**lead with one's chin** |LĒD with wunz CHIN| *v* To leave oneself vulnerable; to act without sufficient forethought; to act incautiously. ORIGINS: From the sport of boxing, in which leaving one's chin unprotected is dangerous.

**push one's luck** |PŎŎSH wunz LUK| *v* To risk previous accomplishments or successes by pursuing a risky path, either through actions or words. USAGE INFO: Sometimes used as an imperative, as in "Don't push your luck" to warn *sb* who is on the edge of making a serious mistake, tactical error, etc.

**put one's ass on the line** |PŎŎT wunz AS ahn *thu* LĪN| *v* To take on responsibility; to accept responsibility for *st*; to take a huge risk. ORIGINS: From slang **ass** meaning "one's person," extended from slang **ass**, used to refer to the rear end or buttocks, and slang **on the line** from gambling jargon meaning "at stake." USAGE ALERT: The inclusion of the word **ass** in the phrase will render it objectionable in some contexts and to some people.

**shoot one's wad** |SHŪT wunz WAHD| *v* To make a total commitment to *sb/st*; to wear out (used either of oneself or one's resources). ORIGINS: From shooting jargon meaning "the plug holding the powder."

**shoot the works** |SHŪT *thu* WURKZ| *v* To make a total commitment of all one's resources.

**stick one's neck out** |stik wunz NEK out| *v* To go beyond one's area of expertise or comfort zone; to interfere in things that aren't one's concern; to take a risk. ORIGINS: From the necessary stretching out of the neck prior to a head being chopped off.

**throw a hail Mary** |THRŌ u hāl MER ē| *v* To make a last-ditch effort that has little chance, but is the only opportunity for success. ORIGINS: From Catholic prayer called "Hail Mary" used in basketball and football jargon for a long throw in the final seconds of the quarter or game that is only likely to succeed with the aid of divine help, but if it does, may tie or win the game (or at least help assuage the loser's egos).

**Non-Slang Synonyms:** chance, put in jeopardy, take a risk, <u>**dare**</u>, <u>**gamble**</u>, <u>**go out of one's depth**</u>, <u>**leap before looking**</u>, <u>**play with fire**</u>, <u>**run the risk**</u>, <u>**skate on thin ice**</u>, <u>**take the plunge**</u>, **brave**, **venture**, **wager**

See also Qualities of People and Things > Terrible, Unpleasant, Problematic, Irritating People and Things > 7 Risky People or Things, page 406.

# FAIL

## 1 To Fall Short

**peter out** |PĒ tur out| *v* To fall short of expectations; to fail before reaching a successful conclusion; to tire.

**poop out** |PŪP out| *v* To collapse; to stop from exhaustion; to stop functioning. ORIGINS: From slang poop meaning "to tire."

**run on empty** |run ahn EMP tē| *v* To be reaching the end of one's reserves of strength, patience, energy, money, or some other necessary item. ORIGINS: From the full–empty dichotomy presented by a gas gauge in a vehicle.

**run out of gas/steam** |run out uv GAS / run out uv STĒM| *v* To become too exhausted to continue *st*. ORIGINS: By analogy to a motorized engine that cannot run without fuel.

**Non-Slang Synonyms:** come to nothing, fall short, give out, lessen, <u>**choke**</u>, <u>**clutch**</u>, <u>**run dry**</u>, **abate**, **diminish**, **ebb**, **fade**, **recede**, **taper off**, **wane**

## 2 To Fail

**can't cut the mustard** |KANT kut *thu* MUS turd| *v* To fail to perform adequately; to be unable to attain the set standard. USAGE INFO: More often found in the negative than the positive: you rarely, if ever, hear of people who *can* cut the mustard.

**crap out** |krap OUT| *v* To stop working properly or at all. ORIGINS: By extension of the gambling jargon **crap out**, meaning "make a losing throw in the game of craps." USAGE ALERT: Some people may misconstrue this term as being related to excrement.

**crater** |KRĀ tur| *v* To fail; to be ruined. ORIGINS: Figurative use based on SE **crater**, meaning "a depression or pit."

**fall down on the job** |FAWL DOUN ahn *thu* JAHB| *v* To fail to meet expectations; to fail to come through with required elements.

**fall flat** |fawl FLAT| *v* To fail completely. ORIGINS: From the concept conveyed by the literal meaning of the SE words.

**fall on one's ass** |FAWL ahn wunz AS| *v* To fail completely; to fail completely and be publicly humiliated as well. ORIGINS: From the concept conveyed by the literal meaning of the SE words. From slang **ass** meaning "the rear end or buttocks." USAGE ALERT: The inclusion of the word **ass** will make this phrase objectionable in some contexts and to some people.

**fall (flat) on one's face** |FAWL ahn wunz FĀS / fawl FLAT ahn wunz FĀS| *v* To fail completely; to fail completely and be publicly humiliated as well. ORIGINS: From the concept conveyed by the literal meaning of the SE words.

**fizzle (out)** |FIZ ul / FIZ ul out| *v* To fail; to slowly succumb to failure. ORIGINS: From the slang fizzle meaning "to fail" and (leak) out, calling to mind the sound of a slow air leak from a tire.

**flop** |flahp| *v* To fail, particularly of a performance or a string of performances.

**flunk (out)** |flungk / FLUNGK OUT| *v* To fail an examination; to be dismissed from a school for academic failure.

**give out** |GIV OUT| *v* To fail; to give up; to stop functioning.

**go pfft** |gō PFFT| *v* To fizzle; to fail. ORIGINS: Perhaps referring to a failed firecracker that does not explode.

**go west** |gō WEST| *v* To fail; to die; to end. ORIGINS: From the sun setting in the west. *See* GO SOUTH.

**not get to first base** |naht get tū FURST BĀS| *v* To fail to make a promising beginning; to be unsuccessful in gaining initial success. ORIGINS: From baseball jargon in which getting to first base is the first step in scoring a run. USAGE INFO: Distinguish from not get to first base with *sb*, meaning "to receive a rebuff before having the opportunity to kiss."

**tank** |tangk| *v* To decline or fail suddenly. ORIGINS: From a play on words, involving SE **tank** meaning "a swimming pool" and the slang expression take a dive meaning "to purposely lose."

NON-SLANG SYNONYMS: be defeated, end, fail, go wrong, run aground, slip, turn out badly, **back the wrong horse**, **fall through**, **flounder** (*flounder* is found here because it is sometimes mistakenly used when *founder* is meant), **lose big**, **come to grief**, **founder**, **miscarry**

## 3 To Fail Utterly and Completely

**crash and burn** |KRASH und BURN| *v* To fail completely; to wipe out (fail). ORIGINS: From repeated incidents in airplane and car crashes. USAGE INFO: Usually depicts a more catastrophic event than simply crashing.

**fold** |fold| *v* To shut down operations; to fail completely.

**go belly up** |gō BEL lē up| *v* To die; to be ruined financially. ORIGINS: From the floating position of a dead fish. USAGE INFO: When speaking of finances, used more often of a business than of a personal financial failure.

**go down in flames** |gō doun in FLĀMZ| *v* To fail completely and suddenly. ORIGINS: Description of an aircraft falling to the ground and burning. USAGE INFO: *See* GO UP IN FLAMES.

**go down like a lead balloon** |gō DOUN līk u LED bu LŪN| *v* To fail. ORIGINS: From the conception of a (hot-air) balloon made of lead.

**go down the drain** |GŌ doun *thu* DRĀN| *v* To become irretrievably lost or destroyed; to be wasted. ORIGINS: The conception is of an emptying sink or bathtub.

**go down the tubes** |GŌ doun *thu* TŪB(Z)| *v* To fail completely; to collapse.

**go over like a lead balloon** |gō Ō vur līk u LED bu LŪN| *v* To fail. ORIGINS: From the conception of a (hot-air) balloon made of lead. USAGE INFO: Often used for the reception of an idea or proposal.

**go up in flames** |gō up in FLĀMZ| *v* To fail completely and suddenly. ORIGINS: Reference to the behavior of fire in a burning building. USAGE INFO: *See* GO DOWN IN FLAMES.

NON-SLANG SYNONYMS: come to nothing, go out of business, meet with disaster, **crash**, **hit bottom**, **lose one's shirt**, **come to naught**, **terminate**

# 4 To Cause to End

**bag it** |BAG it| *v* To stop doing *st*; to abandon a project.

**choke (*st*) off** |CHŌK AWF / CHŌK *st* AWF | *v* To stop in midstream; to end suddenly, as if by choking. ORIGINS: From SE **choke**; the reference is to a dog, stopped short by a choke collar.

**deep-six** |DĒP SIKS| *v* To abandon; to get rid of. ORIGINS: From nautical jargon **deep six** meaning "to throw overboard," which itself derives from the use of the sea as a grave and the conventional depth of a dug grave being six feet.

**pack it in** |PAK it in| *v* To close down work for the moment or the day; to give up on a project. ORIGINS: From the common need to pack up materials that one has been working with. USAGE INFO: *See* PACK IT IN!

**pull the plug on** |PŎŎL *thu* PLUG ahn| *v* To purposely bring about the end of *st*; to stop a project or enterprise prior to completion.

**punt** |punt| *v* To stop doing *st*; to give up on *st*. ORIGINS: From football, in which—on fourth down—a team will often punt the ball to the other team when they feel they are out of options, thus ending their drive for a touchdown or field goal.

**put paid to** |pŏŏt PĀD tū| *v* To stop the progress or possibility of *st* immediately and without warning; to terminate; to quell *sb*'s plans. ORIGINS: From SE **pay off**

meaning "to take revenge." USAGE INFO: Originally British only, but now showing up in US journalism, for example.

**put the kibosh on** |pŏŏt *thu* ku BAHSH ahn| *v* To spoil; to ruin; to prevent.

**put the skids on** |pŏŏt *thu* SKIDZ ahn| *v* To bring to an end. ORIGINS: From SE **skid** meaning "to brake a wheel" in order to stop a vehicle.

**scratch** |skrach| *v* To get rid of; to give up on. ORIGINS: From SE **scratch** meaning "to take a dog or horse out of a race in which it was scheduled to run."

**scrub** |skrub| *v* To cancel.

**scupper** |SKUP ur| *v* To put an end to; to call off. ORIGINS: From SE **scupper** meaning "to pour down the drain (of a boat)."

**take a dive** |tāk u DĪV| *v* To purposely lose a fight; to fail. ORIGINS: From boxing, referring to the boxer who "dives" to the floor without actually having been knocked out.

**throw** |thrō| *v* To deliberately lose a competition. ORIGINS: From professional sports and the SE term **throw away**.

**NON-SLANG SYNONYMS:** end, finish, kill, sabotage, shut down, axe, call it a day, call it quits, pack it in, torpedo, wind up, abort, annihilate, dismantle, eradicate

# 5 A Failure

**bust-up**[1] |BUST up| *n* A financial collapse. ORIGINS: The slang verb **bust** means "break" and a bust-up is the result of "breaking the bank."

**clunker** |KLUNGK ur| *n* A person, speech, product, or other item that is a complete flop; a failure. ORIGINS: Since **clunker** also refers to a badly working piece of machinery, often an aging automobile that may make "clunking" noises, so possibly by extension from that.

**crackup, crack-up** |KRAK up| *n* A collapse; a failure; a vehicle crash; a mental breakdown. ORIGINS: From SE **crack** meaning "to break."

**crash** |krash| *n* A sudden failure. ORIGINS: Perhaps originating with the stock market crash of 1929 and repopularized by computer jargon **crash**, indicating a failure of the hard drive.

**cross-up** |KRAWS up| *n* A complete failure; an instance of confusion. ORIGINS: Likely related to the idiom "get one's signals crossed."

**curtains** |KUR tunz| *n* Complete ruin; death. ORIGINS: From the drawing or dropping of the curtain at the end of a theatrical performance. USAGE INFO: Often in the phrase "It's curtains for...."

**end of the line** |END uv *thu* LĪN| *n* The final part of something; the moment at which there is no going back. ORIGINS: Possibly from railway jargon, in which the end of the line is the termination of the service.

**epic fail** |EP ik fāl| *n* A disastrous or total defeat.

**lights out** |LĪTS out| *n* The end of something. ORIGINS: Possibly by extension of the saying "lights out" in military quarters, summer camps, dormitories, etc. to designate a prescribed bedtime.

**meltdown** |MELT doun| *v* A breakdown: either an emotional breakdown or complete and sudden devastating collapse of some project, plan, enterprise, or situation. ORIGINS: From atomic energy jargon, **meltdown** means "severe overheating of the core of a nuclear reactor, leading to the core melting and radiation escaping."

**muck-up** |muk UP| *n* Something spoiled or ruined.

**no go** |NŌ gō| *n* A failed attempt; a prohibition.

**no joy** |nō JOI| *n* No success. ORIGINS: From military aviation jargon, especially in radar location of targets.

**NON-SLANG SYNONYMS:** collapse, defeat, loss, sinking ship, total loss, **bomb**, **fiasco**, **flop**, **loser**, **mess**, **misadventure**, **rout**

## GOING PLACES

The trope of forward motion for progress is evident in this collection of slang, but there are a couple of interesting variations in the conception when things aren't doing well.

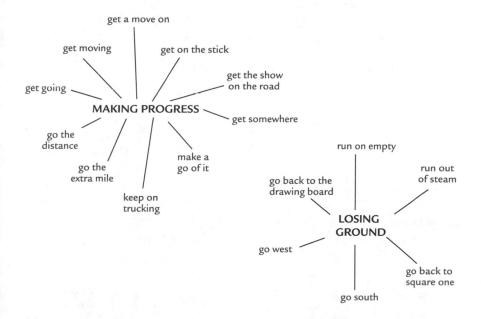

## UP THE DOWN STAIRCASE

Up is the road to progress and down is a losing proposition, right? Interestingly, it's not so simple. One can make progress by going down, and one can lose ground, whether one goes up or down.

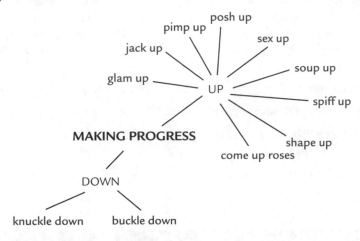

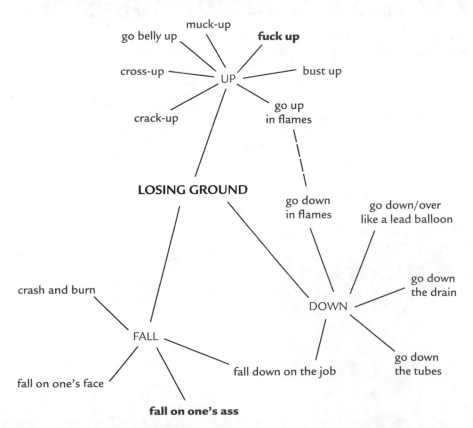

# Thinking

Slang treats brains as well as brawn, and this chapter looks at some of the brainy activities that slang has something to say about. The sections are:

*To Believe*
*To Understand*
*To Evaluate*
*To Know*
*To Find Out*

## TO BELIEVE

**buy** |bī| *v* To accept completely.

**eat** *st* **up** |ĒT *st* UP| *v* To accept completely.

**fall for** *st* |fawl fawr *st*| *v* To be fooled into accepting/believing *st* meant to deceive.

**go along with** |gō u LAWNG with| *v* To agree to, but perhaps reluctantly or tentatively.

**gobble down** |GAWB ul DOUN| *v* To accept quickly and easily, without taking time for consideration or reflection.

**gulp down** |GULP DOUN| *v* To accept quickly and easily, without taking time for consideration or reflection.

**lap** *st* **up**² |LAP *st* UP| *v* To accept *st* eagerly and without question.

**sign up for** |sīn UP fawr| *v* To leap past the consideration stage and declare oneself all in.

**swallow** |SWAHL ō| *v* To accept a (false/deceptive) story.

**swallow hook, line, and sinker** |swahl ō HŎOK LĪN und SINGK ur| *v* To accept in every respect, ignoring every warning sign.

**take the bait** |TĀK *thu* BĀT| *v* To accept a deceptive story; to fall for a scheme.

Non-Slang Synonyms: accept, believe, be convinced, consider honest, credit, give credence to, place one's faith in, put confidence in, rely on, trust; **set store by**; **accredit**, **give credence to**, **give weight to**

# TO UNDERSTAND

**catch on (to)** |kach AHN / kach AHN tū| *v* To come to understand.

**click²** |klik| *v* To become interpretable or clear. ORIGINS: From the behavior of things fitting perfectly, for example, the sound that a metal piece makes when "clicking" into place.

**cotton on (to)** |kaht'n AHN / kaht'n AHN tū| *v* To realize; to recognize; to arrive at understanding. ORIGINS: By extension of the meaning of slang **cotton to**. USAGE INFO: Can also mean "to become attached to."

**dig²** |dig| *v* To pay close attention to; to understand. ORIGINS: Jazz jargon.

**get a line on** |get u LĪN ahn| *v* To secure information about; to understand. ORIGINS: From slang **line** meaning "a useful piece of information, often obtained confidentially."

**get it¹** |GET it| *v* To receive and comprehend the message or material.

**get it in one** |get it in WUN| *v* To succeed in grasping the issue at hand quickly or in the first attempt. USAGE INFO: Can be used for someone grasping some non-obvious dimension of a situation or succeeding in a difficult feat of brain power.

**get the drift** |get *thu* DRIFT| *v* To understand another's words; to understand just the main points, but not the subtleties; to infer the whole story from subtle clues.

**get the hang of** |get *thu* HANG uv| *v* To learn how to (follow a procedure; use a tool; etc.); to become familiar with. ORIGINS: Was originally applied to learning to use a tool.

**get the idea** |get thē ī DĒ u| *v* To understand another's words; to understand just the overarching point, but not the subtleties; to infer the whole story from subtle clues.

**get the message** |get *thu* MES ij| *v* To understand fully what someone is trying to communicate.

**get the picture** |get *thu* PIK chur| *v* To understand; to appreciate the situation.

**get wise to** |get WĪZ tū| *v* To come to understand; to come to realize something that was previously not understood or was being actively concealed.

**grok** |grahk| *v* To understand thoroughly; to experience completely. ORIGINS: Coined by Robert A. Heinlein in his novel *Stranger in a Strange Land* (1961).

**latch on(to)** |lach AHN / lach AHN tū| *v* Come to understand; grasp mentally.

**nail³** |nāl| *v* To achieve understanding of. ORIGINS: From SE **nail** meaning "to make secure." USAGE INFO: Often in phrases like "nail the concept."

**pick up on** |pik UP ahn| *v* To catch on to; to come to understand; to grasp.

**read** *sb/st* **(like a book)** |RĒD *sb/st* / RĒD *sb/st* līk u BŎŎK| *v* To grasp *sb's* thoughts or feelings without having to be told; to discern where *sb's* coming from.

**see where** *sb's* **coming from** |SĒ wer *sb's* KUM ing frum| *v* To understand another's viewpoint.

**suss (out)** |SUS out| *v* To grasp; to understand; to figure out. ORIGINS: Shortened form of SE suspect.

**tumble to** |TUM bul tū| *v* Figure out; discover.

NON-SLANG SYNONYMS: appreciate, comprehend, figure out, grasp, interpret, learn, make sense of, master, recognize, understand, **get**, **be conscious of**, **deduce**, **discern**, **fathom**, **infer**, **take in**

# TO EVALUATE

**eyeball** |Ī bawl| *v* To examine thoroughly; give a long stare; inspect. ORIGINS: From the role of the SE eye in many types of evaluation.

**gander** |GAN dur| *v* To look inquisitively. ORIGINS: From the behavior of the SE gander, stretching out one's long neck to view something.

**gawk** |gawk| *v* To stare stupidly; to gape.

**get a load of** *sb/st* |get u LŌD uv *sb/st*| *v* To take a look at; examine.

**get an eyeful** |get an Ī ful| *v* To obtain a full view of *st*; to see something surprising.

**give** *sb* **the once-over** |GIV *sb* thu wuns Ō vur| *v* To examine; to evaluate; to give a quick appraisal to. ORIGINS: From the slang noun once-over meaning "a quick glance." USAGE INFO: Differences in meaning depend on whether the focus is on *over*, in which case it tends toward thoroughness, or the focus is on *once*, which emphasizes speed and, perhaps, superficiality.

**give** *sb/st* **the up-and-down** |GIV *sb/st* thu up und DOUN| *v* To take a thorough look at; to scrutinize. ORIGINS: From slang the up-and-down meaning "a scrutinizing look; a look," based on how one's eyes would move in such a look.

**have a look-see, looksee** |hav u LŎŎK sē| *v* To examine briefly; to quickly survey; to glance at.

**keep a tab on** |kēp u TAB ahn| *v* Watch with vigilance; keep a record of the actions of; keep under surveillance.

**keep one's eyes peeled\*** |kēp wunz ĪZ PĒLD| *v* To stay visually alert; to be on guard. ORIGINS: The reference is to not allowing one's eyelids (peels/skins) to cover one's eyes, as they would if one fell asleep.
• keep one's eyes skinned |kēp wunz ĪZ SKIND|

**keep tabs on** |kēp TABS ahn| *v* Watch with vigilance; keep a record of the actions of; keep under surveillance.

**kick the tires** |kik *thu* TĪ urz| *v* To examine; to check out before making a purchase. ORIGINS: In what some say is a fairly useless attempt to check for quality, people will sometimes kick the tires of a used car. **Kick the tires** has become a generalized term for making an assessment of something.

**peep** *sb/st* |pēp *sb/st*| *v* To have a look at; to check out. USAGE INFO: Notice that unlike SE peep, the preposition at is not used, e.g., "peep this."

**pipe** |pīp| *v* To notice; to take a look at; to look over.

**rubberneck** |RUB bur nek| *v* To look or nose around in an obvious and unsubtle way; to snoop; to collect information about.

**scope out** |skōp OUT| *v* To examine or investigate: to research. ORIGINS: From Greek **skopos** meaning one's goal or target.

**take a squint at** |tāk u SKWINT at| *v* To examine. ORIGINS: From SE squint meaning "to screw up one's eyes in order to take a careful look."

NON-SLANG SYNONYMS: check, evaluate, look over, rank, rate, review, weigh, <u>check out</u>, <u>size up</u>, **appraise**, **assess**, **take** *st's* **measure**, **value**

# TO KNOW

**know** *st* **backwards (and forwards)** |NŌ *st* BAK wurdz / NŌ *st* BAK wurd zund FAWR wurdz| *v* To know perfectly; to have complete command of; to have mastered *st*.

**know** *st* **inside out** |NŌ *st* IN sīd OUT| *v* To know perfectly; to have complete command of; to have mastered *st*.

**know** *st* **like the back of one's hand** |NŌ *st* līk *thu* BAK uv wunz HAND| *v* To know intimately; to have a complete understanding of.

**know the score** |NŌ *thu* SKAWR| *v* To have a grasp of an entire situation with all its ramifications; to understand the full situation. ORIGINS: From sports competitions.

NON-SLANG SYNONYMS: be acquainted with, know, <u>be on top of</u>, <u>have down pat</u>, **be cognizant of**, **be conversant in**, **be informed about**, **be master of**, **be versed in**, **have knowledge of**

# TO FIND OUT

**ferret out** |FER it out| *v* Discover through painstaking searching. ORIGINS: In the fifteenth century, partially-tamed ferrets were used to keep down the rat population and to flush rabbits from their warrens, leading eventually to the slang use.

**nose** *st* **out** |NŌZ *st* out| *v* To discover something by detective work; to uncover something difficult to trace or purposely hidden. ORIGINS: From slang nose meaning "detective." USAGE INFO: Different from nose out which means "to win or best by a very small margin."

**poke one's nose into** *st* |PŌK wunz NŌZ in tū *st*| *v* To interfere in; to demonstrate nosy interest in; to snoop; to investigate what is not one's business.

**sniff** *st* **out** |snif *st* OUT| *v* To uncover *st*. ORIGINS: From comparison with an animal seeking its prey.

**stick one's nose into** *st* |STIK wunz NŌZ in tū *st*| *v* See POKE ONE'S NOSE INTO *ST*.

NON-SLANG SYNONYMS: detect, determine, find out, reveal, uncover, **ascertain,** **divine, perceive, unearth, unmask**

## THE EYES HAVE IT! OR MAYBE IT'S THE NOSE...

There are different ways to ascertain information, and when we speak slangily, we privilege the eyes for evaluation, but the nose for making new discoveries.

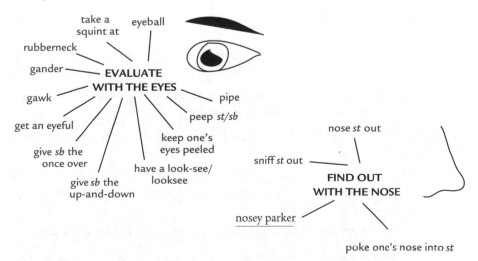

# Money $$

Money is central to most people's lives—reflected in the fact that we use both *bread,* the "staff of life" and *dough,* the stuff from which bread is made, to refer to it. This chapter is organized with the following subsections:

*Amount*
1 Small Amount
2 Some
3 Large Amount

*Cost*
1 Free
2 Cheap
3 Expensive

*Wealth*
1 Poor
2 Rich

*Payment*
1 Pay
2 Avoid Paying

*Ways to Get Money*
1 Beg
2 Make a Profit
3 Overcharge

# AMOUNT

## 1 Small Amount

**chicken feed** |CHIK un fēd| *n* A very small amount of money; small change. ORIGINS: From the very small size of grain required to make food digestible for poultry.

**hay** |hā| *n* A very small amount of money. USAGE INFO: Often appears in the phrase "that ain't hay" to indicate a notable sum of money.

**peanuts** |PĒ nuts| *n* A very small amount, especially of money; anything insignificant.

**shoestring** |SHŪ string| *n* A very small sum of money; a barely adequate amount of money. USAGE INFO: Often occurs in the phrase "on a shoestring" meaning "on a very small budget."

NON-SLANG SYNONYMS: mite, small change, **pin money**, **paltry sum**, **pittance**

# 2 Some

**bucks** |buks| *n* Unspecified amount of money in bills. ORIGINS: By extension from slang buck meaning "a dollar."

**coin** |koin| *n* Unspecified amount of money in change.

**cold cash** |KŌLD KASH| *n* Ready money.

**dinero** |di NER ō| *n* An unspecified amount of money. ORIGINS: From Spanish dinero meaning "money."

**dough** |dō| *n* An unspecified amount of money. USAGE INFO: Both dough and bread are used to refer to money in the US.

**gelt** |gelt| *n* An unspecified amount of money. ORIGINS: From Yiddish gelt meaning "money" or German gelt meaning "gold."

**green(backs)** |grēn / GRĒN baks| *n* An amount of money in bills. ORIGINS: From the color of US paper money.

**hard cash** |HAHRD KASH| *n* Immediately accessible sum of money in bills and coins. ORIGINS: *Hard* may refer to its tangible existence in paper and metal. USAGE INFO: In contrast to a check or other forms of payment.

**kopecks** |KŌ peks| *n* An unspecified amount of money. ORIGINS: From Russian kopeika meaning a Russian unit of currency. USAGE INFO: Used in very general terms, as in, "I don't have enough kopecks."

**loot** |lūt| *n* An unspecified amount of money or property, not necessarily gained by stealing. ORIGINS: From SE loot meaning "stolen goods" derived from a Hindi word meaning plunder.

**mazuma** |mu ZŪ mu| *n* Unspecified amount of money. ORIGINS: From Hebrew through Yiddish mazume meaning "cash."

**moola, moolah** |MŪ lah| *n* An unspecified amount of money.

**shekels** |SHEK ulz| *n* An unspecified amount of money. ORIGINS: From Hebrew shekel, a coin.

NON-SLANG SYNONYMS: capital, cash, funds, means, resources, **bread**, **pocket money**, **wherewithal**

USAGE INFO: Since peso(s) is standard in Spanish, either the first or second language of many Americans, but foreign to other Americans, trying to find a place for it in this hierarchy isn't possible. Nevertheless, it is used similarly.

# 3 Large Amount

**big bucks** |BIG BUKS| *n* An unspecified, large amount of money. USAGE INFO: Because money is SE, while bucks is slang, big bucks is slangier than big money.

**big money** |BIG MUN ē| *n* An unspecified, large amount of money. USAGE INFO: Because money is SE, while bucks is slang, big bucks is slangier than big money.

**boodle** |BŪ dul| *n* A large but unspecified amount of money. ORIGINS: Thought to be from Dutch **boedel** meaning "one's estate."

**bundle** |BUN dul| *n* A large amount of money.

**cool million** |KŪL MIL yun| *n* A million dollars. ORIGINS: Cool seems to be emphasizing the sizeable amount. USAGE INFO: Cool can be used with other large sums, but usually only amounts formed by a one and following zeroes (hundred, thousand, million, etc.), and not less than a hundred, unless one is being ironic.

**deep pockets** |dēp PAH kits| *n* A person with a large, steady amount of money. ORIGINS: From imagining someone reaching down into extensive pockets and bringing up more and more money.

**gravy** |GRĀV ē| *n* Money or profit acquired easily, especially tips or bonuses. ORIGINS: As **gravy** is used to adorn a food item that is very good in itself, like meat or a potato, tips, and bonuses that are considered gravy come in addition to good salary arrangements.

**megabucks** |ME gu buks| *n* A million dollars or a large unspecified amount of money; the name of a number of US state lotteries in which large amounts of money can be won.

**mint** |mint| *n* A large amount of money. ORIGINS: Figurative application of SE mint meaning the place where coins are manufactured.

**nice hunk/piece of change** |NĪS HUNGK uv CHĀNJ / NĪS pēs uv CHĀNJ| *n* A large amount of money.

**pile** |pīl| *n* A large amount of money.

**tidy sum** |TĪ dē SUM| *n* A large amount of money.

NON-SLANG SYNONYMS: fortune, king's ransom, riches, treasure, wealth, **small fortune**, **affluence**, **opulence**

# COST

## 1 Free

**free lunch** |frē LUNCH| *n* Something obtained without the usual fee, transaction, exchange. ORIGINS: Free lunches were provided for paying customers at taverns in the nineteenth century. The term was popularized with the saying "There Ain't No Such Thing As A Free Lunch" (abbreviated with the acronym TANSTAAFL) by Robert Heinlein in a science fiction novel *The Moon Is a Harsh Mistress* (1966) and by economist Milton Friedman.

**free ride** |frē RĪD| *n* An (undeserved) easy time; something obtained without the expected or usual effort or cost.

**freebee, freebie** |FRĒ bē| *n* A free sample, promotion, or other item given without charge. ORIGINS: From SE free.

**giveaway, give-away** |GIV u wā| *n* Free samples.

NON-SLANG SYNONYMS—NOUNS: gift, handout, **free pass**

**comp** |kahmp| *adj* Received without charge. ORIGINS: Short for SE **complimentary**. Complimentary tickets are given to VIPs and sometimes to friends and family of stars. They are also used to fill out an audience that might otherwise be lacking, in a move called **papering the house**, meaning "filling up an audience by giving away (paper) tickets."

**giveaway, give-away** |GIV u wā| *adj* Free; without charge.

NON-SLANG SYNONYMS—ADJECTIVES: complimentary, costless, gratis, unpaid, **gratuitous**, **unrecompensed**

**for free** |fawr FRĒ| *adv* Essentially as a gift, with no recompense; with no strings attached.

**for nothing** |fawr NU thing| *adv* Essentially as a gift, with no recompense; with no strings attached.

**on the house** |ahn *thu* HOUS| *adv* Provided by the owner at no charge. ORIGINS: From SE **house** meaning "the establishment" whether a restaurant, bar, tavern, etc.

NON-SLANG SYNONYMS—ADVERBS: without charge

## 2 Cheap

**steal, a** |u STĒL| *n* An item offered for a price that is judged to be far less than its true value.

NON-SLANG SYNONYMS—NOUNS: a bargain, a good value, **a buy**

**cheapo**[1] |CHĒ pō| *adj* Selling for a very small amount of money. ORIGINS: From SE **cheap**.

**dime-a-dozen** |DĪM u DUZ un| *adj* Of limited value; common. ORIGINS: By extension of SE meaning of literal cost, to "inexpensive," and then to "cheap or low quality."

**dirt cheap** |DIRT CHĒP| *adj* Extremely inexpensive. USAGE INFO: Also **cheap as dirt**. This phrase may or may not imply that the product offered at that price is inferior or worthless.

NON-SLANG SYNONYMS—ADJECTIVES: competitive, economical, inexpensive, low-cost, reasonable, **bargain basement**, **cheap**, **cut-rate**, **low-end**, **depreciated**, **downmarket**

**for a song** |fawr u SAHNG| *adv* For very little money; at a low price; cheaply.

NON-SLANG SYNONYMS: at a discount, economically, inexpensively, on sale

## 3 Expensive

**costing an arm and a leg** |KAWST ing an AHRM und u LEG| *adj* Offered for an extremely high price. ORIGINS: Figurative image of enormous sacrifices required for a purchase.

**high end** |HĪ end| *adj* Extremely expensive and valuable.

**pricey, pricy** |PRĪ sē| *adj* Expensive.

**steep** |stēp| *adv* Over-priced; very expensive.

**stiff** |stif| *adj* A very high price, judged to be excessive.

NON-SLANG SYNONYMS: costly, expensive, overpriced, **big-ticket**, **up market**, **upscale**, **dear**, **exorbitant**

# WEALTH

## 1 Poor

**belly up** |BEL ē up| *adj* Bankrupt; failed; dead. ORIGINS: From the floating position of a dead fish. USAGE INFO: Often in the slang phrase go belly up, which is used more frequently of a business than of a personal financial failure. *See* GO BELLY UP.

**bust(ed)**[1] |bust / BUS tid| *adj* Bankrupt. ORIGINS: Equivalent to informal **broke** meaning "having no money," just as the past participle forms slang busted and SE **broken** are synonyms for "damaged in such a way as to render non-functional." In each case, the form of *bust* is the more slangy word.

**cleaned out** |klēnd OUT| *adj* Broke. ORIGINS: Figurative use of SE clean.

**down-and-out** |doun und OUT| *adj* Poor and homeless. ORIGINS: From the situation of being both "*down* in the gutter" and "*out* of luck."

**feeling the pinch** |FĒL ing *thu* PINCH| *adj* To experience the effects of reduced income. ORIGINS: Metaphorical application of SE **pinch**, as also in penny-pinching.

**flat broke** |FLAT BRŌK| *adj* Totally out of money. ORIGINS: From slang flat meaning "completely" and slang broke meaning "out of money."

**hard up** |HAHRD up| *adj* In need of funds; poor.

**in hock** |in hock| *adj* In debt. ORIGINS: From hock meaning "a pledge in a pawnshop."

**in the red** |in *thu* RED| *adj* Broke; in debt. ORIGINS: From the one-time accounting practice of using red ink for losses and black ink for profits.

**piss-poor**[1] |PIS pŏŏr| *adj* Having very little money or other property. ORIGINS: From slang **piss** meaning "urine" and slang suffix -head, used here as an intensifier. USAGE ALERT: The inclusion of the word **piss** in the phrase will render it objectionable in some contexts and to some people.

**stone-broke/stony-broke** |STŌN BRŌK / STŌN ē BRŌK| *adj* Having no money.

**strapped (for cash)** |strapt / STRAPT fawr KASH| *adj* Broke.

**tapped out** |TAPT out| *adj* Broke; unable to place any more bets. ORIGINS: From slang tap out meaning "to reach the end of one's money."

**washed out** |WAWSHT out| *adj* Exhausted; worn out.

**wiped out** |WĪPT OUT| *adj* Financially ruined; broke.

**without a bean** |with OUT u BĒN| *adj* Penniless.

**without a pot to piss in** |with out u pot tū PIS in| *adj* Extremely poor. ORIGINS: From slang **piss**, meaning "urine." USAGE ALERT: The inclusion of the word **piss** in the phrase, plus the overall reference to excretion, will render this phrase objectionable in some contexts and to some people.

**without a red cent** |with out u RED SENT| *adj* Broke. ORIGINS: From red cent meaning "a trivial amount of money," possibly deriving from the reddish cast of a penny, due to its being made with copper.

NON-SLANG SYNONYMS: badly off, down on one's luck, in debt, needy, penniless, poor, short of money/cash, **broke**, **beggared**, **destitute**, **impecunious**, **impoverished**, **in reduced circumstances**, **indigent**, **insolvent**, **penurious**, **poverty-stricken**, **underprivileged**, **unprosperous**

# 2 Rich

**RFR** Really fucking rich.

**flush** |flush| *adj* Having lots of money. ORIGINS: From SE flush meaning "overflowing."

**heeled** |hēld| *adj* Rich; moneyed. ORIGINS: By shortening of SE **well-heeled**.

**high on/off the hog** |HĪ ahn *thu* HAWG / HĪ awf *thu* HAWG| *adj* Living well; being extremely comfortable. ORIGINS: From the location on a pig of the best cuts of meat, such as bacon and chops, as opposed to the lower portions like trotters and jowls.

**in clover** |in CLŌ vur| *adj* In very comfortable circumstances. ORIGINS: By comparison of wealthy people to cattle who favor clover, reportedly because it is tasty and fattening.

**in the black** |in *thu* BLAK| *adj* Making a profit; doing well. ORIGINS: From the one-time accounting practice of using red ink for losses and black ink for profits.

**in the money** |in *thu* MUN ē| *adj* Rich; wealthy. ORIGINS: From the horse-racing expression, "to run in the money," used of horses that place first, second, or third, thereby gaining a payoff for those who bet on them.

**loaded** |LŌD ed| *adj* Rich; possessing a lot of money.

**rolling in dough/it** |RŌL ing in DŌ / RŌL ing in it| *adj* Extremely wealthy. ORIGINS: The idea is that *sb* has so much money that it would fill a room enough that they could roll around in it.

**rolling in money** |RŌL ing in MUN ē| *adj* Extremely wealthy. ORIGINS: The idea is that *sb* has so much money that it would fill a room enough that s/he could roll around in it. USAGE INFO: Rolling in money, in which no word by itself is slang, is therefore less slangy than rolling in dough, in which dough by itself is slang.

**sitting pretty** |SIT ing PRIT ē| *adj* Doing well, financially or in general.

**stinking of money** |STINGK uv MUN ē| *adj* Having lots of money.

**worth a bundle** |WURTH u BUN dul| *adj* Having a high value.

**NON-SLANG SYNONYMS:** have money in the bank, well-heeled, well-to-do, <u>flush</u>, <u>made of money</u>, <u>on easy street</u>, <u>pick up the bill/check/tab</u>, <u>upscale</u>, <u>well-off</u>, <u>moneyed</u>

## THE INS AND OUTS OF MONEY

Slang reveals a hierarchy through prepositions: as Heidi Klum suggests on "Project Runway," it's better to be *in* than *out*.

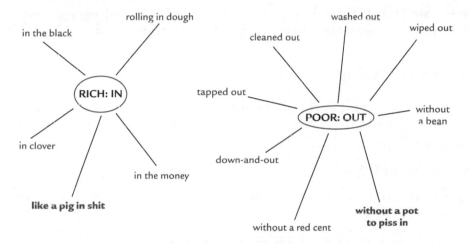

in the black
rolling in dough
in clover
in the money
**like a pig in shit**

RICH: IN

washed out
wiped out
cleaned out
tapped out
without a bean
down-and-out
without a red cent
**without a pot to piss in**

POOR: OUT

## PAYMENT

## 1 Pay

**ante (up)** |AN tē / AN tē up| *v* To pay. ORIGINS: From the practice in poker of making an initial bet as the first step in participating in a round.

**come across (with)** |kum u KRAWS / kum u KRAWS with| *v* To do or pay what's expected (reluctantly); to acquiesce and do what is required of one.

**come through with** |kum THRŪ with| *v* To deliver; to do what is wanted or required in a situation.

**cough up** |KAWF up| *v* To hand over (money), usually unwillingly or under duress; to relinquish; to confess.

**fork out/over** |FAWRK out / FAWRK ō vur| *v* To give out; to hand over, often reluctantly or under duress. ORIGINS: From slang forks meaning "hands."

**kick in** |kik IN| *v* To contribute a share in a group project (usually money); to take effect.

**plunk down** |PLUNGK DOUN| *v* To pay. ORIGINS: From the sound of the money (presumably including some coins) hitting the table or counter. USAGE INFO: Also means "to wager."

**pony up** |PŌ nē up| *v* To pay a debt that's due. ORIGINS: From slang pony meaning "money."

**shell out** |SHEL OUT| *v* To hand over money.

NON-SLANG SYNONYMS: lay out, pay, **chip in**, **dish out**, **foot the bill**, **pay out**, **bear the expense**, **compensate**, **disburse**, **expend**, **remit**, **remunerate**

## 2 Avoid Paying

**beat** |bēt| *v* To cheat by not paying. USAGE INFO: Beat can also be used for other forms of cheating and defrauding.

**diddle** |DID'l| *v* To cheat or swindle.

**do** *sb* **out of** |DŪ *sb* OUT uv| *v* To cheat or swindle *sb*.

**stiff** |stif| *v* To refuse to pay; to fail to pay without acknowledgment that one is doing so.

NON-SLANG SYNONYMS: defraud, **bilk**, **rook**, **shirk**, **swindle**

# WAYS TO GET MONEY

## 1 Beg

**bum** |bum| *v* To beg. ORIGINS: From the informal **bum**, meaning "vagrant or tramp." USAGE INFO: Unlike beg, bum does not require a preposition. Compare: "to beg for a meal"; "to bum a meal."

**cadge** |kadj| *v* To beg. ORIGINS: Possibly a back-formation from the noun cadger, meaning "a peddler." USAGE INFO: Cadge does not require a preposition: "cadge a meal."

**grub** |grub| *v* To scrounge; to beg. ORIGINS: From SE grub meaning "to root in the dirt" extended to the search through garbage and other leavings.

**hit** *sb* **up** |hit *sb* UP| *v* Ask or beg for something, especially money.

**mooch** |MŪCH| *v* To obtain or try to obtain by begging. USAGE INFO: Often used of a friend trying to get some trivial item or small amount of money from another friend rather than of situations of deep and serious need and deprivation.

**put the bite on** |pŏŏt *thu* BĪT ahn| *v* To try to get money from *sb*; to beg.

**put the touch on** |pŏŏt *thu* TOUCH ahn| *v* To try to get or borrow money.

**schmooze, shmooze** |shmūz| *v* To use flattery and ingratiation as a modus operandi; to become intimate for self-serving ends. ORIGINS: From Yiddish **shmuesn**.

**scrounge** |skrounj| *v* To obtain by begging or borrowing, usually from friends and with no serious intent to repay.

**sponge** |spahnj| *v* To beg, usually from one's friends and usually with no intention of repaying.

**touch** *sb* **for** |TOUCH *sb* fawr| *v* To beg for a loan.

NON-SLANG SYNONYMS: beg, pass the hat, **freeload**, **panhandle**, **touch**, seek **charity**, **solicit alms**

## 2  Make a Profit

**cash in**[1] |KASH in| *v* To make a profit, especially by exploiting circumstances. USAGE INFO: Because it may carry the implication of exploitation, this phrase may imply criticism.

**clean up** |KLĒN up| *v* To make a large profit (in a short time). ORIGINS: Figurative use of SE **clean up**.

**hit it big** |hit it BIG| *v* To have an important success, financial or otherwise.

**in the money, be** |bē in *thu* MUN ē| *v* To profit by winning a wager. ORIGINS: From the horse-racing expression, "to run in the money," used of horses that place first, second, or third, thereby gaining a payoff for those who bet on them.

**line one's pockets** |līn wunz PAH kits| *v* To accept a bribe or other illicit funds; to make a large profit.

**make a bundle** |māk u BUN dul| *v* To earn a great deal of money. ORIGINS: Slang **bundle** means "a roll of bills."

**make a fast buck** |māk u fast BUK| *v* To enjoy a quick financial success.

**make a killing** |māk u KIL ing| *v* To clear a large profit by taking some kind of gamble; to make a great deal of money very easily. ORIGINS: From slang **killing** meaning "a great success, usually financial."

**make it big** |māk it BIG| *v* To enjoy a notable success.

**make out like a bandit** |māk out līk u BAN dit| *v* To make a very large profit. ORIGINS: The analogy to the bandit, who takes money without having to earn it, may suggest that the profit in question comes very easily.

**pull in** |POŎL in| *v* To earn. USAGE INFO: Used with a "straight tone" for large sums and sarcastically of small sums.

**rake it in** |RĀK it in| *v* To make a very large amount of money. ORIGINS: Presents the idea of having such large piles of money (like leaves) that a rake is the most effective way to move them.

**shake the money tree** |SHĀK *thu* MUN ē trē| *v* To earn or come into a great deal of money. ORIGINS: From the fantasy that money could "grow on trees."

**NON-SLANG SYNONYMS:** bring home, bring in, earn, make a profit, make money, take in, **clear**, **make**, **pocket**, **pull in/down**, **realize**

# 3 Overcharge

**gip, gyp** |jip| *v* To cheat; to deceive; to avoid paying one's debts. ORIGINS: From the SE word **gypsy**. USAGE INFO: This word is considered an ethnic slur, but especially with the g-i-p spelling, many people who use it are unaware of the origins. USAGE ALERT: People who know that this word stereotypes Gypsies will unlikely find it objectionable.

**gouge** |gouj| *v* To exact or extort a large amount of money; to swindle. ORIGINS: By extension of SE **gouge** meaning "to dig deep into something."

**nick** |nik| *v* To cheat by overcharging; to steal.

**rip off** |RIP awf| *v* To defraud; to swindle; to cheat; to steal from, often by charging an excessive amount.

**sell *sb* a lemon** |SEL *sb* u LEM un| *v* To sell defective or damaged goods. ORIGINS: From slang **lemon** meaning "anything disappointing."

**soak** |sōk| *v* To cheat; to overcharge.

**NON-SLANG SYNONYMS:** cheat, overcharge, **pad**

## CLEAN AND DIRTY MONEY

If you follow the logic of slang having to do with money, it's better for the pocketbook if you are dirty, rather than clean.

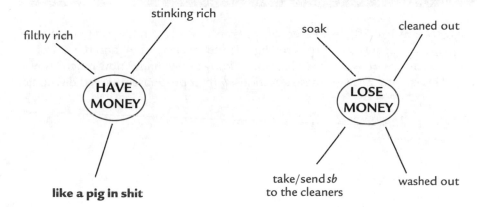

# Quantity, Size, and Number

On a scale of 1 to 10, the interest of speakers of American English in numbers and amounts scores an 11 (pax to Nigel Tufnel of *Spinal Tap*), and there are many occasions on which people want to know: how many? how much? how big? This chapter answers these questions with appropriately named divisions:

*How Many?*
  1 Zero
  2 A Large Number

*How Much?*
  1 None; Nothing at All
  2 A Small Amount
  3 A Large Amount
  4 Having a Large Amount
  5 All

*How Big?*
  1 Small
  2 Large

# HOW MANY?

## 1 Zero

**goose egg** |GŪS eg| *n* Zero; nothing; no points. ORIGINS: From the similarity in shape of the egg to a zero, possibly influenced by the cricket jargon **duck's egg** to indicate a score of nothing.

**nix** |niks| *n* None. ORIGINS: From German **nichts** meaning "none."

**zilch** |zilch| *n* Nothing.

**zip** |zip| *n* Nothing.

NON-SLANG SYNONYMS: none, nothing, zero, **cipher**, **naught**, **ought**, **void**

# 2  A Large Number

**TDM** Too damn many.

**bazillion** |bu ZIL yun| *n* An unspecified, exceedingly large amount. ORIGINS: One of a group of made up numbers ending in *-illion* with pretty indistinguishable meanings, although additional elements may signal even larger amounts (i.e., a bazillion may be larger than a zillion).

**gadzillion** |gad ZIL yun| *n* An unspecified, exceedingly large amount. ORIGINS: One of a group of made up numbers ending in *-illion* with pretty indistinguishable meanings, although additional prefixes may be indicating even larger amounts (i.e., a gadzillion may be larger than a zillion).

**gajillion** |gu JIL yun| *n See* GADZILLION.

**gazillion** |gu ZIL yun| *n See* GADZILLION.

**jillion** |JIL yun| *n* An unspecified, exceedingly large amount. ORIGINS: One of a group of made up numbers ending in *-illion* with pretty indistinguishable meanings, although additional prefixes may be indicating even larger amounts (i.e., a gajillion may be larger than a jillion).

**mucho** |MŪ chō| *n* Many. ORIGINS: From Spanish **mucho** meaning "many."

**squillion** |SKWIL yun| *n* An unspecified, exceedingly large amount. ORIGINS: One of a group of made up numbers ending in *-illion* with pretty indistinguishable meanings; for example, squillion, jillion, and zillion.

**umpteen** |UMP TĒN| *n* Dozens; i.e., a number of teens. ORIGINS: Said by some to have a military origin in WWI, with the nonspecific um replacing a specific number (e.g., four or seven) in order to maintain secrecy in communications.

**zillion** |ZIL yun| *n* An unspecified, exceedingly large amount. ORIGINS: One of a group of made up numbers ending in *-illion* with pretty indistinguishable meanings, although additional prefixes may be indicating even larger amounts (i.e., a bazillion or gadzillion may be larger than a zillion).

**NON-SLANG SYNONYMS:** Since aside from *mucho,* these numbers are all imaginary in the sense that they are made up, there are no non-slang synonyms, because all non-slang numbers are real, even the imaginary ones, such as *i*.

# HOW MUCH?

## 1 None; Nothing at All

**NADT** Not a damn thing.

**damn-all** |DAM awl| *n* Nothing at all. ORIGINS: By extension from SE **damn**, which literally means "Send (it) to hell." USAGE INFO: **Damn-all** is used for emphasis, as in "I've had damn-all to eat today." USAGE ALERT: This term with **damn** will be objectionable in some contexts and to some people.

**diddley-shit, diddly-shit** |DID lē shit| *n* A small or worthless amount, particularly of money; nothing at all. ORIGINS: From slang diddley meaning "anything insignificant" and an extension of slang **shit** meaning "excrement" to use as an intensifier. USAGE INFO: Often used in constructions with an (implied) double negative: "I don't have diddley-shit." Abbreviated use with just the first word, spelled in any of the two ways: "I don't have diddley." USAGE ALERT: The use of **shit** will make this phrase objectionable in some situations and to some people.

**diddly-squat, diddlysquat** |DID lē skwaht| *n* Nothing at all. ORIGINS: Euphemism for **diddley-shit**. USAGE INFO: Often used in constructions with an (implied) double negative, as in "He doesn't have diddly-squat." Abbreviated by using just diddly or just squat. USAGE ALERT: The euphemism squat in this phrase will soften it somewhat, but it may still be objectionable in some contexts and to some people.

**doodley-squat, doodleysquat** |DŪD lē skwaht| *n* Nothing at all. ORIGINS: A variant euphemism for **diddley-shit**. USAGE INFO: Often used in constructions with an (implied) double negative, as in "He doesn't have doodly-squat." Abbreviated use with just squat. USAGE ALERT: The euphemism squat in this phrase will soften it somewhat, but it may still be objectionable in some contexts and to some people.

**doodly-shit, doodley-shit** |DŪD lē shit| *n* A small or worthless amount, particularly of money; nothing at all. ORIGINS: Variation on slang diddley meaning "anything insignificant" and an extension of slang **shit** meaning "excrement" to be an intensifier. USAGE INFO: Often used in constructions with an (implied) double negative: "I don't have doodley-shit." "I don't have doodley" is heard much less frequently than "I don't have diddley" (with whichever spelling). USAGE ALERT: The use of **shit** will make this phrase objectionable in some situations and to some people.

**fuck-all** |FUK awl| *n* Nothing at all. ORIGINS: From slang **fuck** meaning "to engage in sexual intercourse." USAGE INFO: Used emphatically, as in "The will was read today, and I got fuck-all." USAGE ALERT: This term with **fuck** will be objectionable in some contexts and to some people.

**jack (shit)** |jak / jak SHIT| *n* Nothing at all. ORIGINS: From slang jack meaning "fool," a shortening of SE jackass, and slang **shit** used as an intensifier. USAGE INFO: Often used in constructions with an (implied) double negative: "You don't know jackshit" or abbreviated to "You don't know jack." USAGE ALERT: The inclusion of **shit** will make this word objectionable in some situations and to some people.

**squat** |skwaht| *n* Nothing at all. ORIGINS: Shortened form of slang diddl(e)ysquat or doodl(e)ysquat meaning "nothing at all." USAGE INFO: Often used in a construction with a disguised double negative, as in "I don't have squat." Usually used of money or more generally of possessions.

**nada** |NAH du| *n* Nothing. ORIGINS: Spanish nada meaning "nothing."

NON-SLANG SYNONYMS: none, not any, not anything, nothing, **not a bit**, **not a thing**

# 2 A Small Amount

**beans** |bēnz| *n* A small amount. USAGE INFO: Often in the phrase "I don't know beans about...."

**dollop** |DAH lup| *n* A large lump or portion; a small amount. ORIGINS: Related to Norwegian **dolp** meaning "a lump."

**dribs and drabs** |DRIBZ und drabz| *n* Small amounts (at irregular intervals).

**fat lot** |FAT LAHT| *n* Used sarcastically to mean "very little."

**glob** |glahb| *n* A roundish lump of something semi-solid; an indeterminate smallish amount. ORIGINS: From Middle English **globbe** meaning "a large mass," but related to **globe**.

**gob** |gahb| *n* A small lump of something mushy or slimy.

**lick** |lik| *n* A small amount. USAGE INFO: Used with *a* as in, "he hasn't got a lick of sense."

**nibble** |NIB ul| *n* A very small amount, used especially of food.

**skosh** |skōsh| *adj* A small amount; a little bit. ORIGINS: From Japanese **sukoshi**, through American servicemen stationed in Japan.

**small beer** |smawl BER| *n* A small or worthless amount. ORIGINS: From SE **small beer** meaning "weak or inferior beer."

**small potatoes** |smawl pu TĀ tōz| *n* An insignificant amount.

**smidgen** |SMIJ un| *n* A very small quantity.

**spot** |spaht| *n* A small amount of.

**tad** |tad| *n* A very small quantity.

NON-SLANG SYNONYMS: bit, chunk, dose, few, fragment, part, portion, sample, serving, some, taste, **mite**, **modicum**, **moiety**, **morsel**, **particle**, **scarcity**

# 3 A Large Amount

**a \<noun\> and a half** |u \<noun\> and u HAF| *n* A great amount of whatever is referenced.

**bags** |BAGZ| *n* A great deal. ORIGINS: From SE **bag** in reference to the day's kill collected by hunters. Its use spread during WWI.

**beaucoup** |bō KŪ| *adj* A lot; a large quantity of. ORIGINS: From the French **beaucoup** meaning "many." It became popular during the Vietnam War, during which US soldiers came in contact with speakers of French or French/Vietnamese pidgin.

**bellyful** |BEL ē ful| *n* More than enough, specifically of something unpleasant.

**bushels** |BŌOSH ulz| *n* A large, unspecified amount; a great deal. ORIGINS: From the SE unit of measure, a **bushel**.

**buttload** |BUT lōd| *n* A large quantity. ORIGINS: On the model of the more oft-heard slang **shitload**, meaning "an unspecified large amount." At the same time, **buttload** is, in fact, a synonym for **shit**. From slang **butt** meaning "the rear end or buttocks" and acting as a euphemism for **ass**. USAGE ALERT: Because it mentions the human rear end or buttocks, refers to excrement, and presents a graphic image, this term will be considered objectionable in some contexts and by some people.

**gobs** |gahbz| *n* A large amount (often of money).

**heaps** |HĒPS| *n* A large amount; a great deal. ORIGINS: From SE **heap**.

**loads** |LŌDZ| *n* A large amount.

**lots** |LAHTS| *n* A large amount.

**no end** |nō END| *n* A large amount of; lots. Used with *of* to modify a word or phrase as in "gave him no end of encouragement."

**oceans** |Ō shunz| *n* A very large amount.

**oodles** |Ū dulz| *n* A great many; a large number or amount.

**piles** |pīlz| *n* A large amount.

**rafts** |rafts| *n* A vast amount.

**reams** |rēmz| *n* Vast amounts. ORIGINS: From SE **reams** meaning "500 sheets of paper" applied to other amounts and other items.

**scads** |scadz| *n* A large amount.

**shedload** |SHED lōd| *n* A very large amount. ORIGINS: Extended from slang **loads** meaning "lots" with SE **shed** meaning "a small storage building." Originally British; use now spreading. USAGE INFO: Now used as a euphemism for slang **shitload** meaning "a very large amount." USAGE ALERT: Because of the phonetic similarity to **shitload** and the fact that it is used by some people as a euphemism, people may assume that it is in all cases.

**shitload** |SHIT lōd| *n* A very large amount. ORIGINS: From **shit** meaning "excrement" plus SE **load**. USAGE ALERT: Because it includes **shit**, this word will be objectionable in some contexts and to some people.

**slathers** |SLA*TH* urz| *n* Large amounts, often of something spreadable. ORIGINS: From SE **slather** meaning "to squander." USAGE INFO: Was primarily British, but spreading, especially in US food writing, where it is most often used to refer to mayonnaise, butter, jam, frosting, as well as to other items in large quantities.

**slew** |slū| *n* A large number or amount. ORIGINS: From the Irish **sluagh** meaning "crowd."

**slue** |slū| *n See* SLEW.

**stacks** |stāks| *n* A large amount.

**tons** |tūns| *n* A great deal.

**wads** |wads| *n* A large amount.

**whole lot** |HŌL LAHT| *n* With *a*: (a whole lot)—a great many; a large number or amount; with *the*: (the whole lot)—everything.

NON-SLANG SYNONYMS: good deal, great deal, mass, plenty, <u>acres</u>, **lots**, **abundance**, **bounty**, **galore** (used following the noun), **plethora**, **profusion**

# 4 Having a Large Amount

**bursting at the seams with** |BUR sting at *thu* SĒMZ with| *adj* Extremely full of; containing an extraordinary number of. ORIGINS: From the results of overloading a bag with too many or too heavy items.

**chock-a-block/choc-a-block with** |CHAHK u BLAHK with| *adj* Crammed full; jammed full; stuffed. ORIGINS: From nautical jargon referring to a situation in which hoisting tackle have reached their limits.

**filthy with <noun>** |FIL thē with <noun>| *adj* Full of; overloaded with. ORIGINS: From slang use of filthy as an intensifier. USAGE INFO: An example is the phrase "filthy with money."

**loaded with <noun/pronoun>** |LŌD ed with <noun/pronoun>| *adj* Having a large amount of. USAGE INFO: Takes a plural or uncountable noun (like *money*).

**lousy with <noun/pronoun>** |LOU zē with <noun/pronoun>| *adj* Having a great deal of. ORIGINS: From WWI military slang when soldiers in the trenches were lousy with lice. USAGE INFO: Takes a plural or uncountable noun (like *money*).

**stinking with <noun/pronoun>** |STING king with <noun/pronoun>| *adj* Having or owning a large amount. ORIGINS: From SE <u>stinking</u> meaning "having a strong, unpleasant smell." USAGE INFO: Often used in connection with money.

**up the ass** |up *thē* AS| *adj* In excess; in extremely large amounts; many. ORIGINS: From slang **ass** meaning "the rear end or buttocks." USAGE ALERT: The inclusion of the word **ass** in the phrase will render it objectionable in some contexts and to some people.

up the gazoo |up *thu* gu ZŪ| *adj* In excess; in extremely large amounts; many. ORIGINS: Euphemism for **up the ass**, but, oddly, with more specificity, because gazoo is a slang term for SE anus. The euphemism gazoo in this phrase will soften it somewhat for most people, who don't know it's meaning, but it may still be objectionable in some contexts and to some people.

up the wazoo |up *thu* wah ZŪ| *adj* In excess; in extremely large amounts; many. ORIGINS: Euphemism for **up the ass**, but, oddly, with more specificity, because wazoo is a slang term for SE anus. The euphemism wazoo in this phrase will soften it somewhat for most people, who don't know it's meaning, but it may still be objectionable in some contexts and to some people.

up to here with <noun/pronoun> |up tū HIR with <noun/pronoun>| *adj* Possessing in very large amount; possessing in excess. USAGE INFO: Can be an unemotional statement of quantity, as in "You don't have to rush in to buy it: we're up to here with them." The phrase can also mean "having such a large quantity that I'm fed-up," as in "I'm up to here with this constant bickering."

**up to the ass with <noun/pronoun>** |up tū thē AS with <noun/pronoun>| *adj* Possessing in very large amount; possessing in excess. ORIGINS: As an indicator of the height of <whatever it is> stacked around one, this phrase gives a slightly less graphic image than the similar **up the ass** and its euphemistic forms. From slang **ass** to refer to the rear end or buttocks. USAGE ALERT: The inclusion of the word **ass** in the phrase will render it objectionable in some contexts and to some people.

up to the eyeballs with <noun/pronoun> |up tū thē Ī bawls with <noun/pronoun>| *adj* Possessing in very large amount; possessing in excess. ORIGINS: As an indicator of the height of <whatever it is> stacked around one, this phrase gives a less graphic image than the very similar **up the ass** and its euphemisms, while suggesting a larger amount than **up to the ass with <noun/pronoun>**.

wall-to-wall with |WAWL tū WAWL with| *adj* Present everywhere; all around. ORIGINS: From the description of a carpet installation that covers the whole floor.

NON-SLANG SYNONYMS: crammed with, filled with, full of, more than enough, overflowing with, packed with, jam-packed with, brimming with, in excess, replete with, teaming with

# 5 All

**full monte, monty** |FUL mahn tē| *n* Everything. ORIGINS: Unknown. Popularized by the film *The Full Monty* (1997).

**lot, the** |*thu* LAHT| *n* All of whatever it is.

**whole bag of tricks** |HŌL bag uv TRIKS| *n* Everything. USAGE INFO: Often with *the*.

**whole ball of wax** |HŌL bawl uv WAKS| *n* Everything. USAGE INFO: Often with *the*.

**whole enchilada** |HŌL en chu LAH du| *n* Everything. USAGE INFO: Often with *the*

**whole hog** |HŌL HAWG| *n* Everything. ORIGINS: From slang go the whole hog meaning "to do st thoroughly." USAGE INFO: Often with *the*.

**whole kit and caboodle** |HŌL kit und ku BŪ dul| *n* Everything. ORIGINS: From slang whole kit meaning "the entire lot" and caboodle meaning "a large, unsorted collection." USAGE INFO: Often with *the*.

**whole lot** |HŌL LAHT| *n* With *a*: (a whole lot)—a great many; a large number or amount; with *the*: (the whole lot)—everything.

**whole megillah** |HŌL mu GIL u| *n* Everything. ORIGINS: From slang megillah meaning "a long complicated story," from Hebrew **megillah** meaning the Old Testament books of Song of Songs, Ruth, Lamentations, Ecclesiastes, and Esther, which have special liturgical significance in celebrating Jewish festivals. USAGE INFO: Often with *the*.

**whole nine yards** |HŌL NĪN YAHRDZ| *n* Everything. USAGE INFO: Often with *the*.

**whole schmeer, schmear** |HŌL SHMIR| *n* Everything. USAGE INFO: Often with *the*.

**whole schmegegge, schmegeggy** |HŌL shma GEG / HŌL shma GEG ē| *n* Everything. ORIGINS: From a Yiddish word that means "nonsense" (and sometimes, "a contemptible or incompetent person"). USAGE INFO: Often with *the*.

**whole shebang** |HŌL shu BANG| *n* Everything. ORIGINS: From US military jargon shebang for tents where a soldier's possessions were stored. USAGE INFO: Often with *the*.

**whole shooting match** |HŌL SHŪT ing mach| *n* Everything. USAGE INFO: Often with *the*.

**works (the)** |*thu* WURKZ| *n* Everything; the whole lot. USAGE INFO: This phrase can also mean "a sampling of everything available" as in "a pizza with the works."

**NON-SLANG SYNONYMS:** all, everything, sum, **grand total**, **entirety**, **sum total**

# HOW BIG?

## 1 Small

**bitty*** |BIT ē| *adj* Little, small; insignificant. ORIGINS: Diminutive of SE **bit**. USAGE INFO: Bitty is often combined into little bitty or itty bitty; bitsy may be combined to form itsy bitsy. Reduplication is common for small things, e.g., teensy-weensy and the children's finger-play song "The Eensy-Weensy Spider."
• bitsy |BIT sē|

**dinky, dinkey** |DING kē| *adj* Tiny. ORIGINS: From Scotttish **dink** meaning "smart, neat," extended in railway jargon to name a small locomotive and in journalism jargon to name a 300-word piece of writing.

**itty-bitty** |IT ē BIT ē| *adj* Little, small; insignificant. ORIGINS: Probably related to SE **little**. USAGE INFO: Also itsy-bitsy. *See* BITTY.

**measly** |MĒZ lē| *adj* Contemptibly small.

**teeny(-weeny)*** |TĒ nē / TĒ nē WĒ nē| *adj* Very small.
• teensy(-weensy) |TĒN sē / TĒN sē WĒn sē|

**NON-SLANG SYNONYMS:** little, mini, petite, short, small, **pint-sized**, **pocket-sized**, **runty**, **shrimpy**, **diminutive**, **microscopic**, **miniature**, **minuscule**, **minute**

## 2 Large

**daddy of all** |DA dē uv awl| *adj* Especially large, problematic, impressive, etc. ORIGINS: From the father as the head of the family in a paternalistic society. USAGE INFO: *See* GRANDDADDY; MOTHER OF ALL.

**ginormous** |gi NAWR mus| *adj* Very large. ORIGINS: A portmanteau word formed from SE **gigantic** and **enormous**.

**granddaddy, grandaddy** |GRAN dad ē| *adj* The earliest; most respected; most outstanding; or largest of its kind. ORIGINS: From the role and circumstances of grandfathers in many families; having the largest size is an extension of the other traits.

**hefty** |HEF tē| *adj* A large size or amount. ORIGINS: From SE **heft** meaning "weight; heaviness."

**hulking** |HUL king| *adj* Of massive size; large and unwieldy; big. ORIGINS: From SE **hulk** meaning "a large person."

**humongous, humungous** |hū MAHN gus / hū MUN gus| *adj* Extraordinarily large; enormous; monstrous. ORIGINS: Thought to derive from SE **huge**, monstrous, and tremendous.

**jumbo** |JUM bō| *adj* A large, clumsy person. ORIGINS: Contrary to some suggestions, it seems that the term was used of people before being popularized with circus master P.T. Barnum's application of it to a large elephant in 1828.

**mega** |ME gu| *adj* Very large.

**monster** |MAHN stur| *adj* Very large; enormous.

**mother of all** |MU *thur* uv awl| *adj* A situation, problem, delay, etc. that is especially large, difficult, critical, etc. USAGE INFO: *See* DADDY OF ALL and GRANDDADDY.

**whopping** |WAHP ing| *adj* Enormous.

NON-SLANG SYNONYMS: big, broad, bulky, enormous, giant, grand, great, gross, huge, large, roomy, sizable, **gigantic**, **super**, **colossal**, **grandiose**, **immeasurable**, **immense**, **massive**, **monumental**, **mountainous**, **stupendous**, **substantial**, **vast**, **voluminous**

# Speed and Travel

From the foot speed of Usain Bolt of Jamaica or Dash Parr of *The Incredibles* (2004) to the races of NASCAR and the feats of NASA, ever-increasing speed holds a fascination for many. In addition, many of us like to move fast ourselves and appreciate technology that helps us zip around. This chapter is divided as follows:

*Moving Along*
  1 To Speed in a Vehicle
  2 To Move or Dance Very Fast
  3 To Go Very Fast
  4 To Move Quickly and Effortlessly
  5 To Depart in a Hurry
  6 To Escape
  7 To Go Away

*How Fast?*
  1 Fast—Adjective and Adverb

# MOVING ALONG

Most non-slang synonyms don't make all the distinctions shown shown here, so non-slang synonyms for the first three divisions are grouped after To Go Very Fast.

## 1 To Speed in a Vehicle

**barrel (along)** |BER ul / BER ul u LAWNG| *v* To move swiftly (in a motor vehicle). ORIGINS: From the SE **barrel into**, referring to a barrel rolling downhill. USAGE ALERT: Barrel through and barrel ahead also refer to speedy progress, but are more often used of situations that do not involve vehicular travel, for example, "barrel through an examination"; "barrel ahead with the treaty signing."

**belt (along)** |belt / BELT u LAWNG| *v* To move with great speed or to hurry, usually in a vehicle.

**burn rubber** |BURN RUB ur| *v* To speed in a car, especially accelerating from a standstill to a very high speed. ORIGINS: From the effect on rubber tires caused by such driving.

**firewall** |FĪR wawl| *v* To accelerate maximally.

**floor it** |FLAWR it| *v* To go really fast (in a vehicle). ORIGINS: From the action of someone driving a vehicle and pushing the accelerator pedal all the way down (to the floor).

**give her the gun** |GIV her *thu* GUN| *v* To press hard on a vehicle's accelerator pedal; to drive a vehicle very fast. ORIGINS: From slang verb gun meaning "to rev an engine," which is done by pressing the accelerator.

**let her rip** |LET hur RIP| *v* To set *st* in motion; to run *st* going at full speed. ORIGINS: Generalized from its use in steamboat races. At one time, it was customary to use the feminine singular pronoun to refer to ships and other vessels. USAGE INFO: Usually said quickly enough that the |h| is lost from the pronunciation.

**put the pedal to the metal** |poot *thu* PET'l tū *thu* MET'l| *v* Move really quickly. ORIGINS: From vehicles in which the accelerator pedal makes the vehicle go at maximum speed when pushed as far down (to the metal of the floor) as possible.

**step on the gas** |STEP ahn *thu* GAS| *v* To move at very high speed (usually in a vehicle). ORIGINS: From the action of stepping on the accelerator pedal, also called the "gas pedal," to increase a car's speed. USAGE INFO: Also used as an imperative.

**step on it** |STEP ahn it| *v* To move at very high speed (usually in a vehicle). ORIGINS: "It" refers to the accelerator. From the action of stepping on the accelerator pedal, also called the "gas pedal," to increase a car's speed. USAGE INFO: Also used as an imperative.

**NON-SLANG SYNONYMS:** See after To Go Very Fast.

## 2 To Move or Dance Very Fast

**boogie** |BOO gē| *v* To dance or move quickly. ORIGINS: From the dance called the boogie-woogie.

**hoof (it)** |hoof / HOOF it| *v* To go by foot, walking or running; to dance. ORIGINS: From slang hoof meaning "the human foot."

**NON-SLANG SYNONYMS:** See after To Go Very Fast.

# 3 To Go Very Fast

go flat-out |gō FLAT out| *v* To move at top speed.

go full blast |GŌ ful blast| *v* To move forward with as much speed as possible. USAGE INFO: Also used of doing anything to the maximum level possible: as loud as possible; turned up to full power; with all of one's might; etc.

go great guns |GŌ grāt GUNZ| *v* To progress well; to advance with great speed.

**go like a bat out of hell** |GŌ līk u BAT out uv HEL| *v* To go very fast. ORIGINS: Figurative use of SE **hell** meaning "the alternative to heaven; the realm of the devil." USAGE ALERT: The mention of **hell** will make use of this expression objectionable in some contexts and to some people.

go like a shot |GŌ līk u SHAHT| *v* To do something quickly. ORIGINS: The comparison is to a bullet shot out of a gun.

go like blazes |GŌ līk BLĀ zuz| *v* To go very fast. ORIGINS: Euphemism for **go like hell**. From slang **hell** as an intensifier. USAGE ALERT: Euphemisms may still be objectionable in some contexts and to some people.

go like gangbusters |GŌ līk GANG bus turz| *v* To achieve great success; forging ahead easily and without problems. ORIGINS: From a radio drama *Gangbusters* (1936–1957) featuring officers of the law who "busted" criminal gangs.

go like greased lightning |gō līk GRĒST LĪT ning| *v* To act very quickly. ORIGINS: The idea is that lightning would be even faster if grease was applied to it.

**go like hell** |gō līk HEL| *v* To go very fast. ORIGINS: Figurative use of SE hell meaning "the alternative to heaven; the realm of the devil." USAGE ALERT: The inclusion of **hell** will make this expression objectionable in some contexts and to some people.

go like nobody's business |gō līk NŌ bu dēz BIZ nis| *v* To go very quickly; to go very well. ORIGINS: From slang **nobody's business** meaning "something extraordinary."

go like sixty |gō līk SIK stē| *v* To go at a great speed; to do with great force or energy. ORIGINS: Possibly a comparison to the force/energy that sixty people could bring to bear.

go like the deuce |gō līk *thu* DŪS| *v* To go very fast; to do with great investment of effort. ORIGINS: Euphemism for **go like hell**, SE hell being the place where the devil resides and **deuce** being a euphemism for **devil**. USAGE ALERT: The inclusion of deuce will make this expression objectionable in some contexts and to some people, but usually less so than **devil**.

**go like the devil** |gō līk *thu* DEV ul| *v* To go very fast; to do with great investment of effort. ORIGINS: Euphemism for **go like hell**, SE hell being the place where the devil resides. USAGE ALERT: The inclusion of **devil** will make this expression objectionable in some contexts and to some people.

**haul ass** |HAWL AS| v To move really quickly; to rush; to work really hard. ORIGINS: From SE **haul** and slang **ass** referring to the whole person as in the phrase "get your ass over here." Extended from slang **ass** to refer to the rear end or buttocks. USAGE ALERT: The inclusion of the word **ass** in the phrase will render it objectionable in some contexts and to some people.

**hop to it** |hahp TŪ it| v To hurry; to make an energetic start on st; to get to work.

**hump** |hump| v To move really quickly; to hurry; to travel at great speed.

**look alive** |lŏŏk u LĪV| v To hurry. USAGE INFO: Often used as an imperative.

**make it snappy** |MĀK it SNAP ē| v To be quick; to hurry.

**nip** |nip| v To move quickly. USAGE INFO: Combined with a number of prepositions to form the phrases: nip along, nip into, nip out, etc.

**pour it on** |PAWR it ahn| v To move at maximum speed; to exert maximum effort.

**scoot** |skūt| v To move along at a good pace.

**scorch**² |skawrch| v To move at great speed.

**shake a leg** |SHĀK u leg| v To hurry. USAGE INFO: Often used as an imperative.

**stir one's stumps** |STIR wunz STUMPS| v To get moving; to set off briskly.

**zap**² |zap| v To move swiftly.

**zing along** |ZING u LAWNG| v To move really quickly and energetically.

**NON-SLANG SYNONYMS:** be quick, cover ground, gallop, go fast, go like the wind, hurry, race, run, rush, speed, **go like lightning**, **hustle**, **open the throttle**, **career**, **gather momentum**, **hasten**, **make haste**

## 4 To Move Quickly and Effortlessly

**breeze** |brēz| v To move swiftly and effortlessly. ORIGINS: From analogy to the movement of unimpeded wind.

**streak** |strēk| v To move with great speed; to move so fast that one's image is blurred to viewers.

**waltz** |waltz| v To move briskly.

**whiz, whizz** |wiz| v To move rapidly.

**zip** |zip| v To move really quickly.

**zoom** |zūm| v To move really quickly.

**NON-SLANG SYNONYMS:** cruise, flash, flow, fly, glide, sail, shoot, skate, skim, slide, soar, sweep

## 5 To Depart in a Hurry

**beat it** |BĒT it| *v* To leave in a hurry. ORIGINS: Possibly from a combination of SE beat a path and reference to the sound of rapidly retreating footsteps beating the floor/pavement.

**blow²** |blō| *v* To leave; to depart speedily. ORIGINS: May be by analogy with the blowing of the wind. USAGE INFO: Often incorporated in longer slang phrases, such as blow the joint, blow out of town.

**book (it)** |BŎŎK it| *v* To move quickly, especially when leaving. ORIGINS: From bookity-book, an obsolete slang word meaning "to run fast."

**bug out** |bug out| *v* To leave or take off; to run away. ORIGINS: A reference to a flitting insect. USAGE ALERT: Another meaning of bug out, which extends the idea of a bug as irritating or annoying, is "to go insane; to be driven mad."

**clear off/out** |KLIR awf / KLIR out| *v* To leave in a hurry; to depart. ORIGINS: By extension of SE clear, with the idea that one will "clear" a place of one's presence. USAGE INFO: Can be used as an imperative to signal dismissal.

**hightail (it)** |HĪ tāl / HĪ tāl it| *v* To go as quickly as possible; to flee.

**make tracks** |māk TRAKS| *v* To depart really quickly; to run away. ORIGINS: The tracks are the footprints left by the runner.

**scoot** |skūt| *v* To move along at a good pace.

**skedaddle** |ski DAD ul| *v* To leave in haste; to flee.

**skip out** |skip OUT| *v* To leave; to depart in a hurry.

**skip town** |SKIP TOUN| *v* To leave without a trace; to depart without warning.

**split** |split| *v* To leave; to depart in a hurry.

**take a powder** |tāk u POU dur| *v* To run away.

NON-SLANG SYNONYMS: flee, run away, **bolt**, **cut loose**, **cut out**, **dash**, **fly**, **hotfoot**, **make off**, **make tracks**, **run like a bunny**, **rush**, **scamper**

## 6 To Escape

**blow the coop** |BLŌ *thu* KŪP| *v* To leave suddenly; to escape from prison.

**break out** |BRĀK out| *v* To leave, escape. USAGE INFO: **Break out** is SE when referring to escaping from jail. It is likely to be considered slang when said, say, to one's employer in the course of suddenly leaving one's job.

**bust out** |BUST out| *v* To escape (particularly, from prison). USAGE INFO: Synonymous with **break out**, but more slangy.

**do a bunk** |dū u BUNK| *v* To run away; to escape.

**fly the coop** |FLĪ *thu* KŪP| *v* To leave suddenly; to escape from prison.

**go on the lam** |gō ahn *thu* LAM| *v* To run away, often to escape from the police and a possible jail sentence. ORIGINS: From slang lam meaning "to run away." Repopularized by, for example, *The Simpsons* episode "Marge on the Lam" (1993).

**leg it** |LEG it| *v* To run away; to escape on foot. ORIGINS: From slang leg meaning "to run."

**light out** |LĪT OUT| *v* To set off hastily; to hurry away; to escape.

**make a break for it** |māk u BRĀK fawr it| *v* To try to escape; to attempt to leave (often from prison).

**make oneself scarce** |māk wun self SKERS| *v* To escape; to leave quickly.

**take it on the lam** |TĀK it ahn *thu* LAM| *v* To run away, often to escape from the police and a possible jail sentence. ORIGINS: From slang lam meaning "to run away." Re-popularized by, for example, *The Simpsons* episode "Marge on the Lam" (1993).

NON-SLANG SYNONYMS: escape, flee, get away with, run away, steal away, **cut and run**, **go scot-free**, **make a getaway**, **skip bail**, **elude**, **evade**, **take flight**

## 7 To Go Away

**hit the road** |hit *thu* RŌD| *v* To leave on a trip; to set out. USAGE INFO: Can be used as an imperative to send someone away.

**push off** |PŎŌSH awf| *v* To leave; to depart. ORIGINS: From the action of boaters pushing off from the dock.

**shove off** |SHUV ahf| *v* To leave; to depart. ORIGINS: From the action of boaters pushing off from the dock. USAGE INFO: Harsher than the similar phrase push off!

**take oneself off** |TĀK wun self AWF| *v* To leave; to depart.

**truck** |truk| *v* To move on steadily; to travel on.

NON-SLANG SYNONYMS: depart, exit, go away, leave, move on, remove oneself, retire, set out, **head out**, **split**, **embark**, **sally forth**, **take leave**, **withdraw**

# HOW FAST?

**FTASB** Faster than a speeding bullet.

**PDQ** Pretty damn quick.

## 1 Fast—Adjective and Adverb

**double-quick** |DU bul kwik| *adj* Extremely fast. ORIGINS: From SE **double** and SE **quick**.

**hell-bent for leather** |HEL bent fawr LE*TH* ur| *adj* Moving really quickly; traveling at break-neck speed. ORIGINS: From the sport of horseback riding, with the word **leather** referring to the harness. Figurative use of SE **hell** meaning "the alternative to heaven; the realm of the devil." USAGE INFO: There is a related phrase **hell for leather**. USAGE ALERT: The inclusion of the word **hell** in the phrase will render it objectionable in some contexts and to some people.

**lickety-split** |LIK i tē SPLIT| *adj* With great speed.

**like nobody's business** |līk NŌ bu dēz BIZ nis| *adv* Very quickly; very well.

**on the double** |ahn *th*u DU bul| *adv* Very quickly. ORIGINS: From military jargon **double time** meaning "twice as fast as usual."

NON-SLANG SYNONYMS: fast, hastily, hurriedly, quickly, rapidly, **at full tilt**, **in a jiffy**, **in nothing flat**, **pronto**, **speedily**, **apace**, **expeditiously**, **fleetly**, **posthaste**, **swiftly**

# TEACHING
# WITH SLANG

# LANGUAGE REGISTERS

The different levels of language formality are called *registers*. Registers are best thought of not as slices but as ranges of language use because each of us adapts our language in myriad subtle ways in response to the circumstances in which we use words. There are at least five interconnected domains that we respond to by adapting our language.

| AUDIENCE | We communicate differently about exactly the same topic with different people depending on our social relationship to them (boss, brother-in-law, neighbor), whether we have interacted before, their ages, and what/how much we know about them. |
| --- | --- |
| MODE & GENRE | We communicate differently in person and out loud than we do at a distance (say, over the phone) or in writing. And in either case, genre matters: instant messaging differs from e-mail, differs from a typed or handwritten personal letter, differs from a report or a speech. Genre may also give us a particular structure or specific words to say. |
| TOPIC & DICTION | We also communicate differently about different topics. Even with the same audience and genre, our comments on the economy would likely be shaped differently on several fronts from our comments on our favorite movie, band, or flavor of Ben and Jerry's. In addition, topic may influence audience and genre. |
| PURPOSE | We communicate in order to express ourselves, teach, persuade, explain, amuse, console, engage, and for many other reasons. Our current purpose will impact our choice of genre, topics, etc., and will, in turn, be influenced by audience. |
| SITUATION | All the factors that make up our internal and external context such as how we feel physically and emotionally, the time of day and season, who else is present, what other activities may be taking place, whether the situation is formal or informal, intimate or impersonal, private or public, the cultural milieu, and the language we are using (including whether it's our first language or a non-native language) also contribute to our communication choices. |

For the purpose of this book, the following categories are used:

**FORMAL** designates language in its most rule-based uses, with limits on genre, diction, grammar, and syntax. *Formal* covers much of language use that is found in religious, ceremonial, legislative, and business settings; in serious meetings with doctors, lawyers, and bankers; and in academic writing, among other uses. But if you have experience with two or more of these formal discourse situations, you know that no two are exactly alike and that formality means different things in the different settings.

NO REGISTER designates language that fits in anywhere. No matter how formal or informal one's discourse is, one uses words like *and, the, my, your,* etc. These words do not belong to any particular register of language and can be freely combined with language of any register.

<u>INFORMAL</u> language loosens the strictures on genre, diction, grammar, and syntax imposed by formal language, but the experts seem to find that there is a level of informality without slang, as well as an even more informal level that includes slang. In this book, we use *informal* to name a level in between slang and formal. If you think about informal with your immediate family versus informal with older relatives or family friends versus informal with friends your own age when family isn't present, you'll have some idea of the range that informal can cover.

SLANG is nonstandard and nontechnical English, used informally and widely (that is, it is not limited to a particular region, like dialect, or a particular group, like argot or jargon), most often as a choice when one or more Standard English words are available. It is sometimes used playfully, sometimes outspokenly, and often to add emotional intensity to discourse. Levels within slang can be demonstrated with this example: a slang word formed of two SE words (**big money**) is generally not as slangy (for lack of a better term) as a slang word formed of an SE word and a slang word (**big bucks**). Other factors also influence how slangy a word is.

**POTENTIALLY OBJECTIONABLE/OFFENSIVE (PO) SLANG** is a subset of slang that may offend people specifically because it has phrases with PO words and forms of those words, regardless of the meaning of what is said. Because it can have such a different impact from other slang, it is treated separately, almost as if it were a separate register, in this book. There are some set categories that are included in PO slang, which include:

- body parts related to sexuality and excretion
- body functions related to sexuality and excretion
- names for God used for purposes other than addressing God in prayer or stating facts about God
- words that embody evil as conceived by various religions, including *devil* and *hell*
- racial or ethnic slurs

# THE EDUCATIONAL VALUE OF POTENTIALLY OFFENSIVE LANGUAGE

Because this book aims to be instructional as well as a reference, but contains words that are categorized as swear words and/or obscene language, I think it's important to address how this material can fit into an educational setting. Let me start with three brief anecdotes:

A family that lives down the street from me came to the United States from the former Yugoslavia. In an English language class for refugees, in response to a discussion about the English word *chorus*, the mother explained the (innocent) meaning of a word in her native language that is pronounced |hawr|. The teacher, concerned that a discussion of the meaning of the English word *whore* might offend someone in the class, refused to explain what its meaning was, but told my neighbor never to say it. She only discovered its meaning years later, when she saw it used in context in a book.

In early 2009, Vogue model Liskula Cohen brought a defamation lawsuit against Google for a blog on their site that referred to her as "skanky." If words wield that much power, then it is essential to know their meanings and impact in order to make knowledgeable choices about using them.

Another neighbor worked in an office in which a non-native speaker of English was also employed. One day the non-native speaker asked my neighbor about another co-worker, "Is he an *old fart* or a *son of a bitch?*" Clearly the person was trying to get a clearer idea of the meaning of these phrases in order to distinguish them and understand precise meanings.

Language can fail to communicate when people who are trying to make meaning together have different levels of knowledge about a word. This book aims to explain—in as much as it is possible to do so without a specific context to reference—how language is likely to be understood by an informed audience.

# CONSIDERING OFFENSIVE LANGUAGE

In general, there are three ways that language can be objectionable or offensive:

1) **Diction**, when the very words used are considered objectionable or offensive, regardless of the meaning made. Examples are the words that are referred to as PO (potentially objectionable/offensive words) in this book.
2) **Tone**, when the tone of a communication is insulting or abusive.
3) **Meaning**, when words express something that is objectionable or offensive.

In addition, tone can both make otherwise innocent words offensive as well as undercut the offense of the words' literal meaning through sarcasm or irony. On the other hand, there are some particular contexts in which words that are otherwise considered offensive or objectionable can often be used without causing offense or raising objections:

- reporting a true incident ("Someone just called me a twat" is surely different than "You're a twat!")
- saying something of oneself, particularly in apology ("Oh I'm so sorry: I'm such a damn fool!" seems different than "You're such a damn fool!")
- speaking of something contrary to fact ("I'm not the type to say 'it's over: fuck you!' after the first misunderstanding." is arguably different than "Fuck you!")
- creating a fiction by putting words in the mouth of a character

It is interesting to note that the Federal Communications Commission (FCC) tolerated Bono's use of **fucking** as an adjective (he either said "this is really, really, fucking brilliant" or "this is fucking great" during the broadcast of the 2003 Golden Globe Awards). The FCC judged that while it might be "crude and offensive," Bono's use of fucking did not "describe or depict sexual and excretory functions and organs" and therefore was not obscene.

But the FCC does not address the psychology involved: because of the way our brains process information, hearing the word *fucking*—even though it may turn out by the end of the sentence to be used in a way that does not mean "sexual and excretory functions and organs"—may well trigger those meanings in the listener's mind as the sentence continues to unfold and the listener works to make sense of what is being said.

Perhaps this is one point at which people who have no problem with hearing and using this sort of language and those who do have a problem differ: It stands to reason that people whose minds pull up the meaning "feces" every time they hear **shit!**—and so on for every other picturesque PO word—might find this distracting and irritating in a way that other people—whose brains may activate differently—may not immediately understand. Perhaps considering the possibility that we're wired differently may help people better understand each other's language choices: both the desire to not hear offensive material and the desire to express oneself with the vocabulary one is accustomed to use.

# TALKING ABOUT LANGUAGE CHOICES

This book offers opportunities for turning the question of language choice and slang to instructional purposes by making available a wide range of register choices, providing a context in which students' language choices can be addressed in a gentle and objective way. As an instructor, you can refer students to the book's definitions rather than having to define words yourself if doing so would be uncomfortable, and use the origins, usage info, and usage alerts to discuss the repercussions of various choices.

You can use the categories in the article "Language Registers" on page 587, or use this simplified approach to discussing language context:

- **where** we are
- **what** we're communicating about
- **whom** we're communicating with or to
- **when** we're communicating
- **why** we're communicating

# Using a Dictionary and a Thesaurus

This combined dictionary and thesaurus provides a good opportunity to discuss different types of reference books and how they can best serve various needs. If it would be
helpful, the dictionary can be related to receptive language—finding out more about
language that we hear and read, while the thesaurus can be linked to expressive language—helping us make choices of words to use in our speaking and writing. If you are
teaching non-native speakers, this is a book that they may not initially be able to use
every facet of, but can grow into. For best results, start with entry words, pronunciations using the pronunciation key on page xix, and definitions. Reviewing the styles for
the registers and the pronunciation key will be helpful.

# Synonyms

Synonyms can have widely varying meanings. For example, for an adjective that names a
personal trait, like *smart*, you may find a synonym that's derisive (know-it-all), a synonym
that's laudatory (intellectual), and a synonym that's playful (smarty pants) and the
impact of which is largely dependent on context and tone, etc. It's important for students
to know that there are no true synonyms: each word, by virtue of its sound, its etymology,
its history of use, and its length, is unique.

You can invite students to choose a group of synonyms and focus on a particular
word in that group to explain (using the categories listed previously and any others that
might be pertinent) how and why it is distinct from the other choices available.

# Irony and Litotes

It is more likely that students use litotes |lī TŌ tēz| than that they have ever heard
the word. *Litotes* is a figure of speech in which a double negative is used for a positive.
Usually one of the negatives is a word like *not* or *no* or *never* and the other negative is
a noun or adjective that is an antonym of the noun or adjective meant. For example,
if someone attends a fantastic party and when asked about it says, "It wasn't bad,"
meaning "It was fabulous," that's an example of litotes. Because litotes involves saying
the opposite of what is meant, it is an example of verbal irony.

These slang terms

- no joke
- no picnic
- no tea party and
- not too shabby (explained under the listing for shabby)

are all examples of litotes.

Ask students to volunteer other examples.

# Contronyms

Many slang words are **contronyms**, words that have two opposing meanings. An
example is *bad* which has a Standard English meaning of "very unpleasant" and a slang
meaning of "truly outstanding." As a result, the meaning of slang words like **badass**
can't be interpreted without context.

Challenge students to search through the dictionary section to discover contronyms.
Individuals or groups can each cover several letters and share their findings.

## Portmanteau Words

As explained in the entry for frabjous, portmanteau words are words built from two or more other words, but not joined in their entirety, as compound words are. Examples include:

- fantabulous
- ginormous
- grungy and possibly
- contraption

Invite students to locate other words, both slang and Standard English, that were created in this way.

## Suffixes

A number of slang words have several possible forms for one grammatical function. Examples like awful(ly) or **damn(ed)** can be used to initiate a discussion of some of the grammatical differences between informal language and formal language.

## Slang and Rhyme

While the US doesn't have rhyming slang in the sense of Cockney slang, in which rhyming phrases are used as substitutes for the phrases meant, we do have slang that rhymes. Here's a collection of slang in the body of the book that has repeated sounds:

| | |
|---|---|
| big wig | **hell's bells** |
| blah-blaher | holy guacamole |
| boo-boo | holy mol(e)y |
| choc(k)-a-block | **in deep doo-doo** |
| clap trap | name of the game |
| **doo-doo head** | nitty-gritty |
| dum-dum | nitwit |
| fat cat | put the pedal to the metal |
| hard row to hoe | ring-ding |
| **have a shitfit** | wheeler-dealer |
| have the screaming meemies | yo-yo |
| heebie-jeebies | |

American slang also has some synonyms that rhyme:

- buckle down/knuckle down
- buckle under/knuckle under
- bum/scum/crumb
- doofus/goofus
- give *sb* the poop/give *sb* the scoop
- hitch/glitch
- ratty/tatty

An interesting set of slang words would rhyme except that the first syllable has an *i* while the second has an *a:*

- dribs and drabs
- fiddle faddle
- kiss ass
- jim-jams

Challenge students to find rhymes and other sound patterns in Standard English words and phrases. You might wish to have separate categories for words with reduplication, also called *perfect rhyme* (*dum-dum*), as opposed to words with strong rhyme (*fat cat*) or weak rhyme (*heebie-jeebies*).

# Slang Riffs

Some slang is a series of variations on a theme—a riff on some underlying take on things or syntactical pattern. Some riffs become obvious when you place words in alphabetical order, and others when you group words by meaning in a thesaurus. Here are a few that don't come to the fore in either arrangement because the shared element comes at the end of the word:

- addlehead, blockhead, bonehead, bubblehead, **butthead,** chowderhead, chucklehead, cluckhead, **dickhead, doo-doo head**, dumbhead, egghead, fathead, fluffhead, **fuckhead**, hardhead, jughead, knucklehead, lardhead, lunkhead, meathead, muddlehead, musclehead, muttonhead, pinhead, **pisshead,** pointy-head, rattlehead, saphead, **shithead**, stupidhead, thickhead

Less obvious—because it's related to meaning rather than the words that make up the slang phrase—is the connection of excitement and drug abuse the lurks behind the words hyped, keyed up, jim-jams, and jitters.

Challenge students to find riffs in sland and Standard English.

# Self-Expression vs. Communication

Ask students to debate three views of language (or other views that they would like to offer), rewording the definitions if necessary:

VIEW 1: Language is communicative, and as such should be shaped for the audience in order to be as effective as possible.

VIEW 2: Language is a personal expression, and as such should not be inhibited by any constraints, particularly external ones, because to do so would infringe the expression of self.

VIEW 3: Language is sometimes communicative and sometimes expressive and it is up to language users to negotiate language use in each situation, depending on the context.

# Awfully, Frightfully, Fiendishly Useful Intensifiers

Sometimes we want to strengthen the meaning or the emotional intensity of our communication. This can be accomplished in a number of ways. One way is to use intensifiers. Intensifiers are words that increase the intensity of the language they are added to.

It is possible to intensify language without changing the register, and it is also possible to intensify language and change its register at the same time. Such is the power of slang that adding a slang intensifier renders an entire communication as slang. For example, "I'm going to bed" is a bland sentence that could fit in anywhere: The words are of the type that we call *no register*. Look what happens with the addition of one word:

1. Fuck, I'm going to bed!
2. I'm fucking going to bed.
3. I'm going to fucking bed.

It doesn't matter how inoffensive the rest of the words are: One bit of slang changes the entire feel of a communication. Also note that in the first case **fuck** is a sentence modifying adverb, in the second, an adverb modifying a verb, and in the third, an adjective—but the meaning is pretty much the same in all three cases. Despite the placement in sentences two and three, **fucking** really isn't being used to modify the verb or the noun: it's adding emotional intensity to the whole sentence, just as the sentence modifier does.

Interestingly, this does not work in the other direction: Adding a formal word to a slang communication or changing one slang word to a formal word while another slang word remains, does not render the sentence formal.

He's a damned newbie. → He's a damned neophyte.

There are four main ways to make language more extreme across registers. One can:

• substitute a different word or phrase with a more extreme meaning
• add an intensifying element to the sentence, such as an adjective, adverb, or a prepositional phrase
• add a slang prefix, suffix, or infix to a word, or
• use a comparison, for example, a simile

You can find examples of alternate words or phrases with intensified meaning throughout the thesaurus, but particularly in sections in which different levels of intensity are explicitly treated, such as the section on Anger (pages 292–304). Modifiers (pages 271–282 and 286–290), Prefixes and Suffixes (pages 284–285), and Comparisons (pages 283–284) are dealt with in the Communication section. There are examples of words with infixes, but since they are not treated in the body of the book, we'll address them briefly here.

Infixes are word parts that can be added into the middle of a word to intensify it. Examples are **-goddamn-** or **-goddam-** and **-fucking-** or **-fuckin'-**. When an infix is added to a word, at least one of its syllables is stressed, in addition to the stressed syllables in the host word. Examples of slang with infixes include **abso-fucking-lutely** and **abso-goddamn-lutely**.

The chart on the next page shows various ways to intensify and moderate concepts in English. Examples are given for each register. We can see from the chart that most intensifiers are adverbs. Notice that all the potentially offensive (PO) words are divorced from any literal meaning they might have in other contexts, and simply serve to lend additional intensity (and often a negative spin) to whatever is being said.

Ask students to suggest other examples of intensifiers and how they work in slang and Standard English.

# HOW CAN YOU INTENSIFY LANGUAGE?

| | FORMAL | NO REGISTER | INFORMAL | SLANG | PO SLANG |
|---|---|---|---|---|---|
| **WAYS TO MAKE LANGUAGE EXTREME** | | | | | |
| **USE A DIFFERENT WORD OR PHRASE** | *irate →* *apoplectic* | angry → furious | put out → ranting and raving | steamed → hacked off | pissed → rip shit |
| **ADD A(N)...** | | | | | |
| **ADJECTIVE** | *exceptional* *utter* | extreme | mighty | gosh awful   infernal<br>holy   stinking | kick-ass |
| **ADVERB** | *quite simply* (as in *simply delicious*) | absolutely<br>completely<br>extremely<br>most...of<br>all very | madly<br>seriously | all-fired   frightfully<br>awfully   to the max<br>fiendishly   wicked | damn(ed)   fucking<br>effing   goddamn(ed)<br>freaking   hell of a<br>fricking   pissing<br>frigging |
| **ADVERBIAL PHRASE** | | | in Heaven's name<br>in the world | the deuce<br>the dickens<br>the heck | the devil<br>the fuck<br>the hell |
| **PREFIX** | | extra- super-<br>ultra- | | holy | piss- |
| **SUFFIX** | | -est | | -tacular   -tastic | -ass(ed) |
| **INFIX** | | | | abso-bloomin'-lutely | -fucking-   -goddamn-<br>-fuckin'-   -goddam- |
| **USE A SIMILE** | | | | like anything<br>like crazy<br>like mad | like hell<br>like the devil |
| **USE A COMPARATIVE** | | greater than<br>more than | | than heck<br>as____ as all creation<br>as____ as all get out<br>as____ as blazes<br>as____ as heck | as____ as a bastard<br>as____ as a bitch |

# NOTES

# NOTES